Theory & Practice
of
Experiential Education

Karen Warren, Ph.D.
Denise Mitten, Ph.D.
TA Loeffler, Ph.D.

EDITORS

ASSOCIATION FOR EXPERIENTIAL EDUCATION

Association for Experiential Education
3775 Iris Avenue, Suite 4
Boulder, CO 80301-2043
303.440.8844 • 866.522.8337
www.aee.org

ISBN: 978-0-929361-17-8

This publication is sold with the understanding that the
publisher is not engaged in providing psychological, medical, training,
or other professional services. Its contents is not intended
as a definitive guide, but as a resource.

▼ ▼ ▼

Cover art, *Radiant Forest,* by Roderick MacIver, founder of Heron Dance,
a 501 (c) 3 nonprofit dedicated to exploring the beauty and mystery of the
natural world through art and words. www.herondance.org

Published and printed in the United States.

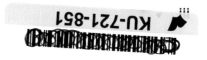
Contents

▼ ▼ ▼

▾ ▾ ▾

▾ ▾ ▾

▼ ▼ ▼

Psychological & Educational Foundations 213

▾ ▾ ▾

▾ ▾ ▾

▾ ▾ ▾

Theory Into Practice 467

▾ ▾ ▾

▾ ▾ ▾

Acknowledgments

▾ ▾ ▾

The editors of this book are like the cutting edge of a splitting wedge: We led the process but were backed by the weight, support, and experience of many people. We would like to acknowledge some of the people on whose shoulders we've stood as practitioners, researchers, and theory generators, as well as those who have contributed directly to this or previous editions of this book. The risk in acknowledging people in this format is that we inadvertently will leave some people off the list. We apologize in advance. The editors would like to thank and express their gratitude to the following people:

- The previous editors of the first three editions of this book, Richard Kraft, Mitchell Sakofs, Karen Warren, and Jasper Hunt, Jr., for setting the foundation on which this book was built.

- The authors who contributed their writing to this volume for skillfully enriching the dialogue about theory and practice in experiential education. Their work is a springboard to further define and articulate the ways we use experiential education in all settings.

- The Association for Experiential Education for its support of both this book and the *Journal of Experiential Education* (JEE), where many of the chapters in this book originated.

- The past and current editors of the *Journal of Experiential Education,* who selected and shaped the original articles.

- The AEE Publications Review Committee, which provided constructive feedback to help guide our process of creating the book.

- The Association for Experiential Education Director of Publications, Natalie Kurylko, for her commitment to this project, her magnificent editing, her timely feedback, and her ability to keep us moving through and across critical plateaus.

- Rebecca Carver, who was helpful in the early stages of this book and whose work on theory in experiential education inspired us. Sadly, on April 29, 2006, at the age of 39, Rebecca lost her year-long fight with breast cancer.

- Each other, for making the book creation process one of commitment, critical thinking, and fun.

Karen Warren would like to thank the following people:

- My mentors in the Association for Experiential Education, who have supported my involvement in AEE and, together, have helped me try to impact the theory and practice of experiential education.
- The Women in Experiential Education Professional Group of AEE, who have for 25 years provided a "home" for me in AEE.
- My students, who have kept me on my growing edge as an educator, a critical thinker, and a scholar. Their inspirational curiosity about experiential education and teaching to transgress has been a significant impetus for my work on this book.
- Finally, but most importantly, my partner Sue Tippett, and daughters Amelia Yeye Tarren and Anna Xin Xin Tarren, for helping me balance my personal and professional life and giving me a reason for making a difference in the world.

Denise Mitten is thankful for:

- My family and especially my daughter, Lauren, who continually inspires me to grow, learn, and create. Motherhood is a wonderful experiential learning environment!
- All of the people with whom I have shared outdoor trips. I have learned much about experiential education theory and practice from trip participants and the many talented guides with whom I worked at Woodswomen, Inc.
- Naomi Ross, Jean Illsley Clarke, and Marilyn Peterson—all generous mentors.
- Wonderful colleagues at AEE, including Christian Itin, folks in the WPG, TAPG, and others who have provided guidance and inspiration over the years.
- Our natural environments, which offer me so much nourishment and opportunities for growth.

TA Loeffler would like to thank the following people:

- My teachers and professors, who used experiential education with passion and creativity and so rekindled my love of learning, which had almost been snuffed out by traditional education.
- My mentors, both inside and outside AEE, who through their lives and work have supported my development as an outdoor professional and scholar.
- My family, for their love and support through this and many big challenges.
- Those who take the risk to sail far from the harbour, climb high above the clouds, and leave the safety of the eddy.

Karen Warren, Denise Mitten, & TA Loeffler, November 2008

Introduction

▾ ▾ ▾

An ounce of experience is better than a ton of theory simply because it is only in experience that theory has vital and verifiable significance.
–John Dewey

In the early days of the Association for Experiential Education, it was often noted that experiential education was experience rich but theory poor. In 1985, the first edition of the original *Theory of Experiential Education* book arrived on practitioners' bookshelves to help rectify this dilemma. Essentially the book was a compilation of photocopies of various theory-based articles—many different fonts and styles pulled together under one cover. We are pleased to introduce the 4th edition of this book, which we have re-titled *Theory & Practice of Experiential Education*. Much like the evolution in the publishing sophistication of the book, theory in experiential education has become more refined since that first edition.

The relationship between theory and practice in experiential education rests on a profound creative tension. As we become more theory based in the application of experiential education, it is essential to maintain the delicate balance between theory and practice. Theory informs practice, while practice tests and refines theory. This book is an attempt to offer the richness of theory that clarifies practice.

The editors of this edition of the book, like most experiential educators of the 70s and 80s, started in practice. But we also were passionate about analyzing, critiquing, and thinking about what grounded our practice. By the mid-80s we were steeped in theory, both creating theory and sorting through the theories that informed our work. It was an exciting time to make use of ideas from other disciplines, create alignments, and be part of an emerging profession. With this evolution there was an important imperative to test theory and begin to amass evidence-based research about the efficacy of experiential education. While great strides have been made, there still remain abundant opportunities for research. In the past few years, several significant research symposiums hosted within and outside of AEE have been excellent forums to showcase and share research that has contributed new theories in experiential education. As a note, this volume focuses on theory and practice and, while the editors agree that research is intimately entwined with theory, the growth of pertinent and useful articles on theory and practice leave the former research section for another much-needed book.

We have witnessed some key developments in the theory of experiential education and have attempted to make this edition reflective of this evolution. The following is a discussion of the changes we have seen that are mirrored in the pages of this volume.

Over the past 30 years the terms experiential education and experiential learning have often been used interchangeably. The writings contained in this new edition aim to clearly define the difference. More sophistication in the use of these terms allows an articulation of the differences and their intended meaning. The distinction is important. Experiential education has been defined as both a philosophy and a methodology while experiential learning may be thought of as the process. In experiential education, a teacher or leader intentionally uses experiential learning (the process of the student encountering direct experience) to move toward a specific learning outcome. Experiential education methodology is often so compelling that some practitioners ignore the philosophical underpinnings. The editors of this book embrace the concept of experiential education as both a philosophy and a methodology. We believe that experiential education has strong philosophical foundations and draws from a number of disciplines. As a result, the reader will find chapters that draw on philosophical, psychological, social justice, and various educational foundations. Methodology and philosophy intersect as we bring theory to practice.

A number of authors included in this book and in other resources cite the Association for Experiential Education's definition of experiential education (see www.aee.org). Many educators over the years have conversed to formalize this definition, which is widely used today. As we suspect that the dialogue about definitions will continue in the future, we started this edition with a section entitled "What is Experiential Education?" We believe the collection of articles in this section shows some of the breadth and depth of experiential education, while serving as an underpinning for the chapters that follow. While impossible to create a collection that embodies the full range of experiential education, we have attempted to broaden the scope of the chapters presented beyond the original outdoor adventure roots of the AEE, while still holding true to this foundation. It was not an easy task, as there is a large quantity of material, both new and old, to choose from and many gaps to fill. As Pema Chödrön suggests, we "started where we were" with the previous book, becoming familiar with its strengths, weaknesses, with articles that would remain, and articles that would be removed. This process resulted in a "wish list" of topics not covered in previous editions of this book that are now part of the fabric of experiential education. As a result, chapters on topics such as multiple intelligence theory, constructivism, brain-based learning theory, educational reform, and facilitation analysis among others have been added.

To those who believe that experiential education is a panacea with the potential to cure what ails education today, the new chapters that critique how experiential education is articulated and practiced will be an exciting addition. Analyses using critical thinking orientations can only strengthen how experiential education is theorized and practiced. Further, an international perspective offered by various chapter authors (with native English spellings) allows the reader to see more global interpretations of experiential education.

We see this book as an excellent teaching resource for undergraduate and graduate courses about education theory and courses specifically in experiential education. As educators, we have consistently found that students and practitioners are enthused about the practice of experiential education, that researchers are excited by the evidence that proves the validity of that practice, and that theorists call for us to understand "on whose shoulders we stand" and how we ground our work in theoretical foundations. This book attempts to be a valuable tool for all of these groups. Some of the classic chapters retained from previous editions give the reader a sense of both the timelessness and progression of ideas about experiential education. As more students pursue studies in experiential education, there is an increased need to provide background, context, theory, and teaching resources. We hope that educators will make this book their own by using the articles that work for their teaching style and students in an order that fits their course progression.

There is immense vitality in the constant change, theory testing, and empirical growth in experiential education ideas. As editors we have used this book to take a snapshot of that growth. As educators we look to our students to continue to expand ideas through critical analysis, reflection, writing, and discourse. Any book about theory and practice in experiential education is a work in progress; as such, we hope that subsequent generations of experiential educators will continue to "write the book" on the theory and practice of experiential education.

What Is Experiential Education?

▾ ▾ ▾

What Is
Experiential Education?

▾ ▾ ▾

Steve Chapman, Pam McPhee, & Bill Proudman

How many times have I been asked the "What is Experiential Education?" question by a person unfamiliar with the field, only to find myself looking at my feet in a paralyzed state before finally coming up with some sort of circuitous answer which inevitably starts with the comment that experiential education is not easy to define in a few words. Yes, there are whole books written on the topic, but the questioner is not typically looking for a book, just a straightforward answer. As editor of the *Journal,* I would often like to say, "Here, just take a look at this brief article." But when has there been an article in the *Journal* that deals with this? I have to go all the way back to a 1981 essay by Laura Joplin, entitled "On Defining Experiential Education" (Vol. 4, No. I, pp. 17–20). I find it hard to believe that nothing has changed in over a decade: Are experiential educators avoiding basic definitional questions? I wonder…. I have not seen a direct attempt to address this topic come across my editor's desk in five years.

Who should be writing this sort of essay? My answer is "each and every experiential educator." But that is not practical for the *Journal.* So where does one start? Surely not with those who use lots of long and hard-to-follow academic words; they would likely confuse my naive questioner. If things have changed, maybe one should search beyond familiar authors who have written at length? Yet it seems it should be people with a good deal of experience in the field, and people who are reflective of what they are doing and why—at least this seems

This chapter originally was published in the *Journal of Experiential Education*, with the following citation:

Chapman, S., McPhee, P., & Proudman, B. (1992). What is experiential education? *Journal of Experiential Education, 15*(2), 16–23.

a sensible start if one is asking that the subtleties of the definitional question be dealt with in a short space. Moreover, it seems highly unlikely, given the history, that just one answer could or would ever satisfy everyone.

This sort of reasoning led Karen Warren, the publications representative on the AEE Board, and me to approach a number of people with the request to tackle this question—experienced and reflective practitioners who have not written on the topic previously. We were not asking for ultimate answers, just a willingness to take on the challenge of re-opening the question with their personal thoughts and feelings. The following three essays comprise the initial response. There are many other perspectives, but hopefully these efforts will provide some valuable ideas and re-open the debate. The field cannot afford to avoid this issue if it is to evolve and develop in relation to the rapid social and educational changes that confront us all.

What Is the Question?

Steve Chapman

People sometimes ask me for a definition of "experiential education." One would think that, as the director of a department of that name and a practitioner for about 15 years, I should be able to answer those questions easily. The truth is, I can't. It isn't really that I don't know. I'm just not always sure what people are asking. Rather than try to define experiential education, I will just reflect on my own experience. My background is in school programs, but perhaps my experience in that arena can also shed light elsewhere. Several commonly asked questions help frame my thoughts.

"Oh, experiential education! That's ropes courses, right?" Experiential education cannot be understood simply as a particular set of activities. Yes, outdoor adventures, new games, and ropes courses all are linked to "experiential education" in the minds of many people. Yet as valuable as backpacking, rock climbing, canoe trips, and ropes courses are, they comprise only a small part of the potential arena. Cross-cultural homestays, community service projects, urban adventure programs, work-study programs, internships, cooperative education approaches in the classroom—all these (along with much more) provide great opportunities for students to become directly and enthusiastically engaged in real learning.

"What is it your students learn out there?" Sometimes people want a definition of experiential education to be presented in terms of content, just as science, history, and math usually are. Actually, experiential approaches are better understood in terms of style, and any topic can be explored using such techniques. Whatever is being studied, the point is to place students into a different, more direct relationship with the material. Students are actively engaged—exploring things for themselves—rather than being told answers to questions.

Although practitioners often cite their particular favorite outcomes (i.e., development of self-confidence), experiential approaches are not restricted to a specific set of goals or domains.

"Students need to be active rather than passive. Is that what you mean?" That depends on what you mean by active. Typical field trips seldom represent what I am talking about. When students are asked to absorb seemingly irrelevant information while walking through a zoo, their senses may become just as dulled as if they were completing classroom worksheets. Active mode refers to how the students' *minds* are used, not their legs. I can as easily run a bogus program in the woods as I can in the classroom, carefully explaining the workings of the world to everyone around me.

The adventure aspect of activities is not necessarily the focus. One issue for me is precisely the degree to which many people currently equate experiential education with various high-adrenalin, high-challenge, highly physical ventures. Perhaps the role of adventure programs—Outward Bound and the like—-in the most recent surge of the experiential education movement accounts for this confusion. Group initiative problems, wilderness programs, rock climbing, and ropes courses are especially fun and motivating. But if used thoughtlessly, they become mere diversions—fun, but educationally pointless.

"I've heard experiential education deals with material that is more 'real.' Is that the key?" Well, it comes closer than defining it by content or by the mere presence of adrenalin. But what does "real" mean in this context? Surely simulations are not out of bounds just because they are fake. It is the question under consideration that must be real; students must perceive it to be relevant, and the activity must provide a worthy vehicle for approaching the issue.

The truth of a metaphor is not measured literally, after all. Getting a group over a specially constructed "challenge wall" is a common and effective initiative problem, but how many of us must actually help someone over a 15-foot plywood wall on our way to work each morning? Similarly, a mock trial can be a great example of an experiential approach, though the question may be about a fictional circumstance (i.e., "Is Jack, in the novel *Lord of the Flies,* guilty of murder?").

"If experiential education is supposed to be student-centered, what is the role of the teacher?" The description that works best for me is "providing minimum necessary structure." In other words, the teacher's role is to give just enough assistance for students to be successful, but no more. If the teacher carries out the role properly, students will accomplish more than they ever could on their own. Yet if the approach is truly student-centered, they may not be aware the teacher had a role at all.

Another critical role for the teacher is to help students make connections. I think most of us would agree that students must eventually understand the point of an experience for it to be educative, and that point seldom emerges fully developed on its own. Some argue that the teacher's primary role is to guide an effective "debriefing" discussion (Kjol & Weber, 1990). Getting full value from even the best metaphors requires closure, and that takes a good guide.

Others suggest that the leader's principal function is to create the experience in the first place. With some combination of insight, skill, and input from the group, the best facilitators can create experiences so analogous to real-life situations that the key points are bound to emerge from within the group's discussion (Gass, 1991). But whether through actively leading a good closing discussion, or by crafting a group's activities so carefully in the first place that the group will naturally process them well, the role of the leader in helping students make connections is essential.

Finally, a fundamental role of the teacher is to be intentional—to have an objective and then to teach toward it. Ropes courses, new games, and tent-camping are just tools, like lectures and textbooks; they do not themselves represent the goal. I like to compare the teaching process to setting a trap. The ultimate goal is to create a situation from which "springs" some revelation—some meaningful insight—for the students. A thoughtful, intentional approach allows the teacher to recognize and develop many seemingly unrelated elements of a course or experience.

For me, the art of teaching has much to do with the ability to develop many disparate pieces of experience—to bring them into place while resisting the temptation to make the points for students. Only when many elements are put together can the trap be sprung. Then all the pieces suddenly fall into place and students have important insights—they suddenly "get it." The teacher must understand the point of activities in these terms in order to set a good trap and must intentionally teach toward that climactic moment.

"Are there particular arenas in which experiential techniques are especially effective?" Though my own schooling suggested otherwise, my adult life has shown that there are many right ways to do most things. Solutions to problems are right if they work. Of course, they are better if they are more efficient or more elegant or otherwise more satisfactory, but there are multiple ways to be right. I believe this principle should lie at the heart of experiential education.

In terms of achieving particular outcomes, I think experiential techniques are especially effective when trying to address community issues. For example, mainstream schooling offers plenty of practice in competition, and until recently, the more cooperative approaches have been largely ignored. If I want to encourage an understanding of the power of cooperation, I must have my students do more than discuss it. They must experience it—feel it. For many of my students, the experience of what real community feels like has been more important than their experience of adventure or personal accomplishment.

An example comes to mind. A ninth-grade boy was struggling with muscular dystrophy, yet wanted very much to join his peers on the five-day backpacking trip that serves as our upper school's orientation program. He did so, but walked with such an unusual gait that the leader asked him quite often if she could check his feet for blisters. The extra attention embarrassed him, but a peer suggested that every time this student took off his shoes and socks to check, they all should do the same. It was an important moment. I imagine that for this student, his personal accomplishment reigns supreme. But for another in the group, that spontaneous act of understanding and compassion represented the most significant event of the trip.

"So ... what is experiential education?" It is an approach that has students actively engaged in exploring questions they find relevant and meaningful, and has them trusting that feeling, as well as thinking, can lead to knowledge. Teachers are cast as coaches and are largely removed from their roles as interpreters of reality, purveyors of truth, mediators between students and the world. They are asked to believe that students can draw valid and meaningful conclusions from their own experiences. Learning in this way ultimately proves more meaningful than just relying on other people's conclusions about others' lives.

Asking the Question
Pam McPhee

Of all things that might be true about experiential education, the one thing that is unassailably true is that you can't find out by defining it.

—John Huie

Having started with this disclaimer, let me follow with descriptive events, experiences that eventually led me on a personal quest: "What is experiential education and what is the use of defining it anyway?"

I have often wondered, How could I spend an average of five hours a day for 180 days in front of the same teacher and not remember who he or she was? So maybe elementary school was a while ago. How about the fact that the average college course and minimum studying time consist of 126 hours and I cannot even list the courses I had in college. Contrast this with the fact that I can remember many of the different influences that the Greeks and Romans had on modern day architecture—thanks to a trip with Janny Campbell to New York City to photograph the buildings (two trips to be exact, because we forgot to put film in the camera the first time). Or that in fourth grade, I understood what propaganda was by bringing in empty cereal boxes from the breakfast table. Now don't get me wrong, I do not want to equate memory with learning. However, I do want to stress the impact of "direct first-hand learning opportunities" (Dewey, 1938).

If you have not read *Experience and Education* by John Dewey (1938), do it. It won't give you many answers, but it sure will start you thinking about what constitutes an "educational" experience. And that is the point. If we do not ask ourselves the question, "What is experiential education?," we are in peril of being "technicians implementing techniques rather than educators who teach through the understanding of their trade" (Peters, 1970). The definition is not the answer; rather, it is the asking of the question that encourages learning. It is important to see knowledge not only in a consumptive manner (i.e., "If I learn this, how will it help me get the things I want,") but also in terms of the intrinsic appreciation of knowing.

> And we know that of all the issues in education, the issue of relevance is the phoniest.
> If life were as predictable and small as the talkers of politics would have it, then the rel-
> evance would be a consideration. But life is large and surprising and mysterious, and
> we don't know what we need to know.... A student should know that he [*sic*] needs to
> learn everything he can, and he should suppose he needs to know more than he can
> learn. (Wendall Berry)

The risk of defining experiential education is that once done, the definition is available for those to regurgitate it at will—a written sentence copied and lost between the yellowing pages of one's notebook. The value is the asking of the question, the ever-elusive attempt to understand, not solely to be better learners and educators, but for the excellence that is intrinsic to it.

Experiental Education As Emotionally Engaged Learning
Bill Proudman

I believe that experiential education, as promoted by the Association for Experiential Education (AEE), is at an exciting crossroads. We must choose between refining our craft as a unique teaching and learning *process* that is applicable in many learning environments, and defining experiential education as simply a set of activities (usually active and taking place outdoors). My purpose in this essay is to argue for the process-oriented path. It is time to shift our educational paradigm to be more inclusive of multiple cultures and perspectives. One place to start is in examining what experiential education is not.

Experiential education is not simply "learning by doing." Living could be described as learning by doing. Often, this is not education, but simply a routine, prescribed pattern of social conditioning that teaches us to stay in predetermined boxes for fear of being labeled as outside of the norm.

I have grown tired of listening to professionals describe their "experiential stuff" in terms of what their students are doing, which usually means doing something outdoors with an emphasis on physical, adventurous activity. Experiential education is not simply a matter of replacing flag football in the physical education curriculum with a ropes course. The introduction of a tool such as a ropes course does not guarantee that the learning will be experiential. I have seen good educators make flag football more "experiential" than a ropes course.

Good experiential learning combines direct experience that is meaningful to the student with guided reflection and analysis. It is a challenging, active, student-centered process that impels students toward opportunities for taking initiative, responsibility, and decision making. An experiential approach allows numerous opportunities for the student to connect the head with the body, heart, spirit, and soul. Whatever the activity, it is the learning and teaching *process* that defines whether a learning experience is experiential. Further, an experiential learning process can be conducted almost anywhere and with any type of activity or learning medium.

Experiential education engages the learner emotionally. Students are so immersed in the learning that they are often uninterested in separating themselves from the learning experience. It is real and they are a part of it. Rather than describing experiential learning as "hands-on" learning (an insensitive and offensive term connoting that one must have hands to learn experientially), maybe we should think of experiential education as emotionally engaged learning.

Experiential Education as a Set of Relationships

The experiential process can best be described as a series of critical relationships: the learner to self, the learner to teacher, and the learner to the learning environment. All three relationships are important and are present to varying degrees during the learning experience. These relationships are two-way and highly dynamic.

Learner to Self: This relationship involves the learner making sense out of the experience. The learner controls this outcome and is ultimately responsible for the learning and growth that takes place. The learner processes new experiences, information, and values within a personal and holistic framework. The opportunity for guided and structured reflection is a valuable element of the experiential learning process. Examples of this learner-to-self relationship in action include activities such as structured journaling and small-group processing that specifically ask the student to engage in self-reflection and introspection.

Learner to Teacher: This relationship is a crucial one, both because of the learner-teacher interaction and because the teacher is responsible for designing and creating the parameters within which the learners will interact with their learning environment. The teacher's role is to define the boundaries to ensure a safe learning environment (physically, emotionally, intellectually) within which a student can become totally immersed. The teacher's role is to provide opportunities for students to make sense of their experiences and to fit them into their ever-changing views of self and the world. It is an atmosphere where mistakes are expected as part of the learning process.

As Keith King (a former AEE Practitioner of the Year) has often said, "Teachers are responsible to, rather than for, their students." The teacher's primary role is that of problem poser, mediator, and coach.

For example, I once designed and led a student-planned, eighth-grade class trip where the students worked with one another throughout the course of the school year to decide where the five-day trip would go and what it would involve. I first articulated a series of planning guidelines, consisting of elements such as mandatory activity components (e.g., need to incorporate service, physical adventure); budget guidelines; and a planning schedule outlining steps and issues to be decided. Over the school year, small subcommittees worked on and reported back to the class about the trip. The class worked within this framework of guidelines and were accountable for the various deadlines prescribed within the planning outline. The planning process itself became as meaningful and significant a learning experience as the trip. Once the trip guidelines were articulated to the students, I simply acted as a mediator and coach.

Learner to Learning Environment: The learning environment is a broad concept that includes the content material being covered, the people and their relationships directly and indirectly involved with the learner, and the surrounding physical environment. Each context looks very different depending on who the learner is. This relationship involves multiple layers, all interacting in differing ways and intensities with the learner. It is obvious that different learners have different learning experiences. Take, for instance, the varying reactions students have to the same learning environment.

During a recent urban exploration, a group of Euro-American adult students, who were doing a neighborhood investigation in a predominantly African-American section of the city, were invited into a church where they experienced a cultural celebration that was different from their own. The students reacted differently to the environment, partly as a result of their own social conditioning and their perceived stereotypes previously developed about that culture. It led to interesting follow-up discussions amongst the students that allowed their differing perceptions to requestion their cultural stereotypes and attitudes, and resulted in powerful discussions on American racism.

Too often teachers are so focused on the activity (and their own learning experiences as a student in that activity) that they blindly assume their students will have similar experiences. Besides being myopic, it also is a culturally biased perspective that negates other cultural and personal interpretations. As experiential educators involved with process, we need to be ever aware of how our own cultural conditioning colors our interpretations of others' learning experiences.

Experiential Education as Methodology

Simple participation in a prescribed set of learning experiences does not make something experiential. The experiential methodology is not linear, cyclical, or even patterned. It is a series of working principles, all of which are equally important and must be present to varying degrees at some time during experiential learning. These principles are required no matter what activity the student is engaged in or where learning takes place.

1. *Mixture of Content and Process*: Often, experiential educators are considered to be too process-oriented at the expense of content and/or theory. We need a conscious mixing of content and process. Theory is the critical glue that holds powerful learning experiences together. Edward Demming, the management guru who transformed Japanese corporations, once said that experience was meaningless without theory.

2. *Absence of Excessive Teacher Judgment:* If the teacher truly believes in the experiential process, the teacher will create the safe working boundaries for students and then get out of the way. Responsibility cannot be nurtured in the learner if the teacher creates or expects the learner to learn for the teacher's (or someone else's) sake. While this does not mean that students get whatever they want, I am advocating that within the teacher-defined boundaries, students should have full run of the premises.

   Each person is a product of his or her cultural environment. Each person is conditioned over time to react in certain ways to given situations. It is critical that teachers recognize the effects of their conditioning in order to allow students to have their own experiences minus teacher judgment.

   As an example, I have experienced teachers excitedly telling students exactly where to place their hands and feet while on a climbing wall, under the guise of helping the student succeed and "get to the top." But this approach raises several critical questions: Whose experience is it? Whose definition of success is being used? What is the goal of the activity for the student? How invested is the teacher in guaranteeing a certain student outcome? Too often, teachers allow their unconscious conditioning to interfere with opportunities for student self-discovery.

3. *Engaged in Purposeful Endeavors:* There needs to be meaning for the student in the learning. It needs to be personally relevant. The teacher works in the program design phase to identify opportunities for students to find meaningful interpretations of their experiences. This can be a daunting task for the educator, as this means highly personalized instruction. However, the necessary paradigm shift here is to recognize the learner as a self-teacher, or to view a group of learners as providing mentoring and coaching for each other.

A workshop on valuing cultural diversity provides an example of engaging in purposeful endeavors. In this instance, the students are given early opportunities to engage in one-to-one talking/listening dyads as a means to articulate their own personal goals after the workshop parameters are identified (the facilitators' assumptions about the workshop content, the group operating agreements, and the workshop goals). The dyad process gives students an opportunity to assess what they wish to get from the experience in their own terms without critical feedback from the teacher or another student. Dyads give students the opportunity to be listened to rather than to be questioned or evaluated by others.

4. *Encouraging the Big-Picture Perspective:* Experiential methodology provides opportunities for the students to see and feel their relationships with the broader world. It opens doors to limitless relationships and develops in the students an appreciation, understanding, and involvement with ideas, other people, and environments that can be both similar and different from the students' own experiences. Students need opportunities to better understand and interact with complex systems and environments in order to understand firsthand the interconnectedness of all things and their place in the web.

For example, I recently worked with a group of educators and wanted to have them experience firsthand the ways in which persons who are members of underrepresented segments of American society have to conform silently to the norms of the groups who have received preferential treatment from being on the upside of the power chart. Two volunteers were blindfolded for the duration of a problem-solving activity. The well-intentioned group generally ignored the two and simply "packaged" them for the purposes of completing the problem at hand. The two blindfolded members were not involved with planning, weren't asked to volunteer their ideas and opinions, and, in the words of one of the sightless group members, were made to feel "stupid and worthless."

Following the experience, group members shared their feelings and perceptions. Light bulbs came on for many. The processing resulted in a powerful discussion about the obvious and subtle forms of institutional and internalized oppression around issues of gender, physical ability, sexual orientation, age, ethnicity, and class. It was a transformational moment for many in the group and acted as an invitation for the group to explore many of the personal ramifications of oppression.

5. *Teaching With Multiple Learning Styles:* David Kolb's experiential learning model is a good touchstone here (Kolb, 1976). Experiential learning is not simply the active, doing part. Rather, Kolb's model describes a learning cycle that emphasizes that for a person to learn experientially, a teaching routine must include a cycle of all four

learning styles: concrete experience, reflective observation, abstract conceptualization, and active experimentation.

It makes sense that if experiential education professes to address the whole person, then it should teach in a routine that touches all four learning styles. Again, the implication is that experiential learning is not simply a process of adventurous physical activity with some discussion thrown in at the end.

6. *The Role of Reflection:* Piling one experience on top of a previous experience is really no different than the worst childhood nightmares of rote learning in school. The need to mix experience with associated content and guided reflection is critical. The dissonance created in this mixing allows the learner opportunities to bring the theory to life and gain valuable insights about one's self and one's interactions with the world at large.

7. *Creating Emotional Investment:* This element provides one of the major differences that I see between other forms of significant learning and what experiential educators often facilitate. I believe that any experiential learning model that does not recognize the importance of emotional investment diminishes its potential effectiveness for the learner in the long run. The process needs to engage the learner to a point where what is being learned and experienced strikes a critical, central chord within the learner. Learners' motivations to continue are no longer based on what they have to do because someone or something else tells them they must. Rather, they are fully immersed and engaged in *their* learning experience.

The teacher's challenge is to create a physically and emotionally safe environment (in the eyes of the students) so as to encourage emotional investment. There must not be teacher judgment or a dismissal of the learner's feelings. It means creating an environment where people are fully valued and appreciated.

In working with groups, I make a regular practice to verbally remind students that they are in control of deciding how or even if they wish to be involved with the learning experiences. Giving students true power to make meaningful, self-determined choices within a teaching/learning context is extremely important to validating each student as a competent, capable member of a group, and developing a climate of mutual trust, respect, and regard for each person.

Often, as a facilitator, I have to introduce and model this concept in a number of ways because individuals' conditioning and experiences have negated their own inner voices. The net effect is that the atmosphere of trust and acceptance allows students the space to determine their own level of emotional investment.

8. *The Re-Examination of Values:* When students feel valued and fully appreciated, there is a greater likelihood that they will re-examine and explore their own values.

The creation of a safe environment for students is initiated by the teacher through clearly defined educational parameters (group working agreements, activity learning goals, a big-picture design plan, etc.) Creating opportunities for personal transformational growth is a hallmark of meaningful experiential education.

9. *The Presence of Meaningful Relationships:* Learning is not an abstract process. It is fully embraced when it is experienced as a series of relationships: learner to self, learner to teacher, and learner to learning environment. Learning that takes place without reference to relationships is not experiential as it does not allow learners an opportunity to see how they fit into the bigger picture.

10. *Learning Outside of One's Perceived Comfort Zone:* A learner often needs to be challenged in order to be stretched by a new experience. While experiential learning need not start from a place of discomfort, learning is enhanced when students are given the opportunity to operate outside of their own perceived comfort zones. By comfort zone, I am referring not only to the physical environment but also to the social environment (i.e., being accountable for one's actions and owning the consequences).

In Summary

Experiential education is transformational. A well-conceived and well-led experiential learning endeavor does not just happen to the student. Meaningful education is not something that can be easily packaged. While society tempts many educators to market a cookbook approach, I believe that experiential educators, like all good educators, are artists using a palette of tools and abilities that are ever expanding and changing. As artists, it is dangerous to become complacent about how we define and perform our work.

Experiential educators need to continue to grapple with the questions of just what is experiential education and, similarly, what is good teaching. Let's continue to push the edges of our emerging profession. Let's also recognize that if we truly subscribe to the idea of lifelong learning, then our understanding and definition of experiential education will also change and expand.

I am reminded of the simple phrase, "The best way to learn something is to teach it." Here's to all of our students who have given us, as teachers, the gift of continued learning. May our journeys continue to be enriched.

References

Dewey, J. (1938). *Experience and education.* New York: Macmillan.

Gass, M. A. (1991). Enhancing metaphor development in adventure therapy programs. *Journal of Experiential Education,* 14(2),6–13.

Kjol, R., & Weber, J. (1990). The 4th Fire: Adventure based counseling with juvenile sex offenders. *Journal of Experiential Education,* 13(3), 18–22.

Kolb, D. A. (1976). Management and the learning process. *California Management Review,* Spring.

Peters, R. S. (1970). *Education and the educated man.* London: Society of Philosophy on Education.

On Defining
Experiential Education

▾ ▾ ▾

Laura Joplin

The premise of this paper is that all learning is experiential.This means that anytime a person learns, he must "experience" the subject—significantly identify with, seriously interact with, form a personal relationship with, etc. Many educational settings only partially promote learning. Those aspects that yield learning can be defined by an experiential model, whether intended or not. Much that is done under the guise of education does not involve learning. Likewise, though all learning is experiential, not all of it is deliberately planned or takes place through an educational institution or setting. This paper is designed to define or identify those aspects of education that are experiential (i.e., those portions of experiential learning which are deliberately planned). This paper includes two approaches to defining experiential education:

1. A five-stage model generalized from reviewing the processes and components of those programs calling themselves experiential;
2. A review of eight characteristics developed by comparing experiential and nonexperiential programs and describing the implicit and explicit assumptions in the experiential programs.

The Five-Stage Model

Beyond particular agency and client-related tasks, experiential programs begin with two responsibilities for their program design: providing an experience for the learner and

This chapter originally was published in the *Journal of Experiential Education*, with the following citation: Joplin, L. (1981). On defining experiential education. *Journal of Experiential Education, 4*(1), 17–20.

facilitating the reflection on that experience. Experience alone is insufficient to be called experiential education, and it is the reflection process that turns experience into experiential education. The process is often called an "action-reflection" cycle. The process is generally referred to as cycle, ongoing and ever-building, with the later stages being dependent on the earlier stages. Most program descriptions and experiential educators hold these statements as "givens" in defining experiential education.

The five-stage model was developed to communicate an experiential action strategy to teachers as they planned their courses. The intent was to enable teachers to more deliberately design their courses and thus increase the experiential nature of those designs.

Briefly stated, the five-stage model is organized around a central, hurricane-like cycle, which is illustrated as challenging action. It is preceded by a focus and followed by a debrief. Encompassing all is the environment of support and feedback. The five stages are one complete cycle, where completion of the fifth stage is concurrent with commencing the first stage of the following cycle.

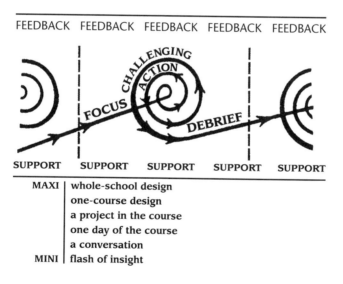

MAXI	whole-school design
	one-course design
	a project in the course
	one day of the course
	a conversation
MINI	flash of insight

The model is both "maxi" and "mini" in scope. A one-semester course could be viewed through the five stages of the model, and also have the limitless repetitions within the whole course. Following the initial premise that all learning is experiential, every time a person "learns," these five stages are involved in one way or another. Thus, interpretation of each of the stages for anyone situation is very dependent upon the degree of or "mini" that is under study. A flash of insight would be describable in these terms. The initial purpose of the model, however, is to enable teachers to design courses and course components. Thus, the model is intentionally simple. For purposes of defining learning, the model is far from appropriate and should not be scrutinized for its relation to learning theory. Rather, the model should be viewed so that regardless of what mental processes and brain functions may be involved, these five stages remain the responsibility of the facilitator of learning.

Focus is the first stage of the cycle. Focus includes presenting the task and isolating the attention of the learner for concentration. It defines the subject of study and prepares the student for encountering the challenging action that is to follow. A good focusing stage is specific enough to orient the student, but not too specific so as to rule out unplanned learning. Most experiential programs expect and intend students to learn things that their fellow learners did not learn: It is the nature of individualized education. Focus facilitates that by helping the learner prepare for what s/he views as important. Focus also works to tell the student what the course and/or teacher holds as important and thus explains the expectations placed on him.

The actions in the focus stage are dependent upon the activity to follow as well as the activity rating on the "maxi-mini" scale. Focus actions may include meeting as a group and having each member his expectations, desires, or needs. It may also include having students use learning contracts. Reading an article relevant to the ensuing action is focusing, as well as the teacher's explanation for the next class activity. Focus can also be indirect, such as when a rock-climbing instructor opens a packsack and begins laying out an array of climbing paraphernalia.

Action is the hurricane stage of the model. This stage places the learner in a stressful or jeopardy-like situation where s/he is unable to avoid the problem presented, often in an unfamiliar environment requiring new skills or the use of new knowledge. Action may be physical, mental, emotional, spiritual, or of any other dimension. Action involves the student with the subject, occupying much of his attention and energy in sorting, ordering, analyzing, moving, struggling, emoting, embracing, etc. The action phase gives the learner great responsibility.

Different actions—such as wilderness experiences, environmental education, and internship programs—have often become confused or synonymous with experiential education. The design of the action component should not be confused with the educational approach being used. All of these, and many more, can be characterized by the same model or philosophy. Recent work in brain research promises the most complete description of action as it relates to the brain's operations. Leslie A. Hart, in *How the Brain Works,* has explained that the brain is innately active. The brain is "on" when it is actively choosing, ordering, making decisions, etc. The brain is not "on" when someone is attempting to pour information into it. Therefore, to design an action component for experiential programs, it is mandatory that the student and his/her brain be given responsibility in the learning process.

Reading a book is a challenging action for an experiential program, *if* it gets the student responsible for processing the information within it. The student can be given such responsibilities as choosing the book to read on a teacher-assigned topic; defining the reason for reading the book; searching for an answer to a problem in a book; using the book as a reference; or defending a personally held value position.

Another cross-reference for defining action is the use of "original sources." Watching a film of someone rock climbing is far different from climbing the rock oneself. Similarly, reading about business administration is much different from interning in a business office. A history class studying the United Nations might take the dramatic field trip and visit that august facility in New York. However, original sources for studying the United Nations could also be interviewing people about its current activities or reading newspaper clippings during a time of great debate on it. Textbooks are a supposedly efficient means of giving information to students, however textbooks innately deny much responsibility to the student. The textbook author decides which source s/he will cite, what the correct references are, and the important points of the topic. All of this denies the student and his/her brain the opportunity and necessity of deciding, sorting, or actively pursuing information.

The overarching strategy that helps implement these ideas of original sources and a brain that is "on" is student responsibility. A student climbing a rock is allowed to succeed and fail on his own; indeed, he must do it on his own. In a classroom, a student must be given the freedom to fail. A teacher who leads the student through an has not given the student the responsibility for that action phase. Increasing student responsibility does not mean leaving a student to struggle with a problem that is beyond his capacity or background preparation. The problem must be appropriate to the learner, and it is the teacher's responsibility to design it accordingly.

Using a student-responsibility schema requires great faith in the learner. Students often express great anger and resentment when first introduced into a responsibility-oriented experiential situation. Tricks to get teachers to assume their overly helpful habits will be tried by many students: students will often exclaim that they are unable to solve the problem. The teacher's only assurance in this situation is his own experience and faith that the student can master the task. The teacher needs to gain faith in the students as more capable than many educational situations accept. The stages of support and feedback in the model mediate the student's anxiety and the teacher's responses.

Support and feedback exist throughout the learning experience, maxi and mini. Adequate support enables the student to continue to try. Adequate feedback will ensure that the student has the necessary information to be able to move ahead.

Support provides security and caring in a manner that stimulates the learner to challenge himself and to experiment. Support demonstrates that the learner is not working alone but has human responsiveness that accepts personal risk taking. Support is implemented in many subtle and obvious ways. Support is demonstrating interest in the learner's situation and letting him know that help is available if needed. Having the group share individual frustrations will help each member see that his/her feelings are not unique. Support can be physical, verbal, or written.

Feedback provides information to the student about what he has been doing. It can include comments about how the student works, his manner of interactions, or the substance of his work. Feedback works best with an equalization of power between learner and facilitator. The teacher should distinguish between those ideas that the teacher holds as true, and those ideas that the teacher believes most professionals in the field hold as true. The areas given to student discretion should be made clear. Feedback is also more easily understood the more specific it is. Specific examples help clarify the meaning, especially those coming from mutually experienced activities.

The fifth stage in the model is *debrief.* Here, the learning is recognized, articulated, and evaluated. The teacher is responsible for seeing that the actions previously taken do not drift along unquestioned, unrealized, unintegrated, or unorganized. Debrief helps the student learn from experience. Debrief is a sorting and ordering of information, often involving personal perceptions and beliefs. In experiential learning—as opposed to experiential education—debrief may occur within the individual. However, in experiential education, debrief needs to be made public. It can be made public through group discussion, writing of themes or summary papers, sharing of personal journals, doing a class project, or a class presentation. It is the publicly verifiable articulation that makes experience and experiential learning capable of inclusion and acceptance by the educational institutions. The public nature of debrief also ensures that the learner's conclusions are verified and mirrored against a greater body of perception than his alone. The process of reflecting on the past often includes decisions about what needs to be done next or how it should have been done initially. The public nature of debrief helps turn these comments into focusing agents for the next five-stage cycle.

This five-stage model presents the general actions and responsibilities that a teacher maintains through experiential education. The nature of the actions chosen by a teacher at each stage of the model can be further clarified by looking at the overarching characteristics on experiential programs. The descriptors to be presented have one unifying parameter: They are based on an "involved" paradigm.

Experiential education is based on the assumption that all knowing must begin with the individual's relationship to the topic. The involved paradigm explains that everything is connected to everything else. Therefore, to learn, we must investigate those relations. Among other things, this necessitates including personal perceptions and values. The process of learning may involve being as objective as possible in any given situation. However, the innate subjectivity that characterizes all knowing must be recognized and accounted for in our learning systems. Following are eight characteristics that further clarify how this involved paradigm is characterized in educational settings.

Eight Characteristics

- *Student based rather than teacher based.* Learning starts with the student's perceptions and current awareness. Much of typical course design attempts to start with an orderly format based on the teacher's ideas or the ideas of the textbook author or the school board. These starting points and the content organization may or may not be relevant to the learner. Experiential education starts with the student and goes at his pace of learning. It does necessitate some latitude given for including unplanned topics and not including all that might otherwise be covered. Though less teacher-decided material may be covered, more material may be learned because of the student-oriented process.

- *Personal, not impersonal, nature.* The learner as a feeling, valuing, perceiving being is stressed. Experiential education starts with the individual's relationship to the subject of study. How a student feels about a subject is valued along with the student's prowess or factual recall. The relationship of educational experiences to personal growth is allowed to be incorporated into the classroom. There are degrees of psychological change that are not appropriate to the classroom. However, the ordinary maturing process of a person often accompanies and affects increasing knowledge. Thus, the person who is learning is as important as the subject that is being studied.

- *Process and product orientation.* Experiential education stresses how a student arrives at an answer as well as how that answer may be. The product of the study is valued within the context of the thought and work processes behind it. This is especially important in the evaluation process. Student evaluation is commonly a "products only" evaluation. Experiential educators also need to assess a student's ideas developing processes, and work strategies. These are readily monitored by student journals. The process of idea investigation can be viewed by looking at the reasons a student chose a book, why it was finished instead of being put aside, and how the ideas within it relate to his/her problem of study.

- *Evaluation for internal and external reasons.* Much of educational evaluation is done for agents external to the student's learning experience, such as parents, school boards, entrance to other educational programs, etc. Evaluation in experiential education also includes evaluation as a learning experience. Evaluation is not something that is only "done to" the student. Students can be encouraged to develop self-evaluation skills and take part in the monitoring of their learning. Competence in evaluation skills is done for agents external to the student's learning experience, such as parents, school boards, entrance to other educational programs, etc. Evaluation in experiential education also includes evaluation as a learning experience. Evaluation is not something that is only "done to" the student. Students can be encouraged to develop self-evaluation skills and take part in the monitoring of their learning. Competence in evaluation skills can help a student become more of an independent, self-directed learner. Students participating in their own evaluation increase their responsibility.

- *Holistic understanding and component analysis.* Experiential education includes both the explanation of phenomena through statistical equations and describing the variety and depth of the qualities of the subject. Narrative descriptions, interviews, personal reports, inventories, questionnaires, or group discussions can provide information. Representing the complexity of situations is stressed over the simple summation.

- *Organized around experience.* Direct experience provides the substance from which learners develop personal meaning. Since the learning starts with the learner's experience, the subject organization must start there also. A problem or thematic approach can provide a strong organization for experiential education. Rather than building from the simple to the complex, experiential situations start with a complex experience and analyze it as the follow-up study. Enlisting student participation in choosing from a set of topics to be covered, as well as the order of study, helps the teacher organize the course around the student's experience.

- *Perception based rather than theory based.* Experiential learning emphasizes a student's ability to justify or explain a subject, rather than to recite an expert's testimony. His ability to articulate and argue his position in the light of conflicting theories, facts, and firsthand encounters will be the test and learning medium. Expert testimony is one source for investigating an idea. Experiential education stresses knowing the subject from the ground up, starting with the student's perception and moving to the expert testimony as verifier of views.

- *Individual based rather than group based.* Experiential education stresses the individual's development in a self-referenced fashion. Group comparisons or norm ratings are useful as supplemental information. Norm-referenced grading can be a part of experiential education, especially for target audiences such as school systems and college entrance boards. However, the emphasis and goal within experiential education is toward monitoring the individual's growth and the development of self-awareness. Group identity and socialization skills are often involved in experiential programs. The emphasis is, however, on the individual's relationship and role within the group, and that person's awareness of group functioning and his/her part in it.

These eight characteristics and the five-stage model taken together can provide the stimulus and home base for a teacher's course-design endeavors. They are intrinsically individually based, for teachers as well as learners. How a teacher implements the ideas will depend on that person's characteristics, perceptions, and goals. The model necessitates that the teacher be a learner along with the student. The model demands continual responsiveness that can only work when the teacher is an active perceiver and learner in the situation. Deliberate exploration of these ideas can help a teacher know him/herself, his goals for his/her students, and his/her ability to implement the type of experiential program that s/he desires.

Learning at the Edge: Can Experiential Education Contribute to Educational Reform?

▾ ▾ ▾

Anne Lindsay & Alan Ewert

Stuart and Linda are high school teachers, and they have a problem. For a number of years, they have been offering experiential education activities within their classes. They have had little success in convincing other teachers to incorporate these activities into other classrooms. Why can't the teachers see the value in experiential education activities and incorporate them into parts of the curriculum? Why is it that "mainstream" teachers seem so tied to conventional teaching styles and unwilling to try something different? After all, don't we all have the same goal—that of providing students with high-quality and relevant learning opportunities?

Introduction

Despite an increasing body of literature that is generally supportive of the efficacy of experiential approaches to learning, the idea has never been fully embraced by mainstream educational organizations. This paper explores the reasons for this lack of acceptance by comparing and contrasting experiential education (EE) and mainstream education (MS). The discussion reviews contemporary literature in the fields of EE and MS and is supplemented by the professional experiences of the authors. As such, the perspective underlying this paper is a general one and may not fully represent all the educational opportunities present in both fields.

The foundation for the discussion of EE is largely taken from an outdoor experiential

This chapter originally was published in the *Journal of Experiential Education*, with the following citation:

Lindsay, A., and Ewert, A. (1999). Learning at the edge: Can experiential education contribute to educational reform? *Journal of Experiential Education, 22*(1), 12–19 perspective. The discussion of MS focuses on the public school systems in the United States and Canada. The purpose of this paper is to explore and describe the relationship between the two fields and discuss implications for the future of this relationship. For example, the discussion considers the current trend toward adapting EE activities such as ropes courses into schools and corporate settings, and questions whether society would be better served by EE being further incorporated into MS or whether it should remain an educational approach that is relatively distinct and separate from MS.

Finally, we acknowledge that no single characterization of any educational tradition fully reflects the complexity that an educational system assumes in practice. Thus, while we present mainstream and experiential education in generalized terms, it is recognized that much variation exists. As such, numerous exceptions to the examples presented can be found.

Foundations of Experiential and Mainstream Education

Experiential Education. According to Knapp (1994), the foundations of EE date back to the beginning of the century and share a common philosophical base with both outdoor education and the progressive education movement that originated with Dewey. This philosophical heritage established the focus on the learner as the center of learning and the value and validity of individual experience. From an EE perspective, this emphasis on individual experience was further refined and developed by Kurt Hahn and resulted in the development of Outward Bound and similar educational institutions (Smith, Roland, Havens, & Hoyt, 1992).

Today EE is frequently characterized as a practice-oriented process. Crosby (1995) argues that experiential educators function within a structure of beliefs and assumptions that are essentially philosophical in nature. Joplin (1995) furthers this characterization of EE by identifying a number of unique qualities. These qualities include the following: (a) patterns of learning are holistic rather than reductionistic; (b) learning is based on direct experience rather than abstractions; (c) learning starts where the learner is rather than where the teacher wants to be; (d) how something is learned (process) is viewed as equally important as what is learned (product); and (e) learning often takes place outside the classroom and in an outdoor environment. Carver (1996) identifies similar characteristics and points to essential values underpinning EE. These include compassion, communication, individuality, and responsibility.

Taken together, these characteristics illustrate the underlying commitment to the legitimacy of *personal and individual growth* that is central to the philosophy of EE. That is, activities and approaches that typify the EE approach are usually not the ends but rather the means to achieving personal growth and development.

Mainstream Education. The original intent of the American and Canadian public school systems was that all citizens should receive a basic education in order to become better individuals and better members of society. The decision whether to seek an education, and in what form, eventually moved outside the purview of the family or the Church and into that of the state or province. Not surprisingly, the early curriculum of the public schools consisted of the skills necessary to serve the economic and political needs of a new nation, namely literacy and numeracy. It also included a strong emphasis on building character and moral virtue (Jennings, 1997).

Certainly the American public school system has changed from these early beginnings, but at least in one way it continues to reflect them, namely the pervasive similarities of schools across the 50 states and, to a lesser extent, the Canadian provinces (Goodlad, 1984; Longstreet & Shane, 1993; Metz, 1998). *Conformity to shared common values* was the vision of the early school promoters—a commitment that has lasted to this day (Tyack & Hansot, 1982).

Clearly, EE and MS have distinctively different foundations. The question remains as to how these two educational traditions compare today. The following section takes a comparative look at contemporary practices in experiential and mainstream education.

Comparing and Contrasting Experiential and Mainstream Education

To compare these two educational traditions, this paper follows the approach used by Lempert (1996). This work compared what he termed "democratic experiential education" with traditional university education by describing particular features of the educational process for both models. In our case, we chose to examine seven elements common to most, if not all, models of education. These elements are goals, the concept of knowledge, the grouping of students, the organization of communication, the organization of the topic, resources, and evaluation strategies. A summary of this comparison is provided in Table 1.

Educational Goals. Discussions of the purposes of MS have typically identified four major goals (Lindsay, 1998). These are: (a) academic-related goals such as reading skills; (b) civic, social, and moral development, such as citizenship training; (c) vocational preparation; and (d) individual development. Although similar goals are recognized in EE, individual development and growth often receive particular attention. This focus on individual growth and development is often accomplished through the enhancement of personal dignity, individual and group problem-solving skills, increased trust between students, self-awareness, team-building, and learning to work cooperatively in a group setting (Smith, Roland, Havens, & Hoyt, 1992). Additional goals for many EE programs are the development of specific physical skills and decision-making abilities. Moreover, the setting of goals by students themselves is also considered a valuable aim of EE. Although the goals of EE typically focus on the development of the individual, implicit in this focus is the broader vision of individuals learning to contribute to the larger community and society.

Table 1.
Comparisons of Mainstream Education and Experiential Education on Seven Parameters

PARAMETER	Experiential Education	Mainstream Education
GOALS	Legitimacy of personal and individual growth: Individual development contributes to the larger community and society	Conformity to shared common values, deterministic: To teach students about societal activity rather than ways of living this activity
CONCEPTS OF KNOWLEDGE	Knowledge does not represent a single view of reality; holistic with the deliberate inclusion of all domains (physical, emotional, cognitive, etc.) into learning	Separation of the physical, social, aesthetic, and affective components from the intellectual part of learning
TEACHING STRATEGIES (Grouping of Students)	Usually small group environments using shared group experiences as a teaching foundation; learning outcomes are often student-directed rather than teacher-directed	Usually large single groups; Student functioning is often independent of other students; students usually only responsible to the teacher and their own work
TEACHING STRATEGIES (Organization of Communication)	Self-organized and task-dependent; Teacher acts as both facilitator and instructor; intra-group communication deemed critical to success	IRE Pattern (initiate, respond, evaluate): directed to and from teacher by the teacher
TEACHING STRATEGIES (Organization of Topic)	Constructivist approach; transfer of knowledge to other areas in student's life	Transmissional model of teaching; often little transfer of knowledge to areas outside the specific subject
RESOURCES	Uses settings outside of classroom; direct experiences are an important component of the learning experience	The experiences and thoughts of others; highly restricted by needs of curriculum
EVALUATION STRATEGIES	Often self-appraisal; focused on task accomplishment	By reference to criteria external to the student's own control or authority

In contrast, the goals of MS do not often directly focus on individual development as the means to social improvement. Rather MS goals emphasize the preparation of responsible citizens, improvement of social conditions, and promotion of cultural unity (Jennings, 1997). As Martin (1997) explains, the mainstream system aims to teach students *about* societal activity rather than ways of *living* that societal activity. With reference to cultural diversity, she suggests that "It is too easy for school to instruct children about it [issues related to cultural diversity] without ever teaching them to be active and constructive participants in living [cultural diversity]—let alone how to make the world a better place for themselves and their progeny" (p. 263). Jennings notes that the enhancement and enrichment of individual life is a goal of MS, but one that is often undervalued and given little attention. In summary, while the goals of both EE and MS involve educating individuals to participate in a democratic society, MS focuses on imparting *a body of common knowledge*, while EE tends to focus on creating educational opportunities for *individual growth and development.*

The Concept of Knowledge. There are a number of attributes associated with how information is presented and organized that are characteristic of EE and provide insight into the way knowledge is conceptualized in the field of experiential education (Proudman, 1995). These attributes include the following:

- There are often multiple truths and multiple-learning styles presented in EE settings with the learner's past experience and personal knowledge deemed critical to learning (Brookfield, 1996), and the learner is usually subject to individual interpretations of reality. Related to this is the framework presented by Kolb (1984), which suggests four learning approaches used in EE: concrete experiences, reflective observations, abstract conceptualizations (i.e., linkages to other components of an individual's life), and active experimentation. Knowledge is "developed" by the learner rather than presented by the teacher.

- Learning is active, both physically and mentally, and is often outside of an individual's comfort zone. In addition, the learner is encouraged to assume responsibility for the acquisition of knowledge and how it is contextualized and organized. Assuming this responsibility also promotes a heightened competency regarding learning and gaining knowledge.

- Activities and experiences, rather than cognitive manipulations, tend to be the primary venues of how knowledge is gained. As such, cognitive knowledge is seen as inextricable from social and emotional knowledge; all develop together in an interdependent process. An important component of these activities is their authenticity and relevancy. Abstract examples are deemed less useful in the EE situation.

Taken as a whole, knowledge gained through an EE setting does not assume a single view of the world, of society, or of human behavior that is inherently right or true. Moreover, knowledge is not seen as a commodity that can be automatically handed from one to another, but rather must be constructed by each individual. Furthermore, in EE, all domains of knowledge, including physical, spiritual, cognitive, emotional, and social, are seen as inextricably connected.

In contrast, the concept of knowledge central to MS is reflected in its organization and is fundamental to the life of the institution. The Greeks invented the classical view of classification in which all knowledge is organized into mutually exclusive categories with clearly defined boundaries (Gardner, 1987). In the same way that they organized the natural world, educational content was categorized into the classical curriculum of the trivium (grammar, rhetoric, logic) and the quadrivium (arithmetic, geometry, music, astronomy). Although the nature and number of these curricular subjects has evolved and changed, the legacy has remained, with the disciplinary partitioning of knowledge being the fundamental organizational structure of MS. For example, students move from lab to gym to classroom across the time blocks of the day, each representing a different subject. Moreover, not only is cognitive knowledge divided into its traditional disciplines, such as math and biology, but it is segregated from physical, social, aesthetic, and affective knowledge. Activity across these non-intellectual domains is typically restricted or even excluded from classroom exercises. Thus, at least in one sense, MS tends to reflect our long-standing Western notion of classification and segregation of the structure of knowledge.

Teaching strategies are the ways teachers or instructors organize the components of a learning event. Three types of strategies comprise the basic framework for most teaching and student learning. These strategies include the physical organization or grouping of students, the communicative organization of the learning event, and the organization of the topic of the lesson.

Organizing Students. In EE settings, the emphasis is placed on *small groups* (10 or less), dyads (pairs), or individuals. Students often are empowered to form their own groups and given responsibility for the management of that group. Moreover, EE instructors often pay a great deal of attention to the stages of group development (Ewert & Heywood, 1991). Instructors evaluate the level of development of a group through a variety of group indicators such as group/individual expectations, individual "fit" within the group, and the level of responsibility an individual assumes for the functioning of the group. Indeed, often a primary function of EE is to facilitate group development.

In the early classrooms of North American public schools, children of varying ages were all grouped together, usually in a single room. There was no fixed policy on grouping or group size. However, the move to make classrooms as efficient as factories, in what Callahan (1962) called "the cult of efficiency," introduced the organization of students by age into the public school system. Today, one of the most definitive features of the public school is its grouping of students by age into *large groups* (20–30) in which students function independently. The group is arranged to face the teacher, who is often positioned behind a desk or lectern. Students are typically seated in individual desks where they function either within an activity involving the whole group simultaneously or in independent tasks performed at their own speed (Goodlad, 1984). Small groups and dyadic activities are used, but the large group is still the major organizational device in MS. Unfortunately, Goodlad's (1984) study is now 15 years old. However, his study was remarkably comprehensive (Page, 1984) and to date has not been replicated. Furthermore, as Goodman (1995) observed, "Despite the impassioned rhetoric of school reform, the ways of educating children have remained remarkably durable."

Organizing Communication. It is axiomatic in EE that a primary role of the instructor is to facilitate students' communication with each other, rather than exclusively with the teacher. In the case of EE, communication typically occurs between students, between the student and instructor, and within the student him/herself. Within the context of this last point, the interface between the intra-communication or "self-talk" of the individual and EE often lies in the challenging and personally relevant tasks required. An individual often receives direct and immediate feedback as to his or her level of efficacy and strength of motivation to achieve a particular task. Thus, in EE, communication is often organized *for and by the task* rather than the instructor.

In MS classrooms, lines of communication usually run through the teacher, who controls who speaks, when s/he speaks, and what s/he speaks about. This pattern has been extensively researched. It is described as the *IRE pattern* consisting of the teacher initiating a response (I), the student responding (R), and the teacher evaluating (E) the response and is considered to be a representative characteristic of most classroom talk (Drew & Sorjonen, 1997).

Organization of the Topic. The organization of topic has often served to define the field of EE. That is, EE has been defined as "a process through which a learner constructs knowledge, skill, and value from direct experiences" (Wurdinger, 1996, p. 60), a definition mirrored in other work (e.g., DeLay, 1996; Priest & Gass, 1997).

Joplin (1995) suggests that EE can be thought of as a five-stage model. The stages of this model include focus, action, support, feedback, and debriefing. In this case, the focus phase serves to present the task, to define the subject, and prepare the student. The action stage involves the student with the subject in personally meaningful and important ways. Support and feedback provide the student with necessary security, as well as personally relevant information. The debriefing stage provides the learner with an ordering and synthesis of information for both the present situation and future scenarios.

Two interventions run throughout the entire activity. These are (a) providing enough support to ensure students continue to confront the challenges of the activity, and (b) providing enough feedback to help the students visualize and understand their own progress through the activity. Joplin's (1995) model shares many similarities with other descriptions of the process of teaching experientially (Carver, 1996; Durian, Owens, & Owen, 1995). The approach owes much to the work of Dewey, Lewin, and Piaget. It is generally known as a *constructivist approach* and is grounded in Dewey's placement of experience at the heart of acquiring knowledge. An important component of the approach is the explicit attention paid to the transfer of learning, or helping learners to connect the experiential learning activity to that of their everyday world (Priest & Gass, 1997).

Topic development in public school classrooms is frequently organized according to a *transmissional* model of teaching (Miller & Seller, 1990), an approach sometimes referred to as behaviorism (DeLay, 1996). This model is characterized by the prior definition of learning outcomes in the form of measurable skills and facts, the exclusion of prior learning by students, the telling of the knowledge that is the objective of the lesson by the teacher, and the use of external motivation such as grades for learning (Lauritzen & Jaeger, 1997). Goodlad's (1984) study found that a transmissional approach typified the vast majority of teaching activity in American classrooms and termed this approach "instructing in the sense of telling" (p. 229), with student responses limited to facts that address teacher-directed questions, and feedback to responses rarely being supportive, corrective, or "some other meaningful acknowledgment" (p. 229). Goodlad reported that less than one percent of teaching time was devoted to eliciting open-ended responses from students. Exceptions to the transmissional approach do exist in MS education, especially in subject areas such as vocational education, drama, and music. However, these subjects are typically seen as marginal and are often the first to be eliminated under budget constraints.

One noteworthy feature of the transmissional approach in MS is that the transfer of learning from a lesson to other contexts is often noticeably absent. As Goodlad (1984) observed, making tasks relevant to students, involving students in setting their own goals, and providing opportunities for connecting knowledge to other experiences and transferring knowledge to other contexts are part of the rhetoric but not the practice of many MS teachers.

Resources for Teaching. Essential to the EE setting is the triad of student, instructor, and setting. Of these, much of EE pedagogy focuses on the student. That is, the student is not only the object *of* learning but also the vehicle *for* learning. Thus, students and their past experiences become critical to the "meaning-making" of the learning activity. Instructors are usually viewed as facilitators of the learning experience rather than the "fountainheads of knowledge." In addition, EE often takes place *through* an outdoor or natural environmental setting rather than simply *in* the outdoor setting. Another resource extensively used in EE is the group, with the group being able to provide individuals with feedback, support systems, challenges, and learning environments whereby they can "test" different social, physical, or emotional skills. Learning in EE depends on a variety of social, as well as physical, resources requiring the integrated involvement of *knowledge across domains* and activity that is predominantly *multisensory*.

In contrast, one of the most notable symbols of North American public schools since its early days has been the spellers and readers around which learning and teaching have focused. In general, such texts have functioned to standardize and homogenize values across

American children contributing to "a minimal core of shared knowledge and values" (Bartine, 1992, p. 42). Not only is there little evidence of diversity within these materials, the methods used with them provide no room for the ideas or interests of individual children or teachers.

Goodlad's study (1984) concluded that teaching in American schools focused on the facts as found in the textbooks and not on more critical or creative skills such as drawing conclusions, applying knowledge, or creative writing. As Joplin (1995) put it, textbooks are regarded as an efficient means of communicating information to students but, in reality, deny or restrict responsibility for learning as well as opportunities for active involvement in the learning process. Goodlad argued that "[There] is a general failure to view subjects and subject matter as turf on which to experience the struggles and satisfactions of personal development" (p. 237), thus pointing to the fact that it is usually the experiences and thoughts of *others* that form the curricular content of a public school education.

A second characteristic of the resources for teaching and learning is the limited and repetitious menu of activity for students. As Goodlad's (1984) study revealed, students in public school classrooms are consistently engaged in writing, listening, or preparing for an assignment. But what passes for writing is often filling in blanks on worksheets or writing short narratives. Activities seldom involve building, drawing, performing, role playing, physical movement, hands-on activity, or making things. School activity is frequently *restricted to the cognitive domain and within a limited range of sensory experience.*

Evaluation Strategies. Evaluation in EE serves two major purposes. The first is identifying individual growth as defined by the student and includes changes in such variables as self-concept, levels of trust, and communication skills. The second is externally related outputs, such as reduction in recidivism rates or higher GPAs (e.g., student orientation programs). In either case, success in EE programs is often determined by the *fulfilment of individual student needs* as opposed to externally defined criteria for success. Moreover, evaluation in EE is also used for the development of theory, program improvement, measuring effectiveness, and marketing (Flor, 1995). It should be noted, however, that in a growing number of cases, debriefing sessions and instructor feedback to the group often take the place of a structured evaluation protocol. Thus, in many cases the question remains, "What did the student actually learn?"

Whereas evaluation in EE does not usually assume a predominant role in program delivery, evaluation in MS assumes a much higher level of importance. As Longstreet and Shane (1993) explain, "There is an impression among educators that everyone involved in education is either about to be evaluated, going through evaluation, or just finishing up an evaluation" (p. 152). In contrast to the multidimensional purpose of evaluation in EE, evaluation in MS has become primarily focused on the costs and benefits of the system to society. Two forms of evaluation have been increasingly used to perform this task. One approach uses criterion-based evaluation where objectives and the relevant standards are set by a group of experts, such as teachers and curriculum specialists, which, in turn, form the basis for the system of numerical or letter grades that typify MS student evaluation. The second involves a body of tests normed and standardized across the entire population. The notion of evaluation *by reference to criteria external to the student's own control* or authority is a long-standing approach and is a force that continues to gain strength in MS.

Conclusions

There are a number of cases of EE being incorporated into public schools (Williamson, 1995). Despite these examples, Raffan (1995) suggests that even in the realm of "practice teaching" for future school teachers, the elements of the experiential learning cycle (i.e., focus, action, feedback, support, and reflection) are seldom seen. Despite an increasing body of support for the efficacy of learning in an experiential approach, it still enjoys limited support in MS practice.

What is clear in comparing EE and MS is how these two traditions fundamentally differ in a variety of ways. MS is directed by criteria external to the learner and defined by the larger society. It is characterized by strategies that direct and measure student performance according to normative values. It depends on views, knowledge, and learning that are relatively compartmentalized. In stark contrast are some of the qualities of EE. These include the attempt to individualize, rather than normalize, student learning and evaluation. In general, EE views both knowledge and learning as fundamentally holistic, while not denying certain occasions where specific skill development is needed and appropriate.

The qualities inherent in MS are valued across broad segments of our society, and it is not our intent to downplay them. However, many calls for reform of MS have been critical of the non-humanistic values inherent in the system and have called for practices that would promote a more humanistic approach. EE, with its longstanding humanist traditions and its focus on individual growth within a broader social and civic framework, would speak directly to this segment of the current educational reform debate.

For despite much activity and apparent change, reform of MS has been slow and has often appeared as more rhetoric than reality. Cuban (1990) states that change through educational reform has often been superficial rather than fundamental. Pogrow (1996) goes so far as to describe efforts to reform MS as perennial failures. A number of scholars would argue that moving toward more humanistic approaches in MS is still a long way from reality (Apple, 1998; Fore, 1998; Goodman, 1995; Waters, 1998). Our comparison of EE and MS illustrates the marked differences between these two educational traditions and suggests one reason why EE has not found ready acceptance in MS. The history of MS reform helps further illustrate the difficulties that proponents of EE will continue to encounter in attempting to work within a MS milieu.

Where does this leave the relationship between EE and MS? First, although major inroads by EE into MS curriculum seem unlikely, Goodlad (1984) reports that there are a number of localized developments that provide exceptional results. Consequently, we would argue that partnerships between MS and EE that are present and flourishing should be supported and encouraged. However, our comparison of the two traditions (MS and EE) also makes us wary of just such a collaboration. First, we have concerns that EE activities such as ropes courses will be adopted into MS settings without the necessary understanding of the foundations and underlying processes that guide these activities. In this case, we suspect that much of the value to individual students from such activities could be diminished and the subsequent perceived efficacy of these learning activities placed in jeopardy.

In addition, we are concerned not only that EE activities and learning experiences will be used without proper reference to the process and foundations of EE, but also that there will be a reduced emphasis on risk management and individual protection. This is not to say that MS educators are uncaring or unconcerned, but rather that EE has developed a body of knowledge and procedures regarding the use of risk in the educational context that precludes a quick check-list or simple signing of a waiver.

Moreover, this risk extends to both the physical and the emotional needs of the individual, often in situations unfamiliar to the MS educator and ones for which s/he is not adequately trained. As such, we recommend that experiential educators should be an integral part of any collaborative effort between MS and EE, in order to protect the integrity and efficacy of these activities.

We also see a second and perhaps more important role that EE could play in contributing to educational reform. This argument is based on the work of Coleman (1987) and speaks to what he calls the "social capital" in young people. Coleman (1987) defined social capital as "the norms, the social networks, and the relationships between adults and children that are of value for the children's growing up" (p. 36). Coleman believes that the responsibility of socializing young people has moved from the family to the school, a task for which schools are poorly prepared. He argues that new institutional structures should be designed outside of the MS structure to provide for this socialization of our young people.

As we see it, the development of the social capital that Coleman (1987) suggests is essential to the health and education of young people and is a central and well-established goal within the EE tradition. Therefore, we recommend that EE continue to offer its programs outside of mainstream settings. Reinforcing this belief, we would posit that EE is ideally suited to provide an effective and alternative educational structure outside of MS for the socialization and education of our youth. Rather than trying to force fit EE philosophies and techniques into mainstream education, EE should continue to develop its own "niche" in the broader educational context.

Thus, can EE contribute to educational reform in North America? We believe it can, but not by becoming subsumed by it. Despite the urging by some to become more "mainstream" (e.g., Michalec, 1993), the differences between the two traditions are great enough to suggest that, at best, we might only expect an uneasy alliance. To return to our opening vignette, we suggest that Linda and Stuart reconsider their commitment to their relationship with their mainstream counterparts. We believe that retaining its independence from MS is an integral and important part of a role that EE can play in contributing to the future socialization and education of our young people.

References

Apple, M. (1998). Are markets and standards democratic? *Educational Researcher, 27*(6): 24–28.

Bartine, D. (1992). *Reading, criticism and culture: Theory and teaching in the United States and England, 1820-1950.* Columbia, SC: University of South Carolina.

Brookfield, S. (1996). Experiential pedagogy: Grounding teaching in students' learning. *Journal of Experiential Education, 19*(2), 62–68.

Callahan, R. (1962). *Education and the cult of efficiency: The social forces that shape American education.* Chicago: University of Chicago.

Carver, R. (1996). Theory for practice: A framework for thinking about experiential education. *Journal of Experiential Education, 19*(1), 8–13.

Coleman, J. (1987). Families and schools. *Educational Researcher, 16*, 32–38.

Crosby, A. (1995). A critical look: The philosophical foundations of experiential education. In K. Warren, M. Sakofs, & J. Hunt, Jr. (Eds.), *The theory of experiential education* (3rd ed.) (pp. 3–13). Dubuque, IA: Kendall/Hunt.

Cuban, L. (1990). A fundamental puzzle of school reform. In A. Liebermann (Ed.), *Schools as collaborative cultures: Creating the future now* (pp. 71–77). New York: Falmer Press.

DeLay, R. (1996). Forming knowledge: Constructivist learning and experiential education. *Journal of Experiential Education, 19*(2), 76–81.

Drew, P., & Sorjonen, M. (1997). Institutional dialogue. In T. Van Dijk (Ed.), *Discourse as social interaction* (Vol. 2, pp. 92–118). London: SAGE Publications.

Durian, G., Owens, T., & Owen, S. (1995). Experiential education: A search for common roots. In: R. Kraft & J. Kielsmeier (Eds.), *Experiential learning in schools and higher education* (pp. 17–25). Dubuque, IA: Kendall/Hunt.

Ewert, A., & Heywood, J. (1991). Group development in the natural environment: Expectations, outcomes and techniques. *Environment and Behavior, 23*(5), 592–615.

Flor, R. (1995). An introduction to research and evaluation in practice. R. Kraft & J. Kielsmeier (Eds.). *Experiential learning in schools and higher education* (pp. 404–409). Dubuque, IA: Kendall/Hunt.

Fore, L. (1998). Curriculum control: Using discourse and structure to manage educational reform. *Journal of Curriculum Studies, 30*(5): 559–576.

Gardner, H. (1987). *The mind's new science: A history of the cognitive revolution.* New York: Basic Books.

Goodlad, J. (1984). *A place called school.* New York: McGraw-Hill.

Goodman, J. (1995). Change without difference: School restructuring in historical perspective. *Harvard Educational Review, 65*(1): 1–29.

Jennings, J. (1997). Do we still need public schools? In F. Schultz (Ed.), *Education 97/98* (24th ed.) (pp. 6–11). Guilford, CT: Dushkin/ McGraw-Hill.

Joplin, L. (1995). On defining experiential education. In K. Warren, M. Sakofs, & J. Hunt, Jr. (Eds.), *The theory of experiential education* (3rd ed.) *(pp. 15–22).* Dubuque, IA: Kendall/Hunt.

Knapp, C. (1994). Progressivism never died—it just moved outside: What can experiential educators learn from the past. *Journal of Experiential Education, 17*(2): 8–12.

Kolb, D. A. (1984). *Experiential learning: Experience as the source of learning and development.* Englewood Cliffs, NJ: Prentice-Hall, Inc.

Lauritzen, C., & Jaeger, M. (1997). *Integrating learning through story: The narrative curriculum.* Albany, NY: Delmar.

Lempert, D. (1996). *Escape from the ivory tower: Student adventures in democratic experiential education.* San Francisco: Jossey-Bass.

Lindsay, A. (1998). *The educational forum: Competing influences reflect different visions of quality of life.* Paper delivered at the Second Annual Conference of the International Society for Quality of Life Studies, Williamsburg, VA, December 3–6, 1998.

Longstreet, W., & Shane, H. (1993). *Curriculum for a new millennium*. Boston: Allyn & Bacon.

Martin, J.R. (1997). A philosophy of education for the Year 2000. In F. Schultz (Ed.), *Education 97/98* (24th ed.) (pp. 261–264). Guilford, CT: Dushkin/McGraw-Hill.

Metz, M. (1998, April). *Veiled inequalities: The hidden effects of community social class on high school teachers' perspectives and practices.* Paper presented at the annual meeting of the American Educational Researchers' Association, San Diego, CA.

Michalec, P. (1993). The future of experiential education as a profession. In R. Kraft & J. Kielsmeier (Eds.), *Experiential learning in schools and higher education* (pp. 32–39). Dubuque, IA: Kendall/Hunt.

Miller, J. P., & Seller, W. (1990). *Curriculum: Perspectives and practice.* Toronto, ON: Copp Clark.

Page, H. (1984). Two perspectives on the crisis in education. *Journal of Experiential Education, 7*(1), 36–39.

Pogrow, S. (1996). Reforming the wannabe reformers. *Phi Delta Kappan, 77*(10): 656-663.

Priest, S., & Gass, M. (1997). *Effective leadership in adventure programming.* Champaign, IL: Human Kinetics.

Proudman, B. (1995). AEE adopts definition. *AEE Horizon, 15*, 1.

Raffan, J. (1995). Experiential education and teacher education. *Journal of Experiential Education, 18*(3), 117–119.

Smith, T., Roland, C., Havens, M., & Hoyt, J. (1992). *The theory and practice of challenge education.* Dubuque, IA: Kendall/Hunt.

Tyack, D. & Hansot, E. (1982). *Managers of virtue: Public school leadership in America 1820-1980.* New York: Basic Books.

Waters, G. (1998). Critical evaluation for education reform. *Education Policy Analysis Archives, 6*(30). Electronic/Unpaged.

Williamson, J. (1995). Designing experiential curricula. In R. Kraft, & J. Kielsmeier (Eds.). *Experiential Learning in Schools and Higher Education* (pp. 26–39). Dubuque, IA: Kendall/Hunt.

Wurdinger, S. (1996). The theory and pedagogy of experiential education: A critical look at teaching practices. *Journal of Experiential Education, 19*(2), 60–61.

Service Learning as Experiential Education's Bridge to Mainstream Education

▾ ▾ ▾

Jason Berv

Over the last 25 years there has emerged a solid body of literature on experiential education, and there has been a resurgence in experiential education methods employed in the broader field of education. Despite the increasing acceptance of experiential education methods, however, they have largely been confined to programs and practices outside of mainstream education, often to be found in wilderness settings and approached in ways that have little explicit connection to the primary curriculum of schools. There is significant value in experiential programs of this sort, but an even greater benefit is being lost by not seeking to vitalize the curriculum in schools with experiential education methods that promote self-directed learners and incorporate a broad variety of learning styles.

In this paper I intend to: (a) to show what can be achieved by using service learning to bring experiential methods into the schools, and (b) to indicate some directions in which schools might go to recapture the role of experiential education as a catalyst for social change. In so doing, I also want to suggest that experiential educators not limit their educational goals solely on the benefits to individual students, but consider social and societal benefits as well.

This chapter originally was published in the *Journal of Experiential Education*, with the following citation:
Berv, J. (1998). Service learning as experiential education's bridge to mainstream education. *Journal of Experiential Education, 21*(3), 119–123.

The Case for Service Learning as a Bridge to Mainstream Education

Service learning provides a hopeful model for bridging experiential pedagogy with mainstream educational environments. Equally important, it brings a strong community orientation and infuses a broader societal dimension into experiential education (Conrad and Hedin, 1995; Levison, 1986; Shumer, 1992, 1993).

Service-learning programs have proliferated in the last decade and have begun to carve out a place in more traditional school settings. However, while some of the best service-learning programs are fully integrated into a (discipline-based) class, others remain extracurricular programs. Such adjunct programs call themselves service learning, but in fact, they usually lack the supervised activity, the academic links, and the reflection necessary to correctly be either service learning or experiential education. For this reason, a more detailed definition of service-learning programs may be useful. Kraft (1996) offers a helpful set of criteria. He writes,

> When they are carefully tied to curricular objectives, contain academic content, involve
> the student in reflection, and contain an evaluative component, they can be considered
> service learning. If these components are missing, they fit more comfortably into com-
> munity-based learning or volunteerism. (p. 140)

This distinction is essential, both for the integrity of the emerging field of service learning and for understanding the argument that I am advancing about the promise of service learning. What follows is a brief look at some compelling arguments in support of quality service learning from several educational perspectives.

The Philosophical Rationale for Service Learning— Preparation of Democratic Citizens

The philosophy of Kurt Hahn offers an overt connection between experiential education and the broader aim of preparation of youth for active participation in society (Sakofs, Armstrong, Proudman, et al., 1995). For Hahn, the purpose of education, in addition to the development of certain character traits such as courage and physical fortitude, was to inculcate in the student certain values that would be important for living within a community. These values included compassion and service to others. Kraft (1992) writes that "It is the hope and promise of service learning that the next generation of children will learn citizenship by actively politicking in their local communities, … and that service learning … will continue to transform … the societies in which we live" (p. 11).

Also addressing themselves to this point, Nathan and Kielsmeier (1995) have spoken of service learning as "the sleeping giant of school reform."

We reject the often-stated assertion that the fundamental task of school is to prepare students for the work force. In a democratic society, one of the basic purposes of public schools is to prepare students for active, informed citizenship. Part of being a responsible citizen is knowing how to get and keep a job, but an equally important part of citizenship is working to build a better world. (p. 71)

Couto (1996) reinforces this point by grounding service learning in the traditions of liberal education. He writes, "Service learning, when done properly, infuses the humanist traditions of ... education with the call of the progressive tradition for democratic practice and reform" (p. 80). Education for a democratic society requires certain skills and dispositions that are best taught through experiential means in the context of service learning. To wit, how is one to teach a student truly to understand social responsibility only through texts and essays or other conventional means? And if we delegate the learning of these skills and dispositions to programs outside of our traditional school settings, then what are we saying about the importance of democratic values?

Thus, there is a compelling rationale for the introduction of experiential education methods in schools to foster democratic competencies in students. Varlotta (1997, pp. 70-71) provides a helpful picture of how service learning can be utilized for this purpose. She writes:

There are "certain things a democracy must teach, employing its full authority to do so: citizenship is first among them." This charge can be met when service learning practitioners follow these ... principles:

(1) Use service learning to teach and practice "citizenship."

(2) Demonstrate how service learning (re)connects the often severed relationship between rights and responsibilities.

(3) Investigate, through service learning, the discriminatory behaviors perpetuated by social injustices.

(4) Promote student "empowerment" by encouraging students to plan their own service-learning projects.

(5) Teach citizenship, not charity. Citizens serve themselves even when they work for "public interest" and the "public good."

The Policy Rationale for Service Learning— Curricular and Pedagogical Innovation

Some recent literature on school reform provides grounds for optimism that there are ways to effectively reconcile experiential education methods and mainstream education. As Westheimer, Kahne, and Gerstein (1992) point out, the growing acceptance of the need for systemic school reform has created an atmosphere conducive to experiential education and the benefits that can accrue from incorporating experiential education methods into more traditional settings. Specifically, they suggest that experiential education can play a significant role in (a) "unifying a highly fragmented curriculum," (b) revitalizing pedagogy, and (c) better serving at-risk student populations. Rather than keeping experiential education on the fringes, incorporating it into the traditional educational setting seems to hold much promise for addressing these three themes that recur in much of the reform-minded literature. (Sarason, 1982; Sizer, 1984; Tyack and Cuban, 1996) Thus, discussions of school reform may provide an opportunity for educators to embrace experiential methods generally, and service-learning methods specifically, for less philosophical and more practical reasons. Yet practice and philosophy ultimately converge in the sphere of better teaching and learning for all.

The Psychological Rationale for Service Learning— Epistemological Evidence

Within the context of school reform and bridging experiential and mainstream education, there is also an attempt to situate experiential education methods within the findings of contemporary educational and psychological research on learning. Fouhey and Saltmarsh (1996) build on the work of feminist scholars, who have suggested that there are some "ways of knowing," typically embraced by girls and women that are not valued in our schools. "Connected knowing," a term coined for this alternative approach, can be accessed much more readily in contexts that employ experiential education methods. "Connected knowing," Fouhey and Saltmarsh write, "legitimizes learning that takes place outside the classroom, recognizes multiple learning styles, and values learning based in experience" (p. 82). This point is reinforced by the work on multiple intelligences (Gardner, 1983; Lazear, 1991), which suggests that student success can be enhanced by providing opportunities for students to express their knowledge and understanding through a variety of modes and "intelligences." Thus, by incorporating experiential education methods in our schools through service learning, we can reduce the male-normative bias in traditional education, increase motivation and achievement by appealing to a broader array of students' learning styles, and reinvigorate curriculum by connecting more explicitly the school and the lived experiences of students.

Similarly powerful conclusions can be drawn from the research on constructivist learning, which at its root is about the ways in which individuals construct knowledge and understanding. In the preface to *In Search of Understanding: The Case for Constructivist Learning*, Fosnot (1993) writes that this new approach to learning draws on "a synthesis of current work in cognitive psychology, philosophy, and anthropology, [and] defines knowledge as temporary, developmental, socially and culturally mediated, and thus, non-objective" (p. vii). She goes on to enumerate five overarching principles of a constructivist pedagogy, which are "(1) posing problems of emerging relevance to learners; (2) structuring learning around 'big ideas' or primary concepts; (3) seeking and valuing students' points of view; (4) adapting curriculum to address students' suppositions; and (5) assessing student learning in the context of teaching" (p. viii). What is striking about this list is its resemblance to the experiential education concepts proposed by Dewey (1916; 1938) for mainstream education over 60 years ago. Perhaps now, with the support of research in other disciplines, Dewey's notion of experience in education can be more fully realized.

In view of the growing constructivist movement, Delay (1996) made explicit the connection between constructivist learning and experiential education. He contends that the methods of experiential education actually are best understood within the framework of a constructivist pedagogy, and that there is great congruence in the two theoretical approaches.

Possible Directions for Enhancing the Power of Experiential Education in Schools

In light of the mounting evidence for the value of service learning, how are schools to implement or improve a program of service learning? What follows are a few suggestions, derived from two among the many notable examples in current practice, for how a school can more effectively ground its curriculum in experiential education methods and give a significant role to service learning in accomplishing educational goals.

For proponents of service learning seeking to develop or improve a school-based program, some recent innovative approaches can be instructive. Outward Bound USA, for example, formed a coalition with Harvard Graduate School of Education and several public schools, and together they have created an organization called Expeditionary Learning Outward Bound (Sakofs et al., 1995). In its initial proposal, Outward Bound listed five areas of priority for its work with schools, among them a commitment to service learning (McQuillan, 1994). Using this priority to inform the development of new curriculum, Expeditionary Learning seeks to provide its students with enriched learning opportunities through extended "expeditions" that will supplement the traditional curriculum. These "expeditions" might take students into the wilderness or into the community to explore a question or problem that requires students to draw on many academic disciplines. A recent example from the Rocky Mountain School for Expeditionary Learning had middle school students serving meals at a Denver homeless shelter, raising money for famine relief, and teaching principles of nutrition to elementary school students, all in the context of learning about the nature of famines in Africa. Kurt Hahn's influence can be discerned clearly in this service-oriented approach to public education.

I am not suggesting that other schools and other educators should simply replicate an Expeditionary Learning curriculum. Rather, I want to call attention to what differentiates Expeditionary Learning schools from many other public schools. The commitment to experiential learning is explicit in the documents that guide the operation of the school and inform the curriculum. Experiential methods and service learning have a prominent place in the foundational values and the design principles of the redesigned schools. It is in this way that Expeditionary Learning can serve as a model for other public schools.

The Eagle Rock School, a private enterprise in Estes Park, Colorado, sponsored by the American Honda Education Corporation, has sought to do much the same thing as Expeditionary Learning. It differs only in that it is in a residential setting that is outside of the public school system, which in some ways places experiential education methods and service learning more centrally in the curriculum (Burkhardt, nd).

Eagle Rock's mission statement, "An Eagle Rock student has the desire and is prepared to make a difference in the world," sets the context for the eight themes of the program. Among these themes is "service to others." Similarly, in the "Ten Commitments" that students are asked to address and progress toward, there are included "serve the Eagle Rock and other communities," "become a steward of the planet," "increase capacity to exercise leadership for justice," and "practice citizenship and democratic living."

As impressive as these commitments are, they mean little without putting them into practice. And Eagle Rock does this, often by fully integrating service learning into the educational objectives and the curriculum. For example, an interdisciplinary course from a recent term had students learning American Government, Civics, and Mathematics, while helping to build the interior of a medical clinic in the local community. All Eagle Rock students have an individualized learning plan, part of which requires each student to design and participate in a service-learning project *(Eagle Rock School Curriculum Guide, 1997)*. To assist students with this, and with all of their academic goals, Eagle Rock has a detailed document explaining the standards, concepts, and goals for each academic area, including service learning. In these ways, students come to see service learning as an integral part of the curriculum, rather than some adjunct pursuit, and the school has articulated a public vision of the role of a rich service-learning experience in the education of its students.

These schools that embrace service-learning principles espouse values that are consistent with educating for democracy. In my view, this is the result of a mission-driven process. Both Expeditionary Learning and Eagle Rock have clear and explicit mission statements that place service learning, and the democratic values that this implies, at the heart of their educational project. And, I would add, they beg the question: "Do our public schools have *any* guiding principles?" Chubb and Moe (1990) have underscored this point in their oft-cited work on school reform. "When schools lack mission, when there is no meaningful way of saying what it is they are supposed to accomplish—how is it possible, even in principle, to design an effective organization? Effective for what?" (p. 55). It is in this arena that I believe service-learning programs and educators can take the lead and point to more meaningful and socially responsive and responsible education.

I have tried to argue in these pages that much of the power of service learning is derived from its effective organizing principles, which I suggest are, at minimum, social responsibility, democratic values, and inclusive pedagogy. So where can we go from here? I want to suggest that, in the name of meaningful school reform, those empathetic to the aims of experiential education should encourage their school or learning community to engage all key constituents in a discussion of their program's mission and how it can and should inform daily practice. This recommendation is supported by the research of the National Service Learning Cooperative (1998), which lists the first of its five essential elements for implementing service learning as "effective service learning is connected to and relevant to the [organization's] mission" (p. 21).

If there is not an existing mission statement, begin the process. There are, of course, no guarantees that this process will be easy. And it would be foolhardy to assume that a mission statement alone will ensure high ideals or success, but a meaningful and inclusive discussion of a school's educational goals should provide many avenues for bringing service learning and experiential education methods into the mainstream. As these discussions yield appropriate opportunities to promote service learning, the attributes of a robust service-learning program should guide subsequent efforts.

Conclusion

As Dewey intended it, experiential education is nothing more or less than sound pedagogy intended to maximize the learning and growth of all participants. The preponderance of literature on experiential education exacerbates the rift between experiential methods and traditional educational settings. Most efforts that seek to bridge the two approaches appear to have little or no overarching moral or social ends and take an individual, rather than a societal, view of education. Those approaches that seek to address moral education or democratic education, on the other hand, may fail to account for the tremendous role that experiential education methods can play in socially transformative education (Kraft, 1992).

The type of experience-based curricula of Expeditionary Learning or of Eagle Rock School, particularly in light of its clientele of at-risk youth, brings into sharp focus certain elements of education as social activism, while clearly articulating a role for experiential education methods in mainstream education. In all schools that wholeheartedly embrace service-learning principles, there is also a practical attempt at schooling to which one can compare the educational vision of Dewey, evaluate the benefits of constructivist learning, and assess the value of promoting a variety of learning styles.

Service learning, in the way that Expeditionary Learning and Eagle Rock have conceived of it, holds tremendous potential to transform public education. To do so, however, we must first recognize the benefits that can be had from implementing experiential education methods in more traditional settings. Through the incorporation of connected knowing, multiple intelligences, and the use of constructivist approaches, experiential education can provide a more inclusive and meaningful educational experience. Taking a cue from Dewey, if we strive for a democratic society, then we must educate our students so that they are able to contribute to that society. Surely the best way to do this is to involve them more directly in the functions and functioning of the communities in which they live.

It is in the context of the larger social environment in which experiential education is to deliver most fully on its promise, and so it is in this context that its role in schools will be most fruitfully conceived. If we are to reap the transformative effects of experiential education, if experiential education as a field is to mature, we must move beyond those conceptions that describe experiential education as primarily an individual endeavor, with individual rewards, to a broader view of the systemic and societal benefits available through experience-based education. Without this progression in the way we think of and talk about experiential education, experiential educators are confining themselves to a marginal role in mainstream education. Yet, if we are to return to the philosophical roots of experiential education and recognize the power of making experience more central in the education of youth through service learning, we will begin to see students who have been given the skills and the understanding to bring democracy into full bloom.

References

Burkhardt, R. (n.d.) *Promotional materials for Eagle Rock School.* Unpublished manuscript.

Chubb, J., & Moe, T. (1990). *Politics, markets and America's schools.* Washington, DC: The Brookings Institution.

Conrad, D., & Hedin, D. (1995). School-based community service: What we know from research and theory. In R. Kraft & J. Kielsmeier (Eds.), *Experiential learning in schools and higher education* (pp. 73–82). Dubuque, IA: Kendall/Hunt.

Couto, R.(1996). Service learning: Integrating community issues and the curriculum. In T. Becker & R. Couto (Eds.), *Teaching democracy by being democratic* (pp. 79–104). Westport, CT: Praeger.

DeLay, R. B., (1996). Forming knowledge: Constructivist learning and experiential education. *Journal of Experiential Education*, *19*(2), 76–81.

Dewey, J. (1916). *Democracy and education*. New York: The Free Press.

Dewey, J. (1938). *Experience and education*. New York: Macmillan.

Eagle Rock School curriculum guide. (1997). Unpublished manuscript.

Fostnot, C. T. (1993) Preface. In J. G. Brooks & M. G.Brooks, *In Search of Understanding: The case for constructivist classrooms* (pp. vii-viii). Alexandria, VA: Association for Supervision and Curriculum Development.

Fouhey, H., & Saltmarsh, J. (1996). Outward Bound and community service learning: An experiment in connected knowing. *Journal of Experiential Education*, *19*(2), 82–89.

Gardner, H. (1983). *Frames of mind: The theory of multiple intelligences.* New York: Basic Books.

Kraft, R. J. (1992). Closed classrooms, high mountains and strange lands: An inquiry into culture and caring. *Journal of Experiential Education*, *15*(3), 8–15.

Kraft, R. J. (1996). Service learning: An introduction to its theory, practice, and effects. *Education and Urban Society*, *28*(2), 131–159.

Lazear, D. (1991). *Seven ways of knowing: Teaching for multiple intelligences*. Arlington Heights, IL: Skylight Publishing.

Levison, L. (1986). *Community service programs in independent schools*. Boston, MA: National Association of Independent Schools.

McQuillan, P. (1994). *An assessment of Outward Bound USA's urban/education initiative*. Unpublished manuscript.

Nathan, J., & Kielsmeier, J. (1995). The sleeping giant of school reform. In R. Kraft & J. Kielsmeier (Eds.), *Experiential learning in schools and higher education* (pp. 67–72). Dubuque, IA: Kendall/Hunt.

National Service Learning Cooperative. (1998). *Essential elements of service-learning*. Roseville, MN: National Youth Leadership Council.

Sakofs, M., Armstrong, G., Proudman, S., Howard, J., & Clark, T. (1995). Developing a teacher development model: A work in progress. *Journal of Experiential Education*, *18*(3), 128–132.

Sarason, S.B. (1982). *The culture of the school and the problem of change (2nd edition)*. Boston: Allyn and Bacon.

Shumer, Robert (1992). *Service-learning and the power of participation: Schools, communities, and learning*. Unpublished manuscript.

Shumer, R. (1993). *Academic learning + experiential learning = complete learning*. Unpublished manuscript.

Sizer, T. (1984). *Horace's compromise: The dilemma of the American high school*. Boston: Houghton Mifflin.

Tyack, D., & Cuban, L. (1995). *Tinkering toward utopia: A century of public school reform*. Cambridge, MA: Harvard University Press.

Varlotta, L. (1997). A critique of service-learning's definitions, continuums, and paradigms: A move towards a discourse-praxis community. *Educational Foundations*, *11*(3), 53–85.

Westheimer, J., Kahne, J., & Gerstein, A. (1992). School reform for the nineties: Opportunities and obstacles for experiential education. *Journal of Experiential Education*, *15*(2), 44–49.

Toward an Ecological Paradigm in Adventure Programming

▾ ▾ ▾

Almut Beringer

Many forms of adventure therapy, in particular wilderness therapy, rely on challenges in the outdoors to achieve objectives of client change. While nature is drawn on as a medium for therapy and healing, some adventure therapists give nature little if any mention when it comes to explaining therapeutic success. The dominant paradigm in psychology and psychotherapy provides insights as to why the contributions of nature in the curative relationship are, at times, marginalized. To more fully understand why and how adventure therapy works, the role of nature as a force in human development needs to be considered. It is proposed that ecotherapy and nature-guided therapy are viable alternative theoretical frameworks for adventure therapy. Ecotherapy and nature-guided therapy provide a critical perspective on adventure and wilderness therapy in that they recognize a social, cultural, and environmental/ecological context to human well-being and behavior. Furthermore, they explicitly acknowledge the potential healing power of natural environments and natural features. Adventure therapy and wilderness therapy may be revisioned in light of ecotherapy and nature-guided healing.

Miles and Priest's *Adventure Programming* (1999), a standard textbook in adventure learning and therapy, reflects assumptions regarding the natural worlds and the context for adventure that are common and widespread in the fields of adventure learning and experiential education. At a time when planetary sustainability and sustainable development are

This chapter originally was published in the *Journal of Experiential Education*, with the following citation:
Beringer, A. (2004). Toward an ecological paradigm in adventure programming. *Journal of Experiential Education, 27*(1), 51–66.

becoming mainstream, normative principles, these assumptions provide opportunity for rethinking the relationship between adventure and natural environments. In short, natural settings have long provided the medium and opportunity for adventure learning and therapy. Yet theoretical frameworks and explanatory models of why and how adventure programming works rarely give sufficient credit to how simply "being in nature" can contribute to personal development, healing, and therapeutic success. The author explores some of the reasons why natural environments may have been neglected as a force in human development in adventure programming research, theory, and practice. Further, the author proposes an alternative framework: an ecological paradigm that not only recognizes the web of relationships between clients/students, therapists/instructors and adventure, but which also recognizes that all adventure learning occurs in biophysical environments.

The underlying conceptualizations in *Adventure Programming* suggest a deep divide between adventure programming and environmental issues. For instance, environmental matters are considered "extensions of" rather than fundamental issues in adventure programming (Section 10) and the natural setting is limited to "wilderness" (Section 8). This may be interpreted as an invitation to reflect on how natural environments are conceived in adventure programming circles, and to investigate the conceptual, empirical, theoretical, and practical aspects of the relationship between adventure programming and natural environments. This chapter provides an analysis of several understandings of natural settings that seem prevalent in adventure programming, and traces some of the reasons why these understandings may be dominant in the field.

Where is Nature? One View of Adventure Therapy

In *Adventure as Therapy*, Gillis and Ringer define adventure therapy as:

> [T]he deliberate, strategic combination of adventure activities with therapeutic change processes with the goal of making lasting changes in the lives of participants. Adventure provides the concrete, action-based, experiential medium for therapy. The specific activity is (ideally) chosen to achieve a particular therapeutic goal. (p.29)

Many adventure therapists and programmers, regardless if they are academics and/or practitioners, accept this definition without hesitation or concern, agreeing that adventure therapy is a form of psychological intervention that relies on activities with managed risk, deliberately selected by the therapist, which the client perceives as adventure. The psychological and/or physical challenge that arouses a state of heightened awareness in the client, the uncertain outcome, the group activity, the unusual settings (e.g., the wilderness or a ropes course), and the immediate feedback regarding the client's behavior, which the challenge affords, all contribute to the intended therapeutic success.

Immediately following this definition, Gillis and Ringer (1999) provide two examples to illustrate this view of adventure therapy. It is their choice of examples in relation to their conceptualization of adventure therapy that creates tensions and that raises issues regarding the place and role of the natural worlds within adventure therapy:

> The specific activity is (ideally) chosen to achieve a particular therapeutic goal. For example, having two persons who have difficulties in their relationship, such as a father and son or husband and wife, paddle a canoe will require them to cooperate in order to be successful. A 14-day backpacking trip for a group of adjudicated youth provides a self-contained purposeful therapeutic community where tasks such as erecting tents, reading a compass, or cooking a meal provide challenges in communication and discipline which can be utilized for therapeutic outcomes. These are just small examples of how adventure can be programmed for therapeutic ends. (p. 29)

The examples, indeed, highlight the elements that make up adventure therapy as described: the challenging activity (canoeing, backpacking); the small group transformed into a community that serves as a therapeutic tool; the therapist's or therapists' deliberately chosen activities (journeying, camping, navigating), which provide immediate feedback to the clients if not carried out correctly (e.g., getting cold and wet, losing one's way, or going hungry). What is striking is the setting where these therapeutic interventions occur and the venues that make the adventure possible: The relationship therapy intervention is a river journey, the youth-at-risk program an extended backpacking trip. Both these interventions are outdoor experiences that rely on specific places and particular natural environments to be carried out. It seems the river journey, as well as the extended hike, are fundamental and profound components of the therapeutic intervention. They are essential aspects of the therapeutic experience without which the therapy in each case would not be possible. Yet in Gillis and Ringer's (1999) definition of adventure therapy, the natural component to the intervention receives no mention. The outdoors, the setting, the environments, and the natural worlds, which contextualize the adventure in which outdoor adventure therapy is embedded, remain invisible. The potential contribution of the natural setting to therapeutic success is unacknowledged and hence, also un-theorized.

Gillis and Ringer's (1999) definition of adventure therapy fails to mention the settings or environments for adventure—*any* setting or environment, be it natural (e.g., wilderness), urban, artificial (e.g., an indoor climbing wall) or constructed (e.g., a ropes course). It also fails to highlight the interpersonal dimensions (group, client-therapist relationship), focusing instead on adventurous activities. Given this, it is disconcerting that the examples they provide are exclusively outdoor adventure therapy; outdoor adventure therapy that would not have been possible if there had not been a river, or a backcountry for the intervention to take place. The question arises why neither the authors, nor the reviewers of the chapter, seem to have noticed this discrepancy. Even the editors, Miles and Priest (1999, p. xiii), differentiate between outdoor pursuits, initiative activities and ropes or challenge courses in their examples of adventurous activities. Furthermore, one of the editors has written on "wilderness as healing place" (Miles, 1987, p. 4).

This apparent tension between activity, human elements, and setting, especially natural setting, opens up questions to ask, such as why the oversight of the natural components in adventure therapy might have occurred, and whether or not the neglect of nature in the curative relationship is repeated in wider adventure therapy circles. Ibbott (1999) confirms that ignoring nature as an element of therapy and healing seems to be quite common in adventure therapy. Gillis and Ringer's (1999) understanding is not an isolated incident, apparently reflecting a tendency in the field. In the review of accurate nomenclature in adventure or wilderness therapy, Ibbott (p. 7) states, "It is worth noting that many of the terms used fail to recognize that it is the wilderness that is the vital therapeutic component." Before exploring why the natural setting may not be consciously considered as vital to the therapeutic process and success, a brief reflection on nature.

On Nature

References to nature and the natural environment are somewhat sensitive issues, for several reasons. First, the term "nature" has many and varied meanings and connotations, and has undergone developments and interpretation over time (Chambers, 1984; Evernden, 1992; Soper, 1995). Further, nature is notoriously difficult to define (Seddon, 1997). As such, the use of the term requires outlining or at least demarcating its interpretation. Secondly, philosophers of nature and philosophers of perception point out that if indeed there is such a thing as nature "out there"—a notion which is itself contested—all we can ever have is a subjective representation (or construction) of it. This is so because in the human process of perception, physiology and cognition are intertwined to such an extent that our sensual impressions of the world "out there" always result in interpretations (Beard, 2002; Chambers, 1984; Timms, 2001). Therefore, even if two people view the same scene, what they see may be quite different—the subjective interpretation of what is "out there" will be influenced by cultural and individual factors (see Meinig, 1979; Tuan, 1974, 1977; see also Kaplan & Kaplan, 1989).

The author does not wish to delve into the philosophical debate as to whether or not we can ever know if there is indeed a nature "out there" and what it may be (see, for instance, Chambers, 1984). She acknowledges, however, that such epistemological analysis would surely have several interesting implications for ontological positions within adventure therapy, and subsequent practice. Rather, in the remainder of this paper, the author resorts to the common sense interpretation of nature as the natural world, or worlds; as the green environment, or environments; as the biophysical, material environment. This can take the form of pristine environments (wilderness), semi-natural (e.g., parks), and human-altered environments (urban, artificial, constructed environments). As such, nature includes the spectrum from wilderness to cultural landscapes. For simplicity of discussion, the notion of artificially created natural environments is left out (see Beard, 2002). The point is to alert adventure therapists and programmers to natural environments in their varied and many types.

Nature and the Environment in Adventure Programming

A comprehensive literature review on the question of how nature is conceptualized and represented in adventure learning and programming is beyond the scope of this paper. It will have to suffice to draw on selected examples from within adventure learning and therapy to balance Gillis and Ringer's (1999) interpretation. The strand of wilderness therapy, in particular, has long acknowledged the power of natural settings in the therapeutic endeavor, as the following three quotes indicate:

> Many programs today use wilderness therapeutic goals of one sort or another. Undoubtedly, both the experiences planned and facilitated by the program leaders and *the [wilderness] environment itself* [italics added] contribute to the healing effect of wilderness experience. (Miles, 1987, p. 4)

> [W]ilderness therapy involves the use of traditional therapy techniques, especially those for group therapy, *in out-of-door settings,* [italics added] utilizing outdoor adventure pursuits and other activities to enhance growth. (Davis-Berman & Berman, 1994, p. 13)

> *The natural world of wilderness,* [italics added] adventure and the outdoors [italics added] has a significant therapeutic role to play in the personal, social and spiritual development of human beings. (Ibbott, 1999, p. 7)

McKenzie (2000), too, includes the setting as one of the explanatory factors in her literature review on why adventure education works. However, the therapeutic-curative potential of natural environments, in particular wilderness environments, is not attributed to the inherent qualities of such environments and their psychological effects (Chenery, 2000; Kaplan & Talbot, 1983; Miles, 1987; Taylor, 1999) but is largely attributed to the state of dissonance created by participants being in an unfamiliar environment, which provides immediate feedback. Only in conclusion to her discussion (and with just one sentence) does McKenzie (p. 20) mention that, "[f]inally, the aesthetic and spiritual qualities of the wilderness environment are considered by some to facilitate personal restoration...and transformation..." The lack of research on the role of the physical environment in achieving therapeutic or educational outcomes (McKenzie, p. 20) is probably one reason why the effect of the natural setting is considered primarily in anthropocentric terms (i.e., wilderness is different from so-called normal, human-mediated environments). Yet the lack of such research is also a reflection of worldviews within adventure education and programming which exclude the natural worlds.

Noticeable in this review is that McKenzie (2000) discusses the physical setting first, out of a total of six factors as to why adventure education works (the remaining five being activities, processing, the group, instructors, and the participant). Whether or not this is deliberate is hard to tell; the effect on the reader is to give the physical environment prominence over those human aspects of adventure education that often receive more, if not sole, attention in attempting to understand and explain adventure programming and therapy.

Another attempt at understanding the potential effects of adventure learning, its power and dynamics, is, once again, more careless regarding the treatment of nature. In a widely cited meta-analysis of 96 studies in outdoor education and adventure programming, Hattie, Marsh, Neill, and Richards (1997) categorized outcomes. Given the traditional focus on personal and social development in adventure programming, not surprisingly, the authors of this research list 39 categories, out of a total of 40, concerning these personal and interpersonal domains. Only the last category makes reference to the biophysical environment in the form of "environmental awareness."

While the ranking of outcomes may be disconcerting, but not surprising, it is interesting to note the authors' findings as they succeed in stepping out of their preconceived notions of what an adventure program might achieve. They write: "In adventure programs, the highest ranking of importance for participants is the enjoyment of nature" (Hattie et al., 1997, p. 76). Taking this finding into account, the authors conclude: "It may be that a model based on enhancing environmental concerns and relationship with nature could be valuable in explaining the substantial changes that can result from adventure programs" (Hattie et al., p. 76). Here, Hattie et al., allude to the healing powers of the natural worlds, which have long been known, and which are now being documented empirically (see Frumkin, 2001). Therapeutic success in the outdoors might, in part, be due to human-environment dynamics, which can only be understood and explained via a theoretical framework that encompasses intrapersonal, human-human, and human-nature relationships, and which awaits further empirical study and analysis (see DeLay, 1996; Taylor, 1999).

These alternative explanatory models, which include and explicitly make reference to natural environments and their potential contributions to the therapeutic endeavor, are to date, still marginal and underrepresented in the adventure programming literature (see, e.g.,

Nichols, 2000; cf. Amesberger, n.d.; Barrett & Greenaway, 1995). How can the relative absence of nature in understanding the power and success of outdoor adventure learning and programming be explained and/or justified, given research on the restorative and therapeutic effects of natural environments, in general, and the differential effects of certain environments, in particular (see Frumkin, 2001; Kaplan & Kaplan, 1989; Kaplan & Talbot, 1983; Ulrich, 1981, 1983, 1984; Ulrich, Simons, & Losito, 1991)? The reasons for the anthropocentric bias in adventure learning and programming are rooted in disciplinary perspectives, theoretical frameworks, and research assumptions and paradigms within psychology. These paradigms within psychology have profoundly affected adventure learning and programming. The next section explores some of these paradigms.

Disciplinary Paradigms in Psychology

The therapeutic use of the outdoors has a long and cross-cultural history. Adventure programming has grown out of the social sciences rather than the environmental sciences. Many adventure therapy practitioners are trained in psychology, psychotherapy and/or social work rather than having a background in the environmental studies disciplines. Consequently, formative influences in adventure therapy have come from disciplinary paradigms in psychology rather than perspectives that honor non-human life and that study human-nature relationships.

Psychology concerns itself with intra- and interpersonal phenomena; as such, the natural worlds have traditionally been considered to be beyond the scope of concern and study in this discipline (Kidner, 1994). Nature is the research object and task for the natural sciences. Whether or not it is cognitive, behavioral experimental, or clinical psychology, environmental aspects have been regarded as complicating rather than illuminating human phenomena and the study of human beings. Rather than potentially improving understanding and prediction of human behavior and its underlying thought, feeling and spiritual processes, analyzing situational and contextual elements to human activity have been seen to confound or "pollute" psychological investigations. As Kidner writes, reflecting on why psychology has commented so little on environmentally destructive human behaviors and pro-environment behavior changes:

> The psychological image of the person, and, to a considerable extent, the experience of personhood, are today based on a reduced form of the self—one largely shorn of intuition, spirituality, and relatedness to natural context. Overwhelmingly, psychology has adopted, with little critical reflection, the same anthropocentric, individualistic ideology that, I have argued, has resulted in the current environmental crisis. (p. 372)

Such an intellectual climate of "subjectivist reduction[ism]" (Kidner, p. 363) has made possible Skinnerian behaviorism and studying rats in artificial clinical laboratory settings with the view of understanding human behavior in "real life." How much is adventure learning and programming being influenced by such views?

A notable exception to the absence of relationships in psychology, and the reduction of human beings to atomistic, individual units (Kidner, 1994) is social psychology. To some extent, social psychology acknowledges that human beings are, at all times, defined by, and contextualized in, relationships, and that the "atomistic individuation" celebrated in mainstream psychology is just one view of self and personhood, and, when considered cross-culturally, an uncommon one (Kidner, 1994). Thus, the relational self, a conceptualization of self and personhood not as isolated individual, but as a being networked in and held by relations, becomes a real alternative. Yet, again, due to disciplinary worldviews that are blind to the natural worlds, the relational self in psychology is characterized and defined by human-human relationships alone (Kidner, 1994; Gilsdorf, 2000). In contrast, the "ecological self" (Mathews, 1991) is a notion that cherishes both human-human and human-nature relationships. In mainstream psychology, including environmental psychology, human-nature relationships are not considered foundational and existential. An ontology and epistemology that includes nature is, to date, still a marginal proposal at best. Nature is neither seen as a context nor as a force for human life, activity, and development (see Kidner, 1994; Fisher, 2002).

Psychological theories of human development built on research in the aforementioned paradigm are highly questionable from the perspective of ecopsychology and human-nature relationships. Given that we cannot escape nature, the biophysical environment of life on Earth, and given the lack of a "naturalistic" or nature-based ontology and epistemology in psychology, one can argue that all theories of human development are probably in need of revision. Several psychologists have recognized this and are addressing some of these shortcomings (Fisher, 2002; Roszak, Gomes, & Kanner, 1995; Winter, 1996; see also Hillman, 1975). Why nature is often not thought of as part of the curative relationship in adventure therapy now becomes clear: Many adventure therapists will have been influenced by the individualistic, reductionist paradigms prevalent in psychology during their psychology, social work, and/or psychotherapy training and professional development.

Given that nature is beyond the scope of the discipline, the condition and health of natural environments has not been an issue for most psychologists, social workers, and/or psychotherapists. Consequently, concern over the state of local, regional, and/or the global environments is largely absent or marginalized as "extensions" in adventure programming research, theory, and practice. Responsibility for the physical settings on which adventure learning and programming relies, and establishing a "give-and-take" contractual relationship with natural environments, is something not widely debated in the field (see Amesberger, n.d.). This does not deny that some adventure programs and adventure practitioners who are sensitive to environmental issues include environmental components in their programs and/or lead pro-environment lifestyles.

In the individualistic paradigm championed by mainstream psychology, it is difficult to see that individual pathologies and social problems might not only be rooted in individual histories, but also in social relationships and concern over the state of the world. Barrows (1998), for instance, highlights how mental health issues and behavioral challenges in youth are linked to, and can be traced back to, concerns over the welfare of the planet. At least in some adolescents, substance abuse and/or delinquent behavior is not only an individual or family problem, but is mixed with pessimism for the future and despair for the world (see Barrows, 1998).

Psychotherapy, on the whole, has been fairly complacent in healing the world and in recognizing the link between individual and societal, or world, pathology. Hence, the integral connection between individual healing to world healing has rarely been made. Hillman and Ventura (1992), for instance, question why despite over a hundred years of psychotherapy, the world seems to be getting worse. In a review of Hillman and Ventura's book, Fideler remarks:

> Psychotherapy, with Freud and Jung, started off in part dealing with the sickness of civi-
> lization, but today everything is reduced to the individual. The individual is supposed to
> cope, get in touch with his [sic] feelings, and...become assimilated to a system that is
> itself pathological and dysfunctional. *The effect of psychotherapy's underlying assumptions*
> *is to help the individual cope by focusing his* [sic] *energies inward and, in effect, anesthetizing*
> *the passions and discontent which could otherwise be directed at the problems of the world*
> [italics added]. (Fideler, 1993, p. 72–73)

Hillman and Ventura's (1992) and Fideler's (1993) critique that psychotherapy might be focusing too much on the individual and her/his healing, to the detriment of conceiving healing in a larger systemic context, is something for adventure programmers to contemplate (see also Goldberg, 2000). Just as psychotherapy has moved toward healing adolescent behaviors in a family context, so might it move next to contextualizing individual issues in larger social and environmental concerns. Outdoor adventure therapy, in particular, might be well placed to set directions, practicing as it does, in the larger ecological context, the outdoors.

In sum, the disciplinary paradigm of psychology has relegated the study of nature to the natural sciences; has negated the context and force of human-nature relationships in human development and behavior; has, if at all, considered nature as the backdrop for human endeavors; and has not considered the environmental crisis as an issue of concern for research and theory. Thus, adventure therapists may overlook nature as a context/setting and force in therapy, and may limit the curative relationship to the client-therapist-challenge activities triad. How explanatory models might be expanded to address the ecological context of therapy, and whether or not templates exist to do so, is the question for the final section of this article.

Ecotherapy

The question of how unconscious disciplinary assumptions and tacit understandings might be brought into conscious awareness and made transparent, to then be reflected upon, changed and/or transcended is in itself an intriguing question for psychology. How might adventure programmers, in particular, and psychologists, in general, become aware of the fact that they may be caught in certain disciplinary paradigms that do not necessarily serve the best, or their intended purpose of healing and growth? Transformative experiences, in which personal reality does not match with accepted theory, resulting in internal cognitive-emotional dissonance, are one avenue. Another avenue is interdisciplinary exchange. Deborah Winter, a psychologist, illustrates the power of both avenues in the introduction to her book, *Ecological Psychology* (1996). Confronted with a polluted river, Winter awoke to how the physical world interpenetrates human civilization; on weekend walks with her partner, a geologist, she discovers the world of rocks and dirt as significant to human life and development.

Psychologists know that internal dissonance can be dealt with in at least two ways: one, by transforming one's belief, values, ideologies, worldviews and/or lifestyles; or two, by suppressing and denying the dissonance, to the best of one's capability. Adventure programming as a field, seems yet to have seriously considered the notion, paraphrasing Winter (1996, p. xv), that there is no easy separation between the human and natural worlds, and between the organic and inorganic worlds. Whether or not the issue of human-nature relationships in adventure programming will be accepted as a dissonance, to be resolved or denied, remains to be seen. Responses to Hattie et al.'s (1997) conclusion, such as Nichols' (2000) research agenda for adventure education, which does not mention the setting or human-nature relationships as focus for empirical work, leave room for doubt as to whether or not adventure programming is open to transformation.

Interdisciplinary discourse, and analysis between adventure programming and environmental studies, can help highlight particular disciplinary perceptions, and can alert practitioners to the fact that disciplinary perspectives are always partial and selective (see Chambers, 1984; Gilsdorf, 2000). This might help adventure educators and programmers see, like Winter (1996), that nature is not a mere backdrop for more fascinating beings engaged in challenging activities, but that nature has value in and of itself. Recognizing inherent value may then be followed by accepting responsibility to respect and protect environments (see the environmental education literature for more detail on this point). This would then lead facilitators to think, not only about which activities may be appropriate for which clientele and for which therapeutic endeavor, but also to further question which activity or activities are appropriate, and in which environment(s). Which types of adventure stimulate participants' enjoyment of nature? Those challenge activities that can detract from the environment/ setting, and those that focus attention on participants' surroundings, are issues that can become central to adventure programming. Practitioners may reject this as complicating adventure programming practice. However, such questions are an important step toward respecting and drawing on the healing potential of natural settings. While somewhat intangible, Hattie et al.'s (1997) findings suggest that these aspects of adventure education cannot be underestimated in achieving positive outcomes.

Nature-guided therapy (Berger, 2003; Burns, 1998), and ecotherapy (Clinebell, 1996) are alternative therapeutic modalities that can serve clients, practitioners, and researchers in adventure learning and programming. Both healing modalities explicitly recognize that human contact with natural worlds can have very positive psychological and/or physical effects (for more details, see Frumkin, 2001; Ulrich 1981, 1983, 1984; Ulrich et al., 1991). When the natural worlds are included in theoretical frameworks to help conceptualize and explain why adventure education and programming works, alternative research agendas and, ultimately, theories will emerge that reflect a corrected understanding of the potential power of adventure programming.

Conclusion

All human activities, including education, therapy, and healing, occur embedded in relationships; in social, as well as human-nature relationships. At times, these relationships are neglected, disregarded, or refuted, leading to pathology visible in personal, societal, and/or environmental crises. Whether or not nature is a wilderness, a seminatural park, a cultural landscape (such as the Australian Alps or Scottish Highlands), or an urban setting like the inner-city, it affects our outer and inner life profoundly (Frumkin, 2001; Kaplan & Kaplan, 1989; Tuan, 1974, 1977, 1993; Ulrich, 1981, 1983, 1984; Ulrich et al., 1991; see also Lopez, 1988). Given this, and given that the individualistic, atomistic conceptualization of the self is one probable cause of the environmental crisis (e.g., Kidner, 1994), the relational or ecological self—the self embedded in, and defined by, human and nature relationships—is a more viable conceptualization for our time (see also Mathews, 1991). Adventure learning and programming is well positioned to champion such an ecological redefinition of self and personhood, working, as it does, not only with intimate therapist-client/instructor-student relationships, but also with group relations in the outdoors.

An ecological adventure education, and an ecological adventure psychology, bring forth fascinating and challenging research questions regarding the interplay of intra- and interpersonal with human-nature dynamics in human development, growth, and healing. Eco-adventure programming would bring forth new forms of educational and therapeutic practice; forms of practice that would not only be therapeutic for the client, but which, at the same time, would be therapeutic to the discipline as well as for the world and the Earth. Ultimately, all adventure programming—be it a river trip, an indoor climbing wall, or a ropes course—is eco-adventure programming in that it cannot be divorced from its biophysical setting. Adventure programming committed to healing individuals and the planet would welcome the ecological systems perspective outlined in this article.

Author Note: This article is based on a paper presented at *Whose Journeys? International Outdoor Education Conference,* Buckingham Chilterns University College, High Wycombe, England, April 8–10, 2002, and published under the title *Toward an Ecotherapy Framework in Adventure Therapy* in the *Journeys'* Conference Proceedings. An article on the same topic, co-authored with Peter Martin, appeared in the *Journal of Adventure Education and Outdoor Learning* in 2003. I thank colleagues at La Trobe University, Bendigo, in particular Peter Martin.

References

Amesberger, G. (n.d.). *Theoretical considerations and practical impacts of therapeutic concepts in the outdoors focussing on systematic and environmental perspectives.* Retrieved October 6, 1999, from http://www.eioaee.org/articles/Amesberger.html

Barrett, J., & Greenaway, R. (1995). *Why adventure?* Coventry, England: Foundation for Outdoor Adventure.

Barrows, A. (1998). Crying for the manatees. *ReVision, 20*(4), 9–17.

Beard, C. (2002, April). *The circle and the square: Nature and artificial environments.* Paper presented at Whose Journeys? International Conference, Buckinghamshire Chilterns University College, High Wycombe, England.

Berger, R. (2003, April). *Nature therapy.* Paper presented at the 3rd International Adventure Therapy Conference, Victoria, British Columbia, Canada.

Burns, G. (1998). *Nature-guided therapy.* Philadelphia: Brunner/Mazel.

Chambers, D. W. (1984). *Imagining nature.* Geelong, Victoria, Australia: Deakin University.

Chenery, M. F. (2000). *Sleeping in the quiet of Mt. Jim: A study of the wilderness therapy programs of The Outdoor Experience.* Bendigo, Victoria, Australia: La Trobe University.

Clinebell, H. (1996). *Ecotherapy.* Minneapolis: Fortress Press.

Davis-Berman, J., & Berman, D. S. (1994). *Wilderness therapy: Foundations,theory and research.* Dubuque, IA: Kendall/Hunt.

DeLay, R. (1996). *Constructing the uninhabited home: Participant experience of nature during and follow-ing a wilderness program.* Unpublished manuscript, University of Alberta, Edmonton, Canada.

Evernden, N. (1992). *The social creation of nature.* Baltimore, MD: The Johns Hopkins University Press.

Fideler, D. (1993). [Review of the book *We've had a hundred years of psychotherapy—and the world's getting worse*]. *Gnosis, 28,* 72–73.

Fisher, A. (2002). *Radical ecopsychology.* Albany, NY: State University of New York Press.

Frumkin, H. (2001). Beyond toxicity: Human health and the natural environment. *American Journal of Preventative Medicine, 20*(3), 234–240.

Gillis, H. L., & Ringer, M. (1999). Adventure as therapy. In J. C. Miles & S. Priest (Eds.), *Adventure programming* (2nd ed., pp. 29–37). State College, PA: Venture.

Gilsdorf, R. (2000, March). *Experience-adventure-therapy: An inquiry into professional identity.* Keynote address presented at the 2nd International Adventure Therapy Conference, Augsburg, Germany.

Goldberg, C. (2000). A humanistic psychology for the new millennium. *The Journal of Psychology, 134*(6), 677.

Hattie, J., Marsh, H. W., Neill, J. T., & Richards, G. E. (1997). Adventure education and Outward Bound: Out-of-class effects that have a lasting effect. *Review of Educational Research, 67,* 43–87.

Hillman, J. (1975). *Re-visioning psychology.* New York: Harper & Row.

Hillman, J., & Ventura, M. (1992). *We've had a hundred years of psychotherapy—and the world's getting worse.* San Francisco: Harper San Francisco.

Ibbott, K. (1999). Wilderness therapy. *Psychotherapy in Australia, 5*(2), 6–10.

Kaplan, R., & Kaplan, S. (1989). *The experience of nature: a psychological perspective.* Cambridge, MA: Cambridge University Press.

Kaplan, S., & Talbot, J. F. (1983). Psychological benefits of a wilderness experience. In I. Altman & J. F. Wohlwill (Eds.), *Behavior and the natural environment.* (pp. 163–203). New York: Plenum.

Kidner, D. (1994). Why psychology is mute about the environmental crisis. *Environmental Ethics, 16*(4), 359–376.

Lopez, B. H. (1988). Landscape and narrative. In B. H. Lopez (Ed.), *Crossing open ground* (pp. 61–71). New York: Charles Scribner's Sons.

Mathews, F. (1991). *The ecological self.* London: Routledge.

McKenzie, M. (2000). How are adventure education program outcomes achieved? A review of the literature. *Australian Journal of Outdoor Education, 5*(1), 19–27.

Meinig, D. W. (1979). The beholding eye. In D. W. Meinig (Ed.), *The interpretation of ordinary landscapes* (pp. 33–48). New York: Oxford University Press.

Miles, J. C. (1987). Wilderness as healing place. *Journal of Experiential Education, 10*(3), 4–10.

Miles, J. C., & Priest, S. (Eds.). (1999). *Adventure programming* (2nd ed.). State College, PA: Venture.

Nichols, G. (2000). A research agenda for adventure education. *Australian Journal of Outdoor Education, 4*(2), 22–31.

Roszak, T., Gomes, M. E., & Kanner, A. D. (1995). *Ecopsychology.* San Francisco: Sierra Club.

Seddon, G. (1997). The nature of Nature. In G. Seddon (Ed.), *Landprints* (pp. 7–14). Cambridge, England: Cambridge University Press.

Soper, K. (1995). *What is nature?* Oxford, England: Blackwell.

Taylor, S. (1999). *An exploration of wilderness effects: a phenomenological inquiry.* Retrieved November 15, 2000, from http://www.c-zone.net/taylors/#G

Timms, P. (2001). *Making nature: Six walks in the bush.* Crows Nest, New South Wales, Australia: Allen & Unwin.

Tuan, Y. F. (1974). *Topophilia.* New York: Columbia University Press.

Tuan, Y. F. (1977). *Space and place: The perspective of experience.* Minneapolis, MN: University of Minnesota Press.

Tuan, Y. F. (1993). *Passing strange and wonderful: Aesthetics, nature, and culture.* Washington, DC: Island Press.

Ulrich, R. S. (1981). Natural versus urban scenes: Some psychophysiological effects. *Environment and Behavior, 13*(5), 523–556.

Ulrich, R. S. (1983). Aesthetic and affective response to natural environment. *Human Behavior and Environment: Advances in Theory and Research, 6,* 85–125.

Ulrich, R. S. (1984). View through a window may influence recovery from surgery. *Science, 224*(4647), 420–421.

Ulrich, R. S., Simons, R. F., & Losito, B. D. (1991). Stress recovery during exposure to natural and urban environments. *Journal of Environmental Psychology, 11*(3), 201–230.

Winter, D. D. (1996). *Ecological psychology.* New York: Harper-Collins College.

Speech, Silence, & the Embodied Experience of Place

▾ ▾ ▾

Brian Wattchow

The acclaimed North American nature writer Barry Lopez, in his influential book *Arctic Dreams: Imagination and Desire in a Northern Landscape* (1986), relays the following story. He asked an Inuit man what it was like to encounter a new place. The man's response illustrates the key themes I wish to discuss in this chapter on the relationships between speech, silence, and an embodied sense of place.

> "I listen." That's all. I listen he meant, to what the land is saying. "I walk around it and strain my senses in appreciation of it for a long time before I, myself, ever speak a word."
>
> (Lopez, 1986, p. 257)

The Inuit man in Lopez's story strives to set aside any preconceptions, theory, and expectations about the encounter with place as he listens to the land. His intention is to be obedient to the land before he can ever be ready to speak. He must allow himself to hear the voices that come from the land before he is ready to put words to his experience. Then, when he finally speaks, the land has become meaningful to him as a place. Encountering the land as place relies upon the experiential encounter with a particular location and making it meaningful through the act of reflection and representation in language. It is the reciprocal nature of this embodied knowing and speaking (or writing) of the experience of place that I wish to explore here.

Language and Experience

Place has received significant theoretical attention in human geography and philosophy since the 1970s. It has been a consistent theme among nature writers and poets for much longer, and its origins can be traced to the Romantic Movement, beginning in the 18th century. But an explicit place-based approach in education is a much more recent phenomenon (Gruenwald, 2003; Orr, 1992; Thomashow, 1996; Woodhouse & Knapp, 2000). It may be that the recent interest in place-based education is re-engaging with an old idea—the value of direct experience—usually via field trips, with local places (Knapp, 2005). Why is it necessary to consider the importance of sense of place and place attachment in education? Park (1995) answered this question simply and decisively when he wrote, "A sense of place is a fundamental human need" (p. 320). In his highly influential book *Place and Placelessness*, Relph (1976) demonstrated how places serve as "sources of security and identity" (p. 6), and how the homogenising influence of modern practices (particularly in engineering, agriculture, and architecture and—I might add—education) can result in the experience of displacement or rootlessness. Educating for a responsiveness to place assumes that at least part of education is about preparing people "to live and work to sustain the cultural and ecological integrity of the places they inhabit" (Woodhouse & Knapp, 2000, p. 4).

If educators are to continue to refine the pedagogy of place-based approaches, crucial questions about the relationship between embodied learning, reflection, and the spoken and written representations of learners' experiences must be addressed. These present experiential educators with formidable challenges. What is the relationship between experience, language, and place? What is the status of silence as a form of listening in the reflective process? If participants' experiences cannot be clearly articulated, how are they legitimised? In this chapter I argue that these concerns centre on the roles that language, silence, and the body play in experiential education and that they require our renewed interest.

Over the last 17 years I have been working with university undergraduate experiential outdoor education students in Australia. I recently completed a doctoral research program that inquired into the lived experiences of those students whilst on paddling journeys on the river systems of southeastern Australia (Wattchow, 2006). The research analysed written work that undergraduates had completed at the time of the experiences and collected contemporary interview data. A placed-based inquiry framework was developed based on the work of Raffan (1992; 1993) on the "land as teacher," and van Manen's (1997) work on action-sensitive pedagogy. A number of curious statements were made by participants that compelled me to return to the issues I have introduced here—the embodiment of place, the role of silence, and issues relating to the interpretation and representation of experience. Take, for example, the following quotation from one of the participants in the study, where she described her response to an encounter with a slow-flowing, meandering section of a river on its floodplain.

> It can be like being with somebody you love—overwhelming, intense and moving. The
> sun and wind on my skin, my senses alive and alert and aware, when my mind is at

peace or racing, my breath catching in my throat with fear or exultation, or flowing easily, when my heart beats steadily or pounds furiously, when my chest tightens with emotion I cannot express and I feel I might explode with the enormity of my feelings, when I am brought to tears by the ecstasy and beauty of a place, of just being there, of experiencing it, of sharing it or keeping to myself. I don't know what these feelings symbolise or mean. In many ways I am afraid I might destroy them by analysing them and reducing them to words.

Another participant expressed an even greater level of caution and confusion about the relationship between experience, place, and rational reflection.

The problem that I've been contemplating revolves around the fact that because I can't define the good in what I feel, I find I can't therefore trust in it. I've stumbled across a range of experiences that have felt intrinsically special. In reflection though, doubt creeps in, undermining their importance, leaving me hollow inside.

Numerous other study participants made similar statements. Essentially, all came to the same conclusion: that there are aspects of felt or embodied experiences in the outdoors that elude our literal attempts to "process" them through either our verbalisations or writings. Yet the ability to articulate experience is a typical demand in experiential education pedagogy (Joplin, 1995). Furthermore, and here is the compelling point for experiential educators, the participants in the research seem to suggest that sensing a deep connection with an outdoor place, such as a river, can be diminished and even endangered through the act of attempting to represent it in language (Csordas, 1999). Paradoxically, it is through their writings and articulations that participants are able to recall the importance of the tacit and, perhaps, unspeakable dimensions of embodied experiences.

According to Abram (1996), drawing upon the French philosopher Maurice Merleau-Ponty's investigations into perception and embodiment, humans are in a "silent conversation that [we] carry on with things, a continuous dialogue that unfolds far below [our] verbal awareness" (p. 52). In this view the human body becomes a fundamental structure of experience. It is continually responsive to its environment and is responsible for its environment: "Movements are learned when the body has understood them, and this understanding can be described as a set of invisible threads which run out between the body and the world with which the body is familiar" (Seamon, 1979, p. 47). The outdoors might "speak to us" but we either cannot find the words to say what it is we are "hearing," or we drown its subtle voice with our clumsy attempts to rationalise what we think we have just experienced.

Paying attention to statements from participants such as those quoted earlier can reignite an interest in a longstanding debate within experiential education about whether the mountains (or rivers) should be left to speak for themselves (James, 1980), or whether it requires the careful guidance of a facilitator to assist the learner in defining the meaning of an outdoor encounter. More than 20 years on this debate about direct experience versus facilitation is far from being resolved.

Place or Placelessness

A focus on place in experiential outdoor programs provides ways of understanding how humans relate to particular locations such as rivers. The experience of places is fundamental to the experience of the world. Humans are constantly recreating themselves and learning their place in the world, Relph (1976) argues, through recreating their place. Place then is participatory. It is inherently experiential. There is an unavoidable reciprocity between people and places. "The word 'place' is best applied," writes Relph (1992), "to those fragments of human environments where meanings, activities and a specific landscape are all implicated and enfolded by each other" (p. 37). When facilitators present an outdoor place as an arena for physical adventure, or as a social laboratory, or even as a pristine wilderness, they fail respond to ecological and cultural particularities that give that locality richer and more diverse meanings as a place.

According to David Orr (1992), educators have failed to see much significance in understanding, or attempting to teach the concept of place. He explains that "Place is nebulous to educators because to a great extent we are deplaced people for whom immediate places are no longer sources of food, water, livelihood, energy, materials, friends, recreation or sacred inspiration" (p. 126). The typical curriculum, according to Orr, is based upon abstraction, which disconnects people from "tangible experience, real problems, and the places where we live and work" (p. 126). Experiential educators challenge many of the assumptions and practices found in the "typical" classroom and curriculum, yet rely upon abstraction and transferability of experience. Joplin (1995) has suggested that "experiential programs begin with two responsibilities: providing an experience for the learner, and facilitating the reflection upon that experience" (p. 15). The ability to frame or frontload and then later guide reflection upon and the verbalisation of the meanings of experiences is considered a cornerstone of experiential education theory and practice. It is argued that facilitators need to work with participants so that they can recognise, evaluate, and articulate their learning in order that it may be generalised and drawn upon in the future (Dewey, 1938; Joplin, 1995). Do these core principles of experiential education pose a challenge to both the role of the learner's body in experience and to the ability to respond to place?

Silencing the Body and Place

At the heart of the matter are the development of connections between the learner's embodied experience of place, how s/he interprets those experiences, and how s/he then attempts to represent those experiences in language. I will now discuss how contemporary practices in experiential education risk silencing, or ignoring, the body and place, and suggest some responses that educators might consider that both recognise and respond to this pedagogical challenge.

The educational philosophies of John Dewey (1859–1952) are often cited as a source of inspiration for the experiential education movement. Dewey's main concern in education was for learners to engage in an emancipatory, democratic learning experience rather than to be passive and disengaged in a learning environment controlled by others. Hunt (1995), paraphrasing Dewey, describes the "primary experience" of the learner as the encounter with "the immediate, tangible, and moving world which presents itself to the senses ... the raw materials from which knowledge can begin" (p. 26). Dewey's philosophy of experience and education continues to serve educators well, warning us about the potential dangers of separating the knower from the known and highlighting the sensing body in its environment as the genesis of all learning.

The real educational significance of experience according to Dewey, however, came through "secondary experience." This reflective experience would take the "gross, macroscopic, and crude materials furnished by primary experience and seek to make them precise, microscopic and refined" (Hunt, 1995, p. 27). For Dewey, this was where knowledge, reconstructed as "growth," was forged. He elaborated a scientific method for experience in education, which was controlled and sequential and included learners finding themselves in "felt difficulty," perhaps as demonstrated by the participant quotations presented earlier in this chapter. As a response to this feeling of difficulty the learner must articulate a problem that requires a solution. The learner then generates a hypothesis that is tested and confirmed or disconfirmed (Crosby, 1995). The result is knowledge that could be called upon in later applications. For Dewey (1938),

> ... education in order to accomplish its ends both for the individual learner and for the society must be based upon experience—which is always the actual life-experience of some individual.... The education system must move one way or another, either backward to the intellectual and moral standards of a pre-scientific age or forward to ever greater utilization of scientific method in development of the possibilities of growing, expanding experience. (p. 89)

Dewey's faith in science, human growth and progress is clear. His methods have been adapted and their application in outdoor education (which is one of many subject areas that draws heavily upon experiential pedagogies) has become commonplace. His vision for education was as an experimental science that provided the "best tool for understanding the world in which we live" (Hutchinson, 1998, p. 41). Many experiential learning cycles have been developed in the wake of Dewey's radical educational philosophy. Most notably, Kolb (1984) proposed a four-stage model during which the learner cycled through concrete experience, reflective observation, abstract conceptualisation, and active experimentation. Kolb argued that while the sequence was important, different learners may enter the cycle at different points based upon their preferred learning styles.

I will focus briefly here on Joplin's "hurricane-like" model, primarily due to its popularity in current practice and because it reveals particularly interesting assumptions in relation to embodiment and learning. These learning models have attempted to provide a sequence and a structure to experiential learning encounters, which can often feel fuzzy, messy, and unpredictable for both educator and learner. Joplin's *Experiential Learning Cycle* reworks Dewey's scientific method, and involves a process of leading individuals and groups through challenging activities in a series of pre-emptive and predictable stages.

1. **A Focus Stage:** This stage presents the challenge and "isolates the attention of the learner for concentration" (Joplin, 1995, p. 17).

2. **An Action Stage:** This stage places the learner in a "stressful or jeopardy-like situation where he [*sic*] is unable to avoid the problem presented, often in an unfamiliar environment requiring new skills and knowledge" (p. 17). It becomes "mandatory that the student and his [*sic*] brain be given responsibility for the learning process" (p. 17). Calling upon brain research to justify this stage, Joplin argues that the "brain is 'on' when it is actively choosing, ordering, making decisions" (p. 17).

3. **A Support/Feedback Stage:** Support and encouragement assist the learner in persisting with the challenging task. Joplin expects that "adequate feedback will ensure that the student has the necessary information to be able to move ahead" (p. 18).

4. **The Debrief Stage:** "Here, the learning is recognized, articulated, and evaluated" (p. 19). In this process it is the teacher's responsibility to ensure that the actions previously taken are not left to "drift along unquestioned, unrealised, unintegrated, or unorganised" (p. 19).

Joplin (1995) draws an important distinction between experiential learning, where the "debrief may occur *within* [my emphasis] the individual" (p. 19), and experiential education, where learning must be articulated and made public. The learner's interpretation of his/her experience is "tested" and critiqued in a theorising of the experiential encounter. She goes on to argue that it is through this process of public verification that experiential learning becomes experiential education, and thus becomes acceptable to educational institutions. In Joplin's pedagogy, it is the relationship between the experience *within*, and the necessity for articulation and public verification of that experience that I find problematic. Such an approach may take the learner more deeply into the world of his/her own experience, or rather a verbalised version of it, but it may not move the learner more deeply into his/her experience of the world.

Furthermore, such a pedagogic approach extends Dewey's allegiance to rationalism and, although it may be argued that it is a form of active teaching that "adds visual, tactile, kinesthetic and socio-emotional qualities to the conceptual ones that prevail in conventional classroom teaching, it is *not* primarily concerned with students' experiencing" (Hovelynck, 2001, p. 8). The distinction made here by Hovelynck is crucial for experiential outdoor education and ultimately for the ability to respond to place, which I have already introduced and defined as an embodied, participatory phenomenon. When educators fail to consider experience as dynamic, unfolding and dependent upon its relationship with place, it becomes possible to view the learner's experience as concrete-like, and open to control and manipulation. Experience then becomes objectified, verified, and accounted for in public. To experience (the verb) has wholly different connotations.

> The verb implies that experiences cannot be programmed. Facilitators may program activities, but the experience will necessarily be co-constructed by all involved in the activity, and the facilitation of this process requires a focus on what participants bring to this activity rather than on the activity itself. (Hovelynck, 2001, pp. 8–9)

Much of the neo-industrial and technical language of facilitation, such as "front loading", "framing," "funnelling," (Priest and Gass, 1997) and metaphorically "tooling" ourselves up for facilitation sessions (Boyle and Cotton, 1999), are derivative of Luckner and Nadler's (1992) *Processing the Adventure Experience*. The inherent danger in these approaches is that they potentially draw us away from recognising what is most essential to the nature of experience. They continue to prioritise cognition over embodied experience and the dualistic separation of mind over body. The corporeal body, the entity most fundamental to experiencing, becomes marginalised and silenced.

There are two problems here. First, what is often "produced" as a result of the "processing" in a reflective debriefing session is always a public version of what learners consider is acceptable to say when their peers, teacher, and others are listening. What learners say may even be "corrected" in this setting where the facilitator acts as a "gatekeeper" (Brown, 2002), subtly managing (often subconsciously) who speaks, whose versions of events are endorsed, and whose are not, and who often summarises the meaning of the experience for the participants. For some of the learners, at least, their experience of being processed in the debrief might be one of, as the poet Ted Hughes (2003) put it: "As your speech sharpened/My silence widened" (p. 432). The second problem occurs when the learner cannot "find the words" for what s/he is feeling and therefore cannot express them in a public hearing that claims to articulate the educational value of the experience. The implicit message to the learner is that those feelings that cannot be articulated are less worthy, or not worthy at all, of being considered educational. This scenario where the learner begins to doubt his/her own learning, was nicely encapsulated in the participant quotation I used earlier in this chapter when the student wrote, "because I can't define the good in what I feel I find I can't therefore trust in it."

In the learning situations outlined above, embodied learning can all too easily be de-legitimised. Take, for example, the hierarchical structuring of facilitation techniques outlined by Priest and Gass (1997). "Letting the experience speak for itself" (p. 181), the experience *within* as Joplin called it, is considered the *least* sophisticated of approaches. At this level, according to the authors, learners are considered to potentially "have a good time and possibly become proficient at new skills, but they are less likely to have learned anything about themselves, how to relate to others, or how to resolve certain issues confronting them in their lives" (Priest and Gass, 1997, p. 181). Within the many levels of facilitation techniques that Priest and Gass (1997) endorse, all of them require increasingly sophisticated skill in predicting, managing, and articulating learners' experiences. This brings up a third problem: Because few educators and facilitators are professionally trained as counsellors, they may not be critically reflective about the language they draw upon in facilitation sessions, and have limited life experiences through which to empathise with the learners' experiences. Inevitably, though well intentioned, there is a tendency for facilitation strategies and techniques to become formulaic. Warren (1998) has previously warned about the "one-size-fits-all" approach to facilitation; in particular, the use of metaphors familiar to the facilitator that may not be appropriate for all learners given the potential diversity of gender and cultural backgrounds. The pendulum has swung a long way from allowing the learner to become immersed in his/her experiences to one where his/her experiences are increasingly linguistically managed by the educator or facilitator.

Such a hyper-rationalisation of experience in education has become entrenched, but critics continue to emerge. Martha Bell (1993) argues that Dewey's "promotion of scientific logic can be seen to reinforce linear, cause-effect, 'either-or' terms of facts and knowledge" that gives "a false sense of the unity of knowledge, its objective nature and the ability to 'discover reality'" (p. 21). Chris Loynes (2002) has referred to the facilitation style I have outlined above as "the algorithmic paradigm" of experiential outdoor education. Such an approach, he argues, is epitomized by its commitment to a modernist tradition that promotes a scientific rationale, a production-line metaphor that renders learning a product and thus a marketable commodity.

> The production line approach tempts the provider and the client to consider participants as objects, resource or labour, manufactured to fulfil their potential as a cog in a machine rather than as a human being. The positivist approach reinforces the idea that this object can be manipulated to a formula. Likewise it tempts the facilitator to focus on certain learning objectives to the exclusion of others. The result, pushed to the extreme, is a participant who is oppressed rather than empowered by their managed experience.
> (Loynes, 2002, p. 116)

When this kind of production line approach is deployed in experiential education, experience may not count unless it can be articulated and publicly validated, unless it can be "captured." The practices of some experiential educators dismiss and silence the role of the learner's body and thus endanger the learner's potential to acknowledge the worthiness of his/her embodied sense of place. I am not arguing that experiential educators should abandon their attempts to assist learners in making sense of their experiences. I am saying that unless educators can accept that even though they may carefully design programs that make certain experiences possible (and even probable), there will always be significant and worthwhile aspects of learners' experiences that forever escape attempts to articulate them. Unless this is recognised, experiential pedagogies will continue to serve as a denial of the embodied qualities of experience and, by association, the ability to respond to place.

Language Severs

My intent to this point has been to critique some of the taken-for-granted practices of contemporary experiential education pedagogy. I intend no disrespect to the ideas and practices of those authors whose works I have examined. On the contrary, as a result of their efforts the learner in an experiential program is likely to be greatly advantaged compared to the learner as a disengaged receiver of skills and content that has been pre-arranged by the instructor, teacher, or educational institution. I have strived to show how a desire to both articulate in public, and to generalise from that experience, is problematic for a pedagogy that is responsive to the body and to place. This idea can be further explored by considering the assumptions we make about language and the 'crisis of representation' of human experience (i.e., how problematic it is when various versions of experience come to be articulated and accepted as truths when many other versions are possible and may also compete for that same status). As a result of the 'crisis of representation' we may well ask, "Can any articulated version of experience be accepted as a truth?"

It has been argued that language traps us in a world of linguistic and discursive representations of experience. Language severs us from the direct, primordial, and sensory origins of our experiences in the more-than-human world (Abram, 1996). Elements of postmodern theory have informed us that people "construct" the places they experience through their culture and language, and that these places are little more than the inscriptions made for them. For example, consider the ways that participants in my research study (Wattchow, 2006) describe experiencing paddling river rapids. River rapids represent a very different kind of river place to the calm water sections of rivers described by participants in the earlier quotations, where they struggled to find words for their experiences. By contrast the faster and rougher waters of the rapids elicited a sudden rush of familiar terms from participants. But what exactly are they saying when they describe "scouting" a rapid so that they can "shoot" it, or "run" it, or "play" on it? What representation of the river are they calling up when they say that the river "sucked them down," "swallowed" or "engulfed" them, "churned" and "trashed" them, and finally "spat" them out? For the outdoor adventurer, the river seems to have become a monster that must be "shot" before it can be mastered. This articulated version of experience is shared among the canoeing community, but may ignore local ecology and cultural history, and thus could lead to negative consequences for waterways. The river is experienced as an action-oriented adversary to be mastered rather than as a multifaceted environment to be appreciated and explored.

It is, therefore, possible that learners' embodied knowing can be ignored or discredited in the effort to articulate their experiences, and that the language used and developed through various activities can sever participants from a richer and more diverse experience of place. What can experiential educators do to maintain learners' sense of connections with their bodies and to the places that their experiences take them? We must strive to maintain the delicate tension that ties learners' embodiment of outdoor places with their subjective interpretations of those experiences that are inevitably filtered through layers of culture. Neill (2002) has described the uneasy relationship between experience and facilitation as a "vital tension" for experiential educators. I am deliberately arguing that we need to extend that tension to include the physical locations on the Earth where experiential learning takes place—whether it be a classroom, laboratory, town, farm, river, or mountain, as we strive to assist learners in their efforts to reflect upon and represent their experiences. This requires a renewed sensitivity to speech and silence, a *poesis* of lived local experience. Our task is not to abandon language and literacy, but becomes one of taking up the "word, with all of its potency, and patiently, carefully, writing language back into the land" (Abram, 1996, p. 273).

Poetic Language Speaks "Earth"

There are many pedagogic possibilities for exploring the mutualism of mind-body-place. For many years Outward Bound and other programs have utilised solos late in programs to provide learners time for introspective reflection on the unspeakable tacit dimensions of experience. Such programs have designed a learning space (which ultimately may become a place for participants) where each learner can *think* about the experience while also *feeling* the weight of its significance. Similarly, I know of programs that utilise art, craft, and drama performance as alternative ways of attempting to widen the possibilities for learners to make sense of their experiences and to represent them. To their credit, Priest and Gass (1997) introduce a range of nonverbal strategies that experiential educators might utilise, but the discussion of them is brief and I feel that this typifies how experiential educators continue to overwhelmingly favour and rely upon verbal and literal approaches to facilitation. I do not intend to elaborate on these nonverbal possibilities here as my purpose in this chapter has largely been to deal with issues relating to language, the body, and experience, and this is the theme that I will to continue to explore.

How then might experiential educators assist participants in taking up language and beginning to speak and write it patiently and carefully back into the land and back into experience? For the German philosopher Martin Heidegger, being in the world was to be found in the act of dwelling in place. For Heidegger, sense of place is historical and linguistic and requires constant interpretation and reinterpretation, telling and retelling. But if writing and speaking severs us from our immediate situation, asks Jonathon Bate, "then how can it speak to the condition of ecological belonging?" (2000, p. 251). Heidegger replies with the other half of the paradox:

> There is a special kind of writing, called poetry, which has the peculiar power to speak
>
> 'earth'. Poetry is the song of the earth. (cited in Bate, 2000, p. 251)

Bate (2000) argues that poetry, and we recall that the ancient origins of poetry are in speech, story, and performance in oral cultures, allows us to step outside the technological frame to awaken "the momentary wonder of unconcealment" (p. 258). "For Heidegger," Bate continues, "poetry can, quite literally, save the earth" (p. 258). As Heidegger writes, in his famous essay *Poetically Man Dwells* (2000),

> Poetry builds up the very nature of dwelling. Poetry and dwelling not only do not exclude
>
> each other; on the contrary, poetry and dwelling belong together, each calling for the
>
> other" (p. 93).

For Pinn (2003), poetry offers an intensity of language that is nondualistic, vulnerable, and brings us close to a sense of embodied experience. It can "provide an enfolding of self with place, of the outer with the inner" (p. 45). The potential of poetry and poetics has begun to attract attention in discussions of qualitative research methodologies (Brady, 2005; Stewart, 2005). It offers a way of pursuing knowing and knowledge that has been "ignored and formally discounted" (Brady, 2005, p. 981), suppressed, and relegated to the margins (Pinn, 2003, pp. 45–46). A poetic response to the representation of experiencing can "exceed and complement more conventional strategies" (Brady, 2005, p. 982). It is "tied to the context of the immediate and the immanent, to the processes of 'being there' and sensual saturation" (Brady, 2005, p. 991). One of the participants in my research study chose a poetic style of writing in an attempt to convey his response to an evening solo paddle on a calm, unthreatening section of an inland river.

> I think of and feel
> Gravity, Slope, Time and Energy,
> Life around.
>
> Moon shadow
> Moon reflection,
> On the boat,
> On the water,
> On the forest,
> On the bow wave
>
> Stars pass behind treetops
> I feel the speed of the river
> I travel at the river's pace.
>
> _____
>
> The bow gurgles, a frog sings
> Gently, the bow nudges the shore,
> All I hear now is the forest, river and me
> The life I surround and am

While even such an eloquent poem is still limited in its ability to represent an experience, it provides a different kind of representation than we might normally encourage or expect in a facilitated session. To begin to appreciate the powerful possibilities of bringing a poetic sensibility to language as a way that learners can reflect upon their experiences, we might ask some questions of ourselves as readers and listeners of this poetic story. How is the more-than-human world present in the poem? How does place speak its way into the learner's experience? How does the poem ask us to be silent and to empathise with—rather than attempt to rationalise—the learner's experience? And, finally, we might do well to ask ourselves, in our role as facilitator, if we can add anything to such a delicate dance with words, experience, and place.

The *poetising* of experience does not refer to a particular type of poetry, such as verse-making (van Manen, 1997). Nor, when I use the word "poet," am I referring to the skilful ability to write in a particular way. Rather, I am recognising that each learner has a certain way of being in the world, as Heidegger put it, where language can express much more of the complexity of human experience when we cease to think of it as a neutral conduit of our ideas or as the only means by which humans construct experience. A poetic approach to language, the body, and place recognises the inferences of a storyline, the significance of the setting where the words were first spoken or written, and the necessity of silence before, between, and after words. In taking this approach, we restore the possibility that we can acknowledge a sensuous, embodied feeling for place in language. The fleshy perimeters of the body become osmotic with the flesh of the world (Merleau-Ponty, 2002), and we strive to get close to this feeling through our speaking, writing and yes, through our silences. Silence may take many forms. It may be the silence required in a facilitation session that accepts the learner's attempt to articulate his/her experience without correction or refinement. It may be the kind of silence that is required to suspend, if only for a while, the preprogrammed learning agenda that attempts to anticipate the learner's needs. Finally, it may be the kind of patient silence, as demonstrated in the opening story borrowed from Lopez (1986), that is required to listen deeply to a place.

This renewed attitude to the complexities of speech and silence begins with an expectation that multiple attempts and genres will be required as we try to assist others in making sense of their experiences. I am not arguing that the pedagogic possibilities of either poetic or other nonverbal approaches to facilitation should replace the Deweyian logic of rational reflection as it is currently used in experiential education. Rather, I have attempted to argue for balancing conventional approaches with alternative genres of reflective practice that clearly legitimise the significance of embodiment and place in *all* learning.

Drawing on many genres of reflection may foster an open attempt to avoid the temptation to neatly "capture" and objectify learners' experiences. In a more humble admission of the role we perform as experiential educators, we may also realise that there will be aspects of the learners' experiences where our most articulate response is to say nothing at all. Perhaps this is what is required for us to speak and write as true educators of experience in the world. We recognise that indeed the mountains and the rivers do speak to us, if only we pause to listen. Perhaps then, with this renewed humility, we might briefly penetrate beneath the layers of our assumptions—which inevitably colour our interpretations—and feel our feet touch lightly down upon the reality of the Earth.

References

Abram, D. (1996). *The spell of the sensuous: Perception and language in a more-than-human world.* New York: Vintage Books.

Bate, J. (2000). *The song of the earth.* London: Picador.

Bell, M. (1993). What constitutes experience? *Journal of Experiential Education, 16*(1), 19–24.

Boyle, I., & Cotton, W. (1999). Debriefing tools to enhance reflection and learning, *Proceedings: Eleventh National Outdoor Education Conference, Murdoch University, January 11–15* (pp. 27–30). Greenwood, WA: COEAWA.

Brady, I. (2005). Poetics for a planet: Discourse on some problems of being-in-place. In N. Denzin & Y. Lincoln (Eds.), *The Sage handbook of qualitative research* (3rd ed.) (pp. 979–1025). San Francisco: Sage.

Brown, M. (2002). *Interaction and social order in adventure education facilitation sessions,* Unpublished doctoral dissertation, The University of Queensland.

Csordas, T. (1999). Embodiment and cultural phenomenology: In H. F. Haber, & G. Weiss (Eds.), Perspectives on embodiment: The intersections of nature and culture (pp. 143–162). New York: Routledge.

Crosby, A. (1995). A critical look: The philosophical foundations of experiential education. In K. Warren, M. Sakofs, & J. Hunt (Eds.), *The theory of experiential education* (pp. 3–13). Dubuque, IA: Kendall/Hunt.

Dewey, J. (1938/1998). *Experience and education* (60th edition). West Lafayette, IN.: Kappa Delta Pi.

Gruenewald, D. (2003). The best of both worlds: A critical pedagogy of place. *Educational Researcher, 32*(4), 3–12.

Hovelynck, J. (2001). Beyond didactics: A reconnaissance of experiential learning. *Australian Journal of Outdoor Education, 6*(1), 4–12.

Hughes, T. (2003). Riddle. In *Ted Hughes: Collected poems* (p. 432). London: Faber and Faber.

Hunt, J. (1995). Dewey's philosophical method and its influence on his philosophy of education. In K. Warren, M. Sakofs, & J. Hunt (Eds.), *The theory of experiential education* (pp. 23–32). Dubuque, IA: Kendall/Hunt.

Hutchinson, D. (1998). *Growing up green: Education for ecological renewal.* New York: Teachers College Press.

James, T. (1980). *Can the mountains speak for themselves?* Sourced online (8th September, 2006): [http//www.wilderdom.com/facilitation/Mountains.html].

Joplin, L. (1995). On defining experiential education. In K. Warren, M. Sakofs, & J. Hunt (Eds.), *The theory of experiential education* (pp.15–22). Dubuque, IA: Kendall/Hunt.

Kolb, D. (1984). *Experiential learning*. Englewood Cliffs, NJ: Prentice–Hall.

Knapp, C. (2005). The 'I-Thou' relationship, place-based education, and Aldo Leopold. *Journal of Experiential Education, 27*(3), 277–285.

Lopez, B. (1986). *Arctic dreams: Imagination and desire in a northern landscape*. New York: Picador.

Loynes, C. (2002). The generative paradigm. *Journal of Adventure Education and Outdoor Learning, 2*(2), 113–125.

Luckner, J., & Nadler, R. (1997). *Processing the experience: Strategies to enhance and generalize learning*. Dubuque, IA: Kendall/Hunt.

Neill, J. (2002). *Are the mountains still speaking for themselves? A defining tension 20 years on*. Sourced online (8th September, 2006): [http//www.wilderdom.com/facilitation/Mountains.html].

Merleau-Ponty, M. (2002 edition). *Phenomenology and perception*. London: Routledge.

Orr, D. (1992). *Ecological literacy: Education, and the transition to a postmodern world*. Albany: State University of New York Press.

Pinn, J. (2003). Restor(y)ing a sense of place, self and community. In J. Cameron (Ed.), *Changing Places: Re-imagining Australia* (pp. 38–47). Double Bay, 1360, NSW: Longueville Books.

Priest, S., & Gass, M. (1997). *Effective leadership in adventure programming*, Champaign, IL: Human Kinetics.

Raffan, J. (1992). *Frontier, homeland and sacred space: A collaborative investigation into cross-cultural perceptions of place in the Thelon Game Sanctuary, Northwest Territories*. Unpublished doctoral dissertation, Queen's University, Kingston, Ontario.

Raffan, J. (1993). The experience of place: Exploring land as teacher. *Journal of Experiential Education, 16(1),* 39–45.

Relph, E. (1976). *Place and placelessness*. London: Pion Limited.

Relph, E. (1992). Modernity and the reclamation of place. In Seamon, D. (Ed.), *Dwelling, seeing, and designing: Toward a phenomenological ecology* (pp. 25–40). New York: State University of New York Press.

Seamon, D. (1979). *A geography of the lifeworld: Movement, rest and encounter*. New York: St. Martin's Press.

Stewart, K. (2005). Cultural poesis: The generativity of emergent things. In N. Denzin & Y. Lincoln (Eds.), *The Sage handbook of qualitative research* (3rd ed.) (pp. 1027–1042). San Francisco: Sage.

Thomashow, M. (1996). *Ecological identity: Becoming a reflective environmentalist*. Cambridge, MA: The MIT Press.

van Manen, M. (1997). *Researching lived experience: Human science for an action sensitive pedagogy*. London, Ontario: The Althouse Press.

Warren, K. (1998). A call for race, gender, and class sensitive facilitation in outdoor experiential education. *Journal of Experiential Education, 21*(1), 21–25.

Wattchow, B. (2006). *The experience of river places in outdoor education: A phenomenological study*. Unpublished doctoral dissertation. Monash University, Australia.

Woodhouse, J., & Knapp, C. (2000). *Placed-based curriculum and instruction.* (Eric Document reproduction Service No. EDO-RC-00-6.)

Historical Foundations

▾ ▾ ▾

The Historical Roots of Experiential Education

▾ ▾ ▾

Mary Breunig

I wish to open this chapter with two short vignettes. A friend of mine recently asked me what kind of expectations I had for my students related to their employment postgraduation. He asked me if the program that I teach in was preparing students for teaching in the K-12 classroom, or if the program was alternatively preparing students to serve as wilderness trip guides and leaders, or if the program was offering students a broad-based curriculum related to recreation and leisure theory and practice and thus preparing them for work as recreation professionals. My response to all of his proposed employment prospects for my students was "yes." I responded that the mission and vision of our program was to use recreation and leisure studies curriculum, specifically outdoor recreation curriculum, to prepare students to serve as agents of social and environmental change in the World. My friend's response was an awed "wow," but I was quick to follow up with a confession that I wasn't sure how well we were yet doing with this intended programmatic "end" given that our program was relatively "new." The method for accomplishing this end vision in our outdoor recreation program is to offer an outdoor recreation curriculum that experientially educates students with a set of knowledge, skills, and dispositions that prepares them to serve as agents of social and environmental change in the world (Brock University Calendar, 2008).

Obviously, the program that I teach in is not the only experiential education program doing this. In fact, at a recent annual conference of the Association for Experiential Education (AEE), I was struck by the number of conference workshops and conversations that addressed the importance of intent, aim, and purpose in experiential education. I was particularly intrigued by the diversity of purposes that were being discussed. A large number of these workshops highlighted the potential for experiential education to serve as a vehicle for social change, particularly within academic programs. Given my experience in co-authoring the vision statement for the postsecondary program in which I teach and given my experience at the conference, I felt impelled to revisit the philosophical roots of experiential education in an effort to better understand how the aim of social change has come to the fore.

The discussion that follows—about both the philosophy of experiential education and its modern-day principles and practices—will reveal that experiential education is rooted in the educational ideal of social change. The purpose of this historical overview is to provide the reader with some background of these roots and to additionally compel the reader to consider how well experiential educators fulfil the intended aim of social change.

Experiential Learning and Experiential Education

Experiential learning and experiential education are buzz words within many educational circles. These terms are often used interchangeably. There are numerous published definitions of experiential education (Joplin, 1981; Luckmann, 1996; Itin, 1999). The Association for Experiential Education (2004) defines experiential education as both a philosophy and methodology in which educators purposefully engage with learners in direct experience and focused reflection to increase knowledge, develop skills, and clarify values. Central to this definition is the distinction between experiential education as methodology and experiential education as philosophy. This distinction suggests that there is a difference between experiential learning and experiential education.

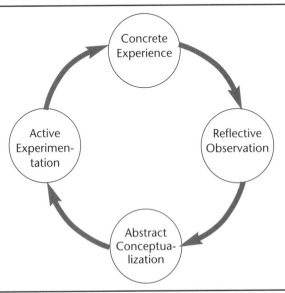

Figure 1. **Experiential Learning Cycle**

David Kolb (1984) provides a useful model to illustrate experiential learning as a cycle (see Figure 1). According to Kolb (1984), experiential learning consists of four distinct segments: "(a) active student involvement in a meaningful and challenging experience, (b) reflection upon the experience individually and in a group, (c) the development of new knowledge about the world, and (d) application of this knowledge to a new situation" (Knapp, 1992, pp. 36–37).

Many experiential education initiatives are based on this learning cycle but do not prescribe an intended learning outcome or aim. Employing the experiential learning cycle without an intended educational aim represents experiential learning as methodology, implying that there is a certain way of teaching that makes the learning experiential.

Experiential education as philosophy employs both methodology (an experiential way of teaching) and philosophy as part of the educative process. Experiential education as philosophy implies that there is an intended aim toward which the experiential learning process is directed. In this sense, the intent of experiential education is just that—an intentional, purposeful approach to teaching and learning.

This next section will provide the reader with a glimpse into the philosophical roots of experiential education theory, with a particular view toward the themes of social change and social justice. It will also highlight the distinctions between experiential education and more "traditional" forms of schooling.

Philosophical Roots

Experiential learning represents one of the earliest forms of education in the Western world. In fact, examples of experience-based learning are found in some of the earliest forms of teaching, including learning passed through storytelling and oral tradition, particularly in First Nations and Native cultures. However, with the advent of the printing press in 1470 and the economic changes resulting from the industrial revolution, the idea of providing a universal and compulsory system of education at the state's expense was born. The first state public school was founded in Europe in the late 1660s by an order requiring student attendance (Good & Teller, 1969). The result was an educational trend that supported what was thought to be a socially efficient means of educating young people to prepare them to enter a work force that was rapidly changing and evolving. More students in schools meant that more efficient means of transmitting information were required. As a result, school curriculum evolved into an assembly line by which economically and socially useful citizens were produced en masse (Pinar, Reynolds, Slattery, & Taubman, 2002). Social utility was the sole means by which school curriculum was judged.

Johann Friedrich Herbart (1776–1841)

In reaction to this "traditional" and supposedly socially efficient approach to teaching and learning, an educational project that focused on the learner and the development of the student's character was also gaining momentum. At the forefront of this educational initiative was the German philosopher Johann Friedrich Herbart. Herbart was influenced by the Italian educator Johann Heinrich Pestalozzi, who believed that students were inherently "good" and should be governed by the principle of love and not fear. Herbart suggested that school curriculum should be developed in accord with the following principles: (a) preparation: teachers take into account students' previous learning experiences; (b) presentation: learning materials are outlined; (c) association: new information is compared with what is already known by the student(s); (d) generalization: rules and general principles are derived from new information; and (e) application: generalizations are applied in practice (Herbart, 1895). The similarities between Herbart's five learning principles and Kolb's (1984) experiential learning cycle in Figure 1 are remarkable. Herbart's first principle, that teachers consider students' previous learning experience, provided the child-centered advocates with further endorsement of the importance of this idea. In the book *On the Education of Man*, Friedrich Wilhelm August Froebel (1826) purported that child-centred, student-initiated play was the best method for both learning and development, providing further evidence of some of the early educational initiatives that provided an "alternative" option to the predominant model of social efficiency.

William James (1842–1910)

This early evidence of the importance of concrete experience led to the development of pragmatism, which represents both a method for analyzing philosophical problems and a theory of meaning that turns away from abstraction toward concrete facts and actions. Charles Sanders Pierce is considered the founder of pragmatism. He and fellow pragmatic William James concluded that humans generate belief through their "habits of action," or that ideas and truths are developed through experience (Noddings, 1995). James considered pragmatism to be both a method for analyzing philosophic problems and a theory of truth. Theories, he felt, are "instruments" that humans use to solve problems and should be judged in terms of their practical consequences for human conduct.

Colonel Francis Parker (1837–1902) and John Dewey (1859–1952)

Colonel Francis Parker, who many regard as the father of progressive education, used the pragmatic educational ideals to argue the case of child-centered curriculum reform. In what became known as the "'Quincy system,' children learned to read, write, spell, and think simultaneously" (Pinar et al., 2002). Progressive education was inaugurated in Quincy, Massachusetts, with Parker's work (Pinar et al., 2002). A more well-known progressivist and colleague of Francis Parker's was John Dewey, who is often regarded as one of the "founders" of experiential education. Dewey believed that the child's experience must form the basis of the school curriculum. He believed that subject matter should not be learned in isolation and maintained the importance of acquainting students and teachers with the conditions of the local community (physical, historical, economic, and occupational) in order to utilize them as educational resources. Dewey believed that the main aim of education was the preparation of individuals to participate in social change (Dewey, 1904; 1938).

Dewey (1916/1944) believed that experience is one means to broaden students' knowledge, bringing awareness to bear and leading in a constructive direction toward "intelligent action." Intelligent action is considered rather than impulsive and is shaped by information garnered from previous experiences while bearing in mind one's goal or purpose (one that serves society) (Dewey, 1916/1944). According to Dewey, the aim of progressive education is "to take part in correcting unfair privilege and unfair deprivation, to perpetuate them" (p. 119).

Dewey's theoretical principles were formulated into a practical application with Kilpatrick's project method. According to Kilpatrick (1918), a project was a wholehearted purposeful activity occurring in a social environment. To achieve a project's aim, students should practice all four aspects of any given project, including purposing, planning, executing, and judging. For Kilpatrick, the project method became an organizing principle of the curriculum. He conceived of the curriculum as a series of experiences in which a child makes his/her own formulation and conclusions, guided by induction (Kilpatrick, 1925). For both Dewey and Kilpatrick, isolated experience was not enough. Experiences needed to be formulated based on both previous experience and the intended outcome of the present experience. Dewey (1938) referred to this as continuity of experience. He further argued that an experience was genuine only when it met the above criteria of continuity and was purposeful and directed toward some intentional end. It is clear that the early work of the progressivists laid the groundwork for our present-day understanding of experiential education and the importance of education as a means for social change.

Maria Montessori (1870–1952) and Rudolf Steiner (1861–1925)

Many school reform efforts were also influenced by progressivism. Numerous educators brought the progressive ideals of experience-based teaching and learning into the classroom. Maria Montessori (The Montessori Method) and Rudolf Steiner (Waldorf School), in particular, deserve mention. According to Montessori, the aim in education is twofold: biological and social. From the biological side, the goal is to foster the natural development of the individual; from the social standpoint, the aim is to prepare the individual for the environment. Discipline, reflection, muscular education, nature in education, and education of the senses and intellect are all important aspects of schooling (Montessori, 1974).

The basic premise of the Waldorf School is that reconstruction of society must begin at school, and education has the potential to develop new understanding and human values appropriate for the times. Waldorf schools, acting upon the insights of Rudolf Steiner, use a curriculum and methodology that fit the child's various stages of development. The schools are based on the concept of free play in a classroom environment that is homelike. Language is developed through songs, poems, and movement games. The schools are full of all natural materials (Toronto Waldorf School, 1972).

Another fundamental insight Steiner brought to education was the intimate relationship between the physical, the psychological, and the spiritual in the human being. In September 1919, the first Waldorf School opened its doors in Stuttgart, Germany, and the first North American school was founded in New York City in 1928 (Toronto Waldorf School, 1972).

It is thanks to the vision and work of these pragmatic and progressive philosophers and educators that the foundation for implementing experiential education in the K-12 school system was laid. In the past quarter-century, the Association for Experiential Education (AEE) and its allied organizations have attempted to bring American public education back to the fundamental proposition that all genuine education comes through experience (Warren, Sakofs, & Hunt, 1995, p. xii). Some of these more recent educational initiatives will be discussed in the section that follows.

Early Experiential Education Initiatives in K-12 Schools

It is hard to say when and where experiential education formally entered the North American school system. This section explores some of the ways in which the above progressive principles influenced the early experiential education initiatives in schools, including: adventure education and the organized camping movement, Outward Bound, K-12 public school initiatives, outdoor and environmental education centers, folk schools, and Quaker schools. It will provide a brief overview of each of these programs as a means to explore the ways in which K-12 experiential school-based initiatives have built upon the educational ideals of the progressivists.

Adventure Education and the Organized Camping Movement

One means by which experiential education entered the modern day K-12 school system was through adventure education. The purpose of adventure education is to bring about an awareness of positive changes in individuals through an outdoor or adventure activity (Priest, 1999). Activities may include hiking, ropes courses, rock-climbing, skiing, snowshoeing, and camping. The organized camping movement of the early 1900s served as a model for the development of many K-12 school programs. Within the camping movement, educators began teaching using expeditions, camping, and challenge activities in North

America as early as 1861 (Raiola & O'Keefe, 1999). YMCA Camp Pinecrest, near Toronto, is one of the oldest youth camps in North America. Pinecrest was established in the early 1900s with a focus on outdoor living skills, environmental education, cultural diversity, and leadership development. The central mission of the camp was to offer opportunities for personal growth and service to others (Hirsch, 1999).

K-12 schools began to adopt the wilderness-trip model used by camps as early as the late 1800s. At the Gunnery School in Connecticut, the whole school went on a two-week, 40-mile journey at the end of the school year. Laura Mattoon was one of many activists in the early 20th century concerned with the instruction and personal growth of young women. She led an expedition in the summer of 1902 to the New Hampshire wilderness with her private girls' school students, integrating the outdoor experience with geological field studies (Raiola & O'Keefe, 1999).

Outward Bound

In 1941, Kurt Hahn established Outward Bound (OB), which represents another example of the application of adventure education in the school environment. Outward Bound, along with Hahn's other educational initiatives—Gordunston School, United World Colleges, Salem Schule, and the Duke of Edinburgh Award Scheme—were all based on the notion that educating youth for the purpose of building moral character was just as important as training the intellect.

The founding of OB was a reaction to the fact that many young British men were dying in lifeboats during World War II. Hahn believed that "character" could be taught to these young men, and character development was what was needed for young people to withstand the harsh and close-quartered living conditions on the lifeboats. Twenty-one years later, the founders of the Colorado OB School raised similar concerns about the character of Americans (James, 1995). Young people in America were seen to be increasingly apathetic and self-centered. The purposes of the OB school were to use the mountains as a classroom to produce "better" people, to build character, and to instil a collective spirit into a group of individuals.

Project Adventure and Expeditionary Learning Outward Bound

As principal of Hamilton-Wenham Junior-Senior High School in Massachusetts in 1970, Jerry Pieh and his colleague Gary Baker were interested in how to "mainstream" the OB process into a secondary public school setting. Their goal was to have the OB process become a part of the standard high-school curriculum. To that end, in 1970 they founded a new program they called Project Adventure (PA). The largest component of the initial program was focused on 10th-grade physical education, but English, history, science, theatre, and counselling were also explored in the context of what came to be known as "adventure activities" (Prouty, 1999). For more than 30 years, Project Adventure has been successfully bringing adventure education into the classroom as an integrated, experience-based approach to teaching academic curricula.

In 1992, Outward Bound further developed its K-12 school-based initiatives with the introduction of the Expeditionary Learning OB program, which represents a proven model for comprehensive school reform for elementary, middle, and high schools. It is based on the following 10 design principles:

1. the primacy of self-discovery;

2. the having of wonderful ideas;

3. the responsibility for learning;

4. intimacy and caring;

5. success and failure;

6. collaboration and competition;

7. diversity and inclusivity;

8. the natural world;

9. solitude and reflection, and

10. service and compassion. (Cousins, 1998)

Now midway into its second decade, Expeditionary Learning OB operates within more than 60 schools throughout the United States. It emphasizes learning by doing, with a particular emphasis on character growth, teamwork, and literacy. It connects academic learning to adventure and service. It provides a framework for educators that informs them about how to teach traditional academic curricula (reading, writing, science, and math) through a challenging set of real-world projects called learning expeditions.

Integrated Programs

Project Adventure and Expeditionary Learning Outward Bound represent just two examples of an integrated approach in the United States. Experiential education exists in a variety of forms within the K-12 school system. In Canada, for example, there exist a number of integrated Environmental Studies Programs (ESPs). Students in these integrated programs spend the full day with one group of peers and one or two teachers for the full school semester. Four or five academic subjects are grouped together and taught by those teachers who have expertise within that particular area of study. A number of these integrated programs that exist in Canadian schools. Ontario has a growing number of integrated environmental studies programs at the secondary level, and in 2000 there were approximately 30 of these in existence (Russell & Burton, 2000).

Outdoor and Environmental Education Centers

Outdoor and environmental education centers in North America represent another setting in which experiential education is employed. These centers are often funded by both state and provincial school boards. A visit to an outdoor center integrates students' classroom learning in science, math, social sciences, and health and physical education with an outdoor experience (Henderson & Potter, 2001). These centers offer traditional outdoor activities and environmental programs, as well as project-based work that integrates academic curricula with outdoor activities.

Many school programs offer adventure-based experiences as extracurricular or "add on" activities: Options include field trips, community service projects, wilderness trips, or even a trip to a city museum that has little or no link to academic curricula. Many outdoor clubs exist within the K-12 public school system, providing camping and outing experiences during non-school hours or holiday breaks. Some schools offer adventure-based experiences as part of the physical education curriculum (Breunig, 2001).

Many of these K-12 school-based initiatives are founded on the principles of progressive education and act upon the ideal that experiential education is both methodology and philosophy. In essence, the ideal would be that the outdoor and experiential activities are the means. The intended educational aim of these initiatives would follow the pragmatic and progressive ideals of social change, preparation for citizenship, an ethic of service, and/or character development. The query that needs to be addressed here is: how successful are the present day K-12 experiential education initiatives at identifying an educational "end" and at achieving that intended end? Is the aim of experiential education as a means for social change being achieved as a result of these K-12 educational initiatives? Are these initiatives staying true to their philosophical roots? Are programs employing experiential education as both methodology and philosophy or are K-12 initiatives employing experiential learning and outdoor activities as the sole ends of their programs? While hard to answer, these questions are important ones to ask as part of an examination of experiential education as a potential vehicle for social change.

Folks Schools and Quaker Schools

A number of folk schools established in the United States by Danish-Americans predate the initiatives discussed above. These are discussed here because they were based on an implicit outdoor education context that distinguishes them somewhat from some of the more explicit efforts outlined above. The main mandate of these schools was for people to obtain not only knowledge that was practical, but to obtain the sorts of values that would prepare them to be good citizens. These folk schools were particularly attractive to progressives wanting to bring together economic, political, and educational experiences (Kett, 1994).

In 1786, Friends Seminary opened its doors in New York City. Its name derives from the Quaker belief that "if Friends were to be useful members of society, Quaker schools were needed to teach both basic subjects and the particular viewpoint toward life by which Friends try to live" (New York Yearly Meeting, 1974). It is believed that the "[t]hree R's of reading, writing, and arithmetic should be taught as deliberately as material that educates to the purposes of imagination, reflection, and intuition. A Friends school should so educate experientially that the word and life become one" (Heath, 1979). Experiential education in both folk schools and Quaker schools was reflected in the curricular emphasis on physical activity, hands-on learning experiences that were both useful and practical, and wilderness trip experiences. Service-learning experiences that integrated the curriculum with an intentional social change agenda emphasized the importance of intentional, purposeful action. The intended aim of these experiences was to prepare people to be good citizens and to participate in society, helping to bring about the world that "ought to be" (New York Yearly Meeting, 1974).

Higher Education

This section provides an overview of some of the experiential settings and many of the principles and practices of experiential education involved in higher education. It serves as a reminder of the variety of contexts that comprise experiential education practice. It will be up to the reader to consider in what ways these contexts fulfill the intended aim of experiential education as a vehicle for social change. Hopefully, the reader will feel impelled to examine the educational aim of his/her own practice as a result of this overview.

Experiential Education in Higher Education

L.B. Sharp was one of the early pioneers of camping education and the first person to receive a doctorate in camping education from Columbia University in 1929 (Raiola & O'Keefe, 1999). The Chicago School, Teachers College at Columbia University, and the Laboratory School of the University of Missouri were some of the earliest experience-based colleges and universities influenced by Dewey and other progressivists. The curriculum for these schools focused on primitive life activities, domestic occupation, nature study, and construction work. Reading and writing were closely related to these activities and arithmetic was connected with the activities as far as seemed feasible (Good & Teller, 1969).

In 1974, a large number of college and university professionals met for a conference that led to the development of the Association for Experiential Education (Miner & Boldt, 1981). According to Michael Gass (1999) of the University of New Hampshire, however, most existing university programs have not developed through a general need perceived by higher education professionals, but rather through the self-designed efforts of select individuals at particular institutions. The applications of most early adventure education programs in higher education were varied: student orientation, student development, residential life-training programs, physical education activity classes, outing clubs, and to a lesser extent to enhance academic curricula.

More recently, there has been growth in the degree-granting programs that award both undergraduate and graduate degrees for outdoor education and recreation (e.g., University of Minnesota, State University of New York-Cortland, Brock University, University of New Hampshire) and experiential education (e.g., Prescott College, Minnesota State University-Mankato). Experiential education programs in higher education have just begun to receive external professional acceptance, and perhaps this is an area that represents the greatest growth potential within the industry.

Two additional outdoor schools deserve mention here. The National Outdoor Leadership School (NOLS), founded in 1965, is a nonprofit school, recognized as the international leader in the field of wilderness-based education and outdoor leadership. The main program objectives of NOLS are leadership development, outdoor skills, minimum-impact conservation techniques, and expedition dynamics. Today, NOLS is regarded as the premier wilderness-leader school in the country, with a particular emphasis on technical skill training (Bachert, 1999). The Wilderness Education Association (WEA) is dedicated to certifying wilderness course leaders who are capable in planning, outfitting, conducting, and teaching certification courses of at least four weeks duration in an actual wilderness environment (Teeters & Lupton, 1999).

Higher education, degree-granting programs, and certification programs represent sites of experiential education that may provide great potential in emphasizing the importance of identifying an educational "end" toward which the teaching and learning is directed. At the moment, many of these programs emphasize experiential learning without identifying the potential for experiential education to work toward an intended educational aim. More work needs to be done in this area.

More Recent Offshoots

Although every experiential program, application, setting, and population cannot be mentioned here, there are a number of closely connected experience-based programs that are noteworthy. Mark Lund (1999) makes note of many of these in a paper entitled "Outdoor Education—From the Roots to the New Branches." Those that will be mentioned here include service learning, experience-based training and development, therapeutic recreation, and women's outdoor adventure programs.

Service learning. Service learning provides a bridge between the various forms of experience-based teaching and learning. Service learning is more than simple volunteerism or community service; it is service that is integrated with academic curriculum and is based on real community needs. People providing the service recognize their own learning and the growth gained from engaging in the service project (Breunig, 2001). The Minnesota Department of Education defines community service learning as an instructional strategy in which students are involved in experiential education in real-life settings and where they apply academic knowledge and previous experience to meet real community needs (Minnesota Department of Education, 1992). Service is one of the pillars of Outward Bound, it is a basic tenet of Quakerism, and with the passing of the National Community Service Act of 1990 in the United States (Nathan & Kielsmeier, 1991), service has gained prominence in public education as well as colleges and universities. Adventure-based programs throughout North America incorporate service as a component to their field experiences. Service learning provides a practical means to apply experiential education in working toward social change.

Experience-based training and development. Experience-based training and development (EBTD) emerged in the early 1980s. EBTD goes by many names: corporate adventure training, outdoor management development and, originally, executive challenge programming. EBTD is adventure education used with managers and executives of corporations that focuses specifically on teamwork and group processes. The overall goal of EBTD is to improve workplace performance. Activities include problem-solving initiatives, personality inventories, challenge course elements, and wilderness or high-adventure programming (Miner, 1999).

Therapeutic recreation. Wilderness therapy, also called adventure therapy or therapeutic recreation, emerged from some of the early camping movement programs, including Life Camps, a camp for underprivileged city children under the direction of L.B. Sharp. Adventure therapists have taken adventure education principles and applied them to diverse groups of clinical clients. Adventure therapy is the deliberate, strategic combination of adventure activities with therapeutic change processes with the goal of making lasting changes in the lives of people (Gillis & Ringer, 1999). The use of adventure experiences for therapeutic purposes is documented with such clinical populations as substance abusers, adjudicated youth, and clients served in private practices and psychiatric hospitals (Gillis & Ringer, 1999).

The passage of the Americans with Disabilities Act (ADA) (1990) has increased accessible adventure-based programming as well. Programs that include persons with disabilities and programming adventure for older adults are two areas that have received increased focus as a direct result of ADA. Persons with disabilities are going to private and public facilities to experience the benefits of participation in adventure activities. According to Leo McAvoy and Greg Lais (1999), the most integrated setting is one that enables interaction between persons with and without disabilities. Wilderness Inquiry, Inc. of Minneapolis is one such organization that integrates persons with and without disabilities on wilderness trips. According to the President's Commission on Americans Outdoors, the demand for outdoor recreation is steadily increasing, with 90 percent of Americans seeking enjoyment from the outdoors. The commission also found that the average age of outdoor enthusiasts is steadily climbing (Lucas & Krumpe, n.d.). Consideration needs to be given to designing outdoor programs for this growing population.

Women's outdoor adventure programs. Women's outdoor adventure programs and outdoor programs that support a crosscultural perspective are continuing to grow and develop within the field of experiential education: "Forming networks of women who have found value in the outdoors, promoting adventure options through women's educational, social and cultural organizations, and offering short courses which allow women to sample the wilderness without making a huge time or financial commitment are all possibilities for adventure institutions to pursue to avert inaccessibility" (Warren, 1999). Programs such as Outward Bound, Woodswomen, and Women Outdoors have all experienced success in offering programs for women.

Targeted programs for teaching crosscultural perspectives (Washington & Roberts, 1999), programs for at-risk youth (Davis-Berman & Berman, 1999), and targeted programs for Native populations (Roberts, 1996) are also on the rise.

Many of the contemporary offshoots of experiential education would suggest that there is great potential for these programs to emphasize their capacity to effect social change. For example, using adventure and experiential education as a means to serve a community, enhance therapy, and/or support a crosscultural perspective has great potential to evoke social change in a very tangible way. Further exploration about how to work toward the educational end of social change through meaningful contemporary experiential education initiatives is also worthy of mention.

Conclusion

Despite its early roots in the progressive education movement, experiential education as a practice is still relatively new. This may be in part because experiential education practice has not yet found its way into more mainstream school environments. As future trends are considered within the field of experiential education, educators need to consider how to better mainstream experience-based programs into more traditional schools and environments. It is time for experiential educators to "come inside" and enter the public school system as a means to engage in a more meaningful and integrated experiential education practice.

It is interesting to note how our philosophical roots share the common educational ideal of social change. Herbart, Froebel, James, Parker, Dewey, and Kilpatrick were all dedicated to using education as a means for social change. Hahn developed a number of modern day experiential schools on this same ideal. Montessori, Steiner, and the early K-12 school initiatives that employed experiential education shared this common goal as well. Experiential education has widespread applications and transformative potential as both an educational philosophy and as a vehicle for social change.

One question that I am often asked by students in my fourth-year experiential education course is, "Since educating people to be actively engaged in social change was such a seminal part of pragmatism, progressivism, and experiential education, why is it not employed in practice more globally in the K-12 school system today?" This question reflects the need to develop both the theory and practice of experiential education. I believe educators need to further develop ways of integrating experiential education more fully into various sites of learning. Experiential education needs to continue to explore how to implement a more widespread application beyond the field of adventure education. Identifying and emphasizing the potential of experiential education as a vehicle for social change may be one way to better accomplish that.

Additionally, more work needs to be done to integrate experiential philosophy into a more meaningful classroom practice. It is easy to espouse the theory, but it can be time-consuming and challenging to actually engage in meaningful experiential practice within the classroom. Clearly, we need to better understand our philosophical roots and the transformative potential of experiential education.

References

Association for Experiential Education (2004). *What is experiential education?* Retrieved Feb. 23, 2004, from www.aee.org

Bachert, D. (1999). The national outdoor leadership school: 40,000 wilderness experiences and counting. In J. C. Miles & S. Priest (Eds.), *Adventure Programming* (pp. 85–93). State College, PA: Venture.

Breunig, M. (2001). *A discussion of parallels between experiential education and Quaker education.* Boulder, CO: Association for Experiential Education.

Brock University Calendar (2008). *Outdoor recreation concentration.* Retrieved August 9th, 2008 from http://www.brocku.ca/webcal/2008/undergrad/recl.html#sec11

Cousins, E. (1998). *Reflections on design principles – Expeditionary Learning Outward Bound.* Dubuque, IA: Kendall/Hunt.

Davis-Berman, J. & Berman, D. (1999). The use of adventure-based programs with at-risk youth. In J. C. Miles & S. Priest (Eds.), *Adventure programming* (pp. 365–373). State College, PA: Venture.

Dewey, J. (1904). The relation of theory to practice in education. In M. L. Borrowman (Ed.), *Teacher education in America: A documentary history.* New York: Teachers College Press.

Dewey, J. (1916/1944). *Democracy and education.* New York: Free Press.

Dewey, J. (1938). *Experience and education.* New York: MacMillan.

Froebel, F. (1826). *On the education of man.* Leipzig, Germany: Keilhau.

Gass, M. (1999). Adventure programs in higher education. In J. C. Miles & S. Priest (Eds.), *Adventure programming* (pp. 373–385). State College, PA: Venture.

Gillis, L. & Ringer, M. (1999). In J. C. Miles & S. Priest (Eds.), *Adventure programming* (pp. 29–39). State College, PA: Venture.

Good, H. & Teller, J. (1969). *A history of western Europe*. (3rd ed.). London: The Macmillan Company, Collier-Macmillan Limited.

Heath, D. (1979). *The peculiar mission of a Quaker school.* Pendle Hill, PA: Pendle Hill.

Henderson, B. & Potter, T. (2001). Outdoor adventure education in Canada: Seeking the country way back in. *Canadian Journal of Environmental Education, 6*, 225–242.

Hirsch, J. (1999). Developmental adventure programs. In J. C. Miles & S. Priest (Eds.), *Adventure programming* (pp. 13–29). State College, PA: Venture.

Itin, C. M. (1999). Reasserting the philosophy of experiential education as a vehicle for change in the 21st century. *Journal of Experiential Education, 22*(2), 91–98.

James, T. (1995). Kurt Hahn and the aims of education. In K. Warren, M. Sakofs, & J. S. Hunt Jr. (Eds.), *The theory of experiential education* (pp. 33–45). Boulder, CO: Association for Experiential Education.

Joplin, L. (1981). On defining experiential education. *Journal of Experiential Education, 4*(1), 17–21.

Kett, J. F. (1994). *The pursuit of knowledge under difficulties: From self-improvement of adult education in America,* 1750–1990. Stanford, CA: Stanford University Press.

Kilpatrick, W. (1918). The project method. *Teachers College Record, 19*(4), 319–335.

Kilpatrick, W. (1925). *Foundations of method: Informal talks on teaching*. New York: Macmillan.

Knapp, C. (1992). *Lasting lessons: A teacher's guide to reflecting on experience*. Charleston, WV: ERIC Clearinghouse on Rural Education and Small Schools.

Kolb, D. A. (1984). *Experiential learning*. Englewood Cliffs, NJ.: Prentice Hall.

Lucas, R. & Krumpe, E. (n.d.). *A literature review of the President's Commission on Americans Outdoors.* Retrieved on July 21, 2003, from www.wilderness.net/pubs/167.pdf

Luckmann, C. (1996). Defining experiential education. *Journal of Experiential Education, 19*(1), 6–8.

Lund, M. (1997). *Outdoor education: From the roots to the new branches*. Retrieved July 28, 2003 from www.aartsci.gmcc.ab.ca/courses/peds205ml/outed.html

McAvoy, L. & Lais, G. (1999). In J. C. Miles & S. Priest (Eds.), *Adventure Programming*. (pp. 403–415). State College, PA: Venture.

Miner, J. & Boldt, J. (1981). *Outward Bound USA*. New York: William Morrow and Company.

Miner, T. (1999). Adventure in the workplace. In J. C. Miles & S. Priest (Eds.), *Adventure Programming* (pp. 395–403). State College, PA: Venture.

Minnesota Department of Education (1992). *Model learner outcomes for youth community service.* St. Paul, Minnesota: Department of Education.

Montessori, M. (1974). *The Montessori Method*. New York: Shocken Books.

Nathan, J. & Kielsmeier, J. (1991). The sleeping giant of school reform. *Phi Delta Kappan, 72*(10), 738–742.

New York Yearly Meeting (1974). *Faith and practice*. New York: New York Yearly Meeting of the Religious Society of Friends.

Noddings, N. (1995). *Philosophy of education*. Boulder, CO: Westview Press.

Pinar, W. F., Reynolds, W. M., Slattery, P., & Taubman, P. M. (2002). *Understanding curriculum* (4th ed). New York: Peter Lang Publishing.

Priest, S. (1999). The semantics of adventure programming. In J. C. Miles & S. Priest (Eds.), *Adventure Programming* (pp. 111–115). State College, PA: Venture.

Prouty, D. (1999). Project adventure: A brief history. In J. C. Miles & S. Priest (Eds.), *Adventure Programming* (pp. 93–103). State College, PA: Venture.

Raiola, E. & O'Keefe, M. (1999). Philosophy in practice: A history of adventure programming. In J. C. Miles & S. Priest (Eds.), *Adventure Programming* (pp. 45–55). State College, PA: Venture.

Roberts, N. S. (1996). NAALA in experiential education: Beyond participation. *Journal of Experiential Education, 19*(3), 117–118.

Russell, L. & Burton, J. (2000). A report on an Ontario secondary school integrated environmental studies program. *Canadian Journal of Environmental Education, 5*, 287–304.

Steiner, R. (1996). *Rudolf Steiner in the Waldorf school.* Hudson, NY: Anthroposophic Press.

Teeters, C. E. & Lupton, F. (1999). The wilderness education association: History and change. In J. C. Miles & S. Priest (Eds.), *Adventure Programming* (pp. 77–85). State College, PA: Venture.

Toronto Waldorf School (1970). *Waldorf: Education for tomorrow.* Toronto: The Waldorf School Association of Ontario.

Warren, K. (1999). Women's outdoor adventures. In J. C. Miles & S. Priest (Eds.), *Adventure Programming* (pp. 389–395). State College, PA: Venture.

Warren, K., Sakofs, M., & Hunt, J. (1995). *The theory of experiential education.* Boulder, CO: Association for Experiential Education.

Washington, S. J. & Roberts, N. S. (1999). Adventure education for teaching cross-cultural perspectives. In J. C. Miles & S. Priest (Eds.), *Adventure Programming* (pp. 359–365). State College, PA: Venture.

Webb, D. (1999). Recreational outdoor adventure programs. In J. C. Miles & S. Priest (Eds.), *Adventure Programming* (pp. 3–9). State College, PA: Venture.

Weinstein, M. (Ed.). (2000). *Making a difference college and graduate guide* (8th ed.). St. Paul: Consortium Book Sales and Distribution.

A History of the Association for Experiential Education 1990–2008

▾ ▾ ▾

Daniel Garvey, Denise Mitten, Steve Pace, & Nina S. Roberts

Attempting to write a history of an organization is an interesting and difficult activity. In the words of Bob Seager of the Silver Bullet Band, it's a question of, "what to keep in and what to leave out." Every activity of the Association for Experiential Education (AEE) is important to someone and yet a written history must find a way to create a story that summarizes some of the most important themes that emerge from an infinite number of events and shared experiences.

The authors of this history—Dan Garvey, Denise Mitten, Steve Pace, and Nina Roberts—have come together in an attempt to co-create such a shared account of AEE from 1990 to 2008. The first published history of AEE, authored by Dan Garvey, covered the birth of the organization through 1990 (and is available online at www.aee.org on the Resources page).

Each author has lived through and helped shape AEE's history. We represent almost 100 years of combined affiliation with the association. We are former Board members, Board treasurer, Board presidents, conference presenters, executive director, Accreditation Council member, Professional Group members and leaders, and general custodians of a shared dream to help maintain an association in support of experiential educators around the world.

The history of AEE is important because the association is both a gathering place for people and ideas *and* a movement of activists intent on changing institutions so that they will better serve the common good. Throughout history there have been movements that have attempted to influence society (think John Dewey's progressive education movement or the women's movement). Some movements have more of a lasting impact than others, but almost always a movement's historic significance is written about long after the real creative dust has settled. While accounting for historic impact and significance is important, it is also essential to capture the themes of a movement shortly after the events that formed them occur. In some ways we are writing a history that is more of a journal versus a reflection of outcomes. The journal history approach is relevant because we live in a world of exponential change. We want to share our history now because the events that have shaped AEE could be useful or even vital to others long before a historical impact piece could be authored.

Methods

To create a more complete picture of the events and activities that have shaped the association, we decided to interview people who have had a significant impact on AEE since 1990, many of whom have been involved with the association for more than 18 years. The following 14 individuals were interviewed:

Barbara Baker	Lee Gillis	Mary Anne Scippa
Sylvia Dresser	Sky Gray	Sanford Tollette
Laurie Frank	Pat Hammond	Karen Warren
Mike Gass	Jude Hirsch	Rita Yerkes
Katrina Geurkink	Chris Lupton	

We acknowledge that other key figures may not have been included in this process, yet we feel confident those we did interview have played a significant role in the evolution of the AEE and that their combined statements form the basis of this chapter.

Each interview was conducted over the phone. Though there each one varied slightly based on the personality style of the interviewer and the casual nature of the discussions, all interviewees minimally were asked the following thematic questions:

1. Regarding AEE and your perspective, can you tell us what the two or three most important events have been since 1990?

2. Why were these events important? And what are the long-term consequences of these events for the association?

3. From your perspective, what can you say about the overall feel of our organization?

Each interview was recorded and transcribed or responses were hand-written and later typed. The typed responses were then sent to one of the authors who had not conducted any interviews for a domain analysis in an attempt to reveal major themes. The four primary themes that emerged are: (a) Board Improvement, (b) Social Justice, (c) Accreditation, and (d) Scholarship and Research.

Of the 164 separate comments made by respondents, 158 fit into one of the above four themes. The remaining six comments, outside the above themes, showed no recognizable pattern. After the themes had been suggested, the authors who did the interviews were asked to verify these classifications. These themes represent a consensus of findings by all the authors. We believe our categories adequately cluster the most important historical trends within AEE since 1990.

Board Improvement

As a nonprofit corporation registered in the state of Colorado, AEE is mandated by law to have by-laws and a Board of Directors. AEE's by-laws contain the "rules" that govern the structure and function of the organization and the Board of Directors. A history of Board changes improvement is recorded in the by-law revisions. Each by-law revision is voted on by the membership, requiring a two-thirds majority to pass. In response to membership prodding and their commitment to social justice, a major by-law revision occurred in 1991 and two subsequent revisions in 2002 and 2004. These changes to the by-laws had significant effects upon AEE.

In the 1991 revision, the Board of Directors (BoD) was restructured and expanded with the intention of creating a more participatory and inclusive organizational structure. Prior to 1991, AEE's BoD was elected at large. The entire AEE membership elected directors, but there was no strategic measure to ensure that the various segments of the association were represented on the Board. Thus, it was possible that a majority of the Board members only represented one narrow interest and/or geographic area. Through this by-law change, the BoD came to be composed of five officers of the Board, a representative from each of the Professional Groups, and representatives from predesignated geographic areas. Additionally, the four-year terms for the officers and a mentoring process were established (e.g., treasurer-elect becomes the treasure and then past-treasurer). This restructuring helped some of the more silent and/or marginalized voices in the AEE be heard. The first meeting of this expanded Board took place in 1993.

Over time, each region wanted and got one representative, Special Interest Groups became Professional Groups, and more Professional Groups formed, growing the Board to almost 20 members. Although the 1991 by-law revision had gone a long way toward building a more inclusive Board structure, the sheer size of the Board hindered its effectiveness. With the same intentionality that the founding members used when forming AEE, Board and committee members again looked for a solution. Growing out of the rigorous 2000 strategic planning process, in 2001 a new structure was proposed that would stabilize the size of the Board to what was thought to be manageable. In this new structure, the Board consisted of the five officers, two people elected from candidates put forth by the Professional Groups Council, two representative nominated by the Council of Region Chairs, and two members-at-large. The executive committee was abolished, and instead of having one meeting a year with only the officers meeting and making decisions, now all meetings consisted of the entire Board, a further refinement of power distribution.

As organizations grow, Boards often evolve from being involved in operational activities (and even doing the everyday work of the organization) to a governing function. A move toward truly making AEE's Board a governing Board resulted from a resource Sharon Heinlen, then executive director, shared with Katrina Geurkink, then Board president-elect, at a three-day meeting in 1998 in Boulder, Colorado. After reading Carver's book, *Boards that Make a Difference*, Katrina engaged in tireless education of the Board of Directors, encouraging the adoption of the Carver Governance Model. In November 2000, the Board voted to move ahead with policy governance using the Carver Model.

Next began the long process of Board self-education and policy development. Over the winter of 2000–01, Board members read Carver's book and at the May 2001 Leadership Summit, as well as a special summer meeting with a consultant, the Board worked on creating a policy register. The first version of the policy register was approved by the Board in November 2001. Since then, the Board has worked hard to guide the association by polling AEE members, researching societal and experiential education-related trends, and crafting Ends that reflect the findings of their research (see Figure 1).

The Association for Experiential Education exists so that educators and practitioners have access to a professional learning community dedicated to enriching lives through the philosophy and principles* of experiential education.

*as articulated on the AEE website (www.aee.org)

1. The learning community is inclusive of diverse peoples and professional practices, collaborative with other communities, and accessible within reasonable means.

2. Authoritative information for implementing and advancing the philosophy and practice of experiential education is accessible.

   a. Standards are identified to improve professional practice and to safeguard the well-being of participants.

   b. Research about experiential education is coordinated and conducted.

3. Decision-makers value and support experiential education.

Figure 1. **The AEE Ends Policies, adopted June 8, 2008.**

The model's structure helped provide common language, helped people understand their roles and responsibilities, helped with accountability, and helped make the Board more responsive to both AEE's stakeholders and the world outside AEE. Yet it has also caused its share of growing pains. To quote one interviewee:

> Restructuring the Board was critical and must be included in this chapter. In the 90s there was so much drama, we were spinning our wheels! Using the Carver Model was very healthy in bringing us to new and very positive directions.

Board improvement remains a focus of AEE. The history of this consistent concern for organizational self-renewal and improvement is a reflection of a vigilance to use experiential learning for growth. As the Board improves its functioning, AEE's staff have more support to further the work of the association.

Social Justice

The authors struggled to appropriately list and describe social justice issues within the history of AEE. In one sense it represents a theme similar to the other themes in this chapter and yet social justice colored every theme and must be seen as braided into the very fabric of AEE. While diversity can be defined as recognizing, appreciating, valuing, and utilizing the unique talents and contributions of all individuals, in its broadest context social justice is about the power attached to all of this. More narrowly defined and organizationally focused, social justice is the action behind knowing how to embrace and engage this rich mixture of individual differences and similarities so that it can be applied in the pursuit of organizational objectives.

Bringing the association to its current incarnation hasn't been an easy evolution (conflicting values, sexism, heterosexism, and racism have been barriers to progress). A big step forward was taken in 1991, when the mission of AEE was reworded to include "to contribute to making a more just and compassionate world by transforming education" and the Board adopted a Diversity Statement (see Figure 2). Putting forth these guiding principles of the association has yielded numerous benefits. For instance, it has led to a more diverse group of individuals exploring the opportunities and resources provided by AEE, as well as new agendas and needs being brought to the forefront of the association's work.

The culture at AEE is a microcosm of a community living, practicing, and learning and teaching about social justice. As stated by one interviewee:

> We have and continue to mirror our diverse culture. AEE is a place to come back to and to feel that consciousness. We are more rooted in the humanitarian issues.... Some of my best conversations and some of my best teaching about how to have those hard conversations were at AEE.

Vision
The vision of the Association for Experiential Education is to contribute to making a more just and compassionate world by transforming education.

Mission
The mission of the Association for Experiential Education is to develop and promote experiential education. The association is committed to supporting professional development, theoretical advancement and the evaluation of experiential education worldwide.

Diversity Statement
AEE does not discriminate on the basis of race, religion, gender, sexual orientation, age, physical ability, or professional affiliation in matters of employment or application for membership.

Figure 2. **Guiding principles of the Association for Experiential Education.**

Given the draw of AEE for members who want to make a difference in people's lives and that people do not always agree on the best ways for this to happen, the work has been challenging and emotional. In fact, there is not even agreement among the membership of AEE that social justice is a part of the association's work.

Much of the social justice work in AEE has happened as part of the Professional Groups, some of which are now called Affiliation Groups. Over the past 18 years, these groups have worked on numerous issues. The Schools & Colleges Professional Group has provided opportunities for both AEE members and the educational institutions they serve. Their commitment to social justice is evident in the work they've done in contributing to the creation of greater equity in educational institutions across the country. Members within the Therapeutic Adventure Professional Group (TAPG) have expanded their ways of thinking and doing from a focus on individual clients/populations (such as looking at "self") by exploring the needs of the larger society. For example, TAPG has contributed to enhancing awareness and increasing knowledge of the reality of oppression within specific populations served (e.g., LGBA issues, people with disabilities, at-risk youth) to the intersection of oppression between groups and the effects across society.

The creation of some AEE Professional Groups—WPG (Women's Professional Group), NAALA (Natives, Africans, Asians, Latinos & Allies), LGBA (Lesbian, Gays, Bisexuals & Allies)—has stemmed from concerns about social justice issues. Efforts of the WPG have resulted in having a sliding-scale membership fee and conducting fundraisers so members from lower income brackets can attend conferences and join the association. Given the historic under-representation of women in leadership positions on the Board and committees, mentoring other women members became a substantial effort of the WPG. Due to often inaccurate representations in the outdoor and experiential education literature, women were mentored to write for the *Journal of Experiential Education* (*JEE*) and to present at regional and international conferences. Furthermore, in 1996, *Women's Voices in Experiential Education* (edited by Dr. Karen Warren) was published. Members of the WPG initiated the 1997 "Take Back the Trails" in support of reducing fear and violence against women and girls (organized following the brutal murders of two young outdoorswomen in a wilderness area in 1996). Such initiatives have made the WPG a model for other Professional Groups across the association.

Support for the establishment of NAALA primarily occurred in a more focused manner in 1990 when a "diversity-related" preconference was organized; this was the spark for a new form of activism. The mission of NAALA is "to elevate the consciousness of AEE's membership toward oppression, exploitation and human suffering, and advocating for social and economic justice within experiential education by developing and implementing new strategies for sharing power." The birth of NAALA initially caused commotion because the group members tended to be outspoken and forthright in expressing their needs and desires. Many AEE members were not used to such powerful voices emanating from previously marginalized people and it took a while for some to listen, learn, and understand. As one of the people interviewed recalls: "In 1990 at the St. Paul conference, the formation of NAALA was huge. It was able to happen because AEE took the risk to have an urban conference and that conference committee was determined to include people of color."

In the fall of 1996, NAALA further addressed the multifaceted ingredients of cultural diversity as AEE published a special issue in the *JEE*: "NAALA in Experiential Education: Beyond Participation" (edited by Dr. Nina Roberts). A central message contained in this issue included the realism that people of color can be strong leaders and not just recipients of experiential education services and opportunities.

A pivotal event occurred in 1998 during the Keynote Address at the Annual Conference in Lake Tahoe. The speaker, dressed in traditional Native clothing, referenced a particular Native American heritage as part of her cultural background. Her appearance and several of her vocalizations (both remarks and songs) were controversial among Native members of AEE and their allies. The silent protest that occurred during this keynote session ignited a dialogue among members that would last years to come. While many lessons were learned from that event, and several other momentous events, for AEE members, finding an acceptable balance of understanding and awareness has been an ongoing challenge.

Between 2001 and 2006, NAALA planned a series of workshops in South Dakota. The gatherings were held each summer for five years on the Rosebud Indian Reservation (and Badlands). Fundraising efforts provided scholarships for teachers and students to attend, purchase of equipment for the ropes course on "the Rez", and teaching skills to engage in service-learning initiatives. NAALA did not introduce experiential education into Native communities; it is already there and a fundamental part of Native life. But the NAALA group was able to help bring new tools, both tangible and intangible, to support instruction and learning.

The LGBA began as an informal collaboration of professionals between 1995 and 1996. Key turning points for this group stemmed from two main events. First, in 1991, the WPG hosted a preconference event at the Annual Conference at Lake Junaluska, North Carolina. During this event, an enormous banner of lesbian, gay and bisexual history was posted, for the first time ever, in the hallway of one of the buildings onsite. Second, Colorado passed Proposition #2 in 1991, a highly discriminatory referendum regarding sexual identity. This sparked debate among members about whether to hold events in Colorado. As one interviewee remembers: "When Colorado passed its antigay amendment, AEE had to struggle with how to be a socially just organization … in light of AEE being based in Colorado." This proposition was reversed by the Supreme Court in 1996. A year later, at the 1997 Annual Conference in Asheville, North Carolina, LGBA approached the Board about becoming a Professional Group, the formation of which was officially approved at the 1998 Leadership Summit. Despite Board endorsement, there was resistance. Nobody overtly questioned that LGBA should exist; the push-back was related to organizational structure. Specifically, what actually constitutes a "PG" became the issue. This in turn led to the Board looking more closely at the structure of PG formation as well as Board structure. (Due to a lack of AEE member interest, LGBA disbanded in 2004.)

"Old Folks and Allies" (OFA) formally convened in 2006 at the Annual Conference in Vancouver, British Columbia. There was a growing need within AEE to create space for elders to connect with each other, share their wisdom with those newer to the field, and contribute to the promotion of experiential education through their connections, projects, and initiatives.

The issues relating to social justice remain at the forefront of the AEE mission and, according to one of the interviewees, change is inevitable:

> We've made progress in meeting our vision around justice and creating a just and more compassionate world. The number of women and people of color who have received AEE awards has been a huge change over the last decade. With race and gender being key issues in our field and, of course others, we've been paying much closer attention to this for all the right reasons.

While progress has been made, it is the belief of the authors of this chapter that AEE must grow, maintain, and promote a social justice consciousness at every level of the association. This will have a profound impact on the difference we, as professionals, can make in the world at large. This includes striving to ensure that we all hold ourselves accountable for being ambassadors of social justice in all its shapes and forms.

Accreditation

Since the founding of the association in the 1970s, AEE members have been interested in sharing information about how to best conduct adventure activities. Throughout the years, countless discussions and meetings about this topic have taken place during annual and regional conferences. These meetings have allowed the leadership of AEE to obtain valuable information from members and member organizations about the need for standards in the field of adventure education. (For more about the birth of the AEE Accreditation Program, reference the first history of AEE and/or the Acknowledgments section of the *Manual of Accreditation Standards for Adventure Programs, 4th edition,* both of which are available online at www.aee.org).

In 1992, Mike Gass and Jed Williamson brought together a group of 12 adventure education experts at the Merrowvista Education Center in Ossipee, New Hampshire. The purpose of the meeting was to create the framework for an accreditation program that would codify the expectations for safe practices within adventure education. Present at the meeting were representatives from what were then—and today remain—some of the most important outdoor programs in the industry: Outward Bound, NOLS, Project Adventure, and others. This initial group envisioned an objective process to evaluate program compliance with a set of standards. The resulting evaluations would be shared with the public so potential clients could make informed decisions concerning the relative safety and worthiness of a program or organization. Creating an accreditation program was a monumental task. As one interviewee recalls: "When I was on the Board in the early 90s, a significant and risky step at the time was accreditation.... It was an attempt to make ... EE more professional and for AEE to have a part in that professionalization."

While accidents can occur in even the best-run programs, there were, and unfortunately still are, programs in operation that are not well informed regarding risk management. Every time a poorly operated program has a serious injury or fatality, families experience tragedy and excellent programs with no connection to the accident suffer a disabling loss of public trust. The AEE Accreditation Program has been successful in elevating the standards of care within adventure education. As of 2008, more than 50 programs have successfully gone through the AEE accreditation process. These accredited programs serve as models for others within the field.

Two AEE publications have greatly influenced adventure education best practices both in the United States and internationally. To date, more than 700 copies of the *AEE Manual of Accreditation Standards for Adventure Programs* have been sold in the United States and abroad, and hundreds more issued to land managers, affiliated organizations, accredited programs, and programs considering accreditation. This publication represents best practices within the adventure education field. In addition, approximately 900 copies of the first edition of *Administrative Practices of AEE Accredited Programs* have been sold, and a second edition, published in November 2007, has seen wide distribution. This book details the administrative practices of 16 AEE-accredited programs, providing valuable information on how to create and implement safe and effective programs.

One of the most important aspects of the accreditation process is the opportunity for programs to be evaluated by well-trained professionals in the adventure education field. More than 100 professionals have been trained as AEE accreditation reviewers. This cadre of trained volunteers provides a vital service. One interviewee summed up the impact of the accreditation process with the following statement:

> Accreditation is one of the greatest accomplishments of the association. Some people were very skeptical and said we'd be in over our heads and would struggle to succeed. We worked on standards that didn't exist. Accreditation and these standards became accepted even among people and organizations that did not belong to AEE.... This continues to be a valued membership service and also tells the broader world about the standards in our field.

Adventure education attracts leaders who are independent thinkers. The strong commitment these early leaders had for this project led them to spend countless hours distilling the principles behind risk management practices into standards. The standards formed the underpinnings of accreditation and the guidance of the two attorneys cannot be underestimated: Betty van der Smissen and Reb Gregg chiseled out a desirable set of standards and helped create today's Accreditation Program. The success of AEE's Accreditation Program is proof of adventure education's evolving professionalism. Although the issue of peer standards and certification has been part of the discussion within AEE almost from the beginning, the last 18 years could be coined the "era of accreditation."

Currently, under the guidance of Paul Smith, the President of the Catherine Freer Wilderness Therapy Program, work is being done through TAPG and the Accreditation Council to broaden and refine the standards that apply to therapeutic adventure programs. As there are practitioners of experiential education in many fields, it will be interesting to observe how the AEE's Accreditation Program grows and evolves to support the needs of practitioners and the public in these other fields.

Scholarship and Research

Over the decades, the members and scholars involved with AEE's Professional Groups have pushed the association to enhance and build the AEE research agenda. In the early 1990s, this push spawned two AEE committees: the Journal Advisory Committee and the Publications Advisory Committee. These two groups worked to formulate policies, create standards, set high expectations, and support high-quality publications and research efforts throughout the association. The need for research standards was evident because there was early criticism among professionals and scholars from other disciplines that research on experiential education was "not rigorous." Back then, some universities would not accept *Journal of Experiential Education* (*JEE*) manuscripts as part of the review, tenure, and promotion portfolio for faculty. During his tenure as *JEE* editor, Alan Ewert worked to rectify this situation by methodically increasing the scholarship of the journal. Today, the *JEE* is a respected, peer-reviewed, scholarly journal presenting scientific and conceptual inquiries into the study and practice of experiential education and its various subfields.

While the academic arena has been clear in its desire for AEE to be involved in research and scholarship throughout the years, member surveys conducted in recent years reveal that more and more of AEE's members also want the association to be involved in forwarding research that validates experiential education. As one interviewee put it: "Research gives more credibility to our field. To have credibility, we need decent research."

To that end, AEE currently provides support to two initiatives. Eight years ago, a handful of AEE leaders realized the need and value of having a research symposium where the work of its members could be supported and recognized. This took the shape of the Symposium on Experiential Education Research (SEER), held each year in conjunction with the Annual International Conference. At SEER, a select group of veteran and novice researchers are given the chance to present their projects and share their findings. As one of those interviewed said: "The Research Symposium, with Alan Ewert's leadership, added to scholarship at the conference and brings credibility to the association."

The association's newest research-focused effort is the Council on Research & Evaluation (CORE). The concept of CORE was inspired by a group of dedicated and passionate researchers and practitioners who were concerned about validating experiential practices in both education and therapy in order to support programs that were being threatened politically and financially. This group, which has met annually since 2005 at the Project Adventure/AEE-sponsored Research & Evaluation of Adventure Programming (REAP) Symposium, pledged to move forward with a Task Force in April 2007 to develop the CORE plan, an initiative that has been led by Bobbi Beale. In November 2007, at the Annual International AEE Conference in Little Rock, Arkansas, the official council was launched. CORE's vision includes facilitating the validation and advancement of experiential education by identifying and promoting research, evaluation, and evidence-based practices. CORE intends to do this by providing access to resources and support through technology, education, and networking opportunities. CORE was designed to provide a unifying structure, a communications hub, and administrative support for several existing AEE subgroups that have strong ties to research, including REAP and SEER. In addition, CORE will be working with existing AEE Professional Groups to strengthen internal alliances, as well as identifying potential external alliances with similar concerns and needs.

We also feel it is important to recognize the member donations that have made small pools of money available for research. One such fund was endowed by Simon Priest and has since been discontinued. In 2005, the Betty van der Smissen Grant Fund was established as a temporary restricted grant fund to support new research or innovative projects that will advance the field of adventure education.

In the broadest sense, research and the dissemination of research findings are about making the value of experiential education available to the largest audience possible. Publications such as the *JEE*, symposiums like SEER and REAP, and councils like CORE are the AEE initiatives that accomplish the latter by doing the former. To quote one interviewee: "This work can help create a level of broader public awareness of what we have to offer. In order to support our members, we must broaden our spectrum and share our work."

Closing Thoughts

Perhaps the most important fact about AEE is that it remains an important gathering point for information and affiliation relating to experiential education. In the 35 years since the inception of AEE, the landscape of education has changed in profound ways. We have witnessed the creative educational reform movements of the 1960s and 1970s and the back-to-basic notions of A Nation at Risk espoused by mainstream education of the 1980s and 1990s. Now we attempt to measure students, teacher effectiveness, and community investment through the No Child Left Behind mandates. In every era, successive generations of experiential educators have helped to influence the discussion and the aims of education and learning. AEE remains part of one of the most vital educational movements because the association holds one truth to be self-evident: If one cares about all our constituents, including students, patients, clients, and others, then one must trust them to take responsibility for their development and be ready to assist them in their quest for fulfillment.

The history of AEE is the accumulated stories of people who have attempted to be of service to others. AEE has evolved from an association organized out of the trunk of its first executive director's car to a professional organization with a talented staff and many volunteer leaders working effectively to improve the many fields that use experiential education.

The actual historic impact of the AEE remains to be written; its vision, however, is as relevant now as at any other time in our history. The future of the AEE is a dream to be realized. The current Ends Policies of the association define the dreams, which are in the process of being realized.

Sketch of a Moving Spirit:
Kurt Hahn

▾ ▾ ▾

Thomas James

Someone said once that Kurt Hahn was the "moving spirit" of Outward Bound when it began in Britain during World War II. Imported to the United States two decades later, Outward Bound, in turn, became a moving spirit of the experiential education movement. Now history has left the man behind—Hahn died nearly a decade ago—but his ideals are as ubiquitous in experiential education as is neoclassical architecture in Washington, DC. What was once innovation has become assumption, shaping and defining our vision. To ask about Hahn's ideals today is really to ask about ourselves as teachers and learners, whether in Outward Bound, in other experiential programs, or in the mainstream of American education. The answers we find should help us to understand, among other things, the meaning of our careers as educators. Work from the dream outward, Carl Jung once said. If we use history to probe the core of idealism that sustains much of experiential education as we practice it, we cannot help but encounter the man who founded Outward Bound in 1941.

"Moving Spirit" is a better designation than "Founder." What Kurt Hahn caused to happen was larger than the program he created to prevent men from dying in lifeboats when their ships were sunk by German U-boats in the North Atlantic. It was larger than the educational methods he applied to solve the problem at hand. It was, above all, a renewal of social vision.

This chapter originally was published in the *Journal of Experiential Education*, with the following citation:
James, T. (1980). Sketch of a moving spirit: Kurt Hahn. *Journal of Experiential Education, 3*(1), 17–22.

Not a hero himself, Hahn infused others with a sense of heroic quest. He was an educator—the word comes from Latin roots meaning "to lead out." As a leader, he left enough unsaid that the people working with him were able to add their vision to the common pursuit. In each of the schools with which he was associated, not to mention the smaller programs he brought into being through the years, there was always in the minds of those who were close to him, a sensation of having within their grasp a unifying aspiration with the power to strengthen individuals and transform social life. Kurt Hahn instilled a pervasive culture of aspiration that remains the essence of Outward Bound and a crucial part of experiential education to this day.

From where did this culture of aspiration come? What went into it that made it so compelling?

We might begin to address these questions by looking for the origins of Outward Bound in 1913 instead of 1941. In the summer of 1913 as an Oxford student vacationing with a friend in Scotland, recuperating from a lingering illness a result of the sunstroke he had suffered a few years before Kurt Hahn outlined his idea for a school based on principles set forth in Plato's *Republic.* This was without doubt an audacious, some would say foolish, act of the imagination. Hahn believed that the most extremely utopian conception or society ever formulated should be applied, purely and simply, to create a school in the modern world. He was 28 years old and had never run a school, nor even taught in one. The ideal school he imagined never came into being, but it exerted a profound influence on all his subsequent efforts as an educator and statesman. He launched Salem School, in Germany, in 1920; Gordonstoun School, in Scotland, in 1934; Outward Bound, in Wales, in 1941; and Atlantic College, in England, in 1962.

The main point is worth repeating. Though the youthful fantasy of a Platonic school never came into being, its influence crops up everywhere in the institutions he built and in the people he drew to his cause. In *English Progressive Schools,* Robert Skidelsky analyzes Hahn's debt to Plato as follows:

> Plato was a political reformer who sought to recall the Athenians to the old civic virtues eroded, as he saw it, by democratic enthusiasm and soft living. His aim was to educate a class of leaders in a "healthy pasture" remote from the corrupting environment, whose task it would be to regenerate society. Hahn must have been haunted by similar visions of decay as, inspired by these ideas, he drew up a plan in 1913 for a school modeled on Platonic principles. The war that broke out a year later and ended in the collapse of Germany was to give them a new urgency to convert what might have remained a purely academic speculation into an active campaign for social and political regeneration.

"Always Bringing Out the Best in People"
By John S. Holden

Kurt Hahn was visiting our house in 1968 when Lyndon Johnson announced that he would not run for President again. At almost the same time, we heard of the tragedy of Martin Luther King. We watched the riots on television. Hahn was there when I took a phone call from one of our students who was doing volunteer work for the Southern Christian Leadership Conference in Washington. Here was "Whitey" in the Black stronghold. His description was far more graphic than what we were able to see on television. The conversation was cut off when the boy said he couldn't stand the tear gas any more.

In spite of this graphic warning, Hahn left our house the next day for Los Angeles. He went right to the Watts area to confer with a black man who had organized the youth there to carry out projects in their neighborhoods to make better living conditions for themselves and their families. He wasn't afraid of the Watts riots.

Except for the lifelong sunstroke affliction that kept him out of bright sunlight, Hahn had the greatest courage, both physical and mental. He wasn't afraid of jogging in the dark along the road during an April thaw when he visited us. He wasn't bothered by the fall he experienced on the way back to the house—just embarrassed and wanting a clothes brush to remove the mud from his suit. He always jogged in the dark, and that was neither the first nor the last fall he lived through. He showed us another example of his courage one time when he was guiding us around Gordonstoun School in Scotland. We came to the watchtower manned by the boys every time there was a storm at sea. I think he was 81 years old at the time, and all his life he had been afflicted with unusual clumsiness. He called himself a physical illiterate. Nevertheless, he had to lead us up the steel ladder into the tower. I stayed close below him as he fumbled and almost slipped on his way up. The trip down was even more hair-raising.

At times I couldn't help thinking that this was the most unlikely man to have started the Outward Bound Movement. But, as I listened to his talk about Salem, about Gordonstoun, about Atlantic College, and about Outward Bound, I realized that he was always moving in the same direction, always bringing out the best in people, always stretching himself to the limit, and always demanding that same stretch in the people working with him.

The last time I saw him was in Cambridge, Massachusetts, after he had returned from Watts. He was full of optimism and hope, uplifted from his meeting with the black man who had calmed multitudes in the California ghettos by giving young people something that they could be proud of doing. Hahn was full of plans to bring together from all over the world the leaders of mountain rescue, Red Cross, water safety, firemen, and ski patrols. Prince Phillip was to foot the bill for this great conclave, which actually did take place in England the following year. Behind this was the theory: teach them to save lives and they'll never be willing to kill.

Kurt Hahn told us one of his favorite stories once as we were leaving the chapel at Gordonstoun. Prince Phillip, who had attended as a student, never returned to his old school until long after World War II when he was already very famous, married to Princess Elizabeth, soon to be Queen of England. Of course, there was great excitement. All the staff and his old teachers gathered around him as he toured the grounds. Suddenly, the Prince disappeared. There was speculation about where he had gone. To the chapel? To his old stand at the watchtower? When Prince Phillip returned, he smiled and said he had gone to see if the pigpen he had built in his student days was still there.

I'm glad we knew Kurt Hahn personally. He made it quite clear to us that the physical aspects of Outward Bound were secondary to the really important things. In his talk, he brought out the thinking part, the serving part, the spiritual part. As a warden of the Eskdale Outward Bound School put it, the aim was to arm students "against the enemies—fear, defeatism, apathy, selfishness. It was thus as much a moral as a practical training." Hahn was disgusted with any article or movie that didn't emphasize this more subtle and more important part of humankind.

It takes little digging to find precisely the same intentions in the founding of Outward Bound in 1941. Men were dying in lifeboats; the English nation despaired of its strength and will to face the coming onslaught of the Nazis. Twenty-one years later, the founders of the Colorado Outward Bound School raised similar concerns about the character of Americans. It had been reported that an alarming percentage of American prisoners of war in Korea had collaborated with the enemy. Americans were overweight, deluged by material goods and technology; the young were seen to be increasingly apathetic and often violently self-centered. In that year, 1962, Outward Bound took a hundred boys into the mountains and tried to teach them something about self-discovery. The purpose of the school could easily have been stated in the Platonic terms used by Hahn in 1921 to describe the purpose of Salem School: "to train citizens who would not shirk from leadership and who could, if called upon, make independent decisions, put right action before expediency and the common cause before personal ambition."

The Colorado Outward Bound School was not started to teach people how to live in the mountains. The idea was to use the mountains as a classroom to produce better people, to build character, to instill that intensity of individual and collective aspiration on which the entire society depends for its survival. Kurt Hahn summarized the school's idealism when he said that the goal was to ensure survival of an enterprising curiosity, an undefeatable spirit, tenacity in pursuit, readiness for sensible self-denial, and, above all, compassion." Another summary appeared in an article published in 1962 by the school's founding president, F. Charles Froelicher:

> Without self-discovery, a person may still have self-confidence, but it is a self-confidence built on ignorance and it melts in the face of heavy burdens. Self-discovery is the end product of a great challenge mastered, when the mind commands the body to do the seemingly impossible, when strength and courage are summoned to extraordinary limits for the sake of something outside the self—a principle, an onerous task, another human life.

Outward Bound places unusual emphasis on physical challenge, not as an end in itself, but as an instrument for training the will to strive for mastery. There is also the insistent use of action, instead of states of mind, to describe the reality of the individual. Education is tied unequivocally to experience, to what one does and not so much to one's attitudes and opinions. A thread running from Plato through Hahn and through Outward Bound is the responsibility of individuals to make their personal goals consonant with social necessity. Not only is the part subordinated to the whole, but the part cannot even understand its own identity, its relations, and its responsibility, until it has grasped the nature of the whole. This explains the connection between self-discovery and self-sacrifice in Froelicher's statement and it also shows where Hahn parted company with many others in the English Progressive School Movement who saw his stance as threatening to individual freedom. Having stood up to Hitler before being exiled from Nazi Germany in 1933, Hahn believed in individual freedom, but he believed that students should be impelled into experiences that would teach them the bonds of social life necessary to protect such freedom. He took from Plato the idea that a human being cannot achieve perfection without becoming part of a perfect society—that is, without creating social harmony to sustain the harmonious life of the individual. This is the overall structure of the argument in the *Republic* and it is also the most important lesson of an Outward Bound course, the lesson without which personal development is of questionable value. In a small group, the patrol, and in a "healthy pasture" away from the degenerate ways of the world, the individual student comes to grips with what must be done to create a just society, within which a human being might aspire to perfection. Here is the true, unadvertised peak climb of an Outward Bound course. An inner transformation precedes outward conquest. This is why Hahn placed compassion above all other values of Outward Bound, for it among all emotions is capable of reconciling individual strength with collective need.

The prospect of wholeness, the possibility, at least, of human life becoming an equilibrium sustained by harmony and balance, is what makes this form of education even thinkable. Skidelsky again offers a lucid analysis of the source of Hahn's thinking:

> The second idea which Hahn assimilated was Plato's notion that the principle of perfection was harmony and balance. The perfection of the body, he held, depends upon a harmony of its elements.... Virtue (the health of the soul) is the harmony or balance between the various faculties of the psyche: reason, the appetites, and spirit. Virtue in the state is the harmony between its functional elements: thinkers, soldiers, and artisans. The same principle can be extended indefinitely—to relations between men, relations between states, and so on.

This passage sheds some light on Hahn's interest in giving his students experiences that would complement their strengths and weaknesses. In his speeches, he said he wanted to turn introverts inside out and extroverts outside in. He wanted the poor to help the rich break their "enervating sense of privilege" and the rich to help the poor in building a true "aristocracy of talent." The schools he founded sent bookworms to the playing field and jocks to the reading room. He did not produce outstanding athletes, but his students exhibited consistently high levels of fitness, accomplishment, and social spirit. He said he valued mastery in the sphere of one's weakness over performance in the sphere of one's strength. To carry forward into Outward Bound today, the program is not meant to turn out virtuosos in any sense. Hahn would have liked what the Colorado staff call "ruthless compassion," the breaking of strong students by forcing them to keep a slow pace with the weaker members of the group. He would also have been happy with the not-quite-so ruthless encouragement of the weaker members to press beyond their limits.

If the miniature society that results is full of conflict, as is often the case in an Outward Bound patrol of widely differing abilities, we may find solace in the words of H. L. Brereton, Hahn's Director of Studies at Gordonstoun. In his book called *Gordonstoun*, Brereton accepts the life of aspiration, of struggling for a goal that always lies beyond the grasp of the society striving for it. He recommends that we follow Plato's use of a "fluid definition" of where we are in relation to the ideal form. Conflict is valuable, both for the group and for the individual, because of the inevitable conflict we can avoid complacent but narrow successes and reach after an elusive but much broader achievement." Brereton goes on:

> It is the nature of a society trying to develop wholeness that it should be a sort of active debate, or even conflict. Plato demands that we accept complexity and the conflicts which result from it, not as avoidable but as a necessary condition of health.

In a very real sense, Outward Bound and other experiential education programs are still trying to answer the questions posed by Socrates in the *Republic:* "What are we to do? ... Where shall we discover a disposition that is at once gentle and greatspirited? What then, is our education?" Brereton speaks for all of us when he says, "We must seek to make the tough compassionate and the timid enterprising." He shows how this view, coming from Hahn, stands next to other educational priorities:

> Hahn, in his broadcast talk just after Gordonstoun was opened in 1934, said that there were three views of education, which he called the Ionian, the Spartan, and the Platonic. The first believes that the individual ought to be nurtured and humored regardless of the interests of the community. According to the second, the individual may and should be neglected for the benefit of the State. The third, the Platonic view, believes that any nation is a slovenly guardian of its own interests if it does not do all it can to make the individual citizen discover his own powers. And it further believes that the individual becomes a cripple from his or her own point of view if he or she is not qualified by education to serve the community.

The preceding paragraphs only scratch the surface of Plato's influence on Hahn. They do not begin to record his debt to other thinkers—Rousseau, Goethe, Max Weber, William James, to name a few of the major one—whose ideas reach Outward Bound and experiential education in one form or another through Hahn. William James, for example, in *The Moral*

Equivalent of War, asked if it is not possible in time of peace to build the kind of social spirit and productivity one takes for granted in time of war. Hahn saw Outward Bound as an answer to that question. Goethe wrote of an education that would need to occur in a place apart, a "Pedagogical Province," so that individuals could be strengthened and given skills to survive, individually and collectively, in the debilitating environment of human society as we know it. This has much in common with Plato's notion of a "healthy pasture," and it is the sine qua non of most adventure programs operating in the outdoors.

Like any idealist in education, Hahn was profoundly indebted to Rousseau, both for the idea that awakening an individual's collective concern is the key to healthy personal development, and for Rousseau's assumption that Nature is an educator in its own right, more akin to the true nature of a human being than is the society that humans have built for themselves. Hahn also drew heavily from the experience of the English school movement at the beginning of this century. But his genius was in applying ideas to emphasize the interdependence of the community as a whole, rather than a disproportionate excellence of some of its parts. A man of aphorisms more than of systematic theory, of aspiration more than of exact analysis, he lived out the aphorism of another great educator, Pestalozzi, who said, "To reach a worthy goal is better than to propound much wisdom."

If Hahn had been only an idealist, if he had not applied his ideals to the humdrum of educational programs—including Outward Bound—then we might be better off leaving him to his rest. As it is, however, his practical concerns are still concerns of Outward Bound and of experiential education.

First, for instance, Hahn asked his students to pledge themselves to a "training plan" that established personal goals and a code of responsibility. Outward Bound instructors make a similar appeal to their students today, though not in the detailed terms used by Hahn at Salem and Gordonstoun, and it is a crucial aspect of the Outward Bound experience. It is no exaggeration to say that the individual commitment of the student, the expressed desire to accomplish a worthy goal by means of the course, becomes, in effect, the moral basis of the community. It becomes the foundation both of compassion and of achievement, and it is, in addition, the ultimate source of value for the Outward Bound pin and certificate. These are not mere objects. At best, they come to represent the energy and determination that have been invested in them all along by students. They signify the pledge, the willingness to press beyond limits, the membership each student earns in a community of seekers. There are times when everyone wants to turn away from it all, just blast away from the cajoling of instructors and other students, but comes back because of the persistent lure of that self-imposed challenge, and the dishonor of withdrawing from it. The pledge imposes a necessary code of responsibility on people who have grown accustomed to a far different set of rules in our time. If the program taps previously undiscovered resources of courage and mutual support in the face of crisis among its students, even in what appear to be trivial situations like cooking a meal or getting up at an early hour, at least it will have opened the door to the revitalization of social life that Hahn had in mind. It will have started its students thinking about living up to an aspiration they have come to realize is possible.

A second concern that Hahn incorporated into all his educational programs had to do with compressing time. From Salem onward, he woke his students early, exercised them, controlled their activities. Even their time to relax and their time to be alone were strictly regulated. As one writer has pointed out cynically, every molder of character wants to control as much of the environment as possible. But on the positive side, this form of education, if it is handled sensitively to foster growth instead of merely to control, can be remarkably effective in leading students out of apathy and self-indulgence. The conflict that arises can be dealt with constructively so that it causes both the individual and the group to confront what must be done to meet collective goals without trampling on the rights of the individual. Any discussion of freedom that ignores this conflict has little basis in reality. Every Outward Bound instructor—indeed, every educator—has probably asked at one time or another: "Is it necessary to make such an incursion into the personal domain of students, their private world of choice and motivation and meaning, in order to give them a learning experience?" When they ask this, they are in effect arguing with Kurt Hahn, and Hahn's answer would be: "Yes, but if it is done gently and with a caring spirit, it will not be such an incursion after all." The structuring of time is a critical factor in influencing behavior. To slow Outward Bound down, to shift its focus from action to sensibility and individual well-being apart from the needs of the group, would be to leave out an element *("impelled* into experience") that Hahn saw as essential to the program.

Third, a centrally important element that Hahn brought to Outward Bound was adventure—with all the risk it entails. He believed that education should cultivate a passion for life and that this can be accomplished only through experience, a shared sense of moment in the journey toward an exciting goal. Mountaineering and sailing were integral parts of his program at Gordonstoun, and he made space in all his programs for student initiative—an expedition, a project, a sailing voyage. Hahn welcomed powerful emotions, such as awe, fear, exultant triumph. Part of his lifelong aspiration, part of the "whole" he sought through programs like Outward Bound, was that the experience accessible to any human being, at any level of ability, could be charged with joy and wonder in the doing. But the corollary is that he saw adventure in a social perspective, as an event of community life and not a private thrill. The adventure of the individual is always mediated to some extent by the values and needs of the group. This is why, almost 40 years after the program was founded, Outward Bound retains an unusual world-view among the outdoor programs that have sprung up around it. Everyone touts adventure nowadays, but in Outward Bound the adventurer must still break down and learn to serve his companions. The experience is individual; the pledge and the challenge are individual; the achievement necessarily belongs to all. Hahn saw his schools as a "countervailing force" against the declining values of the world at large. Perhaps among outdoor programs, Outward Bound is a countervailing force against narcissism and self-centered virtuosity.

Fourth, Hahn understood the educational value of working with small groups of students. He probably took this idea from military organization as it came into the youth movements of the late 19th century, especially the Scouting movement of Lord Baden-Powell in England. Oddly enough, military jargon persists in Outward Bound to this day in terms such as patrol, resupply, debriefing, and reconnaissance. Hahn saw small groups as a way to develop the natural leadership abilities he thought were present in most people, but were suppressed by the dependency, passivity, and bureaucratic impersonality of modern life. Such groups place heavy social pressures on individual initiative, yet at the same time they require it absolutely. Small groups require tremendous amounts of energy to reach the consensus necessary to meet objectives. In a wilderness environment, effective group dynamics are paramount to survival; they rank in importance with technical skills. Natural leaders emerge when the group must solve real problems instead of playing games with an unnatural reward system. A genuine community begins to appear on a small scale—at least the possibility is there. If it happens, each of the separate selves may glimpse an aspiration worth fighting for back home. At its worst, the small group is a troublesome obstacle to the fine experience any wilderness has to offer; but at its best, it opens a new dimension not accessible to solitary escapists, no matter how intense their devotion to the outdoors.

The fifth concern, which could be seen as encompassing all the rest, was Hahn's dedication to community service. It is possible to make a case that the Outward Bound concept was born when the headmaster of Gordonstoun looked around him during the 1930s and saw that the boys in Hopeman Village, near the school, were in terrible physical condition and that they fell into delinquent ways as soon as they reached puberty. Hahn believed the school should serve the community around it, so he allowed a few of his boys to go out on a project to teach the kids how to take care of themselves. The project grew, along with many other service projects he set up, ranging from craftsmanship to landscaping to rescue service. By the time he started developing a program to help sailors acquire the fortitude to survive in lifeboats at sea, Kurt Hahn already had an extensive outreach program from his school, including sailboats, mountaineering gear, tools, and other paraphernalia. As Hahn saw it, the link between individual and school depended for its meaning upon the link between school and society. The notion came into Outward Bound in the form of rescue service, and it has since been applied to diverse needs in communities and the natural environment.

These are a few of the ideas that Kurt Hahn brought to Outward Bound and to experiential education. Perhaps another writer would spend more time enumerating the man's limitations. I believe I have done enough by depicting Hahn's aspiration in a way that is true to the scale in which he envisioned it. Much more could be said about him that would be relevant to American education today. For example, his practice of hiring people who disagreed with him, and then challenging them to challenge him, is a tradition that ought to be perpetuated, even when the resulting conflict is painful. A more thorough inquiry into Hahn's life would undoubtedly turn up other treasures. But such an inquiry would eventually miss the point. The point is that he started Outward Bound with an immense aspiration that gave meaning to the program far beyond the needs being addressed at the time. The task facing Outward Bound and experiential education is to retrace some of that aspiration in the minds of all who come into contact with the programs. If this is done, other elements will fit readily within the whole. Instructional objectives, systems, models, policies, procedures, formats, evaluation schemes—all can play a part, alongside the irreplaceable devotion of staff, once we have come to terms with the essential nature of our business. All are a hollow shell without that recognition.

The staff of experiential education programs enter each course with a large store of technical skill and, in the outdoors, wilderness experience behind them. No student will ever see it all, but it helps to define their world throughout the course. In the same way, the social vision of staff can help to bring a world of dignity and compassion into being, if they are gentle and high-spirited enough. Each course, each student, each moment is an opportunity to use the mountains and other experiential "classrooms" to find the only mountain really worth climbing. This may sound wildly idealistic, but it is not out of keeping with the origins of Outward Bound or with the aims of experiential education. It is the tacit code that unifies and justifies the endeavors of all of us.

Dancing on the Shores of the Future:
The 1998 Kurt Hahn Address

▾ ▾ ▾

Rita Yerkes

Rita Yerkes is the 16th recipient of the Kurt Hahn Award. The following is her Kurt Hahn Address, delivered at the Association for Experiential Education International Conference held November 1998 in Tahoe, Nevada. Prior to the speech, each person in the reception hall was given a bead. The significance of the bead becomes evident at the close of Dr. Yerkes' speech.

I would like to begin by thanking the Association for Experiential Education and acknowledging the past Kurt Hahn recipients who may be with us tonight. Please stand if you are in the audience so that we may thank you again for your many contributions to our association and to experiential education. I would also like to say thank you to the Women's Professional Group for the many opportunities they have given to me during the past 18 years. Special thanks to Craig Dobkin and Michael Gass for our years at Towson State University and to my many students who have taught me much more than I could have ever shared with them. Most of all, I would like to thank my family, Wilma, Ray, Lisa, Bill, Clay, Bradley, Abbie and Julia, Ben, Nell, and Roxanne, who have supported and continue to support my many adventures in experiential education.

It was some 18 years ago that I attended my first AEE Conference and sat in an auditorium much like this one. As I look around the room I see many friends and colleagues whom I have come to know over the years. I would like to start with an informal poll.

This chapter originally was published in the *Journal of Experiential Education*, with the following citation:

Yerkes, R. (1999). 1998 Kurt Hahn address: Dancing on the shores of the future. *Journal of Experiential Education, 22*(1), 20–23.

How many of you have been involved with the association for 26 years? 20 years? 15 years? 1–10 years? Less than one year?

As we celebrate our 26th year of the Association for Experiential Education, it is a time to reflect where we have been as individuals, as an association, where we are now, and where we may journey on the "shores of the future." Come now and share a reflective journey with me.

As an adventurous young child, I loved the thrill of challenge experiences and learning by doing. I did not understand or accept the message that those challenge experiences were only for my many brothers to do. You see, I was a child filled with the joy to be all that I could be.

Future experiential educator

It was only later, as I turned 12, that voices told me to leave challenges and adventures to others. It left me confused. Societal messages grew stronger to leave my joy for the outdoors and "learning by doing" in order to do what "society" expected from young girls at the time.

These societal expectations were not comfortable for me, but there did not seem to be other role models that I could look to and identify with. It was a lonely time. I wonder if similar experiences happen to other young people on their journey today? Questions like "Where do I fit?" "Where do I fit at home?" "Where do I fit at school?" "Where do I fit at work?" "Where do I fit in experiential education?" "Where do I fit in the world?"

Even much later as a young graduate student and experiential educator, I had little access to the many that had gone before me and shared the same struggle. I continued to ask myself, "Where do I fit?" Although I was given a few mentors to look up to, they did not seem to fit my profile. I kept asking my instructors: Who were the people who went before us to create experiential education opportunities? Were there any women and minorities in this field? The response was that they did not know, but thought it would be a good project for someone to do.

So with a valued friend, I set out on a journey to search and reflect. What we found was that there were many experiential education mentors and leaders, forgotten in time, and with it, important leaders and roots of experiential education.

So come with me now and meet a few of those who went before us; perhaps, some whom you have never met before. Let us reflect on their contributions to experiential education and how they have empowered us, like Kurt Hahn, on our experiential education journey—now and into the future.

In 1902, a woman from New York City developed the first camp for girls, Camp Kehonka. Laura Mattoon was to girls as Kurt Hahn was to boys; in fact, they seem to even look alike.

Mattoon was a private school teacher, schooled at Wesley College and taught that anyone could change society for the better. When she graduated she could not get a job because, at that time, it was not appropriate for women to work outside of the home. She started Camp Kehonka using experiential education to educate girls about how they could contribute to and change society. She created opportunities for girls to fully participate in experiential activities by creating clothing called bloomers so that they could move freely. Her camp was about creating a learning environment that fostered student-centered learning, creativity, social justice, and service to others. Mattoon also helped to create the American Camping Association, which has many parallels to the Association for Experiential Education.

Top row: Laura Mattoon, Kurt Hahn
Bottom row: Juliette Low, Abbie Graham

Perhaps the best known to young women was Juliette Low, who in 1912 founded the Girl Scouts. Juliette Low had a vision of creating an organization so that girls could serve their communities and develop leadership skills. Many of our women outdoor leaders today have received their first exposure to outdoor experiential education through the Girl Scouts.

Abbie Graham (1933), a private camp director, author of *The Girls' Camp*, wrote inspirational writings for girls in the outdoors. She captured the essence of providing experiential education opportunities to girls and women when she wrote,

> Eve did not, from the very beginning, like the program set up; no chance to express herself. She did not want to do flowers, she wanted to do trees. In every group there were people doing things on their own initiative which was a surprise to "the management"...
> In such persons lie the imaginative possibilities for group living. (p. 73)

The journey of experiential education is a long and distinguished one. Many have made their contributions to the field. It is only when we take the time to remember, acknowledge, and learn from those who went before us that we can really say there is a home for everyone with us.

The educators mentioned here tonight empower us through their example and accomplishments to meet the many challenges ahead. They have shown us the many ways to practice inclusion. They have empowered us over the years to prepare well for the next millennium by:

- Valuing all people for what they bring to the experience.

- Creating spaces for all to explore their potential and our own inclusivity.

- Recognizing that we each need safe harbors for reflection, so that when we return we can really work together regardless of our differences.

- Celebrating our many special interests, while remembering the common thread we all share; learning through experience.

- Mentoring younger colleagues to pursue their careers and stay in this field.

- Empowering those of us who can make a difference in administration to create opportunities and salaries so young colleagues can stay in experiential education; they are our greatest investment!

- Revisiting our commitment to service learning.

- Continuing the contributions of research and literature that create the body of knowledge that supports and acknowledges our profession and methodology.

- Promoting standards of practice and accreditation efforts.

- Supporting the AEE "Touch the Future" fundraising campaign.

- Finding new ways to reach mainstream education with our methodology.

- Finding a good and balanced place for oneself; taking care of our personal relationships with significant others who sacrifice so much so that we can do the work we do.

As we read the business literature today, there seems to be a new priority in achieving balance in both work and personal life. I came across this quote:

> Seek beauty, give service, pursue knowledge, be trustworthy, hold on to your health, glorify work, be happy.

Looks like something we would read in an executive development team-building session today. The interesting thing to note is it came from the Campfire Girls Organization mission statement in 1916 (p. 4). Yes, we have come a long way together, we have much to celebrate, and we have much more work to do.

So join with me in an invitation that was shared with me by my students and which we pass along to you today. Please take out the bead that was given to you by our Service Crew this evening. Please hold it in the palm of your hand, take a moment to reflect on what is meaningful to you in experiential education—it can be a memory, an event, or a mentor who made a difference to you and others in your life. Then sometime during the conference or after when you get home, pass it on with your energy to another. That's what we do every day in experiential education ... pass it on ... enabling others, making a difference in the life journey that we all share.

As Kurt Hahn (1962) stated:

> The young today are surrounded by tempting declines which affect the adult world—the decline of fitness, due to modern methods of moving about; decline of memory and imagination, due to the confused restlessness of modern life; decline of skill and care, due to the weakened tradition of modern life; decline of self discipline, due to stimulants and tranquilizers. Worst of all, the decline of compassion.... (p. 52–53)

As we speed toward the next millennium in a world dominated by high tech, disengagement, people longing for a sense of community and challenges beyond our imagination, experiential education in its many forms has an important role to play. So now join hands with me and with each other.

Together we have wonderful opportunities of challenge, spirit, and compassion to offer. Together we empower each other.

Together we empower our clients and students.

Together we empower our communities.

Together we empower the world that we all share.

Yes, we have many experiential education dances to dance together on the shores of the future....

Thank you, and good evening.

References

Campfire Girls, Inc. (1913). *The book of the Camp Fire Girls.* New York: Brooks Press.

Choate, A., & Ferris, H. (Eds.). (1928). Juliette Low and the Girl Scouts. New York: *Girls Scouts*, Inc. Doubleday, Doran & Co.

Hahn, K. (1962, July). State of the young in England. *The Listener*, Vol. b.

Graham, A. (1933). *The girls' camp.* New York: The Women's Press.

Miranda, W. (1987, February). The genteel radicals. *Camping Magazine.*

Rohrs, H. (1970). *Kurt Hahn.* London: Routledge and Kegan Paul.

Paul Petzoldt's Perspective: The Final 20 Years

▾ ▾ ▾

Mark Wagstaff & Christine Cashel

Paul Petzoldt, who died in 1999, was one of the early pioneers in outdoor education who saw the future need for trained outdoor leaders. Petzoldt honed his ability to teach outdoor leadership education throughout a lifetime of guiding, teaching, and writing. In an effort to foster the outdoor profession's rich tradition, portions of unpublished manuscripts, journals, notes, and letters written by Petzoldt served as sources for this article. These unpublished records were written during the last 20 years of his life and focus on the process of training outdoor leaders to conduct educational expeditions. The authors chose three interconnected, recurring themes out of a larger body of work that address refinements in Petzoldt's philosophy and methods made over the final 20 years of his life. These refinements include: (a) crucial components in the first 24 hours of an educational expedition, (b) the "grasshopper teaching" method and, (c) judgment and decision-making.

"Now a promise made is a debt unpaid, and the trail has its own stern code. In the days to come, though my lips were numb, in my heart how I cursed that load" (Service, 1916; The Cremation of Sam McGee). Paul Petzoldt recited this passage to emphasize that outdoor leaders must make a deep commitment to the groups they lead. Paul Petzoldt died in 1999, and for most of his life he sought to develop, define, and teach outdoor leadership skills (Ringholz, 1997). He used subtle (an expressive smile), and not so subtle (kicking "billy cans" in the fire)

This chapter originally was published in the *Journal of Experiential Education*, with the following citation:
Wagstaff, M., Cashel, C. (2001). Paul Petzoldt's perspective: The final 20 years. *Journal of Experiential Education, 24*(3), 160–165.

methods to make his points. No one who learned from him ever forgot the experience. Since his first climb of the Grand Teton in 1924, he developed a desire to teach people as well as guide them through the mountains. As a climber he developed the American climbing commands and the sliding middleman technique to free climbers from being roped continuously. His strength and prowess on rock and snow are legendary (Ringholz, 1997). In every experience, with every person, he refined his understanding of outdoor leadership. During the 1932 K2 expedition he experimented with energy conservation techniques. That expedition also reinforced his belief that poor group dynamics can cause failure to reach a goal. "Expedition behavior," a well-documented tenet of leading groups in the outdoors (Drury & Bonney, 1992; Petzoldt, 1974, 1984), was a direct outcome of the 1932 climb (personal conversation).

Paul Petzoldt played an integral role in the development of outdoor leadership in the United States (Ringholz, 1997). Petzoldt held the position of chief instructor for the first Outward Bound School. He left behind one of the most successful outdoor leadership schools in the world, the National Outdoor Leadership School (NOLS). After NOLS, he helped launch the Wilderness Education Association (WEA), and in his last few years he formed the Paul Petzoldt Leadership School for youth. He passionately recorded his ideas on outdoor leadership until his death. Petzoldt did not consciously use written theory about education or group development models. Instead, he was a true experiential educator whose theory came from practice. He would try an idea in the field, write it down, think about it, modify it and try it again.

Little has been published about Petzoldt's thoughts during the last 20 years of his life. Petzoldt's books, *The Wilderness Handbook* (1974), *Petzoldt's Teton Trails* (1976), and *The New Wilderness Handbook* (1984), provided the general public its first real exposure to his written word. Following these seminal works, Petzoldt continued to teach, analyze, refine, and write. Boxes of old field journals, unfinished manuscripts, letters, speeches, and personal notes were pulled from the basement of his home in Maine after his death. These unpublished, historical gems provide a window into his thoughts over the last two decades of his life. Three interconnected, recurring themes were gleaned from these writings that demonstrated his unceasing drive to explain effective training methods. These themes were aspects of leadership and teaching that are important in the planning and execution of an educational expedition. Petzoldt drilled these themes into potential leaders and instructors. They were: (a) the crucial components in the first 24 hours of an educational expedition, (b) the "grasshopper teaching method" and, (c) judgment and decision-making. He emphasized these themes with one simple goal in mind—train leaders to take participants into the outdoors safely and enjoyably. Paul Petzoldt's lifelong commitment to outdoor leadership did not waver from this goal. The following are some of his ideas taken from his unpublished field journals, manuscripts, and speeches.

The First 24 Hours

Ask any outdoor leader about the most intense teaching times in a course and you will probably hear that the first day or two are the toughest. So much is happening. Group members meet each other and gear is issued. The environment and course elements produce student stress. There is an urgency to get to the field and get started. While programs differ in intent and duration, the priorities that instructors establish in the first 24 hours are critical to the success of the program. Petzoldt said it this way, "The first day of any outdoor leadership education program will be a difficult one. There is a temptation for the Instructor [*sic*] to try to give decision-making [*sic*] education before going to the field—and perhaps some is necessary. That which is not absolutely necessary should be postponed till actually in the field" (Petzoldt, n.d.). The emphasis Petzoldt placed on not overloading the student with information was central to tone setting. He believed that students should learn from experience as a predictable progression unfolds on an educational expedition. Effective teaching requires setting a firm foundation of expectations, parameters, and behavior balanced with the logistics of living in the wilderness. Petzoldt had a clear vision of what instructors should focus on during a course start. He did not care how neat and tidy students were in the beginning. He believed that students should get to the field quickly and instructors should begin the shakedown. He recorded his thoughts this way:

> The first day we have done a lot in order to get the expedition started and we've started to develop judgment among the students. If some students are disturbed by fragmented and incomplete teaching of subjects, it may be necessary to explain that education in the outdoors is a continuing process, that subjects are not learned all at once, as chapters are written in a book. They will be learning a little bit about every subject the entire time that they are in the field. Hopefully this will eliminate dissatisfaction with only partial explanations of the various things that they are doing. (Petzoldt, n.d.)

Petzoldt simplified the task of curriculum management by focusing on four priorities. He stressed that these priorities should be considered each day in the field. He stated his perspective by the following, when giving advice to a field instructor:

> First we must make decisions (I suggest you take your students along with you on your thinking process and decision-making—thinking out loud to them) for the day considering our four priorities that we take into consideration with every decision:

The first day the leader will need to emphasize the following:

1. The safety of the individual.

2. The conservation of the environment.

3. The protection of the equipment.

4. Expedition behavior.

The safety of the individual. This concerns many aspects of safety such as avoiding blisters, sunburn, insect bites, chilling the body, overheating the body, fatigue, sprained muscles or being separated from the group.

The conservation of the environment. This concerns disposal of human waste, littering, disturbing flora and fauna, polluting water, causing fire, or causing erosion.

Protection of the equipment. This concerns keeping equipment dry, avoiding loss of equipment and damage to equipment the first day and night of use. [*sic*]

Expedition behavior. This concerns loud and boisterous noises, meeting horses, cycles, hikers on trails, avoiding disturbing other users, obeying laws, rules, regulations, avoid disturbing wild life, avoiding conflict within your group, and promoting enjoyment and fun.

Every day we must give priority to making decisions concerning the previously described four areas. Then, after that is done, the rest of our time we will teach the decision making process concerning other aspects of outdoor leadership. (Petzoldt, n.d.)

These priorities shaped the outline of the first day and influenced information shared with students prior to arrival at a course. For example, Petzoldt resisted the temptation to give a full-blown lecture on expedition behavior at the beginning of a trip. He provided information on a "need to know basis" until he could discuss the concept in more detail.

As part of setting tone and expectations, Petzoldt emphasized the necessity of explaining the educational process. As Petzoldt alluded to earlier, students can become disturbed or distressed by not knowing the exact plan and all the facts associated with a subject. In Petzoldt's later years, he spent significant time in the field with college students, university professors, and seasoned outdoor professionals while teaching WEA courses. Therefore, to deal with these populations he included in his tone-setting strategy the following advice for instructors:

Explain that there may be many ways to do outdoor skills and teach outdoor leadership. We know one way, one method that has proven to be effective and to accomplish our goals and this way, our way is the one we will teach and use on this expedition. This in no way says ours is the most effective, programmatic or productive way. We know of no 'best' ways—since any method can be improved as we hope our method improves and changes to be even more productive in the future.

What we wish to do for you is to teach you our proven way and encourage the development and improvement of your judgment so you can adjust the learning you receive here to the unique situations you will confront later with your own groups in different environments, with different people and with different expeditions purposes.

Therefore to make our learning most efficient and effective we ask your help in accepting our methods and our teaching on this one and only expedition. After this program or course you will have complete freedom, on your own judgment, to change what we have taught, add it to your past methods of outdoorsmanship—or dismiss it all together and go back to your previous methods you think more productive.

This understanding about not arguing about mythical 'best' ways will be difficult for some to understand or cooperate in keeping their arguments to themselves, especially those with experience who came to the program thinking they know the 'best' ways. It will be a blow to some egos to not try and enforce their methods that they think 'right' and 'better' or 'only' ways. (Petzoldt, n.d.)

In order to weave the four priorities throughout a course and build on concepts and skills, Petzoldt believed that a specific style of teaching was needed. Like the students Petzoldt taught in the field, he also found that new instructors were accustomed to teaching information in large chunks, such as the 50-minute college classroom lecture. For example, at the beginning of a course most assume that "how to pack a backpack" should be taught. An instructor will gather the students and give a 45-minute lecture and demonstration on the intricacies of backpacking. The lecture/discussion might be followed by having students pack their own backpacks. Petzoldt gives this advice for the first day on the trail:

Hopefully the group can reach camp without time out for a backpacking lesson. Let them struggle with their packs. Let the packs be sloppy. The first day we must get to the first camp and have time to prepare shelter and food and teach what is essential. We will probably not have time to go into details of how to pack a pack and carry a pack and put a pack on the back or other teachings. All that comes later.

It will probably be necessary to slow down the scout at the head of the line because most people have not been on educational programs. They've been on destination-oriented hikes and they have a habit of going as fast as possible to reach a destination. We probably can't give much of an explanation the first day. We may explain that the first day we want to take a leisurely pace to arrive without fatigue and without blisters. If anything happens along the way appropriate for educational illustrations we will use opportunity teaching. Opportunity teaching will count for a great deal of the education and even on the first day we can seize any opportunity that might develop. (Petzoldt, n.d.)

The "Grasshopper Teaching" Method

As described above, Petzoldt used opportunity teaching to convey information on the first day of a course. Petzoldt spent a significant amount of time in his later years attempting to articulate to instructors what the ideal teaching method was for an outdoor leadership course. He coined the term "grasshopper method" as a preferred teaching methodology. The grasshopper method of teaching allows an instructor to "hop" from one subject to another as circumstances allow. He wanted an introduction to the subject, a demonstration, and practical application in close time sequence for optimal learning of outdoorsmanship (Petzoldt, 1984). This term, grasshopper method, was one of many colorful analogies that Petzoldt coined to grab the students' attention. He was a master at it! The following are his thoughts on the grasshopper method:

This is teaching what is necessary, it is realistic and under actual conditions—the most effective type of leadership teaching. However, it is fragmented, a little of this subject, a little of that subject, a little of this skill and a little of that skill.

Thus, the teaching will be throughout the entire educational expedition. Fragmentation of learning and actual experience will be furthered by "opportunity" teaching. That is taking advantage of situations that present an unusual opportunity to teach knowledge, judgment and skills pertaining to a present and actual situation. This situation itself may present a solution based upon many subjects and parts of several skills.

This type of leadership education we call the grasshopper method is a necessary and practical method of leadership education in the field. The method places a burden on the instructor to keep track of what is taught concerning each subject by the "grasshopper method" of jumping from one subject to another as opportunity and necessity dictates. The instructor must make sure before the educational program is finished to teach and give the experience concerning the subject not covered by the necessary day to day teaching and the opportunity teaching combined. (Petzoldt, n.d.)

What is important to understand about Petzoldt's teaching method was his attempt to formalize the process in order to present an entire curriculum. Outdoor leadership could be taught using this "hop scotch" approach of presenting information. It should be noted that the grasshopper method is actually an extension of his original thoughts on opportunity teaching. "It is very effective to use actual situations for demonstrating various facts of outdoorsmanship. Any opportunity that arises on the trail or at the campsite can trigger on-the-spot teaching" (Petzoldt, 1974, p. 268). Petzoldt was trying to explain that the grasshopper method was a more sophisticated adaptation of opportunity teaching or what is commonly known as the "teachable moment." The grasshopper method was Petzoldt's way of saying that instructors must systematically link teachable moments to present a complete curriculum. If the instructor could understand and apply this concept, the propensity to share too much information would not exist during the first 24 hours. More importantly, Petzoldt believed that if instructors could role model this methodology, the students would then begin to develop the necessary skills and knowledge to demonstrate judgment.

Petzoldt qualified his experience with the grasshopper method when he stated this warning to instructors. "The explanation of the difference in teaching will need to be explained and illustrated over and over and again and again before the college upperclassman, the college graduate and even the college professor, so ingrained in our educational system, can understand or apply this method" (Petzoldt, n.d.). Petzoldt went on to explain the necessity to frame the grasshopper method for the unsuspecting student:

The instructor teaching outdoor leadership under actual conditions in the field must understand how such teaching is different in method and purpose from classroom teaching. Classroom teaching generally consists of giving information by voice, reading or artificial visual aids. Though the purpose of such teaching is supposed to be effectively translated into field conditions that is not what actually takes place. The main purpose to the student will be to memorize material so he can make a grade and pass a course by being able to speak or write the memorized material. Seldom and sometimes it never needs to be translated into decision making with real people under real circumstances.

The most effective teaching in the field though, it is fragmented to solve daily necessities and opportunity situations should not be translated into memory for the regurgitation of that memory but must be translated into decisions—decisions that are translated into action. (Petzoldt, n.d.)

Judgment/Decision-Making Skills

The final theme pulled from Petzoldt's work was the importance of developing judgment and decision-making skills. Petzoldt wrote tirelessly on these concepts the last 20 years of his life, and came into contact with a new generation of students with prior outdoor leadership experience. Petzoldt's experience showed him that a participant's prior experience sometimes, hinders further development in decision-making skills. This was not a new topic for Petzoldt. He broached the subject in his first book, *Wilderness Handbook* (Petzoldt, 1974). "Dealing with the 'expert' who has had some experience and wants to publicize his knowledge presents a problem. He finds it more interesting to question than to listen" (Petzoldt, 1974, p. 265). He was constantly confronted with individuals who had preconceived notions of how things must be done in the outdoors. What was unique about his last 20 years was his consistent exposure to college students and university instructors on WEA trips. Petzoldt was working with students not only with technical skills but also with preexisting leadership skills:

> Since most outdoor trips made by the students have been 'running' trips to reach a goal and return with little or no time allowed for education and decision-making it will be difficult for many students with previous experience to adjust to the educational trip. The instructors will need to mix the necessary learning with physical activity concerning necessary skills along with explaining why it is necessary to not follow the running, exhausting habits of most outdoor trips previously experienced by the students.
>
> The difference between the educational trip and the running exhausting, goal-oriented trip must be understood. The relaxed, enjoyable, comfortable educational expedition will be difficult for the running, stress goal-oriented experience students have previously accepted as outdoor leadership education.
>
> Many students will start the outdoor leadership education program with ideas, truths, prejudices, and habits that hinder programmatic learning based on demonstrable situation. The teacher, instructor cannot erase these traits by words. Argument will be counter productive. (Petzoldt, n.d.)

The underlying theme for the first day and throughout the entire course is judgment/decision-making. Confronting student attitudes and preconceived notions are just a few of the several factors an instructor must address. Instructors must also think out loud and explain the "whys" of their decisions once the student's mind is open. Petzoldt struggled to articulate how to use and teach judgment/decision-making. He believed the foundation for quality outdoor leadership was judgment and decision-making. Petzoldt professed that instructors could help students develop quality judgment and decision-making skills. To him, it was the decision-making and judgment ability that separated effective from non-effective instructors. Petzoldt's experience showed him that students schooled through traditional education tended to be dualistic thinkers. Petzoldt explained judgment this way:

> First we need to understand between ourselves what is meant by the word judgment as it relates to the wild outdoors. Judgment is the process of using previous learning and experience to make a decision and execute decisions. Therefore all the information and experience presented in the program is for the purpose of making and executing decisions in similar circumstances in the future. However, these future situations will never be exactly the same as those circumstances where the teaching takes place. Therefore the decisions will be somewhat different to fit into different circumstances such as different people, different environment, different weather, different purpose, etc.
>
> Teaching judgment under actual realistic conditions in actual environments with actual people gives a vast combination of decision-making experiences that the student can remember to apply to his future leadership. If the student memorizes the decisions and methods used, he [sic] may be able to describe the process in words and speech to pass an exam. However, if the learning is to be effective in the future, the memorized response will not be adequate. Decisions will not be the same and the executions will not be the same as the memorized process.
>
> How then do we teach the student this ability to have judgment in these future situations? One method is to be sure the student knows what we call the 'Whys' in relation to making and executing the decisions in the particular situation under which we are teaching.
>
> Why are we teaching the subject?
> Why are we teaching it now?
> Why is our decision working?
> Why does it apply to our purpose?
> Why is it being done the way it is being done?
> Why, Why, Why? (Petzoldt, n.d.)

Judgment decision-making, according to Petzoldt, was the combination of information available at the moment combined with past experience to yield a decision. All decisions should reduce the odds of injury or loss to people, conserve the environment, and protect equipment needed for the expedition. Petzoldt attempted to emphasize the importance of judgment by making a comparison to the average person's attitude toward technical skills:

> Skill level is not the most important part of outdoor leadership. Having judgment is the most important aspect. Another important aspect is knowing one's limitations and knowing one's ability. Having judgment to accept leadership within one's limitations [*sic*]. Since faulty planning is responsible for about 75% of deaths, accidents, search and rescue and plain unrewarding trips [*sic*]. Being taught the knowledge and judgment of how to plan a trip is indispensable to trip leadership. This is generally not considered a 'skill.' Skill in the outdoors is interpreted by most outdoorsmen [*sic*] to mean experience in physical activities such as biking, climbing, canoeing, etc.
>
> Judgment and ability to plan and execute expedition behavior and judgment on how to use and still conserve the environment are far more important than the 'skills' unless you consider all the above 'skills', which is not the tendency of the average person. (Petzoldt, n.d.)

Petzoldt sometimes would say that judgment is the result of previous bad decisions. Therefore, it is important to give students information and reasons why decisions are made. The leader can accomplish this by thinking out loud. The process of thinking out loud at the beginning of a course is a crucial step in the development of a student's judgment. Petzoldt thought that future judgments would be more sound if the "whys" of past decisions were clear.

Summary

Paul Petzoldt was one of the early pioneers in outdoor education that saw a future need for trained outdoor leaders (Ringholz, 1997). He spent the majority of his life searching for ways to move groups through the wilderness safely and enjoyably. Was he successful in his quest? Certainly we must admire any educator who stayed focused and true to his/her calling. What Petzoldt had was a true calling to develop methods necessary to meet his seemingly simple goal. The amount of material that he wrote in his lifetime and in big, scrawling longhand during the last 20 years of his life was testimony to his commitment. He refused to end the search of finding more effective ways to teach future outdoor leaders. A diminishing community of first generation outdoor leaders who learned directly from Paul Petzoldt can still be found in the field. However, scores of second and third generation outdoor leaders who may have heard of Petzoldt or maybe even heard him speak in his later years have now moved into industry leadership positions. They enjoyed his story-telling ability but to experience his methods firsthand no longer exists.

Paul Petzoldt did not use theory. He made theory by learning from his rich experience. In the 1960s and 1970s he recognized that outdoor leaders had to take better care of the environment and testified during the Wilderness Act hearings for better education about the environment. He put low-impact camping methods into his curriculum despite his past guiding practices of leaving cans in the backcountry. He was willing to change and tinker with ideas and equipment as technology emerged. He never stayed fixed on one idea as "the truth." Petzoldt would simply say, "Rules are for fools." It was instructor judgment that dictated all appropriate decisions. Petzoldt believed that the methodology used on an educational expedition must be different from other types of expeditions. Like a grasshopper, the instructor will hop from subject to subject as opportunities arise while systematically covering a curriculum. Instructors must also explain the "whys" of every decision so the student could comprehend on a deeper level. He understood the importance of setting a strong tone and tried to help leaders through a very intensive time at course start by giving them a system of priorities to guide their decisions.

While his central ideas have remained the same over the years, Petzoldt's perspective was subject to refinement during the last 20 years of his life. We should harbor the valuable lessons that have been passed down in our rich tradition of outdoor leadership. It is a privilege to share pieces of Petzoldt's work with outdoor professionals so his legacy will not be lost. Petzoldt actively paved our future until the very day he died. He left us with a perspective that continues to merit discussion. What remained unchanged for Petzoldt, and for us, today, was the "burden of the load"—the outdoor leader's commitment to the group must run deep.

The authors would like to thank Virginia Petzoldt and Kelly Munson for making Paul Petzoldt's personal journals and writing available.

References

Drury, J. K., & Bonney, B. F. (1992). *The backcountry classroom: Lesson plans for teaching in the wilderness.* Merrillville, IN: ICS Books.

Petzoldt, P. K. (1974). *The wilderness handbook.* New York: WW Norton & Co.

Petzoldt, P. K. (1976). *Petzoldt's Teton tales.* Salt Lake City: Wasatch.

Petzoldt, P. K. (1984). *The new wilderness handbook.* New York: WW Norton & Co.

Ringholz, R. C. (1997). *On belay: The life of legendary mountaineer Paul Petzoldt.* Seattle, WA: The Mountaineers.

Service, R. (1916). *The spell of the Yukon.* New York: G. P. Putnam's Sons.

Philosophical Foundations

▼ ▼ ▼

Reasserting the Philosophy of Experiential Education as a Vehicle for Change in the 21st Century

▼ ▼ ▼

Christian M. Itin

The nature of experiential learning is fairly well understood and agreed upon. Stehno (1986), in reviewing seven models of experiential learning, indicated that each includes: (a) action that creates an experience, (b) reflection on the action and experience, (c) abstractions drawn from the reflection, and (d) application of the abstraction to a new experience or action. However, there has often been a good deal of confusion between the terms experiential learning and experiential education. Many authors have used these terms interchangeably making meaningful discussions difficult (Kolb, 1984; Kraft, 1986). Meaningful discussions have been further hampered in that the terms have been used to describe many different teaching approaches, including field work experiences, internships, previous work experience, outdoor education, adventure education, vocational education, lab work, simulations, and games (Crowe & Adams, 1979; Wurdinger, 1994). The terms experiential education and experiential learning have often been used synonymously with these other terms. This paper, drawing on the philosophical roots of John Dewey and Kurt Hahn, will reassert the argument that experiential education is best understood as a philosophy of education. A clear distinction between experiential learning and experiential education will be made and the central tenets of the philosophy will be presented. A model for conceptualizing the operationalizing of the philosophy will be presented. Finally, the benefits of conceptualizing experiential education as a philosophy will be explored. Particular attention will be given to how experiential education can be a part of educational reform.

This chapter originally was published in the *Journal of Experiential Education*, with the following citation:

Itin, C. M. (1999). Reasserting the philosophy of experiential education as a vehicle for change in the 21st century. *Journal of Experiential Education, 22*(2), 91–98.

Defining Experiential Learning

The first step needed in exploring this topic is to develop clear working definitions of experiential learning and experiential education so that distinctions can be made. In the literature the terms "experiential learning" and "experiential education" have often been used interchangeably (Kolb, 1984; Kraft, 1986). Some definitions of the terms have mirrored each other. Chickering (1976, p. 63)) stated that "[Experiential] learning...occurs when changes in judgments, feelings, knowledge or skills result for a particular person from living through an event or events." The definition of experiential education from the Association for Experiential Education (1994, p. 1) states, "Experiential education is a process through which a learner constructs knowledge, skill and value from direct experience." The fact that nearly identical definitions have been ascribed to experiential learning and experiential education only serves to cloud the discussion. It is important to begin with an understanding of what experiential learning is and what experiential education is and how they relate to each other.

Learning is best considered as the process of change that occurs for the individual. Learning is an individual experience. Education, on the other hand, is best considered as a transactive process between an educator and student. This transactive experience may also include the larger institutional forces (e.g., the educational system). Learning and education are different constructs and, given this, experiential learning and experiential education are different constructs as well. Experiential learning is best considered in Chickering's (1976) or AEE's (1994) definitions as changes in the individual based on direct experience. Drawing on Stehno's (1986) work mentioneded earlier, experiential learning involves action, reflection, abstraction, and application. So experiential learning is best considered as the change in an individual that results from reflection on a direct experience and results in new abstractions and applications. Experiential learning rests within the student and does not necessarily require a teacher. Experiential education will certainly seek to take advantage and maximize the opportunities for experiential learning. However, any definition of experiential education must include or make clear the transactive component between teacher and learner which is absent from the definition of experiential learning. Finally, a definition of experiential education must consider the larger system level issues of education such as the socio-political-economic elements in the learning environment. Experiential education cannot simply be about the experience of the individual as this defines experiential learning.

Voices of the Philosophy of Experiential Education

Before defining experiential education, it will be helpful to consider some of the central voices that have articulated the philosophy of experiential education. No discussion of experiential education would be complete without considering the writings of John Dewey. Dewey's writing reflected the progressive education movement in the United States. In Dewey's (1916) seminal work, *Democracy and Education*, he introduced the place of experience in education. Dewey's concern was linking experience with reflection, which was essentially linking understanding with doing. It was insufficient to simply know without doing and impossible to fully understand without doing. In this early work Dewey was, in essence, outlining the nature of experiential learning.

Dewey further clarified his thinking on experiential education in *Experience and Education*. The progressive education movement was concerned with "the place and meaning of subject-matter and of organization within experience" (Dewey, 1938, p. 7). At the core of Dewey's thinking was an understanding that education was not simply the transmission of facts but the education of the entire person for participation in a democratic society (Kraft, 1986). Education was seen as the central part of preparation for participation in a community. Dewey viewed the educational process as involving the teacher and learner engaged in purposive experience (Dewey, 1938).

If Dewey's writings represent the progressive education movement in the United States, then Kurt Hahn's thinking represents the progressive education movement in England. Kraft (1986, p. 15) states, "No discussion of the theory of experiential education would be complete without some recognition being given to Kurt Hahn, the founder of the Outward Bound movement." Hahn, while most remembered for his contribution to Outward Bound, founded three other schools and several other programs (James, 1995). In developing all these programs, Hahn took many of his ideas from Plato in terms of the development of the citizen and particularly the citizen's ability to serve the community (James, 1995). "Hahn saw service to one's neighbor and in the cause of peace as major aspects of any educational program" (Kraft, 1986, p. 15). James (1995, p. 88) cited Hahn in 1921 as stating that the purpose of his Salem School was "to train citizens who would not shirk from leadership and who could, if called upon, make independent decisions, put right action before expediency, and the common cause before personal ambition." Like Dewey, Hahn was concerned with the democratic process and the place of education in this process. Both were reflecting the ideals and ideology of the progressive education movement.

Hahn saw it as the "foremost task of education to ensure the survival of these qualities: an enterprising curiosity, an undefeatable spirit, tenacity in pursuit, readiness for sensible self-denial, and above all, compassion" (HIOBS, 1990, p. 71). He was concerned with the use of experience as a means to develop the whole person (James, 1995). James indicated four central elements in Hahn's approach to education. They were: (a) using a "training plan" in which students would contract around specific personal goals and a code of responsibility; (b) structuring the use of time to gently impel students into action; (c) placing difficult challenges before students that involved a perceived level of risk and adventure; and (d) using the group to mirror a mini-community and using shared experiences to help them begin to work together. Hahn clearly approached education as a transactive process between educator and student that used experience within a larger sociopolitical process.

Yet another philosophical voice that lays the historical tradition for the philosophy of experiential education is Paulo Freire, "a Brazilian educator whose theory of adult education [was] set within a larger framework of radical social change" (Merriam, 1987, p. 194). The social concern of Freire was the liberation and democratization of the Brazilian people. Freire developed much of his thinking while teaching adult literacy. Freire (1973, p. 43) "rejected the hypothesis of a purely mechanistic literacy program and considered the problem of teaching adults how to read in relation to the awakening of their consciousness." For Freire, the educator engages in a collaborative dialogue about concrete situations with the student. The action of education includes reflection. Like Dewey and Hahn, Freire saw education as a process that could not be separated from the larger issues of a person in a sociopolitical environment. His theory of "conscientization" is about raising the critical consciousness of individuals through education so that they will be better able to participate in the democratic political process (Freire, 1973). For Freire, education is about the content to be taught, the process by which it is taught, and the resulting consequences for the person within their social context. Freire was concerned with the moral and ethical implications of education, in particular those associated with the teacher dominating the educational process.

Paulo Freire (1993) has referred to traditional education as the banking approach to education, in that the teacher deposits information into the student, so that the student can then withdraw information when requested. Traditional education rests on the premise that the teacher has the information and imparts this information to students and then evaluates the students' performance (Richan, 1994). By extension, traditional education is based on the teacher being in a power position in relation to the student in terms of the possession of knowledge and the evaluation of learning. This traditional approach to education can be seen across the educational process from preschool to doctoral programs.

While Freire's ideas are most often cited in radical or critical pedagogical thought, his ideas are consistent with Dewey and Hahn, whose ideas are considered representative of pragmatic thought. All three are concerned with increasing the capabilities (self-efficacy) of individuals to participate in the democratic process (political awareness and action). Each of the voices cited expressed a concern for understanding the subject matter within experience (experiential learning), which can really be seen as developing a critical understanding. Each is also concerned with a purposeful process that involves the teacher actively engaging the student in experience. Lastly, each has some concern for reducing the power relationship between students and the teacher.

Defining the Philosophy of Experiential Education

Drawing upon the authors cited above and building on the work of the Association for Experiential Education's Principles of Experiential Education, Itin (1997, p. 6) has put forth the following definition of the philosophy of experiential education:

> Experiential education is a holistic philosophy, where carefully chosen experiences supported by reflection, critical analysis, and synthesis, are structured to require the learner to take initiative, make decisions, and be accountable for the results, through actively posing questions, investigating, experimenting, being curious, solving problems, assuming responsibility, being creative, constructing meaning, and integrating previously developed knowledge. Learners are engaged intellectually, emotionally, socially, politically, spiritually, and physically in an uncertain environment where the learner may experience success, failure, adventure, and risk taking. The learning usually involves interaction between learners, learner and educator, and learner and environment. It challenges the learner to explore issues of values, relationship, diversity, inclusion, and community. The educator's primary roles include selecting suitable experiences, posing problems, setting boundaries, supporting learners, insuring physical and emotional safety, facilitating the learning process, guiding reflection, and providing the necessary information. The results of the learning form the basis of future experience and learning.

This definition makes clear (a) the place of experience and (b) the transactive nature of experiential education that is interactive between learners, between learner and teacher, and between the learner and his/her environment. It must be understood that these transactions are viewed as experiences and parts of the experience within this philosophy. In addressing the interaction between various system levels, attention is given to the larger socio-political-economic levels that affect education. The philosophy's concern for promoting and exploring certain values provides further evidence of a view of education that understands the larger system level issues within education. This definition of experiential education clearly directs attention to a way of thinking about the educational process that supports experiential learning, but is much more than experiential learning. It makes clear that the principles of experiential learning fit within experiential education, but that experiential education is not just about the changes in the individual. Finally, the ideas of Dewey, Hahn, and Freire can all be seen in this definition.

The philosophy of experiential education makes clear the concern with developing the competency of the learner to integrate what is being learned with the actions that are required. A central premise of the philosophy is that the teacher is responsible for presenting opportunities for experiences, helping students utilize these experiences, establishing the learning environment, placing boundaries on the learning objectives, sharing necessary information and facilitating learning. Teachers have knowledge that is valuable and that students want and require, and the philosophy of experiential education makes clear the context within which this knowledge is disseminated. Experiential education impels teachers into facilitating the experiential learning process for students. In the philosophy of experiential education, the learner actively engages in co-creating with the teacher the educational process. The learning is not a separate experience, but involves the entire person within the context of the learning environment where the learner is challenged to move beyond what is known. The learning is evaluated mutually by the learner and the teacher. Finally, the philosophy makes clear that the experiential education is a purposeful process aimed at increasing the capacity of the student to understand, utilize, and affect his or her experience in the world and ultimately this is for participation in a democratic process (Chapman, McPhee, & Proudman, 1995; Itin, 1997; Kolb, 1984).

This philosophy of experiential education can be clearly seen in the work by Ira Shor, which builds directly off the ideas of Dewey and Freire (Shor & Freire, 1987). Shor (1992, pp. 16–17) outlined what he referred to as empowerment-based education when he wrote:

> The teacher leads and directs this curriculum, but does so democratically with the participation of the students, balancing the need for structure with the need for openness. The teacher brings lesson plans, learning methods, personal experience, and academic knowledge to class but negotiates the curriculum with the students and begins with their language, themes, and understandings. To be democratic implies orienting subject matter to student culture—their interests, needs, speech, and perceptions—while creating a negotiable openness in class where the students' input jointly creates the learning process. To be critical in such a democratic curriculum means to examine all subjects and the learning process with systematic depth: to connect students individually to larger historical and social issues; to encourage students to examine how their experience relates to academic knowledge, to power, and to inequality in society; and to approach received wisdom and the status quo with questions.

A critical piece that Shor brings to this discussion is an acknowledgement that the teacher shares power with the students and responsibility for the curriculum yet does not abdicate their responsibility and authority for the curriculum; the teacher remains purposeful in the process. Of importance in Shor's conceptualization is that neither the teacher nor the students dominate the process, but each brings their skills, talents, and resources to the educational process. Shor has suggested that empowerment-based education should be seen as student-centered, but not necessarily student directed. The distinction rests in recognizing that teachers contribute to the direction of the educational process in a student-centered process. The hallmark of the philosophy of experiential education is that the teacher and student(s) create the educational process through their transaction and interaction. Furthermore, this dynamic exchange becomes a critical part of the process. Finally, this dynamic transaction is an experience and must be viewed as part of the experience that is utilized in the experiential educational process. When a teacher introduces an experience (e.g., a service-learning opportunity), the position of the teacher, the way it is introduced, and where the students are in their readiness to accept the experience are all a part of the process.

Dewey, Hahn, and Freire were all concerned with the preparation of individuals to participate in a democratic society. As such they were concerned with developing the capacity of individuals to take action and recognizing that education is a political process. The choice of what is taught and not taught must be understood in a political context. Experiential education recognizes Shor (1992, p. 13) when he said, "All forms of education are political because they can enable or inhibit the questioning habits of students, thus developing or disabling their critical relation to knowledge, schooling, and society." Education cannot be neutral; by not paying attention to the political aspects of education, it by default supports the dominant paradigm which is currently informing the socio-political-economic aspects of the educational system. A major component of the philosophy of experiential education is the participation of the student in the learning process so that the student can participate in the democratic-social process. The educational process must mirror those results that society desires. In other words, the content being taught is as important as the process by which it is taught and the context in which it is taught. If we want to develop critically thinking, self-motivated, problem-solving individuals who participate actively in their communities, we must have an educational system and educational approaches that model and support this.

A New Model of the Philosophy of Experiential Education

A philosophy is only useful if it can be translated into action. One step in explicating the philosophy of experiential education is through developing a model of the process. All models are, by definition, idealized visions or representations that help one examine the key principles within a theory. A person can certainly practice the philosophy of experiential education without fully manifesting the ideal vision. A teacher or student can actualize specific aspects of the philosophy without actualizing all of them. The intent of laying out any model

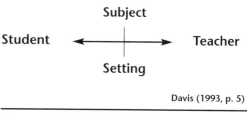

Davis (1993, p. 5)

***Figure 1*. Davis' model of teaching.**

is to illustrate the interrelationship between the principles. The intent of this model is to provide the reader with a holistic picture of how the philosophy of experiential education might look in practice.

James Davis (1993) has presented a beginning framework for conceptualizing the transactive process between teacher and student. He presents his model in relation to teaching stating that, "Teaching in this model is defined as the interaction of the student and a teacher over a subject.... The model is enclosed in a box to represent the setting where teaching takes place" (p. 6). The strength of Davis' model is that it outlines the essential systems within the educational context and it provides a useful beginning framework for an experiential education model.

The philosophy of experiential education enhances Davis' model by making it clear that the relationship between teacher and student is transactive rather then interactive. This is to say that there is an exchange between teacher and student, not simply interaction. Transaction assumes interaction, but adds to it an exchange (Germain & Gitterman, 1980). In a transactive model, the teacher brings information to the process, but so does the student. Teachers and students not only interact, but they exchange knowledge. Students learn from teachers, and teachers learn from students. Similarly students learn from the environment, but they also affect or change the environment. The educational process does more than take place within a setting; it interacts and transacts with numerous environmental aspects. The environment would include not only the setting (the context in which teaching takes place), but also the larger socio-political-economic systems, the multiple students in the class, and any other system that impacts the teaching-learning process.

A second more extensive model, the Diamond Model, can be constructed by drawing upon the definition of experiential education and the model presented by Davis (see Figure 2). In this model, the experiential learning process is clearly visible for both the student and the teacher. The teacher and student share a common experience in terms of the teaching process, although how the process is interpreted is defined by the teacher or students, based on their own reflection upon it. The transactive process, which is a part of the experience, between four principle systems (teacher, student, subject, and learning environment) is also seen in the model by directional arrows (which show that information flows both ways). At the core of the model is a teaching process, which not only marks a shared concrete experience but also indicates how the teacher seeks to encourage the transactive process, that is how the experience is used to guide the educational process. This model does not dictate or reflect a specific teaching approach or strategy; rather, it allows for the many possible approaches that might be used within this model. What is critical in the use of any approach or strategy is that the teaching approaches must include experience, must use the experiences, including the transactive process, and the experiential learning process. Furthermore, this model of experiential education does not reflect any single expression of the philosophy. As was stated in the beginning

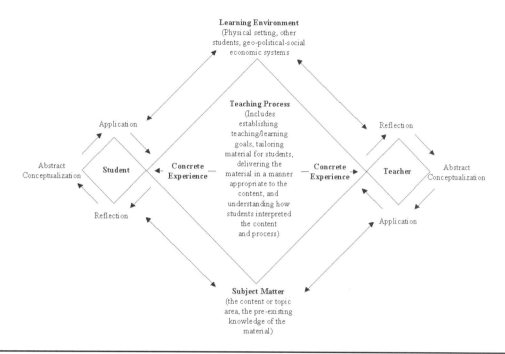

Figure 2. **The diamond model of the philosophy of experiential education.**

of this article, often those who engage in service learning, cooperative learning, adventure-based education, and many other areas will refer to their teaching approach as experiential education, in essence defining experiential education as their approach. In reality these are simply expressions of the philosophy of experiential education in action, or provide evidence of the philosophy of experiential education.

The philosophy of experiential education does not dictate a particular teaching method but rather, it speaks to a way of thinking about the teaching–learning transaction. Davis (1993) has explicated five teaching strategies: (a) training and coaching—draws upon behavioral theory and involves setting clear and measurable objectives, sequencing activities, and providing timely feedback; (b) lecturing and explaining—draws upon cognitive learning theory and focuses on the delivery of content; (c) inquiry and discovery—grows out of the work of Dewey and is concerned with directly immersing students in problems to be solved and learning how to think; (d) groups and teams—grows out of group communication theory and centers on using groups to facilitate learning; and (e) experience and reflection—draws upon the work of Dewey and is concerned with directly involving students in work, service, fieldwork, or other concrete experiences. Davis' work does a good job of conceptualizing the range of strategies that exist, and it should be clear to the reader that there are multiple specific approaches within each of these strategies.

The strategies that Davis (1993) outlined can be used individually or combined together and integrated within the model of experiential education presented. Lecturing and explaining would be legitimate teaching methods as long as the teacher is utilizing experience, the transactions available, and other elements of the philosophy (e.g., Does the lecture set the student up for a service-learning experience? Are students given an opportunity to interact in relation to the content presented?). An educational process that only utilizes lecturing and explaining is likely not taking advantage of all the experiences possible (i.e., all the transactions available). What is critical in this discussion is that the dualistic perspective is rejected in this model. In many previous discussions about experiential education, the philosophy was linked to a single teaching strategy or approach (Beck, 1988; Conti, 1978; Hadley, 1975; Kotze, 1985). Furthermore, this earlier work approached experiential education from a dualistic perspective and stated that various approaches employed either were experiential or they were not. By conceptualizing experiential education as a philosophy, it becomes possible to reject this dualistic thinking. Philosophy is best considered as a way of thinking or a process of constructing arguments around thinking (Honderich, 1995). Therefore experiential education as a philosophy becomes a way of thinking about the educational process. This allows a teacher to utilize lecture and explaining strategies and still approach them from within a framework of experiential education.

A Practical Example of the Philosophy in Action

One way to visualize the philosophy of experiential education in action is to take a subject matter and explore how it might be taught from the philosophy of experiential education. One such example would be a basic college research methods course. Often research is primarily taught from what Freire (1993) would call a "banking approach" to education. The teacher often seeks to deposit large amounts of information into the students with the support of a textbook. A series of tests are the only measures used to determine how well the students have mastered the material. A major part of the justification for this approach in teaching research is that there is a great deal of specialized language and procedures that must be mastered to ensure the students understand the rigors of the scientific method.

The philosophy of experiential education would direct teachers toward providing more opportunities for students to interact with the subject matter, the environment, other students, and the teacher. It is not sufficient that students master the content if they do not understand how to apply it in the real world. One way this might occur is to provide an opportunity for students to conduct or participate in a research project. A number of teaching strategies might be used to accomplish or support this type of project. The use of lectures might be targeted at helping the students to make connections between their projects and the material. The students might work in groups or teams to conduct the project. Training or coaching strategies might be used in helping students develop the technical skills used in research. Inquiry and discovery methods might be used to help students conduct an actual literature search, design a research method, conduct an analysis, and make conclusions. The banking approach encourages students to know the steps, while an approach informed by the philosophy of experiential education would be aimed at knowing the steps, understanding their purpose, and actually conducting the steps. Transactions with the environment could be encouraged by inviting students to engage in research projects, which involve the community. Students could interact with each other not only by doing the project as small groups, but also by sharing the results of their projects. These are just some of the ways that the philosophy of experiential education might influence how a basic college research course is taught. It should be clear to the reader that there are ways that this course could utilize more experiences or allow the experience to lead the educational objectives even more. What should be clear is that we are talking about the degree to which the tenets of the philosophy are operationalized, and this is done differentially depending on the setting, the teacher, and the students.

Operationalizing the philosophy does come with a price. Clearly this type of general approach demands more from the teacher in terms of meeting the unique learning needs of the particular students in the class. The teacher can not simply depend on a lecture-alone approach and repeat it year in and year out. The teacher must assess the learning needs of the students, select appropriate teaching strategies to meet the students' needs, and be willing to use multiple teaching strategies to make it an educational experience. This takes time, energy, and other resources that might be difficult for a teacher to muster. This raises major institutional challenges to teachers who seek to operationalize the philosophy of experiential education. Large classes are often a major obstacle to a teacher's ability to develop meaningful transactions with students (Itin, 1997). In a class of 30–40 students, a teacher is seriously hampered in creating relationships required for meaningful educational transactions. Another obstacle faced by teachers seeking to operationalize this philosophy is reluctance on the part of students (Itin, 1997). Most students have not been formally made familiar with being engaged in an educational process that involves their active engagement and participation. The dynamics of a lack of familiarity coupled with large class size may at first appear as resistance on the part of students. The operationalization of the philosophy of experiential education cannot occur without both a personal investment on the part of the teacher and the institutional supports necessary.

Conclusion

When experiential education is correctly conceptualized as a philosophy of education, it allows for much broader discussions that include a number of important areas. First, it allows for the discussion of the range of approaches and strategies that can be utilized and how they can be linked within this philosophical framework. Next, it allows for the clear distinction between experiential learning, which is correctly seen as a learning strategy. This distinction allows for more accurate and clear communication, which should facilitate professional understanding. If those who support experiential learning and education cannot be clear in their communication, how can they possibly influence those who don't support it? Finally, if experiential education is correctly identified as a philosophy, it allows for the various expressions of this philosophy (service learning, cooperative learning, adventure-based, problem-based, action learning, etc.) to be linked together under this single philosophy. This provides a method of bringing those together who promote these various expressions and to argue for educational reform that would support experiential education in all settings.

The philosophy of experiential education, as expressed in this article, pushes those who support it toward educational reforms, which would in turn, further promote the philosophy. If we can bring together those who support the various expressions of this philosophy and these individuals can speak a common language, there is a greater chance that reform can be successfully engaged in. If educational reform is sought, then the discussion cannot remain at the level of teaching/learning methods. There is empirical evidence of the effectiveness of individual teaching strategies informed by the philosophy of experiential education (Boud, 1985; Christian, 1982; Conti, 1978; Davenport & Davenport, 1986; Kotze, 1985; Land, 1987; Reese, 1993) which has been ignored by many in education. A part of the reason that the evidence has remained ignored is that the approaches have remained relatively separate and splintered. Those who talk about adult learning do not necessarily talk to (or consult the literature of) those who talk about service learning. Those who speak about problem-based education do not talk to those who support adventure-based education. These areas, as stated earlier, are all expressions of the philosophy of experiential education, and yet they have remained somewhat isolated academically and practically. If educational reform is a goal of those who embrace the philosophy of experiential education, then coming together is a first step toward working together to argue for this reform. There is power in numbers and if those who employ the philosophy of experiential education come together there will be more voices speaking of change.

On the practical level, viewing the teaching and learning strategies as expressions of the philosophy of experiential education allows educators to adopt, modify, blend, and integrate the strategies in a meaningful way. Educators often use a variety of strategies, but because they are not well linked theoretically, they may come across in a disjointed way to students. The teacher who primarily uses lecture and then engages in a critical thinking exercise may use the activity poorly. Also the students might not be well prepared to use the experience, or the experience may be poorly fit into the curriculum. The philosophy of experiential education allows teachers to meaningfully link different strategies as expressions of the basic philosophy. If the teacher approaches the educational process from an experiential perspective, then the activities can be more easily linked.

As we move into the 21st century, it becomes increasingly clear that the current educational paradigm that guides the educational process from kindergarten through doctoral programs is not working. Numerous approaches have been put forth to transform education at all levels. Many of these approaches are informed by the philosophy of experiential education. If we can link these various approaches together as expressions of the philosophy of experiential education, perhaps we can advance the educational reforms needed. Furthermore, as we move into the 21st century, it becomes increasingly clear that we must develop citizens who can actively participate in a democratic process and, in doing so, work toward creating a just and compassionate world. The philosophy of experiential education is what is needed to help develop a community that actively involves all in cooperatively solving problems and contributing to the greater good of society.

This article has laid out an argument that experiential education is best viewed as a philosophy of education rather than an approach or specific teaching strategy. The philosophy has been explicated and a model of this philosophy in action has been presented. Some of the obstacles to the operationalization of this philosophy also have been presented, as have the reasons for accepting experiential education as a philosophy were presented and how this philosophy might help transform education for the 21st century. It is this author's hope that this article helps expand the discussion about what experiential education is, how it can be used, where it fits in, and how we might join together under it to advance educational reform.

References

Association for Experiential Education (AEE) (1994). *AEE definition of experiential education.* Boulder, CO: Association for Experiential Education.

Beck, J. E. (1988). Testing a personal construct theory model of the experiential learning process. *Small Group Behavior*, *19*(3), 342–362.

Boud, D. (1985). *Problem-based learning in education for the professions.* Sydney: Herdsa.

Chapman, S., McPhee, P., & Proudman, B. (1995). What is experiential education? In K. Warren, M. Sakofs, & J. S. Hunt Jr. (Eds.), *The theory of experiential education* (3rd ed.)(pp. 235–247). Dubuque, IA: Kendall/Hunt.

Chickering, A. (1976). Developmental change as a major outcome. In M. Keeton, (Ed.), *Experiential learning* (pp. 62–107). San Francisco, CA: Jossey Bass.

Christian, A. C. (1982). A comparative study of the andragogical-pedagogical orientation of military and civilian personnel. *Dissertation Abstracts International, 44*(03), 643A.

Conti, G. J. (1978). Principles of adult learning scale: An instrument for measuring teacher behavior related to the collaborative teaching-learning mode. *Dissertation Abstracts International*, 39(12), 7111A.

Crowe, M. R., & Adams, K. A. (1979). *The current status of assessing experiential education programs.* Columbus, OH: The National Center for Research in Vocational Education, The Ohio State University.

Davenport, J., & Davenport, J. A. (1986). Andragogical-pedagogical orientation and its relationship to selected variables among university students. *College Student Journal, 20*(2), 130-138.

Davis, J. R. (1993). *Better teaching, more learning.* Phoenix, AZ: Oryx Press.

Dewey, J. (1916). *Democracy and education.* New York: Macmillan.

Dewey, J. (1938). *Experience and education.* New York: Macmillan.

Freire, P. (1973). *Education for critical consciousness.* New York: Seabury Press.

Freire, P. (1993). *Pedagogy of the oppressed* (M. B. Ramos, Trans.). New York: Continuum. (Original work published 1970).

Germain, C. B., & Gitterman, A. (1980). *The life model of social work practice.* New York: Columbia University Press.

Hadley, H. N. (1975). Development of an instrument to determine adult educators' orientation: Andragogical or pedagogical. *Dissertation Abstracts International, 35*(12), 7595A.

Honderich, T. (1995). *The Oxford companion to philosophy.* New York: Oxford University Press.

Hurricane Island Outward Bound School (HIOBS). (1990). *Readings.* Rockland, ME: HIOBS.

Itin, C. M. (1997). The orientation of social work faculty to the philosophy of experiential education in the classroom (Doctoral dissertation, University of Denver, 1997). *Dissertations Abstracts International,* 5804A, 1449.

James, T. (1995). Sketch of a moving spirit: Kurt Hahn. In K. Warren, M. Sakofs, & J. S. Hunt Jr. (Eds.), *The theory of experiential education* (3rd ed.) (pp. 75-95). Dubuque, IA: Kendall/Hunt.

Kolb, D. A. (1984). *Experiential learning: Experience as the source of learning and development.* Englewood Cliffs, NJ: Prentice-Hall.

Kotze, D. A. (1985). Factors associated with utilization of an experience-based approach to classroom instruction (innovation, adaptation, learning, technology). *Dissertation Abstracts International, 46*(10), 2905A.

Kraft, R. J. (1986). Toward a theory of experiential education. In R. Kraft & M. Sakofs (Eds.). *The theory of experiential education* (2nd ed.) (pp. 7-38). Boulder, CO: Association for Experiential Education.

Kraft, R. J., & Kielsmeier, J. (1995). *Experiential learning in schools and higher education.* Dubuque, IA: Kendall/Hunt.

Land, H. (1987). Pathways to learning: Using experiential exercises in teaching practice with special populations. *Journal of Teaching Social Work, 1*(2), 87-96.

Merriam, S. B. (1987). Adult learning and theory building: A review. *Adult Education Quarterly, 37*(4), 187–198.

Reese, T. H. (1993). Adult learning research and effective college teaching: Perceptions and practice (effective teaching). *Dissertation Abstracts International, 54*(08), 2915A.

Richan, W. C. (1994). Empowering social work students. In L. Gutiérrez & P. Nurius (Eds.), *Education and research for empowerment practice* (pp. 59-71). Seattle, WA: Center for Policy and Practice Research, School of Social Work, University of Washington.

Shor, I. (1992). *Empowering education: Critical teaching for social change.* Chicago: University of Chicago Press.

Shor, I., and Freire, P. (1987). *A pedagogy for liberation.* Massachusetts: Gergin and Garvey.

Stehno, J. J. (1986). *The application and integration of experiential education in higher education.* Carbondale, IL: Southern Illinois University, Touch of Nature Environmental Center. (ERIC Document Reproduction Service No. ED 285–465).

Wurdinger, S. D. (1994). *Philosophical issues in adventure education.* Dubuque, IA: Kendall/Hunt.

Theory for Practice: A Framework for Thinking About Experiential Education

▼ ▼ ▼

Rebecca Carver

The purpose of this article is to present a lens for looking at experiential education that allows us to view it as a comprehensive entity without getting overwhelmed by the complexity of its interwoven parts. Theory of experiential education has been developed in several areas including philosophy, psychology, and sociology (Warren et al., 1995). The framework that I present draws on these disciplines as well as anthropology, cognitive science, and research on education reform. It belongs to no one camp. It is grounded in the wisdom that shapes the voices and actions of experiential educators in a broad variety of settings.

The interdisciplinary framework is needed because experiential education is an interdisciplinary field, and if we are to benefit from our collective wisdom, we must be able to share and integrate what has been learned both in different settings and from the perspectives of different traditions. The framework is designed to help people stay focused on topics of experiential education while viewing them from several angles. So, for instance, it could be used to organize thoughts about such topics as "challenge by choice" or "learning communities" in a manner that maintains the coherence of these ideas and points to the interrelatedness of ideas that stem from ethical, psychological, social, educational, political, physical, and legal considerations.

·

This chapter originally was published in the *Journal of Experiential Education*, with the following citation:
Carver, R. (1996). Theory for practice: A framework for thinking about experiential education. *Journal of Experiential Education, 19*(1), 8–13.

Where Does This Framework Come From?

The framework is based on field research, a literature review, and consultations with practitioners. The bulk of the field work took place over a period of two years during which I observed programs, reviewed documents, and interviewed participants and staff. Some observations were made from the perspective of an outsider while others were conducted while I was a participant, student, teacher, facilitator, or director of a program. The literature review began with a critical look at writings that specifically address the theory and practice of experiential education. Based on the initial results of this process and the preliminary findings of my field research, I expanded the scope of my literature review to cover topics in other fields that appeared to be relevant. As an example, I included literature on constructivism and constructivist education after it became apparent that a significant part of experiential education is the participant process of collectively constructing knowledge.

At the 1994 International Conference of the Association for Experiential Education, I held a session that served as a place for checking the validity of my model. Approximately 25 participants generated lists of what they believed to form the essence of experiential education. They were then shown my framework and asked to critically assess its validity[1]. Other than suggestions for minor changes (such as making more explicit what I had not shown in the diagram), feedback was positive.

How This Paper Is Organized

The goal of this paper is to introduce a conceptual framework that can (a) serve practitioners as a basis for developing formative evaluations, (b) shed light on connections between a variety of experiential education programs that on the surface appear to have little in common, and (c) allow theorists to locate their work and that of their colleagues in a context that facilitates communication across disciplines.

The remainder of this paper is divided into sections that respectively address the following questions: What is experiential education? What are the pedagogical principles? What is the nature of student experience? What is the role of the teacher? How does this fit together to form a framework for looking at experiential education? How can we use this framework?

What Is Experiential Education?

Quite simply, experiential education is education (the leading of students through a process of learning) that makes conscious application of the students' experiences by integrating them into the curriculum. Experience involves any combination of senses (i.e., touch,

---

[1] The model I presented included a theory of implementation as well as the conceptual framework.

smell, hearing, sight, taste), emotions (e.g., pleasure, excitement, anxiety, fear, hurt, empathy, attachment), physical condition (e.g., temperature, strength, energy level), and cognition (e.g., constructing knowledge, establishing beliefs, solving problems).

Experiential education is holistic in the sense that it addresses students in their entirety—as thinking, feeling, physical, emotional, spiritual, and social beings. Students are viewed as valuable resources for their own education, the education of others, and the well-being of the communities of which they are members. Although formal educators become senior members of learning communities, students share in the process of teaching, and teachers actively continue to learn from their experiences with the group.

Since the teacher is a guide, she needs to have a map of the terrain in order to be effective and not risk putting the group in unnecessary danger. The terrain includes the social dynamics of the group; the physical, emotional, and psychological conditions of group members; the level of development that the group and its members have obtained (socially, physically, academically, etc.); the nature and condition of the environment; its location (geographic, political, or otherwise); and the resources available to the group. A gifted educator can show the group how it can use the experiences of its members to build tools and vehicles for meeting challenges that lead toward personal and social responsibility, self-confidence, self reliance, interdependence, and individual satisfaction.

There are several types of experiential education including (but not limited to):

- Wilderness-based adventure travel, ropes courses, and initiatives
- Job-training internships and apprenticeships
- Survival training and rescue training
- Service learning and programs focused on advocacy
- Art education and production
- Media production (newspapers, television, radio)
- Academic-oriented programs
- Community-based support programs (with a primary goal of providing youth with a safe environment and stable support system for day-to-day living; life skills)
- Early education programs
- T-groups (training groups; interpersonal dynamics workshops)

The purpose for listing the above categories is to show the breadth of experiential education opportunities, and to get people starting to think—or at least wonder—about the kinship among categories that may on the surface seem unrelated to one another. The common elements that underlie their differences are at the core of what experiential education is all about.

Pedagogy

When I started looking for the salient features of experiential education, the first characteristics that came to mind were pedagogical principles that are commonly employed.

Effective educators try to choose methods of teaching that are appropriate for specific situations, taking into consideration the goals of the educational experience, the nature of the content that is going to be covered, and the learning styles of students. So, although there are pedagogical principles that are common among experiential education programs and that are believed by practitioners to be central to the "experiential" method of teaching, the list is not comprehensive and there is no formula for how and when to combine these principles with each other or other forms of teaching.

Having said that, the following four pedagogical principles stand out as salient features of experiential education:

- **Authenticity:** Activities and consequences are understood by participants as relevant to their lives. Rewards are naturally occurring and directly affect the experience of the student (e.g. personal satisfaction) Students can identify reasons for participating in activities. Assessment is formative. The programs provide meaningful experiences within the context of the students' outlook on life.

- **Active learning:** Students are physically and/or mentally engaged in the active process of learning. These activities are used to address social, physical, and emotional as well as cognitive development. The difference between mentally active learning and passive learning is that the former requires students to internalize the thought processes necessary for problem solving—searching for explanations, figuring out ways of understanding, using imagination and being creative—whereas the latter involves accepting what is said and remembering it, so it can be repeated later.

- **Drawing on student experience:** Students are guided in the process of building understandings of phenomena, events, human nature, etc. by thinking about what they have experienced (e.g., what happened to them, how they felt, how they reacted, what resulted, what they observed). Educators create activities that provide opportunities for students to experience what it is like to interact with specific situations. They draw both on experiences students bring with them to a program and those that are shared by participants in the program.

- **Providing mechanisms for connecting experience to future opportunity:** Students develop habits, memories, skills, and knowledge that will be useful to them in the future. The formal process of getting students to reflect on their participation in activities or to reflect on their potential roles as community members is meant to make these experiences relevant to their future endeavors.

Teachers facilitate processes in which students participate in the construction of knowledge.[2] There may be times when teachers share their expertise with students, but unlike a model of education where students are seen as passive recipients of knowledge, students in experiential education programs are treated as active participants in their own education. They are encouraged to take the initiative to seek and learn from the expertise of those around them.[3]

Student Experience

Values shape the goals of educational programs, and the goals in turn affect the experiences of students. Experiential education programs tend to value caring, compassion, communication, critical thinking, respect for self and others, individuality, and responsibility. Responsibility includes enabling people to respond, and creating a culture in which they hold each other and themselves accountable. Caring and compassion involve attending to the emotional, spiritual, mental, and physical well-being of oneself and others, as well as attending to other aspects of one's environment.

The sub-goals of experiential education programs usually fall into three categories. Student experience can be understood in terms of development along the interrelated dimensions that respectively correspond with these categories of sub-goals. The dimensions, described below are: Agency, Belonging, and Competence.[4] Together, changes along these dimensions—the ABC of student experience—are at the heart of what students experience during a program and how it affects them (see Table 1).

The Role of the Teacher

A great deal has already been said about the role of the teacher. The teacher uses the pedagogical principles and attends to the experiences of students as described above.

Since student experience results from interactions between the students and their environments (Dewey, 1938), the role of the teacher is to cultivate environments in which students can develop ABC.[5] Cultivating an environment involves establishing and nurturing the development of a physical and social context for learning. Teachers introduce resources into the learning environment and make decisions about how resources are perceived,

---

[2] See Duffy and Jonassen (1992) for an introduction to "Constructivism."

[3] See Rogoff (1994) for information about Learning Communities and learning as participation.

[4] These are closely related to dimensions identified by Connell and Wellborn (1991) as essential to the development of a healthy self-concept.

[5] If you only read one piece of literature on experiential education, I suggest *Experience and Education* by John Dewey (1938).

Table 1. *The ABC of Student Experience*

A "A" represents the developing of students' personal **agency**—allowing students to become more powerful change agents in their lives and communities; increasing students' recognition and appreciation of the extent to which the locus of control for their lives is within themselves, and enabling them to use this as a source of power to generate activity.

B "B" refers to developing and maintaining a community in which students (and staff) share a sense of **belonging**—see themselves as members with rights and responsibilities, power and vulnerability; learn to act responsibly, considering the best interests of themselves, other individuals, and the group as a whole.

C "C" stands for competence, referring to the development of student **competence** (which usually coincides with the development of teacher competence) in a wide variety of areas (cognitive, physical, musical, social, etc.). Developing competence means learning skills, acquiring knowledge, and attaining the ability to apply what is learned.

distributed, and utilized. In addition to physical resources, these include time, space, authority, language, reputation, etc.

Teachers, as senior members of learning communities, are role models and influence the experiences of students by the way they react, respond, and take action in the combination of settings in which they are viewed by students. In addition to modeling behavior, their responses to student behavior affect student experience.

It should also be noted that since the teacher is also a student, the development of Agency, Belonging, and Competence among teachers is part of the healthy functioning of an organization devoted to experiential education.

A Framework for Thinking About Experiential Education

First, let me summarize what has been said above. Experiential education promotes the development of student agency, belonging, and competence by introducing resources and behaviors that allow for active learning, drawing on student experience, authenticity, and connecting lessons to the future in a learning environment that usually values caring, compassion, responsibility, accountability, individuality, creativity, and critical thinking.

Figure 1 is a drawing of the framework. Student experience, viewed as both a process and an outcome, is at its center. Student experience is located in the context of a learning environment that is characterized by the nature of the student experience, program characteristics,

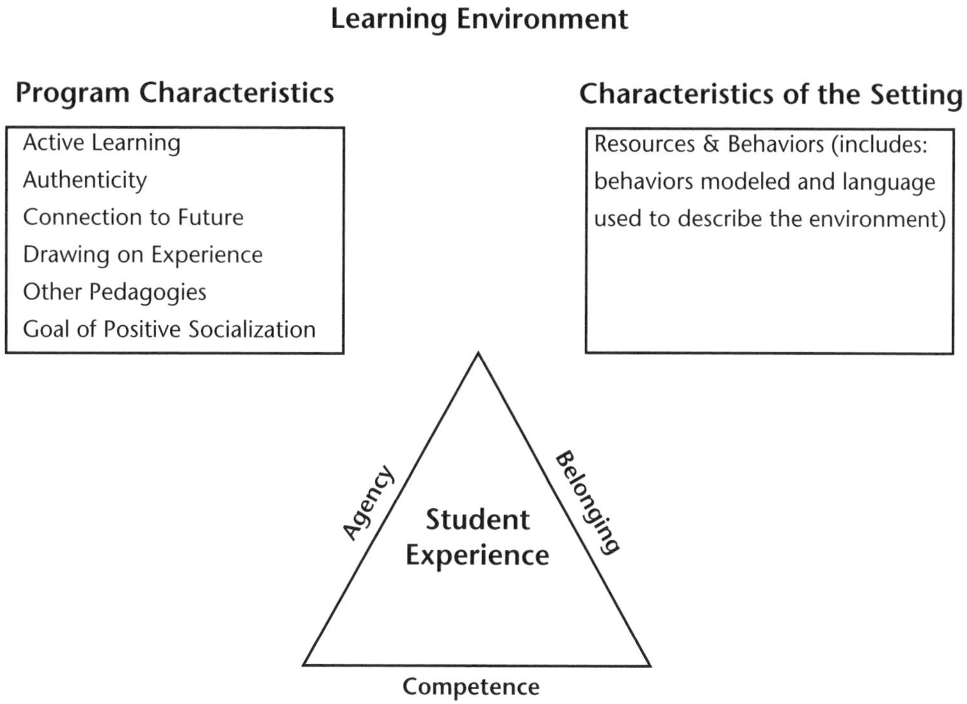

Learning Environment

Program Characteristics

Active Learning
Authenticity
Connection to Future
Drawing on Experience
Other Pedagogies
Goal of Positive Socialization

Characteristics of the Setting

Resources & Behaviors (includes: behaviors modeled and language used to describe the environment)

Agency

Belonging

Student Experience

Competence

Figure 2. **Conceptual framework.**

and more general characteristics of the environment. Program characteristics include both the pedagogical principles that are commonly employed and the goal of "positive socialization," which refers to a process of doing what is in the best interest of both the individual participants and the communities of which they are members. Values, such as those listed above (e.g., compassion and critical thinking), guide decisions about this process. The values also guide decisions about the use of resources and behaviors in cultivating the learning environment.

The Utility of the Framework

The framework is primarily a tool for organizing and communicating ideas about program development and evaluation with colleagues. The framework is not an evaluation instrument and it does not provide a recipe for developing programs. It does provide a structure for thinking about overarching goals, specific objectives, activities, qualifications of staff, selection of students, expectations for student experience, and potential changes for programs and organizations.

My recommendation to program staff interested in using this framework is to start by brainstorming a list of features that you consider to be most salient for the program in question. These features can include goals, values, activities, outcomes … anything you can think of. Next, try to make a list of values that are associated with the program including any values that came up in the brainstorming session but also any other values that come to mind. Try to be specific. If creativity is valued, for instance, ask what is meant by "creativity." Set aside the list of values for future reference. Now, draw a copy of Figure 1 on a big piece of paper. Return to the list of features that you have identified as salient and see where they fit on the framework. Use the framework as a map for locating the features and investigating how they relate to one another. Think about the aspects of ABC that are a focus for your program. Are they in sync with the values that you've identified? What pedagogical principles do you have in place? Are there any pedagogical principles that are over- or under-utilized? How do your decisions about pedagogical principles, resources, and behaviors affect the development of ABC? Thoughtfully answering the above questions can be the start of a formative evaluation and process of program development.

The framework provides a way to look at the whole picture but it does not give a lot of detail about any of the concepts that collectively constitute its substance. At the start, I suggest using your common sense, relying on your experience, and sharing with each other what your perceptions are of the various concepts and how they interact with each other in your setting. When you are ready to look more precisely at what is known about specific topics, consult references and people that can help you learn how the elements on which you choose to focus fit into the broader contexts of categories in which they fall. For instance, if you decide to (a) identify the types of competence that participants develop, (b) establish objectives for what you would like them to accomplish in these areas, and (c) devise mechanisms for assessing whether or not these competencies are developed, you might want to learn about multiple intelligences theory (see Gardner, 1993) and/or empowerment evaluation (see Fetterman et. al., 1996). On the other hand, if you are interested in focusing on how to strengthen the effectiveness of instructors, you might begin by looking at their use of pedagogical principles, resources (including themselves, each other, time, space, authority, language, and tradition), and characteristic behaviors (responses to a variety of situations including both the mundane and the most challenging), then establish what research might be helpful to support your program development. Keep in mind that we live in an era of information overload and there are a multitude of directions in which you can go as part of a search for better understanding the concepts in the framework. An outside consultant may be able to help you identify some of the possibilities so you can more easily decide which would be most fruitful to explore.

A second way that the framework can be used is to help build alliances among practitioners whose work may, on the surface, seem to be unrelated. It turns out that some of the same challenges faced by preschool teachers are faced by college professors, and some of the fundamental goals of art teachers are shared by rock-climbing instructors, but it can be difficult to identify the common ground. The framework provides a structure and vocabulary for opening dialogues. It can be used to help people articulate the underlying features of programs in terms of the ABC goals of student experience, the pedagogical principles employed, how values affect decisions about resources, staff behavior, and what is desirable for a learning environment. Doing so allows practitioners from different fields to learn from each other, see their own work from a broader perspective, understand how they can support each other's efforts, and/or work together to accomplish shared goals.

The framework can also be used to hold up a window through which practitioners and theorists can look together at their work and the work of others. It seems that every well-established group of experiential education programs (such as service learning or wilderness therapy) has its own culture in which vocabulary is selected for framing discussions about experiential education. Similarly, theory rooted in the tradition of academic disciplines is focused and limited by boundaries that pertain to the specific fields in which the theories emerge. So, it is often as if the psychologist, philosopher, and anthropologist are sitting in the same house but looking at the world through three separate windows. Sometimes there is overlap in what they see but their perspectives are different. The framework illustrated as Figure 1 is designed to provide a window for practitioners of all kinds of experiential education and theorists from all disciplines to use so we can see how their ideas fit together. That should make visible the interactions among theories and practices, which in turn can increase or challenge the clarity of each person's perspective.

This window, like any other, is limited by its framework, but this framework is based on the common elements of a wide range of experiential education programs as understood from the perspectives of participants, staff, evaluators, advocates, and theorists from several disciplines. It may always be a work in progress. Constructive criticism is welcome.

Acknowledgments

I wish to acknowledge the contributions of Mindy Carver and Michael Pease who each provided several hours of thoughtful consultation. I also want to thank those who participated in the 1994 AEE International Conference session titled "What is Experiential Education?" and the many people who have either read and commented on my work, shared in provocative conversation that pushed my thinking forward, and/or allowed me to observe them in action.

References

Connell, J. & Wellborn, J. (1991). Competence, autonomy and relatedness: A motivational analysis of self-system processes. In Megan R. Gunnar and L. Alan Sroufe (Eds.), *Self Processes and Development: The Minnesota Symposia on Child Development.* Hillsdale, NJ: Lawrence Earlbaum Associates.

Dewey, J. (1938). *Experience & education.* New York: MacMillan.

Duffy, T. M. & Jonassen, D.H. (Eds.). (1992). *Constructivism and the technology of instruction: A conversation.* Hillsdale, NJ: Lawrence Earlbaum Associates.

Fetterman, D. M. , Kaftarian, S. J. & Wandersman, A. (Eds.) (1996).*Empowerment evaluation: Knowledge and tools for self-assessment & accountability.* Thousand Oaks, CA: Sage.

Gardner, H. (1993). *Frames of mind: The theory of multiple intelligences.* New York: Basic Books.

Rogoff, B. (1994). *Developing understanding of the idea of communities of learners.* Mind, Culture, and Activity, Vol. 1, No. 4.

Warren, K. , Sakofs, M. & Hunt, J. S. Jr., (Eds.). (1995). *The theory of experiential education.* Dubuque, IA: Kendall/Hunt.

A Critical Look:
The Philosophical Foundations
of Experiential Education

▾ ▾ ▾

April Crosby

I had participated in experiential learning as student and as teacher numerous times, but I was not officially introduced to the concept or to its many organized schools, camps, and activities until very recently. When I did become aware, I approached it in the way consistent with my training—skeptically. I found myself questioning all the assumptions and values of experiential education, and I found myself, as some advocates of experiential education would say we all are, unable to really look at it until I had put it into a context that means something to me. In my case this context was philosophical, and I began to look at experiential education as a philosophy of education that would include assumptions and value judgments. I investigated experiential education as a philosophy of education in a long line of such evolving philosophies, and I examined it in light of this line. I found it has a very interesting place in line.

Before I go on, I must make some ideas clear. It is important to see that a philosophy of education, or a theory of education, is based on more general beliefs than may appear in the theory. These are the preconceptions or underlying assumptions of a theory, and until they are seen to be the basis of a theory, and accepted, the theory is unfounded. Some are of the school of thought about experiential education that it is *activity,* not theory, and second, that nothing should be written about experiential education because it threatens its action

This chapter originally was published in the *Journal of Experiential Education*, with the following citation:
Crosby, A. (1981). A critical look: The philosophical foundations of experiential education. *Journal of Experiential Education, 4*(1), 9–15.

orientation and tends to rigidify it. But even if you only "do" experiential education, there are presuppositions you are acting on. What I want to clarify here is that any theory (or action) of education is based on more general theories of epistemology, and those in turn are based on assumptions about metaphysics.

Epistemology is, roughly, the study of how and what we know. It deals with such questions as whether we know via our sense or our reason, or some combination of the two, and whether we know objects of reason (like higher mathematics, for which there is no action or experiential route) with more certainty than we may know things that we learn through our senses. We might think this because information we get from our senses is sometimes mistaken, as when an object in the far distance appears small when in fact it is large. Epistemology is also concerned with the objects of knowledge: Can we know only things that we can tangibly experience, like rocks and tables, or can we know that a non-tangible object, like love, or perhaps God, exists? Some, of course, would say that we have equally reliable experience of God as we do of tables, but for others, this claim raises the question of what do we mean by "experience?" Epistemology is a field that examines many of the underlying assumptions that may be made by people working in the field of experiential education.

Also, epistemology is concerned with such distinctions as that between "belief" and "knowledge." Do we say we *knew* the world was flat but now we *know* it is round? We might say we "know" the true things and "believe" the things that may be proven false, or the things that aren't available for proof, as some would say of the existence of God. The point I am trying to make here is how epistemology, or ideas about how we might learn about the world, is based on what we feel and think to be the case about that world, and hence, it is based on metaphysics.

Metaphysics is, roughly, the study of the way the world is. Aristotle said it is the study of things that don't change, for the most part. It is investigation into what is real; for instance, why does time seem to speed up and slow down? The clock measures objective time while we feel it pass subjectively. Which is real? Is there objectivity at all? Should there be? Is it a handy concept for explaining things, or is it a troublesome ideal that gets in the way? What are the organizing principles in the world? Is history headed in a certain direction, toward a specific actualization toward which we progress, as Christians believe we are headed toward the Kingdom of God and Marxists believe we are headed toward a classless society? Or do we go in cycles of reincarnation, as the Hindus say? Are all of these merely subjective human constructs? Does the world change, or is the change an illusion? Is there ever novelty in the world? These are some of the issues in metaphysics, and clearly theories about how and what we learn about the world would have to entail certain things about that world itself. This is what I mean when I say that philosophy of education, or any activity in the field of education, is based on an epistemology, and therefore, on a metaphysic.

What I found when I did investigations about the philosophical underpinnings of experiential education is that those assumptions underlying experiential education are much more reliable than those underlying more traditional theories of education, and I want to explain what I mean by that. One thing it implies is that students educated according to these assumptions are better prepared to deal with the world than are students educated according to traditional epistemologies. I must say one more thing before going on, however: that is that I am aware that not all people who do experiential education agree on what experiential education is, or what a statement of its theory or values would be. What I mean by experiential education is a very general belief that learning will happen more effectively if the learner is as involved as possible, using as many of his faculties as possible, in the learning; and that this involvement is maximized if the student has something that matters to him at stake. How you get the learner to have something at stake is another issue, and it is, I think, the most controversial question I've encountered in connection with experiential education, but I'm not concerned with it here.

Back to the philosophical underpinnings of experiential education. I want to cursorily review the history of the philosophy of education to show how I think experiential education and some of its philosophical assumptions developed, and why I think it is epistemologically sound.

History

An early theory of education was illustrated by the Sophists, who were teachers in ancient Greece. We think of them as flourishing prior to what we call the golden age of classical Greece, though they were still extant then. These men charged fees for their tutelage, and leading citizens of Athens would pay handsome sums to have their sons taught by them. The teaching consisted primarily of reciting opinions on profound subjects, and helping students to learn to recite these opinions equally persuasively. Students learned answers to questions such as "What is virtue?", "What is piety?", "What is the nature of the beautiful?", and others. We can call this theory the "pouring theory" of education, because the teachers had the learning which they could pour into the students as if they were vessels. Once the students had the learning, they too could recite definitions and theories on deep subjects.

We can see the epistemological and metaphysical assumptions of this educational practice even more easily if we look at another modern counterpoint: the way the catechism is taught in very orthodox Roman Catholic church schools. There, children are given books that pose questions and also give answers. The children learn to recite the specified answers and are said to know their catechism. According to this, we could know that God exists whether or not we have experienced Him, and we know that He, the utmost Reality, does not change.

That's why these answers need not change, and why the method of teaching need not change. The children are learning about an unchanging reality, and those who know can tell those who don't yet know the truth about it. Because of the nature of the *object* of knowledge, in this case God (which is a metaphysical principle), the subjectivity of the learner is not relevant. What is true of God is simply true of Him, not true for me not for you, or true in different ways.

The Sophists also thought that way about the objects of knowledge. Each knew the final word about things that did not need debate. A curious thing is that the Sophists disagreed among themselves, just as our religious leaders might also disagree about what they think is absolute. A father sent his sons to the Sophist with the most prestige, or to the Sophist who would make his son the most influential orator, or, if he were a thinking father, to the Sophist with whom he agreed. In any event, learners were the uninformed who could be filled up with knowledge as if it were soup and one could get it all.

This model of education changed radically with the teacher Socrates (470399 B.C.) He taught by asking questions, not reciting answers, and he asked many questions of the Sophists that they couldn't answer because their opinions couldn't stand up under scrutiny. Socrates was asking about *their* underlying assumptions and they frequently got confused. They were not used to discussion.

As a teacher, Socrates made two major methodological changes from the Sophists. First, he believed that the students had something to contribute to the learning, and he elicited that; second, he believed that the *process* of becoming educated was the important thing, rather than arriving at a final static state, and he practiced that. He taught by beginning where the students were and leading them, through discussion, to examine their own ideas. He taught that the educated person was the one who questions all through life; that learning is a lifestyle, and this style he called "tending the soul." These beliefs and practices sound much closer to those of experiential education than do those of the Sophists.

However, according to Plato, who recorded the conversations of Socrates, the true goal of this search for knowledge is knowledge of the Forms (or what we might call essences) and these were Objective Reality. According to Plato, dialectic discussion is the epistemological tool by which we can learn of The Forms, the metaphysical principles of Reality. Plato says in the *Republic* that this true knowledge of absolutes is not achievable by most of us because of our limited capacity to learn from dialectic. Most of us are doomed to forever mistake images and the sensible objects around us as the highest Reality. Any learning of which we are capable is gained by reflection on our own beliefs, and this is accomplished best by critical discussion with others. Plato also pointed out, accurately, that most of us are hesitant to have our beliefs and assumptions questioned and therefore, learning is usually painful.

Let's look at Plato's epistemological and metaphysical assumptions. Although few students would ever know them, Socrates tried to lead knowledge of the Forms, or absolutes.

There was an essence or Form of virtue, and of beauty, and of other less profound things, each of which was a true, perfect, and unchanging model of that quality or Thing. The Forms existed, in some sense, and functioned as paradigms.

Why would he arrive at such an idea of absolutes? He saw that all we have available to us through experience are *particular* beautiful things yet we say that one is more or less beautiful as if we had some knowledge of an absolute standard of Beauty to which we compare all individual cases. Or, take the idea of a chair. We all know more or less what a chair is, but if you were asked to define it, would you include four legs? Bean bag chairs have no legs at all, and some chairs have three. Would you include that it is used for sitting? If I sit on a table, does that make it a chair? Perhaps you would specify that it has to be *intended* for sitting. Well, is a bicycle seat a chair? We can imagine someone stopping us by saying, "That's not a chair!" when we start to sit on something that might break. Plato saw that although not many of us can articulate what the essence of "chair" is, there *must* be one, because despite differing and changing definitions, we all know what a chair is.

The same is true of Virtue. We may think we know what it is until we are forced to define it. Most likely, even if we don't claim to be able to define it, we could recognize particular cases we would call acts of virtue, and cases we would say clearly are not. Plato watched people wrestle with these things and it made him propose that objective absolutes do exist, but we are just in very hazy touch with them. We can get closer to the metaphysical realities by the epistemological method of reflective and critical dialogue about our theories. This is accomplished in education by asking students to set forth their ideas, which are then examined.

We may call the Socratic philosophy of education the "midwifery theory" because Socrates saw the role of the teacher as that of a midwife: helping give birth to the knowledge that is already within the student; the teacher simply assists with delivery. The goal is persons who can continue to express and examine their own and others' ideas. Socrates saw such constant intellectual exercise as a way of life.

Philosophy of education went through another evolution with Aristotle, (384322 B.C.). In metaphysics, Aristotle rejected Plato's theory of the Forms as Reality because he saw too many problems with trying to defend their existence. Besides, Aristotle's background was as a biologist and he saw the universe in terms of growth and change as a biologist would. Reality as unchanging Forms made no sense to him. He believed that the organizing metaphysical principle was one of change: The world can be explained in terms of things changing from what they *potentially* are to their state of being *actually* realized. For example, acorns always become oak trees, oak trees may become tables, that table may become firewood, or decay into the earth again, etc. Aristotle's Reality was one which took into account change, and the change is from potentiality to actuality. The actualization of a thing depends on its species. For example, the full actualization of a colt is a beautifully running horse because it is the highest function of a horse to run. The fully actualized human being, according to Aristotle, is the one who thinks most fully because thinking is the function of the human species, peculiar to it only.

At this point we can see how the metaphysical principles of potentiality, actuality, and the change from one to the next would influence education theory. Young men were taught to use the highest function of their species, their cognitive minds, in order to become fully realized humans. This led to obvious trouble with ethical questions. We can see that a man who is most highly developed *mentally* might not be what we think of as a *morally* developed man. Aristotle never solves this dilemma very satisfactorily, but he begins to answer with a distinction between "theoretical wisdom," which is the highest function of our minds, and "practical wisdom," which is the highest human potential in the social or moral realm. This is the distinction between "theoria" and "praxis," and Aristotle seems to say that theoria is the higher goal for man.

We can see that by the end of Plato and Aristotle's time, Western intellectual thought had developed a twofold bifurcation: the distinction between Reality and the sensible world, and the distinction between theory and practice. In each case, there is an implied value judgment in favor of the former, but for neither philosopher was attainment of highest knowledge readily possible for man. Very few people could truly know the Forms, said Plato; and the life of pure theoria was not possible for man, said Aristotle. Hence, the search for knowledge in its true form was frustrating.

Western intellectual thought, and the philosophy of education with it, thus inherited a problem of the separation between:

Knowing Mind ⟷ **Knowing Mind**
(subject) **(object)**

The object of knowledge may be a substance like the Forms, for Plato; or a process like theoria, for Aristotle. The problem of epistemology and therefore, education, becomes: How do we get the knowing mind in touch with its object of knowledge, the world?

The answers to this question fell into two major categories. The Rationalists in the 16th century, led by Descartes in France, thought we could only know with certainty those things that we knew through Reason or thinking alone. This meant logic and mathematics were knowable, but the sensible world that we know through our senses was suspect; 2+2=4 never changes, he thought, but sensual things do. The other epistemological school, led generally by the Scotsman Hume, said we could rely only on sense data, and that mental operations were only compilations and augmentations of what we gain through our senses. He thought, exactly contrary to Descartes, that knowledge gained through purely mental means was suspect, and it led to such unfounded hypotheses as "God." All knowledge must be based on what is empirically available to our senses. The debate between empiricism and rationalism is the most basic epistemological debate in philosophy, and depending where you stand on this issue, radically influences how you would think education is effectively conducted and what its proper subjects are.

Let's examine for a minute the problems that would follow from adhering to either a strict rationalism or a strict empiricism. If we believe with Descartes that the information we gain through our senses is unreliable because it is sometimes misleading, then the only knowledge we can have reliably is that gained from using reason only. That limits us to abstract areas such as math and logic and theoretical subjects. We could not even have certain knowledge of our own bodies, as, after all, amputees often "feel" their nonexistent limbs. While the knowledge we *can* have may be objectively true, it is not very useful for functioning in this human world. If we can't trust our senses, how could we ever check our knowledge of the external world, or of each other? If I perceive that an object in a dim light is a dark blue, and I want to confirm it, so I ask you, the confirmation means little more than my original sense impression. The reason is that if I can't trust my senses, then I can't trust my ears to hear you correctly any more than I can trust my eyes to correctly see the blue. If our senses are unreliable, then checking like this is like buying another copy of the same newspaper to confirm a story. Hence, the predicament that follows from a strict rationalist epistemology is that each individual consciousness is forever locked into itself with no way to verify that the external world (and that includes other people) is really there. Knowledge is limited to fairly useless abstractions.

If, on the other hand, we believe with Hume that knowledge comes from empirical sense data, and all knowledge must be traced back to its empirical evidence for validation, then the mind and what it can know is severely limited in another direction. Hume says we cannot legitimately draw conclusions on the basis of sense data that are not themselves directly evidenced. "God" is not the only concept that immediately goes out the window as unfounded. "Causation" is another one. Hume points out that while we may be able to see billiard ball #1 hit billiard ball #2, and then we see billiard ball #2 move, we never in fact *see* the sensual impression that is "cause." All we *know* is that ball #2 always moves when ball #1 hits it (if ball #2 is not impeded) because that is all we *see.* When we jump to the conclusion that ball #1 *caused* ball #2 to move and from there to the conclusion that causation is an explanation of relationship between events, this is an unfounded mental move. "Causation" is merely a mental construct that is made on the basis of habit, not because there is legitimate evidence for the idea. Hence for the empiricists, our knowledge is grossly limited to what Hume called the "blooming, buzzing confusion" of sensual impressions, and any inferences about what causes them or relates them to each other are baseless. We may know our own sense impressions, but we cannot know what it is out there that *causes* them, or orders them.

Before returning to the implications of all this for education, one more step in the history of epistemology must be discussed. This step is how the German philosopher Kant, in 1787, resolved the rationalist/empiricist debate. Reading Descartes and Hume, Kant saw an impasse. He realized that if we assume that the world is orderly, as both Plato did with his Forms and Aristotle did with his growth model, and if we assume that to gain knowledge of this order, the human mind must in some way find and match that objective order, then there was no way we could ever have knowledge. We would have to be outside our own minds to see if what we thought was right about the world was in fact the way the world was.

So Kant saw that the basic approach of expecting the mind to match the world was an impossible premise: It made knowledge impossible. He revolutionized the whole field by supposing instead that the source of order is not in the external world but in the human mind. That is, we order our world in the very process of perceiving it. We cannot use what we perceive unless it is ordered according to certain categories, (e.g., space, time, and causation). Kant hypothesized that because of the structure of the human mind, we would never receive experience except as already organized by our active, structuring minds. For all we know, the "objective" world may be Hume's "blooming, buzzing confusion," but by the time it is available to us, it is not confused. The point is that any notion of what the objective world is like is of no interest to us and should not be taken as a goal of human knowledge because there is absolutely no way we can get in touch with it. We would have to be gods or at least some consciousness other than humans to see it. The only "objectivity" we can have is knowing that humans all order experience in some of the basic same ways because our minds have the basic same structure. Hence, according to Kant, I cannot imagine experience outside of time and space, and I can count on you not being able to either.

By seeing the mind as the active source of order, rather than some objective unchanging Reality as the order, Kant attempted to solve the problem of certainty. Certainty, Reality, objectivity, etc., all have less rigorous meanings, in a sense. They are reality-for-us, or objectivity-for-us, but that is good enough.

Thanks to Kant, Western thought got beyond this epistemological impasse. (There are lots of problems with Kant's work, but those are other issues.) His theory provides room for both reason and experience to function, and gets us out of the disastrous problem of how to get in touch with that which we want to know.

Years later the American, John Dewey (1859–1952) picked up the debate. We can say that he accepted Kant in that the mind is an active, ordering principle, and in that he accepted the world as we experience it rather than seeking some other Reality.

Dewey noted that not only theoretical problems followed from the split between Reality and the sensible world, and from the split between theoria and praxis, but problems of immediate human concern arose because of them also. One problem was that the emphasis on the intellectual or cognitive side of man (especially noted in Aristotle) alienated man from his immediate environment, and also from his emotional, affective self. The emphasis of the rationalists is overly cerebral. Dewey noted that the unavoidable concerns of human beings are not with some abstract and unattainable Reality, but with prosperity and adversity, success and failure, achievement and frustration, good and bad. In other words, humans are more concerned with questions of value than questions of Reality, and any adequate epistemological and educational theory ought to be geared toward knowing values, rather than toward theoretical abstractions.

Dewey saw that the need to achieve *certainty* led Western thought to theoretical constructs like those of Plato and Descartes, or to the epistemological impoverishment of Hume. Dewey saw clearly enough to see that the goal of certainty must be rejected as a starting point. Man is first and foremost an active and emotive being, said Dewey, and reflection and concern with knowing is secondary learned behavior. Furthermore, it is learned primarily as a result of uncertain or problematic situations.

Therefore, said Dewey, the metaphysical starting point should not be an abstraction, but experience itself: Philosophy should investigate life as humans experience it, not as it might be. We find ourselves in continual transaction with the physical, psychological, mental, spiritual world, and philosophy should be a *systematic investigation into the nature of this experience.* Dewey's systematic investigation led him to see that experience is subject to a pattern: First, it has an immediate, felt, aesthetic quality. Experience is not, at first, reflective, and is not at first, replete with the distinctions that reflection bestows upon it. Then, the distinctive qualities *evolve* from the indeterminate, inchoate, and experience *becomes* determinate and meaningful. Finally, experience is often felt to have a consummation, or what might now be called a closure. Dewey saw that the enemy of experience in this sense is not the intellect but the extremes of diffusion or rigidity, either of which would preclude the movement from the felt aesthetic immediacy to reflective meaningfulness. Human life, concluded Dewey, as felt, is a rhythmic movement from events of doubt and conflict to events of integrity and harmony. When humans face the world and want to know about it, the goal is not to find Reality, but to change the problematic to the integrated and consummated.

Starting with this notion of experience as the metaphysical category of what is, changes in epistemology followed. Gaining knowledge was the process of making determinate the indeterminate experience and the method was the scientific method. The steps are:

1. We find ourselves in a "felt difficulty" and this is the condition for inquiry.

2. We articulate the problem for solution.

3. We form a hypothesis for solution, and deduce the consequences of alternative solutions.

4. We test the hypothesis: we confirm or disconfirm.

5. We have knowledge—that which is warranted through inquiry—and it becomes incorporated as background for further inquiry.

Hence, "Reality" is not that which matches some abstract objective level of being, but that which gives meaning to inquiry, and that which is repeatedly meaningful in inquiry and experience. This method of inquiry is self-correcting, because if something is incorrect, it will make experience meaningless, not meaningful, and will be found out.

And "Truth" is not some abstract, objective reality, but rather "that which works" or "that which explains." Knowledge is primarily instrumental for action, not an end-in-itself.

And "Reason" is not an intuitive light that puts men in touch with certainty and truth, but rather, it is a disposition of conduct to foresee consequences of events, and to use what is foreseen in planning and conducting one's affairs.

And "Mind" refers to an instrumental method of directing change.

For Dewey, the point is to intentionally *use* experience in its dynamic form to divest experience of its indefinite and unintelligible nature, and to bring about consummations in life. The point is to make experience usable.

The difference that Dewey made in metaphysics was to start with the experienced world as reality and not to assume some objective Reality that would require God's vision to see. The difference that follows from this for epistemology is that the knowing tools we have, including pure reason and including empirical data from our senses, are both legitimate tools for knowing our world and functioning intelligently in it. The goal of learning is to know about the world as we experience it, and both theory and practice are components in the scientific method for achieving this knowledge.

All of this, which is Dewey's metaphysical and epistemological starting point in experience *as felt,* rather than as objective, leads to a very clear philosophy of education that is, I think, the foundation of what most people call experiential education. In Dewey's philosophy of education, the goal of education is not the right answer, for that might change. The goal is being able to understand and use our experience, and this is achieved by developing the thought processes with which we examine our experience. In this model, the teacher aids the student in developing an approach to his own experience by structuring the student's experience so that he may move from a challenge to a resolution. The educational process is based on the human experience of movement from difficulty to resolution. After resolution comes reflection on the movement so that what is learned may be generalized and used again.

Early in this article, I said that the assumptions of experiential education are more reliable than those underlying more traditional theories. By "more reliable," I meant more helpful in understanding our world, and why I conclude this is by now, I hope, clear. Inexperiential education, the learner-involved-in-immediate-experience is the object of knowledge, and the activity in, and reflection on, that involvement are the means of knowing. Experiential education attempts to blur the distinction between cognitive and affective learning because experience does not come distinguished this way and is not lived this way.

The paradigm of experiential education, which I encountered in a model designed by Laura Joplin, has the following elements: challenge, support, feedback, and debrief. Dewey's theory of experience begins with a challenge: the "felt difficulty," which must be resolved. It includes support and "feedback" in that the attempts at resolution either work or don't work; they help in making meaning or they increase confusion. For Dewey, "debriefing" consists of reflection on the now resolved difficulty, and is the process of integrating what was learned in a way that makes future experiences more intelligible.

Experiential educators may or may not be familiar with Dewey, or with Einstein, Heisenberg, Godel, and other thinkers whose hypotheses imply how misconceived is an educational process that aims at objectivity. What they do recognize is that education that teaches tools that can be used regardless of whatever is currently called truth is the more lasting accomplishment. The assumptions of this orientation better fit the world as we know it and would appear to still fit as that changes.

In looking at experiential education in this way, I was able to see that it is not unfounded, nor is it anti-intellectual as some critics charge and as some practitioners hope. The philosophy and practice of experiential education are developments that have a heritage, regardless of whether its advocates know, acknowledge, or value it. On the basis of this examination, one is able to see that experiential education "teachers" are subject to a misconception that faced the Sophists even 2,000 years ago: they thought they knew the truth, and that therefore people should behave accordingly.

What Constitutes Experience? Rethinking Theoretical Assumptions

▾ ▾ ▾

Martha Bell

There is a need in our professional discourse for more thinking about how the central concepts that direct what we do are organized. In trying to respond to this need, I find myself in a strange place. Reading and writing theory are not thought to be concrete enough activities to count as experientially exciting, or practical enough to engage the focus of practitioners who would rather be out there "just doing it."[1]

I find reading and writing theory challenging, risky, and nerve-wracking. I find facing big rapids on a river the same. Sometimes I am drained, physically, by the tension of concentrating, of experimenting, and of experiencing adrenalin high on a breakthrough. I feel it in my mind, but I also feel it profoundly in and with my body, just as with paddling the big rapid. I decided to try to persevere with the thinking that I have been doing around the theoretical perspectives in our field, because reading, thinking, and writing have given me an embodied location in which to begin such reflecting, just as I would have for any other "concrete" experience. And this embodied location is also the very site for me of the contradiction in terms that I experience in the field's theories.

---

[1] A note about style: words or phrases with common-sense meanings often have other meanings embedded within them, and I use quotation marks to indicate that I question the taken-for-granted use of such words.

This chapter originally was published in the *Journal of Experiential Education*, with the following citation:

Bell, M. (1993). What constitutes experience? Rethinking theoretical assumptions. *Journal of Experiential Education, 16*(1), 19–24.

When I have worked with groups, I have always thought that actually touching the rock (or the wind, water, sand, snow) is an important, concrete experience of something powerful. The theory organizes the learning process, however, around facilitated, abstract, conceptual, "objective" reflection on that quite subjective, embodied experience. Experiential learning is group-based, a social experience, and yet our traditions call it "personal growth" and "character building" individual changes. Theories or group process acknowledge that there is a group identity or culture (e.g. Mitten, 1966; Phipps, 1991), but there is still no clear sociological analysis informing our theorizing. I am looking for understandings of how social subjectivities are formed through embodied knowing, and I think that what happens in experiential learning could help illustrate this.

I will focus on two important aspects of learning through experience that have not been addressed adequately in the theory: the embodied location of experience and the social organization of the process. In this article I explore more of the reading behind my critical "rethinking" of these two aspects of my practice in the field. I start with a brief reference to Dewey's theory of experience. Part of my aim is to contest the neatness of theories that present all the answers, so I try to work with partial, sometimes convoluted, attempts at thinking about some of these issues. I find it a challenging. but impelling experience.

Theorizing Is a Social Practice

John Dewey cautions that "any theory and set of practices is dogmatic which is not based upon critical examination of its own underlying principles" (p. 22). Ideally, critical examination is not destructive but works to expose everything that defines and directs a situation, to be assessed by all. Often those who were not involved in defining the terms of the situation can then identify what is not useful for them (Henderson, 1989, relates this to recreation programming). Changing what we do as practitioners is hard work when we aim to find new strategies that will be as effective as those we had thought to be "tried and true." Furthermore, being critical of the very principles underlying such strategies in our practice may seem suicidal.

And yet, when theories become so well-established that their premises become "common sense," they are rarely examined critically. They organize our thinking to the extent that we do not even think that they exist. Things known to be common sense are taken for granted as part of "the nature of things." Aspects of theories come to be accepted uncritically as "natural," rather than understood as the result of social forces: certain thinking, meeting certain interests, at a particular time in history, and in a specific context.

As an example, I do not find it useful to think in terms of experience in general. *All* experience does not relate to, or even clarify, *my* experience. We talk about concrete experience, but I do not know what this means. To me experience "exists" through interpretation.

It is produced through the meanings given it. Interpretations of lived experiences are always contextual and specific. Experiences are contingent; interpretations can change. There is no generic clone for "the experience" that applies to everyone. This could only happen if experience was an absolute principle, or if people were clones of each other, without personal situations, social contexts, or historical places in time. In reality people have very different experiences. And yet discussions of experience in this journal commonly take this for granted, as if experience has fixed, inherent meaning.

Just recently this occurred in the theme issue on Theory and Practice. Michael Gass wrote in the editorial that "one of the best functions of experience is that it validates all of the processes that theories support" (p. 7). The process of theorizing that this approach illustrates abstracts real experiences into *a concept of experience* that then does not relate to a context. Experience becomes "it" and is treated like an object that can be expected to do the same thing to us every time. The theory of what experience does then bears no resemblance to the experiences actually occurring in local settings. In fact, the theory is used to shape and direct, or constitute, what does happen, so that it resembles what the theory says is happening. Such theories of experience leave little room for more than one explanation of what is happening. They quickly legitimate the single, linear view as a "model" for others to follow.

This is not new. It is "common" practice in theorizing and is a tool of the Western European intellectual tradition. Abstract thinking is privileged over embodied knowing. Dewey's own writing employs a model for the logical steps of inquiry that he thought were essential to the experience of learning (McDermott, 1973/1981, p. 160–240). Dewey does not take it for granted that experience has fixed, inherent meaning; he specifically theorizes that this is so. It has become common sense to us. His model has been simplified for discussions of the process of experiential education, such as David Kolb's (1984, p. 23).

Laura Joplin's five-stage model is another good example of this approach, and one to which many people point when asked for definitions of our field (1981, p. 17–20). We can then say, "This is what happens in experiential learning!" Experience becomes accepted as a social form through abstract models, and is no longer known as a personally and socially lived reality given contextual meanings. The *concept* in turn informs social relations (Smith, 1984, offers an excellent analysis of how the abstraction of specific activities makes them into social rituals). The social concept of gender also refers to a social relation, an experience of becoming feminine or becoming masculine, and yet now the concept actually serves to inform social behaviors. Sociologists are interested in the ways in which gender is specifically experienced and replicated, rather than just accepting it as a conceptual label.

Theorizing is constructing a set of concepts that are deemed a universally applicable and replicable explanation for what is happening. It is, itself, therefore a social practice used to organize social relations. Standardized social rituals can be replicated so that we come to expect certain practices to symbolize social meanings. In *Experience and Education*, Dewey gives two examples of this: sport and manners. He refers to the social control exerted by common expectations that there are unspoken "rules of the game" that prevail over all. He also refers to the code of social conduct that manners represent. Specific manners may change or differ among people, but "the existence of some form of convention...is a uniform attendant of all social relationships," he writes (p. 59). From these examples, we might refer to social practices in everyday terms, then, as rules and etiquette, which we come to expect as "natural."

Experience, according to Dewey, is also a social relationship. He sees experience as a relationship between the individual and his/her environment, a replicable interaction in which meanings are found. He explores the social aspects of experience in the context of a natural harmony of social consensus. In his time, it was radical enough to propose that experience was separate from an absolute ideal of knowledge and engaged in by an active individual. He would not have thought to question the existence of a social harmony.

In our time, we cannot take for granted a social order governed by natural principles, such as fair play or just deserts. These are socially constructed conventions constituting social relations. As such, they represent the interests of those responsible for their construction, those with the power to define them. Thus theory is constructed, as well, to make sense from a certain perspective. An acknowledgement of this is missing from theorizing about experience today.

Having set up the problem that I see with current theorizing in our field, I will go a bit deeper into some of the areas that have serious limitations for me. First, I will take some time to outline how a critical perspective helps to unravel some of these unaddressed issues. They are present in constituting experiences and knowledges for our students, even though "unstated." Then I will look at some of the assumptions on which our practice might rest.

The most important point to start with is that what were radical ideas in another time are resting on assumptions that are inadequate now to help us understand the complexities of experiential learning situations today.

Being Critical

An obvious question for practitioners and theorists, then, is that if we already think the basic assumptions of our profession make common sense, then what would motivate us to question them? If the principles ground the practice, indeed are validated in concrete practice, as Gass suggests above, then why the need for constant critical examination?

The significance of such questions rests on the invisibility of the person doing the asking. The universality of Western traditions of language and knowledge pivots on an invisible, central "we" that treats everything around it from its own perspective. But "we" are not in the picture.

It helps to go back to the underlying principles of the very structure of knowledge, the ways meaning is constructed through ways of defining reality. Theorists like Dewey, who set out principles of experiential education, based their assumptions upon taken-for-granted tenets about thinking and knowing, which organized their approach to forming theories. Logic, rationality, scientific method, and the discovery of intrinsic meaning were essential to Dewey. In his day these were not seen to be connected to learning, and so it was radical to suggest that there were clear, practical, "scientific" steps making up a learning process. It had been common sense in his time that learning happened when the proper information to be known was imposed on students from above.

However, today his promotion of scientific logic can be seen to reinforce linear, cause-effect, "either-or" terms of facts and knowledge. This gives us a false sense of the unity of knowledge, its objective nature, and the ability to "discover" reality. With enough personal effort, we can ensure our students that they will "discover" who they really are. Or they can "discover" that they can go past their limits. Humanistic definitions of identity involve a firm belief in the perfectibility of humans through their lifespan. Dewey refers to learning as having the same continuity as growth and development (1938, p. 36). Knowledge, identity, and meaning in this perspective are intrinsic to the world and human beings. Yet how often is life straightforward or lived on one level? How often do we find ourselves experiencing, and living, contradictions? Is growth cumulative and developmental as theorists claim? A critical perspective does not accept the liberal humanistic perspective, such as Dewey promotes, as the only overarching explanation for reality.

Constructions of knowledge have also structured our language as a meaning-making system by setting up dichotomies in which the world is categorized. If something is not one, it is "the other." Starting with the self, known internally, the other term juxtaposed in the dichotomy can only be known externally. "The other" is always objectified. If the self is the center, the subject of all experience, then the other is experienced, and denied subjectivity. Western theory of knowledge privileges objectivity as the prerogative of the subject. Dewey's theory of experience also privileges objectivity. His steps to inquiry are based on rational, logical problem solving that takes the central position of the subject for granted. The subject, or author, of Western definitions of rationality was always he with access to the texts and his transmission: masculine, Caucasian, well-educated, and heterosexual. Those not involved in defining the dominant terms can only be objectified, such as women, "other" classes, races, ethnicities, sexual identity groups, and so on. This is not a tangential point. This is where being critical becomes important.

It becomes more apparent that something requires a critical examination when the accepted definitions do not match the lived experiences of "others," when they do not "make sense" to those whose experience is denied by the dominant norm. Those who do not experience "reality" the way "everyone else" does cannot take it for granted. And, when the dissonance is not experienced by "us," it is easier for "us" to take things for granted as "natural," suppressing calls for change.

To go back to Gass' premise above, I would contest his statement by suggesting that one of the best functions of experiences is that they are diverse, cannot be fixed or determined, and may *invalidate* the assumptions that theories rely on. My belief in this comes from my own experience. In this way, experiences of dissonance constantly provide us with the location for critical examination. They put "us" in the picture. However, our own or our students' lived experiences are rarely interpreted as useful in cracking open accepted interpretations or theories when they are not consistent. More often, if they do not fit they are seen to be abnormal, "unique," or otherwise rationalized, while the overarching theory is unchanged.

The Body

One of the reasons that I am active in the outdoors and deliberately choose to take other women into the outdoors is to encourage them to feel strong in their bodies. This may seem like a small point or a self-evident goal. I take into account the way norms of femininity are lived by women in white Western society, so that our bodies become a site of expressing heterosexual attractiveness, and our soft, gentle, and nurturing "nature." I see my desire to allow women to experience a different way to feel in their bodies—harder, alert, and effective in initiative and action—as being a form of resistance to a social code that shapes and directs our bodies and our embodied experiences. And yet, becoming fit and healthy is still sexualized for women so that there are also dominant definitions for an attractive "active woman" (as studies of "feminized" aerobics classes have shown; see MacNeill, 1988). Paradoxically, I may be participating in reinforcing standards of strength and capability for women that again subject us to masculine definitions. What assumptions am I operating from about "ideal" body size and image that limit large or "fat" women?

Bodies seem like unique, personal possessions, or perhaps attributes, and yet there are social expectations and regulations around all of our bodies. As experiential educators, we must be aware of these social forces. We often treat experiential learning as a neutral space, a "leveller." It is common sense that women can do anything that men can do in the outdoors (see Knapp's [1985] and Friedrich and Priest's [1992] calls for a theory of androgyny). And yet this is an argument of human "nature," meant to neutralize gender roles, which are a social code. If we really question this assumption, we would see that women bring with them to the outdoors, or their learning experiences, social practices that shape them and their experiences, no matter how much personal achievement they gain (see Warren, 1985).

I notice that I am writing of all women as if all women experience their physical bodies as socially regulated in the same way as I do. I speak here from conversations with women in groups in the outdoors; I cannot speak for all lesbian women, Maori women, women of color, women with disabilities. Where are they in "our" picture of experiential education?

What I am suggesting is not new; yet my body, as the site of my socially learned practices of (and resistances to) femininity—a large part of my identity—has been invisible in the theory. It is not left out, but remains present as the oppositional term in the mind-body dichotomy. The mind is privileged in the process of reflection. As long as experience is understood through abstract, rational, objective reflection, then, in order to participate, I must also use my mind and ignore my body. Yet my experience happens in the very site of my social identity, the site of the rules and etiquette that define me as a woman (and the site of my training in race, class, and heterosexual practices). If I reflect on it from this "feminized" location of knowing, I risk being objectified as "a body." If I remain distant and detached from it, I cannot question the social assumptions that place restraints on what I am capable of experiencing.

Rethinking the Practice

In seeking to expand a theoretical analysis of experience as socially produced for our students, I think we must make spaces to invite and explore different representations of experience.

This challenges many of the most common aspects of the way this profession is practiced. For example, Ewert reports that the psychological perspective is "the most widely used viewpoint" in the research in outdoor adventure (1987, p. 25). This tradition starts with the assumption that the individual is an autonomous being, in rational control of her/his choices, and following developmental patterns of growth, as if every individual will experience the same things in certain predicted situations. In short, the "psychological" view of the individual decontextualizes our behavior, seeking to produce generalizable knowledge. Critical approaches uncover different and contextual *knowledges*.

One example of this is a consideration of the use of ice-breakers and initiative problems with a new group. I find it problematic to treat "the group" as if it were homogeneous, and there are many ice-breakers/initiatives that require too much intimacy and stress than particular participants may be willing to share at that time. It has been reported that in some women's groups the participants waited until well into the expedition before they disclosed more personal information and built trusting relationships; ice-breakers such as trust falls created more anxiety and not necessarily trust (Mitten, 1986, p. 25–26). A critical view of this might reflect a rethinking of the lived experiences of different women (or members of "other" dominant social categories of identity, such as class, race, age, ability, sexual orientation) and an invitation to a group to openly question social assumptions about consent.

Another example might be a rethinking of the use of debriefing or processing. This component is based on an assumption that the reflection that is integral to Deweyian and other models of the experiential learning cycle actually enables participants to remember and so learn from their experiences. Reflection tends to be treated as memory work, a biological function, in models such as Joplin's (1981)—in which it is taken for granted that an experience can be remembered as it was and learning can be taken away from it—rather than as a social practice. Giroux writes that it is the "memory of the oppressed" that keeps the struggle against relations of power alive, and calls for a broader notion of learning that would "include how the body learns tacitly, how habit translates into sedimented history, and how knowledge itself may block the development of certain subjectivities and ways of experiencing the world" (in Freire, 1985, p. xix–xx). When I sit down with a group to "go around the circle," am I really offering a space for the tensions and contradictions of lived experience, the memories of pain and pleasure, and the confusions in knowing to be expressed?

Memory work can surface "body memories," which, painful in the remembering, bring back to consciousness parts of the body that were risked or abandoned for survival. In outdoor "survival" situations, it is important to understand that representations of experience may come in partial forms because of this history, expressed not in one telling but in many as participants become the subjects of their own embodied knowledge.

How can memory frame identity, contributing to self-awareness and self-knowledge, in ways that affirm, resist, or challenge externally accepted meanings? Perhaps remembering an experience recomposes it so that its meaning changes. This remembering might contest the dis-remembering, or fragmentation, of much of the psychological definitions of the self. Whose memories are privileged in the discourse of "the group" and how am I complicit in this in my practice as facilitator?

One last example: facilitating opportunities for participants to "overcome their fear" may be working against the needs of those participants who want to learn to feel their fear, physically, when appropriate, and respond in a way that does not put them at risk, but allows them act to protect themselves. If the metaphor for overcoming resistance and taking risks is not questioned, it may be used to eliminate resistance that may be essential to struggle against disempowerment. Again, what are the particular and subjective needs of my different participants?

If we take Dewey's philosophy of experience and apply it today, out of the historical moment and social context in which it was theorized, we are limiting the possibilities for lived experience of social relations to emerge described in dissonant, contradictory ways. A critical perspective would allow our students, and each of us, to seek meanings in contexts that intersect at different social moments. Experience might be best remembered in the first telling, the collective telling, the re-telling, and the re-remembering of our bodies, not simply our minds.

We have yet to theorize adequately how many of the experiences that we facilitate actually operate to organize who speaks, who remembers, who trusts, who fears, and in whose interests. These are important questions for exposing the ways in which experience is theoretically constituted, and then dislodging it from the dominant definitions which organize it in practice.[2]

---

[2] I want to acknowledge with appreciation the comments, critique, and support through the many versions of this article from Alan Warner, Daniel Vokey, Karen Warren, and Barbara Williams. Thanks to Chuck Luckmann for helping me to separate the jargon from the ideas.

Experience & Participation: Relating Theories of Learning

▾ ▾ ▾

John Quay

The primary aim of this paper is to continue the task of analyzing and advancing experiential education,[1] a task that has been conducted in this journal since its inception. Notwithstanding the pioneering work of many who have reached beyond previous limits in this exploration in recent times (e.g., Carver, 1996; DeLay, 1996; Haskell, 1999; Hutchison & Bosacki, 2000; Itin, 1999; Lindsay & Ewert, 1999), one area that could benefit from further examination is the relationship between experiential education and other theories of learning. The initial challenge is to locate experiential education amongst the vast range of other theories of learning. The task then involves an exposition of those theories of learning that bear a closer resemblance to experiential education, always cognizant of the opportunity to learn more about experiential education, especially its weaknesses, by understanding the issues of learning confronted through these other theories.

Of especial interest is situated learning. It is a learning theory that provides those involved in experiential education with much to ponder. Situated learning shifts the analytic focus from "the individual as learner to learning as participation in the social world" (Lave & Wenger, 1991,

---

[1] In an effort to avoid confusion, the term experiential education has been used throughout this paper rather than a combination of experiential learning and experiential education (Itin, 1999). When experiential learning is the focus then "learning in experiential education" or a similar phrase will be used.

This chapter originally was published in the *Journal of Experiential Education*, with the following citation:

Quay, J. (2003). Experience and participation: Relating theories of learning. *Journal of Experiential Education, 26*(2), 105–116.

p. 43). Situated learning accounts for the intricate part context plays in learning. It is a point often made in discourses of experiential education, but one that has not tended to influence the dominant theories of learning in experiential education.

Meeting the Relations: Constructivism, Social Constructionism, and Cultural Discourses of Learning

When approaching a study of learning theories it is easy to be overwhelmed by the vast array of possibilities offered. An important strategy that can be used in order to overcome some of this difficulty is to perceive some structure or classification within which different learning theories can be compared and contrasted. Davis, Sumara, and Luce-Kapler (2000) provide a useful classification for just such a purpose, which creates two categories of learning theories based on two broad philosophies: those that are best described via a machine metaphor (which they call complicated), and those that embrace an organic metaphor (which they call complex). Using a machine metaphor to describe learning implies that learning is a simple cause and effect process. It is *mechanical*. Structuring curricula using competencies provides a good example of the pedagogical expression of this metaphor. Davis and his colleagues include within this category behaviorist and mentalist theories of learning. An organic metaphor is much more *holistic* in character and implies that understandings of learning must incorporate the phenomenon in its entirety. It is analogous to the processes of adaptation and evolution. In this way "learning is coming to be understood as a participation in the world, a co-evolution of knower and known that transforms both" (Davis et al., 2000, p. 64). Taken in its entirety, this metaphor moves beyond much of mainstream education as it is conducted in schools, because it requires theorization of the relationship between learner and the school within the learning process (Lindsay & Ewert, 1999).

Assuming the legitimacy of these two broad categories, the task becomes locating experiential education among them. The strength of experiential education is founded upon its theorizing of the "intimate and necessary relation between the processes of actual experience and education" (Dewey, 1938/1963, p. 20). This results in the oft-cited theory of learning in experiential education that encompasses "learning by doing combined with reflection" (Priest & Gass, 1997, p. 136). The goal of education, for Dewey, encompassed "being able to understand and use our experience" (Crosby, 1981, p. 14). Kolb provides a perceptively simple yet conceptually complex definition of experiential education as "the process whereby knowledge is created through the transformation of experience" (Kolb, 1984, p. 38). These are but a few of the definitions or descriptions of experiential education that have been documented by theorists and practitioners. Equally important, underlying the myriad opinions on the processes of experiential education, is an *imperative to adapt, to evolve, and to learn* via our experience.

This thematic understanding of experiential education is supported by other work in the field in which the general trend is toward describing experiential education as a holistic form of education (e.g., Carver, 1996; Hutchison & Bosacki, 2000; Itin, 1999). If a classification of experiential education in this way is acceptable, then it may be further implied that experiential education has a relationship with those other learning theories described by Davis and his colleagues founded in a holistic philosophy: constructivism, social constructionism, and cultural discourses.[2]

Constructivism

Connections between experiential education and constructivism are clearly made in the experiential education literature (e.g., Carver, 1996; DeLay, 1996; Hutchison & Bosacki, 2000). Constructivism espouses the notion that "the learner's basis of meaning is found in his or her direct experience with a dynamic and responsive world," and that "we can only form concepts through our bodily actions" (Davis et al., 2000, p. 65). The historical roots of constructivism reside in Piaget's understanding of knowledge formation and his concept of equilibration (Fosnot, 1996), a genesis also relevant to experiential education theory (Kolb, 1984). According to Fosnot, Piaget theorized that "new experiences sometimes foster contradictions to our present understandings, making them insufficient and thus perturbing and disequilibrating the structure, causing us to accommodate" (Fosnot, p. 13). Learning from the perspective of constructivism is a process of active adaptation, an idea clearly encompassed in experiential education theory (Crosby, 1981; Kolb, 1984; Priest & Gass, 1997).

Social Constructionism

One limitation of constructivism is that it views learning as a process that applies specifically to the individual person: It is ensconced in the realm of psychology. The salient nature of this limitation is revealed when the possibility of a small group of people learning through their social interaction as a collective is considered, aptly described as social constructionism. Social constructionism broadens basic individualistic constructivist understandings of learning, professing that "collectives of persons are capable of actions and understandings that transcend the capabilities of the individuals on their own" (Davis et al., 2000, p. 68). This is a crucial expansion and acknowledges that the system involved in learning is not located purely within individuals, but also encompasses the social world as it exists (e.g., everyday educational settings

---

[2] Within this classification of learning theories associated with a holistic educational philosophy, Davis, Sumara, and Luce-Kapler (2000) also include critical discourses in the same category as cultural discourses. Mention of critical theory was omitted from this paper in order to reduce the level of complexity. Davis et al. (2000) also include ecological theories in this classification, a level beyond cultural discourses, which encompasses phenomena such as the Gaia hypothesis. Again, this category has been omitted from this paper in order to reduce complexity.

"as pairs of students, teacher-learner interactions, and classroom groupings," Davis et al., p. 67). Learning is not solely individual, rather, it "is always collective: embedded in, enabled by, and constrained by the social phenomenon of language; caught up in layers of history and tradition; confined by well established boundaries of acceptability" (Davis et al., p. 67).

Prominent in the theoretical foundations of social constructionism is the work of Vygotsky, who claimed that, "Relations among people genetically underlie all higher functions" (Vygotsky, 1981, p. 163). These relations structure Vygotsky's (1978) "zone of proximal development" (p. 84–91), which is that gap between what a learner can learn on his/her own and what s/he can learn with guidance or through collaboration. We can see that learning involves more than an individual person trying to make sense of the world in isolation. It extends "beyond the skin." The social situation is of important consequence.

Cultural Discourses

While social constructionism views learning as located within the small group, cultural discourses broaden the scope further to embrace learning that occurs at the level of the wider society, thus enabling an understanding of how knowledge is created beyond the individual or small group. Although culture does differ in subtle ways amongst different subgroups within a society, overall, there is a level at which some continuity exists and at which these subtle differences contribute to a larger whole. Culture represents knowledge at the societal level. In effect "individual knowing, collective knowledge, and culture become three nested, self-similar levels of one phenomenon" (Davis et al., 2000, p. 70). This permits understandings of learning that encompass the shift from "the individual's efforts to shape an understanding of the world to the manners in which the world shapes the understanding of the individual" (Davis et al., p. 70). Culture is a central aspect of the context within which both the individual and the small group are situated with respect to learning. It encourages the learner(s) to adapt and evolve while, itself, changes over time in subtle ways in response to the actions of the individuals and small groups.

Vygotsky's zone of proximal development can be interpreted at the level of society as the "distance between the everyday actions of individuals and the historically new form of the societal activity that can be collectively generated as a solution to the double bind potentially embedded in ... everyday actions" (Engeström, 1987, p. 174). In other words, while culture is sometimes viewed as an unchanging monolithic entity, there is an important transformative dimension present.

Relative Problems

Constructivism, social constructionism, and cultural discourses provide a structure within a holistic educational philosophy that allows a deeper analysis of experiential education. It is not the aim to conflate experiential education with any of these other theories. Rather, learning through experience occurs at the level of both the individual (constructivism), the small group (social constructionism), and culture (cultural discourses), an advance on those experiential education theories based purely within constructivism that assume learning as primarily the premise of the individual (e.g., Itin, 1999; Joplin, 1981). The social nature of the experience is well understood in the practice of experiential education. Less well understood is the social constructionist character of many aspects of experiential education. The formal reflective strategies commonly used in experiential education, such as group debriefs and reviews, (which are usually distinguished from the experience, per se) as well many of the more informal aspects of group dynamics, all function in social constructionist terms.

The process of active adaptation, of learning, is identified as being located within a social and cultural world. The importance of this context to learning, which is often stated generally but not theorized, is clearly implicated as foundational. Cultural discourses highlight the need for experiential education to attend more diligently to issues of context, especially in the way it is theorized in models of learning in experiential education. Experience occurs in context; it is situated—a sentiment that Dewey supported when he said, "Experience does not occur in a vacuum. There are sources outside an individual that give rise to experience; it is constantly fed from these springs" (Dewey, 1938/1963, p. 40).

Meeting a Fellow Traveler: Situated Learning

Situated learning provides a more tangible application of these other theories of learning, affording a more detailed structure that assists in the task of analyzing experiential education. It grew, in large part, from the body of work by Soviet psychologist Vygotsky (e.g., 1962, 1978), which was further developed by educational theorists, particularly in the United States. Central to this process was the seminal work of Lave (Lave & Wenger, 1991).

Situated learning can be categorized as holistic, and it has a deep-rooted affinity with social constructionism while also encompassing aspects of cultural discourses. It regards learners as active participants within a social and cultural world that influences, and is influenced by them, as they continue to adapt, to evolve, and to learn. This idea is not foreign to the field of experiential education: "Every genuine experience has an active side which changes in some degree the objective conditions under which experiences are had" (Dewey, 1938/1963, p. 39). Of prime importance in situated learning is the conceptualization of the intimate connection between participation and the social and cultural world within which that participation occurs, a viewpoint often missed in many models of learning in experiential education. Lave and Wenger (1991) begin their approach to theorizing this connection through their refinement of the notion of participation in their concept of *legitimate peripheral participation.* This concept attempts to draw attention to the process of moving from being a newcomer among a group of other practitioners "toward full participation in the sociocultural practices of a community" (Lave & Wenger, p. 29).

Legitimate peripheral participation is understandably a complex concept that requires clarification of its nuances in order to avoid distortions of the meaning intended. The temptation is to dissect the concept into three separate notions resulting in "a set of three contrasting pairs: legitimate versus illegitimate; peripheral versus central; participation versus nonparticipation (Lave & Wenger, 1991, p. 35)." But this is not the aim of Lave and Wenger. They "intend for the concept to be taken as a whole. Each of its aspects is indispensable in defining the others and cannot be considered in isolation" (Lave & Wenger, p. 35). When viewed in its complexity it reveals "a landscape—shapes, degrees, textures—of community membership" (Lave & Wenger, p. 35).

Legitimate peripheral participation communicates that "the required learning takes place not so much through the reification of a curriculum as through modified forms of participation that are structured to open practice to nonmembers" (Wenger, 1998, p. 100). While some reference to the context within which participation occurs is made, more detail is required concerning the social and cultural world in order to more fully reveal the characteristics of this connection. Lave and Wenger (1991) provide this through their concept of *community of practice.* "A community of practice is a set of relations among persons, activity and world, over time, and in relation with other tangential and overlapping communities of practice" (Lave & Wenger, p. 98). This concept provides the anchor, steadfastly situating legitimate peripheral participation in the sociocultural world.

The descriptions of these two concepts reveal the dynamic and complex interplay between learner(s) and context, another version of the sociological conundrum of agent and structure (Archer, 1995). Inherent in relationships of this type is that neither part can be defined fully without reference to the other—the distinction between part and whole is difficult to make. Legitimate peripheral participation and communities of practice are co-determined. This is representative of the notion of being-in-the-world (as opposed to the creation of either one merged concept or two isolated concepts), thus calling into play the existential phenomenologies of Heidegger (1953/1996), and Merleau-Ponty (1962, 1968). In short, both learners and context are inseparable parts of the phenomenon of learning.

Evidently, the focus in situated learning is on participation rather than experience, per se. The highlighting of participation results in a more forceful connection with the world as interconnected communities of practice. Dewey himself supported the importance of participation as connecting the learner and the world, saying that "If the living, experiencing being is an intimate participant in the activities of the world to which it belongs, then knowledge is a mode of participation" (Dewey, 1916/1944, p. 338). This sentiment is also apparent in the work of Lave who claims that "Participation in everyday life may be thought of as a process of changing understanding in practice, that is, as learning" (Lave, 1993, p. 6). Participation and learning are thus equated in a defined way, as experience and education have been (Dewey, 1938/1963).

Problems at Home

The connection between learning and participation highlights two major issues for models of learning in experiential education. In many of these models (e.g., Kolb, 1984) learning has been equated with a stepwise process in which an internalized reflection follows concrete experience resulting in an adaptation revealed in further experience. We step out of experience to reflect and process, then we step back in. Experience exists as a memory to be processed via reflection. These models have strongly influenced pedagogy resulting in the programming of separate tasks: the doing and then the formal reflecting followed by more doing. In this sense, learning in experiential education could be placed within a more mechanistic category of learning theories. Its holistic nature, which we intuitively understand, is not made manifest. In other words, experience and reflection are viewed as such individual "tasks" that they can only be informed by psychology—both sociological and ecological perspectives struggle to find space in models of learning in experiential education. Theories of learning in experiential education lack an "embeddedness" in the world (Hutchinson & Bosacki, 2000).

A by-product of this understanding of learning as an individual and internal process results in the creation of the concept of transfer in order to attempt to deal with the circulation of knowledge in society. This is a concept that does "not acknowledge the fundamental imprint of interested parties, multiple activities, and different goals and circumstances, on what constitutes 'knowing' on a given occasion or across a multitude of events" (Lave, 1993, p. 13). Haskell acknowledges that this transfer "has a social and cultural dimension" that has "not been widely recognized" (Haskell, 2001, p. 136). Transfer, commonly conceived, assumes that knowledge is held in the minds of individuals and thus eminently transportable, rather than being closely bound with all aspects of context. Situated learning highlights the context in which learning takes place—the community of practice—incorporating all aspects of this community and its practice. Experience itself is often commonly understood as knowledge held in context—we have experience *in* something, we participate *in* something. These "somethings" are related to contexts. Transfer cannot be understood apart from the recognition of the importance of context to learning.

Situated learning is able to more fully account for learning as a process that involves more than the individual as learner, revealing the vast gulf between many expressions of experiential education as learning *theory* and experiential education as *practice.* While many theoretical understandings of learning in experiential education focus on the individual and the ways in which he or she constructs understandings of the world internally, the language of the practice of experiential education is replete with references to social interaction and culture. This is especially evident in those areas of education that emphasize experiential processes, such as outdoor education and adventure education (e.g., Gair, 1997; Priest, 1986). Situated learning provides the concepts and theory that support this practice.

Getting to Know You:
Learning as Experience and as Participation

As Lave and Wenger (1991) assert, the ultimate aim of legitimate peripheral participation is eventual full participation. Individuals "move from being at the fringes of a community to engaging in more centralized performances in that community" (Linehan & McCarthy, 2000, p. 437). The central aspect of situated learning is this movement toward a more developed participation. At the center of experiential education is adaptive experience, moving toward future improved experiences via a process that combines experience and reflection. Intrinsic to both of these processes are the questions of who is influencing them and to what ends they are directed. Embedded within these questions are the issues of teaching, power, and ethics. Each of these issues is complex and reveals nuances within the learning theories of experiential education and situated learning. These issues revolve around the similarities and differences that exist between understandings of learning as experience and as participation, and highlight what can be learned via their juxtaposition.

Teaching

In any broad discussion of learning the issue of pedagogy must arise, leading to the question of the place of the teacher in the learning process. When learning is viewed holistically, teaching becomes a much more complex concept than it appears in a mechanical model. Learning may be conceived as "*dependent on* but not *determined* by teaching" (Davis et al., 2000, p. 64). Situated learning "decenters" the teacher by moving "the focus of analysis away from teaching and onto the intricate structuring of a community's learning resources" (Lave & Wenger, 1991, p. 94). No longer is the teacher a person of authority imparting knowledge as information. The teachers in this process are other participants in the community of practice. Learning is viewed as a form of enculturation in a community of practice, an acknowledgement that "the activities of many communities are unfathomable, unless they are viewed from within the culture" (Brown, Collins, & Duguid, 1989, p. 33). Every experience of the learner is educative in some way.

Carver (1996) has applied this understanding of pedagogy to experiential education, describing the role of the teacher in a formally educative context as one who "cultivates environments...for learning" (p. 11). Carver's use of the concept of *cultivation* provides an excellent metaphor as it incorporates notions of growth and creativity. It does not have the technical or authoritative baggage that terms such as design or plan have in educational discourse. The term cultivation itself has its roots in the Latin *cultura* (Heidegger, 1971, p. 147), with the term culture, according to Dewey, meaning "something cultivated, something ripened" (Dewey, 1916/1944, p. 121). In a formal educational setting the teacher manages this process of enculturation and the inherent tensions that exist within a community of practice as a result of people continually learning and changing. Situated learning helps us to see that the formal teacher is also part of the community of practice, and that s/he shares the teaching role with all the other participants in this community. Experiential education highlights the role that the teacher plays in structuring the learning situation, including all those aspects that the teacher can influence which impact upon the experience.

Power

The pathway through legitimate peripheral participation to full participation gives rise to concerns about the issue of power in this process. This raises questions about political structures and the level to which democratic practices exist in communities of practice (Hay, 1996). Participation is intertwined with politics. The issue of power and its relation to pedagogy is clearly dealt with in the work of Freire (1970), whose work has been well referenced within experiential education literature (e.g., Itin, 1999). Freire juxtaposes a more traditional "banking" style pedagogy, with a pedagogy that values the experiences of the learners. Knowledge understood as constructed through experience is impacted by democracy as it values the experiences of the learner as educative. Democracy is also fundamental to situated learning because learning, leading to full participation, is dependent upon access.

Democracy, although a seemingly simple concept, has many facets, some of which support learning via participation and experience more fully than others. Governmental processes that rely on citizens electing representatives to determine policy and action on issues are not as democratic as processes that involve citizens themselves in decision-making about these issues, such as referenda.[3] This more involved form of democracy has been called *participatory democracy* (Barber, 1984). Participatory democracy supports a maximum level of participation for individuals in political affairs. To enable participation, and thus learning, political structures must be democratic, and ideally they should involve participatory democracy. This applies as equally to the classroom as to larger political arenas. The concepts structuring situated learning help to further our understanding of power and politics as they relate to experiential education.

Ethics

When the issue of enculturation is considered in any holistic educational philosophy a fundamental question emerges: What is being cultivated? To answer this question it is necessary to explore issues of morals, values, spirituality, and ethics—all of those seemingly subjective issues that are a part of any learning situation. These issues are present in the experiential education literature to the extent that they represent a prominent theme, gathered under the areas of adventure therapy, service-learning, outdoor education, and environmental education (Beringer, 2000; Haluza-Delay, 2000; Long, 2001; Smith, Strand, & Bunting, 2002). These issues are central to any holistic understanding of participation and experience in these communities of practice.

---

[3] Even referenda rely on elected representatives to make decisions about the wording of questions.

One way of approaching this exploration is to focus on what is identified as good. This is because "the good life" is teleological: Everything we do is directed, consciously or subconsciously, toward its attainment (Aristotle, 1980, 1995; Tuan, 1986). Culture plays an important part in how the question of what is good is understood in any community (Tuan). An understanding of what is being cultivated in any particular community of practice is thus founded upon the relationship among the various interpretations of what is good, as held by those individuals, small groups, and the wider society, which constitute and impact upon the community of practice.[4]

Emergent from within this philosophical question is the more practical ethical question, "How are we to live?"— a question that seems to have much more relevance in discussions of legitimate peripheral participation and communities of practice than those of the more individualistic notions of reflection and concrete experience (Singer, 1993). Dewey made reference to its importance by saying that "the only ultimate value which can be set up is just the process of living itself" (Dewey, 1916/1944, p. 240). This question was clearly broached in the work of Hahn, whose educational philosophy embraced "the morally responsible man [sic]...who is committed to the idea of the good and to justice and who regards professional skill as a part of his task as a citizen in society" (Röhrs, 1970, p. 134). Questioning how we are to live forms an essential aspect of the practice of experiential education, notably in outdoor education and adventure education:

> Most days, for example, involve a "debriefing" session around dinnertime when we talk
> about the day. Part of this will be narrowly practical. Who has blisters? How is everyone
> doing? Who has what questions? But it is also an occasion for reflection on ethical mat-
> ters. The specifics, naturally, vary enormously, but the general pattern is to ask what
> happened today from which we can learn something about how to live.
> (Johnson & Frederickson, 2000, p. 47)

This citation reveals the importance of discussion in any community of practice. Determining how we are to live impacts upon the ethics of discussion itself as a process, as exemplified in discourse ethics (Chambers, 1995; Habermas, 1990).

Addressing the question of how to live is a central driving force in much of the practice of experiential education because of its holistic philosophy. This critical nature of experiential

---

[4] Understandings of what is good in life can obviously be manipulated. This manipulation is an inherent aspect of consumer capitalism, implicating the marketing industry in the charades designed to keep us striving for a materialistic vision of the good life (e.g., Csikszentmihalyi & Rochberg-Halton, 1981; Schor, 1998).

education can help to inform situated learning that can be perceived as promoting the status quo. There are, of course, examples of experiential education practice that exist that do not overtly dwell on issues of such magnitude, however underlying any more specific educational aims in a situation in which learning is conceived as experiential are these fundamental issues. What is being cultivated is given by way of an answer to the question of how we are to live. And any answer to this question cannot be separated from the context, the situation, the community of practice in which it is being asked.

Getting Together

Teaching, power and ethics are issues of a contextual nature that are of utmost importance for learners and learning. They highlight the importance of a theorization of context, of the learner, and of the relationship between them, for any theory of learning that is founded upon participation and experience. Experience, participation, reflection, community of practice: The theoretical structures of situated learning complement those of experiential education and vice-versa, assisting in the development of a better understanding of the learning situation. We can accommodate participation as experience. The challenge becomes recognizing experience as participation.

Conclusion

Investigation of other theories of learning creates windows into the world of experiential education that are, as yet, barely opened. By reflecting on those learning theories that could be described as close cousins of experiential education, much has been revealed about its "personality." Constructivism, social constructionism, and cultural discourses provide a structure that enables the scope of the learning enterprise theorized within experiential education to be more completely analyzed.

Situated learning can also be described as closely allied to experiential education. It provides further insight into those aspects of experiential education that have yet to be fully theorized. The view of experiential education provided through situated learning, via the context of learning (as community of practice), and the activity of learning (as legitimate peripheral participation), is invaluable as it theorizes possibilities for learning in experiential education beyond the way it is often modeled as an internalized process. Understandings of learning in experiential education need to be advanced in order to encompass the practice of experiential education, which is based very firmly in the social and cultural world. Experiential education requires further theorization of the relationship between reflection and concrete experience, beyond the basic fact of the existence of this relation. The sociological and ecological aspects of learning need to be incorporated into the learning theory of experiential education, extending the current psychological focus. And more work is called for to expand the existing models of learning in experiential education in order to incorporate these ideas, many of which have only been, at best, introduced in this paper. The theoretical concepts of situated learning may be of importance in these tasks. These concepts help to provide the intersubjective "we" that connects self and world in the trinity: "I – we – world."

These are not easy challenges. A benchmark for the level of difficulty involved is the many years that philosophers have been occupied with the relationship between experience and reflection. However, as challenges, they provide a suitable direction for further exploration, and many chances to expand our understanding.

References

Archer, M. (1995). *Realist social theory: The morphogenetic approach.* Cambridge, England: Cambridge University Press.

Aristotle. (1980). *The Nichomachean ethics.* Oxford, England: Oxford University Press.

Aristotle. (1995). *Politics* (E. Barker, Trans.). Oxford, England: Oxford University Press.

Barber, B. (1984). *Strong democracy: Participatory politics for a new age.* Los Angeles: University of California Press.

Beringer, A. (2000). In search of the sacred: A conceptual analysis of spirituality. *Journal of Experiential Education, 23*(3), 157-165.

Brown, J., Collins, A., & Duguid, P. (1989). Situated cognition and the culture of learning. *Educational Researcher, 18*(1), 32-42.

Carver, R. (1996). Theory for practice: A framework for thinking about experiential education. *Journal of Experiential Education, 19*(1), 8-13.

Chambers, S. (1995). Discourse and democratic practices. In S. White (Ed.), *The Cambridge companion to Habermas* (pp. 233-259). Cambridge, England: Cambridge University Press.

Crosby, A. (1981). A critical look: The philosophical foundations of experiential education. *Journal of Experiential Education, 4*(1), 9-15.

Csikszentmihalyi, M., & Rochberg-Halton, E. (1981). *The meaning of things: Domestic symbols and the self.* New York: Cambridge University Press.

Davis, B., Sumara, D., & Luce-Kapler, R. (2000). *Engaging minds: Learning and teaching in a complex world.* Mahwah, NJ: Lawrence Erlbaum Associates.

DeLay, R. (1996). Forming knowledge: Constructivist learning and experiential education. *Journal of Experiential Education, 19*(2), 76-81.

Dewey, J. (1916/1944). *Democracy and education: An introduction to the philosophy of education.* New York: The Free Press.

Dewey, J. (1938/1963). *Experience and education.* New York: Collier Books.

Engeström, Y. (1987). *Learning by expanding.* Helsinki, Finland: Orienta-Konsultit Oy.

Fosnot, C. T. (1996). Constructivism: A psychological theory of learning. In C. T. Fosnot (Ed.), *Constructivism: Theory, perspectives, and practice* (pp. 8-33). New York: Teachers College Press.

Freire, P. (1970). *Pedagogy of the oppressed*. London: Penguin.

Gair, N. (1997). *Outdoor education: Theory and practice.* London: Cassell.

Habermas, J. (1990). *Moral consciousness and communicative action* (C. Lenhardt, & S. W.Nicholson, Trans.). Cambridge, MA: MIT Press.

Haluza-Delay, R. (2000). Green fire and religious spirit. *Journal of Experiential Education, 23*(3), 143-149.

Haskell, J. (1999). Ecological journey: An enactive view of the nature of experience. *Journal of Experiential Education, 22*(3), 154-161.

Hay, K. (1996). Legitimate peripheral participation, instructionism, and constructivism: Whose situation is it anyway? In H. McLellan (Ed.), *Situated Learning Perspectives* (pp. 89-99). Englewood Cliffs, NJ: Englewood Technology.

Heidegger, M. (1953/1996). *Being and time* (J. Stambaugh, Trans.). Albany, NY: State University of New York Press. (Original work published 1927)

Heidegger, M. (1971). *Poetry, language, thought* (A. Hofstadter, Trans.). New York: Harper & Row.

Hutchison, D., & Bosacki, S. (2000). Over the edge: Can holistic education contribute to experiential education? *Journal of Experiential Education, 23*(3), 177-182.

Itin, C. (1999). Reasserting the philosophy of experiential education as a vehicle for change in the 21st century. *Journal of Experiential Education, 22*(2), 91-98.

Johnson, B. L., & Frederickson, L. M. (2000). "What's in a good life?" Searching for ethical wisdom in the wilderness. *Journal of Experiential Education, 23*(1), 43-50.

Joplin, L. (1981). On defining experiential education. *Journal of Experiential Education, 4*(1), 17-20.

Kolb, D. (1984). *Experiential education: Experience as the source of learning and development.* Englewood Cliffs, NJ: Prentice Hall.

Lave, J. (1993). The practice of learning. In S. Chaiklin, & J. Lave (Eds.), *Understanding practice: Perspectives on activity and context* (pp. 3-32). Cambridge, England: Cambridge University Press.

Lave, J., & Wenger, E. (1991). *Situated learning: Legitimate peripheral participation.* Cambridge, England: Cambridge University Press.

Lindsay, A., & Ewert, A. (1999). Learning at the edge: Can experiential education contribute to educational reform? *Journal of Experiential Education, 22*(1), 12-19.

Linehan, C., & McCarthy, J. (2000). Positioning in practice: Understanding participation in the social world. *Journal for the Theory of Social Behavior, 30*(4), 435-453.

Long, A. (2001). Learning the ropes: Exploring the meaning and value of experiential education for girls at risk. *Journal of Experiential Education, 24*(2), 100-108.

Merleau-Ponty, M. (1962). *Phenomenology of perception* (C. Smith, Trans.). London: Routledge. (Original work published 1945)

Merleau-Ponty, M. (1968). *The visible and the invisible* (A. Lingis, Trans.). Evanston, IL: Northwestern University Press. (Original work published 1964)

Priest, S. (1986). Redefining outdoor education: A matter of many relationships. *Journal of Environmental Education, 17*(3), 13-15.

Priest, S., & Gass, M. (1997). *Effective leadership in adventure programming*. Champaign, IL: Human Kinetics.

Röhrs, H. (1970). The educational thought of Kurt Hahn. In H. Röhrs (Ed.), *Kurt Hahn* (pp. 123-136). London: Routledge & Kegan Paul.

Schor, J. (1998). *The overspent American: Upscaling, downshifting, and the new consumer*. New York: Basic Books.

Singer, P. (1993). *How are we to live? Ethics in an age of self-interest*. Milsons Point, New South Wales, Australia: Random House Australia.

Smith, C., Strand, S., & Bunting, C. (2002). The influence of challenge course participation on moral and ethical reasoning. *Journal of Experiential Education, 25*(2), 278-280.

Tuan, Y. (1986). *The good life*. Madison, WI: University of Wisconsin Press.

Vygotsky, L. (1962). *Thought and language*. Cambridge, MA: MIT Press.

Vygotsky, L. (1978). *Mind in society: The development of higher psychological processes*. Cambridge, MA: Harvard University Press.

Vygotsky, L. (1981). The genesis of higher mental functions. In J. Wertsch (Ed.), *The concept of activity in Soviet psychology* (pp. 144-188). Armonk, NY: Sharpe.

Wenger, E. (1998). *Communities of practice: Learning, meaning and identity*. Cambridge, England: Cambridge University Press.

Forming Knowledge: Constructivist Learning & Experiential Education

▼ ▼ ▼

Randolph DeLay

The teens talked about why they did not make the top of the peak. It looked like it was going to storm, said one. That's the reason, others agreed. No way, said Ryan. "We knew weather might blow in and still we got up late." After further discussion the rest of the group agreed and suggested other contributing factors. The discussion then turned to taking responsibility and not blaming outside things. Janene said that was like when she blames her mother for when she gets grounded.

The participants in this example are engaging in reflection upon their experience. In the process, they are making new connections between their present and prior experiences, generalizing and applying principles from one context to other contexts. The participants are constructing knowledge.

Simmons (1995) equates experiential education and constructivist learning theories yet gives only a cursory explanation. Like me, many experiential educators, especially in the environmental and adventure education fields, may have little or no background in the study of pedagogy. I was trained as a wildlife biologist and recreation leader. It was an easy slide

This chapter originally was published in the *Journal of Experiential Education*, with the following citation:

DeLay, R. (1996). Forming knowledge: Constructivist learning and experiential education. *Journal of Experiential Education, 19*(2), 76–81.

into outdoor education—that fascinating field astride multiple worlds. I have now spent a decade teaching/leading adventure and environmental programs; it is from this context that I will share examples. Although I believe that many experiential educators do not have formal training in education, I also feel our field is particularly adept at accessing practitioners' common-sense knowledge.

In this paper, after a brief critique of behaviorist pedagogical assumptions, I want to present constructivist learning theory as a framework for understanding experiential education. I hope to walk a line between being a practitioner and trying to explain academic theories that I am finding useful in developing my pedagogical practice. Constructivist learning theories present an epistemological foundation for what practitioners understand is occurring in experiential education.

A Brief Critique of the Predominant Approach

The "program" of a wilderness trip and most types of experiential education is a form of curriculum. According to Goodson (1990) the prevailing ideology among many curriculum thinkers, planners, and researchers is "curriculum as prescription." It develops from a belief that every ingredient of a course of study can be defined and the appropriate parts taught in a uniform, systematic sequence. This rather deterministic view tends to assume the teacher (program leader) as the giver of knowledge and the students (participants) as the passive recipients of a common knowledge set.

While all schools of learning theory would suggest that behavior changes through learning, the issue is who is the agent in the learning? A common assumption is the behaviorist notion that students learn because teachers teach, or that the program did something to the person. As one trip participant once told me, "It's like you're trying to open my head and pour in your stuff." Most experiential educators would roundly deny a behaviorist orientation. Yet elements of this stance may be evident in the way many programs are organized or how program leaders describe the expected program outcomes.

Behaviorism has dominated curriculum development and research (Goodson, 1990; Robottom & Hart, 1995). Simmons (1995, p. 124) writes that behaviorism "views education as a matter of applying appropriate external methods and techniques (as stimuli) to evoke the appropriate response: e.g., socially acceptable behavior, recall of information, skill acquisition, etc." Robertson (1994), focusing on environmental education, criticizes the emphasis of research in that field as deterministic, assuming that a "treatment" will effect change and ignoring the learner's prior knowledge, experiences, and cognitive processing of the content. The same criticisms could apply to research in experiential education.

As a practitioner I find much of the published research in environmental and adventure education of limited usefulness for many of the same reasons cited above. The problem boils down to basic assumptions about the nature of human beings and the way we know and learn; most of the research is founded on a different epistemology than that from which I instruct. As Robottom and Hart (1995) criticize, the effort to set rigorous and statistically significant research designs bounds a holistic experience into concrete, but isolated, dimensions, despite the fact that they are not fragmented in everyday life. The research loses much of its practicality for a practitioner and helps little in understanding how the individual is experiencing the program and forming the base of knowledge with which to make present and later decisions. Studies that view experiential programs like a medical 'treatment' ignore the learner's role and make her or him a passive recipient of program delivery. Constructivist learning theory may provide a more grounded epistemological framework for studying the processes of experiential learning.

Constructivist Learning Theory

In contrast to behaviorist models of learning and teaching, constructivist learning theories squarely place the action of learning with the learner. In the example at the beginning of this article, the experience was used by the participants to learn something. Many a lesson could have been drawn from that experience, and undoubtedly different members of the group drew different meaning from the experience. Constructivists contend that participants work to make meaning out of their experience, adapting and altering the educative event to fit past versions of their worldview and that this process should be important in educational research (Von Glaserfeld, 1995). "Consider that although any view of education will point to something that changes as a consequence of an educative event, behaviorist and classical views take the product as evidence of the process" (Robertson, 1994 p. 22).

Knapp (1992, p. 49) points out two foundational beliefs of experiential education: "1) that learning is not limited to the classroom and, 2) that helping students make meaning is what learning is all about." Experiential education is based on the assumption that people learn from experience. While this may seem self-evident, not all experience is educative. As most practitioners will attest, the how of actively teaching so that learning comes from learner experience is a difficult maneuver.

A leading proponent of the stance known as "radical constructivism," Von Glaserfeld (1991, 1995) suggests knowledge is not a precise representation of the world. Instead, knowledge is a construction erected by the individual to "fit" with his or her experience of the world. Two people will understand their experience of an event, and the event itself, in different ways. As a simple example, one person may understand dusk as the absence of light, another as an increase in darkness. The one may conceive dusk as something s/he cannot see in and insist a flashlight is necessary, while another may suggest dusk is not so bad and respond by adjusting his/her expectations to see objects in sharp detail. Darkness is interpreted differently by those who grow up with electric lights or in the night-as-dangerous city streets.

Constructs are ways in which individuals and groups organize experience into categories (Robertson, 1994). The shaping of knowledge is a process of construction. Learning, in the constructivist view, is like a builder remodeling a house. New experience is the raw material and is added to the old experience; the learner is the carpenter. Behaviorist teaching, to utilize a similar metaphor, would be like trying to plop a fully formed building into the individual. Even if that were possible, how could the person ever meaningfully connect that edifice with any other discombobulated pieces of knowledge s/he possesses? Like "Jeopardy," the game show, the pieces of knowledge would be disassociated and meaningless.

Von Glaserfeld (1995) attributes the philosophical roots of constructivism to skepticism: There is no certain knowledge of the real world because, as part of this world, we can never get outside it to see if what we think we know is actually empirical reality. Kant resolved this impasse by supposing that order is imposed in the mind. In the process of perceiving the world, the mind categorizes and organizes. Radical constructivists reject the idea that knowledge is an exact representation of a world as it exists prior to being experienced by the person. There may be an independent reality out there, but we only know the way we see and feel and understand and perceive. Von Glaserfeld (1991, p. 17) explains this perspective: "I have never said there is no [ontological] world, only that I can't know it." To oversimplify, ontology is the branch of philosophy that deals with being or the nature of reality. Epistemology is the study of the origin, methods, nature, and limits of knowledge and learning. Constructivism, as a way of knowing the world, blurs the epistemology-ontology distinction.

In my mind, Von Glaserfeld's comment makes the radical constructivist view palatable. For an individual (or a society), the construction proves its worth by how well it "fits" experience. For Von Glaserfeld (1991, p. 20), constructivism must go beyond the "mere proclamation that the world we experience is a world we construct" and show how it is useful or works in managing our lives. It should be understood that interpretation of experience is influenced by social constructions and personal interpretation. Therefore, the knowledge developed from their experience by individuals will always be directed in certain ways and should not be taken as "the way things always are." The risk is real, for example, for a nervous participant top-roped on an indoor climbing wall.

The constructivist position, summarized (Millar, 1989, p. 589), holds "that the process of eliciting, clarification, and construction of new ideas takes place internally, within the learner's own head." Pedagogically speaking, then, students learn not because teachers teach (the "open head, insert knowledge" assumption), but because they have taken prior knowledge and reworked it in light of new information and experience. These are the twin processes of *assimilation* and *accommodation* as described by Piaget. The first process is new experience incorporated into prior knowledge; the latter term refers to new experience that fundamentally alters prior knowledge (Robertson, 1994). Piagetian theory asserts that direct experience gives meaning and form to the process of learning (Ausubel, 1978). Construction of knowledge is not a process abstracted from prior experience of the individual. To talk about "nature," for example, individuals need an experience of nature. Their knowledge will differ if that experience is through the television, the grass springing through the sidewalk cracks, or a pristine wilderness.

Von Glaserfeld terms his approach "radical constructivism" to differentiate it from "naïve," or "trivial" constructivism. This latter approach is perhaps best represented in the science education field and focuses on "misconceptions" (i.e., Lisowski & Disinger, 1991). It is founded on the assumption that the learner may be mistaken in his/her formation of new knowledge (say, the law of gravity) and needs to learn the "right" concept. Thus, trivial constructivism posits a singular construction that fits reality. Trivial constructivism, while recognizing the agency of the learner in forming knowledge, still postulates an external reality knowable by all individuals in the same way. For example, an experiential educator may assume every participant faced and dealt with challenge on a peak ascent or in the conflicts of group living. Yet participants may deny that it was a challenge. Radical constructivism recognizes the genuinely different experiences the participants have even in the same event, and the different knowledge they form from the experience.

It is for such reasons that I asserted above that many experiential programs have a latent behavioralism embedded in the program or teaching styles. Consider the following example from the literature. Miles (1991) asserts that adventure-based wilderness programming begins in an "encounter" of place or activity and should help people understand the meaning or significance of nature to the individual and broader society. But to do this most effectively, adventure leaders must plan accordingly:

> The outdoor educator must place the wilderness experience in context for students, prepare them for their encounter with nature and then transfer the lessons learned in that encounter back to the students' home environment... Such effort (is required) if the outdoor experience is to be more than a pleasant interlude from the rigors of the classroom [or everyday life] (Miles, 1991, p. 7).

While Miles portrays the necessary steps to assure some transfer of learning, notice who is doing the work in the above quote: the teacher teaches so that the student goes away changed? A wilderness leader who assumes everyone should encounter nature the same way (never mind probably holding different constructions of "nature") would be something other than a constructivist.

Robertson (1994, p. 25) summarizes, "To learn meaningfully, individuals [must choose to] relate new knowledge to relevant concepts and propositions that they already know."

Experiential programs need to take account of the prior history of the participant. Lack of contextualizing hinders participant growth and learning. The learner's own knowledge and prior experience are the most important ingredient in new knowledge construction and must be respected (Ausubel, 1978). In effective education the student takes ultimate responsibility for his or her own learning; the teacher's role is as facilitator—to assist engagement with prior experience in order to assimilate or accommodate. On the other hand, this also assumes that the learner is self-consciously aware of their knowledge already held.

The Social Context of Knowledge

Construction of knowledge is ·also situated within an historical and cultural context—the social world in which the individual participates. The process of knowledge construction is a combination of the influence of social structures and individual role. "Living in a similar culture, we come to share constructs with others in our group, although the implications of these constructs may not be identical" (Bannister and Fransella, 1980, p. 105–106). These social constructions are often unexamined by the individual, what Berger and Luckmann (1966) call "taken-for-granted knowledge." Schutz (1973, p. 45) notes that such knowledge is often "incoherent, only partially clear and not at all free from contradiction." Awareness of this condition indicates the difficulty that will occur in attempting to investigate these constructs. Still, both students and teachers should probe the understandings of a phenomenon. As Robertson (1994, p. 27) explains, "teachers, so that they might better relate to each student's understandings, and students, that they might take a more active role in engaging their own understandings."

For example, in my own research, I found that months after a wilderness trip experience the teen participants were conceptualizing nature and the natural world in ways counterproductive to caring for their home environment (DeLay, 1996). Not surprisingly, they conceived of nature as a place undisturbed, unfamiliar, "out there," with few or no people, and without human-made things. Therefore, in these teens' minds there was no nature at home and therefore no real reason to care for the environment outside the wilderness. In addition, the teens with the most wilderness-tripping experience were the most emphatic to suggest there was no "nature" to be found at home. The upshot of this research was to remind me as an instructor to investigate my student's conceptions in order to help them connect outdoor program experiences meaningfully with their home experience.

Education for Social Change

To function as a group in the wilderness and to decide what camping practices to use requires making choices about constructed knowledge and values. Some critics argue that constructivism is relativistic. The argument typically runs thus: constructivism, rebelling against the notion that "the way things are" is objectively observable without bias on the observer's part, has emphasized the multiplicity of realities. This becomes "accept *any* perspective."

Ravn (1991) notes that constructivism can be liberating in that if reality is not fixed then present circumstances can be changed. "The point that social institutions are the constructions of a community of human agents implies that those same human beings possess the power to radically change those institutions" (p. 97). But Ravn also criticizes constructivist writing as relativist—there is rarely an attempt to draw a line in the spectrum of acceptable constructions. The consequences of such relativism are frightening. Consider such disconcerting examples as female circumcision/mutilation, and the moral outrage of the Holocaust, which some now say did not occur. In a completely relativist argument, both views must be acceptable. Whose perspective is right? Everyone's? Only mine?

The important question in this discussion is how to choose among alternative constructions. Von Glaserfeld (1991) believes that individual conceptual schemes will be reinforced or eliminated through social interaction—whether the knowledge fits experiential reality, including that of the social group. This is similar to the Piagetian notion of adaptation wherein constructions evolve in their environment and the ones that persist are those naturally selected by their fitness. However, this evolution of the common social stock of knowledge seems to ignore the intentional moral agency of human beings. Von Glaserfeld does modify his position somewhat. For him, ethics are the option to change our construction when we don't like what we have created.

Ravn's (1991) solution to the dilemma of choosing among alternative constructions is to tolerate ideas and roles in proportion to their closeness to an optimal condition. Ravn suggests the optimal condition is when "people feel part of the larger whole as well encouraged to accept others pursuing their own paths in experiencing this larger wholeness" (p. 103). Rather than a singular construction of reality, a range of constructions in a similar direction is appropriate; "unity in diversity," Ravn concludes.

According to Fay (1986), the way out of this impasse of how to choose among constructions is to analyze the context in which the construction was formed. Education, as a pre-eminent social institution, is traditionally a transmitter and maintainer of culture. According to critical theorists such as Fay, society is structured in certain ways that are oppressive. An individual needs to understand how s/he is oppressed before choices can be well-made. Not all constructions are equally valuable or beneficial. Education that incorporates a critical analysis, although still accepting the notion that knowledge is constructed by the learners, could serve to liberate people from social constraints that hinder them from living full and satisfying lives (Fay, 1986; Robottom and Hart, 1995).

In the end, we need to make choices based on our understandings. Whether or not there are absolutes is irrelevant since we cannot get outside our interpreted experience.

Yet if there is always a twinge of doubt in knowing that one "knows," the door remains open to listening to others, negotiating shared understandings and, presumably, forming knowledge constructions that work better. Experiential programs do this, for example, when leaders allow the group to develop ways of interaction, then leaders allow the group to develop ways of interaction, then facilitate community meetings to refine or reform these group norms. Because participants have only experienced a limited spectrum of opportunities, the leader's responsibility is to help with appropriate knowledge formation and decision-making by sharing of the leader's own experience. In this context, the leader's beliefs on group living or minimum impact camping, for example, are not universal absolutes but his or her construction of the optimal life.

Constructivism in Experiential Practice

Some problems with the constructivist approach exist. First, the "trivialness" of some constructivist writing has been mentioned. An emphasis on the "right" conceptions would still place the experiential educator in the role of convincing people of what they should have gotten from a particular experience. Second, educational structures and political exigencies may have difficulty understanding pedagogical practices founded on radical constructivist understandings of learning. Experiential practitioners face this difficulty regularly.

Third, Von Glaserfeld's description of radical constructivism strongly emphasizes rational processes as the way of knowing and learning. The focus is on thinking and the mind is objictified instead of embodied. This is a serious weakness, and may reflect our societal emphases on rationalism and empiricism. Experiential educators understand that participants rely heavily on feelings and sensations in the learning process. Experiential education has been called "emotionally engaged learning" (Proudman, 1991). A sense of connection or closeness to something, a place of fatigue and dampness, the stress of a challenge are all part of the way in which participants may "know" nature (DeLay, 1996). Constructivist teaching should beware the trap of privileging the rational as that may lead to "head knowledge" rather than knowledge meaningful in action. For example, knowing objectively about pollution is not as impactful as seeing it; litter often makes an impact on wilderness trip participants, even though it is often ecologically inconsequential.

Finally, individuals can also learn unconsciously. If learning occurs unconsciously, it implies that the learner does not always choose how the construction of new knowledge will occur, which is a major tenet of the constructivist approach (Robertson, 1993; Von Glaserfeld, 1995). It also lays responsibility more heavily on the leader to facilitate experience so that the learner will not develop unintended messages (e.g., the mountain is to be conquered or not making the summit is a personal failure).

So how does a teacher use experience to promote educational outcomes? An immediate note of caution comes to mind. Experiential education is not a series of activities done to a learner. Nor should simulations and games supplant experience of "the real thing." Learning is a process. Teachers must recognize they do not have ultimate control over the outcome. The learner is actively engaged in his or her knowledge construction. In giving up the illusion of control, teachers are actually better able to help learners understand the best present theories in a subject (especially given the rapid propagation of knowledge), and develop the flexibility of higher order thinking and knowledge construction (Von Glaserfeld, 1995). As many experiential educators insist, education should help people learn how to learn and to think on their own.

Constructivist learning theories suggest that the learner is the active agent in his or her knowledge formation. This re-emphasizes the importance of reflection during and after an experience in order for participants to see relevance and form connections between this experience and their broader lifeworld. It also suggests that participants should be alerted beforehand to the possibility of learning something that applies to different contexts. Participants who expect to learn something about, say, facing fears, are more likely to get something from their ropes course experience.

In conclusion, process is not all. Content does matter. Something will be taught and learned. Individuals do not simply experience, they experience something. Therefore, experiential educators have an obligation to help participants consider the world through which they travel. Von Glaserfeld (1995) asserts that teachers have a role in guiding, and even "constraining," the possible knowledge constructions. The ethics of this guidance must, of course, be considered carefully. But constructivism should not be seen as justifying acceptance of all potential constructions with equal valuation. Leaders must also carefully probe their own knowledge and the intent of the program elements as participants experience them. But in the end, under a constructivist epistemology, it is understood that programs do not change people; participants do the changing. In the example at the beginning of this article, rather than the peak teaching the participants, the participants used the peak climb to learn something.

Constructivism, as a theory of learning or knowing seems to have considerable practicality for experiential educators. Understanding how people develop their specific conceptualizations would logically have important ramifications to educators. It also provides a theoretical justification for experiential pedagogy. Since the processes are internal, it is at this point that teaching moves out of the purview of the technician and becomes an art form; the educator strives to deal with the uncertainty of another's mental workings and help the learner develop conceptions that fit and form their experiential reality.

References

Ausubel, D.P. (1978). *Educational psychology: A cognitive view.* New York: Holt, Rinehart and Winston.

Bannister, D. & Fransella, F. (1980). *Inquiring man: The psychology of personal constructs.* New York: Penquin Books.

Berger, P. L. & Luckmann, T. (1966). *The social construction of reality.* Toronto: Doubleday.

Delay, A. B. (1996). Constructing the uninhabited home: Participants' experience of nature during and following a wilderness trip. Unpublished Master's thesis. University of Alberta, Edmonton, Alberta.

Fay, B. (1986). How people change themselves: The relationship between critical theory and its audience. In W. J. Smyth (Ed.), *Reflection in Action* (pp. 55–92). Victoria, Australia: Deakin University Press.

Goodson, I. F. (1990) Studying curriculum: Towards a social constructivist perspective. *Journal of Curriculum Studies, 22*(4), 299–312.

Knapp, C. E. (1992). *Lasting lessons: A teacher's guide to reflecting on experience.* Charleston, WV: ERIC.

Lisowski, M. & Disinger, J. F. (1991). The effect of field-based instruction on student understanding of ecological concepts. *Journal of Environmental Education, 23*(1), 19–23.

Miles, J. (1991). Teaching in wilderness. *Journal of Environmental Education, 22*(4), 5–9.

Millar, R. (1989). Constructive criticisms. *International Journal of Science Education, 11*, 587–596.

Proudman, B. (1992). Experiential education as emotionally-engaged learning. *Journal of Experiential Education, 15*(2),19–23

Ravn, I. (1991). What should guide reality construction? In F. Steier (Ed.). *Research and reflexivity* (pp. 96–109). Newbury Park, CA: Sage.

Robottom, I. & Hart, P. (1995). Behaviourist EE research: Environmentalism as individualism. *Journal of Environmental Education, 26*(2), 5–9.

Robertson, A. (1994). Toward constructivist research in environmental education. *Journal of Environmental Education 25*(2), 21–31.

Schutz, A. (1973). *Collected papers 1: The problem of social reality.* The Hague: Nijhoff.

Simmons, S. (1995). The teacher education consortium: A new network for professional development in experiential education. *Journal of Experiential Education, 18*(3),120–127.

Von Glaserfeld, E. (1991). Knowing without metaphysics: Aspects of the radical constructivist position. In F. Steier (Ed.), *Research and Reflexivity* (pp. 12–29). Newbury Park, CA: Sage Publications.

Von Glaserfeld, E. (1995). *Radical constructivism: A way of knowing and learning.* Bristol, UK: Falmer Press.

Dewey's Philosophical Method & Its Influence on His Philosophy of Education

▼ ▼ ▼

Jasper S. Hunt, Jr.

The thesis of this paper is that John Dewey developed a philosophical method and that his philosophy of education presupposes this method. I want to show that: given his way of doing philosophy, it would have been impossible for Dewey to have espoused any other philosophy of education than the one he developed.

The paper will proceed by first outlining Dewey's method of philosophy. This will be done by focusing in on two fundamental ideas of his entire philosophy. These are Dewey's attack on any form of philosophical dualism and his category of experience. The final section of the paper will show how Dewey's philosophy of education comes directly from his basic philosophical method.

Attack on Dualism

As a young graduate student of philosophy at Johns Hopkins University between 1882 and 1884, Dewey was confronted by a philosophical corpus that seemed to draw its very lifeblood from philosophical dualism.

This chapter originally was published in the *Journal of Experiential Education*, with the following citation:

Hunt, J. S., Jr. (1981). Dewey's philosophical method and its influence on his philosophy of education. *Journal of Experiential Education, 4*(1), 29–34.

In epistemology, the lines were drawn between the rationalists and the empiricists. On the American philosophical scene, this contrast was made evident to Dewey by the diverse views of Chauncy Wright and Charles Peirce. Although both Wright and Peirce were empirical in their methods, they reached different positions, with Wright maintaining a rigid empiricism and Peirce becoming, eventually, more of a rationalist. Dewey was also confronted by William James, who termed himself a radical empiricist but who sought at the same time to defend religious sources of knowledge.

In metaphysics, the battle lines were established between the materialists and the idealists. On the one hand, Dewey was confronted by the philosophy of Ralph Waldo Emerson, who explicitly advocated an idealistic view of metaphysics. Dewey was also familiar with the work of Auguste Comte and his resulting rejection of metaphysics and adoption of materialism. Dewey quotes Bertrand Russell as an example of the attempt to create dualisms in metaphysics. Russell says that mathematics "finds a habitation eternally standing, where our ideals are fully satisfied and our best hopes are not thwarted."[1]

It should be pointed out here that Dewey was himself a metaphysical idealist as a young man. Morton White points out that Dewey turned toward Hegelian idealism as a reaction against British empiricism.[2] Indeed, Paul Conkin says that "Dewey had learned to hate the atomistic sensationalism of British empiricism."[3] But Dewey's exposure to the scientific thought of Chauncy Wright and Charles Peirce led him away from the dominant influence of idealism.

The ultimate dualism Dewey fought was the separation of the human from the natural. Dewey saw this separation as having disastrous results both in epistemology and in metaphysics. In epistemology, it resulted in either an empirical skepticism, which said that all man could know truly was his own sensations, or else a rigid scientism, which said that all man could know was the phenomenal world.

In metaphysics, dualism resulted in either a denigration of the world of being, in favor of the world of becoming, or the opposite. Dewey's main concern was that these dualisms resulted in an ontological fragmentation, that is, a fragmentation of being, with negative results in practical affairs. Dewey refers to the opposites in metaphysics as either total objectivism or else total subjectivism. He was critical of both, as evidenced by the following quote:

> But philosophical dualism is but a formulated recognition of an impasse in life; an
>
> impotence in interaction, inability to make effective transition, limitation of power to

---

[1] John Dewey, *Experience and Nature* (LaSalle, 1925) p. 51. Henceforth referred to as E.N.

[2] Morton White, *Science and Sentiment in America: Philosophical Thought from Jonathan Edwards to John Dewey.* (New York, 1972) pp. 269–273.

[3] Paul K. Conkin, *Puritans and Pragmatists: Eight Eminent American Thinkers.* (Bloomington, 1968) p. 350.

regulate and thereby to understand. Capricious pragmatism based on exaltation of personal desire; consolatory estheticism based on capacity for wringing contemplative enjoyment from even the tragedies of the outward spectacle; refugee idealism based on rendering thought omnipotent in the degree in it is ineffective in concrete affairs; these forms of subjectivism register an acceptance of whatever obstacles at the time prevent the active participation of the self in the ongoing course of events.[4]

This quote shows the stress Dewey laid on the practically bad results of such philosophical dualism as subjectivism or objectivism. Indeed, dualism says Dewey renders man "impotent."

Dewey refers to philosophical dualism by means of a technical term. He calls the attempt to create dualisms both in epistemology and metaphysics the "fallacy of selective emphasis."[5] This fallacy consists in the efforts of philosophers to take a particular aspect of knowledge or reality and to universalize it to a superior status of reality or knowledge. Dewey illustrates the fallacy of selective emphasis by entering into the metaphysical conflict between being and becoming. Dewey refers to the "precarious" and "stable" aspects of existence.[6] He argues that ever since the days of Heraclitus and Parmenides metaphysics has tended to focus on either the world of the precarious or else of the stable at the expense of the reality of the other. Dewey rejects the idea that the world is either in a state of total flux or of total being. The fallacy of selective emphasis is also seen in epistemology by the old conflict between rational and empirical sources of knowledge. He refers to both epistemological systems as falling under the heading of the fallacy of selective emphasis.

The Category of Experience

Dewey was not content to simply criticize the prevailing tendency of philosophy to fall into the fallacy of selective emphasis and thereby create dualisms. Dewey saw his major philosophical task as dealing with this fundamental issue and hopefully solving it. Dewey does not attempt to solve the problems of dualism by entering into the old dialectical arguments directly. Indeed, he rejects the attempt to enter directly into the conflicts outlined above both in epistemology and in metaphysics. He says, "I know of no route by which dialectical argument can answer such objections. They arise from associations with words and cannot be dealt with argumentatively."[7]

---

[4] John Dewey, E.N. p. 198.

[5] John Dewey, E.N. p. 24.

[6] John Dewey, E.N. p. 37–66.

[7] John Dewey, E.N. p. 1.

Dewey's resolution to these problems rests in his analysis of experience. The word "experience" is a technical term for Dewey and contains within it the seeds of his entire philosophy. Evidence for this claim can be seen simply by reading the titles of three of his most influential works. These are *Art as Experience, Experience and Nature,* and *Experience and Education.*

It is with the category of experience that Dewey enters directly into the conflicts that he inherited philosophically. Dewey terms the method of basing philosophical inquiry upon experience as "empirical naturalism."[8] The empirical naturalist is attempting to make a bridge between the human and the natural, the rational and the empirical, and the material and the idealistic. Dewey wants empirical naturalism to render the old philosophical dualisms obsolete, rather than refute them directly. He simply abandons these terms and approaches philosophy from a new perspective-the perspective of experience.

It is at this point that a critical aspect of Dewey's philosophical method comes into play. In his analysis of experience as the base for philosophical method, Dewey distinguishes between two different but interconnected aspects of all experience. These are the "primary" and "secondary" parts of all experience. These two terms serve as the base by which Dewey later reconciles the dualisms in epistemology and metaphysics. They will also play a pivotal role in his philosophy of education.

Primary experience for Dewey refers to the immediate, tangible, and moving world that presents itself to the senses. Dewey refers to primary experience as "gross, macroscopic, crude."[9] When British empiricism refers to sensation as the basis for all knowledge, it is referring to the primary aspect of experience. Primary experience provides the raw materials from which knowledge can begin. When Dewey refers to his method as empirical naturalism, we see the primary aspect of experience at work. His method begins with the world of primary experience. It is explicitly empirical in its method in that it has as its starting point the world presented to the senses. But Dewey goes on to explain that primary experience is essentially "non cognitive."[10] Primary experience is the starting point in his method, but it is not the end point. It is not the stopping point because of its non-cognitive nature. Dewey does begin his entire method on the empirical immediacy presented to man.

Secondary experience (also called reflective experience) for Dewey refers to what happens after a primary experience is had. Reflective experience takes the "gross, macroscopic, and crude" materials furnished by primary experience and seeks to make them precise, microscopic, and refined. The work of reflective experience is to take the data provided by primary experience and order and arrange them. In effect, reflective experience is that part of

---

[8] John Dewey, E.N. p. 1.

[9] John Dewey, E.N. p. 6.

[10] John Dewey, E.N. p. 23.

all experience which temporarily removes itself from the immediacy of empiricism. Secondary experiences, says Dewey, *"explain* the primary objects, they enable us to grasp them with *understanding* instead of just having sense contact with them."[11]

Dewey illustrates the distinction between primary and secondary experience by looking at the work of the modern scientist. The scientist does not have a series of disconnected sensory experiences. He does not sit and stare steadily at his instruments. In short, the scientist does not rest content with primary experience. The scientist takes the data derived from primary experience and reflects upon them. He removes himself from the immediacy of primary experience and reflects upon the information conveyed by the primary experience. The ultimate goal of the secondary experience in science is to take the data and reflect upon them such a way as to be able to make predictive statements about future experiences in the form of the hypothesis.

The category of experience in empirical naturalism seeks to unite the primary and the secondary into a single unity. As Dewey says:

> What empirical method expects of philosophy is two things: First, that refined methods and products be traced back to their origins in primary experience, in all of its heterogeneity and fullness; so that the needs and problems out of which they arise and which they have to satisfy be acknowledged. Secondly, that the secondary methods and conclusions be brought back to the things of ordinary experience, all of their coarseness and crudity, for verification.[12]

In the opening section of this paper, I argued that the foundation of Dewey's method rested upon his rejection of philosophical dualism and his adaptation of experience as the base for empirical naturalism. I also pointed out that this method had implications both in epistemology and in metaphysics. In epistemology, I contrasted the positions of Chauncy Wright and Charles Peirce as immediate precursors of Dewey. Extrapolating from Dewey, we can see how both the fallacy of selective emphasis and the category of experience attempt an answer to the empiricism-versus-rationalism dialectic. In the primary aspect of experience, we see Dewey adopting empiricism and its method of basing knowledge on the senses and on the data provided by the senses. In the idea of reflective experience, we see Dewey making room for the method of rationalism. The fallacy of selective emphasis refuses to focus exclusively upon the primary aspect of knowledge. It also refuses to focus exclusively upon the reflective, or rational, nature of knowledge. In short, by beginning from experience in the first

---

[11] John Dewey, E.N. p. 7.

[12] John Dewey, E.N. p. 23.

place, Dewey avoids the dualisms, while at the same time allowing for the combined roles of empirical and rational knowledge.

There are obvious metaphysical implications in Dewey's epistemological method. I contrasted Ralph Waldo Emerson with Auguste Comte as representing idealism and materialism in the opening section of this paper. Dewey refers to metaphysics "as a statement of the generic traits manifested by existence of all kinds without regard to their differentiation into physicaland mental."[13] Later, Dewey also says of metaphysics that "Qualitative individuality and constant relations, contingency and need, movement and arrest are common traits of all existence."[14] The point to be gained here is that metaphysics for Dewey is *not* an attempt to discover some aspect of being, either materialistic or idealistic, and then elevate that aspect to a status of the really real at the expense of the other aspects of reality. Dewey sides neither with Emerson nor with Comte in this matter. Rather, his answer to the really real question rests in his notion of the "generic traits manifested by existence" lying *within* experience. Again, the fallacy of selective emphasis comes into play and saves Dewey from metaphysical dualism. By beginning from experience as the basis for metaphysics, Dewey allows for the reality of both the material and the ideal as "generic" traits within experience. What is ultimately real for Dewey is experience.

Philosophy of Education

Richard Bernstein has argued that the heart of Dewey's philosophical endeavor is to be found in his philosophy of education. Bernstein says that according to Dewey, "All philosophy can be conceived of as the philosophy of education."[15] In keeping with the thesis of this paper, that Dewey's philosophy of education presupposes his philosophical method, outlined above, I want to show how the method gives rise to his educational position.

Dewey's attack on dualism in philosophy in general can be seen clearly in his philosophy of education. The opening two sentences in *Experience and Education* make this evident: "Mankind likes to think in terms of extreme opposites. It is given to formulating its beliefs in terms of Either-Ors, between which it recognizes no intermediate possibilities."[16] Dewey connects the epistemological dualism of empiricism and rationalism to educational problems. He says:

---

[13] John Dewey, E.N. p. 334.

[14] John Dewey, E.N. p. 334.

[15] Richard Bernstein, *John Dewey* in *Encyclopedia of Philosophy* (New York, 1967) pp. 383–384, Vol 2

[16] John Dewey, *Experience and Education* (New York, 1938) p. 17. Henceforth referred to as E.E.

Upon the philosophical side, these various dualisms culminate in a sharp demarcation of individual minds from the world, and hence from one another. While the connection of this philosophical position with educational procedure is not so obvious as is that of the points considered in the last three chapters, there are certain educational considerations which correspond to it.[17]

On the one hand Dewey was confronted by an educational philosophy that emphasized a purely rationalistic approach to learning. This school maintained that the main goal of education was to inculcate into students the received ideas and facts of the past.[18] This method of education laid great stress on the ability of the student to sit passively and to commit ideas to memory. It tended to devalue initiative and reward obedience and docility. Dewey contends that a philosophy of education that is based upon a purely rationalistic epistemology necessarily presupposes a separation of the mind from the external world. This method saw the goal of education as purely cognitive and not connected or involved with the environment in which mind existed.[19] Methodologically, we see the rationalistic school of education taking the secondary, or reflective, aspect of experience and elevating it to an idolatrous position. That is, reflective experience was pursued in and for itself at the expense of primary, or empirical experience.

We can see that the opposite educational philosophy drawing from Dewey's method would be to elevate the primary aspect of experience to the sole end of education. This would involve taking the purely empirical element in experience and neglecting the reflective element. One of the most common criticisms of the so-called "progressive" education derived from Dewey, was, and is, that in reacting against the rationalistic elements so dominant in education, the progressives neglected the role of the reflective. Dewey himself explicitly rejects any idea that education should swing from a purely reflective, rationalistic position to a purely empirical, nonreflective mode.[20] Here he is being consistent with his fallacy of selective emphasis in avoiding creating any dualism in his reaction to the educational system he inherited.

Dewey's answer to educational dualism is drawn directly from his philosophical method. Just as metaphysics and epistemology must begin from experience rather than from

---

[17] John Dewey, *Democracy and Education* (New York, 1926) p. 340. Henceforth referred to as D.E.

[18] John Dewey, E.E. p. 17.

[19] John Dewey, D.E. p. 377.

[20] John Dewey, R.E. pp. 20–21.

dialectical bifurcations, so too must education begin from experience. Dewey rejects any idea that education must be completely based upon primary experience or upon secondary experience. Education, according to Dewey, must be based upon experience, period, which involves both the primary and the secondary. In describing the central role of experience in education, Dewey says:

> For one has only to call to mind what is sometimes treated in schools as acquisition of knowledge to realize how lacking it is in any fruitful connection with the ongoing experience of the students—how largely it seems to be believed that the mere appropriation of subject matter which happens to be in books contains knowledge. No matter how true what is learned to those who found it out and in whose experience it functioned, there is nothing which makes it knowledge to the pupils. It might as well be something about Mars or about some fanciful country unless it fructifies in the individual's own life.[21]

Dewey's rejection of philosophical dualism and his adaptation of experience as the basis of education give rise to a central idea in his philosophy of education—the idea of the experiential continuum. Dewey argues that the opposite of dualism is continuity. The educational dualisms that Dewey rejects include such things as the separation of mind and body, authority and freedom, experience and knowledge, and dozens of others. Dewey criticizes all of these dualities because they result in a lack of continuity within experience. By his idea of the experiential continuum within educational experience, Dewey hopes to stop duality before it ever gets started.

Dewey illustrates the need for an experiential continuum in education by contrasting the ideas of authority and freedom in education. The old educational methods that Dewey inherited put almost complete stress upon authority in education. This stress upon authority in education stemmed directly from the presuppositions of rationalism. That is, the student was to learn the ideas of the past that the teacher deemed important. This stress upon authority created a basic schizophrenia in education in a society that claimed to value freedom, democracy, self-direction, and personal responsibility. Dewey argues that the result was that the actual experience of the student under the yoke of education was in no way similar to the basic values espoused by the surrounding culture. Therefore, there was no continuity in the experience of the pupil. What was expected in school was docility, passiveness, and submission to authority. What was expected in the "real world" was aggressiveness, self-initiative, and a democratic response to authority.[22] Dewey argues that the ultimate goal of education

---

[21] John Dewey, D.E. p. 389.

[22] John Dewey, D.E. pp. 95–116.

is to make an experiential continuum where the *process* of education, that is *how* a student learns, is given equal footing with the *content* of education.[23]

Dewey wants to take the primary and reflective aspects of all experience and apply them to education. Dewey does not downplay the important role of subject matter, or reflective experience, in education (as superficial critics have claimed). He does want to get away from the obsessive preoccupation of traditional education with secondary experience. Just as Dewey looks to the work of the modern scientist as an example of his basic philosophical method, so too does he look at the education of the scientist as an example for his views on education. Dewey argues that the old methods of education are incompatible with the education of a good experimental scientist. For Dewey sees the good scientist as having cultivated a keen ability at questioning the world around him, rather than simply committing it to memory. I argued in the philosophical method section of this paper that the ultimate goal of knowledge for the scientist was the formulation of the hypothesis as predictive of future experiences. It can be seen here, drawing from the basic method, that education must stress other ideals than the old methods did in order to produce a good scientist. These ideals must include freedom, inquisitiveness, and experiential continuity, as well as the received materials from the past.

Summary and Conclusion

The goal of this paper was to outline Dewey's basic philosophical method, and then to connect it with his philosophy of education. The basic philosophical method was outlined, starting with Dewey's rejection of metaphysical and epistemological dualism and his adaptation of experience as the starting point for all philosophy. Two other technical terms in Dewey were introduced—the fallacy of selective emphasis, and the primary and secondary aspects of experience. The paper then connected Dewey's philosophy of education with his basic philosophical method. This was done by showing Dewey's rejection of traditional education's obsession with the secondary aspect of experience and the resulting stress upon docility and passivity in the educational process. Dewey's discussion of freedom versus authority in education was used to illustrate the effects of dualism in education. Finally, the important role of Dewey's idea of continuity in education was illustrated using both the freedom/authority example and the training of the experimental scientist.

In conclusion, I want to argue that Dewey offers a coherent and sensible pedagogical theory. I will argue that Dewey's educational philosophy is as relevant today as it was in 1920. Dewey offers a source of inspiration to future and present educators who are confronted by timid and reactionary educators screaming for "back to the basics" and the elevation of a

---

[23] John Dewey, E.E. p. 20.

rationalistic principle of education to a supreme status. Dewey also offers a strong warning to those who, in their zeal for reform, would neglect the role of content in the educational process. One only need look at some products of innovative education who are very much "in touch with their feelings," but who cannot write a coherent sentence.

Dewey demands of professional philosophy the highest standards of the application of his theory. For those of us in the field of educational philosophy, Dewey reminds us that philosophy is not an isolated discipline, disconnected from the issues of everyday life. I am here reminded of the modern professor of ethics who is an expert at doing ethical analysis using modal operators, but who is rendered speechless when asked by a pregnant student if it would be ethical for her to seek an abortion. He is also warning us about the other modern ethics professor who spends long hours in the demonstration picket lines in support of a cause, but who is scared to death when confronted by convincing arguments that he may be less than totally right in his convictions.

In short, Dewey is demanding that philosophers and educators begin and end their work from the category of experience. As Dewey himself said:

> I remarked incidentally that the philosophy in question is, to paraphrase the saying of Lincoln about democracy, one of education of, by, and for experience. Not one of these words, *of, by* or *for*, names anything which is self-evident. Each of them is a challenge to discover and put into operation a principle or order and organization which follows from understanding what educational experience signifies.[24]

---

[24] John Dewey, E.E. p. 29.

References

Brodsky, G. M. (1976). Recent philosophical work on Dewey. *The Southern Journal of Philosophy.*

Brodsky, G. M. (1978) Dewey's enduring vitality. *Human Studies.*

Conkin, P. K. (1968) *Puritans and pragmatists: Eight eminent American thinkers.* Bloomington, IN: Indiana University Press.

Dewey, J. (1926). *Democracy and education.* New York: Macmillan.

Dewey, J. (1929). *Experience and nature.* Lasalle: The Open Court Publishing Co.

Dewey, J. (1934). *Art as experience.* New York: G. P. Putnam.

Dewey, J. (1938). *Experience and education.* New York: Collier.

Edwards, P. (Ed.). (1967). *The encyclopedia of philosophy.* New York: Macmillan. White, M. (1972). *Science and sentiment in America: Philosophical thought from Jonathan*

Edwards to John Dewey. New York: Oxford University Press. White, M. (1973). *Pragmatism and the American mind.* New York: Oxford University Press.

Psychological & Educational Foundations

▼ ▼ ▼

Beyond Learning by Doing: Brain-Based Learning & Experiential Education

▾ ▾ ▾

Jay W. Roberts

In recent years, experiential education initiatives have made many in-roads with the mainstream educational establishment. The success of programs such as Project Adventure and Expeditionary Learning Outward Bound, as well as the proven effectiveness of place-based education initiatives within schools, has been well documented. Additionally, ropes courses, and environmental and outdoor education programs have become prevalent in many school districts across the country. Yet, with all these advances, many barriers still exist between experiential pedagogy and traditional schooling. It remains literally, and figuratively, "outside" the educational establishment. Recent initiatives toward accountability and standards have placed experiential education in the crosshairs of reform-minded politicians and school consultants. "Learning by doing" is often described as process-heavy, devoid of content, and a holdout from 1960s progressivist approaches. E.D. Hirsch, a well-regarded voice in educational theory and practice, has gone so far as to say that the "recent history of American education and controlled observations have shown that learning by doing and its adaptations are among the least effective pedagogies available to the teacher" (Hirsch, 1996, p. 257).

The current position of the field within mainstream education places at a premium attempts to significantly broaden and deepen experiential pedagogy beyond mere "learning by doing." This article will explore the recent emergence of the field of "brain-based learning"

This chapter originally was published in the *Journal of Experiential Education*, with the following citation:

Roberts, J. W. (2002). Beyond learning by doing: The brain compatible approach. *Journal of Experiential Education, 25*(2), 281–285.

and discuss its possibilities and limitations to the field of experiential education. A brief history of the development of brain research in relationship to education will be outlined, followed by a discussion of the key principles of the field. Linkages between these principles and experiential education will be discussed, as will several suggested practical applications of the research. Finally, the benefits of aligning experiential education with brain-based learning will be explored.

The Emergence of Brain-Based Learning

In July of 1989, President George Bush declared the 1990s the "Decade of the Brain." What followed was a revolution in research, articles, books, and television specials on what we know about how the brain functions and learns. The cognitive research and medical advances in particular have been many and remarkable. It could be argued that we have learned more about the brain in the past ten years than the previous 100. Additionally, nearly 90 percent of all neuroscientists who have ever lived are alive today (Brandt & Wolfe, 1998).

While still relatively new as a field of inquiry, researchers have identified several findings from recent brain research of particular interest to educators:

- **Neuroplasticity.** The brain changes physiologically as a result of experience, and these changes happen much quicker than originally thought. The environment in which the brain operates determines to a large degree the functioning ability of the brain (Brandt & Wolfe, 1998).

- **The brain is complex and interconnected.** Just as a city or jazz quartet has many levels of interaction and connectedness, the brain has an infinite number of possible interconnections. In essence, there are no isolated, specialized areas; rather the brain is simultaneously processing a wide variety of information (Caine & Caine, 1994).

- **Every brain is unique.** Our brains are far more individualized in terms of physiology, neural wiring, biochemical balance, and developmental stage than previously thought (Jensen, 2000).

Each of these findings suggests the need for a reconsideration of the way we currently educate. Caution must also be practiced. Much of the current research is new, and steps from research to application are inherently complex and difficult. Already, several researchers have questioned the validity of educational applications of brain research (Bruer, 1997). If nothing else, the sheer volume of new information about how the brain functions and learns forces us to question what we truly "know" about learning and educational practice.

Principles of Brain-Based Learning

Drawing from the findings above, several intriguing principles and practical implications have emerged. The following principles are of particular interest to experiential educators, as they support some long-standing practices within experiential education and also push the envelope of what may be possible in the future.

Principle #1: Pattern and Meaning Making

Research supports the claim that the search for meaning is innate and occurs through patterning (Caine & Caine, 1994). Patterning refers to the meaningful organization and categorization of information (Nummela & Rosengren, 1986). In essence, the brain is designed to search for and integrate new information into existing structures and actively resists "meaningless" patterns (Caine & Caine, 1994). The process is constant and does not stop, regardless of whether or not we have stopped teaching. This principle reinforces many of the practices attributed to experiential learning, including emphasis on context and framing, learner involvement in the teaching of the material, alternating between details and big picture (whole/part), reflection components, and relevancy (i.e., relating information to students' previous experience and learning).

Suggested Application #1: Chunking can be an effective tool for presenting the learner with information in an organized, meaningful way. Look at the following list of letters: IBFVTNOJBLKFJ. Try to memorize them as presented. Now look at the next list of letters: JFK, LBJ, ON, TV, FBI. The second list is much easier to memorize even though it contains the same letters as the first list. They have simply been chunked and arranged in a meaningful way that draws on previous experience and information. Consider how you might chunk small activities (lessons or even directions) and large, multiday experiences. How can you arrange information in a more meaningful, patterned way?

Suggested Application #2: Use a "big picture." Remember that your students do not have the same view of the course, lesson, or program that you do. Provide them with a big picture as soon as possible at the beginning of the experience. Rather than an exhaustive outline or itinerary, the big picture gives your students a taste of what's coming and allows them to begin making patterns, connections, and frames for the experience. Revisit the big picture a few times throughout the experience to further solidify the link. In this regard, it is helpful to have it on a flip chart or other visual aid. Try using a "you are here" map with a movable arrow.

Principle #2: The Brain as a Parallel Processor

The human brain is the ultimate, multitasking machine, constantly doing many things at once. This is because the brain is geared toward survival and is, in actuality, poorly designed for linear, lock-step instruction (Jensen, 2000). Consider how you learned to ride a bicycle. Did you learn by reading a book or hearing a lecture on the separate topics of bike parts, safety, and operation? Not likely. It is more likely you learned through a more dynamic and complex series of experiences. Current research supports the notion that the brain learns best through rich, complex, and multisensory environments, (Jensen 2000). In this sense, the teacher is seen more as an orchestrator of learning environments rather than an instructor of linear lesson plans or even a facilitator of experiences (Deporter, B., Reardon, M., & S. Singer-Nourie, 1999). Practical applications for parallel processing include the use of multimodal instructional techniques (visual, auditory, kinesthetic) and multiple intelligence activities (Gardner, 1985). Simulations and role-plays mimic our natural learning environment and encourage complex processing. Lastly, enriched learning environments can be orchestrated through the components of challenge, novelty, choice, high feedback, social interaction, and active participation (Diamond & Hopson, 1998). If the benefits of enriched, multisensory, complex learning environments continue to be supported by the research, experiential theory and practice can and should play a larger role in the classrooms of the future.

Suggested Application #3: Use the EELDRC (Enroll, Experience, Label, Demonstrate, Review, Celebrate) design frame (Deporter, B., Reardon, M., & S. Singer-Nourie, 1999) to create a dynamic, complex, multisensory lesson plan. In the *Enroll* segment, seek to engage students in the material through intrigue and answering the learner question "What's In It for Me?" Give them a brief *Experience* to immerse them in the new information. Use the *Label* segment to punctuate the most salient points with a "lecturette" or debrief. Provide an opportunity for the participants to *Demonstrate* with the new information to encourage connections and personalization of the material. *Review* the material to cement the big picture and, finally, find a way to *Celebrate* the experience to reinforce positive associations with the learning.

Principle #3: Stress and Threat

Learning is enhanced by challenge and inhibited by threat (Jensen, 2000). Paul MacLean (1978) offers a model for considering this principle through his Triune Brain theory. MacLean categorizes the brain into three main regions or separate brains—the reptilian (or R-complex), the mammalian (or Limbic), and the neo-mammalian (or neo-cortex). The reptilian brain controls physical survival and basic needs (flight or fight responses). This is our most primitive "brain." The second brain, the mammalian, houses both the hippocampus and amygdala that function as primary centers for emotion and memory. Lastly, the most advanced part of our brains, according to MacLean, is our neo-cortex. It is here where we use higher order thinking skills, including synthesizing, logical and operational thinking, speech, and planning for the future (Caine & Caine, 1994).

In this model, the brain has the capacity to "shift" up or down depending on perception of the immediate environment. Perceived threat can force the brain to "downshift" to lower order thinking (Hart, 1983). Yet interestingly, heightened challenge and stress, referred to as eustress, can invite an upshift response into higher order thinking skills in the neo-cortex. Recent research has suggested that the chemical and physiological responses to stress and threat are radically different (Caine & Caine, 1994). Psychological models also support a difference between perceived challenge and threat (Csikszentmihalyi, 1991). This idea is expressed in experiential pedagogy through the concepts of adaptive dissonance and the comfort zone." In both cases, the facilitator or teacher intentionally places the learner in stressful situations to encourage and invite new adaptive behaviors and mental models that may be more successful or effective for the learner. Indeed, John Dewey (1934) himself advocated for this type of learning through his idea of placing learners in "indeterminate situations."

Caine and Caine (1994) suggest that specific learning conditions can create situations of upshifting or downshifting. Downshifting can occur when "prespecified 'correct' outcomes have been established by an external agent; personal meaning is limited; rewards and punishments are externally controlled; restrictive time lines are given; and the work to be done is relatively unfamiliar with little support available"(p. 84). By contrast, to create upshifting conditions "outcomes should be relatively open ended; personal meaning should be maximized; emphasis should be on intrinsic motivation; tasks should have relatively open-ended time lines, and should be manageable and supported" (p. 85). Emotions also play a critical role in both memory encoding and threat perception (LeDoux, 1996). Too little emotion and the brain has a difficult time "tagging" the material for long-term memory. Too much emotion and the situation may be perceived as threatening, causing a downshift in mental functions (Brandt & Wolfe, 1998).

Practical applications of the stress/threat principle are numerous and exciting for the experiential field. Experiential pedagogy, with its emphasis on novelty, interpersonal interaction, challenge by choice, and the use of emotions such as play, fear, and humor, is well suited to address stress/threat balances. Understanding how these brain-based principles can be strengthened by experiential learning opens the possibility for meaningful dialogue with mainstream education.

Suggested Application #4: To lower threat levels early in a program or course, place a strong emphasis on relationship building on both the peer-peer and teacher-student level. Work the group from the "inside-out" by making a conscious effort to spend personal time with as many students as possible. Work the group "outside-in" by facilitating highly interactive experiences such as paired shares, trust exercises, and other relationship-building activities.

Suggested Application #5: Use the 60/40 rule for lesson and activity plans. Sixty percent of course experiences should involve ritual-based activities that are repetitive (like community check-ins, skill progressions, or reflection activities) to allow your participants to experience known activities in an unknown environment. But be sure to make approximately 40 percent of activities novel. The introduction of elements of suspense, surprise, and disorder keep learners engaged and can be an effective way to manage attention spans. For example, a common mistake is to facilitate reflection sessions the same way each time (circle up and do a "go around"). After too many of these debriefs, instructors might notice rolled eyes and whispered resistance (too much ritual, not enough novelty). Mix up reflections by using paired shares, group reports, or silent journaling instead of large group discussion. Students are still reflecting, but the novelty of the design invites re-engagement.

Conclusion

Evidence and research from the field of brain-based learning support much of what experiential educators do. Understanding the human brain's tendency toward pattern and meaning-making reinforces the intentional use of reflection and synthesis in experiential education. Viewing the brain as a parallel processor encourages the creation of enriched environments for learners. Experiential methodology facilitates such enriched environments through challenge, social interaction, feedback, and active participation. Finally, the differences between stress and threat responses support the fields' pedagogical approach, including the effective use of emotion and the importance of novelty and choice. In short, what we are learning about how the brain functions supports much experiential pedagogy and practice. Yet, recent developments in brain research should also push practitioners and theorists toward new questions and research queries. What is the role of emotion in experiential education? How do we define, operationally, the differences between stressful and threatening experiences and responses? How is the mind-body connection supported in current brain research? What part can experiential methodology play in the creation of enriched classroom environments?

In order for experiential education's philosophical underpinnings to become more influential in mainstream education, it must move beyond the taken-for-granted notion of "learning by doing." Using only this limited and shallow definition, experiential education becomes nothing more than activities and events with little to no significance beyond the initial experience. One educator recently told me she calls this the "Innoculation Effect" (shoot 'em up, hope it takes). This was not John Dewey's vision and it cannot be our lasting legacy. Indeed, Dewey (1938) once wrote:

> There is no discipline in the world so severe as the discipline of experience subjected to the tests of intelligent development and direction. Hence the only ground I can see for even a temporary reaction against the standards, aims, and methods of the newer education *is the failure of educators who professedly adopt them to be faithful to them in practice...the greatest danger that attends its future is, I believe, the idea that it is an easy way to follow, so easy that its course may be improvised....* (p. 90, *emphasis added*)

Many experiential educators entered the field after becoming disenchanted with or burned out on mainstream educational practice. Teachers, facilitators, and instructors of all types cite the remarkable changes and results that can occur through experiential learning as evidence that it works. Yet, as a field, experiential education still remains long on practice and short on theory and research. But Dewey reminds us in the passage above that teaching through experience is not easy and practitioners must guard against complacency. The field of brain-based learning is one avenue for helping experiential educators articulate *how* and *why* the methodology is effective. There are likely many other alliances to be explored and care should be taken not to wed the fields' legitimacy with one particular research methodology or approach.

How can experiential educators achieve more legitimacy while holding fast to core principles? Moves toward identifying the philosophical approaches of experiential education should be encouraged (Itin, 1999). Efforts must be made to increase both qualitative and quantitative research that cross into mainstream education. As educators, experiential proponents also have a responsibility to engage with the larger discourses in the field of education. At a recent conference, I was surprised to learn how few experiential education practitioners knew of E.D. Hirsch—one of the strongest critics of progressive approaches and a major figure in the standards-based movement. Hirsch (1996) defines learning by doing as "a phrase once used to characterize the progressivist movement but little used today, possibly because the formulation has been the object of much criticism and even ridicule" (p. 256). With critics like this and few legitimate platforms from which to respond, it is not surprising that experiential education remains largely locked out of our schools. Knowing the latest trends and movements within the fields of education, psychology, and sociology can strengthen the fields' voice and message.

While there is value in experiential education's subversive, outside-the-mainstream persona, the field must also seek ways to come in from the "outside," invite dialogue, and encourage interaction across disciplines. Brain-based learning, as a promising new area of research and study, offers an excellent opportunity to do just that. In the next 20 years, will experiential education be an activity-based program (like field trips, ropes courses, and character education) to be implemented in schools or will it be a broader, pedagogical foundation from which to work? The future depends on how we live that question.

References

Brandt, R., & Wolfe, P. (1998). What do we know from brain research? *Educational Leadership, 56*(3), 8–13.

Bruer, J. T. (1997). "Education and the brain: A bridge too far." *Educational Researcher*, *26*(8), pp. 4–16.

Caine, G., & Caine, R. (1994). *Making connections: Teaching and the human brain*. New York: Addison Wesley.

Csikszentmihalyi, M. (1991*). Flow: The psychology of optimal experience*. New York: Harper Perrenial.

Diamond, M., & Hopson, J. (1998). *Magic trees of the mind.* New York: Penguin Putnam.

Deporter, B., Reardon, M., & S. Singer-Nourie (1999). *Quantum teaching.* Needham Heights, MA: Allyn & Bacon.

Dewey, J. (1938). *Logic: The Theory of Inquiry*. New York: Holt, Rinehart and Winston.

Dewey, J. (1938). *Experience and Education*. New York: MacMillan.

Gardner, H. (1985). *Frames of mind: The theory of multiple intelligences.* New York: Basic Books.

Hart, L. (1983). *Human brain, human learning.* New York: Longman.

Hirsch, E. D. (1996). *The schools we need and why we don't have them*. New York: Doubleday.

Itin, C. (1999). Reasserting the philosophy of experiential education as a vehicle for change in the 21st century. *Journal of Experiential Education*, *22*(2), pp. 91–98.

Jensen, E. (2000). *Brain-based learning.* San Diego, CA: The Brain Store.

LeDoux, J. (1996). *The emotional brain: The mysterious underpinnings of emotional life*. New York: Simon & Schuster.

MaClean, P. D. (1978). "A Mind of Three Minds: Educating the Triune Brain" in (eds.) J. Chall & A. Mirsky, *Education and the brain,* pp. 308–342. University of Chicago Press.

Nummela, R., & Rosengren, T. (1986). "What's happening in students' brains may redefine teaching." *Educational Leadership, 43*(8), pp. 49–53.

Experience, Reflect, Critique: The End of the "Learning Cycles" Era

▾ ▾ ▾

Jayson Seaman

Advocates of outdoor and adventure education would undoubtedly consider their approaches to be robust arenas for experiential learning. For nearly three decades, however, researchers and practitioners have recognized a gap between the transformational learning often witnessed during experiential programs, and the ability of the most common conceptual models and research methods to explain these transformations (e.g., Kraft, 1990; Wichmann, 1980). This has come to be known as the "black box" phenomenon (Baldwin, Persing, & Magnuson, 2004). On the one hand, the persistence of this gap supports the view that experiential learning may simply be "too mysterious a phenomenon to fully comprehend" (Conrad & Hedin, 1981, p. 6). On the other hand, it is possible that this gap in knowledge can be attributed to the fundamental way learning has been conceived within these fields.

Experiential learning is typically described within outdoor and adventure education "as a sequential process consisting of several different components, and learning occurs once one has completed the entire sequence" (Wurdinger & Paxton, 2003, p. 41). Yet the idea that experiential learning is by definition a cycle made up of orderly, sequential steps is neither eternal nor universally shared. This idea has received considerable criticism in the broader education literature, so much so that the editors of *Adult Education Quarterly* recently declared it a hindrance to future scholarship. Observing changes in knowledge, research methods, and historical circumstances, they urged readers to "not be caught up short in our thinking and

This chapter originally was published in the *Journal of Experiential Education*, with the following citation:
Seaman, J. (2008). Experience, reflect, critique: The end of the "Learning Cycles" era. *Journal of Experiential Education, 31*(1), 3–18.

action with unquestioned traditions living on in our work" (Wilson & Hayes, 2002, p. 175). However, the full weight of this criticism has not been acknowledged in the outdoor and adventure education literature; in fact, the opposite seems to be the case. So central is this conception of learning that it underwrites the "first principle" of experiential education: "Experiential learning occurs when carefully chosen experiences are supported by reflection, critical analysis and synthesis" (AEE, n.d.). Given the enduring influence stepwise models have on research and practice in experiential education—even beyond outdoor and adventure education—and given the extent of the criticism they have received elsewhere, it might be prudent to revisit the way learning is unconditionally (albeit often tacitly) defined as a "cycle" or "sequence."

This chapter reviews the existing criticisms of "learning cycles" and adds a historical dimension to the analysis. Historical analysis provides a useful way to assess an idea's strengths and limitations. It does this by showing how ideas arise out of specific historical conditions and are aimed at solving particular problems, and how they often reflect the values, perspectives, and goals of people working to promote them. Historical analysis also raises the possibility that circumstances and purposes may be different today than before, and that continually relying on inherited assumptions in an uncritical way might shortchange the way educators think about, study, and support learning in outdoor and adventure programs.

While the concept of learning cycles has played a valuable formative role in experiential education to this point, I argue here that its original purposes and its limits should be observed more carefully when basing research and program designs on it in the future. This is a matter of some urgency given today's "evidence-based" policy climate (Gass, 2005) and as changing societal demographics and elaborate program goals require innovations in practice and research. The chapter concludes with several ways outdoor and adventure educators in particular can move beyond current conceptual and practical limits.

A History of Ideas

With regards to outdoor and adventure education, commentary on the mechanics of experiential learning is said to begin with Plato (Wurdinger, 1995). Our modern conception of experiential learning, however, derives from more recent influences such as John Dewey's experimental method, Piaget's constructivism, and Kurt Hahn's humanism, along with some combination of behaviorist and cognitive psychology (Hunt, 1990; Kraft, 1990). These underpinnings were formalized as *models* in the mid-20th century when "experiential learning" first piqued institutional interest. The prototypical—and most influential (Vince, 1998)—model is Kolb's (1984) Experiential Learning Cycle (Figure 1).

The ideas and models from this era have been characterized as "constructivist perspectives of experiential learning" (Fenwick, 2001). Labeling these models a *perspective* suggests

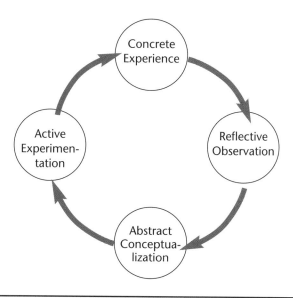

Figure 1. Kolb's (1984) experiential learning cycle.

the possibility of alternatives, and helps mark them off from more established disciplinary traditions. The models comprising this perspective, Fenwick observes, share the assumptions "that learning happens through cognitive reflection, experience can be considered like a bounded object, and an individual 'learner' can be separated from his or her experience to process knowledge from that experience" (pp. 7–8). It is helpful to highlight these assumptions up front to position them as historical artifacts rather than as taken-for-granted truths.

Historical context, theoretical purposes, and ideological commitments. The constructivist perspective of experiential learning developed into a unified set of ideas, if not an ideological movement, in the 1960s and 1970s amidst changing educational and societal trends, not least of which was a large number of adults returning to college through the G.I. Bill (Keeton, 1976). The models developed during this period served two purposes. The first purpose was predominantly administrative. They were explicitly intended to help colleges devise criteria for awarding credit to adults on the basis of prior life experience, as well as to meet the needs of practitioners using simulation games, role plays, and encounter groups as instructional methods (Chickering, 1977; Pearson & Smith, 1985). The second purpose was moral and social. The movement's pioneers expressed concern about "the dizzying rate of change" characterizing modern society (Kolb, 1984, p. 3) and nostalgically sought to reconnect adults with practical life experience while also empowering them to make positive changes in their lives. They unapologetically infused humanistic values into their conception of learning in order to promote "the development of individuals to their full potential as citizens, family members, and human beings" (Kolb, p. 4). In a "hope-filled" manner, they celebrated their commitments to "existential values of personal involvement, and responsibility and humanistic values ... a spirit of inquiry, expanded consciousness and choice, and authenticity in relationships" (Kolb, p. 11).

These two purposes formed a tension, however. The humanistic values of direct experience, free choice, and self-determination needed to be reconciled with the institutional demand for order and predictability, as experiential learning's legitimacy hinged on the ability to convince educational institutions that adults' lifelong "learning can be reliably assessed and certified for college credit" (Kolb, 1984, p. 3). The Commission on Non-Traditional Study was formed in 1971 to address this issue, resulting in the Cooperative Assessment of Experiential Learning (CAEL). CAEL gathered renowned scholars as well as corporate interests such as the Educational Testing Service to survey the status of experiential learning both as an instructional approach and as a general, existential phenomenon that could be assessed and certified (Keeton, 1976). Their task framed by these conflicting humanistic and administrative purposes, advocates needed to reconcile adults' ability to learn on their own with the need to fit experience and knowledge into institutionally recognizable boxes. Problematically for its leaders, interest in experiential learning outpaced the research available to support it on both counts. For example, one contributor to CAEL, sociologist James Coleman (1976), published an influential paper suggesting that learning in everyday situations should be valued alongside school learning. Notably, though, he acknowledged that his comments "far from definitive ... intended primarily to raise issues for serious examination rather than to provide conclusive prescriptions. The investigation of these matters has a long way to go" (p. 58).

Nearly ten years after Coleman's remarks, it appears that there was still a long way to go. Movement leaders Boud, Keough, and Walker (1985) reported that the available "learning theory, despite some hopeful signs, has yet to make any substantial contributions to the kinds of learning tasks with which we are normally faced" and they lamented that "many of our remarks cannot be underpinned by the kinds of research we would hope for" (p. 38). The urgent need under these conditions was to develop a conception of experiential learning predictable enough to incorporate "experience" into pre-established categories, yet open-ended enough to convey the humanistic aims of its advocates. The claim that adult learners should "be able to involve themselves fully, openly, and without bias in new experiences" (Kolb, 1984, p. 30) still had to be balanced against the need to demonstrate how "experience" could be institutionally organized, assessed, and certified. The apparent contradiction entailed in this project was either minimized or disregarded as ideas were codified into models, however. It would ultimately be relieved by defining experience narrowly and by supplying a cognitive mechanism that could satisfy the condition of self-determination while also providing evidence of creditable knowledge.

Experiential learning in two parts. Experiential learning thus took shape not as the research program Coleman called for, but as "both a philosophy and a technique, usually focusing on the relationships between an individual, his or her reflective processes, and something called concrete experience" (Fenwick, 2001, p. 8). As Fenwick notes, the emerging conception of experiential learning consisted of two major aspects. The first was the "here-and-now concrete experience" (Kolb, 1984, p. 21), in which "the learner is directly in touch with the realities being studied" (Keeton, in Kolb, 1984, p. 5). *Experience* in this sense refers to a time-bounded episode of small group interaction, an instructional technique drawn from T-group training methods. This particular conception of experience figured centrally in their conceptual models (Kolb, 1984). The second aspect, individual reflection, was attributed to Lewin, to Dewey, and to Paolo Freire, whose critical views were positioned as the "revolutionary extension of the liberal, humanist perspective" (Kolb, p. 16). The principal aim behind reflection was to accomplish "analytic detachment" (Kolb, p. 9) and "regain our flexibility and creativity in responding to the current situation" (Boud et al., 1985, p. 29).

At first glance, the emancipatory ideals of reflection—something individual adult learners could do "with or without the aid of others" (Boud et al., 1985, p. 26)—seem compelling. Reflection ostensibly provides a means for self-creation in knowledge; finally learners would "have the freedom to make a genuine choice for themselves, rather than conform to the influence of a teacher or other students" (p. 14). But, in keeping with the pressing administrative need to assess and certify adults' experience, reflection also needed to conform to the institutions that would approve and sanction knowledge (Michelson, 1999). For these reasons, reflection could not always be left up to the learner. Boud et al. admit that "there are limits to what each of us can achieve unaided and often the learning process can be considerably accelerated by appropriate support, encouragement, and intervention by others" (p. 36). In order to lay the groundwork for their own proposal, they conceded "that it is useful for learners and teachers to have a model of reflection which points to some of the major processes which they should consider" (p. 26). It is here where the tension is most pronounced. The directiveness of what learners "should" consider, the emphasis on "accelerating" the learning process, and the "intervention" of an instructor were apparently not seen as incongruous with the overriding desire for freedom and autonomy in knowing, expressed quite strongly in the following passage:

> Because we can still learn from our own experience, because we can subject the abstract symbols of the social-knowledge system to the rigors of our own inquiry about these symbols and our own personal experience with them, we are free. This process of choosing to believe is what we feel when we know that we are free to chart the course of our own destiny. (Kolb, 1984, p. 109)

These two contradictory dimensions became conflated into a singular notion of "experiential learning" as graphical models were created, reducing complex processes to a few neat steps. The models do serve useful purposes; a conceptual model such as Kolb's four-stage cycle has tremendous intuitive appeal, adapts handily to various practical applications (e.g., Enns, 1993), and supports a humanistic faith in self-direction. They have also paved the way for modern practices. But, partly because early authors drew eclectically on "theoreticians with quite different backgrounds, motives and incompatible conceptions ... as founders and 'supporters' of experiential learning" (Miettinen, 2000, p. 56), they were able to sidestep the serious epistemological problems surrounding the individual subject versus the social/institutional organization of knowledge. This is a problem that has stayed with us (Bell, 1993; Fox, 2008; Roberts, 2008). At least, it should be recognized that the assumptions behind the constructivist perspective of experiential learning derive more from the prevailing ideological and institutional context of adult education in the 1970s than from focused programs of inquiry about the nature of experiencing, reflecting, and learning.

The constructivist perspective of experiential learning can thus be understood not as a rigorous theory of social and mental processes, but as a set of ideas selected from various disciplinary traditions and training regimens in the attempt to "construct an attractive collection of ideas that can be advocated as a solution to the social problems of our time ..." (Miettinen, 2000, p. 56); which, at the time of its founding, were the administrative needs of higher education institutions and the ideological interests of the human potential movement (Chickering, 1977). Although many of the influential, pioneering authors noted that their claims were not supported by research, today their comments are often cited as foundational without reference to historical context, ideological background, or theoretical purpose (e.g., Wurdinger & Priest, 1999). The perspective has now evolved from a set of practice-driven models with historically specific purposes into a broader belief system underwritten more by liberal-humanist ideology, folk psychology, and administrative interests than by a scientific or epistemological foundation for learning. It has also received considerable criticism in various disciplines such as education, psychology, and philosophy.

Criticisms of the Constructivist Perspective of Experiential Learning

Many of the principles inherent in the constructivist perspective of experiential learning have already received considerable criticism in the outdoor and adventure education literature. Critics in the adult and management education literature—the traditions from which many of these models originated—have focused on more severe methodological and epistemological problems. These challenges will now be reviewed.

Challenges from within outdoor and adventure education. Loynes (2002) argues that the kind of rational, "algorithmic paradigm" sponsored by constructivist models is so pervasive that the field's language, practices, and values largely derive from it, to the exclusion of other alternatives. Bell (1993) observed that many characterizations of experiential education seem preoccupied with individual change and lack "clear sociological analysis" even though "group identity or culture" (p. 19) is thought to be central to learning. Quay (2003) argued that "mechanistic" stepwise models fail to capture the "holistic nature" of experiential learning (p. 108). Similarly, Hovelynck (2001) found outdoor leaders developing "practice theories" that better reflect their work once in the field, suggesting that stepwise models may actually inform practice only superficially. Despite these criticisms, the description of experiential learning as "the change in an individual that results from reflection on a direct experience and results in new abstractions and applications" (Itin, 1999, p. 93) remains remarkably durable as a basic concept.

Methodological challenges. One methodological criticism is that early models such as Kolb's (1984) took theorists' ideas out of context and misapplied them to experiencing and learning, thereby narrowing "experience" to fit preconceived institutional categories and instructional methods. According to Miettinen (2000), this tendency resulted in the conceptual "impoverishment" of "the rich variety and modes of human experience characteristic of various human activities" (p. 61). Since the concept of "learning cycles" is used as both a *definition of learning* and a *formula for practice*, researchers and practitioners are caught in a closed loop, a kind of internally reinforcing logic. Management educators Holman, Pavlica, and Thorpe (1997) note the practical dangers with this logic. Speaking of Kolb, they observe:

> Such has been his influence, that it appears that when managers 'fail to learn' they are
>
> thought by educators to have failed to grasp certain aspects of the learning process (i.e.
>
> the learning cycle), but few question experiential learning theory itself or search for
>
> alternative explanations. (p. 138. See also Wallace, 1996)

Finally, Kolb's description of learning styles, a core concept on which his model is based, has been questioned by different authors. Miettinen (2000) argues that Kolb does not effectively show how the "four different kinds of abilities— *concrete experience abilities* (CE), *reflective observation abilities* (RO), *abstract conceptualizing abilities* (AC) and *active experimentation abilities* (AE)" (Kolb, in Miettinen, p. 61, italics in original)—are related to one another or correspond with phases in a cycle. Miettinen concludes that Kolb's *Learning Styles Inventory* is simply a training tool and should not be considered a typology of underlying learning mechanisms. Research in cognitive science supports Miettinen's critique; Kirschner, Schweller, and Clark (2006) summarize studies showing "that there is little or no correlation between factors that should correlate with the classification of learning styles, and that it [the *Learning Styles Inventory*] does not enjoy a general acceptance of its usefulness, particularly for research purposes" (p. 81). These criticisms suggest that new insights into experiential learning will only come from using tools and concepts from outside the constructivist perspective.

Epistemological challenges. There are also epistemological problems with the notions of *experience* and *reflection* as they are represented in constructivist models. With regards to experience, Holman et al. (1997) explain how the central concept of *direct experience* in constructivist models

> is seen as pure, unproblematic, fully accessible by conscious thought, possessing a presym-
>
> bolic quality which exists prior to the meaning attached to it. The text of experience will
>
> always be able to be read. Its meaning will always be apparent and decipherable. (p. 138)

Miettinen (2000) critiques the notion of direct experience as naïve, noting "the theoretical and epistemological inadequacy of the concept of immediate personal experience" (p. 61) and arguing that there is no such thing as direct experience independent from theories or symbols in the first place (interestingly, there is a lot of evidence that Dewey also held this view. See John Dewey, 1997/1910; 1949). Emerging empirical research in the outdoor and adventure education fields supports this criticism, illustrating how experiencing and learning processes are *mediated* by the physical, social, and discursive conditions of experience (Brown, 2004; Seaman, 2007).

As the radically autonomous learner and the simple "directness" of experience are called into question, reflection as the central act of knowledge production in experiential programs is not easily maintained as a basic principle of learning. Controversially, evidence suggests that conscious reflection may not play as basic a role in experiential learning as previously believed. Research in "social practice" traditions shows how people learn *in* experience, not *from* or *after* it (e.g., Cole, Engeström, & Vasquez, 1997; Engeström, Mietinnen, & Punamaki, 2003). These findings, which are far too numerous to list here, make the sentiment "experience alone is not the key to learning" (Boud et al., 1985, p. 7) simply seem strange, if not misguided.

Furthermore, Michelson (1996) suggests that even if reflection could be conceived as merely a mental exercise, one cannot escape social and cultural meanings when one does it (imagine trying to reflect without using language). The rational emphasis in reflection is itself culturally influenced. For instance, Boud et al. (1985) repeatedly stress that "removing obstructing feelings is a necessary precursor to a rational consideration of events" (p. 26). The presence of obstructing emotions, they write, can "override our rationality to such an extent that we react unawarely and with blurred perceptions" (p. 28). The view that "negative" emotions are suspect rather than serving as crucial insights into the world is a key factor in the argument that experiential learning, as we now know it, is gendered (Fullagar &

Hailstone, 1996; Michelson, 1996). Moreover, such a position is inherently distrustful of sensuous, bodily experience, an ironic situation for a practice that places a premium on physical interaction and engagement with the natural world.

Sociocultural challenges. The constructivist perspective of experiential learning is aligned with Western ideals of individual development. In Kolb's (1984) words, experiential learning is a process of facilitating "growth" and "progress" toward "the highest stages of development" (p. 140), a progression in which learners move "from a state of embeddedness, defensiveness, dependence, and reaction to a state of self-actualization, independence, proaction and self-direction" (p. 140). He takes as his developmental chronology the "ordering of ages at which developmental achievements become possible in the general conditions of contemporary Western culture" (p. 141). This framework, if acknowledged explicitly, could prove instructive to research and program design (cf. Beach, 1999). However, if unrecognized and used uncritically as the basic premise for broad claims about experiencing and learning, the perspective can be considered ethnocentric, as this view encourages a deficit view of developmental differences pertaining to non-Western cultural traditions.

Early research in cultural psychology has been criticized for this very reason, namely that particular forms of abstract reasoning—those common to highly literate societies of European descent—are positioned as a universally advanced developmental state:

> Almost all of the well-known "grand theories" of development have specified a single developmental trajectory, moving toward a pinnacle that resembles the values of the theorist's own community or indeed of the theorist's own life-course. For example, theorists who are extremely literate and have spent many years in school often regard literacy and Euro-American school ways of thinking and acting as central to the goals of successful development, and even as defining "higher" cultural evolution of whole societies. (Rogoff, 2003, p. 18)

Cross-cultural research shows that abstract knowing is not decontextualized, but instead indicates cognitive functioning typical to persons who have participated extensively in institutionalized schooling and middle-class child-rearing practices (Lave, 1993). Cloran (1999) illustrates how the specialized discourse pattern of *observe-reflect-generalize* in particular indicates extensive participation in these practices rather than a universal communicative or cognitive structure. Again, this recognition could prove helpful to research and program design, but its cultural assumptions should be made clear, rather than being kept hidden.

Similar problems can also be seen from a social and political standpoint. The individualism inherent in the constructivist perspective may block efforts to understand mutuality and reciprocity in learning. Michelson (1999) argues:

> Underneath the avowal that community is indispensable is a longing for a unitary, authentic self untouched by the demands of human mutuality.... Experiential learning encourages psychic growth by freeing us from the oppression of other people's choices. Knowles (1990: 42–43) quotes Carl Rogers to the effect that 'I have yet to find the individual who, when he [*sic*] examines his situation deeply ... deliberately chooses to have the integrated direction of himself undertaken by another'. (p. 140)

This individualism may also hinder a deeper understanding of the creativity and spontaneity that arises in face-to-face interaction, as "subjectivities that are potentially multiple, shifting, transgressive, and spontaneous are recast as coherent, stable, rational, and self-regulating" (Fenwick, 2001, p. 32). From this view, it is difficult to see how such individualistic models of learning can adequately support educational approaches strongly claiming "community" and "perspective taking" as desired outcomes (McKenzie, 2000; Wyatt, 1997).

Finally, from an ecological perspective, Bowers (2005) argues that individualist constructivism, which embraces abstract visions of rational, Western progress, intends to "emancipate students from the traditional forms of knowledge that prevent them from entering the modern world" (p. IX)—the world of consumerism. By doing so, it tacitly devalues long-standing cultural traditions as backwards and irrelevant. Elena Michelson argues that this view is also strongly "tied to social relations of capitalism" and has overtones of discipline and external control (in Fenwick, 2001, p. 23). Taken together, these critiques add support to Bowers' (2005) assertion that constructivist theories may unwittingly promote indoctrination by narrowing the broader concepts of *experiencing* and *learning* to fit within preconceived institutional, cultural, and moral frameworks without acknowledging their own function in doing so. In Bowers' argument, the effect is an "illusory state of consciousness" ensuring that "both the teachers and students do not know what they do not know" (p. 110), a condition that is presently leading to cultural and environmental degradation. In outdoor and adventure education, Brookes (2002) has put the problem this way: "Realism and individualism are convenient; they exempt outdoor educators from having to know much about nature (it can be perceived directly) or culture (since meaning comes from within the individual rather than from collective memory)" (p. 415).

Implications of These Critiques

Kirschner et al. (2006) note that an "emphasis on the practical application of what is being learned seems very positive" (p. 84), yet they encourage educators to move past "the fuzzy and unproductive world of ideology—which sometimes hides under the various banners of constructivism—to the sharp and productive world of theory-based research on how people learn" (p. 84). While it is highly doubtful that theory and research could ever be separated from ideology, their assertion that constructivist models of experiential learning are underwritten more by ideology than by research appear to have merit.

In light of these critiques, researchers and practitioners might start to question the definition of experiential learning as a sequence or a cycle. Making continued and unqualified use of this standard definition is problematic for several reasons. First, the most commonly used constructivist models, which have largely become axiomatic with respect to learning in experiential education, were developed under a set of historical circumstances primarily affecting adult education. The extent to which "experience-reflect-learn" patterns apply to experiential learning as it happens with children or as part of compulsory schooling has been taken more as an article of faith than as a proposition that is subject to verification. Researchers might prioritize this issue since it seems central to practice at a very basic level (Russell, 2006).

Second, the tendency of constructivist models to dichotomize individual, social, and environmental aspects of learning remains largely unaddressed. This is especially problematic since social and physical conditions are believed to play a central role in outdoor, adventure, and other experiential programs (Walsh & Golins, 1976). Bereiter (2002) describes one problem with such individual approaches:

> Although cooperation and teamwork are praised, the idea of cooperating in the creation of knowledge never comes to life ... it is hard to deal with the everyday fact of people jointly producing a piece of knowledge that is neither the product of one individual's knowledge or the combination of several individuals' knowledge. Such knowledge is typically an emergent of discourse and cannot be understood at the level of individual interacting minds. (pp. 177–178)

In other words, constructivist models reduce the highly interactive and bodily qualities of outdoor and adventure experiences to secondary elements in an individual's experience, rather than being constitutive *of* experience at a more fundamental level. Researchers equipped with this insight might seek out new methods for studying individuals, groups, and institutions that recognize the complex and multidimensional nature of their relationships.

Third, and in sum, ample empirical research and philosophical argument (e.g., Fenwick, 2001; Rogoff, Paradise, Meija-Arauz, Correa-Chavez, & Angelillo, 2003) suggests that the definition of experiential learning as an orderly series of steps either (a) is false, because alternative links between experience and learning can easily be found that do not follow such a pattern and do not emphasize reflection at all, or (b) represents only a narrow type of experiential learning, and thus pertains only to specific, formal situations. Therefore, adopting other methodological principles can help lead to theoretical and practical insights at a time when both research and practice face new pressures, and when the gap in our knowledge persists.

Conclusion

The intent of this chapter was not to suggest that the routine patterns used in different experiential practices, in which participants engage in an activity then jointly or individually "reflect," should be abandoned. This straightforward approach has unquestionably served many people throughout the years and will probably continue to do so. However, several arguments have been presented against the claim that experiential learning can be fundamentally understood as *equivalent* to these patterns. Moreover, these arguments suggest that the pattern of "experience-reflect-learn" stems from a particular *ideology* of experiential learning, rather than a coherent and broadly applicable *philosophy* or a *theory* of learning. In its time, this framework served a useful purpose. Given changes in knowledge, research methods, participant populations, societal trends, and educational goals, however, it may now be influencing research and practice in unhelpful ways.

One current challenge is to develop conceptions of experiential learning, and methods for studying it, that do not "limit our theorizing and threaten to repress both experiencing and learning processes" (Fenwick, 2001, p. 25). This will require adopting theoretical perspectives that take social and cultural context seriously (cf. Brookes, 2003), that hold promise for guiding instructional practice in increasingly complex applications, and that align with the standards of established scientific and philosophical traditions rather than being based in institutional lore and folk psychology. If experiential education is to play a serious part in the social, educational, and ecological problems of *our* time, it may be worth moving "alternative" perspectives to a more central role in future inquiry and scholarship.

References

AEE. (n.d.). AEE Definition of Experiential Education. Retrieved November 22, 2005, from http://www.aee.org/faq/nfaq.htm#ee

Baldwin, C., Persing, J., & Magnuson, D. (2004). The role of theory, research, and evaluation in adventure education. *Journal of Experiential Education, 25*(3), 167–183.

Beach, K. (1999). Consequential transitions: A sociocultural expedition beyond transfer in education. *Review of Educational Research, 24*, 101–139.

Bell, M. (1993). What constitutes experience? Rethinking theoretical assumptions. *Journal of Experiential Education, 16*(1), 19–24.

Bereiter, C. (2002). *Education and mind in the knowledge age.* Mahwah, NJ: Lawrence Erlbaum and Associates.

Boud, D., Keogh, R., & Walker, D. (1985). Promoting reflection in learning: A model. In D. Boud, R. Keogh & D. Walker (Eds.), *Reflection: Turning experience into learning* (pp. 19–40). New York: Kogan Page.

Bowers, C. A. (2005). *The false promises of constructivist learning theories: A global and ecological critique*. New York: Peter Lang Publishing.

Brookes, A. (2002). Lost in the Australian bush: Outdoor education as curriculum. *Journal of Curriculum Studies, 34*(4), 405–425.

Brookes, A. (2003). A critique of neo-Hahnian outdoor education theory. Part one: Challenges to the concept of 'character building'. *Journal of Adventure Education and Outdoor Learning, 3*(1), 49–62.

Brown, M. (2004). Let's go round the circle: How verbal facilitation can function as a means of direct instruction. *Journal of Experiential Education, 27*(2), 161–175.

Chickering, A. (1977). *Experience and learning: An introduction to experiential learning*. New Rochelle, NY: Change Magazine Press.

Cloran, C. (1999). Contexts for learning. In F. Christie (Ed.), *Pedagogy and the shaping of consciousness: Linguistic and social processes* (pp. 31–65). London: Cassell.

Cole, M., Engeström, Y., & Vasquez, O. (Eds.). (1997). *Mind, culture, and activity: Seminal papers from the Laboratory of Comparative Human Cognition*. New York: Cambridge University Press.

Coleman, J. (1976). Differences between experiential and classroom learning. In M. Keeton (Ed.), *Experiential learning: Rationale, characteristics and assessment* (pp. 49–61). San Francisco, CA: Jossey Bass.

Conrad, D., & Hedin, D. (1981). The impact of experiential education: Summary and implications. *Journal of Experiential Education, 4*(2), 6–20.

Dewey, J. (1997/1910). *How we think*. Mineola, NY: Dover.

Dewey, J., & Bentley, A. F. (1949). *Knowing and the known*. Boston: Beacon.

Engeström, Y., Mietinnen, R., & Punamaki, R. L. (Eds.). (2003). *Perspectives on activity theory*. Cambridge: Cambridge University Press.

Enns, C. Z. (1993). Integrating separate and connected knowing: The experiential learning model. *Teaching of Psychology, 20*(1), 7–13.

Fenwick, T. (2001). Experiential learning: A theoretical critique from five perspectives. Ohio State University: ERIC Clearinghouse on Adult, Career, and Vocational Education.

Fox, K. (2008). Rethinking experience: What do we mean by this word "experience?" *Journal of Experiential Education, 31*(1), 36–54.

Fullagar, S., & Hailstone, S. (1996). Shifting the ground: Feminist theory in the outdoors. *Social Alternatives, 15*(2), 23–27.

Gass, M. (2005). Comprehending the value structures influencing significance and power behind experiential education research. *Journal of Experiential Education, 27*(3), 286–296.

Holman, R., Pavlica, K., & Thorpe, R. (1997). Rethinking Kolb's theory of learning in management education. *Management Learning, 28*(2), 135–148.

Hovelynck, J. (2001). Practice-theories of facilitating experiential learning in Outward Bound: A research report. *Journal of Adventure Education and Outdoor Learning, 1*(2), 53–57.

Hunt, J. (1990). Philosophy of adventure education. In S. Priest & J. C. Miles (Eds.), *Adventure education* (pp. 119–128). State College, PA: Venture Publishing.

Itin, C. (1999). Reasserting the philosophy of experiential education as a vehicle for change in the 21st century. *Journal of Experiential Education, 22*(2), 91–98.

Keeton, M. (Ed.). (1976). *Experiential learning: Rationale, characteristics and assessment*. San Francisco, CA: Jossey Bass.

Kirschner, P. A., Sweller, J., & Clark, R. E. (2006). Why minimal guidance does not work: An analysis of the failure of constructivist, discovery, problem-based, experiential, and inquiry-based teaching. *Educational Psychologist, 41*(2), 75–86.

Kolb, D. (1984). *Experiential learning: Experience as the source of learning and development.* Englewood Cliffs, NJ: Prentice-Hall.

Kraft, R. (1990). Experiential learning. In J. C. Miles & S. Priest (Eds.), *Adventure Education* (pp. 175–183). State College, PA: Venture Publishing.

Lave, J. (1993). Introduction. In S. Chaiklin & J. Lave (Eds.), *Understanding practice: Perspectives on activity and context* (pp. 3–34). Cambridge: Cambridge University Press.

McKenzie, M. (2000). How are adventure education program outcomes achieved? A review of the literature. *Australian Journal of Outdoor Education, 5*(1), 19–28.

Michelson, E. (1996). Usual suspects: Experience, reflection and the (en)gendering of knowledge. *International Journal of Lifelong Education, 15*(6), 438–454.

Michelson, E. (1999). Carnival, paranoia, and experiential learning. *Studies in the Education of Adults, 31*(2), 140–154.

Miettinen, R. (2000). The concept of experiential learning and John Dewey's theory of reflective thought and action. *International Journal of Lifelong Education, 19*(1), 54–72.

Pearson, M., & Smith, D. (1985). Debriefing in experience-based learning. In D. Boud, R. Keough & D. Walker (Eds.), *Reflection: Turning experience into learning* (pp. 69–84). London: RoutledgeFalmer.

Roberts, J. (2008). From experience to neo-experiential education: Variations on a theme. *Journal of Experiential Education, 31*(1), 19–35.

Rogoff, B. (2003). *The cultural nature of human development.* New York: Oxford University Press.

Rogoff, B., Paradise, R., Meija-Arauz, R., Correa-Chavez, M., & Angelillo, C. (2003). Firsthand learning through intent participation. *Annual Review of Psychology, 54*, 175–203.

Russell, K. (2006). Publishing to the choir or digging deep: Implications of a snapshot of experiential education research. *Journal of Experiential Education, 28*(3), 243–247.

Seaman, J. (2007). Taking *things* into account: Learning as kinaesthetically mediated collaboration. *Journal of Adventure Education and Outdoor Learning, 7*(1), 3–20.

Vince, R. (1998). Behind and beyond Kolb's Learning Cycle. *Journal of Management Education, 22*(3), 304–319.

Wallace, M. (1996). When is experiential learning not experiential learning? In G. Claxton (Ed.), *Liberating the learner: Lessons for professional development in education* (pp. 16–31). New York: Routledge.

Walsh, V., & Golins, G. (1976). The exploration of the Outward Bound process. *Unpublished manuscript.*

Wichmann, T. F. (1980). Babies and bath water: Two experiential heresies. *Journal of Experiential Education*, 6–12.

Wilson, A. L., & Hayes, E. R. (2002). From the editors: The problem of (learning in-from-to) experience. *Adult Education Quarterly, 52*(3), 173–175.

Wurdinger, S. (1995). *Philosophical issues in adventure education.* Dubuque, IA: Kendall/Hunt.

Wurdinger, S., & Paxton, T. (2003). Using multiple levels of experience to promote autonomy in adventure education students. *Journal of Adventure Education and Outdoor Learning, 3*(1), 41–48.

Wurdinger, S., & Priest, S. (1999). Integrating theory and application in experiential learning. In J. C. Miles & S. Priest (Eds.), *Adventure Programming* (pp. 187–192). State College, PA: Venture Publishing.

Wyatt, S. (1997). Dialogue, reflection, and community. *Journal of Experiential Education, 20*(2), 80–85.

Positive Psychology & Outdoor Education

▾ ▾ ▾

Dene S. Berman & Jennifer Davis-Berman

Positive psychology is a relatively new movement in the field of psychology that has numerous implications for a wide variety of outdoor education programs, especially those that are therapeutic in nature. With their interest and investment in promoting and enhancing human growth, such programs may benefit from an understanding of this positive frame of reference. This article will review some of the basic tenets of positive psychology before analyzing its applicability as a paradigm for outdoor programs.

Traditionally, psychology has focused on preventing and treating human psychopathology. Clinically, the focus has been to identify and often diagnose deficits in functioning and affect so the clinician might assist the client in reducing these deficits. While there are certainly therapeutic benefits to this approach, it also contributes to a negative paradigm of human functioning, relying on categorizing undesirable symptoms (Asakawa, 2004). This "problem and deficit-focused" paradigm has been widely accepted in the profession of psychology, and has been especially prevalent in the United States since World War II (Seligman & Csikszentmihalyi, 2000).

Positive Psychology

Recent developments in the field of psychology, however, have begun to suggest the adoption of a new paradigm referred to as positive psychology. Positive psychology has as its goal the

---

This chapter originally was published in the *Journal of Experiential Education*, with the following citation:
Berman, D. S., & Davis-Berman, J. (2005), Positive psychology and outdoor education. *Journal of Experiential Education, 28*(1), 17–24.

fostering of excellence through the understanding and enhancement of factors leading to growth. Some of these factors include positive emotions, positive individual traits, and prosocial attitudes (Seligman & Csikszentmihalyi, 2000). Human behavior is seen, through this perspective, as driven by positive human traits. Rather than focus on deficits, positive psychology examines these positive traits and attributes, with an eye toward strengthening them or facilitating their development in clients. These traits are critically important, as they can lead to the development of stable personality and physical states like resiliency (Fredrickson, 2001; Schmidt, 1998), optimism (Seligman, 1990), and even better physical health (Salovey, Rothman, Detweiler, & Steward, 2000) over time. Instead of focusing on decreasing negative symptoms in therapy, a positive psychology approach would focus more on enhancing client strengths.

The "flow" experience has been widely cited and examined as an important part of positive psychology, which has also been discussed in the outdoor literature (e.g., Csikszentmihalyi & Csikszentmihalyi, 1999). According to flow theory, human behavior and action are motivated by a desire to reach a state of flow. In order to experience flow, one must feel that s/he is deeply involved in an experience, highly motivated, cognitively efficient, and truly enjoying the experience (Csikszentmihalyi, 1990). Individuals must feel that their ability to deal with the situation matches the challenges presented in the situation (Massimini, Csikszentmihalyi, & Carli, 1987). The attainment of a flow experience can be seen as a motivator for positive behaviors. An "autotelic" person is one who is motivated intrinsically, and thus, is more likely to pursue and achieve flow experiences (Csikszentmihalyi & Csikszentmihalyi, 1999). Importantly, the quality of an experience is related to both the perceived challenges of the experience and the individual's perceived skill level in dealing with the challenge inherent in the experience.

It seems that positive psychology represents a more growth-oriented model of human functioning than a more deficit-oriented approach. Clinical interventions can be designed to enhance functioning that is already positive, and to facilitate the development and growth of positive personality traits. Those who possess these traits are more likely to succeed in having flow experiences. These flow experiences are like peak experiences, yet their success depends on both the challenge of the situation and the individual's perceived skill level. Given the nature of many outdoor programs, where challenge and skill are often critical factors, the perspective of positive psychology appears to be a natural fit.

Positive Psychology and Outdoor Education

One of the dominant conceptions of motivation for change in many types of outdoor education programs has perhaps best been espoused by Luckner and Nadler (1997). They suggest that people learn and change when they are in a state of dynamic tension. This state is achieved when there is disequilibrium, brought about by an internal conflict. The conflict occurs when there are challenges to a person's perceived sense of safety and security. Thus, change is the result of the person's desire to alleviate a negative internal state. This method of change is often described as taking someone out of his/her comfort zone, which is posited as an essential ingredient for change to occur. The following quote from Luckner and Nadler (1997, p. 24) illustrates this perspective:

> There are conditions or states that people can be placed in, in order to accentuate disequilibrium, dissonance, disorder, frustration, or anxiety. Enhancing these feelings increases the need to order, restructure, or alter one's cognitive map of the world and oneself in an effort to restore equilibrium.... Understanding these conditions and finding ways to create them can increase your ability to promote change.

This model of change bears a striking resemblance to many of psychology's early theories and approaches. For example, Freud suggested that the person has basic needs that often go unfulfilled. The longer these needs go unfulfilled, the greater the urge to satisfy these needs, thereby diminishing an increasingly negative state of being (Hall, 1954).

From a clinical psychology perspective, this traditional approach to creating change should be examined. The current "conventional wisdom" in psychology suggests that clients often need safety, security, and predictability in order to feel free to work on change (e.g., Trull, 2005). In fact, it might even be ethically suspect to encourage clients to experience higher levels of anxiety or perceived risk in order to facilitate change (Canter, 1994).

In addition to ethical concerns, some important clinical issues related to this deficit model of change should be highlighted. First, exposure to perceived risk and anxiety can become debilitating for people, working against the process of change. When participants are in such a state of high anxiety that they feel they are in survival mode, meaningful work on issues or change is unlikely (Davis-Berman & Berman, 2002). Second, anxiety and perception of risk are very subjective experiences. Participants' experience with and tolerance of anxiety vary widely. In fact, for some, the mere experience of being in the outdoor environment may be a big leap out of the "comfort zone." To then employ strategies that increase this tension could be detrimental (Davis-Berman & Berman, 2002). Finally, when participants are placed in situations with little perceived control and high perceived risk, they may change some behaviors in order to cope and better conform, but these changes will probably not be internalized very well. It is through success and experiences of personal control that people generally make positive attributions about the environment, and about their experiences and outcomes in that environment (Seligman, 1990). This is not to say that change doesn't occur as a result of negative circumstances or life events. Anecdotal accounts abound about the experience of turning adversity or even tragedy into life-changing and life-enhancing experiences (e.g., Armstrong & Jenkins, 2003). Naturally occurring positive change resulting from crisis or trauma, however, is quite different from the adoption of this type of paradigm for guiding outdoor programs.

In the field of outdoor education, an alternative perspective has been developed and is exemplified by the assertion that people change for positive reasons, within the context of supportive communities (Mitten, 1999; Warren, 1999). This approach discusses the importance of creating a healthy, supportive community in which people can act on their positive strivings. Communities are created when there is an emergence of conditions such as: working with nature, experiencing the outdoors because of an appreciation of the environment, and safety and sharing with a focus on group members' strengths. Originally conceived as a feminist perspective, compatibility with positive psychology suggests a broader application.

The use of the "flow" model in conceiving and executing outdoor programs is another example of the relevance of positive psychology to outdoor education and therapy programs. This focus on strengths can be seen by examining flow experiences, where the individual experiences a sense of control, concentration, and confidence in his/her perceived ability to be successful. The person who experiences flow is in a state akin to Maslow's (1954) peak experience. In this state, people are fully functioning, have clarity of purpose, and lose themselves in their activities. They are "at one" with what they are doing. However, an activity that leads to flow for one person is not predictive of what will lead to flow for someone else, as flow experiences are unique for each person. It is hard to imagine that these conditions of flow could exist for someone who was experiencing disequilibrium, discomfort, or some of the other negative states that have been associated with the aforementioned models of outdoor education or psychology.

Just as individuals seek out activities that lead to flow experiences (autotelic activities), participants in outdoor education programs are often seeking states of being that are different than those they have in everyday life. These experiences might be best understood and framed by positive theories of change that focus on how people can be helped to become stronger, feel better, develop their uniqueness, and otherwise grow.

Leberman and Martin (2002) recently addressed this issue in the outdoor literature. Using two samples of Outward Bound participants, they looked at the relationship between activities that took participants out of their comfort zones, and the extent to which they related to and learned from those activities, as opposed to perceived learning from activities that were not seen as risky. Their results indicated two interesting findings. First, the activities that took people out of their comfort zones were, for the most part, not those from which they learned the most. And second, the activities from which they learned the most were primarily social, creative, and reflective. These findings certainly are not definitive; nevertheless, they support a more positive model of change, and suggest that participants learned more when in positions of safety.

Shifting Paradigms

It has thus far been suggested that the emphasis on perceived risk and moving participants out of their comfort zones is in need of more examination. Perceived risk is a very subjective experience. Leaders cannot assume that their perceptions are the perceptions of everyone. Even if the majority of participants seem to perceive risk similarly, one cannot assume that these perceptions are the same for all participants.

Another potential consequence of a model that incorporates disequilibrium as a necessary condition of change is that disequilibrium often leads to crisis. In fact, the goal of crisis intervention is the resolution of disequilibrium and a return to the prior state of equilibrium (Dixon, 1979). Without this resolution, emotional reactions like anxiety or other symptoms may emerge.

Many outdoor education programs are intended to work with vulnerable populations. Others are targeted toward people who have been diagnosed with mental health and/or physical health problems. Increasing anxiety or aggravating any other mental health symptoms is not only an undesirable outcome when working with these populations, but it puts participants at added risk.

If the perceived risks of a situation are too high for a participant, the impact can be counterproductive at best, and damaging at worst. This can lead to a difficult situation, as leaders with good intentions may misjudge the impact of a situation on participants, or may not be able to assess the participants' level of anxiety and threat.

It is quite possible that simply participating in an outdoor program represents a dramatic departure from the comfort zone, and that any other push would be harmful. Based on the ideas of positive psychology, this perspective suggests that the greatest amount of change and growth comes from a place of comfort, security and acceptance (Davis-Berman & Berman, 1994). This is consistent with Maslow's (1954) ideas about the hierarchy of human needs; the imperative being that for healthy growth and functioning, the basic needs of security and love must first be met. Safety and security may be especially important when the participants have struggled with mental health problems, or have been victims of abuse or neglect. Interestingly, many outdoor programs cater to troubled youth or special populations, many of whom could be considered to be vulnerable. Many programs with adolescents are particularly harsh, and some are even survivalist in their orientation. This approach may ultimately serve to be quite damaging (Davis-Berman & Berman, 1994).

Consistent with the ideas from positive psychology, outdoor education programs, whose goals are to encourage both personal growth and change, should take steps to try to reduce the perception of risk in programs. Underlying this assumption is the belief that, for many, just participating in a program increases one's sense of threat and instability, and that further threat potentially could be damaging. This is not to say that all perceived risk should be eliminated. The leaders, however, must assess each participant and make the appropriate choices. Although labor intensive, each participant's tolerance for risk and anxiety could be clinically assessed and evaluated prior to the start of the program. Special attention should be paid to participants who report past abuse, instability, and issues related to safety and security in their lives. Empathy on the part of the staff completing this assessment is critical to assessing emotional risk and to designing programs that minimize perceived risk. They should cater the therapeutic program to the needs and capabilities of the participants.

Instead of trying to create change by increasing risk, outdoor educators and therapists can increase motivation by helping to create autotelic experiences. This can be accomplished by helping people enjoy the experience and use skills they develop within a context of friendship and support, in which there is emotional release and the ability to measure oneself against his/her own ideals and others. These activities promote attention to the present moment and activities; there are defined goals and identifiable means for reaching them, and feedback and information about one's striving toward the goals (Csikszentmihalyi & Csikszentmihalyi, 1999). As positive psychology has grown in popularity, the study of success and growth, rather than an emphasis on deficit, has emerged. Similarly, the field of outdoor education should challenge itself to move away from negative models of change to further help people find, develop, and use their gifts.

Discussion

This article is meant to stimulate thinking and conversation among professionals in the outdoor education and outdoor therapy fields. It is hoped that professionals will think about these ideas and apply them clinically, as well as in relation to program development. This article is also meant to stimulate thought and discussion among students, and encourage them to consider varying theoretical paradigms.

Program models should be developed that incorporate the initial assessment of participants. Activities and outdoor modalities should then be chosen to enhance safety, security and the participant's perception of being able to respond well to the program's challenges. Qualitative research should then be conducted that examines the process of creating and fostering an environment in outdoor programs that is supported by the positive psychology paradigm. These kinds of studies would involve asking the participants themselves about the necessary conditions for change. Quantitative studies should then be done to compare programs utilizing more traditional models of change (e.g., Luckner & Nadler, 1997) with approaches built on a positive psychology paradigm to compare both short-term change and the stability of change over time.

References

Armstrong, L., & Jenkins, S. (2003). *Every second counts*. New York: Broadway Books.

Asakawa, K. (2004). Flow experience and autotelic personality in Japanese college students: How do they experience challenges in daily life? *Journal of Happiness Studies, 5,* 123–154.

Canter, M. (1994). *Ethics for psychologists: A commentary on the APA Ethics Code*. Washington, DC: American Psychological Association.

Csikszentmihalyi, M. (1990). *Flow: The psychology of optimal experience*. New York: Harper & Row.

Csikszentmihalyi, M., & Csikszentmihalyi, I. (1999). Adventure and the flow experience. In J. Miles & S. Priest (Eds.), *Adventure programming* (pp. 153–158). State College, PA: Venture.

Davis-Berman, J., & Berman, D. (1994). *Wilderness therapy: Foundations, theory and research*. Dubuque, IA: Kendall/Hunt.

Davis-Berman, J., & Berman, D. (2002). Risk and anxiety in adventure education. *Journal of Experiential Education, 25*(2), 305–310.

Dixon, S. (1979). *Working with people in crisis: Theory and practice*. St. Louis: Mosby.

Hall, C. (1954). *A primer of Freudian psychology*. New York: Mentor Books.

Leberman, S. I., & Martin, A. J. (2002). Does pushing comfort zones produce peak learning experiences? *Australian Journal of Outdoor Education, 7*(1), 71–81.

Luckner, J. L., & Nadler, R. S. (1997). *Processing the experience: Strategies to enhance and generalize learning* (2nd ed.). Dubuque, IA: Kendall/Hunt.

Maslow, A. (1954). *Motivation and personality*. New York: Harper & Row.

Massimini, F., Csikszentmihalyi, M., & Carli, M. (1987). The monitoring of optimal experience: A tool for psychiatric rehabilitation. *Journal of Nervous and Mental Disease, 175,* 545–549.

Mitten, D. (1999). Leadership for community building. In J. Miles & S. Priest (Eds.), *Adventure programming* (pp. 253–264). State College, PA: Venture.

Schmidt, J. (1998). *Overcoming challenges: Exploring the role of action, experience, and opportunity in fostering resilience among adolescents*. Unpublished doctoral dissertation, University of Chicago.

Seligman, M. P. (1990). *Learned optimism: How to change your mind and your life*. New York: Simon & Schuster.

Seligman, M. P., & Csikszentmihalyi, M. (2000). Positive psychology: An introduction. *American Psychologist, 54,* 5–14.

Salovey, P., Rothman, A., Detweiler, J., & Steward, W. (2000). Emotional states and physical health. *American Psychologist, 55,* 110–121.

Trull, T. (2005). *Clinical psychology*. Belmont, CA: Wadsworth/Thomson Learning.

Warren, K. (1999). Women's outdoor adventures. In J. Miles & S. Priest (Eds.), *Adventure programming* (pp. 389–393). State College, PA: Venture.

Promoting Student-Centered Learning in Experiential Education

▾ ▾ ▾

Cheryl A. Estes

Experiential educators claim to value student-centered learning, yet the values, as evidenced in practice, are often teacher-centered. The purpose of this article is to increase awareness of the inconsistencies between espoused values and values in practice effecting teacher-and-student power relationships during the facilitation of experiential programs. The literature review includes related philosophical topics, a summary of what other professionals in the field have written about student-centered facilitation, and an overview of eight generations of facilitation. The author argues that teacher-centered facilitation is problematic in experiential education and justifies increasing the use of student-centered facilitation practices. Suggestions are provided for: (a) establishing forums for dialog about student-centered facilitation, (b) incorporating more student-centered facilitation practices, and (c) considering student-centered learning during program development and facilitator training. The author concludes that the profession's very commitment to integrity necessitates that we, as experiential educators, take action in order to ensure that our programs become more student-centered.

This chapter originally was published in the *Journal of Experiential Education*, with the following citation: Estes, C. A. (2004). Promoting student-centered learning in experiential education. *Journal of Experiential Education, 27*(2), 141–160.

> There is a fundamental question that should be carved in stone over every school
> entrance to remind us all, daily, of a problem we must battle on a continual basis. That
> question: "Who processes the information within?" At the moment, in too many
> classrooms, it is teachers using texts in ignorance of the fundamental educational corol-
> lary to that question: "The extent to which the learner processes the information to be
> acquired is the extent to which it is acquired." (Wigginton, 1986)

Wigginton (1986) strikes at the heart of the problem addressed in this article—for education to be at its best, the learner must be the one who processes the information from
educational experiences. Student reflection on experience is deeply embedded within experiential education paradigms, but incongruence exists between what experiential education
claims to value and what experiential education is in practice. It seems remarkable that one
widely recognized facilitation technique, where the teacher speaks on behalf of the experience (Priest & Gass, 1997), can co-exist with the Association for Experiential Education's
(AEE) definition of experiential education, which includes a number of principles that support
student-centered learning such as, "throughout the experiential learning process, the learner
[italics added] is actively engaged in posing questions, investigating, experimenting, being
curious, solving problems, assuming responsibility, being creative, and constructing meaning"
(AEE, n.d.). On one hand, we claim to value student-centered reflection, yet our values, as
evidenced in practice, are often teacher-centered.

The logic behind the author's claim is as follows: (a) The process of experiential education is commonly considered to be an "action-reflection" cycle (Joplin, 1995, p. 15); and
(b) one of the foremost assumptions of experiential learning is, that it is "student rather than
teacher based" (Joplin, p. 20), and the learner's experience is the valid basis for knowledge
(Crosby, 1995; Joplin, 1995); further, (c) AEE iterates that, "throughout the experiential learning process, the *learner* [italics added] is actively engaged in...being creative and constructing meaning" (AEE, n.d.); however, (d) in practice, experiential educators often assume
authority for directing what students learn during facilitation (e.g., teacher led discussions)
(Bacon, 1983; Bell, 1993; Brown 2002a, 2002b; Estes & Tomb, 1995; Priest, 1996; Vokey, 1987);
thus (e) it is often the teacher, not the student, who has more power during reflection on
experience; and (f) the way that teachers use this power to convey their own messages while
processing experiential activities makes student reflection, as it occurs in practice, more
teacher-centered than student-centered.

Interestingly, while highly skilled experiential educators readily acknowledge this
inconsistency in discussions (personal communication, Mike Gass, November, 2001), it has

been difficult to sustain substantive discourse about the need to examine if and/or how teachers wield power over students during experiential learning. Why is this? The author argues that most experiential educators and students operating in Western educational traditions are socialized into epistemologies that value teachers as authorities, so neither teachers nor students are very aware of this inconsistency. Our socialization causes us to see ourselves as more student-centered than we actually are. That is, teacher-controlled processing of experiential activities fits our world view of what teacher-student relationships *should* look like. Further, it is probable that while experiential educators unintentionally fall into this habit of assuming power over student learning, increased awareness of this problem will promote their desire to engage in conversations directed at increasing the use of student-centered facilitation practices. While generations of facilitation have evolved significantly over the past 40 years (Bacon, 1983, 1987; Doughty, 1991; Gass & Priest, 1993; Itin, 1995; Priest & Gass, 1997; Priest, Gass, & Fitzpatrick, 1999; Priest, Gass, & Gillis, 2000), experiential educators will benefit from critical reflection about where power resides—with the student, with the teacher, or with student-teacher partners in learning—as they facilitate experiential programs. Skilled experiential educators can make conscious choices that empower students to take control of their own learning, and meaningful learning can be increased to the extent that experiential educators can facilitate learning experiences that are more student-centered.

The purpose of this article is to increase awareness of inconsistencies between espoused values and values in practice, effecting teacher and student power relationships during the facilitation of experiential education programs. Awareness is a first step toward meaningful change, and this article is a catalyst for generating more conversations about this issue. Another goal is to increase the use of student-centered facilitation techniques in experiential education and facilitator training programs. This article does not seek to establish the importance of student reflection in experiential learning, as this has been more than adequately covered elsewhere (see Joplin, 1995; Greenaway, 1993; Knapp, 1992; Priest et al., 2000; Sugerman, Doherty, Garvey, & Gass, 2000). The tone of this article is intended to be provocative in order to stimulate discussion. Further, the author admits in advance to certain generalizations and exaggerations for the sake of clarity of argument. My central thesis is supported by a literature review that contains related philosophical topics, a summary of what other professionals in the field have said about student-centered teaching, and discussion about generations of facilitation as they relate to student-centered learning. Suggestions for ways experiential educators can facilitate student-centered learning are included. The article concludes with implications for program development and the training new experiential educators.

Definitions and Key Concepts

The following definitions and key concepts are used in this article:

1. *Facilitation* includes, "anything and everything you [the facilitator] do before, during, or after the learning experiences to enhance people's reflection, integration, and continuation of lasting change" (Priest et al., 2000, p. 19).

2. *Processing* is a guided reflection session that takes place following an experiential activity that typically consists of a circular discussion where the leader poses questions to the participants and restates answers (Brown, 2002b). Other forms of processing include drama, dance, journal writing, and painting (see Greenaway, 1993; Sugerman et al., 2000). Processing is often used interchangeably with facilitation, but for the purposes of this article, *facilitation* refers to the process of guiding students through the entire learning experience. *Processing* refers only to conducting a discussion or activity as a means to reflect upon, learn from, and change as a result of experience (Priest et al., 2000).

3. *Reflection* is a series of sequential steps in a process that a person goes through following an experience, which includes: (a) reorganizing perceptions, (b) forming new relationships, and (c) influencing future thoughts and actions in order to learn from an experience (Sugerman et al., 2000).

4. *Student-centered* (used in conjunction with processing, learning, or teaching) describes a learning process where much of the power during the experience resides with students. In some cases, students and teachers are collaborators, sharing equal power. Student-centered is used in this article in the tradition of the Dewey Laboratory School, where children were involved in group activities that were designed to be similar to how people learned in real life—usefulness and relevance were built into the system (Menand, 2001). Further, student-centered education is appropriate at any age. *Student* is used throughout this article but is interchangeable with other terms including participant and learner.

5. *Teacher-centered* (used in conjunction with the words processing, learning, or teaching) describes a learning process where the power resides with the teacher. Teacher is used interchangeably with other terms including experiential educator, facilitator, instructor, or leader.

Review of Related Literature

Other professionals in the field have written about student-centered facilitation, but to date, the literature has not resulted in sustained conversations aimed at increasing the use of student-centered facilitation practices. The literature review covers three areas: (a) First, there are two related philosophical topics that add clarity to the argument; (b) next, comments of those who have previously questioned the balance of teacher and student power in experiential education are summarized; and (c) thirdly, the results of one study, which examined this situation, are discussed. The literature review concludes with a discussion of eight generations of facilitation as they relate to the student- and teacher-centered concept. Collectively, this literature sets the stage for the action section of this article—increasing awareness of, and sustaining dialog about, student-centered facilitation, and making suggestions for increasing the use of student-centered techniques in experiential education and facilitator training programs.

Related Philosophical Topics

Philosophy is used in this article as a tool to assist experiential educators in becoming better facilitators, and two related philosophical topics help explain why teacher-centered facilitation does not fit within the experiential education paradigm. These topics are presented as: (a) a review of Dewey's philosophy about the importance of experience and the student's role in learning from experience, and (b) an explanation of why epistemologically congruent experiential education programs need to use student-centered facilitation techniques.

Centrality of experience. First, the central role of experience in learning provides a philosophical basis for the experiential education profession. Dewey noted that, "All genuine education comes about through experience" (Dewey, 1938/1988). However, Dewey did not imply that all experiences were equally educative. Whether or not an experience is educative depends upon the quality of the experience, whether or not it is engaging *to the student* [italics added] and if the experience has continuity with the student's further experiences (Dewey, 1938/1988). Dewey was not proposing to elevate "doing" over "thinking," but rather he looked at doing and thinking as just practical distinctions one makes about the learning process as the learner adjusts to tensions that arise when s/he engages in the world (Menand, 2001). Crosby (1995) noted, according to Dewey, the goal of education was for the student to be able to understand and use experience, and this was achieved when students developed the critical thinking skills necessary to examine their experiences. Thus, the teacher's role is to facilitate students' learning by engaging them in experiences that are fundamentally reflective because of their relevance to students' lives. "After resolution comes reflection [by the student], on the movement [experience] so that what is learned may be generalized and used again" (Crosby, p. 79). Further, as Hunt (1995) pointed out, Dewey does not downplay the role of reflection in learning. Dewey does, however, move away from education's traditional preoccupation with the mind and the bias inherent in elevating thinking over doing (Menand, 2001). Thus, the importance of experience, and the student's role in critically reflecting on and learning from experience are clearly expressed and supported through the existing literature.

Epistemological methods. The second topic addressed by the literature explains why epistemologically congruent experiential education must value students' roles in both their experiences and their subsequent reflection on those experiences. Epistemological methods that value the teacher as authority are incongruent with the commitment of experiential education to student-created knowledge. When a teacher directs student reflection by telling them what they learned, students are not expected (or required) to think for themselves about what the experiences could mean. Therefore, they are not empowered to learn *how to learn* from their experiences (Estes & Tomb, 1995). In a similar vein, Vokey (1987) discussed how Outward Bound's uncritical adoption of psychological language and models has compromised its commitment to self-reliance. Vokey noted—to the degree the instructor controls metaphors and student processing, instructors and students are not collaborators in the learning process. Teacher control of what is learned, no matter how well intentioned, conveys a message of control over students rather than student empowerment. Therefore, when in the role of authority, teachers are reinforcing dominant paradigms that lessons are dispensed from teachers rather than discovered by students through a process of meaningful experience and critical reflection.

Questioning the Balance of Teacher and Student Power in Experiential Education

A number of experienced teachers have questioned the balance of power between teacher and student in experiential education (Bacon, 1983; Bell, 1993; Estes & Tomb, 1995; Priest & Gass, 1997; Vokey, 1987). Bacon acknowledged that during debriefing sessions students often say what they think others want to hear; and instructors are so eager to teach about a particular lesson that their eagerness causes them to move too quickly to meet their own goals. This may occur without the instructor having ever determined what the actual effects of the experience were on the needs of the students. As Vokey notes, when teachers coerce people into opinions rather than providing educative experiences they covertly provide appropriate metaphors and language that assume the teacher knows what the students need more than the students themselves. He calls upon Outward Bound to re-examine how "the priorities inherent in the assumptions underlying behavioristic language and models of education concern not empowerment, but control" (Vokey, p. 21).

Bell (1993) observed that when teachers hear someone talk about their experience in ways that do not fit the teacher's existing theories, they often redirect what was said into something that fits what they know. She called for experiential educators to ask hard questions about "Whose memories are privileged in the discourse of 'the group,' and how am I [the teacher] complicit in this in my practice as a facilitator" (Bell, p. 23)? Estes and Tomb (1995) proposed that teacher control and over-intellectualizing in experiential education were taking away from students' self-reliance. Building on his previous work, Priest (1996) called for closer examination of the debriefing component of experiential programs, and its positive and negative effects on participants. His belief was that as experiential educators have been pressured to accomplish more in less time, they have increasingly come to rely on prescriptive approaches that may not meet students' needs and may take away from learning. Priest further speculated:

> Is a prescriptive program truly experientially educative? Because the facilitator has power to decide their agenda for discussion, does specific debriefing prevent truth from arising "within" the learners? Or does it allow the learners to focus more on their issues because the facilitator knows what is best for them? (Priest, p. 40)

Brown (2002a, 2002b) took up these questions in his study on the balance of power during debriefing sessions in one typical adventure program in Australia.

Brown's Study of Social Order During Facilitation in an Adventure Education Program

Brown (2002a, 2002b) utilized conversation-analytic methodology to observe and analyze processing. What he observed was that the teacher created his preferred version of reality through the use of formulations and public re-voicing of ostensibly student-created knowledge during debriefing sessions. Brown observed that the use of paraphrases, widely advocated in experiential education literature, consistently operated as mechanisms that allowed the teacher to create a preferred version of reality from students' answers. The teacher routinely exhibited the following teacher-centered behaviors when he: (a) evaluated student responses as right and wrong, (b) paraphrased students' comments into acceptable answers by stating what "the student really meant," (c) allocated turns at talk, and (d) directed students' talk to the teacher rather than to each other (Brown, 2002a, 2002b). Brown speculated that none of these behaviors appeared to be atypical, and they were likely common in most other adventure programs where talk circles are routinely used. Brown (2002b) concluded, "the explication of how power relationships are built and sustained necessitates a re-evaluation of existing literature on the role of the leader in the facilitation process" (p. 110). He called for experiential educators to "critically reflect on practice with a view to exploring other avenues [than talk circles] for facilitating learning" (Brown, 2002a, p. 293). He concluded that his validation of "what is being done" (in terms of teacher-centered learning) could serve as a precursor to understanding what should be done (in terms of student-centered learning).

Eight Generations of Facilitation and Student-Centered Learning

To date, there are eight recognized generations of facilitation in the experiential education literature, and each generation can be labeled as primarily teacher-centered or student-centered. First, the four earliest generations, similar to those proposed earlier by Bacon (1983), and Doughty (1991), are discussed as one group (Priest & Gass, 1997). A second group, generations five through seven, all tend toward teacher-centered methods (Itin, 1995; Priest & Gass, 1997). Third, the eighth and newest generation, popularized by Priest et al. (1999), returns to a student-centered model after speculation and experimental validation by Priest and Lesperance (1994) that self-facilitation was more effective than teacher-facilitation.

The *first* generation, "letting the experience speak for itself," is identified as appropriate for recreational programs where the primary goal is fun. This generation is primarily student-centered, because the teacher's role is to conduct properly sequenced, well-designed activities, and it is up to the students to derive meaning from their experiences. The second generation, appropriately named, "speaking on behalf of the experience," is a method designed for educational programs. This generation is primarily teacher-centered, and the teacher's role is to provide students with feedback. The teacher tends to tell students what they did well, what they need to work on, what they learned, and how they can apply their knowledge in the future. Priest and Gass (1997) cautioned that this second generation runs the risk of alienating students and hampering learning. The third generation, "debriefing the experience," is a method designed for educational programs that is supposed to circumvent this problem of student alienation. Here, the teacher's role is to ask questions, encourage students to answer and take ownership for thinking about what they have learned. While this generation is ostensibly student-centered, the author argues that, in practice, it often becomes teacher-centered (see the problems observed by Brown, 2002a, in the previous section). The fourth generation, "directly frontloading the experience," is a method designed for educational programs that allows the teacher to focus more on experience and less on intellectualizing about experience. The teacher's role is to highlight or "load" the learning immediately prior to experience by covering key learning points during a pre-activity briefing. The debrief then becomes "direction with reflection," re-emphasizing learning points that occurred throughout the experience. To the degree the teacher decides what students need to learn, and does the loading, this generation is teacher-centered. However, this fourth generation has the potential to be student-centered as well. To the degree that students are involved in deciding what they need to learn, and collaborate with the teacher to frontload their experiences, this fourth generation can be student-centered.

The fifth, sixth, and seventh generations are all teacher-centered methods that involve increasing amounts of client deception for the purpose of accomplishing programmatic goals. Generation *five,* "isomorphically framing the experience;" generation six, "indirectly frontloading the experience" (both described by Priest and Gass, 1997); and generation seven, "using hypnotic language" (described by Itin, 1995), are all considered advanced facilitation techniques best employed by highly trained experiential educators. The ethical application of these generations requires a complete and accurate needs assessment (see Bacon, 1987; Priest & Gass, 1997). Priest and Gass pointed out that in order to make isomorphs effective, the teacher must really know students' setting, language, and background issues. Generations five through seven are designed for use in programs that have specific client goals, which are acknowledged at the front end by the clients (as is the case in some corporate and therapeutic programs). Ethical precautions are in order when applying the fifth, sixth, and seventh generations because they involve varying amounts of student deception (see Hunt, 1986). Experiential educators should seriously consider if student-centered facilitation methods could better accomplish program goals because student-centered methods will likely prove less alienating and may increase the probability that lessons learned will be retained by the students (Priest & Lesperance, 1994).

Priest et al. (1999) popularized the eighth and newest generation, called "self-facilitation." This generation operationalized Greenaway's (1993) proposal that a future generation of facilitation should involve learners as facilitators of their own experiences. Priest and Lesperence (1994) discovered that a corporate group, which chose to self-facilitate by using funneling techniques taught during an experiential program back in the work place, resulted in continually higher gains in postcourse teamwork levels. While this is just one study, it empirically validates Greenaway's idea that student-centered facilitation would be more effective. Experienced facilitators, such as Priest et al. (2000), concluded that an important part of facilitator ethics is respect, which includes "respect[ing] clients' rights to make decisions as well as helping them understand the consequences of their choices" (p. 17). The eighth generation represents a way to keep the increased focus on the value of experience from generation four (frontloading), and combine it with the benefits of student-centered facilitation. This is accomplished by empowering students to be responsible, at least in part, for deciding what needs to be learned and implementing a continuous learning process that can carry over into other life arenas.

Collectively, the literature creates a compelling case that teacher-centered facilitation is a pervasive problem in experiential education. The resolution of this problem requires increased awareness and sustained conversations about teacher and student-centered facilitation practices. The questions that arise, which are subsequently addressed, include: (a) In which forums should this conversation take place? (b) How can we, as experiential educators, incorporate more student-centered practices in our facilitation? and (c) What implications does this information have for program development and facilitator training?

Discussion

One purpose of this article was to make a compelling case for why experiential educators need to use more student-centered facilitation practices. Raising awareness of a problem is the first step toward creating meaningful change. Allow me to raise awareness by answering the following question: Why should experiential educators have more conversations about student-centered learning, even though it is already an explicit value within experiential education?

If we, as experiential educators, want to offer our students the best possible education in the form of experienced-based learning (which arguably provides the *best* form of learning for *life*), we have an obligation to ensure that our programs excel in all respects. To the extent that experiential educators assume power over students by over-controlling their reflection on experience, they devalue both the experience and the students' role in their own learning. The resultant effect is that learning experiences are only a shadow of what they can be. However, we, as experiential educators, can ensure that experienced-based learning excels by utilizing student-centered facilitation techniques. In so doing, experiential educators can facilitate learning that is epistemologically and value congruent. When student-centered techniques are used to both guide the experience, and students' subsequent reflection on experience, experiential education will be at its best. Student autonomy, critical thinking, and self-reliance can be encouraged throughout the action and reflection cycle. Thus, experiential educators consciously using student-centered techniques can ensure that experiential learning is first rate by providing students with more opportunities to take meaningful roles in their own learning. By increasing awareness of this important issue, experiential educators will be empowered to honor—in practice as well as word—the explicit value that experiential education is "student rather than teacher based" (Joplin, 1995, p. 20).

Forums for Dialog About Student-Centered Facilitation

Forums exist for initiating and sustaining conversations aimed at increasing the use of student-centered facilitation practices. International, regional and local conferences provide ideal venues for workshops where interested teachers can engage in dialog about this topic. Further, student-centered facilitation can be a topic for staff training workshops and program debriefs. Workshop-type sessions where teachers have the opportunity to share their views regarding student-centered facilitation practices can be employed. There are many facilitators who, given the opportunity, have a lot to share with others about this topic. In so doing, we can "walk our talk" with regard to ensuring that our experiential programs honor processes through which *learners* [italics added] are actively engaged in all aspects of their learning experience (AEE, n.d.). In addition, the following values, tips, and techniques for incorporating more student-centered facilitation practices in experiential programs can be effective.

Student-Centered Facilitation Techniques

Student-centered learning is not a new idea. In general, it involves reversing traditionally teacher-centered learning and places students at the center of the learning process.

Table 1.
Seven Suggestions for Facilitating Student-Centered Experiential Education Programs

1. Recognize that changing from teacher-centered learning to student-centered learning requires both awareness and effort to initiate and sustain dialog about this problem.

2. Promote student-centered learning by embracing values similar to Paulo Freire's approach to education, where teachers and students transform learning into a collaborative process (Shor & Freire, 1987).

3. Rely less on the standard practice of talk circles and more on creative techniques to facilitate student reflection (see Greenaway, 1993; Sugerman et al., 2000).

4. When talk circles are used, experiential educators need to rethink the role of the teacher in verbal facilitation sessions, and recognize the active and influential role that the teacher has in determining what is supposed to be learned (Brown, 2002a, 2002b).

5. Let students have a role in facilitating their own experiences (Priest & Lesperance, 1994; Wilson, 1995). (See Table 2 for specific ideas.)

6. Begin an experiential program by assessing both teachers and students to the extent possible (Bacon, 1983, 1987; Priest & Gass, 1997; Shor, 1989).

7. Use prescriptive and advanced generations of facilitation techniques, including metaphor (Bacon, 1983, 1987), direct frontloading, isomorphic framing, indirect frontloading (Priest & Gass, 1997), and hypnotic language (Itin, 1995), both ethically and only in experiential programs where teachers are highly trained and it is possible to get a complete and accurate needs assessment.

Emerging brain research validates what experiential educators have always known—students learn best through experiential and student-centered approaches (*Understanding the Brain*, 1995). How can teachers make experiential learning more student-centered? The seven suggestions that follow are values, tips, and techniques the author has gathered from personal experiences and the literature (see Table 1 for summary):

1. The *first* suggestion reiterates the need for experiential educators to recognize that a change from teacher to student-centered learning requires both awareness and conscious effort to initiate and sustain dialog about this problem. To further clarify, most experiential educators practicing in developed countries, including the United States, England and Australia, have been socialized and educated in traditional teacher-centered venues. Thus, we are comfortable with students looking to teachers for information, answers, guidance, affirmation, and permission to speak. Wilson (1995) noted she thought she had reached a plateau in excellence in teaching when she could "set a goal for a group, design a structured activity to 'teach' that lesson, and finally process it to make sure they got the point" (p. 279). This is not necessarily bad teaching, but we must acknowledge that it is not student-centered. Thus, re-socialization into student-centered values and methods involves awareness, commitment, conscious effort, practice, reflection on practice, and continuous improvement efforts.

2. A *second* suggestion is for experiential educators to promote student-centered learning by embracing values similar to Paulo Freire's approach to education, where teachers and students transform learning into a collaborative process (Shor & Freire, 1987). The Freire approach is based on the belief that students can find their own authentic voice, and they create knowledge through critical encounters with reality and ideas (Shor, 1989). While an in-depth study of Freire's and Shor's works will certainly provide the reader with greater familiarity of Freire's techniques than is possible within the scope of this article, a summary of their educational values, in the following section, is illuminating.

Freire and Shor's educational values. Freire promotes the use of dialog in place of teacher-led discussion, because through dialog, teachers and students reflect together on what they know, and do not know, and can act critically to transform reality (Shor & Freire, 1987). Dialog implies the absence of authoritarianism and is an epistemological position—in dialog, the teacher does not own the object of study; rather, the students stimulate the teacher's curiosity, and s/he brings enthusiasm to the students. Together, then, they can illuminate the object of learning. Dialog requires that students participate critically in their own education. This does not mean everyone has to speak, but rather students should be listening carefully to both the teacher and to each other. Students should have the right to speak or to pass, because requiring a turn at talk is coercive. Remarks should be addressed to other students, as well as to the teacher. Shor (1989) suggests that teachers encourage this behavior by breaking eye contact with students who are speaking in order to encourage students to address the group more generally. Freire's approach fits well within experiential education, in part, because it requires students to have prior experiential contact with the object of learning before dialog. Further, the material of study, and the process of study, should be mutually developed by the students and the teachers. Freier called this "co-intentionality," and Dewey referred to it as "co-participation" (Shor, 1989).

3. A *third* suggestion is for experiential educators to rely less on the standard practice of talk circles and more on creative techniques to facilitate student reflection. There are three problems with using talk circles for facilitating reflection on experience: (a) Talk circles provide a familiar teacher-centered environment that encourages the teacher to direct the learning process through questioning, validating, paraphrasing, and allocating turns at talk; (b) the emphasis on the importance of circular talk/debriefing in experiential programs has resulted in a decrease in the importance of hands-on experience (Bacon, 1983); and (c) the use of talk, and the accompanying idea that talking about an experience is necessary for learning to occur, separates experience into "doing" and "thinking" parts which often values thinking over doing. Experiential educators can learn about alternatives to talk circles by familiarizing themselves with guides to alternative reflection activities. Greenaway (1993) described many reflection alternatives that do not rely on teacher-led talk sessions, including art, drama, dance, poetry, writing, storytelling, photography, presentations, or repeating the same activity. Sugerman et al. (2000) have prepared a wonderful guidebook to reflective learning that outlines many proven activities that empower students to take an active role in pre- and post-reflection processes.

4. A *fourth* suggestion for experiential educators who choose to use talk circles is to rethink the role of the teacher in verbal facilitation sessions. This will assist the teacher in recognizing the active and influential role they play in determining what is supposed to be learned (Brown, 2002a). Teachers need to be more aware of the tendency for imbalance in knowledge and power relationships that typically occurs during talk circles and consciously do the following: (a) avoid prescribing acceptable student responses; (b) have students restate their own responses when clarity is needed (or, at minimum, get agreement that the teachers' restatement was accurate); (c) genuinely listen to students; and (d) get students to talk to, and listen to, each other by using verbal and nonverbal techniques that encourage these behaviors. For example, the teacher can redirect a student who speaks directly to her to speak to the group instead.

5. A *fifth* suggestion is for experiential educators to let students have a role in facilitating their own experiences. This is especially important in educational environments where teachers are not likely to acquire a complete and accurate needs assessment, which is essential for ethical application of higher generations of facilitation such as frontloading, isomorphic framing, indirect frontloading, and hypnotic language. Also, students in therapeutic programs, where facilitators tend to rely more on prescriptive (teacher-centered) methods, will likely find self-facilitation extremely beneficial. All students, regardless of the experiential program's mission, can benefit from developing self-facilitation skills and becoming self-reliant learners. Wilson (1995) suggested empowering students by: (a) listening to them; (b) allowing them to set individual and group goals; and (c) allowing them to make choices about activities, how to respond to tasks, and when, and when not to undertake an experience (see Table 2 for a list of ideas for student-centered facilitation).

6. A *sixth* suggestion is for experiential educators to begin a program by assessing both teachers and students to the extent possible. A thorough needs assessment provides an important foundation on which to build a program's goal to create a collaborative learning

Table 2.
Suggestions for Students Facilitating, or Co-Facilitating, in Experiential Programs

- Have a student choose a reading to introduce a day, activity, or as a springboard for post-activity reflection.

- Instead of being the authority in the learning process, the teacher can take the role of resource person, guide, cheerleader, and coach (Warren, 1995).

- Let students decide what they need to learn (Wilson, 1995). For example, allow students to set their own individual and group goals.

- Let students co-create metaphors—tell them what an activity entails and ask, "What do you have to do in everyday life that this experience might be similar to?"

- Let students front-load their own experiences by discussing what they need to work on as individuals and as a group. At the end of the experience, have them decide how well they did. Then, let them set their goals for the next experience.

- Use real instead of contrived issues. If it can't be real, create a larger context in which to view the event (Wilson, 1995).

- Listen, listen, listen. Don't be too eager to share your stories, ideas, and what you think students have learned. Have students paraphrase their own statements, or at least get agreement that you have paraphrased correctly. Avoid judging students' comments as right or wrong. Encourage students to talk to each other instead of just to you.

- Teach students how to use funneling to reflect on their experiences. Empower the team to utilize funneling to process their experiences themselves (Priest & Lesperance, 1994**).**

environment. Bacon (1983) noted, "It is always important to know where the students are coming from before trying to lead them somewhere else" (p. 20). Priest and Gass (1997) acknowledged that teachers should always do their homework by finding out about the group's needs and objectives in advance. Shor (1989) pointed out that in order to operationalize a student-centered learning experience the teacher must begin by researching both self andstudents. In so doing, the teacher is assessing what resources and liabilities the teacher and the students bring to the learning environment. Finally, as Sugerman et al. (2000) noted, a part of good, student-centered, practice involves the teacher constantly assessing the group and his/her own reactions while an experience is ongoing.

7. A *seventh* suggestion is for experiential educators onlyto use prescriptive and advanced generations of facilitation techniques, including metaphor (Bacon, 1983, 1987), direct frontloading, isomorphic framing, indirect frontloading (Priest & Gass, 1997), and hypnotic language (Itin, 1995), in experiential programs when teachers are highly trained and it is possible to get a complete and accurate needs assessment. Some have questioned the ethics of these prescriptive facilitation techniques (Hunt, 1986; Priest & Gass, 1997; Wilson, 1995). It is important to emphasize the caution leveled at these generations of facilitation by Priest and Gass (1997): "Without this information [an in-depth assessment of needs as well as an understanding of what the change will mean in the client's life if the change occurs] this approach [indirect frontloading] can be destructive and changes short lived" (p. 215). Priest and Gass further noted that the facilitator *has to really know what s/he is doing* [italics added]. Bacon (1987) also acknowledged, "the metaphor model is active and directive. As a result, its ethical and effective application requires a complete and accurate [student needs] assessment" (p. 14). Hunt cautioned that if experiential educators are going to facilitate learning experiences that involve deceptions, then they had better be both well-intentioned and apply two rules, including (a) willingness to make any deception publicly known, and (b) ask themselves whether or not they would mind if someone did this to them. Therefore, teachers should use these advanced facilitation techniques only when indicated and not as a matter of standard practice.

In summary, these seven suggestions represent a collection of specific actions experiential educators can take to ensure their facilitation practices are more student-centered. These suggestions address, in part, Brown's call for the need for experiential educators to critically reflect on practice with a view toward exploring other avenues besides verbal reflection sessions in order to embrace our espoused values in practice. Further, the field of experiential education, as a whole, should make it a priority to think of ways student-centered facilitation techniques can be incorporated into program development and facilitator training.

Implications for Program Development and Facilitator Training

Most experiential programs engage in continuous improvement efforts and it makes good sense to place student-centered facilitation on programs' agendas. For example, as a part of improvement efforts, teachers could use brainstorming and discussion to: (a) Identify ways that the program and/or teachers are currently using teacher and student-centered facilitation techniques. Ask questions like, "Does teacher or student-centered facilitation best fit with our mission?" and "What are the positive and negative effects of using teacher and student-centered facilitation?" (b) Identify where student-centered techniques fit best within the program. For example, when students are relatively mature, likely to be committed to program goals, and able to take a partnership role in their education, they are an ideal group for student-centered facilitation;

(c) Brainstorm creative ideas for student-centered activities/methods that can be utilized. The ideas outlined in Tables 1 and 2 provide a place to start; and (d) Teachers should practice, share results, reflect, and refine facilitation approaches. Ideally, both teachers and students will grow through this process.

It is especially important to incorporate concepts from student-centered facilitation into experiential educator training programs because it is newly trained teachers who are particularly vulnerable to relying on teacher-centered approaches. To validate this point, visualize facilitators who have recently learned about the wonders of experiential education and advanced facilitation techniques, such as frontloading—they have so much enthusiasm they are ready to tell everyone about the wonderful lessons to be learned. Telling is the easiest and most comfortable technique, because it is very familiar to those socialized within Westernized educational paradigms. While many, if not most, experiential educators eventually arrive at an intuitive awareness of the importance of student-centered learning through years of practice and reflection (see authors Bell, 1993; Brown, 2002a, 2002b; Estes & Tomb, 1995; Greenaway, 1993; Knapp, 1992; Priest & Gass, 1997; Sugerman et al., 2000; Warren, 1995; Wilson, 1995), less experienced teachers are less likely to have this awareness.

Of further concern, experiential educator training often includes an introduction to advanced facilitation techniques. However, a new teacher has little context in which to understand precautions about the ethical application of these techniques. Therefore, it is especially important to include information from the present article and other related literature in training, practice, and feedback at the outset of an experiential educator's career.

Taken together, the ideas in this article present a clear argument for establishing student-centered facilitation as an important issue in experiential education. To the extent that we, as experiential educators, are prepared to sustain dialog about student-centered facilitation, and take conscious steps to incorporate more student-centered practices into our programs, we can increase congruence between values espoused by the profession and the values we practice. Arguably, it is the profession's very commitment to integrity that necessitates sustaining dialog about this important issue.

Conclusions

The author predicts that student-centered facilitation techniques similar to those described in the present article will become more common than talk circles in future experiential education programs. One can trace the evolution of facilitation and reflection, as it relates to the balance of teacher and student power in experiential programs, from student-centered to teacher-centered, and back to student-centered models. Brown's (2002a) study validates what others have speculated—teachers exert a lot of power during debriefing sessions. If experiential educators wish to retain the claim that experiential education is student-centered, and that "the *learner* [italics added] is actively engaged in posing questions, investigating, experimenting, being curious, solving problems, assuming responsibility, being creative, and constructing meaning," (AEE, n.d.) then significant changes in our accepted facilitation practices are in order.

In response to the question, "Does student-centered facilitation really warrant so much attention when it is already an explicit value of the profession?" The author concludes with this thought: While teacher-centered experiential education has learning value, it is not nearly as beneficial as student-centered experiential education. It is clearly time for the profession to raise awareness, increase discussion, and take action in order to resolve the incongruence between what experiential education claims to value and how experience-based learning is delivered in practice.

Author Note

The concept for this article came from a working paper, "Is Cheese Food Really Food?" presented at the International Conference on Outdoor Recreation and Education (ICORE) (Estes & Tomb, 1995). The author wants to thank Steven Tomb, Inara Scott, and Karl Johnson for their time spent discussing these ideas. Also, thanks is due to Mike Brown and others who took the time to track me down and inquire about the ideas presented herein.

References

AEE (n.d.) *Association for Experiential Education's what is experiential education?* Retrieved September 7, 2004, from http://www.aee2.org/customer/pages.php?pageid=47

Bacon, S. (1983). *The conscious use of metaphor in Outward Bound.* Denver, CO: Colorado Outward Bound School.

Bacon, S. (1987). *The evolution of the Outward Bound process.* Greenwich, CT: Outward Bound USA.

Bell, M. (1993). What constitutes experience? Rethinking theoretical assumptions. *Journal of Experiential Education, 16*(1), 19–24.

Brown, M. (2002a). *Interaction and social order in adventure education facilitation sessions.* Unpublished doctoral dissertation, School of Education, The University of Queensland, St. Lucia, Brisbane, Australia.

Brown, M. (2002b). The facilitator as gatekeeper: A critical analysis of social order in facilitation sessions. *Journal of Adventure Education and Outdoor Learning, 2*(2), 101–112.

Crosby, A. (1995). A critical look: The philosophical foundations of experiential education. In K. Warren, M. Sakofs, & J. S. Hunt (Eds.), *The theory of experiential education* (3rd ed., pp. 3–14). Dubuque, IA: Kendall/Hunt.

Dewey, J. (1938/1988). Experience in education. In J. A. Boydston & B. Levine (Eds.), *John Dewey: The later works,* 1925–1953: Vol. 13. 1938–1939 (pp. 1–62). Carbondale, IL: Southern Illinois University Press.

Doughty, S. (1991). Three generations of development training. *Adventure Education and Outdoor Leadership: The Journal of the National Association for Outdoor Education and the Association of Heads of Outdoor Education Centres, 7*(4), 7–9.

Estes, C. A., & Tomb, S. (1995). *Is cheese food really food?* a.k.a. Some conscious alternatives to overprocessing experience. Paper presented at the 1995 International Conference on Outdoor Recreation and Education. (ERIC Document Reproduction Service No. ED404080)

Joplin, L. (1995). On defining experiential education. In K. Warren, M. Sakofs, & J. S. Hunt (Eds.), *The theory of experiential education* (3rd ed., pp. 17–22). Dubuque, IA: Kendall/Hunt.

Gass, M., & Priest, S. (1993). Five generations of facilitated learning from adventure experiences. *Journal of Adventure Education and Outdoor Leadership, 10*(3), 23–25.

Greenaway, R. (1993). *Playback: A guide to reviewing activities.* Edinburgh, Scotland: The Award Scheme Ltd., The Duke of Edinburgh's Award and Endeavour, Scotland.

Hunt, J. S. (1986). *Ethical issues in experiential education.* Boulder, CO: Association for Experiential Education.

Hunt, J. S. (1995). Dewey's philosophical method and its influence on his philosophy of education. In K. Warren, M. Sakofs, & J. S. Hunt (Eds.), *The theory of experiential education* (3rd ed., pp. 23–32). Dubuque, IA: Kendall/Hunt.

Itin, C. (1995). Utilizing hypnotic language in adventure therapy. *The Journal of Experiential Education, 18*(2), 70–75.

Knapp, C. (1992). Lasting lessons: *A teacher's guide to reflecting on experience.* Charleston, WV: Educational Resources Information Center (ERIC).

Menand, L. (2001). *The metaphysical club.* New York: Farrar, Straus and Giroux.

Priest, S. (1996). The effect of two different debriefing approaches on developing self-confidence. *Journal of Experiential Education, 19*(6), 40–42.

Priest, S., & Gass, M. A. (1997). *Effective leadership in adventure programming.* Champaign, IL: Human Kinetics.

Priest, S., Gass, M., & Fitzpatrick, K. (1999). Training corporate managers to facilitate: The next generation of facilitating experiential methodologies. *Journal of Experiential Education, 22*(1), 50–53.

Priest, S., Gass, M., & Gillis, L. (2000). *The essential elements of facilitation.* Dubuque, IA: Kendall/Hunt.

Priest, S., & Lesperance, M. A. (1994). Time series trend analysis in corporate team development. *Journal of Experiential Education, 17*(1), 34–39.

Understanding the brain. (1995). *Education Update, 37*(7), 1, 4–5.

Shor, I. (1989). Developing student autonomy in the classroom. *Equity and Excellence, 24*(3), 35–37.

Shor, I., & Freire, P. (1987). What is the "dialogical method" of teaching? *Journal of Education, 169*(3), 11–31.

Sugerman, D. A., Doherty, K. L., Garvey, D. E., & Gass, M. A. (2000). *Reflective learning: Theory and practice.* Dubuque, IA: Kendall/Hunt.

Vokey, D. (1987). *Outward Bound: In search of foundations.* Unpublished doctoral dissertation, Queen's University, Kingston, Ontario, Canada.

Warren, K. (1995). The student-centered classroom: A model for teaching experiential education theory. In K. Warren, M. Sakofs, & J. S. Hunt (Eds.), *The theory of experiential education* (3rd ed., pp. 249–258). Dubuque, IA: Kendall/Hunt.

Wigginton, E. (1986). *Sometimes a shining moment: The Foxfire experience.* New York: Doubleday.

Wilson, L. (1995). When we want to empower as well as teach. In K. Warren, M. Sakofs, & J. S. Hunt (Eds.), *The theory of experiential education* (3rd ed., pp. 275–283). Dubuque, IA: Kendall/Hunt.

Deepening the Paradigm of Choice: Exploring Choice & Power in Experiential Education

▾ ▾ ▾

Laura Tyson & Katie Asmus

The ability to make conscious, positive choices is one of the most valuable and transferable outcomes of experiential education, and the careful examination of one's practices and beliefs about choice and power is a critical responsibility for educators. Although today the vast majority of adventure education programs start with the declaration that all activities are "Challenge by Choice," relatively little discussion has taken place in the literature or, in our experience, in the field, about the actual practice and techniques of creating an environment in which participants are empowered to make real, self-affirming choices. In the course of our careers, we have come to recognize a fundamental tension between participant choice and some of the most deeply held tenets of adventure education. The inherent contradictions between the two often create conditions that decrease the likelihood of authentic, conscious choices.

While our experiences are primarily in the field of adventure education, most of the concepts presented here are relevant to all forms of experiential education. We will begin by discussing the Western cultural value of choice. We will then examine the history of choice-making practices and theories in experiential education, followed by a reflection on the inherent tensions and challenges of the most common current model, Challenge by Choice. Finally, we will describe the Conscious Choice model developed at The Women's Wilderness Institute, which provides an active process for teaching and facilitating authentic, informed, and self-affirming choice-making practices. Within this framework we will propose a fundamentally different paradigm for the instructor role in the process of facilitating change, including guidelines for the ethical use of power.

The Cultural Value of Choice

The ability to make choices is central to the concept of freedom in Western culture. This is especially true in the United States, where the freedom of individuals to choose their government, lifestyle, and vocation was central to the tenets upon which the country was founded. The traditional political view of choice is that the degree of freedom an individual has is a result of the number of choices available to him or her. This "American Dream" version of freedom holds that if the choices are available, then anyone can make the choices necessary to own a home and be financially successful (Hochschild, 1995).

But the concept of freedom of choice is more complex than it may first appear. Many scholars, including feminist theorists, have deconstructed this idealized view of freedom of choice to show that the ability of an individual to make certain choices is not just a factor of the availability of choices, but the social context in which they occur, and the internal factors of the degree of will, desire, socialization, and habitual or adaptive choices (Hochschild, 1995; Hirschmann, 2003). Feminist theory recognizes that the choosing self, and its desires and ability to act, is itself a result of social construct, and that choices are made within the context of social expectations, media, personal history, and self-perception (Hirschmann, 2003). For instance, can the 10-year-old boy who has watched daily TV advertisements for Game-Boy really be said to independently want a GameBoy? Can another boy, living in poverty, who adaptively chooses not to want the GameBoy because he knows he stands slight chance of getting one really be said *not* to want it? Hirschmann and other theorists make the case that the choices that people will make are based not only on the number of choices available to them, but on the internal process of the choosing self, and the context and environment in which the choice is being made.

The Process of Making Choices

The "yes" or "no" that we hear from participants as they decide whether or not to participate in an activity is just the tip of an iceberg of conscious and unconscious internal processes. The actual decision-making process is complex and draws on an individual's history, habits, self-awareness, social conditioning, beliefs, biochemistry, and temperament.

Personal history and habits play a large role in how individuals identify desires and make choices. As soon as one is born, the process begins of identification of wants and needs, voicing or acting on them, and experiencing the satisfaction or disappointment of the result. For infants, this is a simple, physical, nonverbal process. As one grows older, the process gets increasingly complex, with obstacles and adaptive behaviors that can develop into lifetime patterns. The sequence of recognizing, acting on, and resolving needs can be interrupted or derailed at any point. Messages are often received that what one wants is different than what one "should" want. Attempts to get needs met may be ineffective. The ability to sense one's inner self may be undeveloped. One could be shamed simply for having needs, or deriving pleasure from their satisfaction. Numerous adaptive behaviors result from the interruption of this natural flow of wanting and resolving. One may learn to distance from one's body and feelings, or reach for short-term gratification because of a belief that what is really wanted is unobtainable. Repeated disappointment often leads to forgetting or ignoring what is really wanted. Awareness of the need may still exist, but the voice to act on it could be undeveloped. Adaptive behaviors can also show up as a lack of will, a pattern of making 'bad' choices, or a pattern of complying with, or rebelling against, the expectations of others.

The science of neurobiology has shown that decisions and choices are made as a result of a balance between the rational, thinking cortex of the brain, and the deeper, more emotional and reactive part of the brain that resides in the limbic system. The limbic system is the area of the brain that is concerned with survival, short-term gratification, and emotional needs. Adolescents have a less developed prefrontal cortex, which heightens the likelihood that they will make choices based on emotional cues and immediate needs rather than rational thought (Rosso, Young, Femia, and Yurgelun-Todd, 2004). Recent research also suggests that rather than the old view of emotions as "noise" to be screened out to reach a rational decision, the ability to integrate emotional factors and somatic sensory input with the rational thought of the cortex is a key element in effective decision-making (Bechara, Damasio, and Damasio, 2000).

Stress, an inherent element in many adventure education or group activities, has a large influence on physiological processes that influence choice and decision making (Svenson and Maule, 1993). Reactions to stress, and their subsequent impact on choice-making, vary widely among individuals, and are distinctly different in men and women. Recent research has shown that the commonly described stress response of an adrenaline-driven reaction, with sharpened senses and a sense of excitement, is more common in males than females. Under the same conditions of moderate stress, females are more likely to release acetylcholine and experience an unpleasant, nauseated feeling and a difficulty with verbal expression (Sax, 2005). Other researchers have found that while a certain degree of stress improves learning in male laboratory animals, it inhibits learning in the females due to inhibited growth of neural connections in the hippocampus (Shors, 2001). Further research found that being able to have control over the stressor removed these inhibitions to learning in females (Leuner, 2004).

Gender roles can also impact the choice-making process. For example, in Western Judea-Christian cultures women have a tendency to comply with outside expectations and to set their own needs aside to take care of others, while men and boys are more likely to act in opposition to expectations (Sax, 2005). For women and girls, identity is strongly influenced by the sense of self in relation to others, and maintaining relationships often comes before personal needs. Women and girls may therefore make choices that lead them away from challenges, because being a strong female, or being better than others at something can lead to social difficulties (Pipher, 1994). For boys and men, doing the scary or hard thing is valued, and taking leadership or competing against others raises social status. Boys are often taught to distance themselves from their feelings, internal perceptions, and gut sense in order to make choices that conform to these cultural standards of masculinity (Kindlon & Thompson, 2000).

A History of Choice-Making Practices in Experiential Education

Early roots of the philosophy of choice in experiential education can be seen in the turn-of-the-century camping movement in the United States. Miranda (1996) discusses the impact that the development of women-led girls' camps of the early 1900s had on the basic tenets of outdoor, adventure, and experiential education. Shared leadership, focus on cooperative governance, and nurturing independent thinking all served to honor each individual's abilities and opinions and to empower girls and women to actively participate in decision-making within their camping communities. "Women directors modeled shared leadership in contrast to 'control from the top', a feature in boys' camping they deplored. Girls would learn 'cooperative government', in which campers have a very real part.... We are teaching attitudes of mind more than anything else'" (Mattoon, 1923 as cited in Miranda, 1996, p. 65).

Another advocate for supporting individual choice in education was John Dewey, a well-known and influential educational philosopher in the 1920s and 1930s. Dewey valued educational experiences based on their impact on an individual's ability to positively contribute to society (Neill, 2005). Dewey's philosophy reflected an understanding of the importance of structuring educational experiences to teach critical thinking and reflective skills, and to develop the capacity for making value-based choices that are appropriate for the individual and her/his community.

Kurt Hahn, founder of Outward Bound and several other European schools based in an experiential model of education, has had a strong influence on the philosophies of adventure education. Hahn's philosophy includes the value of *impelling* students into life-changing experiences. Hahn stopped short of forcing students into experiences, but felt that it was a moral imperative for the instructor to "be a force" that would have strong influence on the decisions of the students. Itin (1996) quotes a 1965 address given by Kurt Hahn in which he stated: "It is the sin of the soul to force young people into opinions—indoctrination is of the devil—but it is culpable neglect not to impel young people into experience" (Hahn as cited in Itin, 1996, p.1). The language of *urging* and *impelling* runs deep in the history of adventure education, which, in contrast to the Conscious Choice Model, implies a value of moving people toward action, rather than exploring the process and complexity of choice.

The feminist movement had an impact on adventure education in the 1980s, as leaders in the field began to actively challenge the traditional paradigm. Mitten (1996), founder of Woodswomen, has written extensively on the integration of feminist theory into experiential programming. In Woodswomen's programs, decision-making was shared as much as possible. Supporting choice was a key component of their educational philosophy, through providing participants with options, having a flexible schedule, allowing people their own timing, encouraging rather than pushing participants, giving them information to make informed choices, and intentionally supporting women in defining and making choices for themselves (Mitten, 1996). Woodswomen programs encouraged *authentic risk-taking* through minimizing stress, supporting participants to create their own goals, and ensuring dialogue around risk and choice.

Karl Rohnke, co-founder of Project Adventure, first coined the now-ubiquitous phrase "Challenge by Choice" in the 1980s. Challenge by Choice is a concept that respects participants' choices about if and how they will participate in an experience. Lisson (2000, p. 20) notes, "Challenge by Choice as a concept is much more than an exit strategy.... In its early origins it was designed as a strategy to promote challenge, risk taking, and learning." While the term Challenge by Choice is a protected service mark of Project Adventure, its use has become commonplace in experiential education. A review of marketing literature of various programs reveals a wide interpretation of the phrase. One program proclaims, "Participants are encouraged to go beyond their normal comfort zones, but ultimately each participant determines their level of involvement." Another says, "Respecting challenge by choice means you don't pass on an activity simply because you are unwilling to try or because something seems too hard. The purpose of these activities is to challenge yourself."

More recently, Schoel and Maizell (2002), coined the term "Challenge of Choice," which gives participants a degree of choice in an activity but does not allow nonparticipation. Emphasis is placed on determining one's particular *level* of challenge, rather than simply whether or not to participate.

Discussion has emerged in the literature about the limitations and practice of Challenge by Choice. Itin (1992, 1996) has valued the retention of the impelling principle, and proposed that Challenge by Choice may encourage negative behavior if it remains unchallenged by the instructor. Itin states that the role of the experiential educator is to challenge and influence students to stretch themselves, but he also writes: "When we are real and genuine, when "challenge by choice" is no longer a program dictum, but a reminder to us to be aware of our power, then it becomes real" (Itin, 1996, p. 2).

Neill (2006) recognizes the incongruity between "encouragement" and true choice in his statement that Challenge by Choice is "somewhat at odds with other more subtle intentional and unintentional strategies which serve to design and facilitate programs in ways that coerce, entice, lure, etc. participants into joining in."

Estrellas (1996) argues that the manipulation or intentional use of stress in a program is not beneficial to creating a learning environment. On the other hand, she notes, choice and self-determination in the midst of a certain type of stress can be empowering. She discusses *eustress* or "good stress," which is marked by the presence of self-awareness, self-determination, pleasure in taking on the stress, and choice over one's situation.

Lisson (2000) notes the tendency in Challenge by Choice programs for participants who opt out of an activity to be left out of the group, or with a meaningless role. He advocates for the inclusion of a variety of roles to choose from, each with a meaningful contribution to the group task. Bunting, Haras, and Witt (2006) describe a model for ropes course programs that includes a wide range of clearly defined ways to be involved in the activities. Their research compared the "Inviting Optimum Participation (IOP)" model with a traditional Challenge by Choice approach, and found that the IOP approach elicited lower levels of anxiety, a higher degree of perceived choice, and similar degrees of meaningful involvement.

The Challenges of Challenge by Choice

The shift in experiential education from the "impelling into choice" paradigm to Challenge by Choice has reflected a growing awareness that the freedom to make one's own choices is central to an experience of personal empowerment. Challenge by Choice, as it is currently practiced, often begins and sometimes ends with the declaration that everyone will have a choice about how they want to participate. Practitioners commonly believe that if choice is available, people will make choices that are in their best interest. Yet providing choices or levels of participation to participants is only the first step in supporting participants in making the choices that are in line with their deeper authentic desires. Giving participants the tools to make self-affirming choices, and creating an environmental context in which choice can freely be explored and expressed, is a complex practice that is rarely given full attention. We have identified three common difficulties with the Challenge by Choice model: (1) opposing underlying values of the facilitator and/or program, (2) a contradictory view of the role of the staff, (3) lack of support and education about how to make healthy choices.

Opposing Underlying Values

One of the fundamental difficulties in the implementation of Challenge by Choice occurs when staff or the program philosophy in which they operate verbalize the freedom of everyone to make their own choices but have underlying beliefs or assumptions that value certain choices above others. Every facilitator brings values or expectations to an experience, and when made overt, these can create valuable boundaries and structure for a course (i.e., "Violence or verbal attacks are not okay here.") But if these values are not overt, a climate of tension is created between the verbalized value of free choice and the opposing values defined nonverbally or through indirect actions.

The roots of impelling into experience run deep in adventure education and, whether spoken or not, remain unconsciously embedded in our collective understanding of the role of the leader and the process of change. These key beliefs and assumptions, and the conscious or unconscious ways in which they express them, create the context in which participants' decisions are made. Here are a few common assumptions that we have encountered in adventure education:

- Doing the hard thing, the thing you don't think you can do, and pushing yourself through self-perceived limitations, is what builds confidence, self-esteem, and character.

- Teamwork and moral character mean giving up your own needs or wants for the greater needs of the group.

- Growth comes from going outside of your comfort zone and stretching yourself. Those who don't stretch appreciably will not gain anything from the experience.

The personal history and values of the facilitator also shape the context. For example, if a leader values willful action, and has shaped her or his own identity through that value, s/he may look down on a participant who faces a challenging situation with passive acceptance. If a facilitator holds tightly to her or his assumptions as absolute truths, whether spoken or not, they can easily become the cultural climate of a group. The implication becomes that some choices are more right than others. To make a choice that goes against the values of the cultural climate takes exceptional courage and self-awareness, and those who do not already possess that degree of maturity will make choices in line with these values, whether they are personally appropriate or not.

The Role of the Staff in Creating Change

How the staff sees its role in facilitating change can further heighten the tension created by any disparities between the cultural climate's values and the values of the individuals comprising the culture. Outdoor educators traditionally have been trained to use their facilitation skills to lead groups toward a desired outcome and often see this as their primary role in creating change. For instance, in *The Conscious Use of Metaphor*, Bacon (1983) describes the role of the instructor as (a) assessing the group, (b) determining the appropriate outcome,

(c) applying the appropriate metaphor to move the group toward the desired outcome. The desired outcome is usually a combination of the widely held assumptions defined above and the personal values of the instructor. While the concept of Challenge by Choice may be explained at the beginning of a course, if the practitioner sees his or her role as moving the group or individuals toward a desired outcome, participants are less likely to be empowered to make authentic choices.

The fundamental difficulty with the Challenge by Choice model, as it is commonly practiced, is that the facilitator becomes caught in an uncomfortable tension between verbalizing freedom of choice yet subtly trying to influence participants to make choices in line with his or her own values, the expectations of the program, and the assumptions of contemporary adventure education. We would like to suggest that this subtle or indirect coercion is an unethical use of staff power. In our experience, staff almost always want the best for their participants. A misguided good intention or attachment to a set of beliefs, however, can lead to the manipulation of outcomes in a number of ways. For example, key information may be withheld that is necessary for effective decision-making (i.e., the peak climb will likely take at least eight hours). Participants who make an "unpopular" choice may be given less attention than those who make choices that are in line with the staff's expectations. Certain traits may be valued over others, such as will versus acceptance, or speed versus slowness. Even giving some forms of encouragement ("you can do it") can undermine a participant's trust in her/his self-perception or decision-making ability.

The social power that staff have is tremendous, and a simple lack of awareness of this inherent power differential between staff and participants and its influence on the course and individuals can be detrimental. Staff have the power to choose the route on wilderness trips, to dictate what activities will be done and when, to raise the status of some participants and demote others, to set a light, heavy, kind, or teasing tone, and to ultimately decide who stays and who leaves the course. Staff are also frequently beautiful, handsome, fit, stylishly dressed in the latest outdoor fashion, funny, socially fluid, representative of the dominant culture, and gracefully comfortable in the outdoors and in their position as leader. In short, staff have the power to define the preferred way of being in this little universe, and will model that consciously or unconsciously. One of the most deep-seated human needs is to belong, and if a course culture created by staff values sameness, or certain ideal traits, rather than diversity, participants will mold themselves to fit, rather than express their authentic selves and choices.

Lack of Support and Education Around Choice-Making

The third challenge of the Challenge by Choice model is that many people simply do not have the skills or awareness to identify their wants and needs, and to voice or act on them. What looks on the surface like a positive choice may actually be based on habit, inaccurate self-perception, gender roles, or social conformity. Participants may make a choice that decreases social pressure or satisfies an immediate need but in the process sacrifices a deeper level of their own truth. While most programs tell participants that they can say no to an activity, there are few programs that provide guidance or curriculum that supports participants in making authentic choices. In the next section we will describe how facilitators can attend to the choice-making process.

Deepening the Process: The Conscious Choice Model

The Conscious Choice model outlines principles and actions that support experiential educators in creating an environment in which participants can develop the skills and self-awareness to make positive, self-affirming choices that are appropriate for their stage of development. The model has been developed and practiced at The Women's Wilderness Institute for 10 years, and recognizes that providing participants with choices is only the first step in the development of the internal and social skills that lead to self-awareness and the ability to make self-affirming life decisions. It deepens the dominant paradigm of choice in adventure education by attending to the social context in which choices are made, and providing tools and information to bring awareness and new skills to the choice-making process. The Conscious Choice model provides guidelines and a clear role for the instructor in facilitating change, and pays close attention to the ethical use of staff power.

As with any model, there are underlying values in the Conscious Choice approach. One is the belief that learning to make conscious, self-affirming choices is one of the most transferable and valuable skills that can come out of an experience. Life circumstances are created largely through choices, conscious or not, and the ability to choose the most positive or growth-full direction has huge ramifications for the quality of one's life. Another fundamental value underlying the Conscious Choice model is the belief that within the context of experiential education, accomplishments in themselves are secondary in importance to the learning and self-awareness that comes from the process of consciously engaging with the situation, and the development of an authentic relationship with self and others. The capacity to make positive, self-affirming choices that grows out of this exploration is of primary importance. Practitioners of the Conscious Choice model develop a trust in the inherent wisdom, creativity, and action that arises from authenticity.

What is a conscious choice? All choices are made out of a combination of historical patterns, the meaning that the brain has assigned to previous events and choices, and the individual's current needs and hopes for the future. Unconscious choices are unexamined decisions that follow habits and patterns, beliefs based on interpretations of personal history, and immediate emotional or physical needs. A conscious choice recognizes habits, personal history, social expectation, and internal pressures that may be influencing the choice, sorts through immediate and long-term desires, and then makes a new choice based on the individual's deepest desire for the future. Emotions may inform the choice, but the choice is not driven by an emotional state. Making a choice in one's best interest requires the identification with a layer of self that is deeper than the immediate, "surface" desires. While a conscious choice may be simple or pleasurable, and in line with surface desires, it may also mean taking action that involves discomfort but provides the opportunity for growth or deeper satisfaction.

Making a conscious choice requires:

1. Awareness that a choice exists

2. Belief that one has the power to impact the outcome

3. Understanding of one's values, wants, and needs

4. Ability to distinguish between short-term gratification and long-term goals

5. Information necessary to make informed choices

6. Courage and self-efficacy to voice desires and/or take action

Not everybody has the capacity to recognize desires beyond impulse or immediate gratification. In the Conscious Choice model, practitioners support each person to reach the deepest layer of self-awareness of which they are capable, and then support that choice.

Creating a Choice-Full Environment: The Role of the Facilitator

The tools and techniques of the Conscious Choice model thrive in an environment where the primary facilitative role of the instructor is to support participants in accessing, expressing, and living the most authentic level of themselves that they are capable of reaching. In this paradigm, instructors challenge themselves to drop their assumptions of what people need and their agenda of moving the group to a particular outcome. In place of an expected outcome, there is trust that by facilitating authentic expression and awareness of the choice-making process, what participants most need will emerge. Participants become responsible for creating their outcomes. There are three primary aspects of the role of the facilitator in the Conscious Choice model: (1) authentic leadership, (2) the power-with stance, and (3) engaging participants in the process.

Authentic Leadership

The foundation for all staff interactions in the Conscious Choice model is authentic leadership. Authentic leadership has become a common term, defined in many ways. Our definition includes leadership that comes from one's genuine integrity, curiosity, responsibility, and caring, as well as support for others in connecting with these aspects of themselves. Being an authentic leader is an art form, not a technique (Cashman, 1997). As an authentic leader, the balance of "you" versus "your role" tips heavily toward an honest expression of yourself. It doesn't mean that you abandon the responsibilities of your role as leader. It doesn't mean always saying or acting out exactly what you think and feel. It means being aware of what you think and feel, and then making a conscious choice about what degree of personal sharing is in the participants' best interest. If you can share yourself while owning your perceptions as yours, and not the ultimate truth, you will open up the space for others to respond with their own authenticity.

When you are leading with authenticity you learn to break out of your own habitual choices and listen deeply for your authentic voice. You keep the agreements you've made with the group members and with yourself. When appropriate, you can be vulnerable, you can share your feelings, disappointments, and triumphs. You acknowledge your biases as your own, and approach your group with open-minded curiosity and a nonjudgmental attitude. When things go awry, you don't blame or judge the group members; you simply state feelings and unarguable facts. For example: "When I saw this morning that no one was ready to go at the time we agreed on for the peak climb, I felt sad about missing out on it and afraid that we won't be able to do any of the peak climbs we'd planned for the course. What happened?" Thus, you model the qualities you would like your participants to develop.

We would like to suggest that part of authentic leadership also includes a moral responsibility to genuinely care for the well-being of your participants. Noddings (1992) has explored this concept of an ethic of care for educators. In our definition, caring does not necessarily mean liking each individual, but it does mean caring for the inherent goodness and potential that lies under the personality traits, whether annoying or enjoyable, of each person. This is an essential element of the power-with stance, which we will explore next.

The Power-With Stance

Imagine tugging, pulling, and pushing on a participant to try to get her to move in a certain direction. Now imagine standing side-by-side, hand on her shoulder, aligning yourself with her and viewing the world from her perspective. This is the stance of the Conscious Choice model—the shift from power-over to power-with. Staff often describe shifting to the power-with position as a huge relief. No longer responsible for getting the group or individuals to move in a certain direction, they can focus on being curious, open-minded, and supportive as they empower others to move in their most authentic direction.

The term power-with was first coined by Mary Parker Follett, a turn-of-the-century educator and social theorist. Follett observed that people often resort to power-over "because they cannot wait for the slower process of education" (Follett, 1924). She asks: "What is the central problem of social relations? It is the question of power.... Genuine power can only be grown, it will slip from every arbitrary hand that grasps it; for genuine power is not coercive control, but coactive control. Coercive power is the curse of the universe; coactive power, the enrichment and advancement of every human soul" (Follett, 1924).

Kreisberg (1992) explores the concept of a power-with relationship between teachers and students in the formal classroom, with insight relevant to experiential educators.

> Relationships of domination not only saturate the structures and norms of schools ... but they also lie deep within teachers. The struggle to move beyond relationships of domination is not solely with external forces, it is an internal struggle as well. It means wrestling with our commonsense assumptions about teaching and shaking our taken-for-granted patterns of acting and relating in classrooms. (p. 154)

As we have already discussed, staff have tremendous power to influence and shape a group and the people in it. In the power-with stance, staff use this power to create structure and boundaries for the experience, to assist participants to arrive at their own truths and speak their needs, and to facilitate agreements and respectful relationships within the group. The intention to share power is explicit and participants are engaged in key decisions about the flow of the course. The essential message to participants is "I am here to help you figure out what you want, to balance that with what is possible, and to help you create that experience." The power to influence comes from taking an active role in supporting participants, and from relating to participants from a stance of authenticity, respect, and equality. It also comes from setting structure and boundaries that encourage authentic self-expression. Power-over decisions—those made unilaterally by staff—are reserved for situations that affect the physical or emotional safety of the group, that protect the environment, or that are needed to maintain the basic character of the course.

It takes a focused, conscious effort to honestly share power. There is a strong, usually unspoken assumption for most participants that they will have less power on the course, and that they will have to go along with whatever agenda is set by staff. This is especially true for marginalized groups, including women, non-Anglo participants, GLBT participants, and working-class people who are used to having less power in the dominant culture. Likewise, most staff are used to being able to pull rank and make decisions for the group simply because they are in the staff role. This scenario is so deeply ingrained, for both staff and participants, that it takes explicit, spoken, and conscious effort on the part of staff to share power. Does this mean time-consuming group decision making for every trivial detail? No. But it does mean that staff explain their intention to share decision-making power at the beginning of a course, and frequently remind participants that they have the right to disagree or question a decision.

Maintaining a power-with stance takes practice and a high degree of self-awareness. The following tips may help:

Learn to recognize when you are in a power struggle. You may feel frustrated or ineffective, or notice tightness in your body. You're trying to make something happen that isn't happening. The simplest way out of power struggle is to acknowledge it, engage your curiosity about the situation, and come back to the power-with statement. You may say either to yourself, your co-worker, or, if appropriate, to the group something like, "I'm noticing tightness in my body and I think I fell into wanting you to do X. But my job here is to support you in discovering which decision is ultimately best for you."

Learn to recognize when you're feeling detached. Common signposts may be tiredness, spaciness, irritation, a whatever attitude, or critical thoughts. This stance is usually an indication that you're in a power struggle but have given up. The Conscious Choice model is not about apathy for what the person or group does. It is about remaining engaged with the process and caring passionately that your group comes to a decision that is best for them.

Learn to recognize the power and influence you have on the group and individuals through your behavior and statements. Own your values, beliefs, and feelings as yours, and not a statement of universal truth. For example, a statement as simple as, "Rock climbing is the greatest thing ever," coming from the person in power, sets a tone that would make it an act of courage for a participant to choose not to rock climb, or to not like it. The statement, "I love to climb" is an authentic expression of who you are, rather than a value statement.

Learn to question any situation in which the group or individual does not have a choice about what they are doing, and be open to recognizing when you may be pulling rank. There are many unavoidably choiceless situations on a course, as there are in life. The fact that it is raining, that the course is 14 days long, that you're out of tortillas—those are all choiceless situations. But a struggle may emerge between staff and participants about hiking in the rain. Perhaps they really do have to hike in the rain to meet the resupply time. But maybe tent time today and hiking twice as far tomorrow is an option, even if it seems less desirable to you or less demonstrative of the qualities your program is trying to instill. Be sure that choiceless situations are dictated by safety concerns, environmental ethics, or circumstances beyond your control, rather than by your own agenda.

Recognize messages of discontent, such as passive-aggressive or indirect behavior, as symptoms of not having enough power. We've seen how the frustration of marginalized and oppressed cultures will erupt into violence, and the same thing will happen on a small scale in our groups. When this occurs, ask yourself,

"What are they not getting that they need?" Find out, and make creative agreements to get those needs met (i.e., they have an hour of free time a day, but agree to get going by 8 a.m.). Participants must be actively engaged and buy into the agreement for it to be successful.

Be sure to share relevant information. Information is power. Withholding information so that participants can "be in the moment" is a power-over move.

Engaging Participants in the Process

The attention paid to framing the experience and introducing the concepts of choice and shared power is critical to the Conscious Choice model. Participants' expectations of a directive, challenging facilitator and their need to comply with the agenda is so strong that this reframing is an essential aspect of this new paradigm. The following elements of framing the experience will help to set a collaborative relationship between staff and participants, and prepare them to take responsibility for their experience.

Clarify your role as a leader. "My job here is to help you create an experience that matches what you want and need as closely as possible. I will do everything I can to make sure we are all safe, and will suggest a structure and activities that I've seen work well. But most of all, my job is to help you clarify what you really want out of this, and then help you make choices that will get you there. I also want to help you learn as a group how to meet as many individual needs as possible, as much of the time as possible."

Help the group and individuals clarify their expectations of themselves. Work in your expectations of them (i.e., honesty, integrity, willingness to keep agreements) and find out what they would like from you. Clarify whether you are able to meet those expectations or not. If you agree to something, be sure you do it!

Talk about choices. "There will be lots of times on this course when you will need to make choices—either as individuals or as a group. We'll talk a lot more about how you figure out what you really want."

Develop a shared language for talking about choice. Distinguish between choices that we make out of habit, that may not serve us well in the long run, versus conscious choices—ones that we pay close attention to, which may feel uncomfortable, or have the possibility of getting us closer to whatever it is that we really want. Use terms such as "surface wants" vs. "deeper wants" and, "habit choice" vs. "conscious choice," or whatever terms fit for you and your group.

Redefine challenge as anything that feels awkward, scary, or different, rather than the external challenges that participants usually think of as the challenges of the course. Talk about the opportunity for growth that comes with any attempt to do something differently than one has done it before, whether that is physical or verbal, internal or external.

Redefine teamwork as the challenge of meeting as many individual needs as possible. Many people, especially women, view giving up their needs for the good of the group as the morally superior choice. Redefining teamwork in this way allows for a greater freedom in identifying personal wants, and encourages authentic interaction rather than silent sacrifice or compliance with expectations. Remind participants that in a group setting it's not always possible to meet all needs, but it is still important to identify and express them. Minimize situations or program structures that require everyone to agree on a single course of action, and engage the group members in creative problem solving.

Find out what each participant's intentions are for the course, and how s/he intends to stretch, or not. This gives you something to return to with curiosity if it isn't happening. "I remember you said you wanted this, but you're doing that. I wonder why?" If s/he really does not want to stretch, let that be. Keep checking back in to see if s/he is meeting her/his goal of not stretching, and what it's like for her/him. Remember that growth often happens via unexpected paths.

Celebrate the first conscious choices, however tiny. Especially celebrate the courage that it takes to make an unpopular choice—one that runs counter to spoken or unspoken group consensus. Celebrate the courage that it takes the first time someone disagrees with you or your co-worker.

Attending to the Choice-Making Process: Teaching Skills

An individual's choice-making process involves a mixture of conscious and unconscious factors and patterns. Exploring this process can be a rich pathway to heightened self-awareness and the ability to make self-affirming life decisions. Just as we don't expect our participants to show up already knowing how to belay, it is important not to assume that they know how to make a decision that leads in a direction of growth. Many people have lost or never learned to listen deeply to their intuition, body, and inner-wisdom; to screen out the expectations of others and lifetime habits; to identify the choices that are in line with their deepest wants and needs; or to speak and act on their deeper desires. By providing tools, practical information, and guidance in these skills, and helping participants to explore the conscious and unconscious patterns in their choice-making processes, facilitators can support students in experiencing feelings of empowerment and success to act upon their lives.

There are many ways that instructors can facilitate personal awareness and skills for making conscious choices. Following are a variety of concepts and tools that we use to create a Conscious Choice environment. The length and structure of the program will influence the depth to which the following recommendations can be incorporated.

Recognizing choice points. The first step in facilitating choice awareness is to illuminate when and how choice exists. Essentially, choice exists to some degree in every moment in life. Discussion about what choices are present in that very moment, along with what choices from the past have gotten people to where they are, can be specific and valuable. It is critical for people to be able to realize the correlation between choice and consequences in order to ultimately connect with their personal power.

Exploring personal habits. We often do a contemplative exercise with people where we have them choose one option from a variety of foods to eat. We then discuss why they chose what they did. This simple exercise brings awareness to the variety of ways that choices are made and the interactions between history, habit, knowledge, intuition, and felt sense that underlie our choices.

Exploring social and cultural expectations. We all live within greater contexts of family, culture, peer groups, spiritual traditions, and educational contexts, which all have their own set of values and codes to live by. Discussion and exercises around identifying these different influences can bring a great deal of awareness to what influences choice. Once social and cultural expectations are identified, people can choose which ones they truly identify with, and how they want to navigate living within these different contexts.

Listening deeply to develop inner awareness. By helping participants connect with the body's felt sense, we support people in listening to their own truths. When one learns to listen to the body's cues, wants, fears, uncertainties, and excitements, internal wants are easier to identify.

Distinguishing between frozen fear and excited fear. Some experiences of fear are a strong 'stop' signal from the body, and others are excitement and readiness for a new situation. Helping participants distinguish between frozen or "stop" fear, and tingly or "go" fear is important especially for those who tend to override stop fear or to back away from go fear. Everyone has their own threshold for this highly energized state of fear or excitement, and simply bringing awareness to the tendency to dissociate from the highly charged state can help people to stay present with it and act from a centered place.

Dealing with the what-ifs. It is not uncommon that fear or uncertainty, and their associated thought patterns, will arise when people engage in making conscious choices. Common fears include: "Is this safe?" "Am I good enough?" and "Will others still like me if I fail (or succeed)?" Sometimes simply voicing the fear helps people to take the next step forward. Directly addressing fears and confronting the "what ifs" is a reality-check that often helps to relieve some anxiety and build self-trust that even the worst fear could be overcome.

Filling in the information gaps. Provide as much information as you can to help participants make a choice, and help participants develop awareness of when they need to ask for more information in order to make a choice.

Finding a voice. For some people, verbalizing or acting on their desires can be the scariest step of the process. Challenges in verbalizing wants may show up as giving up/in, speaking softly, using qualifying or apologetic language, or even using a joking tone. Help participants listen for hesitancy, qualifiers, or other communication that sounds uncertain and to restate their needs until they feel satisfied with the strength of their statement.

Share your observations, but own them as your perceptions and not the ultimate truth. For example: "From what I've seen you do so far, and because I've seen other girls about your size do it, I think that you can probably do the peak climb without too much difficulty. But I want to help you make the decision that feels right to you." Note that this is different than a statement that tugs on the person: "I really think you should try it, because I think you can do it."

There are many exercises that can be done to support people in developing choice awareness and choice-making skills, including discussion, art-making, group initiatives, brainstorming, mind-mapping, story-telling, and other body-awareness and value-clarification tools, and creative and expressive exercises.

Social Justice Perspectives

It is interesting to note that much of the evolution of choice-making theory in experiential education has come from working with marginalized groups. While the traditional view of impelling into choice emerged from the early Outward Bound days of working with groups of young white males, Karl Rohnke departed from this model and developed Challenge by Choice as a result of working with urban youth (Neill, 2006).

The Conscious Choice model originated in our work with women who were survivors of traumatic violence. In these cases it was obvious that people who have had choice violently or coercively taken away from them benefit from support to reconnect with an ability to know and trust what they truly want, and to take the steps to voice and act on it. Any subtle power plays, even "encouragement," on the part of the instructor are clearly counterproductive.

The lessons from this population transferred easily to our work with women and girls. Women, we observed, entered new situations and groups expecting to have little power. We frequently heard from participants that they had felt uncomfortable stating a personal need, and often had even forgotten how to recognize their own needs. In essence, we realized, most women and girls tend to give up, misunderstand, or not trust their own needs and power on the same continuum as survivors of trauma, although in more subtle ways.

Who else lies on this continuum? Anybody who is or has been in the position of having less power than others in our society—people of color, adolescents, GLBT individuals, those of lesser socioeconomic status, and even many white males. Ultimately, any participant, male or female, stepping into a program in which there is a whole institution, and one or two staff representing the authority of that institution, who have the power to decide what s/he will eat, what s/he will do, who stays and who goes, is automatically in a position of less power.

What about boys and men? Boys have their own struggles with making self-affirming choices, and we have come to recognize the value of the Conscious Choice model for all genders. While girls may know what they want but have difficulty voicing their needs, boys have often been trained to ignore their feelings and intuition from a much younger age (Kindlon & Thompson, 2000), and so frequently act out of habit or conform to a masculine ideal rather than truly knowing what they want. Boys may automatically choose the difficult or scary physical challenges, along with their accompanying rewards of proud coaches, parents, or staff, rather than notice a deeper need to acknowledge fear or to take a different role. While the Conscious Choice model is especially relevant for disempowered groups, we believe it is also relevant for those who have been in positions of power and privilege. While privilege typically brings more availability of choice, more confidence, and more practice making choices, it does not necessarily mean that the privileged are more aware of their true wants or their habitual patterns of choice.

Conclusion

Facilitation through the Conscious Choice model is not an easy art, and requires a high degree of maturity and self-awareness on the part of the facilitator. Yet as our world becomes more and more consumer-driven, violent, and disengaged from the natural world, it is essential that we adapt our models to utilize the truly transformative potential of experiential education. Conformity to mainstream sociocultural standards is no longer necessarily a demonstration of "good moral character." The world is calling for a way for people, young and old, to learn how to listen to and act on their authentic voice, rather than complying with what is expected. Instead of creating environments where the preferred way of being is to be like the instructors, we must value the wisdom that comes from the full diversity of human experience.

The Conscious Choice model gives a framework for teaching the essential skills of choice-making and authenticity within a context where all essential qualities are equally valued: will and acceptance, heart and mind, speed and slowness, doing and being, extroversion and introversion, masculine and feminine. By shifting to this new paradigm, in which the role of the facilitator is to facilitate what is most authentic for the individual and the group, we believe that experiential education will remain relevant and powerful as we work with increasingly diverse populations in a changing world.

References

Bacon, S. (1983). *The conscious use of metaphor in Outward Bound.* Denver: Colorado Outward Bound School.

Bechara, A., Damasio, H., & Damasio, A., (2000). Emotion, decision making, and the orbitofrontal cortex. *Cerebral Cortex, Vol. 10*(3), 295–307.

Bunting, C., Haras, K., & Witt, P. (2006). Meaningful involvement opportunities in ropes course programs. *Journal of Leisure Research, Vol. 38, No. 3, 339–362.*

Cashman, K. (1997). Authentic leadership. *Innovative Leader. Vol. 6*(11) *fromhttp://www.winstonbrill.com/bril001/html/article_index/articles/301–350/article305_body.html.*

Estrellas, A. (1996). The eustress paradigm: A strategy for decreasing stress in wilderness adventure programming. In Warren, K. (Ed.). *Women's Voices in Experiential Education* (pp. 32–44). Dubuque: Kendall/Hunt.

Follett, M. P. (1924). *Creative experience.* New York: Longman Green (reprinted by Peter Owen in 1951).

Hirschmann, N. (2003). *The Subject of Liberty: Towards a Feminist Theory of Freedom.* Princeton: Princeton University Press.

Hochschild, J. (1995*). Facing up to the American dream: Race, class, and the soul of the nation.* Princeton: Princeton University Press.

Itin, C. (1992). Challenge by choice as professional enabling. *Insight, 1*(1), 2.

Itin, C. (1996). The impelling principle in challenge by choice. *Rocky: Newsletter of the Rocky Mountain Region of the Association for Experiential Education*, 4(3), 6–7.

Kindlon, D. & Thompson, M. (2000). *Raising Cain: Protecting the emotional lives of boys.* New York: Ballantine Books.

Kreisberg, S, 1992. *Transforming power: Domination, empowerment, and education.* Albany: State University of New York Press.

Leuner, B., Mendolia-Loffredo, S., & Shors, T. (2004). Males and females respond differently to controllability and antidepressant treatment. *Journal of Biological Psychiatry, 56*(12), 964–970.

Lisson, B. (2000). Is there a choice in challenge by choice? *Pathways: The Ontario Journal of Outdoor Education, 12*(4), 20–21.

Mitten, D. (1996). A philosophical basis for a women's outdoor adventure program. In Warren, K. (Ed.). *Women's Voices in Experiential Education* (pp. 78–84). Dubuque: Kendall/Hunt.

Neill, J. (2006). *Challenge by Choice*. Retrieved April 8, 2007, from www.wilderdom.com/ABC/ChallengeByChoice.html

Neill, J. (2005). *5- word summary of Dewey's "Experience & Education."* Retrieved April 8, 2007, from http://www.wilderdom.com/experiential/SummaryJohnDeweyExperienceEducation

Neill, J. (2005). *John Dewey, the modern father of experiential education.* Retrieved April 8, 2007, from http://www.wilderdom.com/experiential/ExperientialDewey.html.

Noddings, N. (1992). *The challenge to care in schools: An alternative approach to education.* New York: Teachers College Press.

Pipher, M. (1994). *Reviving Ophelia: Saving the lives of adolescent girls.* New York: Ballantine.

Rosso, I. M., Young, A. D., Femia, L. A. & Yurgelun-Todd, D.A. (2004). Cognitive and emotional components of frontal lobe functioning in childhood and adolescence. *Annals of the New York Academy of Sciences, 1021*, 355–362.

Schoel, J., & Maizell, R. (2002). *Exploring islands of healing: New perspectives on adventure based counseling.* Beverly, MA: Project Adventure.

Sax, L. (2005). *Why gender matters.* NY: Doubleday.

Shors, T. & Associates. (2001). Sex differences and opposite effects of stress of dendritic spine density in the male versus female hippocampus. *Journal of Neuroscience, 21*(16), 6292–97.

Svenson, O., & Maule, A. J., (Eds.). (1993). *Time pressure and stress in human judgment and decision making.* New York: Plenum Press.

Taylor, S. et al (2002). Biobehavioral responses to stress in females: Tend-or-befriend, not fight-or-flight. *Psychological Review, 107*(3), 411–429.

A Contemporary Model of Experiential Education

▾ ▾ ▾

Kate J. Cassidy

In this chapter I propose a model of experiential education founded on the contemporary perspective that truth is not determined by a fixed reality, and that meaning is context dependant, socially and culturally mediated, and influenced by the unique histories of every person. This model breaks experiential education into three key components: community, experience, and learning. The component of community highlights the balance between the individual and the collective and is presented as a foundation for experiential education. The component of experience is made meaningful to both individuals and the collective through involving interdependent roles and multiple ways of interacting with the world. Finally, the component of learning is proposed to include both reflection and interpersonal dialogue to create individual and social meaning. Each of these sections—community, experience, and learning—are presented as an overview, a description of each component based on a mutually negotiated reality, and as theory applied to practice.

Community

People search for feelings of acceptance, belonging, and safety in relationship with others (Baumeister & Leary, 1995; Durkheim, 1933; Gardner, 1991; Maslow, 1954; Nisbet, 1969; Osterman, 2000; Putnam, 2000; Sergiovanni, 1994). When group relationships have an accepting and safe community atmosphere, individuals may feel more comfortable and open to share their skills, abilities, and perceptions with others. When people can engage in this type of open communication in a community, it provides the opportunity for an expanded understanding of self, and of the world for greater learning.

Pluralistic and Reciprocal Community as the Foundation for Experiential Education

Solomon, Battistich, Kim, and Watson (1996) describe a community as "a social organization whose members know, care about and support one another, have common goals and a sense of shared meaning, and to which they actively contribute and feel personally committed" (p. 236). John Dewey wrote:

> No amount of aggregated collective action of itself constitutes a community.... To learn
>
> to be human is to develop through the give and take of communication an effective sense
>
> of being an individually distinctive member of a community; one who understands and
>
> appreciates its beliefs, desires, and methods... (1927/1984, pp. 330–332).

Theorists have long suggested that social interaction is critical to education and the learning process (Bandura, 1977; Dewey, 1958; Johnson & Johnson, 1989; Noddings, 1992; Vygotsky, 1978). Specifically, the social interaction that I call community in this chapter (and highlighted in the quotes above) values individual difference by developing a group process that supports care, difference of opinion, and dialogue; and builds a shared vision by aligning individual and group goals. It is a pluralistic notion of community that does not require similarity or equality, but rather that each individual comes to see and value the other, as Shields (2000) puts it, "despite, or perhaps because of difference" (p. 285). This is in contrast to the historical idea of team or community where similarity, conformity, and boundaries used to exclude others were considered the ideal (Gardner, 1991).

Social interaction within experiential education programs is often thought of in terms of Tuckman's stage model as a basis for group program design and facilitation (Luckner & Nadler, 1997). Bruce W. Tuckman's (1965) model of group development, known by the titles forming, storming, norming, and performing (adjourning was added in 1977), remains one of the most commonly cited models of group development today (Smith, 2005; Worchel, 1994). However, Tuckman (1965) himself acknowledged that the transferability of his model may be limited as it was based primarily on "research dealing with sequential development in therapy groups" (p. 395). In Tuckman's model, as in other traditional models of group development (e.g. Bales, 1950; Fisher, 1970; Mills, 1964; Thelen, 1954), it is commonly suggested that groups move in linear or cyclical fashions from individual issues such as inclusion and orientation through conflict to interpersonal unity and performance. Proposing a more organic view of group dynamics, McCollom (1990) suggests that even "if we cannot say how groups develop . . . we should at least be able to identify general categories of factors that will shape development" (p. 151). I propose that a developed group is in line with the social interaction that I call community in this chapter. The description of community I present here incorporates underlying themes found in group development literature (Cassidy, 2007), but highlights three basic factors that are constantly interacting within groups from a social, cultural, and pragmatic perspective. This pluralistic notion of community, as comprised of three fundamental elements—the individual, the collective, and meaning—are described in detail below.

The individual. Many believe that individual identity is a social product that develops in conjunction with others (Cooley, 1922; Rogers, 1947; Wenger, 1998; Young, 1990). That is to say, people define who they are by the relationships and group histories with which they associate, and come to know themselves through the eyes of those around them. Individuals want their unique essences, backgrounds, and life stories to be recognized and valued (Greene, 1993; hooks, 2003; Napier & Gershenfeld, 2004; Stangor, 2004). They also need to feel that they are comfortable, safe, accepted, competent, and respected members of the groups to which they belong (Baumeister & Leary, 1995; Maslow, 1954; Osterman, 2000). When an individual's background and skills are not recognized, his/her very identity can be negatively impacted. When people feel that they have to defend their self-concept from assault—whether that be a direct attack, or simply a lack of recognition—their ability to learn, grow, and contribute can easily be reduced (hooks, 2003; Maslow, 1954; Wenger, 1998). But when members are recognized for their unique skills and life stories in a community, a space is created for people to feel safe and open to share their perspectives (Greene, 1993). When people are encouraged to speak as they truly are, greater potential for new insight and shared understanding emerges as people can more easily engage in authentic communication (Freire, 1984; Greene, 1993; hooks, 2003; Peck, 1987).

The collective. Individuals are bound together as a collective by group norms and processes. Group norms are expectations, both overt and hidden, about how members will interact with each other while moving toward goals. Three foundational and related norms emerge from the literature as key to a pluralistic community; they are a respect for difference, safe conflict, and care (Mitten, 1989; Warren, 1996). These norms help form a group foundation that encourages open communication between members. The opportunity for authentic communication allows individuals to express themselves and cultivate an effective climate for learning and action (Wilson & Hanna, 1993).

Norms that support the exploration of difference, as well as commonality, are critical for a healthy community in contemporary times (Noddings, 1996; Weisenfeld, 1996; Wheelan, 2005b). When people come together in a group, interaction can easily lean toward the traditional desire for agreement, harmony, and one common truth (Janis, 1982; Young, 1990). When this happens, alternative perspectives can be easily overlooked and eventually silenced (Shields, 2000). Opportunities to support individuals and learn from others are lost when difference of all types are not recognized. People must be open to hearing voices that are not often heard, or are simply different from their own, if the unique presence of each individual is to be truly valued (Greene, 1993). When this happens, there will be a possibility of conflict throughout the life of a group. Effective learning communities include norms and strategies that support the safe and productive management of conflict whenever it might occur (Napier & Gershenfeld, 2004). When individuals feel free to be themselves, and to disagree without concern for retribution, healthy cohesion and trust tend to increase (Mitten & Clement, 2007; Stangor, 2004; Wheelan, 2005a). These conditions can help foster a climate where respect and care between members is possible. The desire to be cared for is primary to being human (Maslow, 1954; Noddings 2002). By approaching others with deep appreciation and a concern for their well-being, communication between people is more likely to be open (Buber, 1970; Napier & Gershenfeld, 2004; Noddings, 1996; Stangor, 2004). When communication is open, people can share their distinct perspectives and perhaps develop a deeper sense of belonging.

Communication is at the root of an effective learning community. When every voice is heard, people best come to know themselves and the world (Dewey, 1916, Greene, 1993). Although events will be seen differently based on each person's unique lens (Greene, 1993), dialogue enables group participants to explore the presuppositions, ideas, beliefs, and feelings that influence their perceptions. An ideal community invites open communication, and listens deeply to foster new insights and shared meaning between individuals.

Meaning. Activity provides the center around which individuals can form as a community. In order to engage in productive activity, a common understanding of where a group is going should exist (Sergiovanni, 1994). A group vision can set this common direction for a community. A vision must be broad to capture where the collective wishes to go, but must include the needs and goals of individual members (Senge, 1994; Stangor, 2004; Toseland & Rivas, 1995). By providing the opportunity for each member of a community to articulate personal goals and influence the hopes and expectations of the group, people can connect what they are about to do with their own understandings and life-story (Wenger, 1998). Without this shared direction, members working from different backgrounds and toward different ends may believe they are a group, but their desire for varied outcomes results in separate or non-meaningful activity. These conditions help establish a shared sense of meaning to cultivate a culture that values the full and effective participation of all community members, regardless of personal identity, experience, or background (Mitten, 1989). In this way it creates fertile conditions for learning and achievement.

Pluralistic and Reciprocal Community: The Role of the Educator

I suggest that developing and maintaining individuals and groups as communities may well become the most important role for the educator in contemporary times. In a global society, it is important for educators to explore with people in communities how all may participate to their greatest potential. I offer a few practical examples.

Figure 1. **The foundation of "community."**

I believe that the educator should model helping people feel comfortable, safe, respected, and cared for. For example whether it be a short- or long-term program, I always try to meet people at the door and welcome them into the room. I find out about new participants' backgrounds at the beginning of a program, and learn what led them to be part of the present group to respect the backgrounds that they bring. I always start with adult learners by addressing comforts, such as where the washroom and water can be located to demonstrate care. If a class or group has been separated for a period of time, I try to do an activity, or spend some time catching up, to allow learners to mentally rejoin the group and feel safe. I believe that these small actions have an impact on establishing and maintaining a respect for the individual.

Groups will establish standards of behavior, or norms, whether they are openly discussed or not. It is often very helpful to bring the process into the open and discuss how the group may best function together. For example, I do this by working with group participants to create community guidelines. Guidelines can cover such things as how people should be treated, how to create the best environment to support dialogue, and how the group wishes to handle the occasional conflict or disagreement so that a member's background, competence, or perspectives on the world are not threatened. From this basis, I plan for periodic community check-ins to reflect on how the group is functioning and to add or adjust guidelines. These actions help a group establish and maintain a healthy group process.

Often people assume that they have the same goals as other group members; however this is often not the case. For example, one person might join a class to learn about the topic, while another person might have joined for social purposes. It is useful for the educator to facilitate a discussion around why the group has assembled. One way I do this is by talking with learners about how we will specifically determine and celebrate success both as individuals and as a collective. As a shared direction is established, I encourage the community to revisit group guidelines and keep them up to date. These actions help create shared meaning that incorporates the needs of individuals and the collective.

Overall, I propose that facilitating a community atmosphere that values each individual, maintains healthy interactions, and directs attention toward a shared group vision that includes individual goals may well be the primary function of an educator in contemporary times. These three key aspects of community are presented in Figure 1. I suggest that this notion of community should form the foundation for experiential education in a diverse and global society.

Experience

The idea that meaning is situated, socially and culturally mediated, and influenced by the unique histories of every person suggests that education may be most successful when located in experience (Dewey, 1938; Lave & Wenger, 1991; Wenger, 1998). Experience can provide an opportunity to engage the whole person by connecting mind, body, and feelings (Dewey, 1938; Martin, Franc, & Zounkova, 2004). It can also provide the social context from which to build shared purpose, language, and understanding with others (Dewey 1938; Lave & Wenger, 1991).

Figure 2. **Educational experience can be enriched by establishing individual and collective meaning through involving interdependent roles, and multiple intelligences.**

Experiences That Value Multiple Ways of Interacting With the World

Experiences provide the space for individuals to express their identity and meet personal goals. In a social context, experiences generally require multiple roles to achieve a collective vision. Theorists suggest that simply being active does not necessarily create an educational experience (Dewey, 1938). Experiences are more likely to be educative when they connect to the unique histories, stories, and differences of each learner (Cassidy, 2001; Dewey, 1938; Greene, 1993; hooks, 2003). As such I suggest that experience should also respect multiple ways of interacting with the world. Currently the dominant Western culture's emphasis on verbal and logical-mathematical intelligence has great influence on educational design and what is valued in society. Experiences that reflect different intelligences are more likely to inspire individual meaning, respect the variety of abilities and roles available within a learning community, create products that reflect different cultural perspectives, and expand the boundaries of language by including other types of interaction and communication (Gardner, 1983; Reiff, 1997). Howard Gardner (1983) suggests that there are at least eight ways of knowing—Linguistic, Musical, Logical-Mathematical, Visual-Spatial, Bodily-Kinesthetic, Interpersonal, Intrapersonal, and Naturalistic. Elliot Eisner (1994) writes of Gardner and his theory, "He has provided not only significant leads for researchers to pursue, but extremely important implications for developing a more equitable approach to education" (p. 560). His theory provides an excellent framework from which to consider the multiple ways of approaching a topic and valuing each learner's way of interacting with the world in experiential education (Cassidy, in press).

Multiple Ways of Interacting With the World: The Role of the Educator

If you accept that learning is situated and jointly negotiated, then historical methods of Western education that emphasize compartmentalized and passive learning come into question. I suggest that respecting and incorporating other ways of knowing, to value multiple roles is important for creating an equitable and pluralistic society. A few examples are offered below.

If I were planning to teach a class of children about India, for example, I might have them locate music that they like from that country, and then use it as the center from which to explore the countries' history, influences, people, industry, or geography. Or, as another example, I might design a team-building adventure around a variety of forms of challenge and reflection, including outdoor challenges and discussion, but also art, music, and drama.

To include multiple roles and ways of knowing in an equitable and holistic manner I suggest that it is important to see the verbal and logical-mathematical bias of dominant Western thinking. I also believe that the educator should be aware of his/her own comfort level with the different ways of interacting with the world in order to ensure that all are considered when designing educational experiences. Overall, I propose that when an educator is constantly alert to the backgrounds and ways in which people interact with the world, s/he is better able to offer experiences that value multiple roles and are respectful and inclusive of multiple intelligences. Three aspects of experience are proposed in Figure 2; these are multiple roles, multiple intelligences, and meaning.

Learning

As people interact with others from different cultures and contexts in contemporary times, there is increasing awareness of multiple ways of living, thinking, and being in this world. This is lending credence to the ideas that truth is not determined by a fixed reality, and that meaning is context dependant, socially and culturally mediated, and influenced by the unique histories of every person (Dewey, 1938; Gredler, 1997; Lave & Wenger, 1991; Schwandt, 2000; Wenger, 1998; Wertsch 1995). Theories that emphasize the pragmatic, situated, and social nature of learning are particularly compatible with this perspective of reality. These theories suggest that learning comes from social engagement, joint negotiation, and a common set of communication tools (artifacts, routines, vocabulary) that carry the accumulated knowledge of the community (Dewey, 1958; Lave & Wenger, 1991; Wenger, 1998). From this perspective I suggest that reflection, but also dialogue with others on shared, meaningful experience, is critical in contemporary times (Bandura, 1977; Boud, Cohen, & Walker, 1993; Dewey, 1958; Johnson & Johnson, 1989, Lave & Wenger, 1991: Vygotsky, 1978; Wenger, 1989).

Adding Dialogue to the Experiential Learning Cycle

Theorists have suggested that it is the process of reflection that allows an experience to become a source for learning (Dewey, 1933; Boud, Cohen, & Walker, 1993; Schön, 1983). Reflection allows individuals to review experiences, connect to feelings, and attend to prior influences that effect understanding. Experiential learning as an action-reflection sequence has been expressed in a number of definitions and models under the name of the experiential learning cycle (see Joplin, 1981; Kolb, 1984). In addition to this, I propose that open communication—or dialogue—is also critical for experiential learning. Dialogue invites people to open up to each other with the objective of really trying to understand the meaning behind what is being said. Ordinary conversation often assumes that people see the world from the same perspective. Dialogue makes the opposite assumption—that everyone is different and sees the world from a unique angle. This type of communication involves uncovering assumptions and may help people better understand how meaning is influenced by each person's unique history (Boud, Cohen, & Walker, 1993; Bohm, 1996; Greene, 1993). Dialogue encourages communication between differences and learning from the flow of meaning between people (Barge, 2002; Bohm, 1996; Stewart, Zediker, & Black, 2004). Dialogue helps bring people together as they come to see their perspective as one part of a cohesive whole

(Barge, 2002; Bohm, 1996; Stewart, Zediker, & Black, 2004). By truly hearing other perspectives, learners expand their understanding of the world by hearing and incorporating other points of view. As such, encouraging dialogue invites a more democratic approach to education that helps overcome oppression (Boud, Keogh, & Walker, 1985; Freire, 1984; Greene, 1993; hooks, 2003).

Creating Shared Space for Learning: The Role of the Educator

Assuming that meaning is context dependant, social, and influenced by the unique histories of every person, it makes sense that the role of the educator should move from one of traditional transmission-style lecturer to one of facilitator and co-learner in contemporary times. I suggest that in these roles the educator can best encourage reflection on experience and draw people into a shared space for dialogue. A few practical examples are offered below.

People reflect in different ways and at different paces. It is often helpful for the facilitator to incorporate activities that encourage people to reflect in other than verbal ways. For example, when working with adventure participants, classroom students, and even staff training teams, I often find that great insight comes from asking participants to create an art piece (collage, sculpture, drawing, song, poem, etc.) that expresses their feelings on, or learning of, a topic. I provide fun materials to help them understand that high-end artistic skills are not needed. Participants often say that the process of reflecting in this manner helps them make connections in creative ways. I also suggest that it is important to remember that some

Figure 3. Opportunities for learning can be enriched by establishing individual and collective meaning through reflection and dialogue.

people take longer to process their thoughts. In a multiday program I always try to ask learners each morning if they have any insights from the activities of the previous day.

To truly encourage dialogue, educators should be aware of their own influence, biases, and power. What the educator says, and how s/he responds to a member's ideas, is often carefully noted by participants. For example, I try not to use summary comments such as "excellent" or "interesting point" when a group member shares a thought, to avoid implying that I am the judge of worth. I propose that true dialogue is more likely to occur when educators believe that they have as much to gain as learners as they have to share as teachers. For this reason I believe that the selection of experience, as well as the reflection and discussion

Figure 4. **In this model, the foundation for experiential education is based in community that addresses the needs of both the individual and the collective.**

Individual	• People want to belong and be accepted. • People want to be acknowledged for who they are, where they come from, and what they bring to the group. • People question whether their needs will be met within the group. • People want roles that they are capable of filling and that allow them to contribute. • People want to have influence in the groups to which they belong. • People want to be able to safely express their ideas, needs, and differences of opinion.
Collective	• Community norms emphasize respect and care for others. • Community norms encourage the expression of commonalities but also differences. • Strategies for conflict resolution are important within healthy communities. • Positive norms form the basis for safe and open communication in a group. • The creation of norms often provides structure that often allows group members to assume much of their own leadership.
Meaning	• A shared vision is the center of community and helps direct efforts toward meaningful goals. • Where possible communities incorporate individuals' personal goals in creating a shared vision. • Establishing this meaning helps individuals and groups move toward goals they care about. • Norms, roles, and procedures are often dynamic as group visions and goals change.
Experience	• Not all experiences are educative. • Educative experiences take into account the unique histories, stories, and differences of every learner. • Unique participants may be more likely to find meaning when experiences provide a variety of points of entry; address different learning styles; provide different roles; respect processes and products that are relevant to different cultures; and provide a variety of ways that individuals can use their skills, and ways of interacting with the world, for the benefit of their community. • Interdependent roles allow participants to learn from others and work toward shared goals.
Learning	• Experience is the stimulus for learning. • Meaning is made as people reflect on experience. • People relate to new experience by how it fits with what past experience has made them, including their social, political, and cultural background. • Language has influence on how people think and share, therefore having an influence on what people experience. • Dialogue with others helps people to consider how their backgrounds shape what they see. • Dialogue with others of different backgrounds encourages critical reflection and helps to expand the possibilities of experience.

Figure 5. **An outline of the main points of the model of community, experience, and learning.**

process, is often best accomplished when the teacher and students engage as co-designers and co-learners. In general I believe that it is important to embrace moments of silence for reflection, ask caring and authentic questions, and to approach every experience with curiosity and a willingness to learn from others.

Overall, I suggest that a shared and meaningful learning space can be more easily created when the educator takes on the role of facilitator and co-learner. I believe that this positions the educator to help individuals within communities engage in the three key aspects of reflection, dialogue, and meaning. This is illustrated in Figure 3.

Conclusion

The freedom to interact openly and listen carefully to others is critical for living in a global society that moves beyond oppression and assimilation, to a place where all voices are represented for inclusive understanding (Freire, 1984; Shields, 2000). It is also important for all ideas, perspectives, and suggestions to be heard for communities to be able to fully tap the diversity, creativity, knowledge, and potential within a group. From this perspective, what seems needed is a model of education that is capable of exploring all viewpoints to reflect a global society where meaning is dynamic. This calls for an approach to education that is social, situated, dialogical, and open ended. Experiential education offers such a framework. In this chapter I presented a model of experiential education that proposes dialogue, experiences that include multiple ways of interacting with the world, and community that values difference be added to traditional ideas of experiential education. In the model presented, pluralistic community acts as the foundation for learning, as illustrated in Figure 4. Communities can contribute positively to members' feelings of belonging and safety as well as their identity development. They offer opportunities for members to use their skills and ways of interacting with the world for the benefit of others, and they provide a context for learning as people have the opportunity to reflect and dialogue with peers. The model of community, experience, and learning is self-reinforcing—each component making the other stronger. See Figure 5 for a summary of the model's main points to help translate theory into practice.

The ideas presented in this chapter suggest that experiential education is an important and valuable method of education in contemporary times if meaning is indeed context dependant, socially and culturally mediated, and influenced by the unique histories of every person. Overall, the model that I present is still very much grounded in the ideas originally put forth by Dewey, who has had much influence on how experiential education has been understood to date. It extends this understanding by centering experiential education in a pluralistic idea of community and building a model based on a pragmatic, social, and cultural perspective of meaning.

References

Bales, R. F. (1950). *Interaction process analysis: A method for the study of small groups.* Reading, MA: Addison-Wesley.

Bandura, A. (1977). *Social learning theory.* New York: General Learning Press.

Barge, K. J. (2002). Enlarging the meaning of group deliberation: From discussion to dialogue. In L. R. Frey, (Ed.) *New Directions in Group Communication* (pp. 159–178). Thousand Oaks, CA: Sage.

Baumeister, R. F., & Leary, M. R., (1995). The need to belong: Desire for interpersonal attachments as a fundamental human motivation. *Psychological Bulletin, 117,* 497–529.

Bohm, D. (1996). *On dialogue* (L. Nichol, trans.). New York: Routledge.

Boud, D., Cohen, R., & Walker, D. (1993), Introduction: Understanding learning from experience. In D. Boud, R. Cohen, & D. Walker, (Eds.) *Using Experience for Learning,* (pp. 1–18). Bristol, PA: SRHE and Open University Press.

Boud, D., Keogh, R., Walker, D. (1985). Promoting reflection in learning: A model. In D. J. Boud, R. Keough, & D. Walker, (Eds.) *Reflection: Turning Experience into Learning,* (pp. 18–40). London: Kogan Page.

Buber, M. (1970). *I and thou* (W. Kaufmann, trans.). New York: Scribner.

Cassidy, K. (2001). Enhancing your experiential program with narrative theory. *Journal of Experiential Education, 24*(1), 22–26.

Cassidy, K. (2007). Tuckman revisited: Proposing a new model of group development for practitioners. *Journal of Experiential Education. 22*(1), 413–417.

Cassidy, K. (in press). Multiple intelligence theory as a framework for program development. In R. H. Stremba & C. Bisson, (Eds.) *Teaching Adventure Education: Theory and Best Practices.* Champaign, IL: Human Kinetics.

Cooley, C. (1922). *Human nature and the social order.* New York: Scribner.

Dewey, J. (1916/1966). *Democracy and education. An introduction to the philosophy of education.* New York: Free Press.

Dewey, J. (1933). *How we think.* New York: Dover Publications.

Dewey, J. (1938). *Experience and education.* New York: Simon and Schuster.

Dewey, J. (1958). *Experience and nature.* New York: Macmillan.

Dewey, J. (1927/1984). The public and its problems., In J. Boydston (ed.), *The later works, vol. 2,* (pp. 330–332). Carbondale, IL: Southern Illinois University Press.

Durkheim, E. (1933). *The division of labor in society.* Simpson, G., trans. New York: The Free Press.

Eisner, E. W. (1994). Commentary: Putting multiple intelligences in context: Some questions and observations. *Teachers College Board Record, 95*(4), 555–560.

Fisher, A. (1970). Decision emergence: Phases in group decision making. *Speech Monographs,* 37, 53–66.

Freire, P. (1984). *Pedagogy of the oppressed.* New York: Continuum.

Gardner, H. (1983). *Frames of mind.* (2nd ed.) New York: Basic Books.

Gardner, J. W. (1991). *Building community.* Washington, DC: Independent Sector.

Gredler, M. E. (1997). *Learning and instruction: Theory into practice* (3rd ed.). Upper Saddle River, NJ: Prentice-Hall.

Greene, M. (1993). The passions of pluralism: Multiculturalism and the expanding community. *Educational Researcher, 22*(1), 13–18.

Hoerr, T. (1996). *Succeeding with multiple intelligences.* St. Louis, MO: The New City School.

hooks, b. (2003). *Teaching community*. New York: Routledge.

Janis, I. L. (1982). *Groupthink (2nd ed.)*. Boston: Houghton-Mifflin.

Johnson, D. W., & Johnson, R. T. (1989). *Leading the cooperative school*. Edina, MN: Interaction Book Company.

Joplin, L. (1981). On defining experiential education. *Journal of Experiential Education*, 4(1), 17–20.

Kolb, D. A. (1984). *Experiential learning*. Englewood Cliffs, NJ: Prentice Hall.

Lave, J. & Wenger, E. (1991). *Situated Learning. Legitimate peripheral participation*, Cambridge: University of Cambridge Press.

Lazar, D. (1999). *Eight ways of teaching*. Arlington Heights, IL: SkyLight Training and Publishing.

Luckner, J. L., & Nadler, R. S. (1997). *Processing the experience: Strategies to enhance and generalize learning*. Dubuque, IA: Kendall/Hunt.

McCollom, M. 1990. Reevaluating group development: A critique of the familiar models. In J. Gillette, & M. McCollom (Eds.) *Groups in context,* (pp.134-154). New York: Addison-Wesley.

Martin, A., Franc, D., & Zounkova, D. (2004). *Outdoor and experiential learning: An holistic and creative approach to programme design*. Burlington, VT: Gower Publishing.

Maslow, A. (1954). *Motivation and personality*. New York: Harper.

Mills, T. M. (1964). *Group transformation: An analysis of a learning group*. Englewood Cliffs, NJ: Prentice-Hall.

Mitten, D. (1989). Healthy expressions of diversity lead to positive group experiences. *Journal of Experiential Education, 12*(3), 17–22.

Mitten, D., & Clemment, K. (2007). Responsibilities for adventure education leaders. In R. Prouty, J. Panicucci, & R. Collinson (Ed.s) *Adventure-Based Programming and Education*. Champaign, IL: Human Kinetics.

Napier, R. W., & Gershenfeld, M. K. (2004). *Groups: theory and experience (7th ed.)*. Boston: Houghton Mufflin.

Nisbet, R. (1969). *Quest for community*. Oxford: Oxford University Press.

Noddings, N. (1992). *The challenge to care in schools: An alternative approach to education*. New York: Teachers College Press.

Noddings, N. (1996). On community. *Educational Theory*, 46(3), 245–267.

Noddings, N. (2002). *Starting at home. Caring and social policy*. Berkeley, CA: University of California Press.

Osterman, K. F. (2000). Students' need for belonging in the school community. *Review of Educational Research, 70*(3), 323–367.

Peck, M. S. (1987). *The different drum*. Ontario, Canada: Touchstone.

Putnam, R. D. (2000). *Bowling alone: the collapse and revival of American community*. New York: Simon & Schuster.

Reiff, J. C. (1997). Multiple intelligences, culture and equitable learning. *Childhood Education, 73*(5), 301–04

Rogers, C. R (1947). Some observations on the organization of personality. *American Psychologist*. 2, 358–368.

Schön, D. (1983). *The reflective practitioner. How professionals think in action,* London: Temple Smith.

Schwandt, Thomas. (2000). Three epistemological stances for qualitative inquiry. In N. K. Denzin & Y. S. Lincoln (Eds.), *Handbook of Qualitative Research 2ed.*, (pp. 189–213), Thousand Oaks: Sage.

Senge, P. (1994). *The fifth discipline: The art and practice of the learning organization*, New York: Doubleday Currency.

Sergiovanni, T. (1994) *Building communities in schools.* San Francisco: Jossey-Bass.

Shields, C. M. (2000). Learning from difference: Considerations for schools as communities. *Curriculum Inquiry, 30*(3), 275–294.

Smith, M. K. (2005) '*Bruce W. Tuckman–forming, storming, norming and performing in groups, the encyclopedia of informed education*, www.infed.org/thinkers/tuckman.htm

Solomon, D., Battistich, V., Kim, D. I. & Watson, M. (1996). Teacher practices associated with students' sense of the classroom as a community. *Social Psychology of Education, 1*(3), 235–267.

Stangor, C. (2004). *Social groups in action and interaction*. New York: Psychology Press.

Stewart, J., Zediker, K. E., & Black, L. (2004). Relationships among philosophies of dialogue. In R. Anderson, L. A. Baxter, & K. N. Cissna (Eds.), *Dialogue: Theorizing Difference in Communication Studies.* Thousand Oaks, CA: Sage.

Thelen, H. A. (1954). *Dynamics of groups at work.* Chicago: The University of Chicago Press.

Toseland, R. W., & Rivas, R. F. (1995). *An introduction to group work and practice* (2nd ed.). Needham Heights, MA: Allyn and Bacon.

Tuckman, B. W. (1965). Developmental sequence in small groups. *Psychological Bulletin*, 63, 384–399.

Tuckman, B. W., & Jensen, M. C. (1977). Stages of small-group development revisited. *Group & Organizational Studies*, 2, 419–427.

Vygotsky, L. S. (1978). *Mind and society: The development of higher mental processes.* Cambridge, MA: Harvard University Press.

Warren, K. (1996). The midwife teacher: Engaging students in the experiential education process. In K. Warren (Ed.), *Women's Voices in Experiential Education*. Dubuque, IA: Kendall/Hunt.

Weisenfeld, E. (1996). The concept of we: A community social psychology myth? *Journal of Community Psychology*, *24*(4), 337–346.

Wenger, E. (1998). *Communities of practice: Learning, meaning and identity.* Cambridge: Cambridge University.

Wertsch, James V. (1995). Sociocultural research in the copyright age, *Culture & Psychology*, *1*, 81–102.

Wheelan, S. A. (2005a). *Group processes: A developmental perspective.* Boston, MA: Allyn & Bacon.

Wheelan, S. A. (2005b). *Creating effective teams.* Thousand Oaks, CA: Sage.

Wilson, G. L., & Hanna, M. S. (1993). *Groups in context: Leadership and participation in small groups.* New York: McGraw-Hill.

Worchel, S. (1994). You can go home again: returning group research to the group context with an eye on development issues. *Small Group Research, 25*, 205–224.

Young, I. M. (1990). *Justice and the politics of difference*. Princeton, NJ: Princeton University Press.

Author's Acknowledgements

I am grateful to Tim O'Connell, Ph.D., for his time in reviewing an early version of this chapter and to Michelle McGinn, Ph.D., for reviewing multiple versions of this chapter and for her helpful suggestions.

Programming the Transfer of Learning in Adventure Education

▾ ▾ ▾

Michael A. Gass

When evaluating the effectiveness of any learning experience, educators have often focused on how learning will serve the student in the future. This concern has become particularly true in the field of adventure education. Whether it has been a young adolescent developing more appropriate social behaviors, a freshman student obtaining a more beneficial educational experience at a university, or another program where adventure is used as a valid educational medium, the credibility of programs using a challenging environment has been based upon the positive effects they have on their students' or clients' futures.

This effect that a particular experience has on future learning experiences is called the transfer of learning or the transfer of training. In our attempts to simplify the essential, most adventure educators call this phenomenon "transfer." Transfer is valuable to many programs in the sense that their success, continuation, and/or livelihood is based on the effect their program has on the future of their students or clients. For example, when describing the value of adventure programming as a milieu used to prevent delinquency, the U.S. Department of Justice states that despite having some plausible theoretical or correlational basis, wilderness programs without follow-up (transfer) into clients' home communities "should be rejected on the basis of their repeated failure to demonstrate effectiveness in reducing delinquency after having been tried and evaluated."

This chapter originally was published in the *Journal of Experiential Education*, with the following citation:
Gass, M. A. (1985). Programming the transfer of learning in adventure education. *Journal of Experiential Education, 8*(3), 18–24.

While transfer is critical to the field of adventure education, probably no other concept is so often misunderstood. Much of the confusion plaguing the transfer of learning has resulted from two main factors. First is the concern that the initial learning usually takes place in an environment (e.g., mountains) quite different from the environment where the student's future learning will occur. Second is the lack of knowledge concerning the variety of methods available to promote transfer. Neither of these problems is limited to adventure education, but there are certain theories, models, and techniques that pertain directly to the field and can assist in eliminating much of the confusion surrounding the topic and enable individuals to strengthen the transfer of their program's goals.

Theories Concerning Transfer

Concerning the application to adventure education, three central learning theories pertaining to transfer exist that explain how the linking of elements from one learning environment to another occurs (see Figure 1). Bruner describes the first two, specific and non-specific transfer, in attempting to show how current learning serves the learner in the future.

> There are two ways in which learning serves the future. One is through its specific applicability to tasks that are highly similar to those we originally learned to perform. Psychologists refer to this specific phenomenon as specific transfer of training; perhaps it should be called the extension of habits or associations. Its utility appears to be limited in the main to what we speak of as skills. A second way in which earlier learning renders later performance more efficient is through what is conveniently called non-specific transfer, or, more accurately, the transfer of principles and attitudes. In essence, it consists of learning, initially, not a skill but a general idea which can then be used as a basis of recognizing subsequent problems as special cases of the idea originally mastered. (1960, p. 17)

The following example from a student's notebook serves to illustrate the use of specific transfer in adventure education:

> Today during the class we learned how to rappel. Initially I was quite frightened, but I ended up catching on to the proper technique and enjoying it quite a bit! One thing that helped me in learning how to rappel was the belaying we did yesterday. With belaying, our left hand is the "feel" hand while the right hand is the "brake" hand. With rappelling, it is the same; our left hand is the "feel" hand and our right hand is used to "brake" our rappel and control our descent.

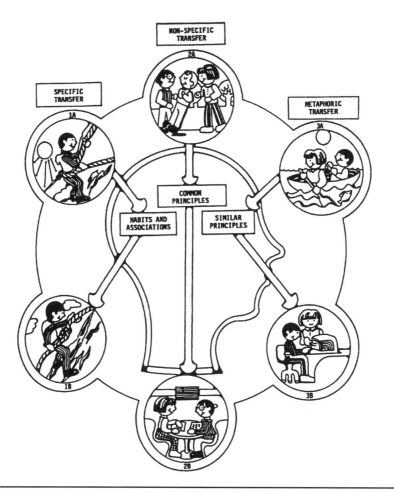

Figure 1. **Three theories of transfer in adventure education. The above diagram illustrates how learning in adventure education is linked to future learning experiences. In the first theory, specific transfer, the learner takes the habits and associations acquired during a previous experience (Diagram 1A— the hand skills of belaying) and applies them to a new experience to assist him in developing a new skill (Diagram 1B—the hand skills of rappelling). In the second theory, non-specific transfer, the learner generalizes the common underlying principles received from a previous experience (Diagram 2A—developing trust from an initiative game) and employs them in a new learning situation (Diagram 2B—developing trust with peers at school). The third theory, metaphoric transfer, shows the learner transferring the similar underlying principles from canoeing (Diagram 3A) to working with other individuals in a business corporation (Diagram 3B).**

In this example, the student's previous experiences of specific hand skills learned while belaying positively affected her ability to learn the necessary and correct hand skills of rappelling. Figure 1 illustrates these events occurring-the initial stage of learning how to belay, the development of the proper and safe habits while belaying, and finally, the use of these skills while rappelling.

The next example from another student's notebook highlights what Bruner describes as non-specific transfer, or the use of common underlying principles in one learning situation to assist the student in a future learning experience:

> [As a result of the wilderness course] I've seen myself developing more trust in my friends at school. The no-discount policy[1] helps me quite a bit, but I think what helped the most was learning how I receive as well as give support to others. I felt that this was the most important thing I learned [while on the wilderness course].

In this second example, the student had the common underlying principles that she learned about developing trust (i.e., receiving and giving support from/to others) from the wilderness course and generalized those principles and attitudes to a new learning situation (i.e., school). This ability to generalize by the learner is crucial for non-specific transfer to occur. Figure 1 shows the connection of two learning situations by common underlying principles or non-specific transfer. In this example, the student, through an initiative such as the Willow Wand Exercise[2] supplemented with a no-discount policy, learns valuable principles and attitudes about developing trust in peer relationships. She takes these principles, generalizes them, and transfers them to a new learning situation, such as developing meaningful relationships at school based on trust.

The third transfer theory associated with adventure learning also requires the student to generalize certain principles from one learning situation to another. While the principles being transferred in this theory are not common or the same in structure, they are similar, analogous, or metaphorical.

The following passage illustrates a student making the connection between the similar underlying principles of canoeing and his group working together:

---

[1] The no-discount policy is a technique from Gestalt psychology used by some adventure programs. It asks that all participants (voluntarily) enter into a "contract" with the other group members, agreeing not to discount their feelings as well as the feelings of the other members in the group. Members of the group are asked to confront any discounting behavior and this will often lead to a group discussion.

[2] The Willow Wand Exercise is an initiative used to introduce the concept of trust to a group in an adventure experience. It often serves as a lead-up activity to a Trust Circle or Trust Fall.

There has been a certain jerkiness in the group. It's like the progress of a canoe. When the people on each side paddle in unison, with each person pulling his weight, the canoe goes forward smoothly. If certain people slack, or if there is a lack of co-ordination, progress becomes jerky. The canoe veers [from] side to side. Time and energy are wasted. (Godfrey, 1980, p. 229)

In this particular situation, the student is not using the principles of efficient canoeing for future aquatic learning experiences. He is instead transferring the concepts or principles of canoeing as metaphors for another learning experience that is similar, yet not the same.

This third type of transfer, metaphoric transfer, is also illustrated in Figure 1. Here the student takes the similar underlying principles mentioned in the example above, generalizes them, and applies them to a future learning experience with similar elements. The future learning experience represented in Figure 1 for metaphoric transfer is a group situation where the necessity of everyone working together efficiently is vital (in this case, working for a business corporation).

Probably the individual who has done the most investigation into the use of metaphoric transfer with adventure learning is Stephen Bacon. In the following passage, he further explains how using experiences that are metaphoric provides a vehicle for the transfer of learning:

The key factor in determining whether experiences are metaphoric is the degree of isomorphism between the metaphoric situation and the real-life situation. Isomorphic means having the same structure. When all the major elements in one experience are represented by corresponding elements in another experience, and when the overall structures of the two experiences are highly similar, then the two experiences are metaphors for each other. This does not imply that the corresponding elements are literally identical; rather, they must be symbolically identical. (Bacon, 1983, p. 4)

A Program Model for Transfer

When reviewing the three transfer-of-learning theories discussed previously, it can be seen that the key to increasing transfer often lies either in the selection or design of appropriate learning activities or in the teaching methodology. One of the major faults of adventure education has been the lack of planning for the transfer in these areas. Transfer must be planned, much in the same manner as an educational objective, or a properly planned learning skill.

Figure 2 portrays the learning process of an adventure program interested in procuring positive transfer for a student.

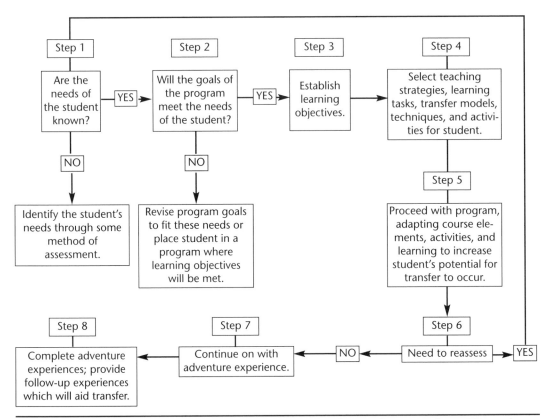

***Figure 2.* Learning process model with an emphasis on the transfer of learning.**

As seen in the model, once the needs of the student and the goals of the program are properly identified and matched, the learning skills, activities, teaching strategies, and transfer models and techniques are planned. A strong emphasis is placed here on providing the connection between the present and future learning environments to increase the amount of transfer that will occur. Note that throughout the program, if the needs of the student change, the model directs the instructor to assess these changes and adapt new learning activities and transfer elements to the student's new behavior. At the completion of the adventure experience, follow-up activities are also used to enhance positive transfer.

Factors/Techniques That Enhance the Transfer of Learning Through Adventure Activities

Given the information in Figure 2 for programming transfer, what are some of the factors or techniques adventure educators can use to assist them in increasing the transfer of their students' learning? (Shown by Step 4 in Figure 2.) Many researchers have presented exhaustive lists of elements that can lead to positive transfer, but some of these are unalterable (e.g., genetic factors concerning intelligence), while others have little application to the "non-traditional" atmosphere where most adventure learning takes place.

As stated in the program model, it is necessary for the adventure educator to select not only the proper transfer of learning theories, but also the techniques and activities involved with the increase of transfer applicable to his/her program. Ten techniques adaptable to the transfer of learning occurring with adventure activities are presented here as examples. However, many other techniques exist and should be selected for their ability to transfer the goals of the specific program and what theory of transfer one is using. (A bibliography is included with this article and sources that address this topic to a greater degree are noted by ***.)

1. *Design conditions for transfer before the course/program/learning activities actually begin.* Several steps can be done prior to a learning experience that can aid in the transfer of learning from an adventure activity. Examples of these steps include:

   a) Identify, develop, or establish a commitment to change in the student.

   b) Have a student set goals for the experience.

   c) Write and set tight learning objectives for the student in the program.

   d) Place the plans and goals made by the student in writing to create a stronger commitment for transferring the learning.

2. *Create elements in the student's learning environment similar to those elements likely to be found in future learning environments.* Learning environments with strong applicability to future experiences have greater potential for a more positive transfer of learning. The following example of a disaffected youth in a wilderness program shows how elements of the program were created to assist him in transferring a behavior, in this case, a greater self-concept, into a subsequent learning environment.

   Throughout the course, Kurt was presented with a variety of challenging tasks. He overcame strong personal fears and doubts and succeeded at many of the tasks that required a great deal of initiative. The staff noticed that after he had developed a stronger belief in himself, he was especially zealous on tasks that required a great deal of trust and responsibility (e.g., belaying). Throughout the course, the staff continued to place Kurt in progressively more difficult situations that demanded a strong, realistic belief in himself as well as other members in the group. Many of the discussions at night were about the relationships between the elements they faced as individuals and as a group in the wilderness and those they would find when they returned to their communities. as individuals and as a group in the wilderness and those they would find when they returned to their communities.

Other learning behaviors are often presented in a similar manner to increase their relevance and application to future learning environments for students. Certain programs have found that by approaching problem-solving and decision-making skills in a general manner, their students succeed in creating elements valuable for future use (Gass, 1985, p. 5).

3. *Provide students with the opportunities to practice the transfer of learning while still in the program.* There was probably no better time for Kurt to practice the skill to be transferred (i.e., an increased self-concept) than during the course. The variety of contexts in which to practice transfer, the number of times Kurt could practice transferring the skill, and the strong support group that developed during this outdoor adventure program all helped Kurt to focus on the generalizing and conceptualizing skills he needed to strengthen the bond that his transfer needed for different learning situations.

4. *Have the consequences of learning be natural—not artificial.* One can think of the consequences of learning as either being natural or artificial. "Natural consequences are those that follow or would follow a given act *unless* some human or human system intervenes. Artificial consequences follow or would follow a given act, if, and only if, some human or human system *anticipates* or responds to the initial act and causes the artificial consequence or modifies a natural consequence" (Darnell, 1983, p. 4).

Superficially viewing the field of outdoor education, one would think that all learning that takes place in the outdoors would have natural consequences. Unfortunately, far too often this is not the case. Whether it has been from an "overly" caring instructor or an overpowering one, too often the student becomes dependent on, is shielded by, or anticipates the instructor as a reinforcer of learning. Once the course is over and the reinforcer (i.e., the instructor) is removed from the student, learning behavior is severely hampered or terminated. In this way, with artificial consequences, the result of learning transfer is extremely limited.

However, if outdoor programs make their students' learning more experiential, natural consequences are more likely to occur. This results in the stronger formation of learning behaviors likely to be available in future learning situations, hence, the increase in the amount of transfer. Some experiential learning techniques that foster the development of natural consequences include relying upon the student's intrinsic rather than some external source of motivation; placing more responsibility for learning on the student (see 8); and not shielding the learner from the consequences of their learning, whether they be positive or negative.

5. *Provide the means for students to internalize their own learning.* The ability for a student to internalize his/her own learning creates the concepts and generalizations central to the transfer process. Adventure educators have differed to a great extent on how this is best accomplished. Many believe that by getting their students to verbalize, or place their own learning into words, the internalization of the concepts to be transferred is increased through self-awareness and reflective thinking (Kaliski, 1979, p. 62). Others feel that conscious efforts such as verbalizing are secondary to other methods of internalization, such as the subconscious development of metaphors for transfer (Bacon, 1983, p. 2).

   All methods that ask students to internalize learning behaviors from adventure programs strongly support the use of *reflection* to aid internalization. It seems that any process an instructor can use that enables the student to identify personal learning leads to a greater applicability of learning for future situations.

   An example of a process often used by adventure education programs that increases transfer through reflection is the "solo" experience. Certain programs feel that such an experience reinforces the learning that occurs in the adventure program and helps students/clients to identify how they are going to use the experience in the future (Gass, 1985, p. 6).

6. *Include past successful alumni in the adventure program.* Sometimes the incorporation of successful alumni in courses or programs assists in the transfer of learning for students/clients. The following example demonstrates how one program uses this technique:

   > By listening to how these alumni used the skills they had learned from the program in their lives, students began to envision how they might use elements of the program in future situations. While not always advisable or possible for some programs, many individuals felt this "vicarious" method of planning future transfer strategies aided in the transfer of learning for students. (Gass, 1985, p. 5)

7. *Include significant others in the learning process.* The inclusion of other individuals closely associated with the student's/client's learning process has often been found to heighten the transfer of learning (Gass, 1985, p. 2). Some of the persons used to fill this vital role have been peers, parents, counselors, social workers, and/or teachers.

The following example illustrates how one program includes significant others in the learning process to provide positive transfer for a student:

> Before Cristina participated on the adventure portion of the family therapy program, several objectives were established for her family, counselor and school teacher—as well as herself. Cristina and her family met with the staff, and other participants and their families prior to the adventure experience in order to familiarize both the students and the parents of the reasons for their participation on the course. Another reason for this meeting was to inform them of possible changes in the student that could occur. The program continued to stay in close contact with Cristina's family in order for them to adjust to and support possible changes in Cristina's personality and behavior.
>
> Cristina also created several goals in a pre-trip meeting with the assistance of a staff member in the areas of personal, family, school and peer development. The contracts were discussed on the course and monitored monthly, with proper adaptations, for the next six months. Cristina's teacher also participated on several portions of the wilderness course, enabling him to support, reinforce and try and use the observable changes during the adventure program with Cristina in the classroom.

8. *When possible, place more responsibility for learning in the program with the students/ clients.* Many programs, especially those invested in teaching adventure education experientially, believe that placing more responsibility with the students in the program not only increases their motivation to learn but also their incentive to apply their learning in future experiences. Examples of this range from some programs involving students in the planning of food menus to other programs that have students organize and conduct an entire adventure experience on their own. Certain programs have implemented strong service components that have a definite focus on future experiences outside of the adventure experience (MacArthur, 1982, pp. 37–38) and enhance the self-responsibility within the student that could lead to a greater transfer of learning.

No matter what techniques programs use to involve their students/clients in the planning and operations of an adventure experience, their involvement should depend on their ability to accept responsibility for learning and their willingness and desire to do so. A person who willingly accepts responsibility for learning will transfer information much more readily than an individual who approaches such a task with a sense of indifference or resentment.

9. *Develop focused processing techniques that facilitate the transfer of learning.* In many adventure education programs, processing/debriefing/facilitating is often used to enrich a student's learning experience. The length and intensity of these debriefings can differ from a quick and informal sharing of the day's occurrences to a lengthy and formalized discussion of a particular incident with a specific set of rules and guidelines. Despite this vast difference in the application of techniques, there are certain general characteristics that, if included in the processing of an experience, will assist in the transfer of learning. Some of these characteristics are:

   a) Present processing sessions based on the student's/client's ability to contribute personally meaningful responses.

   b) Focus on linking the experiences from the present and future learning environments together during the processing session.

   c) When possible, debrief throughout the learning experience and not just at the end of it, allowing the students to continually focus on the future applicability of present learning.

10. *Provide follow-up experiences that aid in the application of transfer.* Once a student begins transferring learning, the presence of follow-up activities (e.g., continued communications, feedback on learning decisions, processes, and choices) serves to heighten transfer abilities. Again, one reason for this might be the positive effects of reflection between learning situations. Reflection gives the student the opportunity to see and evaluate the results of past learning behaviors, garner learner motivation, and plan future learning strategies and directions.

Conclusion

As educators who use the outdoors and challenging situations to help students to learn more efficiently, we all aspire to teach our students something useable—and therein lies the value of our program. But, unless we assist our students in providing their own linkages, bridges, and connections to their learning, the utility of much of the education we care and work so hard to bring about is put away in the equipment room along with the ropes and backpacks. As we strive to become better educators and proponents of the value of adventure education, let us look upon transfer as a device to excite students by showing them the future value of their current learning experiences. This motivation, provided by the opportunity to use their learning again, can furnish one of the strongest incentives for continued learning and the field's success.

References

Bacon, S. (1983). *The conscious use of metaphor in Outward Bound.* Denver, CO: Colorado Outward Bound School.***

Bruner, J. (1960). *The process of education.* New York: Vintage.•

Darnell, D. K. (1983). *On consequences, learning, survival and good life."* An unpublished report. Dept. of Communications, University of Colorado. ***

Gass, M. A. (1985). *Strengthening adventure education by increasing the transfer of learning.* Durham, NH: University of New Hampshire.•

Johnson, G., Bird, T., Little, J. W., & Beville, S. L. (Center for Action Research, Inc.). (1981). *Delinquency prevention: Theories and strategies.* U.S. Dept. of Justice: Office of Juvenile and Delinquency Prevention.•

Kaliski, K. (1979). *The role of the instructor in the Outward Bound process.* Three Lakes, Wisconsin: Honey Lakes Camp.***

MacArthur, R. S. (1982). The changing role of service in Outward Bound. *Journal of Experiential Education, 5(2).* •

Mitzel, H. (Ed.). (1982). *Encyclopedia of Educational Research.* (Vol. 1) (American Educational Research Association) (5th ed.) (pp. 1947–1955). New York: Free Press.•

Rhoades, J. S. (1972). *The problem of individual change in Outward Bound: An application and transfer theory.* Doctoral dissertation. University of Massachusetts.•

Richardson, B. L. (1978). *The transfer of learning from high-risk activities in adventure-based outdoor education programs.* An unpublished report. Northern Illinois University, p. 22.***

Ethics & Spirituality

▼ ▼ ▼

Experiential Education & Spirituality

▾ ▾ ▾

Paul Heintzman

I have heard it said that a hallmark of the 1990s was that we let spirituality out of the closet. I actually think it is still in there, but with the door flung wide open. There has been an increase of writings and ease of discussion even in corporate settings on the importance of a spiritual focus.

Marianne Scippa (2000) made the above comments in her 1999 Kurt Hahn Address titled "Catalysts for change: The healing power of experiential practices." While an earlier edition of this text (Warren, Sakofs, & Hunt, 1995) included republication of a conceptual paper (Fox, 1983) and an empirical study (Stringer & McAvoy, 1992) on the topic of spirituality and experiential education, it is only during the last decade that there has been tremendous growth in the literature on this topic, including a special issue of the *Journal of Experiential Education* on spirituality (Vol. 23, No. 1, 2000). Much of this literature is conceptual (e.g., Haluza-Delay, 2000; Anderson-Hanley, 1997; White, 2000). In a 1994 article, Morgan challenged the assumption that most people who engage in outdoor and adventure recreation have a spiritual relationship with nature. He claimed that this relationship is a myth as there is very little empirical evidence to support it. In 1997 Anderson-Hanley observed that research on experiential education and spirituality was in a state of infancy. In the last decade, however, a number of empirical studies have been published (e.g., Fox, 1997; Fredrickson & Anderson, 1999; Heintzman, 2007a; Loeffler, 2004; Sweatman & Heintzman, 2004) and theoretical models developed (Fox, 1999; Fredrickson & Anderson, 1999; Heintzman, 2002). This chapter will provide an integrative review of recent empirical studies and theoretical models that may be helpful in explaining the relationships between experiential education and spirituality.

Conceptualization of Spirituality and Related Terms

The English word "spirituality" comes from the Latin term *spiritus*, meaning "breath of life" (Elkins, Hedstrom, Hughes, Leaf, & Saunders, 1988) and can be traced to the Greek word *pneuma*, which is used to describe a person's spirit guided by God's spirit (Principe, 1983). In today's multicultural society, however, there are many diverse expressions of spirituality and religion. Based upon scientific and historical scholarship, a panel of more than 20 scholars identified the main criterion for spirituality as "the feelings, thoughts, experiences, and behaviors that arise from a search for the sacred" (Larson, Swyers, & McCullough, 1998, p. 21). The search for the sacred refers to the search for God, a higher power, a larger reality, and/or ultimate truth as perceived by an individual.

The concept of spirituality is similar yet different from the concept of religion. The English word "religion" comes from the Latin word *religio* and is related to the Latin word *legare*, which means to connect or to bind (Paloutzian, 1996). The English word ligament, which means connection, derives from the same root. Thus the etymological background of the word "religion" suggests a reconnecting process, a repairing of brokenness, and a striving for a sense of wholeness (Paloutzian). Scientific and historical scholarship suggests that religion may be characterized by one or both of the following statements, the first of which is the same as the above criterion for spirituality: (a) "The feelings, thoughts, experiences, and behaviors that arise from a search for the sacred;" and/or (b) "A search or quest for non-sacred goals (such as identity, belongingness, meaning, health, or wellness) in a context that has as its primary goal the facilitation of spirituality" (Larson et al., 1998, p. 21). In addition, religion is characterized by (c) "the means and methods (e.g., rituals or prescribed behaviors) of the search that receive validation and support from within an identifiable group of people" (Larson et al., p. 21). This last statement alludes to the five dimensions of religion: religious beliefs (what is believed), religious practice (a set of religious behaviours, e.g., prayer), religious feeling (mental and emotional experience), religious knowledge (information about one's religion) and religious effects (consequences of religion on one's life) (Paloutzian).

Based on the criterion of spirituality and religion identified above (Larson et al., 1998), it can be concluded that spirituality may be experienced within, or outside, the context of religion. When the case of spirituality within the context of religion is considered, an analogy is helpful: Spirituality is like water and religion is like the container that holds the water (Seaward, 2000). In other words, religion is the context within which spirituality may, although not necessarily, be experienced. For example, for some people the Jewish religion may be primarily associated with cultural and social meanings while for other people the Jewish religion is also the container or framework in which their spirituality is developed and nurtured. Based on a theoretical and empirical perspective, Elkins et al. (1988, p. 10) defined spirituality, within or outside the context of religion, as "a way of being and experiencing that comes about through awareness of a transcendent dimension and that is characterized by certain identifiable values in regard to self, others, nature, life, and whatever one considers to be Ultimate."

Although there are different expressions of spirituality and religion, McDonald & Schreyer (1991) made a helpful distinction between the process and content of spirituality. While process and content are intertwined and one cannot occur without the other, content is the particular object of spirituality while process refers to the spiritual activities and functions that a person engages in. Even though the content of different spiritual expressions (e.g., a belief system, content of a prayer) may differ from one spiritual expression to another, the processes (e.g., prayer, meditation) involved in spirituality might be similar across different spiritual expressions.

In addition to the term spirituality, a number of related terms may be found in the literature on experiential education and spirituality. *Spiritual experience* may be defined as "an acute experience of a spiritual nature" where "acute" refers to an "unmistakably noticeable" experience (Chandler, Holden, & Kolander, 1992, p. 170). *Spiritual growth* or *spiritual development* refers to the "process of incorporating spiritual experiences that results ultimately in spiritual transformation" (Chandler et al., p. 170). The assumption underlying this process is that the mere occurrence of spiritual experiences does not necessarily result in spiritual development unless the experiences are dealt with and integrated into one's life. The terms *spiritual health* or *spiritual well-being* originate in the medical wellness and health promotion literature (Westgate, 1996). Within the context of holistic health, spiritual health or spiritual well-being is considered as one component of holistic health that is integrated with the social, emotional, mental, and physical components of holistic health. Hawks (1994) developed the following short but comprehensive definition of spiritual health:

> A high level of faith, hope, and commitment in relation to a well-defined worldview or belief system that provides a sense of meaning and purpose to existence in general, and that offers an ethical path to personal fulfillment which includes connectedness with self, others, and a higher power or larger reality. (p. 6)

Although many definitions of spirituality and the related terms of spiritual experience, spiritual growth, spiritual development, spiritual health, and spiritual well-being exist, most researchers on the topic of experiential education and spirituality let participants self-define these concepts.

Theories Relevant to Experiential Education and Spirituality

Researchers who have studied the relationships between experiential education and spirituality have based their studies upon, alluded to, or confirmed aspects of a variety of theories and theoretical models. Included are the theory of flow (Csikszentmihalyi, 1975), restorative environments theory (Kaplan, 1995), the sense of place concept (Williams & Stewart, 1998), Chandler et al.'s (1992) theoretical model of spiritual wellness, and leisure and well-being theories (Mannell & Kleiber, 1997). The first three of these will be examined briefly here, and the latter two will be explained later in the chapter.

A theory sometimes associated with experiential education and spirituality is the theory of *flow*. Social psychologist Csikszentmihalyi (1975) proposed that flow experiences were intensely absorbing experiences where the challenge of an activity matched the skill level of the individual so that the person lost track of both time and awareness of self. If a person's skills were much higher than the challenges of the activity the person would experience boredom, while if the challenges were much higher than the skills a person would experience anxiety. The flow experience, characterized by a centering of an individual's attention, timelessness, overcoming limits of ordinary experience, and a sense of union, may also be associated with spiritual or transcendental experiences (McDonald & Schreyer, 1991; Williams & Harvey, 2001). Often occurrences of flow are experienced in an outdoors or natural setting, and are normally the result of intense emotional and/or physical challenge (Fredrickson & Anderson, 1999). Both Stringer and McAvoy (1992) and Fredrickson and Anderson have noted the relevance of the theory of flow to the spiritual dimension of wilderness/adventure experiences.

Restorative environments theory (Kaplan & Kaplan, 1989; Kaplan, 1995) is helpful in trying to understand the processes that take place when a person is removed from his/her everyday environment, which is often the case during experiential education activities or programs. Restorative environments are characterized by four features: (a) *being away*, that is, in a conceptually or physically different setting from one's everyday environment; (b) *extent*, which refers to a setting adequately rich and coherent that it can captivate the mind and foster exploration; (c) *fascination*, a form of attention that requires no effort and may focus on content (people, nature) or process (problem-solving, story telling); and (d) *compatibility*, which requires a setting that is congruent with and advances one's purposes or inclinations.

Although a variety of settings exhibit the four features of a restorative environment to differing degrees, natural settings tend to be richly blessed with all four features. Research on restorative environments has documented the greater restorative potential of natural environ-ments in comparison to urban settings or other artificial settings (Kaplan, 1995). As will be explained in more detail later, in a variety of studies related to experiential education, Heintz-man (2007a, 2007b, 2008; Sweatman & Heintzman, 2004) found support for the "being away" feature of this theory, while the fascination and compatibility features were helpful in explain-ing why experiential education participants found natural settings conducive to spirituality.

Another theory that has been used to explore the spiritual meanings associated with experiential education is that of "attachment to place" or "sense of place." These concepts refer to the strong emotional and symbolic connections people tend to form with places and the rich and varied meanings they give these places (Williams & Stewart, 1998). Williams, Patterson, Roggenbuck, and Watson (1992) suggested that natural resources and settings:

> are not only raw materials to be inventoried and molded into a recreation opportunity,
> but also, and more important, places with histories, places that people care about, places
> that for many people embody a sense of belonging and purpose that give meaning to
> life. (p. 44)

Sense of place suggests that spiritual experiences are the result of complex interactions between an individual and the setting, including both the social and physical environment. As explained in more detail later, Fredrickson and Anderson (1999) used sense of place and related concepts of *place attachment*, *sacred space*, and *sense of divine a*s the starting point to explore the relationships between wilderness experience and spirituality.

Spiritual Experience Process Funnel Model

Fox (1999) developed the spiritual experience process funnel model that suggests the wilderness experience can ultimately lead to significant attitude change and the development of new behaviours. This model is based on Fox's (1997) examination of six women's percep-tions of a solitude wilderness experience (modified wilderness quest) in Croajingolong National Park in Australia. She recorded the women's reflections on nature, wilderness soli-tude, spiritual experience, and the significance of participation in a women-only group.

The spiritual experience process funnel uses a grounded theory framework with six themes to explain the spiritual experience process. First, this model suggests that individuals may bring "baggage" into wilderness experiences that may generate a fear of nature. Sec-ond, rationalizing or *accepting these fe*ars may produce feelings of self-control, which in turn can lead to relaxation, a reduction of anxiety and stress, and a sense of being comfortable with nature. Third, when individuals become relaxed and in control, individual or group events such as those involving deep reflection, natural beauty, mystery, or encounters with others may trigger a receptivity and openness to *opportunities for spiritual experience*. Fourth, this spiritual experience may include *intense emotions and feelings* such as awe and wonder, which can lead to connections with nature, the inner life, other people, and a higher power/God. Fifth, these spiritual experiences are *transcendental* in that they can lead to delayed responses such as tranquility and peacefulness that contribute to spiritual growth over time. Sixth, these spiritual experiences may facilitate significant *life transformation* through personal attitudinal and behavioural changes, such as empowerment in family, work, and other relationships, over a period of time. While Fox's model is a starting point, the wilderness experience is very complex and most likely involves more factors than those presented in the model.

Model of Youth Camp Experience and Spirituality

The third and fourth themes of Fox's (1999) model are similar to Sweatman and Heintzman's (2004) model of youth camp experience and spirituality. Sweatman and Heintzman developed their model from a qualitative study that investigated the perceived impact of outdoor residential camp experience on the spirituality of youth. The camp setting facilitated spiritual growth and development as it provided a natural setting as well as an opportunity for the participants to get away from their everyday lives in an urban environment. In the natural environment, experiencing structured and unstructured time alone enhanced spirituality by providing youth with opportunities to reflect on their lives. Social experiences also had an impact on the participants' spirituality by allowing them to develop relationships through formal and informal activities. Finally, the majority of the participants expressed that the camp experience provided them with positive feelings that they associated with their spirituality. Both the Fox, and Sweatman and Heintzman models contain elements of the spiritual process that have been supported by a number of empirical research studies: personal history, solitude, group experiences, intense emotions and feelings, transcendence, and life transformation.

Personal History

Fox's (1999, p. 459) first theme, that "people carry 'baggage' into wilderness adventure experiences which influences perceptions and may generate fears toward nature," is based on the data from her 1997 study: "to reach this comfort zone where spiritual experiences could occur, fears and anxiety had to be overcome, and an environment in which the participants felt safe and protected had to be found" (Fox, 1999, p. 459). Other studies related to experiential education and spirituality have not identified fear as a barrier to spiritual experience for participants (e.g., Heintzman, 2007a, 2007b, 2008). However Heintzman (2007b), in a study of an 8-day experiential environmental education (EEE) course for graduate students, discovered that participants experienced the course from within the context of his/her personal history, the current circumstances of his/her life, and the attitude brought to the course. For example, for one student the course was a celebration of turning 50, for a young married couple the course occurred at a difficult time in their summer when they were depressed, while for another participant the course had many similarities with his everyday life and thus there was a sense of continuity with his daily circumstances. These personal histories and contexts influenced the students' experiences of the course.

All of these participants also noted the importance of their "frame of mind," "conscious choices to accept where I am, appreciate where I am," and the attitude they brought to the course. Thus, Heintzman (2007b) observed that the role of personal history, context, and attitude may be just as important as the actual structure and content of the experiential course in bringing about spiritual outcomes. Consequently, experiential educators need to understand and be sensitive to the personal histories and contexts of each individual.

Solitude

Fox (1997) found that solitude in wilderness was important for the women in her study as it provided them with peace, tranquility, a chance for inner journey, and time for self-reflection. Time spent alone in nature also enhanced the opportunity to listen, watch, explore, and reflect upon nature. Likewise, Fredrickson and Anderson (1999), in a qualitative exploration of women's wilderness experience (a canoe trip in the Boundary Waters Canoe Area Wilderness in Northern Minnesota and a hiking trip in the Grand Canyon), discovered that during periods of solitude, participants contemplated life's deepest questions, which they did not have time to reflect on in everyday life. This solitude left them renewed and rejuvenated. A 24-hour solo was seen by many participants in an EEE course as being extremely beneficial for their spirituality (Heintzman, 2007b). For those who participated in a solo on a men's wilderness canoe trip, time alone was helpful to spiritual well-being (Heintzman, 2007a). Stringer and McAvoy (1992), based on a qualitative study of wilderness adventure programs (a canoeing trip in Northern Ontario and a backpacking trip in the Beartooth Mountains in Wyoming and Montana), noted that the major factor inhibiting spiritual experiences in wilderness was the lack of time alone or not enough free time.

Group Experiences

Stringer and McAvoy (1992) observed that the sharing of different experiences, opinions, and ideas that each participant brought to the group was an important factor that contributed to their spiritual experiences. Fox (1997) found that being in a group facilitated the spiritual experiences of women in wilderness. She discovered that the women experienced a sense of spirituality by being part of an all-women's group and that working as a team with other women enhanced their spiritual experience. Similarly, Fredrickson and Anderson (1999) observed that the aspects related to being part of an all-women's group (i.e., "group trust and emotional support," "sharing common life changes," "non-competitive atmosphere") contributed to the meaningful dimensions of the wilderness trip. In a study of men's wilderness experience and spirituality, Heintzman (2007a) discovered that a variety of social settings on a trip, such as being with the entire group, being with two or three other participants, or being with one other participant, was viewed as important to spiritual well-being. The opportunity to discuss with others, to share stories and personal life experiences, and to have friendship and camaraderie were all helpful to spiritual well-being.

An interesting dimension of group experience is participation in single-gender groups. As noted above, Fox (1997) and Fredrickson and Anderson (1999) found that for the women in their studies being part of a women-only group enhanced the spiritual experience. In Heintzman's (2007a) study of a men's wilderness experience, only some of the men in the group viewed being part of a men-only group as an important factor in enhancing spiritual well-being. In a similar study (Heintzman, 2008), all the participants strongly believed that being part of a men-only group played a very important role in influencing the spiritual outcomes of trip participation. A possible explanation was that the men in the second study (Heintzman, 2008) had a common purpose and interest in spirituality while not all men in the first study (Heintzman, 2007a) were equally committed to the spiritual dimension of their wilderness experience. In both studies those who viewed the men-only group as important to their spiritual well-being believed that such a group provided the opportunity to focus on men's spiritual issues and to be open and vulnerable with each other.

Balance of Solitude and Group Experiences

In some cases, the factors of being with other people and having solitude go together. For example, Heintzman (2007a) found that the variety of social settings on a wilderness trip, such as being alone, being with one other person, and being in a group, along with times to be alone in solitude, were viewed as important to spiritual well-being. While it may seem contradictory that both group experiences and times of solitude are associated with spirituality, it seems that both of these types of experiences in the same wilderness trip may be critical factors in spiritual experience.

The balance of both types of experiences also has been found to be important in youth camp experiences (Sweatman & Heintzman, 2004) and an EEE course (Heintzman, 2007b). In the former, experiencing structured and unstructured time alone influenced participants' spirituality by providing them with opportunities to reflect on their lives, while social experiences also had an impact on the participants' spirituality by allowing them to develop relationships through formal and informal activities. In the latter, a combination of solitude within community was beneficial. The spectrum of social settings, including a 24-hour solo, rowing boats together, group tasks, and corporate spiritual activities all contributed to this combination of solitude within community.

Emotions Associated with Spiritual Experience

The fourth theme in Fox's model suggests that spiritual experiences include intense emotions. For example, Stringer and McAvoy (1992) found that the experiences that were considered to be most spiritual were also identified as the most emotionally intense. The emotions associated with these spiritual experiences tended to be positive and associated with an increased sense of awareness of a greater power, nature, others, and of self. Likewise, many of the women in Fox's (1997) study experienced the emotions of awe and wonderment of nature that contributed to their spiritual experience or a sense of spirituality. In addition, the women experienced a number of feelings associated with spirituality and spiritual experience such as: connectedness, heightened senses, inner calm, joy, inner peace, inner happiness, and elatedness. "Positive feelings" was a theme identified by Sweatman and Heintzman (2004) in their study of youth residential camp experience and spirituality. Positive feelings experienced at camp about oneself and about camp—such as happiness, love, and peace—enhanced participants' emotional well-being, which was closely related to their spirituality. Haluza-Delay (2000) critiqued these types of studies as focusing on pleasant emotional states and urged investigation after the experience to determine participants' life transformation.

Transcendence

Fox's (1999, p. 459) fifth theme is that "spiritual experiences are transcendental, and over time contribute to spiritual growth." Long-lasting feelings of transcendence such as peacefulness, elation, calmness, and tranquility lead to "empowerment, inner strength, inner peace, clarity, contentment, accomplishment, awareness, and connection (to self, womanhood, nature, spirits and other people)" (Fox, p. 459). Similarly, Stringer and McAvoy (1992) observed that most spiritual experiences were accompanied by an increased sense of awareness of self, others, the environment and/or a greater power. This sense of transcendence is reflected in a theme that described the immediate impact of participation in a men's wilderness canoe trip: peacefulness, peace with oneself, and peace with the world (Heintzman, 2007a). A photo elicitation study on the meaning of outdoor adventure experiences for participants in college-based outdoor programs, found that being in the outdoors led to a state of peacefulness or contemplative mindset; it was a place to find peace, calm and stillness (Loeffler, 2004). Several women in Fredrickson and Anderson's (1999) study experienced a "religious-like" or self-transcending experience characterized by feelings of peace and humility that led them to new levels of spiritual experience.

Life Transformation

The spiritual experience process funnel model suggests that wilderness experiences may contribute to spiritual growth over time. Little is known about the long-term impact of wilderness experiences, as most studies on wilderness experience and spirituality have not incorporated a longitudinal dimension but have focused on the immediate experience of the wilderness trip. Haluza-Delay (2000, p. 146) commented that "such studies say little about the consequences of such experiences. Neither Stringer and McAvoy (1992) nor Fredrickson and Anderson (1999) incorporated a longitudinal aspect, so the results of the experiences in participant life transformation are indeterminate." In Stringer and McAvoy's study, posttrip interviews were conducted as soon as possible (3–45 days) after the trip, while in Fredrickson and Anderson's study followupfollow-up interviews were conducted within three weeks of the trip. Nevertheless, Stringer and McAvoy concluded that the experiences appeared to have some impact on participants' lives due to the fact that most participants were able to describe their experiences approximately one month later.

Fox (1999, p. 459) stated that the participants in her study returned home with feelings of "elation, inner happiness, inner strength, inner peace, clarity, pride in self, and an enhanced connection to spirituality, nature and self." Although it was not explained how long after the trip followupfollow-up data were gathered, it was claimed that these positive feelings led to changes in values and behaviours. Feelings of empowerment, clarity, and inner peace led to inner strength and self-control, which impacted both work life and family life in terms of feeling more in control and stronger in regards to relationships, roles, and personal goals.

Heintzman (2007a) examined the longer term impact of wilderness experience for a group of men on a wilderness canoe trip by conducting interviews approximately 5–7 months after the trip and found that the long-term impact of the trip seemed to be primarily associated with the memory and recollection of the experience and less with any specific behavioural change. A study of a different men's wilderness canoe trip involving interviews 8–10 months after the wilderness experience revealed that the development and enhancement of spiritual friendships was the main impact of the canoe trip upon spirituality (Heintzman, 2008). IndepthIn-depth interviews with participants seven months after they participated in an 8-day, EEE course discovered that the course impacted the spirituality, environmental attitudes, and behaviours of each person differently, both in terms of the type of impact and the degree of impact (Heintzman, 2007b). For some the course impacted their lifestyle in terms of environmental behaviours, and for others the impact was upon their attitude. The degree of impact (minimal, dramatic) was partly influenced by the personal history that a participant brought to the course. For example, the degree of impact was less for someone who already was practicing environmentally friendly behaviours than for someone who previously had not.

In a rare study of the life significance of an experiential education program, Daniel (2007) used the significant life experience (SLE) theoretical framework to understand the long-term value of a Christian-based, Outward Bound-type, 20-day wilderness expedition for college students. The sample included 227 people who had participated in this wilderness program at some time between 1976 and 2000. Ninety percent of the participants believed the expedition had made a difference in their lives, and for one-third the significance of the experience increased over time. Life significance was influenced by: (a) how unique the expedition was to the participant; (b) the timing of the expedition in the participant's life; and (c) the extent to which memories of the trip were connected to later life experiences. The solo was identified by 39% of the sample as the most significant trip component. The overarching theme related to life significance was that the expedition encouraged a greater awareness of God, nature, and self (actions, attitudes, behaviours, beliefs, and personal abilities).

Leisure and Spiritual Well-Being Model

Heintzman (2002) developed a model of leisure and spiritual well-being that proposes processes that link leisure experiences with spiritual well-being. This model has relevance to, and may be adapted to, experiential education. Heintzman's model is based upon Chandler et al.'s (1992) theoretical model of spiritual wellness that incorporates two dimensions of spiritual wellness. One dimension ranges from a condition of "repression of the sublime" where one denies or defies the spiritual tendency within oneself to a condition of "spiritual emergency," where one is preoccupied with spirituality to the detriment of the other dimensions of wellness. Spiritual wellness occurs at or near the midpoint of the continuum. The other dimension in the model is a continuum of spiritual development that represents "the process of incorporating spiritual experiences which results ultimately in spiritual transformation" (p. 170). Heintzman's model also incorporated a number of leisure and well-being theories (Mannell & Kleiber, 1997), such as keeping idle hands busy, buffering and coping, personal growth, and identity and affirmation theories, which will be explained in the context of this model.

Heintzman's (2002) model is based on the assumption that leisure experiences may either consciously or unconsciously provide opportunities for "grounding" or "working through" spiritual difficulties, as well as "sensitizing" one to the spiritual. According to Chandler et al. (1992), spiritual growth can be prompted by both spontaneous events and intentional activity. They suggested various counseling techniques that create spiritual awareness and enhance movement toward higher levels of spiritual wellness. For example, in a state of spiritual emergency a person experiences spiritual energy in an amount too great or a form too different for the person to integrate smoothly into their life. If a person is in a state of spiritual emergency, "grounding" slows down the process of spiritual emergence so that the spiritual experience is more likely to be assimilated, which results in spiritual development rather than a chronic state of upheaval.

The notion of grounding is consistent with two different theories of leisure and well-being: keeping idle hands busy theory and buffering and coping theory (Mannell & Kleiber, 1997). The keeping idle hands busy theory suggests that leisure activities and involvements may engage a person in the physical world thereby diverting the person's attention away from his/her spiritual emergency and helping him/her cope with the situation. Activities that connect a person with the earth—which are often used in experiential education—are suggested as types of activities that slow a person down and bring the person back down to physical reality.

Meanwhile, the buffer and coping theory elaborated by Coleman and Iso-Aloha (Coleman, 1993; Coleman & Iso-Aloha, 1993) suggests that leisure indirectly affects well-being and health via its capability of generating coping behaviours in reaction to stressful life events and changes. Leisure participation may facilitate coping with stressful life events by strengthening the buffers of social support and self-determination. Techniques for working through can also be used with people in a condition of spiritual emergency to help them "stay with" the emergency to facilitate its transformation potential. Chandler et al. (1992) recommended that "working through" involves experiential techniques to respond flexibly to the person's needs and states of consciousness. There is little empirical research on the use of these techniques within experiential education. In Fredrickson and Anderson's (1999) study of a women's wilderness experience, all of the women had experienced a major life change prior to participation (deterioration of personal health, major career change, death of a loved one), so the trip provided the opportunity to leave the stresses of everyday life to have an experience of spiritual rejuvenation in the wilderness environment. Many of the women stated that the trip provided the opportunity to regain a sense of meaning and connectedness that they would not have found elsewhere. Elements of the techniques and theories explained above are illustrated in this study: positive interpersonal interactions (the social support component of the buffer and coping theory) and total immersion in the wilderness setting (grounding) contributed to spiritual inspiration.

At the other end of the continuum, if a person consciously or unconsciously represses the spiritual, *sacralization* or *resacralization* activities may move a person toward spiritual wellness. Sacralization is defined as "sensitizing to the spiritual those who have no conscious experience of the spiritual" (Chandler et al., p. 172), while resacralization refers to resensitizing "those who have been spiritually well but have moved, consciously or unconsciously, toward repression," (Chandler et al., p. 172). Resacralization was a term Maslow used to mean "rediscovering a sense of the sacred in everyday life" (Davis, 1996, p. 419). Periods of solitude, or solos, within experiential education programs are examples of opportunities for sacralization or resacralization. Personal growth theories of leisure and well-being are consistent with sacralization and resacralization, as leisure activities can provide the opportunity for people to become the type of people they would like to be (Mannell & Kleiber, 1997). Meditation, relaxation, rhythmic breathwork, creative visualization, imagery, and awareness exercises are common interventions used in counseling and therapy to foster spiritual development through the process of sacrilization. Many of these activities are often used in experiential education (e.g., meditation, see White, 2000).

Adapting Heintzman's (2002) model, experiential education experiences, which involve interplay of time, activity, motivation and setting, can provide contexts in which spirituality is explored rather than repressed, and where spiritual preoccupation due to a spiritual emergency can be addressed. In addition, repeated experiential activities can provide opportunities to translate experiences of a spiritual nature into spiritual development. This model also incorporates restorative environments theory, which includes the features of "being away to a different environment," "extent" (a rich setting that captivates the mind and fosters exploration), "fascination" (a form of attention that requires no effort), and "compatibility" (advances a person's purposes), which are helpful in explaining how specific activities and settings may move a person toward spiritual well-being. The model also suggests that experiential education activities may play both a positive and a negative role in spiritual well-being and development. The following sections examine the empirical research related to each component of this model: activity, motivation, time, and setting.

Activity

Are some experiential education activities more conducive to spiritual experiences than others? Some women in Fredrickson and Anderson's (1999) study of wilderness experience found the physically challenging nature of canoeing and hiking activities to be spiritually inspirational. Stringer and McAvoy (1992) observed that reports of spiritual experiences by participants on a wilderness canoe trip mainly focused on the interconnections between people, while participants on a mountain hiking trip, which generally offered more opportunity for time alone than the canoe trip, tended to describe spiritual experiences involving an awareness and appreciation of the vast, stark beauty of the alpine environment. They also discovered that many different types of activities were spiritual in nature (e.g., swimming, meals, laughing, Earth-awareness exercise).

Likewise, for participants in an EEE course, a wide variety of specific aspects, activities, and experiences enhanced spirituality (Heintzman, 2007b). Furthermore, the types of activities in this EEE course that enhanced spirituality varied from person to person. What was most important was the overall mix of activities, experiences, and elements of the course as the holistic, 24-hour nature of the course led to a spiritual impact (Heintzman, 2007b). While most of the participants in the EEE study found organized spiritual activities (e.g., liturgy, worship time) to be helpful to their spiritual well-being, in a study of men's wilderness experience (Heintzman, 2007a), organized spiritual activities (e.g., Sufi dance, smudging ceremony) were not identified as being important to the participants' spiritual well-being, while structured spiritual discussions were helpful to some but not others. The restorative environment theory's (Kaplan, 1995) compatibility element explains why some activities may be helpful to some people and not others: Spiritual rejuvenation is brought about only when an activity is congruent with the purposes or roles of a person. Flow theory (Csikszentmihalyi, 1975) also provides insight into why some activities are spiritually helpful to some people but not others. Another explanation is the identity and affirmation theory of leisure and well-being, which suggests that leisure provides people with the opportunity to select activities that are congruent with the type of people they are or would like to be (Mannell & Kleiber, 1997).

Some quantitative research suggests that experiential activities can be combined with explicit or overt spiritual activities to bring about spiritual outcomes. In one study 310 college students participated in Outward Bound-type programs that included Christian growth and discipleship activities, as well as team-building, interpersonal challenge, and personal challenge activities (Anderson-Hanley, 1996). Participants in these programs were found to report significantly higher levels of subjective spiritual growth than a wait-listed control group. Griffin (2003) studied the spiritual growth of youth participants in a two-week experience involving overt Christian teaching combined with whitewater rafting, rock climbing, backpacking, and challenge course activities. Through a combination of qualitative and quantitative methods it was determined that spiritual growth could be strengthened through a mixture of spiritual teaching and adventure activities.

Motivation

Whether a person finds a wilderness experience, an experiential activity, or even an organized spiritual activity spiritual may depend on the motivation of the person. For some participants on a men's wilderness trip, the primary motivation for being on the wilderness trip was related to canoeing and not related to spirituality (Heintzman, 2007a). Similarly some of the participants in Stringer and McAvoy's (1992) study of wilderness adventure were not looking for experiences of a spiritual nature. Thus these cases suggest that the motivation of the participant may influence whether or not a person experiences spiritual outcomes. Heintzman (2007b) found that a person's attitude was part of the personal history that a person brought to an experience. One participant stated "I was very much in an attitude of having my hands wide open to just receive what came, so each experience was very full in that regard." Another participant perceptively observed: "If the students were receptive spiritually ... they can be learning ... in any sort of situation and no matter what about the structure of the course.... It is more to do with the student than the teacher ... or the course."

Time

In their study on wilderness adventure, Stringer and McAvoy (1992) discovered that "time off" was viewed as a critical factor in many participants' spiritual experiences; several individuals desired more free time than was provided. In fact, when participants were asked what factors inhibited their spiritual experience, the most significant inhibiting factor was lack of time off or time alone due to leadership responsibilities or insufficient free time scheduled into the structure of the trip. Experiencing structured and unstructured time alone during an outdoor residential camp experience positively influenced the spirituality of youth by providing them with opportunities to reflect on their lives (Sweatman & Heintzman, 2004). In her study of women's wilderness experience, Fox (1997) concluded that structured time for solitude and for being in nature was important for spiritual experience.

Setting

Given that most experiential education activities take place in the natural environment, it is not surprising that the nature setting has been found to be associated with spirituality. Loeffler (2004) found that a spiritual connection with the outdoors was one of the meanings of outdoor adventure experiences for participants in a college-based outdoor program. Participants often used the word "spiritual" to describe the intimate connection they experienced with the natural world due to being on an outdoor trip. Likewise, being immersed in nature was repeatedly mentioned by participants on an EEE course as being helpful to their spiritual well-being (Heintzman, 2007b). Many different reasons were given for the important role of nature (e.g., the beauty, awe, and grandeur of nature; nature was a setting for spiritual practices; feeling the power of nature; being aware of God). Different reasons for nature being associated with spiritual well-being were also offered by men participating in a wilderness experience: For some it was marvellous and awe-inspiring, while for others it produced a sense of being vulnerable (Heintzman, 2007a). The women in Fox's (1997) study viewed nature as powerful, therapeutic, and spiritual. Nature inspired spiritual experiences that were connected to self and nature, wonderment, awe, and natural beauty. Spiritual experiences were enhanced through "contact with nature, appreciation and observation of nature's beauty and power, and through the therapeutic tranquillity, space, solitude and relaxation of nature" (p. 63).

Restorative environments theory (Kaplan, 1995) may explain why nature is conducive to spirituality. First, nature settings are characterized by the extent feature of restorative environments theory (Kaplan); that is, natural ecosystems provide rich settings that captivate, foster exploration, and connect people to a larger world. Second, nature settings allow for soft fascination or attention. This feature of restorative environments theory (Kaplan) suggests that natural features (e.g., sunsets, clouds, mountain vistas) can be observed effortlessly, leaving plenty of opportunity for reflection on spiritual matters.

Given that most studies on experiential education and spirituality have been studies of wilderness experience, it is not surprising that wilderness has been found to be a setting conducive to spiritual outcomes. Stringer and McAvoy (1992) discovered that "wilderness provides [participants] a place to find inner peace and tranquillity, solitude, beauty, and spiritual rekindling...." (p. 18). It also "prompted spontaneous [private] praise and worship, where other kinds of environments wouldn't" (p. 19). Fredrickson and Anderson's (1999) research demonstrated the importance of the contribution of being in *bone fide* wilderness. The biophysical characteristics of the wilderness and direct contact with nature were important in spiritual inspiration and led to a more contemplative and self-reflective experience.

Fredrickson and Anderson Model

Fredrickson and Anderson (1999) suggested a model that has a greater focus upon the setting factors of a wilderness experience than the spiritual experience process funnel model (Fox, 1999). They suggested that while a number of concepts related to the spiritual benefits of wilderness (sense of place, place attachment, sacred space, sense of the divine) emerge from the wilderness setting, there are also more specific setting attributes that trigger meaningful spiritual experiences in wilderness. For the women in their study of wilderness experience, Fredrickson and Anderson observed that it was a unique mix of landscape characteristics and social interactions that make a place spiritually inspirational. In support of wilderness as sacred space with a sense of the divine, Heintzman (2007a, 2007b, 2008) found that nature helped some participants connect with their God, while Loeffler (2004) discovered that the outdoors was a place where the participants could connect with a higher power or purpose. Fredrickson and Anderson speculated that meaningful spiritual experiences may lead to off-site spiritual benefits or spiritual growth that could possibly result in longer term benefits such as a more "psychologically balanced and environmentally sound state of being" (p. 23). While their research is the first step in exploring this model, they recognize that more research is needed, because:

> The way in which individuals react and interpret the natural environment is a multifaceted phenomenon, and the ways in which various individuals derive or attach meaning from various landscapes is equally complex. (p. 35)

Being Away

While Fredrickson and Anderson (1999) discovered that the biophysical characteristics of the wilderness, along with direct contact with nature, were significant, Stringer and McAvoy (1992) observed that the greater opportunities for and enhancement of spiritual experiences in wilderness settings were usually ascribed to the lack of constraints and responsibilities in the wilderness as compared to the participants' everyday lives in or near large urban areas. Thus, Stringer and McAvoy speculated that a different environment, without the usual time and energy constraints, was the operative factor for some participants, and it did not matter whether the environment was wilderness or somewhere else. This explanation is consistent with the "being away to a different environment" feature of the restorative environments theory (Kaplan, 1995) that suggests being in a different place is conducive to renewal and restoration.

The being away dimension of the restorative environments theory is also supported by other studies. A residential camp setting was perceived by youth as beneficial for their spirituality not only because of the natural setting of the camp, but also because this setting provided a place away from their everyday lives, which were dominated by technology, pollution, and busy cities (Sweatman & Heintzman, 2004). Camp offered a nonurban experience, and the majority of interviewees recognized this as a positive change from their urban home community. When asked why the experience was beneficial to their spiritual well-being, the men on wilderness canoe trips most frequently answered that wilderness provided an opportunity to get away from the everyday routine and world, and to focus on the spiritual (Heintzman, 2007a, 2008). Similarly, participants in an EEE course found the 24-hour solo to be beneficial because it allowed them to focus on spirituality, as the solo removed them from the busyness and obligations of their everyday life (Heintzman, 2007b).

Implications for Experiential Education Practice

A number of practical implications arise from the above discussion of empirical research and theoretical models. These implications are summarized in Table 1.

Conclusion

The empirical research and theoretical models reviewed in this chapter suggest that there are a multitude of factors that influence the relationship between experiential education and spirituality. These factors include: the personal history of the participant, opportunities for solitude, group experiences, a balance between solitude and group experiences, activity, motivation, time, nature setting, and being away to a different environment. Thus the relationship between experiential education and spirituality is a complex one and experiential educators need to take all of these factors into consideration when planning for spiritual outcomes such as the emotions associated with spiritual experience, transcendence, and life transformation. Each of the theoretical models presented in this chapter tends to focus on one, or a few, of the experiential education factors associated with spirituality. Fox's (1999) spiritual experience process funnel focuses on the individual, the "baggage" the individual brings to the wilderness experience, and the importance of rationalizing or accepting the fear of nature. Sweatman and Heintzman's (2004) model of youth camp experience and spirituality focuses on how the natural and nonurban setting of the camp, along with time alone and social experiences may lead to spiritual experience. Heintzman's (2002) leisure and spiritual well-being model emphasises activity, motivation, time, and setting. Fredrickson and Anderson's (1999) model focused upon setting factors such as sense of place, place attachment, sacred space, and sense of the divine. As research on experiential education and spirituality is at an early stage,further research is needed to support and refine these models. All of these models are limited in that they do not incorporate all of the factors related to experiential education and spirituality, and thus all of them need to be taken into consideration when trying to understand the relationships between spirituality and experiential education. Furthermore, these models are primarily based on the results of one study (Fox; Sweatman & Heintzman) or are theoretical frameworks for guiding research (Fredrickson & Anderson; Heintzman). Hopefully, future empirical research and theoretical development will lead to the development of a more comprehensive model that provides an integrated, critical synthesis of the multitude of the complex factors related to experiential education that contribute to spiritual

Table 1.
Implications for Experiential Education Practice

1. Integrate structured and unstructured times of solitude within experiential education activities.
2. Provide structured and unstructured opportunities for participants to be together in small or large group settings, as well as introduce activities that build community.
3. Try to maintain a balance of opportunities for solitude and social interaction.
4. Develop experiential education activities with plenty of opportunity for interaction and immersion in the natural world.
5. Pay careful attention to the holistic impact of all the components of an experiential education activity or program taken together; the sum may be more important than the individual components.
6. Because personal histories and contexts play an important role in the impact of experiential education activities, experiential educators need to be very sensitive to the individual needs of each participant. It is important to facilitate spiritual expression within the comfort zone of the participants.
7. Depending on the nature of the experiential education activity and the background of the participants, use tools such as journal writing, meditation, inspirational readings, and group discussions to sensitize participants to the spiritual (i.e., sacrilization).
8. Introduce participants to settings that are different than their everyday world.
9. Because the motivation or the attitude a person brings to an experiential education activity is important, help participants develop an attitude characterized by openness and receptivity.
10. Recognize that the type and degree of spiritual outcomes from an experiential activity will vary from one participant to another.

experience and lead to spiritual growth and development. Additional research on the long-term impact of the relationship between experiential education and spirituality is also desirable. Nevertheless, the empirical research conducted during the last decade has advanced our understanding of the role of spirituality in experiential education, has provided additional support for theories such as the restorative environments theory, and has provided a number of implications (see Table 1) that are helpful to experiential education practitioners who are interested in facilitating spiritual outcomes.

References

Anderson-Hanley, C. (1996). Spiritual well-being, spiritual growth and Outward Bound-type programs: A comparative outcome study. A paper presented at the annual meeting of the Christian Association for Psychological Studies. St. Louis, MO. April, 1996.

Anderson-Hanley, C. (1997). Adventure programming and spirituality: Integration models, methods, and research. *Journal of Experiential Education, 20*(2), 102–108.

Chandler, C. K., Holden, J. M., & Kolander, C. A. (1992). Counseling for spiritual wellness: Theory and practice. *Journal of Counseling and Development, 71*(2), 168–175.

Coleman, D. (1993). Leisure-based social support, leisure dispositions and health. *Journal of Leisure Research, 25*(4), 350–361.

Coleman. D., & Iso-Ahola, S. E . (1993). Leisure and health: The role of social support and self-determination. *Journal of Leisure Research, 25*, 111–128.

Csikszentmihalyi, M. (1975). *Beyond boredom and anxiety: The experience of play in work and games* (pp. 35–54). San Francisco: Jossey-Bass.

Daniel, B. (2007). The life significance of a spiritually oriented, Outward Bound-type wilderness expedition. *Journal of Experiential Education, 29*(3), 386–389.

Davis, J. (1996). An integrated approach to the scientific study of the human spirit. In B.L. Driver, D. Dustin, T. Baltic, G. Elsner, & G. Peterson, (Eds.), *Nature and the human spirit: Toward an expanded land management ethic* (pp. 417–429). State College, PA: Venture.

Elkins, D. N., Hedstrom, L. J., Hughes, L. L., Leaf, J. A., & Saunders, C. (1988). Toward a humanistic-phenomenological spirituality: Definition, description, and measurement. *Journal of Humanistic Psychology, 28*(4), 5–18.

Fox, F. E., (1983). The spiritual core of experiential education. *Journal of Experiential Education, 6*(3), 3–6.

Fox, R. J. (1997). Women, nature and spirituality: A qualitative study exploring women's wilderness experience. In D. Rowe & P. Brown (Eds.), *Proceedings, ANZALS conference 1997* (pp. 59–64). Newcastle, NSW: Australian and New Zealand Association for Leisure Studies, and Department of Leisure and Tourism Studies, The University of Newcastle.

Fox, R. (1999). Enhancing spiritual experience in adventure programs. In J. C. Miles & S. Priest (Eds.), *Adventure Programming* (pp. 455–461). State College, PA: Venture.

Fredrickson, L. M., & Anderson, D. H. (1999). A qualitative exploration of the wilderness experience as a source of spiritual inspiration. *Journal of Environmental Psychology, 19*, 21–39.

Griffin, J. (2003). The effects of an adventure-based program with an explicit spiritual component on the spiritual growth of adolescents. *Journal of Experiential Education, 25*(3), 351.

Haluza-Delay, R. (2000). Green fire and religious spirit. *Journal of Experiential Education, 23*(3), 143–149.

Hawks, S. (1994). Spiritual health: Definition and theory. *Wellness perspectives, 10,* 3–13.

Heintzman, P. (2002) A conceptual model of leisure and spiritual well-being. *Journal of Park and Recreation Administration, 20*(4), 147–169.

Heintzman, P. (2007a). Men's wilderness experience and spirituality: A qualitative study. In R. Burns & K. Robinson (Comps.), *Proceedings of the 2006 Northeastern Recreation Research Symposium* (pp. 216–225) (Gen. Tech. Rep. NRS-P-14). Newton Square, PA: U.S. Department of Agriculture, Forest Services, Northern Research Station.

Heintzman, P. (2007b). Rowing, sailing, reading, discussing, praying: The spiritual and lifestyle impact of an experientially-based, graduate, environmental course. Paper presented at the Trails to Sustainability Conference, May 2007. Kananaskis, AB.

Heintzman, P. (2008). Men's wilderness experience and spirituality: Further explorations. In C. LeBlanc & C. Vogt (Eds.), *Proceedings of the 2007 Northeastern Recreation Research Symposium* (pp. 55–59) (Gen. Tech. Rep. NRS-P-23). Newton Square, PA: U.S. Department of Agriculture, Forest Services, Northern Research Station.

Kaplan, R., & Kaplan, S. (1989). *The experience of nature: A psychological perspective.* Cambridge: Cambridge University Press.

Kaplan, S. (1995). The restorative benefits of nature: Toward an integrative framework. *Journal of Environmental Psychology, 15,* 169–182.

Larson, D. B., Swyers, J. P., & McCullough, M. E. (1998). *Scientific research on spirituality and health: A consensus report.* Rockville, MD: National Institute for Health Care Research.

Loeffler, TA (2004). A photo elicitation study of the meanings of outdoor adventure experiences. *Journal of Leisure Research, 36*(4), 536–556.

Mannell, R. C., & Kleiber, D. A. (1997). *A social psychology of leisure.* State College, PA: Venture.

McDonald, B. L., & Schreyer, R. (1991). Spiritual benefits of leisure participation and leisure settings. In B.L. Driver, P.J. Brown, & G.L. Peterson, (Eds.), Benefits of leisure (pp. 179–194). State College, PA: Venture.

Morgan, G. (1994). The mythologies of outdoor and adventure recreation and the environmental ethos. *Pathways: The Ontario Journal of Outdoor Education, 6*(6), 11–16.

Paloutzian, R.F. (1996). *Invitation to the psychology of religion.* Boston, MA: Allyn & Bacon.

Principe, W. (1983). Toward defining spirituality. *Studies in Religion, 12*(2), 127–141.

Seaward, B. L. (2000). Stress and human spirituality 2000: At the cross roads of physics and metaphysics. *Applied Psychophysiology and Biofeedback, 25*(4), 241–245.

Scippa, M. T. (2000). The 1999 Kurt Hahn Address: Catalysts for change: The healing power of experiential practices. *Journal of Experiential Education, 23*(1), 26–30.

Stringer, L. A., & McAvoy, L. H. (1992). The need for something different: Spirituality and wilderness adventure. *Journal of Experiential Education, 15*(1), 13–21.

Sweatman, M., & Heintzman, P. (2004). The perceived impact of outdoor residential camp experience on the spirituality of youth. *World Leisure Journal, 46*(1), 23–31.

Warren, K., Sakofs, M., & Hunt, J. S. (1995). *The theory of experiential education.* Dubuque, IA: Kendall/Hunt.

Westgate, C. E. (1996, September/October). Spiritual wellness and depression. *Journal of Counseling and Development, 75,* 26–35.

White, W. (2000). Chasing the Buddha: Bringing meditation to experiential education. *Pathways: The Ontario Journal of Outdoor Education, 12*(2), 5–7.

Williams, D., Patterson, M., Roggenbuck, J., & Watson, A. (1992). Beyond the commodity metaphor: Examining emotional and symbolic attachment to place. *Leisure Sciences, 14,* 29–46.

Williams, D. & Stewart, S. I. (1998). Sense of place: An elusive concept that is finding a home in ecosystem management. *Journal of Forestry, 96*(5), 18–23.

Williams, K. & Harvey, D. (2001). Transcendent experience in forest environments. *Journal of Environmental Psychology, 21,* 249–260.

Ethics & Experiential Education
as Professional Practice

▾ ▾ ▾

Jasper S. Hunt, Jr.

This article will argue for giving ethics a central role within the emerging profession of experiential education. I hope to accomplish this by connecting the ethical thought of Alasdair MacIntyre and Aristotle to issues in experiential education in general and the adventure-based wing of experiential education in particular. The danger of allowing experiential education to become a set of techniques devoid of ethical control by practitioners will be outlined. Finally, some thoughts on avoiding this danger will be offered.

Two scenarios will serve to present the type of issues central to this paper:

> You are working as an adventure therapist at a psychiatric hospital. You have a group of patients on the high ropes course. The staff psychiatrist is out with the group, watching as they go through the course. A young man, high up on the course, demands to be lowered to the ground immediately. You work with him psychologically, yet he continues his insistence that he be lowered. You have been trained in the "challenge by choice" method of experiential education (developed by Project Adventure) and you agree to lower the young man. The psychiatrist looks at you and tells you that the young man is at the point of a great psychological breakthrough but that it will be missed if you lower him to the ground. The psychiatrist tells you not to lower the man. You object to the psychiatrist's order. He looks

This chapter originally was published in the *Journal of Experiential Education*, with the following citation:

Hunt, J. S. (1995). Ethics and experiential education as professional practice. *Journal of Experiential Education, 14*(2), 14–18.

at you and reminds you that he is a psychiatrist and that you are merely an employee of the hospital, acting as a technician under his direction, and that, as with all technicians employed by the hospital, you are to follow physician's orders.

The A.B.C. Acme Toy Corporation has contracted with your experiential education program to develop teamwork and group cooperation utilizing adventure-based activities. All employees are told to participate in this new and wonderful event. They show up. One of the initiatives being used is the Trust Fall, starting out with low falls and ending with a high fall back into the arms of one's fellow employees. One woman refuses to do any of the Trust Falls arguing that these activities have nothing to do with making quality toys. The C.E.O. of the corporation steps in and tells the woman that she needs to display her loyalty to the corporation and that if she will not participate in the exercises, her commitment to the A.B.C. Acme corporation will be called into question. The C.E.O. then strongly urges the woman to attempt the falls. The instructor on the spot, although nervous about the coercion of the C.E.O., feels strongly that the C.E.O. is ultimately in charge of his employees and that whether or not coercion is justified with the woman is the C.E.O.'s decision, not the instructor's.

Both of these examples represent an issue of growing importance and controversy in experiential education. At first glance, the ethical issue may appear to be whether it is morally permissible to use coercion in experiential education, and if so, then when. However, there is a deeper, more profound issue in these two situations. It is whether experiential educators are autonomous professional practitioners or technicians operating under the orders of others. Whether the others are psychiatrists, corporate executives, school teachers, or principals, does not matter.

There is no doubt that one of the biggest growth areas for experiential education lies in its potential benefits for executives and business managers, psychiatric patients, public school employees and students, and other groups or organizations with some control over the fates of their members. The ethical issue that is relevant here is what special moral obligations do practitioners have to screen the participants in programs and to *set the moral standards* that govern activities.

One logical possibility is to take the position that experiential educators (I include adventure therapists and other specialists using experiential activities under the heading "educator") are merely technicians providing a service to an organization. It could be argued that it was not within the ropes course instructor's role and responsibility in the psychiatric example to interfere with the psychiatrist and the patient in ethical matters. It is possible that the instructor ought to defer to the judgment of the psychiatrist in all matters involving the welfare of patients. The same logic could be used in the situation involving the *C.E.O.* and the employee.

An alternative possibility would be to argue that the experiential educator is an independent practitioner who is not only *permitted* to intervene in the relationship between the organization and its members, but is *morally obligated* to intervene in that relationship if it is professionally relevant to the experiential educator. Note that in both the psychiatric and corporate situations, there exists an unequal power relationship between the person who sent the group for the experiential activities *(C.E.O.* or psychiatrist) and the group members (employees or patients). The question then becomes, do experiential educators have, in matters involving ethical judgment, a foundation upon which to base a countervailing power relationship against the organization on behalf of participants? If the answer is no, then experiential educators are not really autonomous *professional practitioners* but are, instead, *technicians* providing a service at the command or contract of others. If the answer is yes, then experiential educators become morally obligated to protect the best interests of participants against possible moral harm by others, including C.E.O.s, psychiatrists, and other leading authorities within organizations.

Experiential Education as a Practice

Before further proceeding with the issue of coercion, it is important to this topic to discuss the issue of a practice in some detail. It is my contention that only if experiential education is understood as an autonomous professional practice does it make sense to argue morally for or against the use of coercion. Otherwise, experiential educators may be required to defer to the wishes of others in moral matters like coercion.

The term "practice" is a technical one. It is one of the words that connects all of the ideas in this article together. Philosopher Alasdair MacIntyre (1984) has defined a practice in terms that are useful for the topic at hand:

> By "practice" I am going to mean any coherent and complex form of socially established cooperative human activity through which goods internal to that form of activity are realized in the course of trying to achieve those standards of excellence which are appropriate to, and partially definitive of, that form of activity, with the result that human powers to achieve excellence, and human conceptions of the ends and goods involved are systematically extended. Tic-tac-toe is not an example of a practice in this sense, nor is throwing a football with skill; but the game of football is and so is chess. (p. 187)

Belaying a ropes course is not a practice in MacIntyre's sense, but using a ropes course as an educational or therapeutic modality is. Just as I can be an excellent surgeon or a poor surgeon, so too can I be an excellent experiential educator or a poor one. The goods or "standards of excellence" that are achievable by a surgeon, a football player, or an experiential educator are goods attainable only by those who participate in the practice of medicine, football, or experiential education. Participating in a practice presents the practitioner with the potential of achieving various standards of excellence that are inherent in the specific practices.

The use of the term "goods" is open to a confusion that should be mentioned. MacIntyre makes a distinction between goods that are *internal* to a practice, and goods that are *external* to a practice. Suppose, for illustration, that an experiential education program was to hire an instructor who was primarily seeking employment in order to finance his or her latest mountaineering expedition. The instructor does an adequate job, receives the appropriate pay, and uses the money to go on the expedition. The good that this hypothetical instructor receives is the money. There is no reason for this instructor to do more than the minimum required in order to be paid for the job. Indeed, if the instructor can do less than is called for, and not get caught, then the person still receives the pay and can be called successful. This sort of good achieved by the instructor is what MacIntyre calls a good external to a practice.

Internal goods, on the other hand, are goods that are attained purely because of the excellence achieved by participating in a well-executed practice. An experiential educator pursuing internal goods will receive satisfaction by being recognized as achieving a level of excellence only attainable by participating in the practice. Thus, instructing a ropes course with style and care reaps rewards to the instructor that are not identical to the pay received for the work completed. This does not mean that internal and external goods are mutually exclusive. An experiential educator who is well paid may, at the same time, receive internal goods from a job well done.

Thus, it makes sense to talk about a good or a bad experiential educator. Presumably, what is desired are good educators rather than bad ones. This is where ethics emerges as inherent to the very core of what it means to participate in the practice of experiential education. Practices logically imply standards of excellence for practitioners to measure themselves against. As MacIntyre (1984) argues:

> A practice involves standards of excellence and obedience to rules as well as the achievement of goods. To enter into a practice is to accept the authority of those standards and the inadequacy of my own performance as judged by them. It is to subject my own attitudes, choices, preferences and tastes to the standards which currently and partially define the practices. (p. 190)

I may aspire to achieve excellence as a baseball player, but I do not achieve it if am only able to hit the ball given five strikes, instead of three. The point of MacIntyre's quote is that inherent to achieving the label of "a good baseball player" is the idea that I am only allowed three strikes at bat. Any more than three strikes and I am no longer playing baseball. The three-strike rule provides a standard of excellence by which my performance is judged. If I am to achieve excellence as a baseball player, it will only be possible insofar as I conform to the standards set by the practice of baseball. The goods that I achieve by meeting these standards are the goods internal to the practice of baseball.

The end result of someone who achieves levels of excellence set by a practice is to refer to that individual as a virtuous person. In formulating the definition of virtue, MacIntyre (1984) writes:

> But what does all or any of this have to do with the concept of the virtues? It turns out that we are now in a position to formulate a first, even if partial and tentative definition of a virtue. *A virtue is an acquired human quality, the possession and exercise of which tends to enable us to achieve those goods which are internal to practices and the lack of which effectively prevents us from achieving any such goods.* (p. 191)

The first step, then, in formulating a conception of a virtuous experiential educator is to look at the practices that make experiential education what it is. For a person can only attain the status of a virtuous experiential educator through his/her functioning within the practice. The achievement of goods internal to the practice of experiential education is the key to achieving virtue in this context.

There is often a tendency to restrict discussion of practices to purely technical activities. In other words, a practice could be limited to articulating the standards of excellence purely in terms of such things as the technical and interpersonal skills needed to function as an experiential educator. If this were the case, then virtue in experiential education would be reduced to the mastery of purely technical and interpersonal skills, and the issue of ethics would, therefore, convert to discussion of those matters. One could argue that: I have mastered these skills, therefore, I am a virtuous experiential educator. This argument would be valid as far as it goes. Certainly mastering the technical, internal goods of the practice of experiential education is a vital part of the virtues of the practice. But there is more to virtue than just technical and interpersonal activities.

Aristotle (McKeon, 1941) discusses two kinds of virtue that are very helpful:

> Virtue too is distinguished into kinds in accordance with this difference; for we say that some of the virtues are intellectual and others moral, philosophic wisdom and understanding and practical wisdom being intellectual, liberality and temperance moral.... Virtue, then, being of two kinds, intellectual and moral, intellectual virtue in the main owes both its birth and its growth to teaching (for which reason it requires experience and time), while moral virtue

comes about as a result of habit whence also its name *ethike* is one that is formed by a slight variation from the word *ethos* (habit). (p. 952)

Aristotle makes the distinction between an intellectual and a moral virtue. Knowing how to perform the technical and interpersonal activities of experiential education falls under the umbrella of an intellectual virtue. The intellectual virtues, however, cover only part of the territory of virtue. *A moral virtue is one which must be developed in order that the intellectual virtues be guided and controlled toward their proper ends.* For example, I may achieve the excellence of making good safety judgments about the appropriate use of ropes-course belay techniques when working with various student populations. Suppose, however, that I am lazy and I, therefore, do not use these techniques because they make my job more difficult. My laziness becomes a character flaw within me that gets in the way of my exercising the intellectual (technical) virtue of being a good ropes course facilitator. Unless I develop the moral virtue of industriousness as well as the intellectual virtue of good technical skills, I will never achieve the internal goods of being an experiential educator who utilizes ropes courses. *Without moral virtue I could become an experiential educator, but I could not become a good experiential educator.*

According to Aristotle (McKeon, 1941), therefore, ethics becomes the formation of the right habits needed to guide the intellectual virtues:

> This, then, is the case with the virtues also; by doing the acts that we do in our transactions with other men [humans], we become just or unjust, and by doing the acts that we do in the presence of danger, and being habituated to feel fear or confidence, we become brave or cowardly.... Thus, in one word, states of character arise out of like activities. This is why the activities we exhibit must be of a certain kind; it is because the states of character correspond to the differences between these. It makes no small difference, then, whether we form habits of one kind or another from our very youth; it makes a very great difference, or rather all the difference. (p. 953)

If MacIntyre is right about virtue being a necessary ingredient for achieving goods internal to practices, then the virtues become essential for practitioners to achieve their ends. If Aristotle is right that ethics is the development of right habits needed to guide the intellectual virtues, then it seems reasonable to conclude that in order to have a practice of *good* experiential education, ethics and virtue are needed as inherent to the practice.

This leads to a pivotal question: Is experiential education a practice? Does experiential education at its current state of development meet the definition of a practice articulated by MacIntyre, or is it merely a set of techniques blowing in the wind, to be grabbed and used in any way that an individual or group chooses? One can think of a practice as either a static, completed final product, or one can think of a practice as an emergent element within a larger social context. If one takes the static, final completion route, then it seems clear that experiential education is not a practice. But I will argue that no practice is final and complete. Whether the practice is medicine or baseball or law, they all are changing as appropriate to fit new situations and contexts.

Therefore, my position is that experiential education is on the way to becoming a practice, but that it is not fully there yet. Clearly, most existing programs realize internal goods by adhering to standards of excellence. Experiential educators measure themselves against the rules and standards of the programs in which they operate. The attitudes, choices, preferences, and tastes of individual experiential educators are held in check by the contexts in which they work. For instance, an Outward Bound instructor who engages in sexual relations with his or her students will be censured by Outward Bound. A Project Adventure instructor who coerces and forces unwilling participants into doing activities would also be censured. Every program that I am aware of has standards of excellence that partially define the bounds of acceptable behavior to which educators must adhere.

A critical issue facing experiential educators is whether or not there are universal standards of excellence that are not program specific and that all experiential educators measure themselves against. This issue is extremely controversial. Although controversial, nevertheless, it must be faced. Unless there are standards of moral excellence to which all practitioners must adhere, experiential education cannot be called a practice and the whole argument of this paper collapses. My view is that there are de facto universal moral standards but that these have not been made as explicit as they could be. If the profession is to measure up to MacIntyre's criteria of a practice, then the moral standards must be as dear for experiential educators as they are for physicians, baseball players, and lawyers.

By implication, therefore, if I am correct that experiential education is an emerging professional practice, then the issue of coercion of students is of professional concern to practitioners. This gets the argument going, but it does not resolve it.

Just as there can be disagreement within the practice of experiential education about the details of the technical issues, so, too, can there be disagreement about the moral virtues. It is beyond the scope of this paper to resolve the specifics of coercion as a virtuous or a vicious act. However, the implication of the philosophical argument is that this issue should be dealt with from *within the profession* and that the ethical resolution not be handed over to those who contract for services. It is enough, at this point, if I have convinced readers that the complete welfare of participants is of concern to the professional experiential education practitioner, and that this concern includes both moral as well as technical issues.

Psychiatrists or corporate executives may have the power to order people to show up at an experiential education site in the first place, but that power ends the moment the participant "steps off the bus" and enters into the professional realm of the experiential educator. If coercion of participants, whether under psychiatric care or corporate edict or whatever, is ethically problematic, then the practitioner had better tread very carefully before coercing his or her students into doing experiential activities. Whether the coercion comes from the experiential educator or from some other source, it is still under the professional ethical purview of the practitioner. Failure to recognize this fact could well result in the practitioner not achieving the internal goods open to him or her by participating in the practice of experiential education.

I want to argue that a central new direction must be to scrutinize the virtues necessary for achieving the ends of experiential education in general and the adventure-based wing in particular. This scrutiny can only be accomplished by practitioners being willing to submit themselves to the scrutiny of the community of fellow practitioners.

Experiential educators are notoriously individualistic, and the idea of submitting oneself in one's professional life to the scrutiny of other practitioners' views on professional ethics may be troubling for some. However, MacIntyre is very clear about this necessity. A collegial relationship between practitioners is a special relationship. MacIntyre (1984) writes:

> It belongs to the concept of a practice as I have outlined it—and as we are all familiar with it already in our actual lives, whether we are painters or physicists or quarterbacks or indeed just lovers of good painting or first-rate experiments or a well-thrown pass—*that its goods can only be achieved by subordinating ourselves within the practice in our relationship to other practitioners.* We have to learn to recognize what is due to whom; we have to be prepared to take whatever self-endangering risks are demanded along the way; and we have to listen carefully to what we are told about our own inadequacies and to reply with the same carefulness for the facts. In other words we have to accept as necessary components of any practice with internal goods and standards of excellence the virtues of justice, courage and honesty. For not to accept these ... so far bars us from achieving the standards of excellence or the goods internal to the practice that it renders the practice pointless *except as a device for achieving external goods.* [emphasis added] (p. 191)

To paraphrase, colleagues in a professional practice are part of the fabric that defines what the practice is and, therefore, colleagues are partially definitive of each participant in the practice. This means there is a built-in moral obligation to share one's technical and ethical ideas with one's colleagues in a professional practice. This is in contradistinction to the society at large, where no such obligation exists.

The alternative to practitioners establishing their own ethical parameters is for others, possibly in other professions or government, to establish them. As experiential education becomes more sophisticated in its technical dimensions, so, too, must it become more sophisticated and accountable in the ethical dimension. If MacIntyre is correct about the moral virtues being essential for the achievement of excellence within a practice, then professional experiential education practitioners are obligated to begin to define what is virtuous and what is vicious within the practice. Failure to do this would be to engage in an absurd enterprise. Success in defining virtues and vices will help in the development of experiential education as a sophisticated professional practice.

References

Macintyre, A. (1984). *After virtue.* (2nd ed.). Notre Dame: University of Notre Dame Press.

McKeon, R. (Ed.). (1941). *Nicomachean ethics.* From The Basic Works of Aristotle. New York: Random House.

Challenging Assumptions:
Examining Fundamental Beliefs
That Shape Challenge Course
Programming & Research

▾ ▾ ▾

Brent D. Wolfe & Diane M. Samdahl

In recent years there has been a growing call for introspective examinations to uncover the unquestioned assumptions that ground our areas of study. In leisure studies this was first evidenced in the feminist critique that drew attention to a decidedly male bias in much of our theories and research. This was matched with a corresponding challenge raised by qualitative epistemologies that questioned the premises of positivistic research as a mechanism for studying the rich complexity of people's lives. Poststructuralism, in general, has prompted many fields to step away from an essentialist belief in theories in order to examine the fundamental, unquestioned assumptions upon which those theories are premised.

In this paper we reflectively examine one area of leisure studies—challenge (ropes) courses. By revealing the assumptions that shape practice and research in this field, we also reveal hidden biases that have inadvertently restricted our understanding of challenge courses. When made visible, these assumptions can be openly tested to provide stronger support for, or perhaps meaningful refinements in, the use of challenge courses. This type of critique does not pretend to reveal the "true" or "only" assumptions in an area of study; rather, it is to be judged by the utility of insight it provides into the body of literature it has examined.

This chapter originally was published in the *Journal of Experiential Education*, with the following citation:

Wolfe, B. D., & Samdahl, D. M. (2005). Challenging assumptions: Examining fundamental beliefs that shape challenge course programming and research. *Journal of Experiential Education, 28*(1), 25–43.

Challenge Courses

Since the 1940s, when Kurt Hahn first introduced the use of the outdoors as a learning experience for naval sailors, educators and professionals have praised the benefits of programs involving actual and perceived risk, and the outdoors. Outdoor adventure programs of this type typically fall into two general categories: (a) programs that last from one to three days and are heavily facilitated by a leader, and (b) programs that may last for several days/weeks (often in the wilderness) and test participants' abilities to develop independent or group problem-solving skills. In this paper, the authors focus on a component that can be found in both of these types of programs—challenge (ropes) courses.

Typically, challenge courses are comprised of four independent conditions: (a) socializing games, (b) group initiatives, (c) low elements, and (d) high elements (Priest, n.d.). These activities are presented to participants in a sequenced order by trained facilitators. Not all challenge course encounters incorporate all four of these components; however, some combination of the four will always be present.

Socializing games are designed to introduce group members to one another and introduce the facilitators to the group. During this stage, participants have the opportunity to learn the names and personality characteristics of everyone who will be involved in the events. Games such as Elbow Tag, Giants Wizards and Elves, and name games[1] all can be played during this introductory period.

The second stage, involving group initiative activities, is designed to help the group take steps toward trust and cooperation. These activities involve solving problems in the form of physical obstacles presented by the facilitator(s). Group initiatives can consist of Magic Shoes, The Grid, Turnstile, Group Lap Sit, and Group Knot.

Low elements are the next component in the progression of the challenge course. Low elements are group-oriented activities that occur on or near the ground using preconstructed equipment where group members act as spotters to ensure each others' safety. These activities provide opportunities for group members to think and work together as they solve contrived challenge course problems (e.g., participants are typically asked to move the entire group from point A to point B with some type of limitation placed on them). Presumably participants will develop a sense of trust and grow closer as a team. Low elements can include activities such as Islands, Spider's Web, TP Shuffle, and Nitro Crossing.

The final components of a challenge course are high elements, which usually are suspended 20–40 feet above the ground. These elements are constructed in the trees or on poles

---

[1] Activities listed are examples of potential challenge course activities. We recognize that there are many different activities and the lists in this article are not meant to be exhaustive.

sunk into the ground. Participants wear traditional rock-climbing gear and use an elaborate safety system called a belay, which protects them should they fall. While high elements can focus on teamwork (e.g., Dangle Duo, Group Support), their primary purpose is to encourage individuals to find strength within themselves to do something they thought they could not do. This is premised on the belief that the preceding activities (e.g., socializing games, group initiatives, and low elements) have built confidence and trust, as intended, leaving individuals empowered to overcome the physical and emotional struggles inherent in the high elements. High elements can include the Flying Squirrel, Pamper Pole, and Zip Line.

Research on Challenge Courses

Researchers studying challenge courses have examined outcomes of participation, such as social and personal development. This includes study of the outcomes and values associated with challenge courses (Goldenberg, Klenosky, O'Leary, & Templin, 2000), such as specific benefits for youth including perceived self-efficacy for high-school students (Constantine, 1993); enhanced self-concept for college students (Finkenberg, Shows, & DiNucci, 1994), and adolescents with cerebral palsy (Carlson & Evans, 2001); and resiliency for low-income minority youth (Green, Kleiber, & Tarrant, 2000). Researchers have also examined challenge courses in relation to their ability to facilitate cooperation within families (Burg, 2001) and to enhance teamwork in organizational settings (Bronson, Gibson, Kishar, & Priest, 1992; Priest & Lesperance, 1994).

Methods used in challenge course research. In general, many of these researchers employed quasi-experimental designs with pre- and posttest measurement of the dependent variables. In some instances, researchers collected data via questionnaires administered just prior to the challenge course and within one week after completion of the course (e.g., Constantine, 1993; Finkenberg et al., 1994; Green et al., 2000), while other researchers added a longer six-month follow-up after the intervention (e.g., Bronson et al., 1992; Goldman & Priest, 1990; Priest & Gass, 1997; Priest & Lesperance, 1994). Priest (1995, 1996a, 1998) used a hybrid of this technique, collecting data prior to the intervention, at specific points during the challenge course, and at specific points after completion of the course. When researchers used control groups they were typically comprised of individuals from the same group or organization (Priest, 1995, 1996a); often people in the control group participated in the programmed intervention upon completion of the study.

For research on the effects of challenge courses on social and personal development, researchers have used a variety of existing scales, such as the *Self-Efficacy Scale* (Sherer et al., 1982), *Tennessee Self-Concept Scale* (Roid & Fitts, 1989), *Protective Factors Scale* (Witt, Baker, & Scott, 1996), and the Hope Scale (Snyder et al., 1991). A few instruments unique to challenge course research have been developed or adapted by authors to supplement the above scales (cf. Constantine, 1993; Green et al., 2000). These scales are typically administered before and after the intervention, with researchers comparing pretest results with posttest results. The scales used to measure social and personal development have focused on understanding self-efficacy (Constantine, 1993), encouraging participants to make descriptive statements to portray themselves (Finkenberg et al., 1994), comprehending protective factors (Green et al., 2000), and developing and attaining goals (Robitschek, 1996).

Priest and his colleagues developed many of the instruments used in research on challenge courses with organizational teams, including the *Team Development Inventory* (TDI, used in Bronson et al., 1992, and Priest & Gass, 1997). In 1992, an expert panel convened at the Association for Experiential Education Training and Development Research Conference and created the *Interpersonal Trust Inventory* (ITI) including the partnership, organizational, self and group versions. The ITI has been used extensively (cf. Priest, 1995, 1996b, 1998; Priest & Lesperance, 1994). Both of these instruments measure a dependent variable (e.g., trust, team development) that uses a five-point Likert-type response format. The TDI asks participants to respond to statements such as, *"Team members understand group goals and are committed to them,"* and *"Team members look to each other for consultation on resolving challenges"* (Bronson et al., 1992, p. 51), while the ITI may ask participants to indicate their agreement with statements on five subscales: Acceptance, Believability, Confidentiality, Dependability, and Encouragement (Priest, 1996b, p. 37). These instruments also use modified semantic differentials in which participants are asked to determine which of two bipolar adjectives better represents their organization (cf. Priest, 1996a). Only a few studies examining the impact of challenge courses in organizations have used methods other than (or in addition to) pre- and posttest questionnaires (e.g., interviews; see Bramwell et al., 1997; Klint & Priest, in press; Priest, Gass, & Fitzpatrick, 1999).

Though the challenge course is used as a primary intervention (independent variable) in these studies, published research articles offer few details about the nature of the challenge course activities used in each study. Some studies used only the group initiative activities or low elements (e.g., Priest, 1998; Priest & Gass, 1997; Priest et al., 1999), while others employed group initiatives, low elements, and high elements (e.g., Constantine, 1993; Finkenberg et al., 1994; Goldenberg et al., 2000; Robitschek, 1996). Specific information relating to facilitator training, leadership styles, how these elements were introduced to the group, and how long groups spent on each element is not provided. The challenge courses studied have varied from a five-hour intervention (Constantine, 1993) to weekly activities spread over the course of a semester (Finkenberg et al., 1994). No study provided detail about actual events or interactions that occurred between group members or between the group and the facilitator during the challenge course activities. This lack of detail about implementation makes it impossible to examine, replicate, or critique the exact interventions used in these studies, and the varying time frames over which the challenge course activities took place makes it difficult to compare one study to another.

Reported findings in challenge course research. As previously noted, researchers report positive outcomes for individuals who participate in challenge courses, including enhanced self-efficacy, self-esteem, and resiliency. While almost all of the research related to individuals reports positive outcomes, several authors (cf. Constantine, 1993; Finkenberg et al., 1994; Robitschek, 1996) raised questions related to the transference of behaviors to other life activities, such as career development or vocational functioning (cf. Robitschek, 1996). Similarly, authors have questioned the lingering impact of effects on participants. Luckner (1989) found that gains were maintained for only two months, and Finkenberg et al. (1994) openly questioned the permanence of changes found in their own study. Overall, authors have reported that challenge course programs increase individual participants' self-efficacy, resiliency, and hope; however, questions remain regarding the permanence of these changes and the ability of participants to transfer knowledge from one setting to another.

In organizational settings challenge courses have been associated with increased teamwork and trust. Longitudinal studies show that these outcomes, though statistically significant in many cases, typically are reduced and minimized over the passage of time (Bramwell et al., 1997). However, when follow-up activities occur, participants may demonstrate continued improvement in team functioning for up to six months (Priest & Lesperance, 1994). In that study, Priest and Lesperance used four groups (control, no follow-up, follow-up, and self-facilitating) and compared scores on the TDI over a period of six months. Six months following the intervention authors provided participants in the "no follow-up group," the "follow-up group," and the "self-facilitating group" with the TDI and found that the "no follow-up group" had reverted to pre-intervention levels; however, the "follow-up group" (who elected to conduct its own social gatherings, business meetings, and sub-teams) maintained changes seen immediately following the program. In contrast to these groups, six months following the intervention, the "self-facilitating group" (who chose to learn debriefing techniques used by its facilitator) actually increased their score on the TDI. Based on this, Priest and Lesperance recommended that corporate interventions include self-facilitating follow-up procedures to maximize improvement. While findings from virtually all research related to challenge courses have been highly positive, caution exists when considering how long the changes may last.

The previous review has highlighted representative studies on challenge courses in an attempt to acquaint the reader with this literature, with specific focus on methodological designs commonly used in this body of research. For a more thorough bibliography of research on challenge courses, see Attarian and Holden (2001).

Data Analysis

In an effort to examine the broad body of research in this arena, the authors sought out any study that included at least one of the four activity components Priest (n.d.) identified as necessary for a challenge course. An electronic search using the terms challenge course, ropes course, adventure programs, and experiential education turned up many articles relating to challenge courses. Information was also solicited through electronic "listservs" in an effort to find studies not included in electronic databases. All collected articles were examined; papers that did not report research or that did not include the use of at least one of the components identified by Priest were excluded from analysis. There were 24 articles left for review.

The analysis entailed critically examining these studies in an attempt to uncover the basic assumptions that shaped each study. The first author, having experience as a challenge course facilitator, read each article and highlighted phrases and statements that were represented as factual knowledge; these were statements that the researchers did not ground in theory or existing research but rather stated as if they needed no further validation. Examples include statements like, "A study was conducted to develop better understanding of the range of benefits that result from participating in a ropes course program" (Goldenberg et al., 2000, p. 208), and "Many adventure activities, in which either the actual or perceived risks are elevated, can enhance participants' levels of engagement and their interdependence, thus leading to greater degrees of trusting behaviors" (Priest, 1995, p. 107). In the first example, the focus on "the range of benefits" reveals a fairly common assumption that ropes course participation does produce outcomes that can be classified as "benefits." The second example reveals an assumption about a causal process through which adventure activities bring about engagement, interdependence, and trust. At this point in the analysis there was no judgment about these statements; the intent was simply to find places where assumptions that were derived from outside the study had shaped the nature of the reported research.

After highlighting statements that appeared to reveal assumptions in all 24 articles that reported empirical research on challenge courses, the first author then examined those statements for common beliefs or similarities, and established thematic coding by comparing these statements to one another (see Straus & Corbin, 1990). In a series of ensuing discussions, the authors examined the emerging sets of beliefs in an attempt to determine if they were potentially testable postulates that indeed had been taken for granted. Through this analysis, several assumptions were found to be prevalent throughout the literature. These were grouped into two overriding categories and several smaller subcategories. The larger categories of assumptions included beliefs about: (a) positive outcomes, and (b) transference.

Findings

Two central assumptions emerged from our analysis: (a) that risk and challenge lead to positive outcomes, and (b) that those benefits can be transferred to experiences outside the challenge course. These two beliefs are, in fact, integral to the design and implementation of challenge courses, and they clearly have had a significant impact on the nature of programming and research in this field. However, examination of the literature revealed that these beliefs have been accepted as foundational tenets, and have not been challenged and tested as to their veracity. As such, they are unexamined assumptions that should be articulated and scrutinized to see if (and how) they are influencing the practice and study of challenge courses.

Risk Leads to Positive Outcomes

Foremost among the identified themes was the notion that challenge courses have positive outcomes. Many articles' titles directly state this notion (e.g., "Building Self-Efficacy Through Women-Centered Challenge Course Experiences" [Hart & Silka, 1994]), or imply potential benefits (e.g., "Physical Challenge and the Development of Trust Through Corporate Adventure Training" [Priest, 1998]). Interestingly, though positive outcomes were the focus of most of this research, the studies were not designed in ways that could potentially disprove the value of challenge courses. Thus, positive benefits were an assumption rather than a testable outcome of challenge courses. These assumptions of beneficial outcomes manifested themselves in relation to five types of effects: (a) risk-taking behaviors, (b) general benefits, (c) teamwork, (d) trust, and (e) self-concept.

Risk. The first attribute related to challenge course outcomes involves risk, both real and perceived. Real risks involve the dangers inherent in some of the activities, such as falling off an element 30 feet in the air. Perceived risks involve an individual's perceptions of tasks that face him or her, such as the anxiety created as a result of being asked to crawl through a hole that is smaller than one's body. These facets of risk directly interact with an individual's competence, as represented in Martin and Priest's (1986) Adventure Experience Paradigm. This paradigm is one of the seminal models in adventure education and is still influential in challenge course programming. According to Priest (1992), when an individual's competence is high and risk is low, exploration and experimentation result. As balance is reached between an individual's competence and the level of risk, the participant moves into a state of adventure, culminating in peak adventure when an individual's abilities are equal to the risks presented. As the risks in the situation begin to outweigh an individual's competence, misadventure occurs; and when risks significantly outweigh a participant's competence, devastation and disaster are the outcome. According to Priest (1992):

Misadventure, a minor mishap of acceptable proportions, would take place if the canoe capsized. Although the paddlers might get wet, cut, scraped or bruised, and perhaps embarrassed in front of their friends, they would also recover by drying out or healing their wounds. Here misadventure is a useful educational tool, because people learn from their mistakes: an important part of the adventure experience. Devastation and disaster, however, would involve major losses, neither recoverable nor acceptable, such as drowning or developing a permanent phobia of moving water. While the first four conditions are desirable parts of any recreational adventure experience, the latter one is not. (p. 129)

The quote by Priest illustrates many of the assumptions regarding the value of risk in adventure education. The first assumption is that people need to learn how to deal with risk. This is a central component in all challenge courses, where facilitators are asking the participants to take risks. The risks escalate in terms of presumed danger, from failing at fun simulations in group initiatives to the perceived danger (in spite of safety precautions) of standing on top of a 30-foot pole. Implicit in this approach is an assumption that people need to learn how to deal with risks, and that it is typically beneficial for people to take such risks. We highlight this as an untested assumption because it has not been effectively challenged or framed within theoretical limitations. For example, is it beneficial to encourage juvenile delinquents to engage in more risky behavior? Likewise, is risk-taking a good trait for corporate executives in charge of large sums of other people's money? Yet juvenile delinquents and corporate executives are two key populations for whom challenge courses are designed. The underlying assumption behind challenge courses is that, yes, it is beneficial for participants to engage in perceived risky behavior. Clearly there is a need to examine this belief more closely.

The second assumption seen in relation to risk deals directly with the *Adventure Experience Paradigm* (Martin & Priest, 1986), which assumes that the potential benefits from an adventure experience outweigh the potential risks (except in the case of devastation and disaster). The overt assumption is that participants have the ability to recover from negative situations (such as falling out of a canoe) and learn more about themselves, thereby growing through the process. Inherent in this model is a reliance on the course facilitator to know an individual's limits—how much risk can a person take before falling into devastation and disaster—and to push just far enough for that individual to reach peak adventure. Likewise, the facilitator must know which aspects of an activity are perceived as risky to a participant. For example, what is the risk of falling out of a canoe? The obvious physical danger is injury or drowning; more moderate danger might be seen in the panic associated with loss of secure grounding. But what about perceived risk based entirely on prior misadventures in the water? Or the significant social risk for an adolescent girl when wet clothes reveal her body shape? It is dangerous to assume that the facilitator knows or understands the perceived meaning of a risky activity for all participants, or that the facilitator is capable of turning that risk into benefit. Yet the assumption that everyone will benefit by being put in a risky situation, combined with a reliance on the facilitator to understand risk as it is perceived by the participants, has been a foundational tenet of this field. Priest's (1992) description of the *Adventure Experience Paradigm* glosses over the devastation and disaster component of the model to focus entirely on the benefits of peak adventure. There is no parallel research on devastation and disaster—or on more moderate outcomes such as stigma and discomfort—in participants' challenge course experiences.

The final assumption associated with risks and outcomes is seen in the earlier quote from Priest (1992) as well—the assumption that people will recover from any adverse effects resulting from the challenge course. Without a belief in recovery from misadventure, or in the unlikelihood of devastation and disaster, it would be irresponsible to subject participants to the potential risks of participating in challenge course activities. In a sense, challenge courses require participants to be resilient enough to gain from the experience (yet resiliency is often a goal, not a requirement for participation). People have diverse ways of coping with challenge, and some people are more capable than others of internalizing positive lessons from misadventure. The assumption that all people can recover from traumatic events on the challenge course is very dangerous, yet very prevalent in the literature and in practice.

General benefits. In all of the articles reviewed, not one author questioned the belief that challenge courses are beneficial. Most studies were embedded in a belief that challenge courses produce beneficial outcomes, with the purpose of the study focused on documenting or understanding the parameters of those benefits. There are lengthy discussions of potential group and individual benefits of challenge courses including: improved critical thinking, improved decision-making skills, enhanced communication skills, enhanced trust, enhanced teamwork, enhanced leadership, increased confidence, increased self-esteem, enhanced coordination and agility, and enhanced expression of thoughts and feelings (cf. Goldenberg et al., 2000, p. 210). Many studies report high levels of overall satisfaction among participants of challenge courses.

On the surface, this body of research seems to provide solid, empirical evidence in support of those benefits; however, examining what is not present provides insight into the authors' implicit assumptions. Though outcomes can be positive or negative, the literature reviewed does not contain discussion of the potentially negative outcomes that might occur due to participation in challenge courses. There was no analysis of anxiety or ill feelings created between participants due to the experience. There was no examination of instances where a facilitator's intervention caused more harm than good. Nor was there consideration of the differing impact of challenge course participation in light of the needs and vulnerabilities of different individuals in the group. No intervention is entirely perfect, yet researchers have given little attention to those places where challenge course interventions have faltered or failed even though those instances might produce the best understanding of the intervention itself. By not asking whether the potential benefits apply equally to people of all backgrounds and needs, and by not questioning whether all outcomes are beneficial, this research seems to reify the challenge course model without truly examining or testing it.

This might seem to contradict research that presents documented evidence of the benefits of challenge courses. However, when examined critically, those studies might be capturing the influence of pre-existing assumptions held by the challenge course facilitators and researchers. During the challenge course itself, facilitators establish a discourse that often highlights benefits as they engage participants in discussion about their experiences in each activity. Likewise, researchers implicitly emphasize the likelihood of benefits in the wording of potential outcomes that participants are asked to assess (e.g., assessing group cohesion instead of conflict). Long (2001) showed how participants are socialized into a common, shared meaning through the "ropes course process." Given these factors, it is impossible to know the extent to which documented benefits are a consequence of socialization, and/or expectations that are shaped by the challenge course facilitators and researchers. We found no study that asked questions such as, "Were there any negative outcomes that you experienced as a result of this event?" even though those questions are essential for understanding the full range of potential outcomes that challenge courses might produce.

Of the literature reviewed for this paper, all authors appeared to begin with the assumption that challenge courses are beneficial. This was reflected in the very nature of their questionnaires, so their data were predetermined to document these assumed benefits. More importantly, we don't know what else participants might walk away with, including enhanced fears or emotional scars from activities the researchers thought would produce only benefits.

Teamwork. According to research conducted by Bronson et al. (1992), and a theoretical discussion by Maxwell (1997), challenge courses have increased teamwork between participants in corporate adventure training programs. Implicit in these discussions is an assumption that teamwork is a desirable trait and teams are the best method for solving problems in business and in life (cf. Meyer, 2000; Priest & Lesperance, 1994). But is this necessarily the case? Outside of the challenge course literature there is less support for the belief that teamwork is always a desirable goal, and a greater acknowledgment that individual effort rather than teamwork is often central to success. For example, if teamwork is necessary to progress in the business world, we would expect to see more teams of chief executive officers (CEOs). Likewise, if teams are so ideal, why do we pay homage to people like Donald Trump or Bill Gates, who are portrayed as highly successful individuals and not acknowledge the teams that supported their individual accomplishments? Though teamwork is often desirable, we should exercise more caution before promoting it as a universally preferred trait. One might even argue that teamwork is beneficial primarily for the lower strata of workers in the corporate world and not to those who push their way to the top. The fundamental assumption that we need to build teamwork should be examined and contextualized more completely.

Another aspect of teamwork is the assumption that a group of separate individuals who might or might not know one another should and will join together to achieve team goals. Groups of participants who know one another bring with them a complex history of interactions that have already led to embedded social hierarchies. On the other hand, groups of participants who do not know one another are busy with the social processes of self-presentation and exploration. The assumption that every group of participants will learn enhanced teamwork through challenge courses fails to consider the very real fact that differing personalities do not always mix and individuals sometimes create more conflict than harmony. Yet there is no research documenting interactions and discord that occur between group members.

Related to this is the unchallenged belief that it is in people's best interest to work together in teams. This is an interesting assumption given the prominent attention paid to adolescents and youth-at-risk for whom challenge courses are common interventions. Away from challenge courses, counselors and health educators spend an inordinate amount of effort to help adolescents resist peer pressure and gain the strength to act on their own. There is no discussion in the literature about the conditions under which teamwork should be promoted.[2]

Trust. Closely related to the notion of teamwork is the idea of trust. Conventional wisdom and many different research studies state that challenge courses increase trust among participants (cf. Priest, 1995, 1996a, 1998; Vincent, 1995). According to Priest (1998), "The acquisition and maintenance of trust is critical to the success of a team and goes hand in hand with cooperation and communication" (p. 31).

---

[2] A graphic example comes from the first author's experience as a Certified Therapeutic Recreation Specialist. Working with adolescent residents of a locked residential treatment center, he used low challenge course activities to create a sense of team and community. While unsupervised one evening, two residents tied their bed sheets together, cut through the heavy wire screen in the window and escaped from the facility. One of the residents was captured by the police and returned to the facility. When the first author asked why he had done it, the adolescent replied that he was only doing what he had been taught in groups on teamwork—to work and get along with a person he really didn't like. In this instance, participants had learned teamwork as intended, but the negative fashion with which they used this learning was totally unexpected.

The first assumption related to trust is that trust is a good characteristic to develop; however, the question should be asked, "Are there situations where trust should not be encouraged?" There certainly are situations where trust could be a negative attribute—for example, individuals in abusive relationships who continue to trust their abusers or individuals who must protect vital confidential information. Assuming that trust is a quality that is always good ignores situations where unearned or misplaced trust results in negative outcomes. The literature on challenge courses discusses trust without acknowledging the complexity of social relationships that sometimes make distrust a better course of action.

Another assumption related to trust is that it will be established and reciprocated among challenge course participants. Facilitators encourage group members to trust others in the group through activities such as the "Lap Sit." In this activity, people in the group stand in a tight circle with their hands on the shoulders of the person in front them. When the facilitator gives a command, everyone sits down on the knees of the person behind them. When done correctly (reciprocating trust), the group will support itself in a sitting position. When done incorrectly (non-reciprocating trust), the group will fall to the ground. The Lap Sit is used to encourage participants to trust their teammates—in this case, to trust that your neighbor's lap will be behind you to support you as you blindly shift into a sitting position. Through activities like this, group members are encouraged to believe that trust will be returned. The extent to which participants actually learn to trust, or the benefits of a belief in reciprocated trust, has not been examined.

An underlying assumption in all of this is that trust is necessary for teamwork, communication, and cooperation. This is implicit in the emphasis many challenge course activities place on trust-building as a central goal for the activity. Conventional wisdom and empirical research both imply that challenge courses promote and encourage trust-building. However, it is not uncommon for people to work, communicate, and cooperate with others without necessarily trusting them. While trust may be helpful in some situations, it probably isn't as central to teamwork or success as the challenge course literature implies.

Self-concept. Data exist that apparently document a positive impact of challenge courses on self-concept (cf. Priest, 1996b). Whether integral aspects of self can be measured in pre-/post-test designs using standard instrumentation highlights an implicit assumption in empirical science; some would argue that these scales capture little of what we truly feel or believe about ourselves. While enhanced self-concept has always been assumed to be a worthy goal, recent discussions have begun to challenge this assumption by noting that enhanced views of self are also evident in egotistical or selfish behaviors.

The belief that challenge courses affect self-concept must be examined in conjunction with the prior point about positive and negative outcomes of challenge courses. Of the literature we reviewed, no study examined ways that experiences on a challenge course could undermine self-concept or reaffirm negative beliefs about one's self. The potential for negative feedback can be seen in activities like the Pamper Pole, where participants climb to the top of a 30–40 foot pole and jump off of it attempting to catch a trapeze or ring a bell. Some participants easily clamber to the top, jump off, catch the trapeze or ring the bell, and exclaim to the other participants how easy the activity was, while others struggle and some never make it to the top of the pole. What are the potentially negative consequences on self-concept when a participant does not succeed in an activity that others can perform? This situation presumably is at the heart of "challenge by choice" (cf. Carlson & Evans, 2001; Rhonke, 1989), a philosophy that suggests that participants be allowed to set their own goals in terms of how much of the activity they want to accomplish. Thus, for some participants "success" might be defined by simply climbing partway up the pole. Even though challenge by choice attempts to respect the differing skills and abilities of participants, there has been no examination of how this choice is perceived by challenge course participants. It takes a strong individual to be satisfied with public behavior that one's peers might define as failure. The belief that challenge course activities enhance self-esteem, even when completed only partially, deserves critical examination.

When challenge courses are used to enhance or promote self-concept there is an expectation that this enhanced self-concept will be sustained after the participant leaves the activity. This assumes that temporal or contextual changes that occurred on the challenge course will be manifested more permanently in other social situations, with other individuals, and without the facilitator's overt intervention and validation. The difficulty of changing behaviors or self-concept has fostered entire fields like psychotherapy and social work; the assumption that a challenge course leader can effect this type of change in a few hours, in a group setting that carries an equal probability of "devastation and disaster" certainly needs to be examined more critically.

Benefits Are Transferable

In addition to the previous set of assumptions that challenge courses produce benefits, the authors' analysis of the literature revealed a second set of assumptions that addressed the issue of transference. Both challenge course researchers and practitioners have long believed that lessons and effects from participating in challenge activities will generalize to other facets of participant's lives. Virtually all research conducted on corporate adventure training seeks to show that behaviors demonstrated on the challenge course translate into improved behaviors at work (cf. Bronson et al., 1992; Maxwell, 1997; Priest & Lesperance, 1994; Smith & Priest, in press). Similarly, challenge course research conducted with low-income minority youth (Green et al., 2000), and at-risk youth (Robitschek, 1996) focused on behaviors that adolescents can transfer and practice in other environments. Research has presumably shown that challenge courses increase protective factors in low-income, minority youth (Green et al., 2000), improve the internal locus of control of adults with hearing impairments (Luckner, 1989), and "promote positive growth and change for persons with disabilities" (Herbert, 1996, p. 3). The belief in transference is so strong that the primary purpose of challenge courses, at least when used as an intervention, lies in the impact that occurs when those experiences are transferred into other life contexts.

This belief in transference necessarily builds upon the beliefs presented earlier: that risk produces positive outcomes that are evidenced by teamwork, trust, and self-concept. Clearly, this belief in transference is, therefore, delimited by assumptions that underlie those beliefs about positive benefits. Likewise, evidence about transference is constrained by instruments that ask respondents to focus specifically on potentially beneficial outcomes of the event. But even without these concerns, research into long-term effects of challenge courses has not provided convincing evidence that long-term transference occurs (cf. Constantine, 1993; Finkenberg et al., 1994; Robitschek, 1996). In spite of this lack of evidence, proponents of challenge courses adamantly cling to their belief that challenge interventions produce long-term change in individuals.

Even if transference were to be documented and supported, it would be vulnerable to the concerns we've raised about potentially negative or detrimental outcomes that might occur during challenge activities. Discussions of transference inevitably are framed as the transference of *benefits* that ultimately enhance one's life. But if a notion such as trust can be transferred from the challenge course to the boardroom, couldn't mistrust be transferred just as well? And if challenge courses teach about the reciprocity of trust, isn't there a possibility that they could teach individuals how to take advantage of trust that is given? What happens when a team completes a challenge activity but hides the fact that one member cheated, for example by touching the net in Spider Web, when the rules state that this should cause the entire team to start over? Are we teaching people that cheating is okay if you are not caught? And when an individual's self-concept is undermined or demeaned though group interactions or failure at an activity, are we reinforcing that negative sense of self? There is a great danger to transference unless we are absolutely certain that only the positive outcomes are being carried forward into future situations. Even though a preponderance of challenge course research reports evidence of transference, that work is limited by the researchers' limited focus on potentially positive outcomes. If transference is to be critically examined, researchers and practitioners must allow for the possibility that harmful effects can be transferred too.

Even if one accepts the assumption that skills are learned through participation in a challenge course, the question remains about whether or not those skills *should* be transferred into other settings. We've already addressed this in our earlier discussion of the potentially harmful consequences of risk and trust, if carried forward into the wrong situations. The focus on positive aspects of transference has other unintended consequences as well, forcing a utilitarian goal around recreational activities while overlooking the value of simply having fun.

Conclusion

The authors do not deny the possibility that challenge courses might have the potential to create positive changes as described in the literature; however, research and practice have embraced this belief rather than put it up for critical examination. The structure and design of research has resulted in studies that do not effectively challenge or test the efficacy of challenge courses. Conceivably, any of the assumptions previously described could be proven wrong; taken together, if all of these assumptions fail, there would be little rationale for the continued use of challenge courses. On the other hand, research that tests and supports these assumptions would greatly strengthen the foundation of challenge course programming. Thus, we call for research that allows for the possibility that challenge courses produce no benefits, or negative benefits, and research that examines transference of any and all effects that might stem from participating in a challenge course.

Critical deconstruction of this type can be applied to any field of study. Indeed, all research is premised on assumptions derived from the paradigms that shape the researchers' quest for knowledge. In quantitative research we try to overcome this by setting high standards before we reject the null hypothesis, a procedure premised on skepticism until a preponderance of the evidence proves otherwise. In qualitative research we seek out disconfirming evidence, intentionally challenging emergent themes by looking for data that contradicts them. These are fundamental tenets of the research process because they force us to re-examine and challenge assumptions about what we think we see in our data. In this article, we are simply asking challenge course researchers to do a better job of holding on to that skepticism.

The authors would like to briefly suggest some strategies for addressing the dilemmas we have created by revealing the unfounded assumptions embedded in challenge course research and practice. The first solution is to open this topic up for discussion. Based on the assumption that risk is necessary for positive change—to the assumption that challenge courses produce positive benefits, to the assumption that challenge course facilitators can bring about these changes—researchers and facilitators need to be willing to ask difficult questions about their work. This open discussion should extend beyond published research papers, and it needs to entail practitioners and researchers working together to examine assumptions from both academic and practical perspectives. These discussions must strike at the heart of what challenge courses are all about, and allow for the possibility that challenge activities are not as beneficial as they are claimed to be. In essence, proponents of challenge courses need to put themselves in a situation similar to what they ask of their participants: to accept the risk this challenge raises and to move through the activity with self-reflection that leads to a stronger state of existence. A willingness to question assumptions present in challenge course programs does not diminish or lessen the field; on the contrary, it may lead to a stronger foundation for the profession. If we wish to grow as a field we must change, and to change we must question.

To help us understand assumptions present in challenge course programs, researchers and practitioners would do well to ask those who are directly impacted by challenge courses—the participants. Voices of participants must be made clearer and guide all practical aspects of challenge course design and implementation (see Cassidy, 2001). Simply adding open-ended questions to survey instruments or providing participants with end-of-program evaluations will not be sufficient; we must take the time to interview participants in order to understand their perceptions and experiences. By listening carefully to their stories, we will be better able to see our own beliefs and assumptions that had been invisible to us.

We believe that challenge courses might indeed have the power to facilitate positive growth and change, but also the power to implement or reaffirm negative traits and characteristics as well. Such is the nature of most social contexts. By openly examining the assumptions that shape challenge course research and practice, we will be in a position to design stronger studies capable of producing greater insight into the benefits—and the limitations—of challenge course participation.

References

Attarian, A., & Holden, G. T. (2001). *The research and literature on challenge courses: An annotated bibliography.* Jonas Ridge, NC: Alpine Towers International.

Bramwell, K., Forrester, S., Houle, B., Larocque, J., Villeneuve, L., & Priest, S. (1997). One shot wonders don't work: A casual-comparative case study. *Journal of Adventure Education and Outdoor Leadership, 14*(2), 15–17.

Bronson, J., Gibson, S., Kishar, R., & Priest, S. (1992). Evaluation of team development in a corporate adventure training program. *Journal of Experiential Education, 15(2),* 50–53.

Burg, J. E. (2001). Emerging issues in therapeutic adventure with families. *Journal of Experiential Education, 24(2),* 118–122.

Carlson J. A., & Evans, K. (2001). Whose choice is it? Contemplating challenge-by-choice and diverse abilities. *Journal of Experiential Education, 24*(1), 58–63.

Cassidy, K. (2001). Enhancing your experiential program with narrative theory. *Journal of Experiential Education, 24*(1) 22–26.

Constantine, M. (1993). The effects of a ropes course experience on perceived self-efficacy: A study designed to examine the effects of an adventure program. *Pennsylvania Journal of Health, Physical Education, Recreation, and Dance, 63*(2), 10.

Finkenberg, M. E., Shows, D., & DiNucci, J. M. (1994). Participation in adventure-based activities and self-concepts of college men and women. *Perceptual and Motor Skills, 78,* 1119–1122.

Goldenberg, M. A., Klenosky, D. B., O'Leary, J. T., & Templin, T. J. (2000). A means-end investigation of challenge course experiences. *Journal of Leisure Research, 32,* 208–224.

Goldman K., & Priest, S. (1990). Risk taking transfer in development training. *Journal of Adventure Education and Outdoor Leadership, 7*(4), 32–35.

Green, G. T., Kleiber, D. A., & Tarrant, M. A. (2000). The effect of an adventure-based recreation program on development of resiliency in low income minority youth. *Journal of Park and Recreation Administration, 18,* 76–97.

Hart, L., & Silka, L. (1994). Building self-efficacy through women-centered ropes course experiences. *Women and Therapy, 15*(3/4), 111–127.

Herbert, J. T. (1996). Use of adventure-based counseling programs for persons with disabilities. *Journal of Rehabilitation, 62*(4), 3–9.

Klint, K. A., & Priest S. (in press). Qualitative research on the transfer effectiveness of a corporate adventure training program. *Journal of Adventure Education and Outdoor Leadership.*

Long, A. (2001). Learning the ropes: Exploring the meaning and value of experiential education for girls at risk. *Journal of Experiential Education, 24(2),* 100–108.

Luckner, J. L. (1989). Altering locus of control of individuals with hearing impairments by outdoor-adventure courses. *Journal of Rehabilitation, 55*(2), 62–67.

Martin, P., & Priest, S. (1986). Understanding the adventure experience. *Journal of Adventure Education, 3*(1), 18–21.

Maxwell, J. (1997). Increasing work group effectiveness: Combining corporate adventure training with traditional team building methods. *Journal of Experiential Education, 20*(1), 26–33.

Meyer, B. B. (2000). The ropes and challenge course: A quasi-experimental examination. *Perceptual and Motor Skills, 90,* 1249–1257.

Priest, S. (1992). Factor exploration and confirmation for the dimensions of an adventure experience. *Journal of Leisure Research, 24,* 127–139.

Priest, S. (1995). The effect of belaying and belayer type on the development of interpersonal partnership trust in rock climbing. *Journal of Experiential Education, 18*(2), 107–109.

Priest, S. (1996a). Developing organizational trust: Comparing the effects of challenge courses and group initiatives. *Journal of Experiential Education, 19*(1), 40–42.

Priest, S. (1996b). The effect of two different debriefing approaches on developing self-confidence. *Journal of Experiential Education, 19*(1), 40–42.

Priest, S. (1998). Physical challenge and the development of trust through corporate adventure training. *Journal of Experiential Education, 21*(1), 31–34.

Priest, S. (n.d.). Retrieved June 6, 2003, from http://www.tarrak.com/EXP/exp.htm

Priest, S., & Gass, M. (1997). An examination of "problem-solving" versus "solution-focused" facilitation styles in a corporate setting. *Journal of Experiential Education, 20*(1), 34–39.

Priest, S., Gass, M., & Fitzpatrick, K. (1999). Training corporate managers to facilitate: The next generation of facilitating experiential methodologies? *Journal of Experiential Education, 22*(1), 50–53.

Priest, S., & Lesperance, M. A. (1994). Time series trends in corporate team development.
Journal of Experiential Education, 17(1), 34–39.

Rhonke, K. (1989). *Cowstails and cobras* II. Dubuque, IA: Kendall/Hunt.

Robitschek, C. (1996). At-risk youth and hope: Incorporating a challenge course into a summer
program. *The Career Development Quarterly, 45,* 163–169.

Roid, G. H., & Fitts, W. H. (1989). *Tennessee Self-Concept Scale, Revised: manual.* Los Angeles: Western
Psychological Services.

Sherer, M., Maddux, J., Mercandante, B., Prentice-Dunn, S., Jacob, B., & Rogers, R. (1982). The self-
efficacy scale: Construction and validation. *Psychological Reports, 51*(2), 663–671.

Smith, R., & Priest, S. (in press). Barriers to transference from corporate adventure training to the
workplace. *Journal of Adventure Education and Outdoor Leadership.*

Snyder, C. R., Harris, C., Anderson, J. R., Holleran, S. A., Irving, L. M., Sigmon, S. T., et al., (1991).
The will and the ways: Development and validation of an individual-differences measure of hope.
Journal of Personality and Social Psychology, 60, 570–585.

Straus, A., & Corbin, J. (1990). *Basics of qualitative research: Grounded theory procedures and techniques*
(2nd ed.). Newbury Park, CA: Sage.

Vincent, S. M. (1995). Emotional safety in adventure therapy programs: Can it be defined?
Journal of Experiential Education, 18(2), 76–81.

Witt, P. A., Baker, D., & Scott, D. (1996). *The Protective Factors Scale.* Unpublished instrument,
Department of Recreation, Park, and Tourism Sciences, Texas A&M University, College Station, TX.

Landfullness in Adventure-Based Programming: Promoting Reconnection to the Land

▾ ▾ ▾

Molly Baker

Let us venture back to the early 20th century, to the glory days of nature study when naturalists, such as Anna Botsford Comstock and Enos Mills, were promoting an "essential nature literacy" that necessitated direct contact with plants and animals in their natural surroundings (Pyle, 2001, p. 19). It was a time when botany walks were common and "a lively, experimental curiosity in plants and animals was nothing unusual; it was simply one component of the engaged citizen's life" (Pyle, 2001, p. 19). Move forward to the mid-1900s, however, and we find Aldo Leopold lamenting the fact that field studies had been succeeded by laboratory biology as the pure form of science, and that memorizing the names of the bumps on the bones of a cat had come to take precedence over gaining an understanding of the native countryside (Leopold, 1953). Leopold observed that our collective relationship to the land had been compromised to the point where we were fast approaching a state of "landlessness." He noted in his Round River essays:

> The problem, then, is how to bring about a striving for harmony with land among a people many of whom have forgotten there is any such thing as land, among whom education and culture have become almost synonymous with landlessness. (Leopold, 1966, p. 210)

This chapter originally was published in the *Journal of Experiential Education*, with the following citation:
Baker, M. (2005) Landfullness in adventure-based programming: Promoting reconnection to the land. *Journal of Experiential Education, 27*(3), 267–276.

Landlessness, according to Leopold, was manifesting itself in two distinct but related ways: the literal loss of places wild and free; and the figurative loss of our collective awareness of, and admiration for, the land.

Before the turn of the 21st century, Lopez spoke to this concept of landlessness, noting that almost four decades later it had reached an unprecedented level. In his book *Rediscovery of North America,* Lopez stated: "We have a way of life that ostracizes the land" (Lopez, 1990, p. 31). As the suburbanization of America evolves at an ever-increasing rate, landscapes are becoming more homogenized and we often find ourselves in "Anywhere, USA" (Hilten & Hilten, 1996). During the past century, our collective environmental literacy has declined dramatically. As noted by Hawken, "That an average adult can recognize one thousand brand names and logos but fewer than ten local plants is not a good sign" (Hawken, 1993, p. 59).

These combined realities—irreversible loss of undeveloped land, plus changes in our national relationship to land—have created the need for reconnection, both on a personal level and national scale. The day has passed when participants can leave adventure-based programs with a sense of accomplishment, but without a sense of their relationship to the land. It seems, then, that as experiential educators it is incumbent upon us to assess whether our students are becoming actively engaged in the landscape or merely passing through it. Simply put, are we promoting *landless* or *landfull* experiences?

Landlessness in Adventure Education

It may be assumed that the environment plays an integral role in adventure-based programming simply because it is there. Oftentimes, however, the land becomes a backdrop surrounding the adventure experience (Baker, 1999; Haluza-Delay, 1999; Miner, 2003). The myriad modern-day forces distracting our awareness from the land can be both overwhelming and insidious; it is all too easy to divert our attention toward the activity, the group, the gear, the gadgets—to be pulled away by the map, the altimeter, the GPS, by everything but the very landscape that can inspire our travels. The most notable of the many factors that conspire to create a landless trip are traditional programming objectives centered on inter/intrapersonal skill development, coupled with students' tendencies to focus first and foremost on the technical and social aspects. The likelihood of a landless trip increases when instructors demonstrate a higher baseline competence in technical and people skills rather than in land skills; or when they are teaching in new areas where they have limited knowledge of the landscape. Frequently, the extent to which the land is emphasized is dependent more upon the interests and expertise of the individual staff, rather than the mission statement, training or curriculums of the organization.

Granted, an increasing number of adventure-based programs are placing a higher priority on the inclusion of environmental objectives in their curriculums. However, the implementation frequently centers on Leave No Trace (LNT) philosophy, with a handful of natural history classes added whenever possible. Although commendable as a starting point, this approach tends to frame LNT practices as technical skills with natural history curricula becoming disjointed or lacking in context.

The bottom line is that even on a month-long course in a wilderness setting, students' awareness of the land can be limited to its direct impact on their immediate experience (i.e., the weather, a pretty sunset or a breathtaking view). Likewise, they may relate to the landscape solely in terms of negotiating it, whether through route finding, river crossings or campsite selection. When interactions with the land are viewed in this way, students may not consciously relate with the land, and may, instead, become passersby traveling through "Any Woods, USA." The upshot is that landscapes may become interchangeable and the unique aspects of a particular place, along with any potential connections to it, may be lost.

Promoting "Landfull" Experiences

Experiential educators can take a tangible step toward addressing disconnection with the land by promoting "landfull" experiences. If an experience is to be landfull, it necessitates rethinking adventure as we know it today. A landfull adventure is not a journey away, guided by the pull of modern technology and distractions, but rather a journey home, to discover a sense of belonging to the land. As Meyers so aptly describes it in his book, Lime Creek Odyssey:

> We cannot come to know a place by rushing in and rushing out. I often wonder just what it is that people see in the wilderness when they come for a week or two each year. I imagine their spirits are refreshed and their time here is quite pleasant. I know they learn a great deal. But what do they see? I believe there are some things that can only be seen if you stay awhile. Others become visible only to those who gaze at a landscape and think, this is my home. (Meyers, 1989, p. 112)

This notion of discovering home may challenge or even run counter to mission statements and curricula in adventure-based programming. Yet it is vitally important that we provide students with opportunities to develop "land" skills (in the same way we promote leadership and technical skills), if we are to address the need for an "essential nature literacy." As in the glory days of nature study in the early 1900s, the key is for students to discover an engagement with the land that extends beyond simply knowing the names of trees, to include a personal approach of relating to the land. This discovery is not only a site-specific sense of place, but also an ongoing relationship with land that transcends time and place. The essence of landfullness is when the personal process becomes less intentional and more a part of our identity—in other words, relating to the land is a part of who we are.

The question then becomes how to go about promoting landfull experiences. We must recognize that as a society we are not in the habit of relating to land in a direct and intentional way. Accordingly, landfullness necessitates that we move beyond an inevitable awareness or a convenient consciousness of the land. It requires experiencing the land in its entirety through all of the senses, including the emotional/affective —not only as it is today, but also as it was in the past and will be in the future. Most importantly, it requires an intentional exploration of our own interactions with, and relationship to, the land. This act of striving to be intentional is what enables the land to become more than a scenic backdrop; as we actively engage with the land it becomes more integral to our experience. It is through purposeful consideration of our relationship to the land that we develop our own ever-evolving personal process of coming to know a place. Rather than traveling *through* the land, we begin to travel *with* and *in* the land.

The Landfull Framework: Levels of Landfullness

The intent is not to replace traditional goals of personal growth and group development, or to override the curriculum with an environmental agenda, but rather to introduce a landfull approach. The "Landfull Framework" is proposed as a holistic approach to integrating environmental education into adventure-based programming that allows for flexibility based on differences in program type, instructor background and student groups. By using the framework as an ongoing theme, instructors can easily repackage existing environmental studies activities and natural history curricula so that what students may have perceived as isolated classes will be seen as part of a cohesive whole. More specifically, the Landfull Framework:

- Recognizes that people come to know a place in different ways;

- Challenges students to develop an intentional, not merely a convenient, consciousness of the land and to actively consider their relationship to it; and

- Enables students to discover and develop their own definition of landfull that is personally significant, and to become self-directed in moving through the levels of landfullness.

The Landfull Framework consists of four levels: (a) Being Deeply Aware, (b) Interpreting Land History, (c) Sensing Place in the Present, and (d) Connecting to Home (see Figure 1). Although it can be used in a linear progression, it is more effective to mix activities and classes that focus on all four levels consistently throughout the course/trip. When the framework is clearly laid out to students at the outset, they have a shared vocabulary and a mental schematic to support the integration of activities. Moreover, when all levels are integrated, students are able to discover the ways in which they connect to the land sooner. Each level has a specific focus and corresponding questions, as listed on the following pages:

Being Deeply Aware

When a group arrives at the trailhead, participants find themselves at a place on the map that may mean nothing to them personally. In this stage, the focus often is simply on the activity and the group. Using a topographic map analogy, a student's thinking is based on a "summit mentality" and the land is seen as a backdrop, or merely a route to the summit, but little more.

- *Focus:* Increase awareness of one's surroundings.

- *Questions:* Where am I? What's around me? Who is around me?

- *Activities:* Students ground themselves by becoming conscious of the lay of the land on both a micro and macro scale through different activities, such as: (a) *Sensory Awareness* games (e.g., "Meet Your Neighbors"—each student goes off to get acquainted with something that interests them, then have a "party" where everybody introduces his/her "new neighbor" and tells its story); (b) *Mapping Initiatives*—students use ropes on the ground to outline where they are, including the state, park/

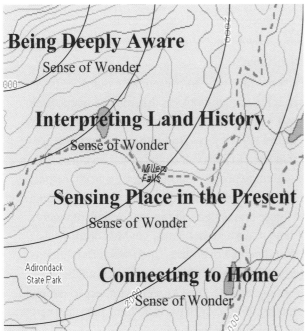

Being Deeply Aware
Where am I?
What's around me?
Who is around me?

**Interpreting Land History:
Natural & Cultural History**
How has this land changed over time?
What & who have lived here in the past?
How did they relate to the land?

Sensing Place in the Present
How is this place unique?
Who lives/passes through this land
  now and what is their relationship
  to it?
What does this place mean to me?

Connecting to Home
How can this place link to other land-
  scapes & experiences with land?
When does the land become home?
When does home become the land?

Figure 1. The Landfull Framework, used to guide the integration of environmental education in adventure-based programming, consists of four areas of landfullness.

forest boundaries, mountain ranges, rivers; (c) *Location Celebrations*—take time out to observe surroundings in an engaging way (e.g., have a birthday party for a tree to celebrate its age, including balloons and singing); and (d) *Art Gallery*—students take turns being the "docent" along the trail by sharing with others the "masterpieces" of artwork they find most intriguing.

Interpreting Land History (Natural and Cultural History)

Reaching this stage, students are somewhat aware of their surroundings, but only through direct observation. At this point, depth can be added to the students' experiences by increasing their knowledge of the area through both natural and cultural history. Instructors may tend to focus more on natural history than on cultural history, perhaps due to lack of knowledge or concerns about perpetuating stereotypes or historical inaccuracies. However, cultural history often creates a more tangible connection to the land than does natural history in students' minds. By highlighting both the natural and cultural history of a place, the likelihood of making the land come alive may be increased. Rather than relaying historical facts and figures, instructors can reveal the story of land and people over time to spark curiosity using the following examples:

- *Focus:* Increase knowledge of the uniqueness of a particular landscape.
- *Questions:* How has this land changed over time? What and who have lived here in the past? How did they relate to the land?
- *Activities:* (a) *Site-Specific Interpretation*—take time to contemplate points of interest, such as cliffs, signs, names on a map, or found objects that may be overlooked as "junk;" (b) *Journaling*—students write their personal land histories (e.g., their story with the land over time); "A Day in the Life Of …"—students write from the perspective of something/somebody that used to live on the land and then guess each others' perspectives; (c) *Role Plays*—identify people/land-use groups from the past and take on roles for a day, for a dinner party, or for a debate at a town meeting; (d) *Skits*—dress up as an historical figure and appear on the trail or in camp with a story to tell (a few leaves and duct tape make a great beard!); (e) Melodrama—as a group, act out the story of the land and people over time, and if no information is available have different groups interpret signs in the landscape and act out their version of what could have been the story); and (f) Time Travel—connect to people from the past through food, gear, and/or stories (e.g., If we were here 100 years ago, what would we be wearing? Eating? What would the land look like?).

Sensing Place in the Present

If land history is the story of land and people over time, sensing place is feeling a part of the stories (Kriesberg, 1999). Sense of place is a dynamic and personal construct that addresses how we assign value to a place and was first applied to landscapes in 1974 by the geographical philosopher Yi-Fu Tuan (1974). Sensing place is the continuous development of a personal connection to a particular place that evolves from not only spending time there, but also from learning about its land history. In addition, one understands how the place is unique and is able to articulate one's connection with, relationship to, and feelings about the place. Using a topographic map analogy, students in this stage have gained appreciation of the entire mountain; they are as aware of the marshes at the base as the peak itself. The following illustrates this:

- *Focus:* Facilitate connections to a place that are personalized and ever-evolving.

- *Questions:* How is this place unique? Who lives/passes through this land now and what is their relationship to it? What does this place mean to me?

- *Activities:* (a) *Mapping*—students draw a map of the route and then add overlays to it, including personal highlights, group benchmarks, and sense-of-place landmarks—aspects of the land that were personally significant; (b) *Topo Naming*—rename terrain features on the map based on your personal experiences and/or impressions of the land; (c) *Solos*—students are given solo time both at the beginning and end of the trip/course to contemplate how their relationship to the land has changed over time; and (d) *Art Gallery*—students are given ample time to find a spot and create a masterpiece that represents their interactions/relationship with the place, and then students explain their creations to the group.

Connecting to Home

The objective of this stage is to enable students to bridge the gap between backcountry and front country. It is this transference of landfullness to everyday life that creates relevance for the land skills developed during the trip/experience. *Connecting to Home* is not a single closure activity to be conducted on the last night in the field, but rather an ongoing effort to develop a conscious awareness of how we relate to the land around us and the role it plays in our everyday lives.

- Focus: Promote the linking of landscapes—the transference from the backcountry to the front country (home).

- Questions: How can this place link to other landscapes and experiences with the land? When does the land become home? When does home become the land?

- Activities: (a) *Water Talk*—discuss the water supply at camp and then have students share where their water comes from at home; (b) *Daily Walk*—link the skill of being an active navigator in the woods to increasing awareness of one's surroundings at home. Have the students draw or map out the route they take to work/school at home, everyday, including significant landmarks along the way; (c) *Time Warp*—students envision what a particular piece of land looked like 50/100 years ago and then consider what their hometown looked like at the same time; (d) *Constellation Myths*—locate a constellation in the night sky during the trip and then discuss where the constellation would be located at home; then create a myth of how it came to be; and (e) *Back Home Discoveries*—parallels of discoveries made on the trip/course are made to home (e.g., a tree on the trail is linked to a tree in the neighborhood; vista on the trails can spur discussion of what is my "vista" from the home/office).

The Sense of Wonder—actively contemplating the land—serves as a catalyst for moving between the levels of the Landfull Framework. For example, when participants spend time in a place and learn about its land history, their sense of wonder, at some point, will be engaged. By learning more about land history, and further wondering about the place, they will begin to contemplate what the place means to them personally, and thus be propelled into the Sensing Place stage. Sense of Wonder refers to the concept introduced by Rachel Carson (1956) in her book *The Sense of Wonder*. It is a state in which one is actively interacting with another entity, whether it be tangible (e.g., a tree), or intangible (e.g., time); this interaction engages the person mentally through the processes of inquiry (e.g., posing questions as in a state of curiosity), and/or physically through the senses (e.g., seeing, hearing, smelling, tasting, and/or touching), and/or emotionally through feelings (e.g., affective sentiments of awe, appreciation, etc.). Sense of Wonder represents the reflection/processing step that is integral to the experiential learning process (Kolb, 1984).

The benefits of teaching from a landfull perspective are numerous. At a minimum it adds a new, and often unexpected, dimension to the expedition. Students may gain an increased knowledge of the landscape, develop an appreciation for the uniqueness of a particular place and/or discover a personal connection to the land. Ultimately, students may be able to transcend a site-specific sense of place by developing an ongoing relationship with the land that is integral to their everyday lives. As a reinterpretation of the "essential nature literacy" that Anna Botsford Comstock, Enos Mills, and Aldo Leopold all strove for in their time, this "landfull" approach is aligned with experiential philosophy. The pull of modernity has existed for centuries, and will continue to disconnect us from the land with greater force and diligence in the future. Striving to actively engage students with places is a sure step toward creating a collective connection to landscapes and a more sustainable future.

References

Baker, M. A. (1999). Sense of place: Connecting people to places. *Interpscan*, *26*(3), 20–21.

Carson, R. (1956). *The sense of wonder*. New York, NY: Harper Collins.

Haluza-Delay, R. (1999). Navigating the terrain: Helping care for the Earth. In J. C. Miles & S. Priest (Eds.), *Adventure Programming* (pp. 445–454). State College, PA: Venture.

Hawken, P. (1993). A Declaration of Sustainability. *Utne Reader*, *59*, 54–61.

Hilten, J., & Hilten, R. F. (1996). A Sense of Place for environmental education and interpretation. *The interpretive sourcebook: The Proceedings of the 1996 National Interpreter's Workshop*, (pp. 59–61). Fort Collins, CO: The National Association for Interpretation.

Kolb, D. A. (1984). *Experiential learning.* Englewood Cliffs, NJ: Prentice-Hall.

Kriesberg, D. (1999). Creating a Sense of Place with children's literature. *The interpretive sourcebook: The Proceedings of the 1999 National Interpreter's Workshop*, (pp. 81–83). Fort Collins, CO: The National Association for Interpretation.

Leopold, A. (1953). *Round River*. New York, NY: Oxford University Press.

Leopold, A. (1966). *A Sand County Almanac with essays on conservation from Round River*. New York, NY: Oxford University Press.

Lopez, B. (1990). *The rediscovery of North America*. Lexington, KY: University Press of Kentucky.

Meyers, S. J. (1989). *Lime Creek Odyssey.* Golden, CO: Fulcrum.

Miner, T. (2003). The role of the environment in adventure and outdoor Education. *Taproot, 13*(4), 6–8.

Pyle, R. M. (2001). The rise and fall of natural history: How a science grew that eclipsed direct experience. *Orion*, *20*(4), 17–23.

Tuan, Y. (1974). *Topophilia: A study of environmental perception, attitudes, and values.* Englewood Cliff, NJ: Prentice-Hall.

Connecting Ethics &
Group Leadership: A Case Study

▾ ▾ ▾

Kate Lehmann

A group of nine women and I embarked on a week-long canoe trip into the Boundary Waters Canoe Area with the outdoor adventure organization, Woodswomen. According to one guide, it was a representative Woodswomen gathering in that the group included women with diverse skills and experiences who came together and evolved in a typical way. After returning home, I began to try to analyze the events and activities of that trip. How was it possible that Woodswomen was able to deliver on their promise that each participant would learn, grow, and have fun on a trip when the individuals came with vastly different experiences? Why did it seem that the group was not being guided and yet the guides had a very strong presence? It is my belief that the effectiveness of Woodswomen's approach is related to the integration of ethical principles with a strong leadership model.

This microcosm of experience involving a small group in an outdoor setting during a finite period is illustrative of the wider and deeper connection between effective leadership and ethics. While there is substantial work that explores this connection on a theoretical level, there is little material that gives concrete examples of how ethics can be a foundation for group leadership models. Woodswomen provides a case study that demonstrates this profound connection as it is actualized in an outdoor group setting.

The theoretical principles for this study come from the work of Robert Terry, an ethicist at the Reflective Leadership Institute at the University of Minnesota, and from the group

This chapter originally was published in the *Journal of Experiential Education*, with the following citation:

Lehmann, K. (1991). Connecting ethics and group leadership: A case study. *Journal of Experiential Education, 14*(3), 45–51.

development and leadership model defined and used by Woodswomen. This research about Woodswomen is not intended as an organizational assessment. Rather, it is a means to explore the connections between ethics and leadership, using a leadership model that seems to be ethical, effective, and adaptable to other organizations or group situations. My conclusions are based on lengthy personal interviews with several Woodswomen guides[1] and Executive Director Denise Mitten. Training materials and personal experiences with Woodswomen also contributed to the study.

Ethical Principles

In a recent lecture at St. Cloud University, Robert Terry (1991) outlined six basic ethical principles that provide the foundation for effective leadership. Rather than focus on a single principle, such as justice or love, as the basis for a model of ethical leadership, Terry seeks to weave the six principles into a whole cloth. Terry maintains these principles are universal in nature but responsive to situations. Each principle is equally important in building an ethical framework. They are interrelated and interdependent, building on each other but also referring back to each other.

At the root, this is a model of leadership grounded in the concept of authenticity. Terry (1991) explains, "What I mean by authenticity is being true and real in yourself and in the world…. True is abstract, real is concrete and so we have to get together what we think is true, in terms of patterns, and the embodiment of that. That is 'live it,' walk your talk." Terry maintains that authenticity is a fundamental condition of being human, it is "presupposed in every human act," even in lying. When we lie, we attempt to convince someone else of something that is not true, all the while knowing what the truth really is. To be inauthentic, or to experience inauthenticity, is to sever or experience a disconnection between appearance and reality. This is the deliberate separation of truth from reality, the ultimate form of dissonance.

Terry (1991) maintains that authenticity is something that we struggle to achieve, calling the experience of authenticity "a liberation … when you feel the alignmentof who you are and what you're about." He recognizes, however, that this is a process rather than an achievement in itself. It is impossible to reach the point of perfect alignment because we can never find absolute truth. Rather, "We have got to struggle with what's true … we have to explore each other's perspectives" and, in so doing, come as close as we can to authenticity.

From the basis of authenticity, Terry (1991) begins building a foundation for leadership with the following ethical principles:

- *Dwelling:* We each "show up" with our histories and our identities and need to accept and agree that it is all right for each of us to be there. If we ignore or deny a

---

[1] Guides were guaranteed anonymity, so the names used in the text are fictitious.

person's experience and history, we have, effectively, denied his or her identity. The principle of dwelling is the foundation for embracing and respecting the diversity of people present in our lives. Leadership, itself a relationship between leader and constituents, seeks to increase both the leader's and the constituent's ability to be present, recognizing the diverse perspectives and talents of each individual.

- *Freedom:* The ability to make choices and decisions is integral to being able to sustain relationships. Based on personal history and preferences, each of us can exercise options. This, however, is predicated on the assumption that we have chosen to "show up" and participate in the social conversation.

- *Justice:* Once we are present and have the ability to make choices, we must agree on how we relate to each other. Justice is based on a principle of fairness that has three aspects: (1) Equality—All who choose to be present are equal in their claims; (2) Equity—The idea that initial inadequacy or unfairness can be addressed; and (3) Adequacy—The methods for addressing issues of equality and equity must be adjusted to consider changes.

- *Participation:* Having determined that we wish to be present and have the ability to make choices within the bounds of justice, we take action to engage, we make a "claim" for our own personal power and take part in the world as ourselves and for ourselves.

- *Love:* Love is the principle that turns people toward each other; it is the recognition that, in our journey, in our conversation, we are in a relationship with each other and that participation is not only for our own sake. The principal aspect of love with which leadership is concerned is caring. This is the notion of "standing with people in their duress, not fixing them."

- *Responsibility:* This clarifies love and maintains adequate boundaries between people by "owning up" to who we are and what we are doing.

Leadership, says Terry (1986), is the "courage to call forth authentic action" in oneself and in others, to increase dwelling, freedom, justice, participation, love, and responsibility. I would add that not only do leaders put forth that call but to be effective on a sustained basis, they must live and encourage others to live according to the principles Terry has outlined. It is through living out the principles that leaders can model a way of being that is an authentic and ethical engagement with the world.

Putting Ethical Principles Into Practice

Woodswomen advocates leadership that is solidly grounded in these particular ethical principles. Leadership style is based on the personal style of the guide and the level of direction is based on the requirements of the situation, thus resulting in an approach that is flexible and adaptive. The role of the guide is to provide an environment in which constituents discover their own power, their own resources, and exercise their own leadership abilities.

The Woodswomen leadership training process relies on an understanding of group formation and development that aligns with the progression of Terry's principles (see Table).

The tasks of leadership relate to the principles as the experience unfolds. The concept of authenticity provides the basis from which the expedition is launched. The initial stages of group formation relate to dwelling and the establishment of freedom and justice as operative ethical principles. If authenticity is the point of departure, then this part of the adventure is analogous to deciding to go on the trip, becoming familiar with gear and with one's traveling companions.

Mid-trip stages of group development relate to participation, love, and responsibility. The adventure is underway as the group travels and each person interacts with others and seeks personal fulfillment. As ethical principles are integrated, the travelers move toward greater authenticity. Thus, authenticity is both the starting point and the destination sought, while the journey is the process of integration and transformation.

Table 1.
The Profession of Ethical Principles With Leader Tasks

Ethical Principles for Leadership	Leader Tasks
First Phases of the Journey	
Dwelling	Encourage openness and honesty, determine expectations, concerns
Freedom	Foster participation in decision making
Justice	Reinforce positive group norms, recognize appropriate contributions
Later Stages of the Journey	
Participation	Involve each person, moderate level of direction according to circumstance
Love	Value each person, help each to achieve personal goals
Responsibility	Encourage individual responsibility, recognize the power of influence

Authenticity

Authenticity, the alignment and integration of truth and reality, is where the journey begins. Woodswomen's approach is to create an atmosphere in which each participant is encouraged to discover her own intrinsic worth and abilities, and to acknowledge her accomplishments. The truth is that, given the knowledge and the skills, women are capable of having a safe, comfortable, challenging but nonstressful outdoor experience. The reality is that many women have not been able to do that or believe that they aren't capable of it. One guide addressed this when asked about what difference having an all-women's group made in the experience of being in the outdoors. She said:

> If there are only women there, we do everything. Then we realize that women can do everything ... it's real powerful. Who's going to carry the canoe? We will. Who's going to use that axe? We will. Who's going to cook? We will. Who's going to drag the canoe up on shore? We will. It's all those little pieces. If it's just us, we will do everything. And that changes their lives because, they can do that, what else can they do!"

The search for authenticity is the general goal of this trip, as it is the goal of integrated, ethical leadership. To enhance people's ability to experience authenticity, leaders can promote values that set the stage or provide the tools for constituents to use on their trip.

Dwelling

Terry's first principle, that of "dwelling," is one of the most significant factors in the Woodswomen model. Dwelling means showing up, and in that, affirming not only one's own history and values but also being prepared to acknowledge the presence and legitimacy of others.

One task of leadership is to encourage and model the idea that it is all right to show up as you are, that the first step toward fully participating in the world is to be present, with all our personal histories, both good and not so good.

Woodswomen programs consistently begin not only with traditional introductions of guides and participants, but also with discussion about participants' expectations and concerns. Guides encourage candor but lead the discussion in a way that avoids extensive or inappropriate personal disclosure.

Understanding and accepting a participant's level of skill, her beliefs and values, also contributes to the group process. Encouraging and supporting members of the group in their efforts to be open about their desires and concerns is critical to the guide being able to conduct a safe and satisfying trip. In addition, determining expectations allows the guide to consider the various individual needs and desires. From this, the guides can then respond by designing a trip experience, in concert with the group, which will attempt to address those wants.

The next step is to recognize that participants are able to make decisions about where they wish to go and how they want to get there.

Freedom

The ability to make choices, freedom, is another building block of the Woodswomen approach to increasing an individual's ownership and involvement in the group experience. Executive Director Denise Mitten has dubbed the process an "affirming-collective process of decision-making (Mitten, undated).

The guide's role in decision-making can be central or peripheral, depending on the decision being made and how long the group has been together. The process of decision making seeks to maximize each individual's freedom to choose within the context of the experience. Initially, the leader will identify that a decision needs to be made and is responsible for providing information about the options available to the group. Group members then can add their information, concerns, and desires. The guide then can discern whether there is a general, common interest or groupings of interest that could be accommodated by breaking into smaller subgroups. The guide also might suggest an alternative way to accommodate varying desires. Even if the resulting decision does not completely fit all individual desires, each person has had an opportunity to be heard.

The affirming-collective decision-making process acknowledges that the guide or leader has information that needs to be shared and has the responsibility to put forth options that meet the criteria of safety. By listening to each of the group members, she can voice what action is to be taken based on the information that has come from the members themselves.

One guide related an anecdote that illustrates that, even in the face of having to go along with a decision that she flatly opposed, she felt her opinion was acknowledged and validated. In this situation, Julia was a participant, rather than a guide. During the trip, a decision had to be made about what route to take: one choice would result in an extremely long day and bring them to the site of ancient pictographs; the other choice would be to forego the pictographs and have a shorter day on the water. Julia was one of only a couple of women who opposed the longer day. She told me:

> It was real clear that I was either going to have to choose to paddle with one of the other
> women alone [and leave the large group] … or I was going to have to change my mind.
> Denise said, "Since that seems to be where we are," recognizing the impasse, "what can
> you get out of the day? What do you want so that you'll feel like you've gotten something
> important too because you're having to give a tremendous amount?" … Now first of all,
> I didn't even think I was giving that much which was a real key piece and then I got to

choose whatever I wanted. Well, I'm not greedy. I thought about it ... and said "What I really want is to bear no responsibility for this decision."... And it was a wonderful day! ...

Since then, Julia has used this approach both in leading group trips and in her work and family life. She said:

We try never to sacrifice individual goals to group goals.... I think that's a key to empowerment, that you don't have to just cave in to somebody else's needs, that you can get your needs met while giving up a piece of what you want. But it recognizes [your] generosity instead of saying, of course you ought to do what other people want.

Shared decision making also contributes to encouraging leadership among participants and creates a situation in which group members can exercise their freedom.

Justice

The affirming-collective decision-making process and program activities are also based on the principle of justice. Justice, says Terry, is the concept of fairness with its subsets of equality, equity, and adequacy.

Equality is demonstrated in the thinking that each participant has equal claim to receiving the benefits promised to her, namely a trip that is safe and fun, and through which she can acquire additional knowledge and skills.

Another aspect of justice is equity. This is operative in two ways: skills training and individual contributions to the tasks of the group. Since there are varying skill levels represented among group members, instruction is available to those who desire to advance their level. Guides provide training to the extent that an individual wishes it. Contributions to the group tasks are also done in an equitable manner based on how an individual wishes and is able to contribute. Tasks are not assigned or rotated. Each person is encouraged to contribute in ways that are appropriate for her/him. This, in turn, acknowledges the diverse interests and talents available in the group. Denise Mitten has written:

Delighting in group diversity is important. Recognize differences.... We look for cues from participants, and when they are extended, we accept them.... Reinforce that a "sunset watcher" can be as important as a "fire builder." Equal is not that we each carry 55 pounds, but rather that we contribute appropriately. One woman may carry a limited amount due to a weak back, but she may cook a little more often, or sing wonderful songs as the group portages. Often, given the space and support, participants will equal out the tasks. (Mitten, 1985)

Finally, the third subprinciple of justice is adequacy. Equality and equity need to be responsive to changes in the situation. As skill levels increase or individual interests and abilities change, new situations may arise. The guide must respond appropriately by altering the amount of direction given to individuals or the group.

For instance, a group that has been together for a few days will need little or no direction in how to set up tents or prepare a meal.

Having acknowledged the right of each person to be present and to make choices, and having established the norms of equality, equity, and adequacy, the group members can now move into interaction and relationship building. This is the journey toward each other as well as farther into themselves.

Participation

Participation is the principle of claiming and exercising power. Participation suggests that, once a person is present (dwelling), accepts their ability to make choices (freedom), and agrees that interaction will be on a playing field leveled by the concept of justice, then they must act. Leaders, says Terry (1991), "act in concert with followers." Followers, or constituents, also must exercise their power; otherwise, lack of participation will result in oppression.

Participation is tied to the stage of group formation and process known as "performing." At this stage, participants are familiar enough with task requirements, such as setting up camp and loading canoes, so that the work gets done smoothly and without much discussion. They have acquired more skills and feel more comfortable with their surroundings. The trust that has been engendered previously allows participants to reach this comfort level. Because of the trust level, more personal information may be shared and friendships begin to form. Mary stressed that once a group has full participation and has reached the performing stage, the guide needs to moderate her behavior accordingly:

> You have to look at what information they do need but not be really directive because people don't need that any more. One of the things we talk about is how, if you're a good guide, you basically get yourself out of the role. You're less and less of that central directive person.

The level of participation of any individual is still a personal decision. Again, Woodswomen stresses that each participant needs to assess her needs and desires and figure out her limits. Neither the organization nor the guide predetermine standards or goals for the participant. Rather, each woman is encouraged to choose her own level of challenge. Julia maintains that:

> Given the choice, most people will stretch more.... In my experience people will choose stuff
> that is amazing to me, that's really out there on the outer edge of what they can do.... Since
> you have permission to quit whenever you want, then you can push yourself further.

Mary concurred, saying:

> It's not assuming that we know what they need to do to build their characters. We don't
> think they need to climb to the top of the rock to build their characters. For some women
> just being there is building their characters incredibly, or going part way up the rock.
> People come from different places and they are their own best judge of where they're
> coming from and what they need to do.

There is a critical distinction between creating a situation in which individuals find and
exercise their own power, and sharing or giving away power. Power is not a commodity in this
model. The guide is not in a position to broker it away. Instead, in fact, the guide is
always in a position, vis-a-vis the group, to exercise power as it is appropriate to the situation.

Love

Recognition of one's own power and the move to act is not done in isolation. Participation means that there is interaction and relationship with others. Terry (1991) says that
love is the act of attending to one another, of "discovering the we-ness of our relationship."
It is finding our similarities and differences. Love tempers power and participation by
acknowledging that there are others involved in this interaction.

One guide, when asked about what an appropriate name for this philosophy of leadership might be, suggested that it is based on unconditional love. It is apparent that caring, as a
principle of love, is of great importance to the success of the Woodswomen group experience.

> I think people want to be respectful, I think people want to love each other [and] want to
> be loved, and we often don't know how to do it. So one of the things that I teach and our
> model embodies is how to do what we want to do anyway. (Mitten, personal interview)

With the onus on the individual to take responsibility for herself, caring is emphasized
that is affirming of the value of the individual rather than "caretaking" or "curing."

On the group interaction level, enabled by genuine care, individuals can begin to differentiate themselves from the group. Differentiation is the healthy expression of oneself
through the sharing of personal information, needs, and desires (Mitten, undated). It is
alright for a participant to risk being or doing something different. Personal goals become as
important as group goals and subgroups may form around a particular interest or activity.

The fear of being different has been mitigated by the expression of genuine care by the guide and by other group members.

Woodswomen maintains that achieving differentiation is critical to reaching the goal of helping women to discover their own power:

> Often in a group where things are assigned all the time and everybody does their own piece, the whole group depends on everybody doing his or her piece at the right time and so there's no room for individuals to say "I am good at that but I don't want to do it any more, I want to do something else." ... We, from the first, talk about having options— all of us can do this or some of us can do that. Right from the beginning we try to instill that sense. Again this goes back to our empowering philosophy, it's not only okay to make a choice different from the group but it will be supported and encouraged if that's what a woman wants to do. So you see how that differentiating stage is really critical to our philosophy. (guide interview)

Responsibility

Robert Terry tells us, "Love needs to be clarified by responsibility ... that is, as long as I don't own up to my piece of the action, love is going to blur what's going on." Each person is responsible for who she is, how she behaves, and what she contributes. This is particularly important in the relationship of guides and participants because of the power difference between them.

Responsibility is a key value in this model. It is fostered by allowing participants to design what they want into the activities. Responsibility is also stressed in relation to how the guide models behavior, leads the group through the experience, and brings it to a close. It is central to the affirming-collective decision-making process and is apparent in the attitude that there is no single right way to do something. A guide told me:

> Everything is a possibility so I think that initially women respond to that by feeling a little cast adrift. They're not going to be told what to do all the time.... We're really reinforcing that women can do things already. They don't have to have instruction about every single thing in order to be able to operate in the woods. So they feel just a little bit like we're not guiding them but they come to realize, and they've commented on that too, that by the middle or end of the trip they've been talking among each other rather than just having participant-guide, guide-participant communication going on.

While there is a focus on participants learning to take responsibility for themselves, there is an equally strong emphasis on the guide's responsibility for her own actions and conducting herself in a manner that is appropriate to the situation. The key component in the leader taking responsibility is the recognition of how powerful a position she is in and the amount of influence a leader can have over members of the group.

One example of how influential the guide can be is in the use of language. Language sets the tone of the trip and influences how participants view their environment and how they react to situations. In essence, language shapes experience.

Since participants are encouraged to choose what constitutes their own challenge, success/failure language is avoided. Mary described an example related to a hiking trip:

> Language is critical. On the North Shore hiking trip, on Saturday, you have three options for hikes. There's a longer hike, a medium hike and a shorter hike. It's really important that when you describe the advantages and disadvantages of each you don't say there's an easy hike and a hard hike because then all of a sudden there's all this value judgement attached to the easy hike like it's taking the easy way out.

In addition, humor is used to try to counteract the use of negative terminology by participants. Mary related to me:

> You know, there are some people who are always dumping on themselves and we can contradict that in a real gentle way. Women learn about being wimps. That's a real common word ... so we say, "Yeah, you know, that stands for Women Improving Muscular Prowess." That just sort of diffuses that as a derogatory term.

The power of language is one example of the influence a guide can have on the atmosphere and tone of the trip. Responsibility then, for the guide, is acknowledging how influential her behavior can be and exercising that power in a manner that promotes individual choice, growth, and responsibility.

At the end of the trip experience, guides have a significant responsibility to perform closure on the trip in some way that is appropriate to that particular group: outright recognition and discussion of the fact that this adventure has come to an end, introducing the topic of returning home, and/or helping to integrate the experience into the guide's and participant's life by seeing the experience in context. The memory of the trip and the skills gained, both technical and personal, can be integrated into the person's life rather than the trip existing in memory as a circumscribed event. This integration is crucial to the development of authenticity, the alignment of truth and reality.

Conclusion

The journey with Woodswomen took us along a route that began and ended with the search for authenticity. Along the way, members of the group underwent various transformations as did the nature of group interaction. At each stage, the guide adapted her leadership style to the circumstance and, on each leg of the journey, ethical principles guided both the leader and the constituent interactions. These principles, upon which Woodswomen has based its program philosophy and approach to group leadership, provide the foundation for a successful group experience.

References

Mitten, D. (1985). A philosophical basis for a women's outdoor adventure program. *Journal of Experiential Education, 8*(2), 20–24.

Mitten, D. (undated). *Meeting the unknown: Women bonding in the wilderness.* Unpublished manuscript.

Terry, R. (1986). *Leadership—A preview of the seventh view.* Hubert Humphrey Institute of Public Affairs.

Terry, R. (1991). *Ethics for the 21st century and beyond.* Lecture broadcast on Minnesota Public Radio.

"Let's Go Round the Circle:" How Verbal Facilitation Can Function as a Means of Direct Instruction

▾ ▾ ▾

Mike Brown

In this chapter, the term facilitation refers to the act of conducting a verbal discussion prior to, or after an activity, with the aim of encouraging students to reflect on what will, or has been, learned from experiences. An overview of the role of the leader/facilitator, as advocated in some widely available adventure education texts, is discussed. This is followed by an outline of the methodological approach that guided the research project. The analysis section highlights how the leader was observed directing and orchestrating the direction of talk through the "common sense" and everyday ways of conducting verbal facilitation sessions. The primary focus of analysis is on the structure of the interaction in these sessions (i.e., a leader-initiated topic for discussion, a student reply, and leader evaluation of this response). Short excerpts of data are used to support and illustrate the claims that are made in regard to the nature of the interaction that is observed in these settings.

The Leader's Role in Conducting Verbal Facilitation Sessions

In much adventure education literature (Brackenreg, Luckner, & Pinch, 1994; Gass, 1990; Knapp, 1990; Luckner & Nadler, 1997; Priest & Gass, 1997; Quinsland & Van Ginkel, 1984) the leader is positioned in a manner that portrays her/him as a guide who assists the program

This chapter originally was published in the *Journal of Experiential Education*, with the following citation:
Brown, M. (2004)."Let's go round the circle:" How verbal facilitation can function as a means of direct instruction. *Journal of Experiential Education, 27*(2), 161–175.

participants in discovering their own meaning of an experience by providing an appropriate framework for discussions. Sugerman, Doherty, Garvey, and Gass (2000) consider that the role of the leader is to "set up an environment where learning through reflection can take place and all participants are able to understand the meaning of the experience for them" (p. 9). Others (Chapman, 1995; Joplin, 1995) maintain that the role for the leader is to help students make connections between an activity and other life situations so that experiences can be given meaning and be integrated into students' lives. In many of these accounts, the role of the leader is idealized, and s/he is seen as a neutral or background figure to the "real" action, which is the student reflecting on, and speaking of, his/her experiences. Chapman maintains that the leader's role is to give just enough assistance for students to be successful, but no more. He argues that if the approach is truly student-centered, students may not be aware the leader had a role at all. He suggests that leaders in adventure education are like coaches who "are largely removed from their roles as interpreters of reality, purveyors of truth, mediators between students and the world" (Chapman, p. 239). Spegel (1996) claims that the elicitation of student-generated responses, coupled with appropriate processing of the activity, allows adventure educators to move "beyond teacher-student rhetoric to enhance deep learning within students" (p. 30). The leader is frequently portrayed as a benevolent guide who is not actively, or at least overtly, involved in directing and orchestrating the student reflection and learning process. Students are apparently free to draw valid and meaningful conclusions from their own experiences.

While numerous commentators have remarked on the role of verbal processing and the leader's role in guiding student "self-discovery," several writers (Bell, 1993; Boud, 1997; Bowles, 1996; Brown, 2002a; Estes & Tomb, 1995) have questioned how verbal facilitation is enacted and how it positions the participants in these sessions. Boud claims that present conceptualizations of facilitation and the role of the facilitator are often based in notions of group relations training and are not sufficiently critically aware of the need to acknowledge diversity in the promotion of learning from experience. They are, he fears, too rooted in the "older humanistic notion of facilitation, or worse, direct instruction" (Boud, p. 1). Both Bell and Bowles express concerns regarding the position adopted in some texts that imply that participants are not "fit to give justice to their own potential" (Bowles, p. 11) and therefore they need prompting by the leader to achieve certain outcomes. Estes and Tomb state that the increasing emphasis on leader-directed processing in adventure education may be devaluing both the learning experience and the promotion of self-reliance among participants. They suggest that over-processing can be problematic as it is the leader rather than the student who decides what was learned and its relative value. They do not doubt the importance of facilitating an experience in order to assist the transfer of learning, but they question how this should occur. Similarly, Proudman (1995) suggests that the leader may take too active a role in achieving particular outcomes:

How interested is the teacher in guaranteeing a certain student outcome? Too often, teachers allow their unconscious conditioning to interfere with opportunities for student self-discovery. (p. 243)

Brown (2002a) argues that the physical structuring of sitting in a circle, and the pre-allocation of student turns at speaking, creates a formal turn-taking system where there are limited options for students to make contributions that fall outside of the topic determined by the leader. In a more recent paper, Brown, (2003) argues that the use of leader paraphrases or summaries of student responses acts as a means to allow the leader to "fix" what the student really meant. In paraphrasing the student's response the leader has a powerful mechanism to articulate a preferred version of events.

What is apparent from a brief review of the literature is the fact that the leader/facilitator has an important role in the facilitation of students' reflection and articulation of their experiences. Irrespective of whether the leader's role is placed in the foreground or cast in the shadows, with little reference to his/her involvement in this student-centered approach to learning, it is only through a detailed study of actual interaction that we can better understand the potential consequences of our individual and collective actions as leaders.

Methodological Approach

Ethnomethodological studies focus on the common-sense and routine knowledge(s) used by participants as they interact in social activities. In examining how people use language in the ongoing process of social interaction, ethnomethodology focuses on understanding the actions that result from talk (Baker, 1997). By examining the common-sense and routine knowledge(s) employed by the participants in these sessions, attention is drawn to how the leader both enables and constrains students to speak about their experiences. Heap (1990) maintains that the importance of ethnomethodological studies is that they can inform us about the structures of phenomena and the consequences of those structures for realizing the leader's ends and objectives. The knowledge that is derived from such studies can therefore make a difference as to how practice is organized, on both a personal and collective level (Heap, 1990). The discussion generated may inform educators regarding the decision to continue or modify current facilitation practices. A detailed analysis of interaction reveals whether it is the student's unmodified contribution, or the leader's version of what is "really" meant, which is admitted as contextually appropriate knowledge. For a detailed explanation of ethnomethodology the reader may wish to consult the following texts: Baker, 1997; Garfinkel, 1967; Heritage, 1984; Maynard and Clayman, 1991.

The data presented for analysis are drawn from transcripts of facilitation sessions that were recorded as part of a larger research project (Brown, 2002b). The students were year-nine boys

(14 years of age) from an Australian independent (private) school. Each group consisted of approximately 15 students and two leaders. The students were participating in a four-day program as part of the school's standard curriculum. The program consisted of a two-day river journey in canoes, and two days of activities at the school's residential camp. Activities in close proximity to the camp included rock climbing, participation on ropes course elements, and a day walk. Most, if not all, of these students had previously participated in the school's sequential outdoor education program. The leaders were specialist outdoor education teachers employed by the school. Both leaders were males. All participants agreed to participate in the study and were aware that the discussions were being recorded. The specific focus of the program was to encourage teamwork by providing activities that required co-operation and communication. Apart from the researcher's presence, no modifications to a "normal" program were enacted. The researcher acted as a participant observer but did not contribute to the discussions.

Analysis

Space constraints do not permit inclusion of the "excerpts" used in the analysis. However, for specific examples of the extracts used in this study, please refer to Table A1 in the Appendix. The transcripts are transcribed according to the notations developed by Jefferson (Hutchby & Wooffitt, 1998). (See Table A2 in the Appendix for notations used in this study.)

Establishment of Topic: Initiation Phase

At the commencement of each facilitation session, the leaders and students assembled and sat in a circle formation. Following any preliminary comments the leader would introduce the topic for discussion and call upon the students to respond. (See Appendix Table A1, *Extracts 1-4*, for examples of leader introductions to these discussions.)

In each of these openings to a discussion, the leader clearly articulated the basis on which the students were to respond. The "rightness" or issue of "best practice" in determining the topic for discussion is obviously open to debate. The important point is *how* these sessions were introduced and framed. The leader's initiation of a particular topic constrains the range of replies that the students may reasonably make. In carefully stipulating boundaries of the topic for discussion in these settings the leader is employing a strategy used by teachers in classrooms that functions to address two central issues in instructional interaction: (a) the leader's concern in getting the right answer from the student, and (b) the student's concern in getting the answer right (French & MacLure, 1979). Our attention will now turn to how the leader responds to student replies.

Leader Evaluations of the Student Replies

The leader responds to the student's reply to the topic for the discussion in a number of clearly identifiable ways. The leader accepts the student's contribution by issuing a straightforward evaluation such as "okay" (see Table A1, *Extract 5*, turns 91 & 93, in the Appendix). In some replies the leader is a little more tentative (i.e., "okay; that's pretty appropriate"). (See *Extract 6*, Table A1 in the Appendix.)

The leader also responds to the student's contribution by paraphrasing or formulating what the student has said (for a detailed discussion of the use of paraphrases, see Brown, 2003). The use of paraphrases or formulations as a means to fix meaning is well established in studies of conversational interaction (Heritage & Watson, 1979, 1980). In formulating the "real" meaning of the students' replies the leader is able to confirm what is relevant for the students in this setting. The student reply provides a resource, particulars of which the leader can either choose to ignore or extend, and treat as newsworthy. Young (1984) argues that in instructional settings, "the formulating practices involved seem aimed less at making the pupil's meanings clearer than at shaping them to conform to the teacher's view" (p. 236). Through the act of formulating the student reply, the leader is in a position to announce what all the students will be held accountable to now know (Baker, 1991a; Heyman, 1986). Formulations also function as a useful mechanism to avoid having to issue a negative evaluation of the student reply. By modifying the student's reply into a more appropriate response in his formulation, the leader is able to correct the student's position without overtly disagreeing with him. In this way, facilitation appears to be a positive experience for both parties. However, as Young (1984) so aptly states:

> We have a practice which, while forming as much a part of the teacher's contribution to
> the dialogue as teacher monologue, passes itself off as a version of the pupil's contribu-
> tion. As such it appears to play a central role in managing the active participation of
> pupils in the verbal appropriation by them of the teacher's "knowledge" in a natural and
> orderly but essentially hidden manner. (p. 235)

What is clear is that the use of a formulation provides the formulator, in this case the leader, with a powerful means to shape the direction of the talk and maintain control over the sense of what is meant (Heritage & Watson, 1979).

The Use of the Initiation-Reply-Evaluation Sequence (I-R-E)

Studies of classrooms, and other sites where instruction occurs, have identified the pervasive use of the *initiation-reply-evaluation* (I-R-E) sequence of interaction between the teacher and students (Baker, 1991b; Heap, 1985; MacBeth, 2000; McHoul, 1978; Mehan, 1979, 1985; Sinclair & Coulthard, 1975). Baker and Freebody (1989) have argued that the I-R-E sequence is the defining form of teacher-student talk. The use of the three-part interactional I-R-E sequence—leader question→student reply→leader evaluation—is the basis for leader-student dialogue in these facilitation sessions. The initiation component need not be explicitly stated at the beginning of each new student turn as it is contained in the leader's opening address at the beginning of the session. Regardless of whether or not the evaluation phase takes the form of a "simple acceptance" ("okay; great") or an extended sequence involving the use of a formulation, the three-part sequence underpins the interaction and is central to understanding how social order is constructed in these settings.

The role of the I-R-E format in educational settings has been extensively discussed in studies of instructional interaction (Baker, 1991b; Heap, 1985; MacBeth, 2000; McHoul, 1978; Mehan, 1979, 1985; Sinclair & Coulthard, 1975). MacBeth (2000) describes this three-part sequence as the "workhorse of direct instruction" (p. 37), while Heap (1983) argues that this three-part sequence is associated with a discourse format that has the task specific use and the pedagogic aim of instruction.

The pervasiveness of the I-R-E sequence can be understood in relation to its role as a device to control student participation and to regulate the construction of knowledge based on the leader's interpretation of contextually appropriate replies (Baker, 1991a). Central to this sequence is the leader's ability to set the topic or pose the question in the introduction. Of particular importance for facilitators of group discussions is an understanding of the role that establishing a question, as a basis for discussion, plays in eliciting particular replies. The request for students to reply to a question is, as Baker and Freebody (1993) state, a "powerful device for directing talk, perhaps even more powerful than a lecture, since students are asked to participate in and legitimate their positioning through questions" (p. 283).

While it is the leader who produces the topic for discussion and certifies the adequacy of the student reply, the students must provide a response in the I-R-E format (Heap, 1985). In providing responses to a topic set by the leader, the students are participating in the accomplishment of a social order (Baker, 1991a). While this is a collaborative production, it does not mitigate the asymmetrical relations that exist in reference to the distribution of knowledge, or more particularly the leader's "knowledge" of the appropriate knowledge that can be produced. By evaluating the student's reply the leader is demonstrating his claim to knowing the "right" answer (Pomerantz, 1984). The leader's ability to evaluate student replies is premised on asking the types of questions to which s/he can reasonably be expected to know the answers; a phenomena which Mehan (1985) describes as the "ubiquity of known-information questions in educational discourse" (p. 127). Stubbs (1983) argues that questioners may ask questions that appear to be asking a student for her/his personal view, when the questioner really has a particular answer in mind. The asking of questions to which the questioner already knows the answer are described as "test" (Baker, 1991b) or "pseudo questions" (Stubbs, 1983) and are distinguished from "real" questions where the questioner is genuinely in search of an answer to a question to which he does not know the answer. In these sessions, the leader asks a series of pseudo-questions on which s/he apparently considers her/himself knowledgeable and therefore is in a position to evaluate the appropriateness of the student reply.

> Teachers' questions are essentially tests of pupils' ability and willingness to move to-
> wards the "official" frame of reference, and what pupils say "has meaning" in the context
> of some body of school knowledge which excludes or transforms what is "irrelevant."
> (Edwards, 1980 p. 248)

The leader's evaluations of students' replies repeatedly reaffirms her/his claim to superior knowledge which, in turn, forms the basis of the knowledge that is produced and admitted
as appropriate in the ensuing discussion. As in other institutions (courts, medical consultations)
the talk in these facilitation sessions is organized to produce a single outcome where the leader's
expert knowledge or claim to prior knowledge warrants closing the talk when that outcome
has been achieved (Edwards, 1980).

The manner in which facilitation is conducted in these settings is similar in form to the
recursive chain of three-part sequences that Drew and Heritage (1992) identified in classroom
instruction. The use of this recursive chain permits the leader and students to collaboratively
build a list of items/values/knowledge(s) that are valued in this setting. In her/his setting of the
topic, the leader establishes the *grid of specifications* for student contributions that functions as
a "wish list" for student replies. Through the ongoing talk the students add items/values/ knowl-
edge(s) that meet the leader's criteria of appropriateness. Through the use of this format the participants are constructing a list of sought-after items, or more particularly, a series of lists of
valued knowledge(s).

While the author has argued that the use of the I-R-E sequence in facilitation serves an
instructional purpose, it also performs a role in the acculturation of students (Baker, 1991a).
Hammersley (1977) makes a similar point when he states that in instructional settings the students, or at least most of them, have learned a form of interaction in which authority and knowledge are bound together. The students "are being socialized into a world in which knowledge
is something known by those 'in authority'" (Hammersley, 1977 p. 83). Young (1984) takes a
stronger position arguing that this three-part format has a "number of features which appear
more consistent with indoctrination than education" (p. 223).

In using the I-R-E format, the leader is able to evaluate the adequacy of a student's reply
and, if necessary, work with the student to produce a modified version of the initial response that
fulfills the criteria for adequacy. This instructional format allows the leader to diagnose the student's (in)competencies as a learner, and if necessary, to instruct her/him through the introduction of more contextually appropriate resources that assist her/him in providing an acceptable
reply. This conceptualization of student-leader interaction is based on an understanding of the
student as being incompetent and not yet able to understand the "real meaning" therefore
requiring the input from the leader to achieve competence (French & MacLure, 1979). The paradox of *competent leader–not yet competent student* interaction is realized in the conflict between

the leader's need to treat the student as sufficiently competent to interpret the requirements of the topic but also as incompetent in regard to her/his ability to provide a contextually appropriate response (MacKay, 1974). In the use of formulations, the leader can be seen to be correcting or modifying the student response so that the student is led to the "right" answer. The paradox of the *competent-incompetent* learner in the adventure education context is alluded to by Bowles (1996). He argues that the form of adventure facilitation advocated in many texts implies that participants in programs are "not fit to give justice to their potential; they must be helped, prompted by 'heteronomous' agents and stimuli, forced if necessary" (p. 11). Hovelynck (1999) has also expressed the concern that facilitators may take too active a role in passing on their own meaning that is to be attached to an activity.

Conclusion

A close reading of interaction from facilitation sessions reveals the mechanisms by which the leader can control these discussions. The analysis challenges practitioners and theorists alike to move beyond current practices and develop new ways in which to allow students to articulate their learning. If, as the author contends, verbal facilitation sessions permit the leader to accept, reject, or modify student contributions, it is pertinent to ask—how is student experience positioned in an approach to facilitation that is structured around the three-part I-R-E sequence? The analysis indicates that by using this form of verbal facilitation the apparent uniqueness of the student's experience turns out to be a managed social accomplishment (Perakyla & Silverman, 1991). As in the more formal classroom setting, facilitators run the risk of not exploring student experience in favor of shaping the student's reply into "the right answer" rather than exploring the student's thinking (Hammersley, 1977). As in studies of classroom interaction, the apparently student-centered talk in facilitation sessions does not mean that the student's knowledge is necessarily valued (Baker & Freebody, 1989). The practice of employing students' knowledge and feelings about various topics/events appears to personalize learning, and renders instruction more student-centered. It has been suggested that the use of such techniques, in what is essentially a leader directed discussion, may only serve to expand the legislative boundaries of instruction into personal and social areas of the student's life (Baker & Freebody, 1989). Thus, the apparent primacy of the learner's experience and the role of the leader advocated in much adventure education literature may not accurately reflect practice, or at least practice when verbal facilitation is conducted where the leader is in a position to set the topic for discussion and evaluate student replies.

How facilitation sessions are structured is a key issue for adventure educators. If instruction is the aim of a particular session (e.g., how to fit a harness), then there is nothing essentially wrong with using the I-R-E format. If, however, adventure educators wish to provide opportunities for students to express and articulate learning that reflects their lived experience, they may wish to explore other ways to facilitate this learning. Perhaps it is time for a more critical consideration of some of the assumptions that underpin current practice. The author has presented a case that suggests that in verbal facilitation sessions there is the opportunity for the establishment of knowledge and power relationships that are in opposition to the claimed aims of experiential educators. It is not suggested that the consequences of these actions are intended by practitioners. However, adventure educators face the danger by not critically examining their practice, of perpetuating a social order in which one member can determine the meaning of experiences for others. What this article *does* reinforce is that adventure education theorists cannot accept conceptions of the leader that idealize him/her as being a neutral, or background figure, who is of little or no consequence to student's self-discovery through experience. It is also argued that students are not necessarily free to draw valid and meaningful conclusions from their own experiences.

Why is it that, as leaders, we consider it necessary to *re-voice* what a student has already said, other than to fix or change the meaning in some way? Why do we feel the need to call on students to answer a question of our choosing and then evaluate the appropriateness of their reply? Whose learning is favored in these sessions and, more importantly, what is being learned? Are we engaging in word games in facilitation sessions or the enculturation of students into our world view? Boud (1997) succinctly summarizes many of these concerns in his call for consideration of the broader context in which facilitation upon an activity takes place:

> "Who establishes the activity for whom?" is often the most fundamental question to be considered. If it is initiated by members of dominant social groups for those that are not members of dominant groups there is inevitably the risk that reflection will merely add to oppressive activities which exist and not expose or confront them. The most likely outcome will be compliance, in which participants go through the motions of reflection without revealing (sometimes even to themselves) what are the real learning issues. (p. 6)

This paper has "problematized" and raised questions in regards to currently observed facilitation practices. The hope is that this article will encourage practitioners and theorists to examine the basis of their actions, actions that if left unquestioned may have unintended consequences for our students. Having highlighted the potential for verbal facilitation to act as a vehicle for direct instruction, one challenge is to move beyond leader-directed approaches, and find new ways in which students can "remain the 'agents' of their experience and their learning" (Hovelynck, 1999 p. 22). The other challenge is to continually critique and reflect on facilitation as it is enacted to ensure that the theory and practice of facilitation continually inform each other in meaningful ways.

References

Baker, C. (1991a). Literacy practices and social relations in classroom reading events. In C. Baker & A. Luke (Eds.), *Towards a critical sociology of reading pedagogy* (pp. 161–188). Amsterdam: John Benjamins.

Baker, C. (1991b). Reading the texts of reading lessons. *Australian Journal of Reading, 14*(1), 5–20.

Baker, C. (1997). Ethnomethodological studies of talk in educational settings. In B. Davies & D. Corson (Eds.), *Encyclopedia of language and education* (Vol. 3 Oral discourse and education, pp. 43–52). Dordrecht, Netherlands: Kluwer Academic.

Baker, C., & Freebody, P. (1989). Talk around text: Constructions of textual and teacher authority in classroom discourse. In S. de Castell, A. Luke, & C. Luke (Eds.), *Language, authority and criticism: Readings on the school textbook* (pp. 263–283). London: Falmer.

Baker, C., & Freebody, P. (1993). The crediting of literate competence in classroom talk. *The Australian Journal of Literacy, 16*(4), 279–294.

Bell, M. (1993). What constitutes experience? Rethinking theoretical assumptions. *Journal of Experiential Education, 16*(1), 19–24.

Boud, D. (1997). *Reflection as a catalyst for change.* Paper presented at the Tenth National Outdoor Education Conference, Sydney, Australia.

Bowles, S. (1996). Techniques and philosophy. *The Journal of Adventure Education and Outdoor Leadership, 13*(2), 7–19.

Brackenreg, M., Luckner, J. L., & Pinch, K. (1994). Essential skills for processing adventure experiences. *Journal of Experiential Education, 17*(3), 45–47.

Brown, M. (2002a). The facilitator as gatekeeper: A critical analysis of social order in facilitation sessions. *Journal of Adventure Education and Outdoor Learning, 2*(2), 101–112.

Brown, M. (2002b). *Interaction and social order in adventure education facilitation sessions.* Unpublished doctoral dissertation, University of Queensland, Brisbane, Australia.

Brown, M. (2003). Paraphrases and summaries: A means of clarification or a vehicle for articulating a preferred version of student accounts? *Australian Journal of Outdoor Education, 7*(2), 25–35.

Chapman, S. (1995). What is the question? In K. Warren, M. Sakofs, & J. S. Hunt, Jr. (Eds.), *The theory of experiential education* (3rd ed., pp. 236–239). Dubuque, IA: Kendall/Hunt.

Drew, P., & Heritage, J. (1992). Analyzing talk at work: An introduction. In P. Drew & J. Heritage (Eds.), *Talk at work: Interaction in institutional settings* (pp. 3–65). Cambridge, England: Cambridge University Press.

Edwards, A. D. (1980). Patterns of power and authority in classroom talk. In P. Woods (Ed.), *Teacher strategies: Explorations in the sociology of the school* (pp. 237–253). London: Croom Helm.

Estes, C. A., & Tomb, S. (1995). *Is cheese food really food? a.k.a. Some conscious alternatives to overprocessing experience.* Paper presented at the 1995 International Conference on Outdoor Recreation and Education. (ERIC Document Reproduction Service No. ED 404 080)

French, P., & MacLure, M. (1979). Getting the right answer and getting the answer right. *Research in Education, 22*, 1–23.

Garfinkel, H. (1967). *Studies in ethnomethodology.* Englewood Cliffs, NJ: Prentice-Hall.

Gass, M. A. (1990). Transfer of learning in adventure education. In J. C. Miles & S. Priest (Eds.), *Adventure education* (pp. 199–208). State College, PA: Venture.

Hammersley, M. (1977). School learning: The cultural resources required by pupils to answer a teacher's question. In P. Woods & M. Hammersley (Eds.), *School experience: Explorations in the sociology of education* (pp. 57–86). London: Croom Helm.

Heap, J. L. (1983). Dialogue: Interpretations of "What do you mean?" *Curriculum Inquiry, 13*(4), 397–417.

Heap, J. L. (1985). Discourse in the production of classroom knowledge: Reading lessons. *Curriculum Inquiry, 15*, 245–279.

Heap, J. L. (1990). Applied ethnomethodology: Looking for the local rationality of reading activities. *Human Studies, 13*, 39–72.

Heritage, J. C. (1984). *Garfinkel and ethnomethodology*. Cambridge, England: Polity Press.

Heritage, J. C., & Watson, D. R. (1979). Formulations as conversational objects. In G. Psathas (Ed.), *Everyday language studies in ethnomethodology* (pp. 123–162). New York: Irvington.

Heritage, J. C., & Watson, D. R. (1980). Aspects of the properties of formulations in natural conversations: Some instances analysed. *Semiotica, 30*(3/4), 245–262.

Heyman, R. D. (1986). Formulating topic in the classroom. *Discourse Processes, 9*, 37–55.

Hovelynck, J. (1999). Facilitating the development of generative metaphors: Re-emphasizing participants' guiding images. *Australian Journal of Outdoor Education, 4*(1), 12–24.

Hutchby, I., & Wooffitt, R. (1998). *Conversation analysis: Principles, practices, and applications*. Malden, MA: Polity Press.

Joplin, L. (1995). On defining experiential education. In K. Warren, M. Sakofs, & J. Hunt, Jr. (Eds.), *The theory of experiential education* (3rd ed., pp. 15–22). Dubuque, IA: Kendall/Hunt.

Knapp, C. E. (1990). Processing the adventure experience. In J. C. Miles & S. Priest (Eds.), *Adventure education* (pp. 189–198). State College, PA: Venture.

Luckner, J. L., & Nadler, R. S. (1997). *Processing the experience: Strategies to enhance and generalize learning* (2nd ed.). Dubuque, IA: Kendall/Hunt.

MacBeth, D. (2000). Classrooms as installations. In S. Hester & D. W. Francis (Eds.), *Local educational order: Ethnomethodological studies of knowledge in action* (Vol. 73, pp. 21–71). Amsterdam: John Benjamins.

MacKay, R. (1974). Conceptions of children and models of socialisation. In R. Turner (Ed.), *Ethnomethodology*. Harmondsworth, England: Penguin.

Maynard, D. W., & Clayman, S. E. (1991). The diversity of ethnomethodology. *Annual Review of Sociology, 17*, 385–418.

McHoul, A. W. (1978). The organization of turns at formal talk in the classroom. *Language in Society, 7*, 183–213.

Mehan, H. (1979). *Learning lessons: Social organization in the classroom*. Cambridge, MA: Harvard University Press.

Mehan, H. (1985). The structure of classroom discourse. In T. A. Van Dijk (Ed.), *Handbook of discourse analysis* (Vol. 3, pp. 120–131). London: Academic Press.

Perakyla, A., & Silverman, D. (1991). Owning experience: Describing the experience of other persons. *Text, 11*(3), 441–480.

Pomerantz, A. (1984). Agreeing and disagreeing with assessments: Some features of preferred/dispreferred turn shapes. In J. M. Atkinson & J. Heritage (Eds.), *Structures of social action: Studies in conversation analysis* (pp. 57–101). Cambridge, England: Cambridge University Press.

Priest, S., & Gass, M. A. (1997). *Effective leadership in adventure programming*. Champaign, IL: Human Kinetics.

Proudman, B. (1995). Experiential education as emotionally engaged learning. In K. Warren, M. Sakofs, & J. S. Hunt, Jr. (Eds.), *The theory of experiential education* (3rd ed., pp. 240–247). Dubuque, IA: Kendall/Hunt.

Quinsland, L. K., & Van Ginkel, A. (1984). How to process experience. *Journal of Experiential Education, 7*(2), 8–13.

Sinclair, J. M., & Coulthard, R. M. (1975). *Towards an analysis of discourse: The English used by teachers and pupils.* London: Oxford University Press.

Spegel, N. (1996). Lawyers learning to survive: The application of adventure-based learning to skills development. *Journal of Professional Legal Education, 14*(1), 25–50.

Stubbs, M. (1983). *Language, schools and classrooms* (2nd ed.). London: Methuen.

Sugerman, D. A., Doherty, K. L., Garvey, D. E., & Gass, M. A. (2000). *Reflective learning: Theory and practice.* Dubuque, IA: Kendall/Hunt.

Young, R. E. (1984). Teaching equals indoctrination: The dominant epistemic practices or our schools. *British Journal of Educational Studies, 22*(3), 220–238.

Appendix

Table A1.
Sample Extracts of Leader Introductions to Discussion

Extract 1

| 1 | L | … we want <u>each</u> person (0.3) to say (0.8) one (0.7) short (0.7) <u>clear</u> (0.7) statement … I want it to be something that's going to be <u>essential</u> (0.8) for (0.4) this group for us (0.8) to have a successful day today (1.5) what do we need … each person needs to say (0.9) something different (1.7) a'right (0.6) and it has to be something to do with our group (0.2) … you need to say why that's important for the group (1.5).… |

Extract 2

| 274 | L | I just want to ah (.) go round the circle one more time (2.0) an' ah I know this is taking a little while but (.) I'm (0.8) quite impressed with (.) the ah discussion that we've had (1.8) I want you to (3.8) <u>tell me</u> (.) what benefit the <u>school</u> is going to get from you having been here for the two days that you've been here so far (1.0) …(0.8) <u>how</u> does the school benefit so this really probably why the school (1.0) why you think the school is running the program now … |

Extract 3

| 1 | L | um (0.7) what I would like you to do is to (1.4) have a good think about today (3.2) and I want you to (1.0) think of <u>one</u> thing (0.8) that people <u>did</u> today or that they did well today (0.8) that would help make the rest of this week (0.8) or for that matter next week (0.5) when you're not canoeing and rock climbing or next term or next year (1.2) or next month at home or (0.8) just something that would make things go better for you (1.3) so things that you saw <u>people</u> (0.8) not just one person doing (1.0) things that you saw people doing that would <u>help</u> things go better (2.0)… |

Table A1. (continued)

Extract 4

104　L　… guys those <u>are</u> (0.5) all fantastic (0.5) bits of feedback for you guys (0.8) um (.) that you've said about yourselves and that's really good (0.8) what I want you to do now (1.2) is ah (.) ha have a really good think (0.8) and think of (.) something that's like one of those things (.) that you could do <u>next</u> week (1.2) to make <u>next</u> week a bit better (1.4)…

Extract 5

90　S1　um (0.5) like people sharing food and stuff (1.2) like (0.4) making dinner a whole lot easier (2.0) so everyone could enjoy a good dinner (1.0)

91　L　okay (2.4)

92　S2　um um (1.4) just the (0.5) ah everyone (1.3) um doing the work without being (0.8) told (1.7) like (0.8) a couple of times (3.2)

93　L　okay (3.1)

Extract 6

16　S1　I'm Len um (1.5) so (.5) teach us about the bush and have fun stuff

17　L　okay so teach ya <u>how</u> to have fun

　　S1　Yeah

18

19　L　okay (1.5) that that's pretty appropriate (2.0)

Table A2.
Examples of Transcript Notations

(0.6)	Number in brackets indicates a pause in tenths of a second.
(.)	A dot enclosed in brackets indicates a pause in talk of less than two-tenths of a second.
=	The equals sign indicates "latching" between utterances.
[ ]	Square brackets between adjacent lines of concurrent talk indicate the onset and end of overlapping talk.
(unclear)	Words within brackets indicate difficulty in accurate transcription. This is the transcriber's best guess at an unclear utterance.
<u>Under</u>	Underlined words indicate speaker emphasis.

Note. Based on notations developed by Jefferson (Hutchby & Wooffitt, 1998).

Social Justice

▾ ▾ ▾

A Call for Race, Gender, & Class-Sensitive Facilitation in Outdoor Experiential Education

▾ ▾ ▾

Karen Warren

Josh Miner, one of the founders of Outward Bound in the U.S., said in the early 1960s,

> Outward Bound has made a great effort to achieve the social "mix" which makes each
> student confront the universality of his [sic] human nature. The schools take the Iowa
> farm-boy and billet him with a San Francisco lawyer's son. They take the heir to a Boston
> fortune and let him paddle with the son of an Arizona Indian. They take the son of a Mis-
> sissippi "poor white" and let him share a litter handle with a boy from the streets of
> Harlem. (1970, p. 204)

As Outward Bound and other experiential education programs begin to become more inclusive of different social groups either through the changing demographics of the U.S. population or the more successful efforts by programs to recruit women/girls, racial minorities, and economically disadvantaged students, a strong imperative for facilitators to be trained in socially just leadership emerges.

Experiential education facilitation is an essential component of the learning cycle. As the field seeks to move away from the power dominance of the white, male, class-privileged,

This chapter originally was published in the *Journal of Experiential Education*, with the following citation:
Warren, K. (1998). A call for race, gender, and class sensitive facilitation in outdoor experiential education. *Journal of Experiential Education, 21*(1), 21–25.

European roots of experiential education (James, 1996), facilitators will need to become more conscious of how their methods can advance or impede social justice. This article will critically examine current philosophies of facilitation in experiential education in an attempt to unveil opportunities for leaders to use more culturally sensitive methods in teaching, training, and counseling. How the uncritical use of methods prevents more equitable outdoor experiential education will be shown. Several of Kurt Hahn's philosophies of practice will be critiqued to show how experiential educators can be analytical about accepted practice in light of social justice. Finally, suggestions about research and practice needed to influence the field of experiential education on social justice issues will be given. Although I will look specifically at outdoor leadership, ideas in this paper will be pertinent to facilitators of other experience-based pursuits.

Limitations of a Methods Approach

In asking facilitators to use socially and culturally sensitive facilitation, we must be acutely aware of the limitations of a methods approach to experiential education. In her insightful article, "Beyond the Methods Fetish: Toward a Humanizing Pedagogy," Lilia Bartolome (1994) cautions against the uncritical use of teaching methods, particularly with students from subordinated cultures. Practitioners who are very proud of their expanding bag of tricks often adopt methods without scrutinizing them for their suitability to oppressed groups.

The current practice of experiential education is in jeopardy of having a highly developed body of methods without the accompanying analysis of how such methodology can contribute to, or impede, social justice. Bartolome urges "a shift from a narrow and mechanistic view of instruction to one that is broader in scope and takes into consideration the socio-historical and political dimensions of education" (p. 176).

Method Traps

I have identified several traps I have seen experiential educators fall into in their uncritical use of methods, especially as it pertains to diversity work.

The "One-Size-Fits-All" Method

The delusive belief that there are generic methods that will work for everyone in a group persists when educators view their learning communities as homogenous groups of students with similar needs. Certainly, a "one-size-fits-all" method of experiential education is simpler to use and seemingly more efficient, but it fails to acknowledge the social differences that exist in every group.

Several authors have shown how the one-size-fits-all method may not be suitable for women's experience. Mack (1996) critiques the current use of metaphors in outdoor experiential education. She maintains that the common practice of using imposed metaphors with clients isn't effective with women. Instead, Mack suggests that metaphors derived from women's own experience be used and that the locus of power in facilitation be transferred to the participant. She concludes by warning against a one-size-fits-all approach even within groups of women,

If an outdoor instructor plans to implement derived metaphoric constructs, it must be acknowledged that the use of metaphors is not appropriate for everyone. Since metaphors require the use of language and not everyone feels comfortable expressing themselves through words and discussion, not all women will respond to the abstract form of metaphor creation.

Rohde (1996) questions the dominant program model of stress challenge for use with female incest survivors. Extrapolated from this work is the question of whether the one-size-fits-all method of facilitating stress challenge experience works well with participants from other oppressed groups. For example, "at risk" youth (who tend to be kids of color in many programs) may respond to stress with instinctive and conditioned behaviors that are counterproductive to their growth. Similar questions need to be asked when the temptation to use a generic method for other subordinated groups arises.

Rote Methods

Programs that run many groups of students through a standard curriculum often fall into this trap. Stagnation is the foe of inclusive programming. The use of ropes courses where instructors use routine teaching progressions and "tried and true" methods is an example of this trap. A repetitious use of the tools of experiential education can cause facilitators to be unthinking or mechanistic in the application of their bag of tricks. Formulaic methods familiar to the facilitator but unexamined as to their cultural appropriateness are problematic.

The most profound example of my own use of rote methods occurred a few years ago with a class I was teaching on women and girls in the outdoors. I decided to use the Spider's Web initiative to build group-bonding and problem-solving skills. As I advanced through my standard safety and educational framing of the activity, I expected outcomes similar to those I had seen for years of using this initiative. Instead, women stood unmoving in front of the web, courageously beginning to speak. As the women assessed the many sized holes in the web, they spoke of conflicting feelings about their bodies and how the initiative would separate them rather than bring them together (Warren, 1996). It was a poignant reminder that accepted methods must be constantly opened to critical examination.

Separating Technique From Theory

Rohnke & Butler (1995) remind adventure experiential educators to "Recognize that your leadership expertise is equally valuable as a burgeoning bag of adventure activities" (p. 4). Methods of facilitation that lack theoretical validation are empty attempts to practice without a sound grounding. This trap is particularly pertinent in cultural diversity work as facilitators attempt to "do the right thing" without an understanding of their own biases or the current anti-bias work theories. Facilitators need training not only in techniques but, more importantly, about the social and cultural backgrounds of their participants and the way their locations in privilege or marginality affect how they teach and facilitate.

For instance, in order to understand the dynamics of a mixed race outdoor program, facilitators need to understand current theories on racial identity development (Tatum, 1997). I have witnessed white facilitators, in the name of inclusivity, break up small groups of students of color who are interacting positively with each other on a course. These facilitators fail to understand that the racial identity development stage of the students of color encourages the students to seek out others who are like them for support.

Choosing Experiences Before Goals

Experiential educators are often exposed to compelling and provocative methods that they are drawn to use due to their novelty or by the fact that the experience was a formative, life-impacting event at one time for them. The result is that the facilitator tries to work that experiential event into the curriculum without regard to the goals of the class or group. For example, outdoor instructors may want to use an overnight solo experience in the curriculum because solos had a particularly powerful impact on them when they were outdoor program students. Or an outdoor leader planning a weekend trip decides the activities and location of the trip before considering what the participants should get out of the trip. This cart-before-the-horse way of creating experiential education curriculum is commonplace. I have often seen educators propose very creative and intense experiential methods that were ultimately contrary to the intentions of their facilitation for that segment of the course or group experience.

With regard to socially just facilitation, the way educators experience the world might be different from their students from oppressed social groups. To use experiences that are important to facilitators but alienating to students who have different norms and behavioral expectations supports this methods trap. As Marchesani & Adams (1992) point out, "Differences in culture or gender are still viewed in relation to the dominant ideas and contributions of those that have traditionally set standards and defined norms of participation" (p. 15).

Social and Cultural Awareness in Facilitation

Facilitators can unveil and articulate the cultural facets of their programs. For instance, the compass was invented by the Chinese; the kayak developed from Inuit skin boats; and many elements of the rope course (e.g., the Burma bridge) are the functional solutions to real-life challenges of people from other cultures.

Facilitation must take into account the linguistic habits of students in relation to their race, class, gender, age and ethnic origin (Shore, 1986). For example, facilitation methods must account for the fact that men use more of the available air time in a discussion than women

(Van Nostrand, 1993), and boys' contributions to dialogue are praised, challenged, and generally validated more highly than girls' (Sadker & Sadker, 1994). Facilitators trained in gender responsiveness will be more able to create equitable sharing in mixed groups. Also, students of other cultures may use more non-verbal ways of knowing and processing experiences (see Delpit, 1995); therefore, facilitators need training to take these differences into account.

Several pillars of Kurt Hahn's educational philosophy that have influenced the outdoor adventure field could be reexamined. Hahn's ideas of service and self-reliance have traditionally set the tone for outdoor experiences, but it may be time to take a new look at these philosophies.

Rethinking Service

Service to the community was one of the pillars of Hahn's educational philosophy that has been maintained to varying extents in experiential education programs today. Robert Greenleaf's (1977) model of servant leadership continues to inform the work of many involved experiential educators. Yet a critical look at how the concept of service is manifested with less-privileged groups reveals some troubling dilemmas.

For racial minorities, particularly African Americans, servitude has a profoundly troublesome history associated with slavery. As bell hooks (1994) points out, this servant-served paradigm has implications for the contemporary dynamics between blacks and whites. To require African Americans to aspire to servant leadership may be antithetical to the harsh realities of their involuntary service in the U.S. that still goes on today in more subtle forms.

For economically less-advantaged students, the existence of a service economy, supported by the work of their families and friends, leads many such students to question the implicit value of service learning. Class issues have been the least recognized of social justice issues in the outdoors. One of Hahn's original educational precepts was to "free the children of rich and influential parents from the paralyzing influence of wealth and privilege" (Ewald, 1970, p. 37). The challenge now is how to include poor and working classes in outdoor adventure, as well as developing class sensitivity about service on courses.

For women, the role of service to others is an encultured part of their everyday lives. To set up programs that focus entirely on service to the outside community then becomes a perpetuation of a role that, while it may be familiar to women, may not offer the greatest avenues for growth. Experiential education facilitators might better be conscious of creating experiences to assist women in learning to be of service to themselves.

While I do not believe that facilitators should discard the idea of service from their programs, I believe the experiential education community needs to critically analyze how service is framed and carried out.

Rethinking Self-Reliance

Another of Hahn's major tenets of educational thought was the development of self-reliance in students. In the U.S., the idea of rugged individualism is added to Hahn's precept, creating a climate in the experiential education field that has focused on individual learning and growth rather than community development (Wyatt, 1997).

Many racial and ethnic groups hold cultural values that place community more prominently than individual accomplishment and dependence on self. For example, Latino(a) students see family as a foundation of emotional and economic security and support. Since family is more important in Hispanic communities than in Angelo communities (Grossman, 1984), the exclusion of family from outdoor courses could be re-examined. One instance of this dynamic happened several years ago when I was in charge of a program in which my Hampshire College students facilitated a camping weekend for Latina girls from a local human services agency. In the process of signing up girls for the weekend, the agency director called me because one of the girls' mother wanted to go on the camping trip with her daughter. Not understanding the cultural values involved, I told the director that it was not appropriate for family members to attend the weekend, even though in retrospect it would have not only been nice to have another adult along but would have responded to the underlying need for cultural inclusion.

Other facilitation practices such as individual demonstrations of competence, solos, and impersonal forms of recognition such as badges, pins, and certificates of accomplishment may be culturally incongruent to the values of people of color, women, and poor/working class students. Practices involving community building, teamwork, shared reflection time, and personal feedback such as praise, hugs, or pats on the back may be more welcoming and effective for some.

Again, I am not advocating for the systematic abolishment of practices of self-reliance in outdoor experiential education, but I think we need to be aware of the alienation of cultural values possible in their unexamined use.

Conclusion

A closer look at social justice manifested in the outdoor experiential education field reveals that there are many outstanding philosophical and practical issues still to be addressed by professionals. The attention to topics of race, class, and gender in staff training and professional preparation programs in the outdoors is imperative. More research on how to effectively train leaders, teachers, and counselors is needed. Qualitative studies that demonstrate the developmental dynamics of social justice work are needed in addition to the growing body of quantitative assessments. Integrating social and cultural competency in outdoor experiential education leadership will quell the silencing about social justice that currently prevails. Therefore, accreditation standards must incorporate social justice as a criteria important to accredited programs, and outdoor experiential education training programs in colleges and universities and in the field itself should include anti-bias leadership education in the curriculum.

In addition, the major outdoor adventure programs will need to take the lead as role models in addressing equity issues outdoors, and not only in recruitment but in the subtle messages leaders of courses can convey about who is welcome in outdoor experiential education. Programs such as Project Adventure's diversity course series and Outward Bound's Connecting with Courage program for adolescent girls are examples of what is possible in anti-bias work in the field. What is missing is a strong network or a forum to share exemplary practices in social justice work between programs.

Many questions still remain. Do we only use culturally sensitive facilitation methods in diverse groups or in all white groups? How can we take the programs to the participants rather than bring the participants to the programs? How is race-, class-, and gender-sensitive leadership different from "standard" practices? How do we train leaders to be self-aware of their conditioned biases and to be equitable outdoor facilitators? These questions and others can only be addressed by experiential educators willing to be critically aware of their own privilege and power, and who have the necessary training in order to be self-reflective about their facilitation practice with regard to social justice.

References

Bartolome, L. (1994). Beyond the methods fetish: Toward a humanizing pedagogy. *Harvard Educational Review, 64*(2), 173–194.

Delpit, L. (1995). *Other people's children: Cultural conflict in the classroom*. New York: The New Press.

Ewald, M. (1970). Salem school 1919–33: Foundation and expansion. In H. Rohrs & H. Tunstall-Behrens (Eds.), *Kurt Hahn*. (pp. 22–38). London: Routledge & Kegan Paul.

Greenleaf, R. (1977). *Servant leadership*. New York: Paulist Press.

Grossman, H. (1984). *Educating Hispanic students: Cultural implications for instruction, classroom management, counseling and assessment*. Springfield, IL: Charles C. Thomas.

hooks, b. (1994). *Teaching to transgress: Education as the practice of freedom*. New York: Routledge.

James, K. (1996). Making change: Recognizing culture. *Journal of Experiential Education, 19*(3), 127–134.

Mack, H. (1996). Inside work, outdoors: Women, metaphor and meaning. In K. Warren (Ed.), *Women's voices in experiential education* (pp. 24-31). Dubuque, IA: Kendall/Hunt.

Marchesani, L. S. & Adams, M. (1992). Dynamics of diversity in the teaching-learning process: A faculty development model for analysis and action. In M. Adams (Ed.), *Promoting diversity in college classrooms: Innovative responses for the curriculum, faculty, and institutions.* San Francisco: Jossey-Bass.

Miner, J. (1970). Outward Bound in the USA. In H. Rohrs & H. Tunstall-Behrens (Eds.), *Kurt Hahn* (pp. 197–208). London: Routledge & Kegan Paul.

Rohde, R. (1996). The value of therapeutic wilderness programs for incest survivors: A look at two dominant program models. In K. Warren (Ed.), *Women's voices in experiential education* (pp. 45–60). Dubuque, IA: Kendall/Hunt.

Rohnke, K. & Butler, S. (1995). *Quicksilver.* Dubuque, IA: Kendall/Hunt.

Sadker, M. & Sadker, D. (1994). *Failing at fairness: How our schools cheat girls.* New York: Touchstone.

Shore, I. (1986). Equality is excellence: Transforming teacher education and the learning process. *Harvard Educational Review,* 56(4), 406–422.

Tatum, B. D. (1997). *"Why are all the black kids sitting together in the cafeteria?" and other conversations* about race. New York: BasicBooks.

Van Nostrand, C. H. (1993). *Gender-responsible leadership.* Newbury Park, CA: Sage.

Warren, K. (Ed.). (1996). *Women's voices in experiential education.* Dubuque, IA: Kendall/Hunt.

Wyatt, S. (1997). Dialogue, reflection, and community. *Journal of Experiential Education, 20*(2), 80–85.

Healthy Expressions of Diversity Lead to Positive Group Experiences

▾ ▾ ▾

Denise Mitten

The expression of diversity is one of the most important features of a healthy group. It is a key to safety, good decisions, participant enjoyment, and trip or expedition success. Recognition of diversity, recognition of people's fears about diversity, and a commitment to encourage participants to express their perspectives and wants is part of the challenging job of a group leader. The typical result in groups where acknowledging and using diversity constructively is a norm, is the ability to set goals and accomplish tasks. Group members will feel validated as individuals and contribute to group discussions and decision making in a positive, constructive manner.

The Value of Diversity

Diversity means variety, distinctness or separateness of being. People can be different or alike in many ways; these include trip or life expectations, cultural background, learning styles, communication styles, political persuasions, interests, race, economic status, spirituality, age, gender, skills, physical condition, sexual preference, educational background, diet preferences, stress tolerance, and goal orientation. Any and all of these aspects can bring people together, have no effect, or keep them apart. As leaders and educators, it is important to realize that we bring all the ways we are different from each other in our cities and towns

This chapter originally was published in the *Journal of Experiential Education*, with the following citation:
Mitten, D. (1989). Healthy expressions of diversity lead to positive group experiences. *Journal of Experiential Education, 12*(3), 17–22.

with us on an outdoor trip. We have a wonderful opportunity to structure an environment where the expression of diversity is welcomed. Some people for the first time in their lives can feel part of a group and can feel that as individuals, each one of them matters to the leader and to the other individuals in the group. People can feel that they can be honest about their trip expectations, talk about important concerns, and feel heard and validated.

In a society that teaches us to minimize differences, it is often difficult to establish a group norm of sharing and celebrating them. Diversity itself is value-free. There is no good or bad diversity. On the other hand, how people perceive others as individuals, including their opinions and behaviors, is often value-laden. Each person brings her or his own history of exposure to differences, including both fears and appreciation of differences, to an outdoor trip.

Historically, many people have been afraid of diversity. Those who have different aspirations may be seen as threats to achieving one's own goals. Some people think that only one kind of person will be liked. Some will not initiate a conversation with someone who is obviously different from them. Many people have learned to minimize the ways in which they differ from others, to look and act like they fit the "mold." It is easy for a norm to be set that everyone has to want the same thing or at least everyone has to say they want the same thing. A common phenomenon in the early 1900s for immigrants to the United States was to completely give up speaking their native tongues and participating in their cultural traditions in order to become as American as possible, so as to be able to achieve success and feel safer. It was not uncommon for people who spoke differently to be ostracized, beaten up, and overlooked for jobs. Many immigrant families refused to teach their children their native language.

A group that does not accept diversity can feel unsafe to its members. They may not say they are tired and need to stop for a rest or that they want to walk slowly and are content to stop short of the summit. Others may not feel it is appropriate to say, "I want to push hard and go all out to reach the summit." People can be worried about violating a norm, stepping on someone's toes, or losing the respect of the trip leader.

Diversity helps build strength in a group just as it does in natural environments. There are a number of ecological principles that apply both to our natural environment and to the human population. Ecological communities with high diversity are healthy, have a greater chance of surviving and continuing to evolve, and are better able to adapt or cope with disasters such as weather, pests, and other catastrophes. Human populations are similar. Positive, diverse groups are more stable, can endure hardships, and.can cope with disasters better than groups that are not diverse or groups where the expression of diversity is not encouraged.

Diversity in personalities can be an asset in a group. One person may think of the details, one person may think about the whole picture, another person may recognize the importance of feelings. We cannot expect each person to embody all the personality qualities that are needed for a successful expedition; however, people who are allowed to express their personalities can come together and create an effective team.

For example, by developing a board of directors that includes a lawyer, bank president, fund raiser, doctor, homemaker, farmer, and business manager, we acknowledge that these people have different skills, are diverse in their interests and competencies, and come together to perform a service or govern a business or organization. It is in the best interest of the organization for the group to express and use this diversity. The goals of the organization can be better accomplished because of the variety of expertise. The healthy expression of this diversity takes place when the chairperson encourages each of the individuals to use his or her talents and expertise to problem-solve for the organization. Conversely, there is not a healthy expression of diversity if the chairperson indicates that the board members are to follow directions and not question decisions. The board members may become apathetic and resign, rebel against the chairperson, or subtly sabotage the organization's goals.

I see diversity among individuals as a useful and a highly desirable aspect of groups. As a leader, I use the group's expression of diversity to attain goals not otherwise possible.

Eliciting the Expression of Diversity

Within the Woodswomen program model,[1] there are helpful tools for working with diversity. Our model has been successful when working with groups on day, weekend, or week-long trips, as well as major expeditions. It has been successful with women's groups, women and children's groups, mixed-gender groups, and men's groups. This approach to the healthy expression of diversity is widely applicable to group settings beyond the specific, outdoor-trip context that is discussed below.

A necessary ingredient in this process is having leaders who are comfortable with themselves and the ways they are different from the perceived norms of society. Accepting one's own self is crucial in helping people embrace their differences and themselves. It is also useful for leaders to know about a number of different lifestyles and perspectives. Leaders are more accessible if a person can chat with them about their interests and hobbies, no matter what they may be.

Some educators are worried about diversity-run-wild. Does embracing diversity mean that there are no rules and the trip is chaotic? What happens if everyone does different things? How will the trip be safe? How will the leader stay in charge? How will programming goals be accomplished?

---

[1] Woodswomen, Inc., is an adventure program for women of all ages that offers wilderness trips. It is working to build a strong international network of outdoors women.

It is important to distinguish between the healthy expression of diversity and the suppression of diversity. Often, in the guise of keeping control of a group or maintaining order, a leader will accidentally suppress diverse perspectives. For example, if a leader knows that one person may want to hike faster than the pace of the group, the leader may choose to ignore that observation and hope that the fast hiker will conform to the pace and be content enough so that there will be no conflict. Often, however, the leader's fear of talking about and working with diverse expectations will lead to the very conflict the leader was trying to avoid. If diversity is stifled in a group, members may become discontent, rebellious, and defiant, and, for example, decide to paddle fast forward in a rapid even though it would be safer to backpaddle. This can lead to unsafe situations.

Many leaders confuse inappropriate rebellion against authority, which comes from people being suppressed, with the expression of diversity. This makes the leaders reluctant to allow the healthy expression of diversity. If a leader is fearful or confused about what the healthy expression of diversity is, then it will be hard for that leader to create the space for its expression.

An example of a situation where the leader missed an opportunity to create the space for participants to express diverse expectations occurred on a leadership course. We were talking about the backpacking trip we were planning for the last five days of our course. One woman did a great job of explaining the alternatives for our hike location. Then she opened up the discussion for questions. Another woman asked about hiking farther than the proposed route. Someone else said she would like that, too. The woman heading the discussion did a common thing: She asked who else wanted to go farther. No one raised a hand. The woman leading the discussion concluded that since "the group" did not want to hike farther, the matter was closed. This situation left the women who spoke up feeling alone. A more appropriate response would be "Pat, Cathy, and perhaps others may want to hike farther. We can certainly explore the option of part of the group hiking farther. What other questions are there about the routes?" After questions about the routes are fielded, go back to the question of what each individual wants to do. I think it is important to keep an open mind and to be sure that as a leader, one guides the group to openly consider both the group's and the individual's options. The final decision will be better accepted by all group members if they believe that the leader explored with them the alternatives that they wanted.

There are ways that groups covertly and overtly discourage or suppress diversity. In a men's group, a participant related a trip experience. Jeff was asked by players on his baseball team to go to the Boundary Water Canoe Wilderness for a week. He thought that would be a great idea. He showed up at the appointed time and off they went. He related that he woke up the first morning scared to death as he was hearing shotgun blasts near his head. He got up to find five dead gulls lying in the water. He was horrified to realize that his comrades had done the shooting and, in fact, were planning to drink and shoot for much of the trip. He said he did not dare to speak up for fear of his life or at least ridicule. Jeff was scared to say he was different or that he did not want to shoot the birds. He said that he was able to confide in his brother-in-law who was also on the trip, so he did not feel totally alone. The other men in my group confirmed that this situation is not unusual. Many had been on trips where they did not agree with the behavior of the most vocal or popular men but felt helpless to speak up.

An optimistic programming model incorporates the idea that it is possible and desirable for group members to be different, have different goals, backgrounds, and strengths, and still enjoy a wilderness trip together, and, in fact, better accomplish group goals than if there were no diversity. This approach emphasizes respect for the individual and the belief that if the individual has a chance to say what s/he wants in a comfortable, supportive environment, and feels s/he is heard, then that person will be a willing, active, and constructive group member. Having a group norm of realizing and acknowledging differences is important be- cause a person who feels uncomfortable or embarrassed about sharing what s/he considers an important part of her/himself, may tend to withdraw and isolate her/himself, especially if she perceives that she will be labeled as "different" from the other group members. That per- son will not be eager to participate in risky situations. Groups with a negative attitude about diversity reinforce people's fear that they will not be accepted if they reveal certain things about themselves. Suppressing themselves can add to low self-esteem and self- denial, making it hard for individuals to trust enough to establish healthy relationships. Of course, wanting to share an aspect of oneself, but having a fear of being ostracized, is different from a situation in which a person may choose not to share of her/himself while establish- ing casual relationships. If people feel secure enough to say what they want or talk about how they are feeling—tired, sick, happy, driven—then, as leaders, we are setting the stage for a successful trip.

Leaders sensitive to the importance of individual expression work hard to reinforce the positive aspects of diversity. They are available to talk and be with the participants in both quiet and direct ways. Leaders use inclusive language and do not make assumptions about who is in the group or what people will want to do, nor do they assume that everyone is the same and thinks in the same way. Spending time with each participant and being obviously supportive to all helps make it safe for participants to approach each other. Humor and frank- ness are also helpful. Leaders meet people where they are, encourage participants to be responsible for their actions, and are not confrontive. They encourage people to say what they want, express their opinions, and feel comfortable about who they are. Leaders encourage a feeling of being included in the group process, which I consider different from "belonging" to a group. It is important that a person retain the feeling of individuality and choice in participating in the group process and group activities. In order to participate fully and to build self-esteem, participants need to consider themselves as individuals who can freely come and go from a group.

There are certain specific steps a leader needs to take in order to elicit the healthy expression of diversity. The stage is set for the group to be receptive to diversity at the initial trip gathering. As the leader meets the group, it is important to make verbal contact with each person. During initial introductions, group members learn about each other and start to learn about and have reactions to the diversity in the group. For example, some women come on a women's trip assuming that since we are all here, we are similar and present for the same reasons. During introductions to one trip, I saw one woman's face drop as she heard another say, "I am so glad to be here with others like me who have left our husbands and children at home. We can have a girls' week out in the woods." The woman whose face dropped felt that this description did not include her and was uncomfortable thinking that she was possibly the only group member who did not have a husband and children. In fact, the group was a diverse mix of women in a variety of personal relationship situations. It was up to the leader to be sure the conversation reflected the group's diversity instead of waiting to see if it happened. People are not used to being direct about differences. The leader can model directness and the participants can learn from this modeling.

At this first meeting, time and emphasis is given equally to each individual's expectations. The leader also creates the space to allow people who do not have expectations to share at the first meeting, to freely voice them any time during the trip, stressing that differences in timing is a normal way that people vary. Within 24 hours, the leader repeats the question regarding expectations to the group to allow for a potential timing difference. During the trip, leaders periodically check in with individuals regarding their expectations.

At the end of the initial meeting, many people may think, "How are we going to make this work? We are all so different." The leader expresses overtly what many people may be thinking by stating in an upbeat, positive tone, "To have different expectations with a diverse group of people is a perfectly normal and healthy occurrence for a group." Continuing in a matter-of-fact tone, the leader says that some individual's expectations will probably change as the trip progresses and invites people to keep her/him posted on their thoughts. The leader emphasizes that one of the goals of the trip is to have fun, which is certainly possible with the great diversity in the group.

Leaders greatly influence trip norms. The leader reinforces the notion that it is valued to say what you think by making a personal connection with each person in a way that gives them permission to be comfortable being who they are on the trip. Leaders can support a positive attitude toward diversity by avoiding disparaging remarks, jokes, and discussions about different groups (i.e., women talking about all men's groups, backpackers talking about canoeing groups, ethnic and racial minorities, etc.).

The example that follows illustrates how to work with diverse expectations rather than suppressing them. A group was scheduled to climb Pisang Peak in the Himalayas. After walking six days to the base of the peak, we were turned back from our attempt by a storm that dropped 12 feet of snow in four days. Because of time constraints, we had to decide whether to attempt the summit again and return to Kathmandu the way we walked in, or abandon the summit and continue our circuit around the Annapurna massif. I asked group members for their preferences. Two women wanted to do the circuit and four wanted to attempt the summit again. At first the women began to make cases for their preferences. However, since it is a strong value for us to encourage participants to meet their individual goals, and in this case it was safe and practical, I suggested we divide into two groups. Groups often resist separating because in our society, we often learn to separate when we are not getting along, not because we have different goals. It is important for leaders to redefine separation to mean that we all get to do what we want and still support and like each other. This is a healthy relationship model for people to learn and to transfer to their personal relationships. If healthy diversity had not been encouraged in this group, it is unlikely group members would have been willing to state their preferences and to part amicably for a portion of the trip. If we had stayed together, it would have been unsafe to attempt a summit with climbers who were ambivalent. In this case, the group divided for a period and rejoined later in the trip.

The leader must be aware of the individuals' goals and expectations before an ambitious endeavor. For example, on a ski mountaineering trip in Colorado, we were to attempt a peak ascent on Day Five. One question I have learned to ask group members is, "What are your goals for the day?" For example, "Do you want to get as far as you can but not necessarily to the top? Do you want to have fun, take pictures, and not focus on the ascent? Do you want to focus on getting to the top?" It is important that each group member be honest with her/himself and the group about her/his goals. The group and individuals have a greater chance of personal success if everyone says what they really want for the day. I ask people these questions in several different ways. A peak ascent is too important and the safety considerations are too great to not do all I can as a leader to get participants to speak up about their desires. In this case, all group members said their goal was to have a fun day and get as far as they could, but not necessarily to the top. In fact, seven out of eight of us went to the top. The eighth woman, 56 years old and on touring skis for only the fourth time, stayed 45 minutes below the summit, resting. The crux is for participants to feel secure enough to be candid about their goals.

If a leader does not deliberately elicit or support the expression of diversity, a variety of scenarios can occur. Here are two illustrations:

A woman related a story where she was on an outdoor educators' course. On Day Two of the trip, the more vocal group members began making fun of "process." It quickly became the norm to not talk about personal concerns. The more vocal members were smoking marijuana. This concerned the participant, but she felt unsupported by the instructors, who were laughing at the jokes. She did not want to risk being ostracized by the group by pushing against the norm to bring up what she perceived as a safety issue.

Two other people reported they went on a guided wilderness trip together expressly to share the experience with each other. On Day Two, the group held a kangaroo court, saying that these two people could not be affectionate on the trip, not because of safety, program or inappropriateness, but because it bothered some of the group members. They were 15 miles up-river from the nearest town, unable to leave the trip, and feeling unsupported by the leader and other participants. The leader, of course, thought she was doing what was in the best interest of the group since during the kangaroo court, it seemed as if the majority of the members said they wanted these two to change.

Individual differences in groups can bring about catastrophes, whatever the setting. The challenge is to encourage the expression of diversity rather than suppress it. By respecting individual differences, we allow and encourage participants to take responsibility for their own health, and well-being. This in turn creates a safe and fun atmosphere in which major goals can be accomplished.

White Awareness & Our Responsibility to End Racism

▼ ▼ ▼

Karen Fox

I was pleased to see the discussion concerning racism and prejudice in the field of experiential education. As a white woman from the United States teaching in Canada, I was also saddened and angered by the comments of Messrs. Pervorse and Garrett because of the lack of attention to the meaning of words, critical thinking standards, and previous work on the meaning, origin, and effect of racism. I believe it is essential that we choose and use words wisely and think critically about emotionally charged issues. I believe it is our professional obligation to express thoughtful and well-reasoned opinions as we develop programs in a multicultural world. I wish to deal only with a few of the issues raised in their argument.

Note: This article discusses white awareness and the responsibility to end racism in the context of a series of short articles in the Horizon, *the newsletter of the Association for Experiential Education (AEE). Although it explicitly responds to previous* Horizon *articles, it goes beyond them to bring a conceptual and critical analysis to these issues from a white perspective. In order to facilitate the reading of this article, the series of articles in the* Horizon *by Arthur Wellington Conquest III, Roberto Velez, and Dan Pervorse and Jim Garrett are reprinted immediately following this article. The Conquest and Velez articles originally appeared in the January 1991* Horizon, *and the Pervorse and Garrett response to them appeared in the May 1991* Horizon.

This chapter originally was published in the *Journal of Experiential Education*, with the following citation:
Fox, K. (1992). White awareness and our responsibility to end racism. *Journal of Experiential Education, 15*(3), 26–30.

The Difference Between Racism and Prejudice

Messrs. Pervorse and Garret use the words prejudice and racism interchangeably throughout their letter. This was unfortunate because the words have very different meanings. The definition given by Messrs. Pervorse and Garrett (see paragraph two of their letter on page 420) is only one aspect of prejudice. "Prejudice" comes from a Latin stem meaning to pre-judge or have a preconceived opinion or feeling which may be favorable or unfavorable. Racism, on the other hand, is the "belief that human races have distinctive characteristics that determine their respective cultures, usually involving the idea that one's own race is superior and has the right to rule others."[1] It is important to note that racism involves the belief in the superiority of one's own race and the involvement of systems of power to promote that belief. Building from results of the Kerner Report, Whitney Young (1970) states:

> Most Americans get awfully uptight about the charge of racism, since most people are not conscious of what racism really is. Racism is not the desire to wake up every morning and lynch a black man from a tall tree. It is not engaging in vulgar epithets. These kinds of people are just fools. It is the day-to-day indignities, the subtle humiliations, that are so devastating. Racism is the assumption of superiority of one group over another, with all the gross arrogance that goes along with it. Racism is a part of us. The Kerner Commission has said that if you have been an observer you have been a racist; if you have stood idly, you are racist. (p. 730)

If one attends carefully to the words and their definition, a distinct difference between requesting representation of an under-represented group (i.e., people of color) and racism (i.e., belief in the superiority of a particular race) emerges. The demands by Messrs. Velez and Conquest were for representation of an underrepresented group and awareness of underlying racist and oppressive behavior patterns of the Association for Experiential Education (AEE), which is dominated by white people. Those demands are not the same as expressing a belief in superiority of one race over the other.

---

[1] I base my definitions and use of words on the Random House Dictionary of the English Language. I have tried to be faithful to the list of definitions for each word since such a strategy supports a more honest and complete discussion of the concepts. Simple definitions are adequate when there is an agreement about an item (e.g., chair, bicycle), but a more comprehensive discussion is needed when we are exploring the meanings of abstract concepts. To that end, it is extremely helpful to use research results and philosophical discussions about racism and prejudice that include context, meaning of words and syntax, and current associations with the concept.

Attending to the Standards of Critical Thinking

Even if one were to agree with the definition of prejudice provided by Messrs. Pervorse and Garrett, they do not support their claim that Messrs. Velez and Conquest "cross the line into racism." Messrs. Velez and Conquest made generalizations (a logical process) from their own experiences with AEE professionals. Making generalizations from experience is not an irrational process. It is instructive to closely examine the structure of the writings of Messrs. Velez and Conquest.

Mr. Velez states that he, himself, had several experiences (notice it was more than one experience) with outdoor educators who were "bigoted and know-it-all." Notice that Mr. Velez does not generalize the label to *all* outdoor educators; he merely says that he was *reluctant* to attend the conference, given these previous experiences. In addition, Mr. Velez does not indicate that he thinks people of color are superior and does not invoke a power structure or system to oppress white people—two of the conditions necessary for racism. Finally, Mr. Velez tests his original generalizations and conclusions by attending the conference.

Mr. Conquest presented an analysis of power structures within AEE and associated organizations. Although one may disagree with his analogy of the plantation, it is a proper use of constructing an argument using analogies. Mr. Conquest supports the analogy by drawing connections between the power relationships on a plantation and the power relationships between personnel roles and functions, (i.e., assistants often serve their bosses with little or no access to power or policy development). In addition, Mr. Conquest merely requests that people of color have control over programs designed for them and about them. He never once indicates that he thinks people of color should have power over white people or that they are superior to white people. He simply states that people of color should have a strong voice and control in programs designed for people of color. As in the case of Mr. Velez, there is no sign of racism (the belief that one race is superior and should have power over another race) in the words of Mr. Conquest. A dialogue using critical thinking skills would address the topic at hand and present evidence to counter the analogy or disprove the supporting evidence.

Furthermore, their generalizations seem warranted (and necessary for their own survival in a world where white people hold the power) given the generations of oppression and violence toward people of color and the barrage of daily reminders of that history. When referring to individuals, we assume the individual has white skin unless so noted. Therefore, we identify black athletes or scholars but not white athletes or scholars. It is implied that the norm or standard is white skin and this leaves people of color excluded. In addition, one only has to watch the nightly news to hear examples of white police officers beating people of color, the low number of people of color represented in positions of power, the high number of people of color in jail, and the higher percentage of infant mortality for children of color, to see the continuation of the racism and prejudice within the institutions of power (Kaufman, 1989; Robson, 1990; Klauda & St. Anthony, 1990; Klauda, 1990; von Sternber, 1990; Weiner, 1990).

Racism and White Privilege

What is missing in the response by Messrs. Pervorse and Garrett is an understanding of racism as a problem for whites (Katz, 1978).[2] It is people with white skin who have access to power structures and do not have to think about the color of their skin. It is part of what Peggy McIntosh (1991) defines as "white privilege." We tend to think of racism as disadvantages for people of color without seeing the corollary aspects that put people with white skin at an advantage. White privilege is an "invisible knapsack" of invisible but important special provisions that can be used when needed. What are these provisions? Ms. McIntosh gives us some examples:

1. I can, if I wish, arrange to be in the company of people of my race most of the time.

2. I can go shopping alone most of the time, pretty well assured that I will not be followed or harassed.

3. I can turn on the television or open to the front page of the paper and see people of my race widely represented.

4. When I am told about our national heritage or about "civilization," I am shown that people of my color made it what it is.

5. I can be sure that my children will be given curricular materials that testify to the existence and excellence of their race.

6. Whether I use checks, credit cards, or cash, I can count on my skin color not to work against the appearance of financial reliability.

7. I can arrange to protect my children most of the time from people who might not like them.

8 I can swear, or dress in second-hand clothes, or not answer letters, without having people attribute these choices to the bad morals, the poverty, or the illiteracy of my race.

9. If a traffic cop pulls me over or if the IRS audits my tax return, I can be sure I haven't been singled out because of my race.

---

[2] See J. H. Katz (1978), *White Awareness: Handbook for Anti-Racism Training*. Katz carefully builds a case for the need of white people's awareness of their own attitudes and behavior that unintentionally and unconsciously still perpetuate racism. In addition, she notes the negative costs for white people when they unknowingly operate from these racist attitudes. Also see E. Lee (1985), *Letters to Marcia: A Teacher's Guide to Anti-Racist Education*. Lee presents the many facets of subtle racism in the school and lesson plans for addressing the various issues.

10. I can speak in public to a powerful male group without putting my race on trial.

11. I am never asked to speak for all the people of my racial group.

12. I can remain oblivious of the language and customs of persons of color who constitute the world's majority without feeling in my culture any penalty for such oblivion.

13. I can go home from most meetings of organizations I belong to feeling somewhat tied in, rather than isolated, out-of-place, outnumbered, unheard, held at a distance, or feared. (p. 5)

White privilege is an elusive subject and the tendency is to avoid facing it because it questions the myth of meritocracy. If these things are true, the United States is not such a free country, one's life is not what one makes it; many doors open for certain people through no virtue of their own.

Even the word "privilege" seems misleading. Privilege is normally considered a favored state, whether earned or conferred. Yet some of the above conditions work to systematically over-empower certain groups. Such privilege simply *confers dominance* because of one's race. There is a difference between earned strength and unearned power conferred systematically. Power from unearned privilege can look like strength when it is in fact permission to escape or to dominate. But not all the aspects of white privilege are damaging. Some, like the expectation that neighbors will be decent to you, or that your race will not be counted against you in court, should be the norm in a just society. Others, like the privilege to ignore less powerful people, distort the humanity of the holders as well as the ignored groups (McIntosh, 1991).

Messrs. Pervorse and Garrett's statement that we (white people) "have done everything we can," is a statement originating in white privilege. It assumes that white lives are morally neutral, normative, average, and ideal; that we white folks can work to allow "them" to be more like "us." The statement implies a power over others, not a power working with others to oppose all forms of oppression. The statement assumes that it is responsible (and good) to act for others and that we can be sure of our own moral intent and wisdom. Such assumptions prevent us from seeing the destructive consequences of our well-intentioned projects. Although many of our projects are meant to "help people of color," these projects can and do inflict more damage and oppression.[3] This is directly related to a lack of interaction with and transfer of power to people of color. The statement leaves people of color in the

---

[3] For an excellent discussion about the costs of racism for the people who have access to the power structures over people of color, see Susan D. Welch (1990), *A Feminist Ethic of Risk*. Welch convincingly argues that many projects developed by white people to help people of color fall short because of a lack of interactive dialogue that acknowledges the damage of oppression, sees the need for ongoing work toward freedom and justice for all people, and conceives of people of color as both victims and courageous fighters of oppression.

role of "victim," not as actors determining their own roles. The statement leaves in place a power structure dominated by white people deciding the fate of people of color. Messrs. Velez and Conquest do not want more charity or programs designed by white people. Messrs. Velez and Conquest are claiming what is rightfully theirs—the power to define their own programs to support the freedom and self-dignity of people of color (Gibson, 1989). Such a commitment from AEE means material changes in structure, number of people of color in positions of power, and content of the programs.

The examples of role models chosen by Messrs. Pervorse and Garrett are also insightful. A study of children who are African-American indicates that African-American children are so inundated with white role models and symbolism that they point to children with dark skin and say they are dirty, ugly, and bad, or even wish they were white. It is the overwhelming whiteness of role models that does not assist a young child of color to imagine that s/he are could obtain a particular level of achievement. It is white people who lack a broad perspective of role models across racial and cultural arenas, not people of color. For instance, how many scientists, scholars, politicians, social activists, or authors of color in American history can one name? In addition, I fail to see the significant relevance of athletic role models to experiential education. There has been a long history of racism in sports. Initially, many of the major sports were closed to people of color. The latest series on racism in a Minneapolis newspaper indicated that athletes of color still encounter racism and many teams do not even promote their games within communities of people of color (Weiner, 1990). The example would have been much more relevant had the examples come from experiential education, education in general, outdoor education, or a similar area.

The Role of Critique by People of Color

The only way white people can understand and know the subtlety of racism is to interact and listen carefully to people of color who are sensitive to the nuances. People of color have an "epistemological privilege" (Narayan, 1988)[4] by virtue of living in two racial worlds and having to survive in a world dominated by white people. People of color must not only maintain their own cultures and dignity but also learn how to relate to white people who are in power and control much of the lives of people of color. We, white people, do not live in a world where we have to be conscious of the color of our skin and hence, must learn this knowledge from listening to people of color. If we, white people, truly want to resist racism

---

[4] For an extensive explanation of epistemic privilege, standpoint epistemology, and methodological humility, see Vma Narayan (1988), *Working across difference: Some considerations on emotions and political practice,* and P. H. Collins (1991), *Learning from the outsider within: The sociological significance of black feminist thought.*

and prejudice, we must learn how we perpetuate it in our systems and practices through ignorance and lack of awareness and attention.

The anger expressed by Messrs. Velez and Conquest reflects generations of oppression, racism, and prejudice that their families, friends, and even they themselves have undergone. The only way to address such subtleties is people of color taking the risk and expressing their righteous anger toward such situations. Although it is not pleasant, those of us who are white must be accountable for that history as well as our own perpetuation of the system because we are the ones who have access to the privilege and power system. Messrs. Velez and Conquest are setting healthy examples in this field by voicing their justified anger at the situation and taking the risk of exposing their own feelings.[5]

We are a long way from being diverse together, and the statements of Messrs. Velez and Conquest indicate we must listen more to people of color. It is people of color who help us see how our actions, even well-intentioned actions, perpetuate racism and prejudice. It is they who will point the way to resolving some of the issues. It is they who have fought racism and prejudice for years. It is we white people who need to listen and hear their anger that there already has been too much damage.

This critique is not to replace the responsibility of white people to speak out against racism, as men need to speak out against sexism. It is not the responsibility of people of color to educate white people about their racist behavior. It is the *responsibility of white people* to acknowledge their access to privilege and power based on skin color, remain accountable for the history of oppression of people of color by white people, and change their attitudes and behaviors as well as work toward justice for all. I agree with Messrs. Garrett and Pervorse that people of color and white people cannot hold others at arm's length. But I fail to see how expressing anger and defining the subtleties of racism and prejudice as seen by people of color is pushing people away. Susan Welch (1990) states:

> It is painful to learn we have caused others harm, either as individuals or as members of a dominant social group. Change occurs when the response to this knowledge is not guilt but repentance, a deep commitment to make amends and to change patterns of behavior. Such changes are not losses but gains, opportunities to live out our love and respect for others. (p. 174)

---

[5] Susan Welch (1990) discusses the privilege of white, middle-class people that allows them to retreat from discussions about racism when righteous anger is expressed concerning the history and effects of racism on people of color.

We cannot stand side by side if one race is not allowed to express its anger.

If AEE is truly opposed to oppression, prejudice, and racism, we must enter into a dialogue with people of color and hear their critique of the plans and actions designed by white people. As a mature and ethical organization, we would invite such critiques and explore their meanings. We must unflinchingly recognize not simply the evil consequences of our thoughtless or greedy actions but also the negative consequences of our attempts to pursue good. We must, in effect, create a matrix of resistance to all forms of injustice. We could start by listening more to the details and suggestions of brave people like Messrs. Velez and Conquest.

▾ ▾ ▾

Diversity: Accepting/Respecting Color
Arthur Wellington Conquest III

It has been more than 25 years since the historic Civil Rights Bill was signed by President Lyndon B. Johnson and the doors of "the dream" were supposed to magically open for people of color (POC) in America. In the name of misleading terms like "integration" and "the melting pot," and at a time when large numbers of POC were being recruited as course participants, POC were lured into the outdoor field with powerless positions such as assistant instructors, urban specialists, and, in rare cases, instructors. In reality, however, the basic foundations of slavery and the plantations it supported remained fixed. Whites, as masters, gave the orders and controlled everything, while POC, as the house servants, accepted their subservient status and did as they were told. This system, unfortunately, continues full-steam ahead today.

As long as POC have to idolize individuals who don't represent or speak for them, then those individuals only serve as wardens of (outdoor) institutions that have POC locked up in economic, political, and mental prisons in America. [About 500,000 POC are literally locked up in prisons.] Malcolm X once said, "If you stick a knife in my back, if you put it in 9 inches and pull it out 6 inches, you haven't done me any favor. If you pull it all the way out, you (still) haven't done me any favor."

While AEE, along with the rest of America, prepares for the drastic changes that will occur with the Workforce 2000, emotionally seductive words like "diversity," "pluralism," and "cultural differences" are being used more frequently. Are these terms code words for "integration" and "affirmative action?" What do these terms mean and are POC going to allow whites, especially white males, to continue to set themselves up as the custodians of their communities? Are these signals specifically designed to distract attention from the conflict, tension, and pressure intrinsic in eliminating prejudice, discrimination, racism?

If white individuals and/or organizations associated with AEE are going to seriously address issues encompassing diversity, then they must begin to embrace the notion that cultural/racial differences as they relate to POC, especially skin color, are on a par with their own. Historically, most things associated with POC in this country are assumed to have less value than those of white people. Jazz vs. classical (European) music is but one example. Even today, all but the most racially healthy whites at some point in their lives have an assumption that POC are somehow tainted and/or inferior. [I see and experience the superior/inferior posture daily—at the 1990 AEE conference in St. Paul, too—and when I refuse to submit, many whites become extremely indignant.]

Diversity must not mean that POC have to reject their cultures and adopt the values of white society to participate as equals within mainstream outdoor institutions. POC should be allowed to accept and like being who they are. Taking this a step further, white outdoor educators must be willing to accept POC's desire to control their own institutions and educate children of color accordingly so they do not feel compelled to define themselves in relation to a society which has not yet come to terms with accepting and respecting color. Diversity is accepting and respecting a colored heart with a colored face, a nation within a nation.

▾ ▾ ▾

The St. Paul Conference Was "Hip!"

Roberto Velez

Reluctantly, I attended the 1990 AEE Annual Conference in St. Paul, Minnesota. I was reluctant because my experiences with elitist, "know-it-all," bigoted, outdoor educators made me apprehensive about the possibility of spending any time with large numbers of them at a conference. But this conference was different for a variety of reasons. First, there were more people of color present than I had expected and many of them ran workshops that addressed their cultures and their oppressive experiences in America. Second, I took part in a "special workshop" made up of about 40 people of color. Together we developed a set of goals for social change and empowerment within the experiential education field. Third, I was inspired and rejuvenated with a sense of hope by brothers like Arthur Conquest and McClellan Hall, who have been "in the fight" for justice and equality in the outdoor education movement for a number of years. Finally, I met a number of sincere white people, such as Rick Hall, who demonstrated throughout the conference that they, too, were willing to stand up and out against racism.

I'm glad I attended the conference and I look forward to the 1991 conference in North Carolina, where I hope to see, talk to, and work with my brothers and sisters again.

▾　▾　▾

Racism and Prejudice in the Field

Dan Pervorse & Jim Garrett

The January 1991 issue of *The AEE Horizon* proved to be quite enlightening and, at the same time, perplexing. It was enlightening to read the many thoughts and viewpoints of the various members, yet at the same time, some of those views caused some anxiety. Two articles in particular, one written by Roberto Velez and the other by Arthur Wellington Conquest III, dealt with the topics of prejudice and racism, particularly as they relate to the experiential education field.

As with both of these gentlemen, we too are concerned about and despise racism and prejudice in any form. This of course includes the form that took shape at the hands of both Mr. Velez and Mr. Conquest. For the purpose of clarification, Webster's Dictionary defines prejudice as "an irrational attitude of hostility directed against an individual, a group, a race, or their supposed characteristics; preconceived judgment or opinion; an opinion or leaning adverse to anything without just grounds or before sufficient knowledge." Additionally, racism is "racial prejudice or discrimination."

Mr. Velez crossed the line into racism from the outset of his letter in the *Horizon*. He stated that he was reluctant to attend the 1990 AEE Annual Conference because of the large numbers of "elitist, 'know-it-all,' bigoted, outdoor educators" who would be there. We are glad that his experience at the conference was much to the contrary of what he expected. However, by making such a statement about any of us, based solely upon his own experiences with others in this field, he fits the above definition of a racist. He is the very epitome of what he is speaking out against. It angers us to be lumped into such a category by him when he has no knowledge of our persons or character. His very words violate the stance that people of color (POC) claim to take against such attitudes.

The letter composed by Mr. Conquest does make a meaningful attempt at addressing these issues in this field. However, this letter also seems to be structured around a foundation of racial prejudice. Mr. Conquest's presupposition that all programs that are directed by whites ("Whites, as masters," giving orders and controlling everything, while POC act "as the house servants") are continuing to perpetuate the slavery and plantation system is basically a gross overexaggeration of reality. We have done what we can in our respective agencies to bring in POC at leadership positions in order to effect necessary changes and to address the pertinent issues of our communities. We are tired of being blamed for the history of discrimination of the past. We don't doubt that POC do, in fact, still face prejudice, but we are not perpetuating it and are tired of POC who point their fingers at us and blame us simply because of our skin color.

Mr. Conquest states that "white outdoor educators must be willing to accept POCs desire to control their own institutions and educate children of color" so that they can deal with their own cultural values. In this same light, POC need to allow us "white outdoor educators" to do the same, without putting us down for doing so. In an effort to delineate and understand their own cultural heritages over the years, some POC have denied the existence and/or importance of a white cultural heritage. Do not deny us the same rights that you so desire for yourselves by labeling our own efforts to grow as being racist. It would be wrong for anyone to deny anyone else of their right to learn and grow and to be involved in their heritage.

There is also another perspective that must not be overlooked. One of the purposes of many experiential education programs is to provide the participants with positive role models. Based on the statement quoted above, is Mr. Conquest suggesting that the only proper role models for children of color are POC (and conversely white role models for white children)? If this were true, then why are Michael Jordan and Larry Bird such powerful role models for many children in this country irrespective of color?

If we are serious about breaking the cycle of racism and prejudice in this field, should we not be setting healthy examples in our own programs? The healthy example that must be promoted is for programs to have a racially and/or culturally diverse program staff. If we perpetuate the idea that the only proper role models for children are those of their own race, we will be guilty of promoting segregation and racism.

Additionally, according to Mr. Conquest, "diversity is accepting and respecting a colored heart with a colored face, a nation within a nation." This definition is too narrow in that it seems to say that diversity is a function of color. Diversity is accepting/respecting differences in others regardless of color (and for that matter sex, age, the way people dress, geographical location, program affiliation, etc.).

One of the main reasons for the existence of AEE is to bring together people from all walks of life who are interested in perpetuating the philosophy and goals of experiential education. In other words, it is to unite people of like minds yet of different life experiences. Those differences are what we would call diversity. Each of us brings something special and truly unique to this organization, regardless of whether our differences flow out of an educational, professional, racial, sexual, or any other, perspective. This is the essence of true diversity.

We agree with Mr. Conquest that terms such as "melting pot" do not describe the true essence of diversity. The melting pot presents a picture of a cauldron where all are boiled together into one large indistinguishable and dysfunctional glob. Much to the contrary, we each need to maintain our uniqueness and our own heritage. But it will only hurt all of us if we continue to segregate and throw bigoted barbs at those who don't fit our particular special interests. POC should not hold others who are different than they, in particular the white male, at arm's length because they don't understand POC issues. How will we gain an understanding of your issues or you of ours if we continue to push each other away? Instead, we need to stand side by side and learn from one another about our differences in order that we all might grow. The beauty of true diversity in AEE is that we are diverse together.

References

Anzaldua, G. (1990). *Making face, making soul-Hacienda caras: Creative and critical perspectives by women of color.* San Francisco, CA: Aunt Lute Foundation.

Gibson, B. (1989). Meeting the interpretive needs of minorities. In the *Proceedings of the* 1989 *National Interpreters Workshop.* St. Paul, MN: National Association of Interpretation.

Katz, J. H. (1978). *White awareness: Handbook for anti-racism training.* Norman, OK: University of Oklahoma Press.

Kaufman, J. (1989, June 18). The color line: Blacks and whites in a divided America (Part I). *The Boston Globe Magazine, 16–59.*

Kaufman, J. (1989, June 25). The color line: Blacks and whites in a divided America (Part II). *The Boston Globe Magazine, 18–49.*

Klauda, P. (1990, June 14). Dark skin perceived as a crime waiting to happen. *Minneapolis Star Tribune,* pp. 1, 17, and 19 A.

Klauda, P., and St. Anthony. (1990, June 15). N. Minneapolis minority neighborhoods get fewer home loans from banks. *Minneapolis Star Tribune,* pp. 1 and 8A.

Lee, E. (1985). *Letters to Marcia: A teacher's guide to anti-racist education.* Toronto, ONT: Cross Cultural Communication Centre.

McAllister, P. (1991). *This river of courage: Generations of women's resistance and action.* Philadelphia, PA: New Society Publishers.

Mcintosh, P. (1991). White privilege: Unpacking the invisible knapsack. *Matrix,* pp. 5–6.

Robson, B. (1990, January). Pride and prejudice. *Minneapolis St. Paul Magazine,* pp. 42–51, and 130.

von Steber, B. (1990, June 15). Minnesota power structure is overwhelmingly white. *Minneapolis Star Tribune,* pp. 1, and 18 and 19 A.

Weiner, J. (1990, June 19). Sports teams slow to reach out to minority fans. *Minneapolis Star Tribune,* pp. 1, 17, and 19 A.

Welch, S. D. (1990). *A feminist ethic of risk.* Minneapolis, MN: Fortress Press.

Young, W. (1970). Exceptional children: Text of a keynote speech. In J. H. Katz *(1978), White awareness: Handbookfor anti-racism training.* Norman, OK: University of Oklahoma Press.

"Borrowing" Activities From Another Culture: A Native American's Perspective

▾ ▾ ▾

Gordon W. A. Oles

The entire spectrum of the wilderness/adventure education experience is a most dynamic phenomenon. Many of the programs and experiences facilitated by adventure education practitioners are exciting, innovative, affective, and effective. Moreover, the profession has not developed to the point where the calcifying effects of organizational rigor mortis threaten to overtake it. There is still room for new ideas. In fact, if a wagging finger were to be pointed, it would have to be directed toward the tendency to jump on a bandwagon whenever an idea, concept, or practice captures one's fancy. It seems that one of the more pervasive bandwagons has been the trend of latching on to the rituals and practices of various Native American tribes and other aboriginal groups.

My concern stems from my experience in working with a number of agencies that conducted wilderness rehabilitation programs for troubled youth. One aspect of the various agencies' programs included sweat lodge ceremonies, giving of names, vision quests, fasts, etc., yet no cultural context was appropriate for the things that they were doing. Additionally, I believe that these agencies and individuals had no right to take these religious activities and put them to use in that setting.

I have had deeply spiritual experiences that I do not share with others, yet they are of profound meaning to me, for the context in which they occurred was appropriate to my

---

This chapter originally was published in the *Journal of Experiential Education*, with the following citation: Oles, G. W. A. (1992). "Borrowing" activities from another culture: A native American's perspective. *Journal of Experiential Education, 15*(3), 20–22.

cultural heritage. There are other events that I share with others of my culture, for we have these experiences in common; however, those who are outsiders must always be excluded.

By attempting to adopt Indian ceremonies into their adventure leadership programs, these well-intentioned but misguided leaders have desecrated things that should have remained sacred and holy. From my perspective as a Native American (who also happens to be an outdoor leader), these contrived, pseudo-Indian activities were tantamount to a non-believer taking the Emblems of Communion and passing them out along the trail as a snack.

What if I were to come into St. Patrick's Cathedral, clad only in moccasins and a breech-clout, and attempt to take the place of the priest? Or suppose that I went into a synagogue on Yom Kippur and sang *Kol Nidre* instead of the cantor? Can you see the incongruity? Even if I say the correct words and do the correct things, I certainly do not have the right to do so, and I would most likely offend the religious sensibilities of those within their respective congregations. It works both ways.

Many non-Indian people within Western society seem to think of Indians as a separate species from them, with a cosmology based upon fear and superstition. Worse, they may view us as curiosities, or as stage props instead of people. In the short story *Sun and Shadow,* Ray Bradbury pointedly demonstrates the cultural insensitivity that far too frequently occurs when Westerners deal with indigenous peoples.

> We must understand each other.... I will not have my alley used because of its pretty shadows, or my sky used because of its sun, or my house used because there is an interesting crack.... We are poor people. Our doors peel paint, our walls are chipped and cracked, our gutters fume in the street, the alleys are all cobbles.... Did you think I knew you were coming and put my boy in his dirtiest clothes? We are *not* a studio! We are people and must be given attention as people. Have I made it clear? (Bradbury, 1953)

Our religious beliefs may seem strange. I will agree they are different from the Western world's cosmology; however, that difference does not make them less valid as a means of expressing reverence for the divine. From a Western viewpoint, land is a commodity to be bought and sold, or to be plundered and conquered. To the Native American, the Earth is our mother. Western thought arrogates to humankind the sole right of reason and being. One Native American perspective takes the viewpoint that all animals are sentient beings. Moreover, the very rocks themselves are alive. Western thought conveniently divides the sacred from the profane; yet in the cosmology of a Native American, one may see the Hand of the Creator in all things; therefore, all is sacred.

How often over the centuries has our religious expression been ridiculed by the West? Yet, at the same time, if *their* religious institutions fail them, many non-Indians think that by adopting some Indian rituals or ceremonies (or a "reasonable facsimile"), they will find their way back to truth and light. *It just isn't going to happen!*

I seriously doubt that Western society is without spiritual meaning, and I cannot subscribe to the notion that the West is morally bankrupt (as yet). All enduring societies must have been built upon a spiritual and moral foundation, or else they would not have endured. In all of these societies that have risen and fallen, there was a spiritual drive that sustained them in their growth. Western society is no exception, though it seems in many cases that this spiritual dimension has been either denied or demythologized.

Western society has had its full complement of culture heroes, but what has it done with them (or to them)? If the heroes have displayed any human failings, they have been unceremoniously removed from their pedestal. Any element of the supernatural was dealt with in just as cavalier a manner. *Consequently, there remains a spiritual void when the culture heroes are dismantled, and we vainly search for their replacement.* It has been popularly stated in Western thought that "God is dead (also the culture heroes)." It must be remembered, however, that it is we who have killed them in our de-eschatological hubris. In Native American mythology, however, the hero remains inviolate; *it is we who must live up to the myth.* Therein lies a critical cultural difference between a Native American perspective and the Western cosmological viewpoint.

Authentic Cultural Contexts

In order for a religious institution to work, it must be founded within the appropriate cultural context. Its adherents then practice their beliefs within that cultural milieu, and do so appropriately with their society's full sanction. For example, the religious ceremonies that are integral to any given tribe will be central frameworks of that tribe's cultural identity. Trying to juxtapose certain ceremonies into Western society would be disturbingly jarring. By the same token, those tribes also recognize the absurdity of trying to do the reverse. Hence, virtually all outsiders and outside distractions are excluded from most activities within the tribal religion, and rightly so. The hero motifs, cosmological perspectives, etc., remain forever intact—a standard that the tribal members strive to attain in their lives.

"Putting new wine into old bottles" is a timeless adage now, even as when it was first uttered. Adventure educators should critically examine the activities that are adopted. Activities must be *authentic* in order to be effective. In this definition of terms, authentic activities must be congruent to one's cultural framework. Therein lies the dilemma. Though people may recognize the value of certain activities (and Native American ceremonies have been perennial favorites), they cannot effectively make use of them if these activities and ceremonies come from a culturally dissimilar framework. To do so would make them appear unnatural and contrived. No amount of "cultural appreciation" or "cultural sensitivity" can make them fit within the Western cosmology, because the necessary perspective is lacking. Nor can elements that have been appropriated (stolen) be of lasting efficacy, for the simple fact that they have been practiced without the proper sanctions. There is neither the cultural precedent, the cultural framework, *nor the authority* to conduct any sort of tribal activity— even when couched with Anglo terminology and even if conducted with the purest motives and even if those conducting these activities are doing them in a manner that is "sensitive" to the feelings of the Native Americans' tribal ceremonies that have been appropriated. In all honesty, I would have to say, "Find your own ceremonies; don't take ours."

Finding Western Cultural Contexts

Within the framework of non-Indian culture, there is a rich legacy that has been bequeathed if people will only look. Western society is not devoid of examples that could be emulated, if only one could look beyond one's cultural myopia. For example, if an individual only went so far as to read the delightful stories that Laura Ingalls Wilder (1976) wrote about her growing up, a very effective program could be developed using the subsistence skills that were once common to America's settlers. Wilder was not alone; there were others who left behind a record of early American life and institutions. Virtually every library has some sort of account of a pioneering family that could be effectively used with further research. A most simplistic example perhaps, but it could be easily incorporated into a program. Wigginton (1974) has done much to preserve America's heritage with the Foxfire efforts. Surely there is much that could be critically examined and incorporated from that source—and numerous others.

The nice thing about this approach is that it is *authentic* in the previously defined sense. Moreover, I doubt that many people's sensibilities would be offended, as might occur with some of the pseudo-quasi-religious-mystic undertones of some "Indian style" activities. Certainly, they would not take on the trappings of the "cigar-store" Indian and the inherent tawdriness that comes from such an unnatural union.

> ... pseudo-Indianism is a passing fad. It cannot last. A sacred pipe torn from the body of
>
> a living heritage soon dies and becomes meaningless. (Hawk, 1990)

This is not to say that sweat baths, solo experiences, quests, walkabouts, and so on are inappropriate for use in programs—just don't couch them in metaphorical contexts that cause them to appear to be something that they could never be. Once something has been shown to be a forgery (despite all the careful attention to authentic details), baseness becomes glaringly apparent.

The Value of Rites and Ceremonies

It seems that there is a need for formal rites or ceremonies to validate human experiences within a society. In Western societies, there are christenings, bar mitzvahs, weddings, graduations, funerals, retirements, etc., all done with much ceremony. They are formalized ways in which each person's place in a Western society is validated. In Native American societies, there are rites and ceremonies as well. Upon closer examination it might well be said that activities of the types under discussion are essential for the complete development of a human being. One example must suffice.

Among many Native American tribes, the training of the young boys to become men was long and thorough. For instance, one of the great Crow chiefs, Plenty Coups, had this to say:

> In all seasons of the year most men were in the rivers before sunrise. Boys had plenty of
>
> teachers here. Sometimes they were hard on us, too. They would often send us into the
>
> water to swim among cakes of floating ice, and the ice taught us to take care of our bod-
>
> ies. Cold toughens a man.... In we plunged amid the floating ice. The more difficulties we
>
> faced, the better for us, since they forced us to use our heads as well as our muscles.
>
> Nothing was overlooked that might lead us to self-reliance or give us courage in the face
>
> of sudden danger. (Linderman, 1967)

As I come to the end of this discourse, I feel it necessary to explain a few things. As a Native American, I felt that I could share some perspectives, but please keep in mind that I have only spoken for myself; I do not speak for my tribe. I certainly do not speak for all Native Americans. Nonetheless, I felt that it was important that I should share some of my feelings with you, so that there may be greater understanding between us.

I have no quarrel with those who see the value of developing men and women among our youth by making use of certain activities such as a solo experience, a fast or vision quest, bathing in a sweat lodge, or whatever other activity has been included within an adventure program.

Native Americans are not the only societies in which these activities occur or have occurred; consequently, we don't have a monopoly on them. What I will always object to is couching these activities in the realm of "Indian lore." I am not a museum specimen; my beliefs are not for sale. I am a human being. Treat me as such.

I realize that many people may strive to do these things because of a desire to emulate certain ideals, but please remember, the Noble Savage has existed only in literature, and perpetuating that myth only perpetuates stereotypical ideas. Romance is very seldom reality.

If you feel that the clients you serve may benefit from a sweat bath, fine, *but* don't say it's a Dakota sweat lodge ceremony. If you feel you want to change your name, fine. Just don't tell me that it's an Indian name. (If it really were your true name, I would hope that you wouldn't tell me.) If you want to fast, go ahead; that's your business. And, if you are in search of a vision from your Creator, please seek earnestly. All I ask is that you keep those things sacred to you. There are numerous models within the Western cultural context that can be deemed to be worthy of emulation: Why be ashamed of them because they originated in Western civilization?

References

Bradbury, R. (1953). *Sun and shadow.* New York: The Forthnightly Publishing Company.

Hawk, W. (1990). *Native American religion and New Age cults.* University of Wisconsin: Symposium on Wisconsin Indians. Linderman, F. B. (1967). *Plenty-Coups, Chief of the Crows.* Lincoln: Bison Books.

Wigginton, E., (Ed.). (1974). *The Foxfire book, vol. 1.* Charlotte: Foxfire.

Wilder, L. I. (1976). *The little house in the big woods.* New York: Scholastic Books.

Gendered Experience:
Social Theory & Experiential Practise

▼ ▼ ▼

Martha Bell

It has been almost 20 years since Joy Hardin's doctoral study of women's outdoor experiential learning first identified psychological insights into women's different experiences as participants. And in 1978, women members of the Association for Experiential Education first raised "women's issues" at the annual general meeting, linking the politics of equal rights for women to professional responsibility and attention to sexist language in the association (Garvey, 1990; Yerkes, 1985). Now the first anthology of women's writing in the field of experiential education has been published (see Warren, 1996b), with chapters that contest dominant narratives[1] overlooking women's participation in the collective meaning-making of experience, women's contributions to the practice of experiential facilitation, and women's visibility in the history of the Association for Experiential Education. Recently, it was noted of the anthology that "some of the chapters are somewhat dated ... [and] have been previously published, some as long ago as the 1980s" (Davis-Berman, 1997, p. 54). Indeed, the continued popularity of the small group of landmark essays published in the 1985 *Journal of Experiential Education* issue, "Experiential Education from the Male and Female Point of View," is notable.

---

[1] Dominant narratives of outdoor experiential education are Cockrell (1991), Ewert (1989), Kraft and Sakofs (1985), Miles and Priest (1990), Miner and Boldt (1981), and Warren, Sakofs, and Hunt (1995).

This chapter originally was published in the *Journal of Experiential Education*, with the following citation:
Bell, M. (1997). Gendered experience: Social theory and experiential practice. *Journal of Experiential Education, 20*(3), 143–151.

Are there so few perspectives on gendered experience in the literature of experiential education that early essays "reclaiming" women's experiences are reprinted with little revision of the ideas (e.g., Mitten, 1996, 1990, 1985; Warren, 1996a, 1990, 1985)? Has the dialogue on the nature of gender and associated social issues not changed in the past decade? And where does the "male point of view" contribute to the issues of gender under discussion?

This essay attempts to answer these questions. It argues that social theory and feminist debates have in fact radically altered investigations into social identities and gender relations. New debates point to ways in which gendered identities are not "stable," but have changing social effects in Western society that inform everyday experiences. Still, contemporary arguments and insights have hardly influenced the literature of outdoor experiential education. Gender-issue discussions more often highlight women's "different" perspectives. It is important to the profession to explore why this might be.

The Politics of Gender

The lack of a study of gender, as opposed to studies of women, is conspicuous in this field as elsewhere gender studies are informing education research. From outdoor recreation, leisure, and sport to psychology, sociology, and philosophy, related literature and research examine gender relations. Why is there little reflection of the new developments within related fields of practice and their disciplines to be found in experiential education?[2]

Disciplinary boundaries are collapsing. Experiential education, itself, has emerged from an interdisciplinary combination of psychology, education, and philosophy. Yet feminist studies have developed gender critiques from within every discipline possible and created a distinctly interdisciplinary research methodology. It is hard to find the influence of feminist theory (beyond the research of psychologist Carol Gilligan) in experiential education, yet it seems inconceivable that there would be no study of the politics of gender informing the development of experiential education.

A selection of literature is analysed here with insights from feminist scholarship on gender. It is hoped that a clear, analytical overview might offer a useful tool through which readers, whether researchers or practitioners, might trace the gender concepts that are taken for granted in theoretical and applied aspects of experiential education. The aim is to bring to the fore what are in fact theoretical problems that no longer make sense in practice.

---

[2] Feminist theorising has been combined with leisure research; useful applications to experiential contexts have been forged (Henderson, 1996; Roberts & Drogin, 1993). In education, feminist pedagogy has been compared with experiential pedagogy (Warren & Rheingold, 1993).

This chapter begins by examining the concept of gender as theorized in competing frameworks, as a factor in personality, as a structural category, and as an identity constituted in social relations. The implications of diverse uses of gender concepts to the literature of experiential education are considered. It is suggested that a closer look at gendering practices[3] in organizing bodily experiences, such as physical and mental challenges, can illustrate how experiences are gendered. Approaches are given for practitioners interested in exploring the gendering dynamics of the lived experiences of their students.

Certain accepted theoretical foundations, surveyed briefly below, already serve to underpin experiential practice in the increasing number of publications that define the profession. However, until practitioners are able to interpret gender debates and the actions that contribute to what are actually discourses[4] of identity and power more clearly, experiential practice will revolve on dated concepts of gender and limited concepts of experience.

Sex, Gender, and the Self

A person's sex is commonly treated as an identifying attribute belonging to every individual. As such, it is considered a variable in psychological research, the aims of which are to establish the nature of the individual self by examining all possible variables and the methods of that typify empirical research in experiential education (Ewert, 1987). Conclusions such as "research findings suggest that the outdoor risk taker is usually relatively young, middle class, and male" (Ewert, 1989, p. 62) code sex as either male or female and align it with other demographic "variables" in a list.

Gender may perhaps be most widely understood as an aspect of personality development and part of the expression of personal identity. The term gender conveys consensually accepted meaning about the universal process of gaining a sense of identification for boys and girls. The developmental process is treated as universal because it is assumed that all human growth occurs in the same way. Accordingly, it is claimed that "people develop a gender identity and understanding of gender roles ... as young as five or six years of age" (Jordan, 1992, p. 62).

---

[3] The term *gendering practices* means the language and actions that organise certain gendered meanings while leaving room for deviation and variation, in that there is not one blanket gender identity to be taken up once and shared by all members of a gender group. Gender identities are achieved in continual, contingent processes (see Connell, 1995; Renold, 1997, for use of the term).

[4] The term *discourse* as used here means a network of meanings derived from ideas, ideology, language, and habits reinforced by social institutions and their routine practices. See Weedon (1987) for more detail.

On the basis of psychology, therefore, it can be argued that sex and gender are conceptually significant to experiential educators in that they both inform the self-identity of participants. Experiential learning is about reflexive, or self-referenced,[5] growth in relation to understandings of the self and other, the self and social groups, and the self and society. Beyond self-awareness and personal change, experiential learning also has emancipatory goals. The empowerment of individuals and groups is about collective reflection and social change. In addition, practitioners' gendered self-identities inform the learning context.

In psychological terms, empowerment is a process of facilitating the development of individuals into whole, moral persons, finding greater purpose to their lives and activities by making choices that allow them to reach for their personal potential as capable, knowing, and integrated human beings. To Jordan (1992, p. 62), when "all participants … are '"given" the power and capability to accomplish personal as well as group goals," they are empowered. Roberts (1996, pp. 234–235) discusses empowerment from meeting physical and mental challenges as resulting in positive experiences and personal benefits for participants, who gain "a sense of self and mission."

Not all experiential educators, however, find psychological terms the most useful basis from which to view the complex relationships between self, other, learning, knowledge, power, and physical activity in the outdoors (e.g., K. Bell, 1990; M. Bell, 1996, 1993a; Davidson, 1994; Lynch, 1991). Empowerment must be linked to consciousness-raising (Kohn, 1991). Reflexive growth is only more powerful than reflection alone when it links growth to a process of becoming conscious of one's identity in a social context.

Gender then may be not a component of, but a central constituent of the self *in formation.* If the sense of self of a participant is changing with new self-knowledge, then gender would be a changing, ongoing process. "Becoming gendered therefore entails a coming to awareness of and to some extent internalizing asymmetries of power and esteem" (Flax, 1990, p. 120–121) as the self is informed by its surrounding context. How the reflexive self in each of us becomes conscious of gender must be of concern to practitioners designing experiential learning.

When gender is treated as a psychological construct rather than a social construct, it is innate and personal, and social relations are simply interpersonal relationships. Psychology generates a discourse of individualism that inhibits social change (Davidson, 1994; Warren & Rheingold, 1993). As its claim to truth is normative, its assumptions displace the possibility of alternate, or indeed emancipatory, explanations.

---

[5] Joplin (1981, p. 20) clarifies the term in this way: "Experiential education stresses the individual's development in a self-referenced fashion." In the context of adventure education, one among many experiential pedagogies, Miles and Priest (1990, p. 1) claim that the "goal of the adventure is to expand the self, to learn and grow and progress toward the realization of human potential."

Arguments such as Phipps' (1988, p. 15), for example, that "the psychological foundations of teaching and learning" offer the most effective principles on which to develop individual students' communication, perception, arousal, and motivation treat individuals as having identical needs in their psychological development. As gender is already fixed in each individual, it is not a part of their learning. But, relying on the same assumptions in recent work when survey data reveal perceived differences between women and men instructors' effectiveness, Phipps cannot explain why a person's gender might emerge as affecting the teaching and learning process and can only indicate that there is a new "variable" to consider: "Are there basic gender differences that come into play?" (Phipps & Claxton, 1997, p. 44). More explanations for the effects of becoming conscious of gender in social contexts might help to illuminate the research findings.

A key text provides another example when it presents "the nature of experience" as wholly encapsulated in a section on "the social psychology of adventure education" with no section on sociology or cultural theory (Miles & Priest, 1990). The only examination of the nature of the self makes no mention of gender, again presumably because while self-concept can be enhanced, gender is seen as a stable feature of the universal self (Klint, 1990; see also Ewert, 1989). The universal self, in social psychology, is stabilised in biology and thus returns to biological sex.

The sex-differences perspective grounds the developmental focus and anchors the theory of sex role socialization. Different gender traits and behaviours are developmental according to sex; they are predetermined by age-related stages of growth differentiated by sex and "learned" early on. Gender analyses in experiential education literature relying on the notion of sex differences commonly start with a list of the traits "associated with" females and those "associated with" males (e.g., Henderson & Bialeschki, 1987; Jordan, 1992; Joyce, 1988; Knapp, 1985; Nolan & Priest, 1993). These lists are then taken as immutable. An example is the concern that "males and females are often caught in their sex roles and respond according to stereotypical patterns" (Knapp, 1985, p. 16). It is a common notion that the "gender trap" can be escaped if its "biological origins" are respected (that is, not questioned) and if individuals simply adopt and "model" the role behaviours of the "opposite" sex (Knapp, 1985, p. 19).

Social psychologists influenced by cultural arguments now accept that social, rather than biological, meanings of gender, rather than sex, influence role socialization.[6] But while they acknowledge that gender roles may be socially constructed, or moulded from concensual

---

[6] This shift among social psychologists is in contrast to past uses of role theory itself, which did not conceptually allow for social categories such as gender to shape roles (Deaux, 1992).

meanings,[7] they do not dispute that sex-based traits are responsible for defining the social meanings with which gender is categorised (Kitzinger, 1992).[8] In experiential education literature, it is therefore sometimes argued that social meanings *map* the gender identities of masculinity and femininity *onto* the existing biological sexes of male and female (e.g., Henderson, 1996; Jordan, 1992). These can be interpreted as attempts to clarify the process of becoming gendered.

Even so, such arguments rarely concede that physiological differences are actually constructed into "two and only two, obviously universal, natural, bipolar, mutually exclusive sexes that *necessarily* correspond to stable gender identity and gendered behaviour" (Birrell & Cole, 1994, p. 375; emphasis added). The problem with a cultural revision of gender role orientation is still that it collapses gender onto sex for its conceptual stability. Sexual difference seems to be a key obstacle for experiential educators.

Gender and Patriarchy

Sexual difference is defined in a competing theoretical explanation in which biological sex is itself treated as a social phenomenon. Social theory argues that gender identity is not predetermined by an essential factor, sex, directing one's earliest psycho-sexual development as a person who is (already) male or female. Social identity is not developed psychologically, concluded at sexual maturity for the adult man or woman, but defined in a plurality of group memberships.

Social identities, then, comprise categorical groups used to stratify contemporary Western society. In this case, sexual difference stratifies society into a gender order, that is, patriarchy. Gender serves to categorise men and women differently through the sexual division of labour and production rather than through the biological imperatives of growing up as girls or boys.

Early social theorists gave a functional explanation for universal social categories. Categories were thought to structure all social behaviour through the institutions of society, and human beings adapted to the stability of categorical structures in family systems. As everyone is born into a family, gender categories could be applied universally.

---

[7] The term *socially constructed* here means the repetitive social moulding of knowledge created by consensual beliefs. While it is not theoretically the same as socialised, it is sometimes substituted by those who want to indicate the "strong," collective effects of socialisation (Kitzinger, 1992). Social construction refers to knowledge; socialisation refers to behaviours in reciprocal role relationships (Deaux, 1992).

[8] Gender schema theory (discussed by Jordan, 1992) is the combination of early sex differences research with beliefs in socialisation, but children are still thought to be predisposed to the behaviour of a sex type.

As feminists have pointed out, the gender system is maintained in the (heterosexual) family through kinship rules that fuse sexuality and gender (Rubin, 1975). Functional sex/gender categories consequently prepare men and women for the social relations of the workplace, that is, the "public" activities of production, without attention to the "private" activities of reproduction (Chodorow, 1978). When treated functionally, the permanence of the gender order and its constituents, such as motherhood, childcare, and family roles, are rarely questioned (e.g., Mitten, 1985), dealing instead with their effects.

Patriarchy, in underpinning society, also actively directs pedagogical practices and principles. The heterosexual family discourse plainly organises adventure-based counselling, another of the many experiential pedagogies, to the point that co-leadership relationships are characterized in one text as modelling "mom and dad" in complementary (gendered and sexualized) roles (Davidson, 1994; see Schoel, Prouty, & Radcliffe, 1988, pp. 155–56).

Gender and Social Relations

In a third theoretical framework, sociocultural studies are further interested in the interaction of gender with culture rather than with society. In a much more complex way than developmental template or gender order, gender and culture continue to interact in every situation and environment in which there are social relations attached to cultural meanings.

Sociologists see gender as an ideology, a set of political interests that "produce" our intentions, actions, social interactions, and exchange values. Essentialism, discussed further below, would be one such ideology, perhaps the most "productive" in terms of current gender issues in experiential education. Sociocultural theorists are specifically interested in the local contexts in which ideological meanings are enacted differently. For example, "the outdoors" is one such local context where particular cultural meanings are produced. Cultural meanings are contingent, less fixed, and negotiated in everyday social relations. The "everyday" in the outdoors may be unfamiliar to students, but routines for outdoor leaders and facilitators are established to professionalise social relations. There is still constant construction *and reconstruction* of masculine and feminine identities "which produce us as social beings" (Renold, 1997, p. 7). In this way, gendered social relations are implicated in continual struggles for power (Connell, 1987, see pp. 54–61) even in the outdoors.

And so there are various explanations available for how "the self" and social interactions are gendered to answer the question posed by Phipps and Claxton. One might conclude that gender identity is innate and predetermined, internalized in the learning of social roles, organized in structural categories, or produced and reproduced in the social relations of everyday actions. Whether one does so depends on one's belief in the primacy of biologically based psychological causes, the salience of socialization, the control of systemic institutions, or the exercise of relations of power. A survey of the literature shows that there is a predominance of the first two explanations, that is, a reliance on the sociopsychological etiology of gender identity in experiential education.

Why Does Gender Matter?

Often the claim is that gender does *not* matter in the outdoors, a "natural" learning environment that can somehow be gender-free. There is powerful appeal in the claim that everyone is treated equally by nature; when learning is experienced in the outdoors, gender does not matter. Yet the nostalgia for gender-free experiences reveals how strongly gender matters in social contexts. Indeed, the claim that "the potential benefits of outdoor experiences for women are often similar to benefits anyone might receive" (Henderson, 1992, p. 50) promises a normalising function for outdoor activities. And it it is clearly lodged in a sociopsychological perspective of the already formed gender identity of those seeking universal benefits.

The "even-handedness of consequences" (Powch, 1994, p. 18) and level-playing-field claims that the outdoors is beyond the social have been criticized as a myth (e.g., Joyce, 1988; Warren, 1985). Nature and the outdoors are social contexts in which meaning is constantly being constructed. The wilderness has been called "the Earth Mother, the Goddess" (Powch, 1994, p. 19), but also called a "male world" (Loeffler, 1995), one "associated with male dominance" (Nolan & Priest, 1993; see also Gray & Patterson, 1995; Jordan, 1990; Knapp, 1985; Lynch, 1991). Gender does matter here, not in an individualistic, psychological orientation or even psychic metaphor, but rather in its power to infuse shared cultural meanings into the local site of experiential learning.

Another local site is social relations themselves, in which gendered identity is constituted. Most of the feminist writing proposes that as women are different from men—in the very nature of their being—they "need" different treatment, leadership, and programming whether or not men are present (e.g., Beale, 1988; Bialeschki, 1992; Cosgriff & Bell, 1990; Johnson, 1990; Jordan, 1992; Joyce, 1988; Mack, 1996; Mitten, 1996, 1992, 1985; Nanschild, 1996; Warren, 1985). Sexual difference is taken up as the solution to the myth of equality, despite feminist critique that exposes the equality-versus-difference opposition as a false construction (Scott, 1988). "Different" is always not equal in such an opposition because, ultimately, identifying women as different in their "essential" natures defines women as "natural"' and forever limited by their (sexed) bodies.

Other analyses hinge on the claim that because women and men are different, men "need" women present in the same groups and programmes so that gender issues are confronted (e.g., Knapp, 1985). Accounts of the first women to participate as students at Outward Bound in the United States (Miner & Boldt, 1981) and the participation of girls with boys in outdoor education (Gray & Patterson, 1995; Humberstone, 1990) credit women and girls with defusing dominant masculine behaviours and attitudes in their groups. The responsibility for "humanising" experiential education contexts and "completing" their "half" of the range of human behaviours (Joyce, 1988, p. 24) again places girls and women in a false position of complementarity. That sexual difference and gender complementarity are essentialized, and undertheorized, indicates the power of gender matters in experiential education.

Gendered Bodies

Significantly, gender matters more in experiential education than in other forms of learning, because experiential pedagogy depends on the performance of bodies and physical achievements (Arnold, 1994; Bell, 1993b). Likewise, gender issues are embodied in both becoming a gendered person and becoming empowered through action. Experiential learning is not simply about changing behaviours, respecting unique needs, or honouring difference, but also constructs gendered behaviours, defines special needs by gender, and reconstitutes sexual difference in active bodily experience. As long as psychobiological explanations rest on developmental difference that "naturalises" gender (as essential), experiential education will also naturalise gendered bodies.

Critical theorists have revisited both social and psychological meta-theories since the 1980s, including accepted explanations for human growth and development, knowledge, pedagogy, experience, and the self (Flax, 1990; Morss, 1996; see Butler, 1990, 1987, for such a revision). They conclude that people participate in actively gendering their own bodies, their activities, and experiences "within a network of deeply entrenched cultural norms" (Butler, 1987, p. 128).

The cultural norms for gendered bodies as sites of power are overlooked in outdoor experiential education contexts (Bell, 1993b; e.g., Maguire & Priest, 1994). Typically, practitioners are encouraged to treat participants as a bundle of feelings, instinctive defenses, and unconscious behaviour patterns (e.g., Nadler & Luckner, 1992, pp. 3–6). Becoming gendered occurs in not only the unconscious with its drives and instincts, but also the socially constituted body with which one enacts one's feelings and fears.

The link for experiential educators is that embodiment is the direct experience of one's own "lived" body within different cultural meanings. That is, embodiment is subjective and social at the same time. It is therefore a site for the lived sense of self and gender *and* cultural expectations of self and gender. Participants cannot experience learning experientially without actually embodying their own coming to consciousness.

The lived sense of self, then, is always located in a person's experience of his/her own socially produced life story. Dewey (1938, p. 89; emphasis added), notes that "education ... must be based on experience—which is always *the actual life-experience of some individual.*"

As such, "the self" can never be disconnected from the constituents of that life experience, that is, the constituents of lived subjective and social identity: gender, class, race, and sexuality. As Warren and Rheingold (1993, p. 29; emphasis added) suggest, "To validate the experience of women and girls, it is crucial to include real issues of *their* lives."

Not only are experiences always gendered, but class, race, and sexualization intersect with gendering practices in forces of social regulation. Moreover, intense personal effort often accompanies the practices necessary for becoming one's gendered, sexual, racial, and economically invested "self" (Bartky, 1990; Foucault, 1980). Learning experiences must take these social and subjective forces into account.

Experiential Practice

How do practitioners sensitive to gendered social relations take gender into account in learning experiences? How does experiential programming construct gendered behaviours and constitute sexual difference in active bodily experience? Rather than repeating the valuable suggestions already available for how to apply socially critical approaches in one's teaching (e.g., Jackson, 1993; McClintock, 1994; Warren & Rheingold, 1993), the focus here is on preparing oneself for a more informed selection of the practical activities offered by other authors.

Primarily, the important point is to examine every pedagogical method, activity, and rationale for ways that it restricts possibilities for gender to be practised in multiple ways. This might seem like a self-evident point, but it is more difficult in practice.

It may be overwhelming to facilitators to know where to start, especially if students come with deep investments in their particular constructions of masculine or feminine self-identity. The following excerpt from an interview in New Zealand hints at the worry that social issues can be confused with a personal agenda; the context is how this outdoor leader responds to gender dynamics.

> Valerie: It's usually not something I talk about explicitly with a group.... I often have a
> dilemma about what concepts or what ideas or what things I should introduce. It's like,
> well, this is their experience.... I can see all this stuff going on now but this is what they
> are focusing on.... Should I draw their attention to this or should I just work with what
> they perceive is important to them?

There is more than one place for facilitators to start when looking for ways to include gender interventions. The first is reading the professional literature carefully for traditional concepts of masculinity and femininity. Comb professional materials for clear definitions of gender concepts and indications of the discipline in which they are theorized. For example, a report on men's and women's experiences in an experiential work programme explains to the reader that the research is grounded in Gilligan's psychological premise that "women have different developmental needs than men" (Kozolanka, 1995, p. 73).

Practise not taking ideas for granted. Find out what developmental needs are, for example, and read a copy of Gilligan's work. Practise deconstructing ideas for generalizations about the "essential" nature of men and women. Note that Kozolanka does not assume that he knows what the women in his study "need," but works from their journals and poses questions based on his reading and his empirical field observations.

The second place to begin is by comparing what you read with your own professional experiences. Keep rigorous field notes as you observe your students and your own practice. Ask yourself where the male point of view contributes to the construction of gender relations. Kozolanka's (1995) research, for instance, discusses gendering practices at the jobsite, but unfortunately then reports only women's experiences of femininity, sexism, and homophobia rather than the men's of masculinity, misogyny, and heterosexism.

When dialogue on sexism and gender oppression falls to women in their workplaces and professional associations (Garvey, 1985; Joyce, 1988, Yerkes, 1985), the logic of essentialism is being used against women. The lack of self-conscious scholarship in experiential education on masculinity or men's experiences (Rasberry, 1991, is the exception) is evidence of the extent to which gender issues are subordinately positioned as "women's issues."

Here is another example, juxtaposing two unsubstantiated generalizations[9] with two empirical observations from the same New Zealand interview.

> It is easy for women to slip into a secondary subservient role to a confident male. (Johnson, 1990, p. 40)

> Women are frequently intimidated by men in mixed programmes ... that require any degree of physical competence. (Nolan & Priest, 1993, p. 14)

> Valerie: I find lots of things here [at the outdoor centre] reinforce the fact that it's not okay for a woman [on staff] to ask for help, because it just reaffirms everyone's opinion that women, you know—we're here as tokens and that really we shouldn't be doing this.

> Valerie: Subtle comments are really common in terms of ... [me] being sort of male.... One of the groups that I've had very recently ... had one quite strong character in the course and

---

[9] These statements are not substantiated with empirical research material, but appear in commentary-type articles for practitioners.

he constantly made comments—Like, he would constantly correct me.... And just make comments like "Oh, any man can do that, you should be able to do that."... And then at the same time as he was saying that, he'd rush in and pick heavy things up for [the other women students] and do stuff. He wouldn't actually let them be physical and competent. And it was really interesting to watch ... how more and more withdrawn the women actually did become.

The juxtaposition of the statements and "lived" realities of a situation helps to draw out ambiguities and contradictions in discussions that fix gendered behaviours in very narrow terms. It becomes clearer that "the same society which urges us to reconsider stereotypes in sex role definition and to 'liberate' ourselves and others from their constraints, also exhibits extraordinary anxiety about the whole matter.... There is something contradictory about cultural attitudes toward gender" (Miranda, 1985, p. 7).

The third suggestion for educators, leaders, and programmers is to examine the discursive power of gender narratives as they operate on the bodies and actions of participants. McClintock (1994, p. 40) suggests that "real people presenting true stories" of their experiences can be an effective emancipatory tool. The collective emphasis is as crucial to this technique as to any other aspect of challenge-based approaches, so that any story told is not just personal but invites recognition of the social constituents of life histories and memories.

Narratives are, however, "more than a story-telling tool" (Renold, 1997, p. 7), but rather, complex discourses that access inclusion and exclusion. As discursive story-lines, especially when collectively generated, narratives of becoming masculine or becoming feminine may be used effectively throughout an adventure or learning experience to reconstruct gendering practices, such as language, as "lived" by students as opposed to applying abstract applications of gender norms. Their "deconstruction" might illustrate ways in which gendered identities, such as being a strong man—or strong woman—are not "stable," but have multiple social effects which people can, or feel unable to, take up or discard.

Gendering practices themselves obviously *effect* the "something contradictory in cultural attitudes," but when dissonance is brought to consciousness, its availability as a site of resistance to dominant narratives may be revealed. Gender narratives do change in ongoing struggle. Professionals might then begin to understand, for example, women of colour who identify first as members of an ethnicity, but also embrace universally woman-centred metaphors of the wilderness (e.g., Asher, Huffaker, & McNally, 1994). Facilitators might forge connections for men, for example, who do not see differences between men, such as men of different class backgrounds or men of different sexualities, as impacting their own lived experiences of masculinity.

In conclusion, the argument here has not been for the "truth" of any one explanation of gender relations and their effects. Varied disciplinary bases within which researchers work will always provide their particular definitions. However, more informed debate on new concepts of gender and the constituents of identity, in order to make clear the internal logic and implications of whatever theoretical perspective is used, will always strengthen a profession intimately involved with powerful narratives of more than just individual learning and growth.

References

Arnold, S. C. (1994). Transforming body image through women's wilderness experiences. In E. Cole, E. Erdman & E. D. Rothblum (Eds.), *Wilderness therapy for women: The power of adventure* (pp. 43–54). New York: Haworth Press.

Asher, S. J., Huffaker, G. Q., & McNally M. (1994). Therapeutic considerations of wilderness experiences for incest and rape survivors. In E. Cole, E. Erdman & E. D. Rothblum (Eds.), *Wilderness therapy for women: The power of adventure* (pp. 161–174). New York: Haworth Press.

Bartky, S. L. (1990). Foucault, femininity and the modernization of patriarchal power. In *Femininity and domination: Studies in the phenomenology of oppression* (pp. 63-82). New York: Routledge.

Beale, V. (1988). Men's journeys & women's journeys: A different story? *Journal of COBWS Education, IV*(1), 7–13.

Bell, K. S. (1990). *Making tracks: Gender relations and tramping.* Unpublished Masters Thesis, University of Canterbury, Christchurch, New Zealand.

Bell, M. (1996). Feminists challenging assumptions about outdoor Leadership. In K. Warren (Ed.), *Women's Voices in Experiential Education* (pp. 141–156). Dubuque, IA: Kendall/Hunt.

Bell, M. (1993a). *Feminist outdoor leadership: Understandings of the complexities of feminist practice as women outdoor leaders.* Unpublished Master's of Education Research Project, University of Toronto, Toronto, Canada.

Bell, M. (1993b). What constitutes experience? Rethinking theoretical assumptions. *Journal of Experiential Education, 16*(1), 19–24.

Bialeschki, M. D. (1992). We said, "why not?"—A historical perspective on women's outdoor pursuits. *Journal of Physical Education, Recreation & Dance, 63*(2), 52–55.

Birrell, S., & Cole, C. L. (1994). Double fault: Renee Richards and the construction and naturalization of difference. In S. Birrell & C. L. Cole (Eds.), *Women, sport and culture* (pp. 373–397). Champaign, IL: Human Kinetics.

Butler, J. (1990). *Gender trouble: Feminism and the subversion of identity.* London: Routledge.

Butler, J. (1987). Variations on sex and gender: Beauvoir, Wittig and Foucault. In S. Benhabib & D. Cornell (Eds.), *Feminism as critique: On the politics of gender* (pp. 128–142). Minneapolis, MN: University of Minnesota Press.

Chodorow, N. (1978). *The reproduction of mothering: Psychoanalysis and the sociology of gender.* Berkeley, CA: University of California Press.

Cockrell, D. (1991). *The wilderness educator: The Wilderness Education Association Curriculum Guide.* Merrillville, IN: ICS Books.

Connell, R. W. (1995). *Masculinities.* St. Leonards: Allen & Unwin.

Connell, R. W. (1987). *Gender & power.* Stanford, CA: Stanford University Press.

Cosgriff, M., & Bell, M. (1990). Women Outdoors New Zealand: Networking to serve women's needs in the outdoors. In NZAHPER (Ed.), *Proceedings of the 1990 Commonwealth and International Conference for Health, Physical Education, Dance, Recreation and Leisure, Vol. 6* (pp. 59–68). Auckland: Conference Organizers.

Davidson, J. (1994). *A feminist poststructuralist reading of adventure outdoor education.* Unpublished Master's Thesis, University of Alberta, Edmonton, Canada.

Davis-Berman, J. (1997). Book review of women's voices in experiential education. *Journal of Experiential Education, 20*(1), 53–54.

Deaux, K. (1992). Personalizing identity and socializing self. In G. M. Breakwell (Ed.), *Social Psychology of Identity and the Self Concept* (pp. 9–33). London: Surrey University Press.

Dewey, J. (1938). *Experience and education.* New York: Collier Books.

Ewert, A. (1989). Outdoor adventure pursuits: Foundations, models, and *theories.* Columbus, OH: Publishing Horizons.

Ewert, A. (1987). Research in outdoor adventure: Overview and analysis. *Bradford Papers Annual, II*, 15–28.

Flax, J. (1990). *Thinking fragments: Psychoanalysis, feminism, & postmodernism in the contemporary West.* Berkeley, CA: University of California Press.

Foucault, M. (1980). *Power/knowledge: Selected interviews & other writings 1972–1977.* Edited by C. Gordon. New York: Pantheon Books.

Garvey, D. (1990). A history of the AEE. In J. C. Miles & S. Priest, *Adventure education* (pp. 75–82). State College, PA: Venture.

Gray, T., & Patterson, J. (1995). Differential gender outcomes for adolescent participants following an extended sojourn to the Australian bush. In L. S. Frank (Ed.), *Association for Experiential Education 23rd Annual International Conference Proceedings* (pp. 106–109). Boulder, CO: Association for Experiential Education.

Henderson, K. A. (1996). Feminist perspectives on outdoor leadership. In K. Warren (Ed.), *Women's Voices in Experiential Education* (pp. 107–117). Dubuque, IO: Kendall/Hunt.

Henderson, K. A. (1992). Breaking with tradition—Women and outdoor pursuits. *Journal of Physical Education, Recreation & Dance, 63*(2), 49–51.

Henderson, K. A., & Bialeschki, M. D. (1987). Viva la diferencia!: Male/female differences can contribute to positive growth in all outdoor learning. *Camping Magazine, 59*(4), 20–22.

Humberstone, B. (1990). Warriors or wimps? Creating alternative forms of physical education. In M. A. Messner & D. F. Sabo (Eds.), *Sport, Men and the Gender Order: Critical Perspectives* (pp. 201–210). Champaign, IL: Human Kinetics.

Jackson, S. J. (1993). The end of the innocence: Learning to critique experience through the media analysis of sport. *Journal of Experiential Education, 16*(3), 40–45.

Johnson, D. (1990). Women in the outdoors. *Journal of Adventure Education and Outdoor Leadership, 7*(3), 38–40.

Joplin, L. (1981). On defining experiential education. *Journal of Experiential Education, 4*(1), 17–20.

Jordan, D. (1992). Effective leadership for girls and women in outdoor recreation. *Journal of Physical Education, Recreation & Dance, 63*(2), 61–64.

Jordan, D. (1990). Snips and snails and puppy dog tails...The use of gender free language in experiential education. *Journal of Experiential Education, 13*(2), 45–49.

Joyce, M. (1988). Rocks & rivers, men & women: Learning from each other at Outward Bound. *Journal of COBWS Education, IV*(1), 22–25.

Kitzinger, C. (1992). The individuated self concept: A critical analysis of social-constructionist writing on individualism. In G. M. Breakwell (Ed.), *Social Psychology of Identity and the Self Concept* (pp. 221–250). London: Surrey University Press.

Klint, K. A. (1990). New directions for inquiry into self-concept and adventure experiences. In J. C. Miles & S. Priest, *Adventure Education* (pp. 163–172). State College, PA: Venture.

Knapp, C. (1985). Escaping the gender trap: The ultimate challenge for experiential educators. *Journal of Experiential Education, 8*(2), 16–19.

Kohn, S. (1991). Specific programmatic strategies to increase empowerment. *Journal of Experiential Education, 14*(1), 6–12.

Kozolanka, K. (1995). Gender and engagement in a jobsite classroom. In B. Horwood (Ed.), *Experience and the Curriculum* (pp. 69–92). Dubuque, IA: Kendall/Hunt.

Kraft, R. & Sakofs, M. (Eds.). (1985). *The theory of experiential education*. Boulder, CO: Association for Experiential Education.

Loeffler, T. A. (1995). Factors influencing women's outdoor leadership career development. *Melpomene Journal, 14*(3), 15–21.

Lynch, P. (1991). *Girls and outdoor education*. Unpublished master's thesis, University of Otago, Dunedin New Zealand.

McClintock, M. (1994). Our lives are our best teaching tools. *Journal of Experiential Education, 17*(2), 40–43.

Mack, H. (1996). Inside work, outdoors: Women, metaphor and meaning. In K. Warren (Ed.), *Women's Voices in Experiential Education* (pp. 24–31). Dubuque, IA: Kendall/Hunt.

Maguire, R., & Priest, S. (1994). The treatment of bulimia nervosa through adventure therapy. *Journal of Experiential Education, 17*(2), 44–48.

Miles, J. C., & Priest, S. (1990). Adventure *education*. State College, PA: Venture.

Miner, J. L., & Boldt, J. (1981). *Outward Bound USA: Learning through experience in adventure-based education*. New York, NY: William Morrow.

Miranda, W. (1985). "Heading for the hills" and the search for gender solidarity. *Journal of Experiential Education, 8*(2), 6-9.

Mitten, D. (1996). A philosophical basis for a women's outdoor adventure program. In K. Warren (Ed.), *Women's Voices in Experiential Education* (pp. 78–84). Dubuque, IA: Kendall/Hunt.

Mitten, D. (1992). Empowering girls and women in the outdoors. *Journal of Physical Education, Recreation & Dance, 63*(2), 56–60.

Mitten, D. (1990). A philosophical basis for a women's outdoor adventure program. *Action, 8*(2), 26–27.

Mitten, D. (1985). A philosophical basis for a women's outdoor adventure program. *Journal of Experiential Education, 8*(2), 20–24.

Morss, J. R. (1996). *Growing critical: Alternatives to developmental psychology*. London: Routledge.

Nadler, R. S., & Luckner, J. L. (1992). *Processing the adventure experience*. Dubuque, IA: Kendall/Hunt.

Nanschild, D. (1996). Women's perceptions and experiences in outdoor recreation. In T. Gray & B. Hallyer (Eds)., *Catalysts for change: Papers from the 10th National Outdoor Education Conference* (pp. 177–182). Sydney: The Outdoor Professionals.

Nolan, T. L., & Priest, S. (1993). Outdoor programmes for women only? *Journal of Adventure Education and Outdoor Leadership, 10*(1), 14–17.

Phipps, M. (1988). The instructor and experiential education in the outdoors. *Journal of Environmental Education, 20*(1), 8–16.

Phipps, M. L., & Claxton, D. B. (1997). An investigation into instructor effectiveness. *Journal of Experiential Education, 20*(1), 40–46.

Powch, I. G. (1994). Wilderness therapy: What makes it empowering for women? In E. Cole, E. Erdman & E. D. Rothblum (Eds.), *Wilderness Therapy for Women: The Power of Adventure* (pp. 11–27). New York: Haworth Press.

Rasberry, G. (1991). Learning to cross the street: A male perspective on feminist theory. *Journal of Experiential Education, 14*(3), 6–11.

Renold, E. (1997). 'All they've got on their brains is football:' Sport, masculinity and the gendered practices of playground relations. *Sport, Education and Society, 2*(1), 5–23.

Roberts, N. S. (1996). Women of color in experiential education: Crossing cultural boundaries. In K. Warren (Ed.), *Women's Voice in Experiential Education* (pp. 226–240). Dubuque, IA: Kendall/Hunt.

Roberts, N. S., & Drogin, E. B. (1993). The outdoor recreation experience: Factors affecting participation of African American women. *Journal of Experiential Education, 16*(1), 14–18.

Rubin, G. (1975). The traffic in women: The political economy of sex. In R. R. Reiter (Ed.), *Toward an Anthropology of Women* (pp. 178–192). New York, NY: Monthly Review Press.

Schoel, J., Prouty, D., & Radcliffe, P. (1988). *Islands of healing: A guide to adventure based counseling*. Hamilton, MA: Project Adventure.

Scott, J. W. (1988). Deconstructing equality-versus-difference: Or, the uses of poststructuralist theory for feminism. *Feminist Studies, 14*(1), 33–50.

Warren, K. (1996a). Women's outdoor adventures: Myth and reality. In K. Warren (Ed.) *Women's Voices in Experiential Education* (pp. 10-17). Dubuque, IA: Kendall/Hunt.

Warren, K. (Ed.). (1996b). *Women's voices in experiential education*. Dubuque, IA: Kendall/Hunt.

Warren, K. (1993). The midwife teacher: Engaging students in the experiential education process. *Journal of Experiential Education, 16*(1), 33–38.

Warren, K. (1990). Women's outdoor adventures. In J. C. Miles & S. Priest, *Adventure Education* (pp. 411–417). State College, PA: Venture.

Warren, K. (1985). Women's outdoor adventures: Myth and reality. *Journal of Experiential Education, 8*(2), 10–14.

Warren, K., & Rheingold, A. (1993). Feminist pedagogy and experiential education: A critical look. *Journal of Experiential Education, 16*(3), 25–31.

Warren, K., Sakofs, M. & Hunt, J. S., Jr. (Eds.). (1995). *The theory of experiential education*. Dubuque, IA: Kendall/Hunt.

Weedon, C. (1987). *Feminist practice and poststructuralist theory*. Oxford: Basil Blackwell.

Yerkes, R. (1985). Guest editorial: We are all in this together. *Journal of Experiential Education, 8*(2), 4–5.

Sharing Lesbian, Gay, & Bisexual Life Experiences Face to Face

▾ ▾ ▾

Mary McClintock

I first experienced a panel presentation on lesbian and gay issues when I was a college student in the mid-Seventies. Members of the campus Lesbian Alliance spoke to dorm groups as part of an effort to improve the climate for lesbians at the women's college I attended. It was both scary and exciting to sit in the dorm living room with other women from my dorm and discuss our concerns as lesbians, heterosexuals, and women who did not want to define their sexual orientation. By the end of the evening, I felt proud to be a lesbian and part of the organization that sponsored the discussion, and relieved that it was possible to talk about myself with other women in the dorm. The dialogue that occurred helped set a context for discussing everyone's concerns, whatever their sexual orientation. Fifteen years later, my experience of hearing a speakers' panel when I was in college was echoed by a student in one of the classes I teach. He said, "Listening to the panel made me feel proud to be a gay man. It was the first time I realized that I could feel good about myself and stand up to the harassment facing in the dorm."

Currently, I am a member of Face to Face, a gay, lesbian, and bisexual speakers' bureau based in Amherst, Massachusetts. We speak to a wide range of groups, including classes in elementary schools through colleges, social service organizations, and religious organizations. We have spoken at several Association for Experiential Education (AEE) Northeast Regional Conferences. Similar speakers' bureaus exist in Boston, San Francisco, and at many

This chapter originally was published in the *Journal of Experiential Education*, with the following citation:

McClintock, M. (1992). Sharing lesbian, gay, and bisexual life experiences face to face. *Journal of Experiential Education, 15*(3), 51–55.

colleges. Speakers volunteer for a number of reasons. I am a member of a speakers' bureau because talking to people about being a lesbian feels like one small thing I can do to make the world a better place for lesbians. I do not want other lesbians to face the discrimination and pain that I have experienced.

This article explores the importance, rationale, process, and effective use of lesbian, gay, and bisexual speakers' panels as an educational tool. Why should experiential educators be familiar with and use these panels? Lesbian, gay, and bisexual people are everywhere, including learning and working as students and staff members of experiential education programs. Homophobia (the fear and hatred of lesbians, gays, and bisexuals) is also everywhere. Like other forms of oppression, homophobia works on many levels, including interpersonal and institutional levels. As students and staff of experiential education programs, we are subjected to jokes and comments about lesbians and gays, harassment, and institutional policies that discriminate against us. All of this serves to hinder our ability to learn as students or work effectively as staff members.

My own experience bears this out. As a staff member of an organization that provided therapeutic wilderness programs for adolescents, I experienced harassment from students with whom I worked and the potential of losing my job if anyone found out I was a lesbian. Prior to my starting work in the program, a gay man on the staff told other staff that he was gay. Right after he disclosed his sexual orientation, the Board of Directors of the organization met and removed "sexual orientation" from the non-discrimination clause in the personnel policy. They decided that they wanted to reserve the right to discriminate against lesbians and gays in hiring. When I learned of this policy, the message to me was clear: being open about being a lesbian could cost me my job. In that job and others where I could not be open about being a lesbian, I found that I was less able to be effective in my work. Hiding something as basic as the identity of my life partner took a tremendous emotional and mental toll. Being emotionally shut down meant that I was less available to my students and my co-workers. I had similar experiences as a student in experiential education programs.

As experiential educators, we spend a great deal of time and energy working to make sure that our students can get the full benefit of our educational programs and that staff can perform their jobs. However, if we do not work to eradicate homophobia and other forms of oppression in our programs, we are essentially saying that it is acceptable for some of our students and co-workers to not receive all that we have to offer and, potentially, to be hurt by our program. I believe that it is essential for all experiential education programs to work on improving their ability to be a setting where lesbians, gays, and bisexuals can be fully affirmed as students and staff members. These beliefs have been echoed by AEE members who have been panelists and participants at lesbian, gay, and bisexual speakers' panels at AEE Regional Conferences.

Speakers' panels are one of the most powerful methods available for educating people about lesbian, gay, and bisexual issues. What exactly is a lesbian, gay, and bisexual speakers' panel? Although the format varies depending on the context of the panel, the basic format consists of an introduction to the panel; each panelist speaking briefly about his/her life as a lesbian, or bisexual person; and a time for questions, answers, and dialogue. On the surface, this design sounds quite simple, and not very experiential or profound. However, I can say honestly that profound experiential education does occur at every panel.

After many years of being a panelist and using panels in the courses I teach on social justice issues, I have begun to examine the question: What makes this form of social justice education so successful? I have come up with a number of possible reasons. First, homophobia is both similar to and different from other social justice issues. An understanding of homophobia's uniqueness with respect to other forms of oppression sheds some light on the power of lesbian, gay, and bisexual speakers' panels. A second key factor in the success of these panels is that they are designed and facilitated in a manner that attends to the emotional safety of both the panelists and the participants. Finally, speakers' panels are grounded in basic principles of adult and experiential learning theory. These principles include an understanding of the importance of personal experience to adult learners and the use of processing discussions to complete the experiential learning cycle. These are all key issues in the success of this form of social justice education.

Homophobia in Relation to Other Forms of Oppression

One of the main ways that homophobia works is through silence and lack of information. From a very young age, many of us are taught not to talk about "that kind of people." For many, the only context in which they hear about lesbians, gays, and bisexuals is whispered jokes and stereotypes or shouted taunts. For most people, there is virtually no accurate information available about lesbians, gays, and bisexuals. Two comments by college students who experienced panel presentations in their classes attest to the lack of accurate information available. A woman in her sixties commented, "Thank you for coming to talk to our class. I never met a lesbian before. I need to think more about this. You are not what I expected a lesbian to be like." A 20-year-old man said, "I used to think fags were all really sick ... but being in this class and hearing the panel made me realize that maybe the stuff people say about gays is like the stuff people say about Jews like me ... maybe it's all lies."

Panels about lesbian, gay, and bisexual issues have similarities to and differences from other forums where members of oppressed social groups speak about their lives. Some other oppressed groups, such as women, Jews, and people of color, have been more visible than lesbians, gays, and bisexuals. Lesbians, gays, and bisexuals are often invisible because many of us do not reveal our identities. Because men of color and women are more visible, they are more likely to be put in an educator role: to be asked questions about the "women's point of view" or the "African American's point of view," etc. Many members of oppressed social groups, especially women and people of color, are tired of being educators and do not want to be in this role. Lesbians, gays, and bisexuals are less likely to have been put in this educator role because of our relative invisibility and because heterosexual people have not been clamoring for education about our lives. While forums of speakers on other social justice issues can be powerful, lesbian, gay, and bisexual speakers' panels are particularly powerful because of these contextual differences.

My experience as a woman and as a lesbian illustrates these differences. I do not feel compelled to speak on panels about my experience of being a woman. There are many opportunities to talk to other people in daily conversations about the issues that concern me. A growing number of written and media materials address women's issues. Many times other people have assumed that I would be an educator or speak about women's issues because they know I am a woman. On some occasions the educator role has been all but forced on me. In contrast, as a lesbian, I choose to speak on panels for a number of reasons. Speaking up is a self-empowering act in a world that continually tells me I should hide and be ashamed of who I am. I speak about my experience of being a lesbian in a homophobic world because it is one way that I can break the silence about our lives. Unless I make a point of saying that I am a lesbian and bringing up lesbian issues, I do not have conversations with people about lesbian issues. Prior to my having taken on a more visible role as a lesbian educator, other people did not assume that I would fulfill this role. Recognizing the difference in my experience as a woman and as a lesbian has helped me understand that educational strategies should not be uniformly used to address all social justice issues.

Creating a Safe Environment for Learning

Lesbian, gay, and bisexual speakers' panels are only successful to the degree that they are capable of creating an atmosphere of emotional safety for panelists and participants. This safety is a crucial condition for everyone to feel able to speak honestly about their experiences and beliefs. A number of design elements and facilitation strategies are used to create a safe atmosphere. One element that contributes to a safe atmosphere is the use of panel members who are not members of the group or students in the class. This serves the dual purpose of not putting pressure on members of the group/class to be "out" (i.e., open/public) as lesbians, gays, or bisexuals, and of allowing students/group members to choose to share their experiences if they wish, but not to force them to take on an "educator" role. It is also crucial that speakers, whether they are outside speakers or speakers from within the group, are speaking voluntarily, that they are not pressured into speaking.

All lesbian, gay, and bisexual speakers' panels should have as part of their format the setting of guidelines for how the panel and participants interact with each other. Commonly used guidelines include the following:

- Everyone agrees to maintain confidentiality about what is said during the session;

- Everyone acknowledges that because there is a general lack of information about the lives of lesbians, gays, and bisexuals, there is no such thing as a "stupid" question; panelists may choose not to answer a particular question, but participants should ask;

- Panelists speak from their own experiences and do not represent all lesbians, gays, and bisexuals, acknowledging that there is a great diversity in lesbians, gays, and bisexuals;

- Participants are requested to speak from their own experience, using statements rather than we, they, you, etc. For example, saying "I, as a student in this school, have experienced ..."rather than "the students in this school believe ..." .

Guidelines are presented as part of the introduction to the panel. The guideline of confidentiality is especially important for many speakers and participants. Some speakers only share their first names and ask that the names of panelists not be revealed because they fear that if their sexual orientations were widely known, they could lose their jobs or their children. Discussing these real concerns often helps participants understand the kind of discrimination we face.

Having a method for participants to ask questions anonymously greatly enhances the sense of emotional safety and, often, allows for a broader range of questions. One way to do this is to pass out index cards at the beginning of the session and have participants write questions on the cards after panelists finish their initial speaking. All participants are asked to either write a question, or write do not have a question" on their cards. The cards can then be collected and responded to by the panelists. It is important that everyone write something or it will be clear who is writing, and the process will not be anonymous. Methods such as guidelines and anonymous questions create a setting that allows panelists and participants to feel safe enough to share their own experiences and hear the experiences of others.

Adult Learning Theory

Adult learning theory helps to explain the success of lesbian, gay, and bisexual speakers' panels. This form of social justice education is particularly appropriate for adult learners. A characteristic common to most adult learners is that they bring a great deal of personal experience to a learning situation. It is common for adult learners to relate their own experiences in a learning setting and to frame new learning in the context of how these experiences can be applied to future situations. Malcolm Knowles, in his book *The Modern Practice of Adult Education* (1980), points out that "adults define themselves largely by their experience" (p. 50). Recognizing this centrality of personal experience, Knowles (p. 50) concludes that adults "are themselves a rich resource for learning" and "have a richer foundation of experience to which to relate new experiences" (and new learnings tend to take on meaning as we are able to relate them to our past experience). Adult learners in particular can benefit from lesbian, gay, and bisexual speakers' panels because they emphasize the sharing of life experiences and facilitate applying the understanding gained to future situations.

Speakers' Panels and Experiential Learning Theory

In many ways, speakers' panels on lesbian, gay, and bisexual issues are not unlike many other forms of experiential education. The core of experiential education is the experiential learning cycle: having an experience, reflecting on the experience, analyzing the experience, and then using that analysis to generalize learnings to future situations. Lesbian, gay, and bisexual speakers' panels provide this type of learning experience for the panelists and for the participants. Although the "experience" varies for panelists and participants, for both it can be an experience that defies social norms. One way in which panels differ from activity-centered experiential education and from panels related to other topics is that they draw primarily upon the life experiences of the panelists and, often, the participants. Sharing life experiences is a valid tool in experiential education related to social justice issues. To paraphrase the feminist saying, "The personal is educational." The individual life experiences of members of oppressed social groups are the reality of social injustice. If reality is not one fixed measurable phenomenon external to people, but is something socially constructed by people, then the telling of life experiences and learning from each others' experience is a way to move from a unjust present reality to a just future reality.

For panelists, the act of articulating life experiences, speaking out loud about one's life, and breaking the silence surrounding lesbian, gay, and bisexual issues is an experience that defies our pervasive invisibility. For participants, meeting lesbians, gays, and bisexuals, hearing them speak about their real-life experiences, and entering into dialogue with panelists allows participants to replace whispered stereotypes with complex human reality. For both panelists and participants, spending time together talking about a subject that is normally taboo is in itself a profound emotional and intellectual experience.

As contexts for panels vary, so do the means in which the experiential learning cycle is completed. In some settings, course instructors or the panelists lead the group through a more formal processing discussion of the experience. As an instructor of a college course on social justice issues, I have facilitated discussions directly following panels. In these discussions, I ask students to reflect on messages they received in the past about lesbians, gays, and bisexuals and relate those messages to what they have just heard from the panel. I also ask them to consider how the experiences related by the panelists fit into the larger context of social justice issues. We discuss how this experience will affect their future interactions with lesbians, gays, and bisexuals.

Not all settings lend themselves to prolonged, formal processing discussions. In settings where the participants are all part of an organization or group, some processing can be built into the question-and-answer period. For example, as a panelist in a presentation to a social service agency, I have asked participants how they previously addressed gay, lesbian, and bisexual issues and individuals in their agency, and how they will change based on what they have heard from panelists. In open forum presentations to groups of unrelated individuals, little formal processing occurs. Panelists weave into their presentations the notion of examining past beliefs and using the experience of hearing the panel to inform their understanding of lesbians, gays, and bisexuals. In this way, panelists model learning from experience rather than directly facilitating such learning.

In addition to the processing discussions facilitated by or demonstrated by panelists or instructors, a great deal of informal processing occurs in discussions among participants and panelists after the presentation. The format and safe atmosphere created by the panelists provides the groundwork for individual participants to continue learning from the experience in the future through conversations with colleagues, friends, and family. All of the above components are key to the success of lesbian, gay, and bisexual speakers' panels. However, above and beyond these components, there is one factor I would emphasize. Crucial to the success of panels is the personal element. Spending an hour or two eye to eye with someone who is a real, live, complex human being goes a long way toward breaking down the myths and stereotypes of lesbians, gays, and bisexuals as sick, unhappy, or perverted people. I often ask participants to think about me, the other panelists, the laughs we have shared, and the serious things we have discussed the next time someone says something hurtful about lesbians, gays, and bisexuals. For heterosexual people, speakers' panels put a human face to an "issue" that for many has been clouded in secrecy. For lesbians, gays, and bisexuals in the audience, panels provide more positive images of how we can live our lives. For everyone, they foster learning and understanding because they are truly "face to face."

References

Knowles, M. (1980). *The modern practice of adult education.* New York: The Adult Education Company.

Wes. (1992). Quotation used by Wes in her work on AIDS, reprinted on buttons by Tickle Graphics. For more information, contact Wes at Box 383, Southington, CT 06489.

Suggested Readings

Alyson, S. (1991). *Young, gay, and proud!* Boston: Alyson Publications.

Blumenfeld, W. (Ed.). (1992). *Homophobia: How we all pay the price.* Boston: Beacon Press.

Blumenfeld, W. J., and Raymond, D. (1988). *Looking at gay and lesbian life.* Boston: Beacon Press.

Cohen, S., and Cohen D. (1989). *When someone you know is gay: High school help line.* New York: Dell.

Hutchins, L., and Kaahumanu, L. (Eds.). *Bi any other name: Bisexual people speak out.* Boston: Alyson Publications.

Integrating Persons With Impairments & Disabilities Into Standard Outdoor Adventure Education Programs

▾ ▾ ▾

Cindy Dillenschneider

It was a beautiful day for paddling. We met at the put-in, prepared our boats, and set out on a day trip. Our group consisted of 10 paddlers of all experience levels and abilities. Each was immersed in his or her own experience: readying boats, watching for birds and alligators, or having lively conversations with friends. Once on the water, some people paddled lazily along the river anticipating the view beyond the next bend while others darted forward and returned, opting for the physical workout of hard paddling. Our guides shepherded us along the river, allowing some to paddle ahead and others to come up slowly from the rear. From the air we would have looked like a multicolored accordion, expanding and contracting as we progressed upstream.

As the midpoint of the day approached and our bellies began to growl from hunger, the guides began to look for an appropriate lunch spot. Certainly it would not be an easy task to find a flat open space among the dense brush, irregular banks, and small marshes. I don't know how long they considered the decision but after some time, one of the guides paddled to a steep 4-foot–high embankment and called us all over. "Lunchtime," he sang out. We pulled in and one-by-one made our way over tree roots and up the slightly eroded bank.

A few minutes later someone pointed out that one of our group members had paddled upstream around the next bend. "No problem," I thought; he was an experienced kayaker who frequently went out on his own. In about 30 minutes our friend returned and sat in his

---

This chapter originally was published in the *Journal of Experiential Education*, with the following citation: Dillenschneider, C. (2007). Integrating persons with impairments and disabilities into standard outdoor adventure education programs. *Journal of Experiential Education, 30*(1), 70–83.

boat floating just offshore behind the cluster of boats tied to the bank. There was no easy place to pull out of the sun or to beach the boat, so he continued to sit. I wondered to myself if he would like to get out of his boat and join us. I didn't mention my thoughts. Our location up the bank would have been profoundly difficult for him to access as he was also a wheelchair user who could not walk.

It did leave me wondering about the following, however: Why did the guides choose to stop here? Were there other places where we could have all enjoyed lunch together? Had the guides talked to our boat-bound member about options prior to stopping? What thoughts did others have about this awkward situation? What knowledge did the guides have about creating inclusive outdoor experiences?

Some of the above questions from that experience and other experiences I have had with inclusive outdoor adventure education programs have led me to the topic for this paper. The main purpose of this paper is to provide some historical background on the topic of how to integrate persons with impairments and disabilities into outdoor adventure education programs, to offer suggestions about how to accommodate for specific differences, to identify principles of inclusion, and to specify criteria for implementing inclusive practices in outdoor adventure education.

The Problem: A Practice of Segregation

In 1977 I performed an extensive search of outdoor programs in the United States looking for Outward Bound-type opportunities for people with disabilities. While I was aware of a century-old tradition of therapeutic outdoor programs in the United States that were based on a residential camping model, this search revealed two fledgling nontherapeutic programs providing outdoor adventure experiences to people with cognitive, physical, and sensory disabilities. These were the Breckenridge Outdoor Education Center in Colorado and Environmental Traveling Companions in California. By the early 1980s, Wilderness Inquiry in Minnesota, and Minnesota Outward Bound began excursions into inclusive design. All programs involved activities such as rock climbing, white-water rafting, kayaking, backpacking, alpine and Nordic skiing, and other outdoor adventure activities. Today, a search on the Internet would reveal outdoor adventure programs throughout the United States and the world that serve people with disabilities. However, the majority of these programs offer segregated experiences and many use social-service style organizations to provide a client base of people with common impairment histories (e.g., post-rehabilitation outdoor adventures for people with spinal cord injuries or outdoor programs for adults with developmental disabilities who reside at a group home). While the increase in the availability of programs represents some improvement and deserves some praise, the fact remains that very few programs offer experiences that integrate people with impairments or disabilities with people without impairments or disabilities.

Historical Perspectives on Disability

In the United States, between the late 1800s and the mid-1970s, it was the norm to separate, from birth to death, individuals who had obvious physical, cognitive, or psychiatric differences. The states maintained schools for deaf and blind individuals, asylums for people with mental illness, and institutions for those who had cognitive impairments. It was also common during this time to institutionalize people with physical disabilities or keep them at home and isolated from their communities (Braddock & Parish, 2001). These historical practices highlight a host of misleading assumptions, including: people with impairments or disabilities are different from the rest of society; they must be provided with separate services; they require therapeutic programs; and people with impairments or disabilities can only engage in activities with their "own kind."

What Is Changing?

In 1980 the World Health Organization (WHO) published The International Classification of Impairments, Disabilities, and Handicaps (ICIDH) in an attempt to create an operative international classification of human function in relation to impairment (World Health Organization, 2001). Over the next two decades the WHO engaged in significant international discourse with, among others, people with disabilities. In May 2001, the World Health Assembly of the WHO approved a significant revision of the original document. The second and final revision, ICIDH-2, resulted in a change of name to the International Classification of Functioning, Disability and Health (ICF) and a change of emphasis from a negative and medicalized view of impairment to a neutral, contextually influenced understanding of health characteristics in complex interactions between environment, society, and bodily function and structure. The final draft of the ICIDH-2 (World Health Organization, 2001) summarizes this change of emphasis in claiming:

> It is the interaction of the health characteristics and the contextual factors that produce disability. This being so, individuals must not be reduced to, or characterized solely in terms of their impairments, activity limitations, or participation restrictions. (pp. 188–189)

For example, instead of referring to a person as a "mentally handicapped person," the classification uses the phrase "person with a problem in learning." ICIDH-2 in essence avoids referring to any person by means of a health condition or disability term, and by using neutral, if not positive, and concrete language throughout (World Health Organization, 2001). "To further address the legitimate concern of systematic labeling of people, the categories in ICIDH-2 are expressed in a neutral way to avoid depreciation, stigmatization and inappropriate connotations" (World Health Organization, 2001, pp.188–189).

In 1990 the president of the United States, George H.W. Bush, signed the Americans with Disabilities Act (ADA) into law. This civil rights legislation is intended to end discriminating practices in employment, public services, public transit, and telecommunications on the basis of disability or perceived disability. Here disability is defined as an "impairment that substantially limits one or more major life activities ... having record of such an impairment [or] ... being regarded as having such an impairment" (Americans with Disabilities Act, 2001, Sec. 3 [2]). Impairments are considered to be physiological or psychological disorders and examples of major life activities include walking, speaking, performing manual labor, learning, and recreating. Under these operational definitions, it is possible for a person to have an impairment without having a disability.

A brief recounting of a story from Martha's Vineyard clarifies this idea. In 1880, the United States census of Martha's Vineyard residents indicated there were 18 deaf individuals in 122 households (1880 Census of Chilmark, Mass., 1998). Because of the high percentage of deaf individuals and their location in the history of Martha's Vineyard, it was common for everyone, hearing and deaf, to know and use sign language (Groce, 1985). At Martha's Vineyard, societal norms existed that were inclusive of signed and verbal communication. Thus, an impairment of deafness did not result in limits to performance of major life activities and therefore did not result in disability. Moreover, for hearing individuals moving into the area, it was a lack of skill in sign language that was regarded as a limitation.

In reference to the current legislation, WHO and the ADA claim that a disability is the result of an impairment in consort with social and environmental contexts. According to WHO and the ADA, a disability is not the impairment itself. The importance of this distinction is that domestic legislative bodies and leading world organizations are beginning to change their views about disabilities, by viewing them less as medical concerns and viewing them more as social concerns. When disability is shifted into the social arena, that shift encourages everyone to view individual difference, including impairment and disability, as part of a continuum of human experience.

Essentially, individual differences are present in 100% of the population. Yet, in contrast to these changes in thought, arbitrary lines of acceptance of and service to clients seem to separate ably perceived individuals from those with obvious impairments. Pertaining to outdoor adventure education and in light of the above, the key query is: What ethical guidance do outdoor adventure educators use when we choose to teach an outdoor skill to one eager student while avoiding teaching the same skill to an equally eager student who may just happen to use a wheelchair?

Relevant Research

The United States census of 2000 reported that approximately 19% of the population between ages 6 and 65 have a disabling condition (U.S. Census Bureau, 2003). Based on evidence cited in *Inclusive Outdoor Programming: A Training Manual* (McAvoy et al., 2003), people with disabilities or impairments desire the same opportunity for adventure as people who are not labeled as having an impairment or disability. The authors go on to state that:

> Research ... indicates that persons with disabilities are no different from anyone else in the kinds of natural settings they prefer.... [They] prefer the same kind of outdoor recreation activities as do those without disabilities ... [and] seek the same kind of challenge and adventure in the outdoors as do those who do not have disabilities. (pp. 4–5)

It is clear that people with impairments and disabilities seek opportunities to socialize with friends, try new and challenging experiences, and recreate with their families.

When an impairment or disability is only part of and not the primary identity of an individual it is imperative for adventure educators to embrace the responsibility of creating programs that provide all participants with an opportunity to function to their fullest abilities. The essential query then becomes: How can this be done? This next section will hopefully serve as a tool for adventure educators to better understand how to navigate the spectrum of individual difference and how to begin to make accommodations for some of these differences.

Navigating the Spectrum of Individual Difference

One way to accommodate individual difference is by identifying categories relating to function and providing accommodation in each functional area when needed. Table 1 provides an illustration of one way to view this process.

While Table 1 provides general suggestions for accommodation that can be applied in most environments, educators need to work directly with an individual student to determine the best ways to apply these suggestions in a given situation. Some students come with individual differences in more than one area. Therefore, learning how to combine some knowledge within each area of difference is important.

To illustrate this concept, I will briefly recount another paddling experience. On this particular trip, our group consisted of three somewhat able-bodied individuals and three individuals with obvious impairments. I say somewhat able-bodied because each of us had our own personal differences: back problems, tendonitis, prior heat injuries, and other "typical" problems of aging outdoor enthusiasts. Each person had differences in mobility, endurance, strength, and health. The three people who had visible physical impairments used wheelchairs. One person who used a wheelchair had a prior spinal cord injury, which resulted in paralysis from the waist down. While he experienced differences in motor control, he was able to launch his boat and manage all aspects of the paddling trip without assistance. Because of his creativity in eliminating barriers to participation, his impairment did

Table 1.
Area of Function With Suggested Accommodations

Area of Function	Suggested Accommodations
Sensing	Ask the student to explain the nature of the sensation difference
Vision	Use bright, contrasting colors, textures, hand-over-hand teaching
Hearing	Use diagrams, written directions, modeling, face the student when speaking, don't cover your mouth when speaking
Touch (cold, heat, pressure, pain)	Anticipate and warn student of temperature concerns and hazards; remove or cover sharp edges; reduce or eliminate friction, and eliminate pressure on bony prominences; ask student to describe any medical concerns related to altered sensation
Body orientation and positioning	Physically guide student through body positioning, slow down instruction, use verbal or visual cues at key positions
Strength and endurance	Provide lightweight equipment, lighten the load, offer shorter route options, take frequent breaks, provide external supports, consider alternative methods of travel
Motor control and balance	Take a slower pace, lower the center of gravity, provide a wide base of support, use equipment that offers greater stability, provide larger gripping surfaces, choose the most accessible environment
Cognitive processing and planning skills	Break complex skills into steps, use concrete language, repetition and practice, multiple senses, partners, slow instruction, provide time for processing, maintain student focus through novelty, provide additional supervision, limit distractions, write down steps processes
Communication	Check frequently for understanding, ask student to demonstrate skill, provide instruction in a variety of means
Emotional control	Limit distractions, speak in calm and supportive tones, provide additional supervision, be observant for increased anxiety, respond quickly to de-escalate frustration, designate time-out areas and procedures to allow self-regulation, set appropriate limits
Health and health maintenance needs	Maintain regular schedules for meals, work, and sleep; learn what health maintenance needs exist and how the student regulates these concerns; understand how well regulated the condition is; carry extra sets of medications; provide opportunity for breaks as needed
Ambulation and mobility	Encourage use of assistive devices, work with student to identify most easily accessed environments, consider alternate route options, ask the student for suggestions, consider alternate methods of travel

not result in a disability on this trip. However, many people benefit from accommodations and it is often hard to know how to begin the process of accommodation for specific conditions. For simplicity, let's look at two individuals' strengths, functional differences, and methods employed to accommodate specific needs. Table 2 provides information on one paddler without and one paddler with apparent disabilities.

Table 2.
Accommodating and Utilizing Areas of Functional Difference

Paddlers	Functional Differences	Areas of Strength	Accommodation and Utilization
Paddler #1	Health Differences: Chronic tendonitis in elbows. Prior heat injury resulting in inability to regulate body temperature through sweating	Experienced paddler and instructor, event organizer/leader, disability awareness, problem-solver, equipment expertise	Lightweight paddle, compression straps for tendonitis, cooling neckerchief and hat, breaks as needed; use to coordinate event, design adapted equipment, assist with accommodations
Paddler #2	Paralysis in four extremities; no sensation of temperature, pressure, and pain below level of paralysis	Desire to paddle, disability awareness, excellent communication skills, willingness to try new ideas, patience, critical thinking ability to evaluate a variety of equipment supports	High-backed seat, lateral support, wedge under seat to limit sliding, removal of footpegs, shoes to prevent injury, hand grip-assist, paddle support; use to test and evaluate new equipment designs and teach disability awareness

While the information in Table 2 only provides descriptions about two members of the group, all paddlers used accommodations for their specific differences. That said, only half the group would have been viewed as having a disability by any onlookers who happened to pass by. More importantly, all paddlers brought specific strengths to the experience. The combined marshalling of strengths and accommodating areas of functional difference allowed the group to set out with common goals, to test adapted equipment designs, and to have fun paddling. This is inherently different from viewing the trip as an experience engaged in by three able-bodied paddlers assisting three "needy" people with disabilities.

Principles for Accommodating All Students

Program staff new to inclusion may find that teaching a diverse clientele is initially somewhat overwhelming. Here are five principles with examples that can assist program staff in accommodating all students including those with impairments or disabilities.

1. Communicate with students about the fundamental activities and environments they will experience (e.g., students should expect to sit in a canoe for up to four hours at a time while assisting with paddling or using map and compass for navigation). Accurate information allows participants to consider their abilities, needs, and goals with correct perspective and to choose program options that suit their abilities. When serving a more diverse portion of the population, it is also important for instructors to anticipate how transitions between environments will affect student functioning. Returning to our original story of paddling on the river, it was the transition between the river and the bank that created an impassible barrier at the lunch stop. Instructors often effectively anticipate the impact of the larger ambient influences (e.g., Is the temperature cold enough to cause hypothermia?). But the interface between the student's body and whatever it contacts is a fundamental environment to which instructors typically pay little attention. Unless the instructors have knowledge specific to impairments and disabilities, it may be difficult to anticipate problem areas. A novice student unfamiliar with the activity or environment may not readily anticipate a problem either. When working with students with sensory perception differences it is important to be especially vigilant in helping them recognize a problematic interface. As an example, a kayaker who does not have sensation in the skin on the heels of his or her feet or on the buttocks can sustain damage to the skin and tissues from pressure or friction; the damage can be severe enough to require hospitalization. The student knows the personal dangers and you can provide accurate information about the environment. Together the student and instructor have the knowledge to anticipate and prevent many problems.

2. Always have the person with the impairment (the student, in this case) assist the instructors in understanding his or her actual needs and strengths. While novices in any outdoor activity will need your guidance, the student who experiences an impairment or disability is the expert in his or her personal needs. Use good communication skills to draw on the individual's experience and knowledge. If the student is experienced in outdoor activities, ask if any assistance or assistive device is needed. If the student is new to outdoor activity find out if assistance is needed in other activities. Ask questions about the type of activities s/he commonly engages in and her/his goals for pursuing the selected outdoor activity. Some impairments or disabilities make communication difficult. In these instances the capacity of the instructor to accurately assess the abilities of a student is compromised. If someone who can enhance communication is available to help, recruit assistance but continue to talk directly to the person with the impairment or disability and use the assistant to help you interpret the answers. Avoid the common mistake of talking to the assistant about the person with whom you are actually trying to communicate. Additionally, as with all students, use observational skills to help you cue in to strengths and possible needs related to cognition, physical ability, and social interaction, but verify the accuracy of your assessment with the student. Work together with your student to determine what assistance is desired, the range of supports available, and what you can provide.

3. Commit to possibility thinking. A combination of hard work, a belief in possibility, and creative thinking can lead to outcomes that initially appear impossible. An experience early in my career cemented possibility thinking into my fundamental makeup as a professional outdoor educator. In 1980 I had the unique experience of assisting Ed Roberts, former head of the California Department of Rehabilitation, on a white-water rafting trip. Mr. Roberts, who had quadriplegia as a result of polio and used a ventilator for breathing, was my raft partner on a class III section of the Stanislaus River. While most outdoor adventure professionals would consider white-water rafting with a person with quadriplegia requiring ventilator-assisted breathing impossible, the positive thinking that the staff of Environmental Traveling Companions engaged in and Mr. Robert's positive thinking helped lead to a very successful trip. Years later I again met with Mr. Roberts and he told me that he enjoyed the entire day without using his respirator because of the flexible movement of the raft on the waves, and this was the only time he could remember in his adult life when he did not use a respirator for an entire day. The power of the experience of white-water rafting with a person who slept each night in an iron lung and watching the instructors take the whole process in stride as if they did this every day was so profound that the word impossible left my vocabulary that day.

4. Provide appropriate, high-quality, and individualized supports. Supports can be provided in all domains: social, emotional, cognitive, and physical. In all cases, supports for clients with impairments or disabilities should be given the same careful consideration as those provided for clients without impairments or disabilities. If one of the goals of an organization is to help participants be respected as fully active and equal members of the group, then supports must be in place that reflect that purpose. These supports must not demean or limit students, especially for the sake of convenience. For instance, when a student requires extended time to perform a task, the instructor may be tempted to perform the task for the student or to be more directive than is necessary. However, taking time to assist rather than direct the student models sensitivity and respect for the individual. The act of patient instruction may go far in setting the tone for interaction within the group.

Adaptations to equipment need equal attention. For decades professional outdoor educators have been quite satisfied to provide duct tape and baling-twine solutions to individual adaptations, and students who have needed adaptations have been gracious in thanking us for sanctioning inclusion. Even the most creative duct tape creations send a message. When high-quality equipment is provided for program participants without impairments, the same high-quality adaptive equipment needs to be provided for program participants with impairments.

If one considers the developments in adapted alpine skiing equipment, for example, one can see significant progress over the last 20 years. In the early 1980s the first adapted alpine ski was, in appearance, a modified sled. And while it allowed people with mobility impairments to ski alongside friends in virtually any terrain, it was still viewed by the public as a sled. Today, adapted alpine ski equipment utilizes standard high-performance alpine skis with standard ski bindings to mount an adapted seat. This design sits the skier up off the ground, allows the skier to load and unload from the lift independently, and permits the skier to ski on the same type of equipment as stand-up skiers. When the public looks at this equipment design, they can easily identify the activity as skiing. A skilled skier using this adapted equipment can carve turns on virtually any terrain, including extreme terrain. This progress in adapted equipment has allowed the public to change its view of mobility-impaired skiers. In order for students with impairments to gain this type of status within the typical outdoor recreation program, attention must be given to the detail and appearance of equipment as well as its function. It is time for the outdoor education industry to advance the range of professionally designed equipment available to enhance the experience of people with impairments.

5. Do no harm. In inclusive groups, instructors may experience more differences in behaviors and social skills, cognitive processing, and physical ability than they would with a group of students without disabilities. It is thus crucial for program coordinators to ensure that field instructors have the background, training, and experience to make appropriate decisions when facilitating outdoor experiences for inclusive groups. It would have been a profoundly different experience that day on the Stanislaus River if Mr. Roberts had been seriously injured as a result of our enthusiasm for trying to make all "things" possible.

Criteria for Inclusive Practices in Outdoor Adventure Education

So, what constitutes inclusive outdoor adventure education practice? First, inclusive practice includes opportunities for individuals with disabilities to be fully involved members of a group, including people with and without disabilities (Wilmshurst, n.d.). To be fully involved means that students with impairments are immersed in the full experience of the activity, not engaged in patronizing activities such as handing out personal flotation devices and then watching as others are instructed in the basics of stroke technique. If inclusion requires additional time, effort, or assistance, then it is up to the practitioner to provide these supports.

Second, in order for integrated experiences to truly be inclusive, individuals with disabilities must be fully respected members of the group (McAvoy et al., 2003). Fully respected members of a group will hold a similar status within a group, not a lower status demonstrated by well-intended but demeaning interactions. Because of the still segregated norms in society, it is very likely that practitioners will need training and practice in how to interact with people with impairments or disabilities in ways that promote respect. Third, an individual with an impairment or disability should have the opportunity to operate at a level of competence and independence based on his or her abilities and strengths. Each participant has very distinct abilities. These abilities should be valued and the person with the disability should be allowed the opportunity to perform at his/her or her highest level without interference from others. While it might be faster to perform a task yourself rather than to wait for a participant to do it, it is unfair to "rob" the individual of an opportunity to demonstrate his or her unique competency.

Fourth, individuals with disabilities should be able to choose from a range of supports that facilitate competence and independence (Wilmshurst, n.d.). The possibility for the participant to choose from a variety of support options may facilitate a more successful outcome for the individual, the group, and the program. The concept of offering a range of supports is similar to the practice of teaching skills or content through a variety of methods and media. Supports that may be provided can be as simple as offering a space near the front of the group during an instructional session, a magnifier for map reading, or offering a water bottle with an integral straw to a participant who has difficulty removing the lid. Many supports are readily available and inexpensive and having them available and creating awareness of options will allow participants to operate at their highest level.

Sociological studies on contact theory cited in the book *Disability, Society, and the Individual* (Smart, 2001) stipulated four conditions that must be present in order to create positive change in the perception of people with disabilities by people without disabilities. These conditions include: (a) there must be equal social status relationships between the individuals with and without impairments or disabilities; (b) interactions must occur under natural and voluntary conditions; (c) interactions should facilitate viewing the person with a disability as an individual; and (d) the group members with and without impairments or disabilities must have a common goal, and it is best if the goal cannot be achieved without cooperation among them.

Hopefully, the above principles, criteria, and conditions can serve as tools for outdoor adventure educators who are striving to conduct outdoor trip experiences that are more inclusive.

Recommendations

The outdoor adventure education industry would do well to meet the interests of people with disabilities or impairments who desire to participate in adventure experiences by continuing to make advances in inclusive program offerings. To do this the fields needs to:

1. Change its thinking, by viewing human difference as a continuum of abilities, to view impairment or disability as only a small part of the identity of any individual, and to believe in the possibility of inclusive offerings.

2. Offer an expanded range of supports to students by utilizing a breadth of teaching methods, program communications, teaching assistance, equipment options, and activity choices.

3. Expand business practices to include matching of participant ability to program offerings, improve staff training in inclusive practices and disability awareness,

provide information about fundamental activities and environments, and market or publicize programs as inclusive or accessible.

4. Ask difficult questions about the industry, including: Who has been left out of outdoor adventure education programs? What is the motivation when access is denied to people based on disability? What will it take to propel the industry forward? What will it take to design and provide inclusive access to outdoor programs? What role do all educators play in this initiative.

Consider the Possibilities

Consider how readily achievable inclusion is in open enrollment programs where participation is voluntary, enrollment is an individual choice, and participants must cooperate to achieve common goals. It is common practice within the outdoor industry to promote full and active involvement of all participants. As outdoor adventure educators, we institute practices that emphasize respect and equal status relationships among our participants. We encourage our students to become self-actualized individuals and to achieve competence. We champion both independent and interdependent accomplishments as necessary for group success. We offer a wide range of supports to students who struggle to learn foreign skills in a foreign environment. We promote and value each individual as complete and unique. We employ the use of group challenges in natural and unmitigated conditions to require group efforts to succeed. We orchestrate and role model socially enhancing interactions between group members. As individual educators and as an industry, we are poised to open our doors to inclusive practices in outdoor adventure education. It is time to believe it is possible and take action.

References

Americans with Disabilities Act of 1990, Pub. L. 101–336, §1 (Sec.3.2.a, b, c). (2001). Retrieved July 22, 2006, from http://www.usdoj.gov/crt/ada/pubs/ada.txt

Braddock, D. L., & Parish, S. L. (2001). An institutional history of disability. In G. L. Albrecht, K. D. Salman, & M. Bury (Eds.), *Handbook of disability studies* (pp. 11–54). Thousand Oaks, CA: Sage.

Groce, N. (1985). *Everyone here spoke sign language: Hereditary deafness on Martha's Vineyard.* Cambridge, MA: Harvard Press.

McAvoy, L., Rynders, J., Smith, J., Scholl, K., Newman, J., Holman, T., et al. (2003). *Inclusive outdoor adventure programming: A training manual.* Unpublished manuscript. University of Minnesota, Minneapolis.

Smart, J. (2001). *Disability, society and the individual.* Gaithersburg, MD: Aspen.

The 1880 Federal Census of Chilmark, Mass., Transcribed by Judy Swan, 1998. Proofed and prepared for the web by Chris Baer. Retrieved July 5, 2006, from http://history.vineyard.net/dukes/cen80c.htm

U.S. Census Bureau. Disability census 2000: Census 2000 brief. (2003). Retrieved March 18, 2006, from http://www.census.gov/prod/2003pubs/ c2kbr-17.pdf

Wilmshurst, Geoff. (n.d.). *Facilitating inclusion and access to outdoor education and recreation programs.* Retrieved July 22, 2006, from http://www.outdoored.com/articles/Article.aspx?ArticleID=162

World Health Organization. Classification, Assessment, Surveys and Terminology Team. (2001). *The international classification of functioning, disability and health.* Geneva, Switzerland.

Theory Into Practice

▾ ▾ ▾

Turning Experiential Education & Critical Pedagogy Theory Into Praxis

▼ ▼ ▼

Mary Breunig

I often hear people say that experiential education is experience rich but theory poor. For me personally, this saying did perhaps ring true during my early years using experiential education, particularly during the period of time when I was leading wilderness trips full time and experience and play were at the heart of my practice.

Now that I teach experiential education in the post-secondary classroom, in the School of Outdoor Recreation, Parks, & Tourism at Lakehead University, Ontario, and have explored experiential education theory and the broader field of education, I have come to realize that experiences that lack intention, purpose, and direction most often simply represent play. Play is fun; but play is not always enough, especially if there is some educational end toward which the practice (experience) is directed. I believe that my students need to more fully consider the aim, intent, and purpose of their practice(s) as a means to responding to the criticism that experiential education is experience rich but theory poor.

I believe that one means to help students accomplish this is through developing their understanding and their location within some of the broader educational theories. It is interesting to note that many educational theories suffer from a converse weakness to that of experiential education. In other words, it is argued that educational theories are theory rich but experience poor (Eisner, 2002), lacking in practical information about instructional strategies

This chapter originally was published in the *Journal of Experiential Education*, with the following citation:

Breunig, M. (2005). Turning experiential education and critical pedagogy theory into praxis. *Journal of Experiential Education, 28*(2), 106–122.

(Gore, 1993). Perhaps there is some value, then, in exploring experiential education alongside other educational theories, as a means to examine the gap between theory and practice.

The purpose of this article is to consider how theory and practice can be employed within the post-secondary experiential education classroom as a means to work toward one of its potential educational aims, the development of a more socially just world (Itin, 1999). This article will also explore and examine the fields of critical pedagogy to help support this argument. Critical pedagogy has numerous educational aims—one that is shared with experiential education is that the purpose of education should be to develop a more socially just world (Kincheloe, 2004).

The overarching purpose of this article will be to explore some of the ways to begin to develop classroom practices that act on the theoretical underpinnings of experiential education and critical pedagogy, and their shared educational aim. One of the underlying assumptions of this article is that by acting on their methodological desires, in essence by "practicing what is preached," experiential educators and critical pedagogues will be better able to work toward one intended educational aim that their theories purport.

Experiential Education

As I was working toward a Masters of Science degree in experiential education, I discovered intellectually what I had known intuitively—that there is value in engaging in purposeful experience as one component of the educative process. In other words, in addition to learning through books, lectures, and more "traditional" methods of teaching and learning, learning may be enhanced through an intentional experience. An experience may assume many forms. It may be as simple as rearranging the chairs into a circle to encourage dialogue between students or it may be more involved such as engaging in a student-directed classroom experience.

I have seen experiential education employed in a math class where students build "geometry town" to experience the mathematical equations they are learning, and in a science lab where students use an egg drop experiment to better understand a physics concept. Experiential education may also include the use of adventure education and/or wilderness trips as a component of the educative process. In this instance, a course on desert ecology may use the desert as a classroom and bring the texts, notebooks, pens, and students into this newly defined classroom setting.

Support for experiential education can be found in the earliest form of learning from the earliest time of humans. From learning being passed through storytelling and oral tradition to Plato's interest in soul, dialogue, and continuing education, experiential education has prevailed as a dominant mode of learning in Western culture (Richards, 1966; Smith, 2002). John Dewey (1938) expressed his belief that subject matter should not be learned in isolation, and that education should begin with student experience and should be contextual. More recently, Paulo Freire (1970) suggested that educational praxis should combine both action and reflection as part of the educative process, rejecting what he called the "banking model" of education, whereby the role of teachers was to deposit knowledge into the "empty" repository of the student mind.

Experiential education today may be best defined as a philosophy and methodology in which educators purposefully engage with learners in direct experience and focused reflection in order to increase knowledge, develop skills, and clarify values (Association for Experiential Education, 2004). The aim(s), goal(s), and purpose(s) of experiential education depend upon where it is being practiced, why it is being practiced, and by whom. Some of the commonly cited goals include: character building (Brookes, 2003), critical thinking (Brookfield, 1996), and a more socially just world (Itin, 1999), among others.

Critical Pedagogy

While pedagogy is most simply conceived of as the study of teaching and learning (Knowles, 1973), the term critical pedagogy embodies notions of how one teaches, what is being taught, and how one learns (Giroux, 1997). Paulo Freire is regarded as the inaugural philosopher of critical pedagogy for his work on recognizing the relationship among education, politics, imperialism, and liberation (McLaren, 2000). "All descriptions of pedagogy—like knowledge in general—are shaped by those who devise them and the values they hold" (Kincheloe, 2004, pp. 5–6). Kincheloe would argue, however, that one commonality between the various descriptions is that a critical pedagogical vision within schools is grounded in the social, cultural, cognitive, economic, and political context that is part of the larger community and society.

This form of critical pedagogy is a way of thinking about, negotiating, and transforming the relationship among classroom teaching, the production of knowledge, the institutional structures of the school, and the social and material relation of the wider community and society. It explores how the project of schooling may be recast in ways that focus teaching on the development of a moral project(s) for education as social transformation (McLaren, 2003). Critical pedagogy, like experiential education, encourages critical thinking and promotes practices that have the potential to transform oppressive institutions or social relations (Keesing-Styles, 2003).

Theory vs. Practice

Theory is often conceived of as an abstract idea or phenomenon. Practice involves an action component that goes beyond the abstraction of theory. In this sense, practice and experience are one and the same. One way to conceive of this is that theory represents knowledge, while practice is the application of that knowledge. One of the key issues still facing the fields of both experiential education and critical pedagogy is their implementation (Estes, 2004; Keesing-Styles, 2003).

There exists a lack of congruence between the pedagogical theories and the actual classroom practices. Freire, an inaugural philosopher of both pedagogies, encourages educators to join him on his professional mission of the search for "unity between theory and practice" (McLaren, 2000, p. 5). Thus, theory informs practice, while experiential and practical knowledge can be employed as a means to understanding and interpreting that theory. This next section will examine the gap that exists between theory and practice within the fields of experiential education and critical pedagogy.

Experiential Education

Many experiential educators identify the lack of congruence between what is theoretically espoused and what is practiced. Kolb (1992) illuminated the gap between what Argyris and Schon (1974) referred to as "theories of action" and "theories in use." For example, Kolb suggested that many experiential education programs emphasize that reflection is an essential element of the experiential learning process and yet practitioners may actually leave little time for debriefing, journaling, group discussion, counseling, or other forms of reflection. "What practitioners actually do in the field in this case, choosing action at the expense of reflection, rather than creating a balance, indicates theory-in-use" (p. 25) rather than theory-in-action. The significant issue here is that, as practitioners, we may say we act a certain way, but the espoused theories-in-action may be quite different from what actually happens in the program. More recently, Estes (2004) concluded that while experiential educators claim to value student-centered learning, these values, as evidenced in practice, are often teacher-centered. Kolb and Estes encourage experiential educators to examine the incongruence between espoused values and values in practice within learning environments.

Critical Pedagogy

As valuable as its contribution has been in placing pedagogy in the forefront of discussion, critical pedagogy still exists more as a theory of pedagogy rather than a practical specification, informing educators about the principles that should govern their work but saying little about how they might actually do it (Osborne, 1990). In fact, the work of many critical theorists has come under a similar criticism to the one that was raised earlier in reference to experiential educators. Eisner (2002) criticizes critical theorists as being more interested in displaying the shortcomings of schooling than providing models toward which schools should aspire. Pinar, Reynolds, Slattery, and Taubman (2002) suggest that greater collaboration between critical scholars and school teachers could further strengthen a critical classroom practice. It is agreed that critical theory continues to be excessively abstract and too far removed from the everyday life of schools.

Giroux (1988) declared that critical educational theory has "been unable to move from criticism to substantive vision" (p. 37). He further illustrates this by maintaining that critical theory has been unable to "posit a theoretical discourse and set of categories for constructing forms of knowledge, classroom social relationships, and visions of the future that give substance to the meaning of critical pedagogy" (Giroux, pp. 37–38).

Gore (1993) argues that, in fact, some of the best writings of critical theorists offer little suggestion of strategies that teachers might use in practice. Furthermore, these writings provide no explication of what attempts are made within these educators' own classrooms to implement the critical pedagogy they espouse. These critiques impel educators, both experiential educators and critical pedagogues, to begin to develop a critical praxis.

Experiential and Critical Praxis

I believe that the potential for experiential education and critical pedagogy to achieve one of their intended aims will be strengthened through examining the ways in which educators can turn the theory of these two pedagogies into purposeful classroom practices. I will take up the notion of praxis as a means to describe classroom practices in this next section of the article. Freire (1970) maintains that praxis involves both action and reflection. From Freire's perspective, there is no final act of knowing. Knowledge has historicity; it is always in the process of being. If absolute knowledge could be attained, the possibility of knowing would disappear for there would no longer be any questions to ask or problems to solve. Praxis, therefore, starts with an abstract idea (theory) or an experience, and incorporates reflection upon that idea or experience and then translates it into purposeful action. Praxis is reflective, active, creative, contextual, purposeful, and socially constructed.

The remainder of this article will be devoted to addressing how to work within some of the aforementioned incongruence and overlap between theory and practice by examining a number of methods to engage in an experiential and critical praxis. More specifically, I will explore some of the ways to begin to develop a praxis that acts on the theoretical underpinnings of experiential education and critical pedagogy, and their shared educational aim that education can be one means to develop a more socially just world.

Giroux (1997) encourages both students and educators to ask themselves the following questions as they begin to practically explore some of the theoretical assumptions that critical pedagogy proffers: (a) What counts as knowledge? (b) How is knowledge produced and legitimized? (c) Whose interests does this knowledge serve? (d) Who has access to knowledge? (e) How is this knowledge distributed within the classroom? (f) What kinds of social relationships within the classroom serve to parallel and reproduce the social relations of production in the wider society? (g) How do the prevailing methods of evaluation serve to legitimize existing forms of knowledge? and (h) What are the contradictions that exist between the ideology embodied in existing forms of knowledge and the objective social reality?

These questions, which examine the role of the dominant ideology in establishing some of the underlying assumptions about teaching and learning, will be explored throughout the remainder of this paper. The discussion that follows will consider experiential education and critical pedagogy theory, suggesting a number of classroom practices that can be employed as a means to examine some of the previous assumptions in relation to the following: the purpose and structure of schools, the curriculum, teaching methodology, the role of teachers, and the role of students within the post-secondary experiential education classroom.

The Purpose and Structure of Schools

As previously stated, one shared educational aim of both experiential education and critical pedagogy is that they both conceive of teaching, learning, and the project of schooling in ways that focus teaching on the development of a moral project(s) for education as social transformation (Itin, 1999; McLaren, 2003). When students query me about my own intent regarding teaching, I tell them that, for me, the purpose of schools is to develop peoples' critical thinking skills as a means to develop a more socially just world. They often ask me how I am able to maintain this ideal when most people believe that the purpose of schools is to prepare people for a growing and changing workforce (Pinar et al., 2002). I tell them that, in my opinion, schools can do both—they can prepare people for future work in the world "that is," while still offering them a vision of what "could be." For me, that vision of what "could be" is the development of a more socially just world.

Schools do more than provide instruction. Schools provide the norms and principles of conduct that are learned through students' varied experiences in schools and in the larger society. These norms and principles are most often associated with the ideologies of the dominant race, gender, religion, and culture of the social class, or group of people that is in control of the material and symbolic wealth of society (Giroux, 1997; McLaren, 2003). Schools act to perpetuate these dominant ways of knowing.

One way for students to begin to become cognizant of this is by asking them to engage in a series of experiential activities that offer counter-hegemonic insights into the dominant ways of knowing that school structures tend to transmit. If hegemony represents not only political and economic control of one social class over others but also the ability of the dominant class to inject its ways of knowing so that those who are oppressed by it begin to accept it as common knowledge (Giroux, 1997), then counter-hegemony offers a vision of what "could be" different if less oppressive ways of knowing and institutions were in place.

I encourage students to discuss the ways in which school structures serve the interests that support the dominant educational and social ideologies. One way to engage students in better understanding and examining the ways in which schools act as agents of socialization and assimilation is by having them do an institutional "hegemony treasure hunt" (Fawcett, Bell, & Russell, 2002). Having students physically explore the school building, with the particular goal of examining assumptions about the purpose of schools and the school structure, is one way for students to begin to employ the theory in practice. Asking students to walk through the faculty hallways, or a hallway with classrooms in it, and hunt for observable artifacts that allow them to examine some of the commonly held institutional assumptions is also educative. Ask students to consider the following: What did you observe? What assumptions do those observations contain about who holds power and who has a "voice?" In what ways do your observations inform your understanding about the purpose of schools, school structures, and school culture? Students can additionally be encouraged to walk down the hallway of the administrative offices considering some of these same questions.

This activity can be done with the specific purpose of examining educational assumptions or can be employed to examine an array of other institutional assumptions including: environmental issues, gender issues, issues related to institutional accessibility, and issues of hierarchy and power, among others.

Curriculum

The content of the curriculum and the methods of pedagogy employed teach lessons (Weiler, 2001). Apple (1990) and Giroux (1988) describe how both the content and form of curriculum are ideological in nature. According to them, the ideals and culture associated with the dominant class were argued to be the ideas and content of schooling. Therefore, knowledge and classroom practices also affirm the values, interests, and concerns of the social class in control of the material and symbolic wealth of society (McLaren, 2003). Eisner (2002) refers to this as the "hidden curriculum." The hidden curriculum consists of the messages given to children not only by school structures but by textbooks, teachers, and other school resources. This curriculum is often believed to serve the interest of the power elite of the school and society, and is therefore inherently unable to support an equitable school system or society (Apple, 1975; Eisner, 2002).

Questioning assumptions about curriculum and its influence on existing forms of public school classroom knowledge, teaching styles, and evaluation will help uncover some of this hidden curriculum. Encouraging students to expand their "treasure hunt" by including an exploration of course content provides one means for them to investigate some of these assumptions. I ask students to look at the syllabi for various courses. I then break students up into small groups and have them share some of the information contained in those syllabi: the required readings, the assessment methods, the "tone" of the writing, and whatever else they read that "speaks" to the curriculum.

I encourage students to stay in the same small groups and explore some of the curricular assumptions within the context of the broader university. I encourage them to visit the university bookstore and the library, asking them to consider what groups or individuals seem to have more representation in curricular material, and what groups or individuals seem to have less representation. I then ask them about the ways in which their discoveries inform our discussion about the influence of the dominant ideology on curriculum and whether or not Giroux's (1997) ideas about the hidden curriculum are valid and accurate.

I additionally ask students about what sources of knowledge are most frequently represented in the curriculum. I ask students to generate a hierarchical list of what sources of knowledge are considered to be the most valid and what sources are considered to be the least valid. I start this activity by asking them if they believe there is value in experience. In my fourth year experiential education course, they inevitably answer "yes, of course." I then ask them how this source of knowledge compares to the knowledge that is contained within a peer-reviewed journal. They then better understand the question and begin to list multiple sources of knowledge that typically include: peer-reviewed journals, non-peer–reviewed journals, textbooks, newspapers, television, peers, parents, and experience, among others. They have a harder time trying to hierarchically list them than they do generating the list once they have started. When I ask them to try to list them hierarchically, I encourage them to consider their findings from the previously described activities, asking them what sources of knowledge seemed to be more valid than other sources based on the course syllabi and the artifacts from their trip to the bookstore and the library.

Critically questioning some of these assumptions about curriculum impels students to appreciate that while there are many sources of knowledge, there are certainly some that are more valued within the university context. They then begin to understand that knowledge is, at least in part, socially constructed, partial, and contextual. With advanced undergraduate students or with master's students, this information can serve as a springboard to discuss some of the broader issues around constructions of truth, reality, and knowledge and the ways in which the broader educational theories of constructivism, postpositivism, and poststructuralism can further inform this conversation.

Teaching Methodology

Teaching methodology represents another source of educational hegemony. Freire (1970) refers to the "banking model" of education whereby the student functions as an open repository to whatever knowledge the teacher chooses to deposit that day. This methodology further supports the dominant educational ideology that silences and marginalizes students' voice and experience. This happens through the belief that the main purpose of schools is to transmit the knowledge necessary for people to enter the workforce and that good teaching involves the transmission of that knowledge through the most socially efficient means (Pinar et al., 2002).

One method to counter the "banking model" of education is the problem-posing (liberatory) method of education espoused by Freire (1970). Within this practice, dialogue is employed as a pedagogical method in juxtaposition to the oppressive monological methods of knowledge transmission. Problem-posing education counters the hierarchical nature of "banking" education by suggesting that education should be co-intentional, involving both teachers and students as subjects. Through dialogue new relationships emerge, that of teacher-student and student-teacher (Freire, 1970).

Within this context, there is opportunity for moving beyond some of the limiting factors of banking education. Changing the classroom setting by moving all of the chairs into a circle is one possibility. This simple act "says" a lot. It places the students and the teacher in a physically mutual relationship. Involving students in the creation of goals, objectives, and expectations of the course is another way to help offset some of the power imbalance inherent in the banking model. Choosing course material that is inclusive and represents some of the aforementioned multiple sources of knowledge is important. This, too, can be done in collaboration with students. The teacher gives structure and direction to this process, encouraging academic rigor and thoughtfulness. "The liberating teacher does not wash his or her hands of the students" (Shor & Freire, 1987, p. 172). Rather, teacher-student and student-teacher are co-creating the methodological practices of the classroom.

Some of these methodological practices may include: experiential activities, small-group work, seminar-style, lecture, student presentation, discussion, and creative expression. In most of my classes, I try to employ a mixed methods approach. I begin by identifying a clear purpose to the lesson and identify related readings. I then try to incorporate mini-lecture, guided discussion or small group work, and an experiential activity as components of each lesson. It is time-consuming, but I do find that students stay engaged and learn more because a mixed methods approach addresses their various learning styles and intelligences.

If multiple "ways of knowing" and multiple sources of knowledge are valued, then multiple methods of assessment and evaluation must also be considered. These may include journals, presentations, and critical reflection papers, in addition to tests and quizzes. They may also include peer, self, and/or teacher evaluation. As students move through my courses and have better preparation and understanding of the student-centered classroom, I provide them with increased options. Students can contract a mark or they can choose to receive only written feedback on their assignments, rewriting as they progress through the course and then negotiating a mutually agreed upon mark with me at the end of the semester.

Role of Teachers as Agents of Social Change

Because education is by nature social, historical, political, and cultural, "there is no way we can talk about some universal, unchanging role for the teacher" (Shor, 1987, p. 211). "Teachers at all levels of schooling represent a potentially powerful force for social change" (Giroux, 1997, p. 28). Teachers can develop pedagogical theories and methods that link self-reflection and understanding with a commitment to change the nature of the larger society. Teaching is, thus, a theoretical, intellectual, and political practice within the critical classroom. Teachers need to work toward becoming more fully "cognizant of the political nature of their practice and assume responsibility for this rather than denying it" (Shor, 1987, p. 211). The teacher as an agent of social change attempts to build coherence and consistency as a classroom virtue, while recognizing that s/he is operating as an agent to either perpetuate the institutional structures and those people who hold power within that structure, or to be critical of the institution and those who hold power as a means to lessen oppression. It is imperative that teachers investigate their "situatedness" within this context, helping to reveal some of the inherent biases and assumptions that play themselves out in classroom practice.

One of the first tasks of the critical educator is to explore her/his own subjectivity and "locate" or situate her/himself within that praxis. This process is both active and reflexive. Subjectivity, in this sense, represents an ongoing construction of the development of the personal lens through which one sees the world, and through which notions of reality and truth are shaped. This lens, alongside the stories that are told and the narratives that give coherence and meaning to life, inform the history that is engaged, the science that is studied, and the rules of grammar that are employed and taught (Simon, 1992). They further inform the texts that are chosen and the material that is presented. The teacher must therefore explore this subjectivity as a means to understanding not only the ways in which s/he teaches (methodology), but also the content that is taught.

I often start my course on experiential education with recognition of my own situatedness and bias by telling students a bit about my upbringing, my background, and my own experiences with teaching and learning. I "locate" myself as someone who is a product of the system. I tell them that although questioning educational assumptions and engaging in counter-hegemonic practices represents a central role in the courses that I teach, I was never particularly good at engaging in this form of praxis myself, as a student. I tell them that I found it hard to question assumptions about teaching, learning, the role of the teacher, and the role of the student when my K-12 school experience prepared me to be silent and passive, and to "brown-nose" the teacher as a means to attaining an "A."

I find that students become more at ease with some of the issues that are being presented in class after I self-disclose in this way. They recognize that it is okay for this "work" to be unsettling, and that it is okay for them to want to know how to be liberated while still maintaining an A average. I encourage students to examine assumptions about my own classroom and my own teaching. When the students and I start to fall back into some of the hegemonic patterns of a more traditional classroom, I encourage them to "name" these and to have the courage to stop the class so that we can examine what is happening. I encourage them to do the same with marking. A good system of marking is one that is regarded as fair and reasonable by those who are being marked, as well as by the person who is doing the marking.

I practically implement some of the theoretical ideals of student-centered learning, including: valuing student voice, promoting and practicing dialogue, shared decision-making, and valuing their previous experiences and their ways of knowing. I also tell them that my role as teacher is different than their role as students because of my, at least presumed, greater maturity of experience (Dewey, 1938). This puts me in the somewhat privileged position of facilitating certain aspects of the course, including: the initial course content, assessment methods, and marks.

Because I take a student-centered approach to teaching and learning in both the second and third-year courses that I teach, by the time students enroll in my fourth-year experiential education course, they have received some preparation to engage in a student-directed classroom. I provide some initial direction to the student-directed experiential education course, but decisions about assessment methods, course content, teaching methodology, and final marks are decided collaboratively by the class. I have learned that certain groups of students need more guidance than other groups when engaging in this process. I provide resources that help to inform their decisions and the minimal structure necessary to encourage success with establishing the content for this 12-week course.

The Role of Students as Agents of Social Change

According to most critical theorists and experiential educators, students are not empty vessels, but rather are individuals with life experience and knowledge, situated within their own cultural, class, racial, historical, and gender contexts (Freire, 1970; hooks, 1994). Students arrive in the critical classroom with their individual expectations, hopes, dreams, diverse backgrounds, and life experiences, including a long history of previous schooling and educational hegemony.

When the role of the student in the critical classroom is thus considered, the assumption is that not only will an educator create a classroom condition that offers students the opportunity to work toward social change, to have a voice in the educational process, to have the knowledge and courage to be critical, and to be interested in and committed to this process, but that students have a responsibility to critically commit themselves to this process. This affords students the opportunity to fulfill their prescribed role (within the critical process) as agents of social change.

Students need to receive adequate preparation for functioning within the critical classroom context. If schools operate in accordance with their established roles in society (Giroux, 1997), it is quite possible that students may operate in the same manner. In other words, many students have been taught from early on that to be a "good student" means to be silent, passive, and accepting; a good student's primary purpose is to learn the knowledge the educator imparts in an unquestioning manner. hooks (1994) reinforces this by maintaining that even during college, the primary lesson was to learn obedience to authority.

Students need to locate themselves within the critical classroom in the same way the teacher does, exploring their own epistemologies and biases. Asking students to write educational autobiographies to explore their experiences with schools and with learning represents one starting point to this process. Encouraging students to share and discuss their autobiographies allows them an opportunity to better understand their various subjectivities and the differing educational experiences of students within the classroom. One common result of this process of "naming" is that students may awake from their passivity and begin to question some of their own previously held assumptions about teaching and learning. It also allows them to see that each individual within the classroom has had different experiences and holds different assumptions about teaching and learning.

I additionally ask students to consider their upbringing, parents, siblings, education, religion, and the values that inform their beliefs and to draw concentric circles that represent, in essence, the lens they employ to view the world. Students are then able to use this lens in describing how they, in part, "see" and interpret information and sources of knowledge. Asking students to read *White Privilege: Unpacking the Invisible Backpack* (McIntosh, 1989), and asking them to unpack their individual "backpack" of privilege allows them to name themselves and relate that to the dominant ideology, locating their "positionality" in relation to that ideology.

Risks and Student-Directed Classrooms

It would be naïve of me to conclude here that the result of this is that students become liberated and begin to take responsibility for their education. The process of naming themselves, questioning educational assumptions, and engaging in student-directed classrooms is full of risk. Some of these risks may result in growth and positive change, or some of these risks may have more negative consequences or may be miseducative. Students and teachers may be empowered or they may feel frightened or threatened.

The risk-taking involved in a student-directed classroom almost always results in students disagreeing with either fellow students or the teacher over not only what texts should be read but how they should be read, and this process of questioning expands to curricular material in its entirety, as well as course assessment methods, methodology, required assignments, and all other aspects of any given course, in any given semester. Simon (1992) warns that this may lead to a number of questions, including: Who will make the decision about not only what we read, but what we write? What process of deliberation will be used and what forms of authority will be invoked?

The teacher needs to be prepared for how unsettling this process can be and needs to act upon her/his somewhat privileged position as facilitator to help guide this process. There is no set of prescriptive practices that describe how to do this. A teacher needs to rely on her/his own experience, her/his mastery of the subject matter, and her/his intuition when choosing to engage students in this process. It may be wise for a teacher who is new to the post-secondary classroom to begin this process slowly, considering ways to make the classroom more student-centered before delving into the complexities of a student-directed classroom experience.

There is also risk when students and teachers engage in the process of naming themselves. The project of naming oneself can provide teachers and students with a language of critique that proffers an understanding of how different subjectivities are positioned within a historically specific range of ideologies and social practices. But what happens when a student's voice expresses a "way of knowing" that bumps up against another student's "way of knowing" and the two are contradictory? Who gets heard? Do voices that express racism, sexism, or elitism have credence if the intent of the critical classroom is to create less oppressive ways of knowing and structures?

There is great potential in incorporating some of the play-based and group dynamics activities familiar to experiential educators to help with this. It is important to be attentive to creating a classroom community that encourages a safe space for teaching and learning, but that also establishes ground rules that discourage further oppression and silencing. Helping students establish their level of comfort with sharing and discussing some of these issues by asking them to engage in a comfort zone activity on the first day of class is one place to start. When students disagree, employing the reflective activity known as fishbowling (Knapp, 1992) will allow students the opportunity to authentically listen to one another when trying to work through some of these differences.

Despite these challenges, the post-secondary experiential education classroom exists as an exciting site of learning. It can provide a foundation upon which to begin to encourage students to engage in a dialogue that analyzes the dominant ideologies and social practices that constitute schools and the larger society. This can provide a means for students to further consider the ways in which they can act as agents of social change in developing a different vision of schools and society, one that can reflect the ideals of a more socially just world.

Conclusion

A challenge to the critical pedagogue is how to incorporate some of these principles and avoid mere tokenism. A simple adjustment to the physical space of the classroom may not lead to greater dialogue and less hierarchy. Students accustomed to some of the comforts of the banking model of education (Freire, 1970) may be unable or unwilling to accept this change in methodology. It is important for an educator to act as facilitator and guide, teacher-student, student-teacher and engage in meaningful praxis with students, while avoiding paternalism. This, too, represents a challenge to critical pedagogy in practice.

There are many other challenges to engaging in this form of classroom praxis, including: lack of student preparation, institutional constraints, student resistance, and the fact that research is often valued over teaching in post-secondary institutions and student-centered teaching requires a lot of time. That said, I believe the advantages to engaging in a more purposeful classroom praxis that acts on the theoretical underpinnings of experiential education and critical pedagogy can be one means to working toward a vision of a more socially just world.

Greater collaboration between theorists and teachers could further strengthen both the theory and the practice of the post-secondary experiential education classroom. It is agreed that critical pedagogy continues to be excessively abstract and too far removed from the everyday life of schools. "There is much to be learned from reflecting on the congruency (or lack thereof) between our methodological desires and practices" (Russell, 2003, p. 131).

This paper provides a vision of what "could be." It proffers ideals on the construction of a post-secondary classroom praxis that emphasizes the potential for classroom practices to reflect pedagogical theory. Shor and Freire (1987) ask, "What kind of teaching could make critical learning happen?" (p. 19). Imparting theoretical knowledge is no longer enough. In turn, an isolated experience that is disconnected to a broader theory or set of ideas is also insufficient. There is great potential in combining the best of both. The post-secondary experiential education classroom provides one site for the pursuit of a critical pedagogical praxis that is rich in both theory and practice.

References

Apple, M. (1975). The hidden curriculum and the nature of conflict. In W. Pinar (Ed.), *Curriculum theorizing: The reconceptualists* (pp. 95–119). Berkeley, CA: McCutchan.

Apple, M. (1990). *Ideology and curriculum* (2nd ed.). New York: Routledge & Kegan Paul.

Argyris, C., & Schon, D. A. (1974). *Theory in practice: Increasing professional effectiveness.* San Francisco: Jossey-Bass.

Association for Experiential Education. (2004). *What is experiential education?* Retrieved February 23, 2004, from www.aee.org

Brookes, A. (2003). A critique of neo-Hahnian theory. Part one: Challenges to the concept of "character building." *Journal of Adventure Education and Outdoor Leadership, 3*(1), 49–62.

Brookfield, S. (1996). Experiential pedagogy: Grounding teaching in students' learning. *Journal of Experiential Education, 19*(2), 62–68.

Dewey, J. (1938). *Experience and education.* New York: Macmillan.

Eisner, E. (2002). *The educational imagination: On the design and evaluation of school programs* (4th ed.). New York: Macmillan.

Estes, C. (2004). Promoting student-centered learning in experiential education. *Journal of Experiential Education, 26*(2), 141–160.

Fawcett, L., Bell, A. C., & Russell, C. L. (2002). Guiding our environmental praxis: Teaching for social and environmental justice. In W. Leal Filho (Ed.), *Teaching sustainability at universities: Towards curriculum greening* (pp. 223–228). New York: Peter Lang.

Freire, P. (1970). *Pedagogy of the oppressed.* New York: Continuum.

Giroux, H. (1988). *Teachers as intellectuals.* Boston: Bergin & Garvey.

Giroux, H. (1997). *Pedagogy and the politics of hope: Theory, culture, and schooling.* Boulder, CO: Westview Press.

Gore, J. M. (1993). *The struggle for pedagogies: Critical and feminist discourses as regimes of truth.* New York: Routledge.

hooks, b. (1994). *Teaching to transgress: Education as the practice of freedom.* New York: Routledge.

Itin, C. M. (1999). Reasserting the philosophy of experiential education as a vehicle for change in the 21st century. *Journal of Experiential Education, 22*(2), 91–98.

Keesing-Styles, L. (2003). The relationship between critical pedagogy and assessment in teacher education. *Radical Pedagogy, 5*(1), 1–20.

Kincheloe, J. L. (2004). *Critical pedagogy.* New York: Peter Lang.

Knapp, C. (1992). *Lasting lessons: A teacher's guide to reflecting on experience.* Charleston, WV: ERIC.

Knowles, M. (1973). *The adult learner: A neglected species.* Houston, TX: Gulf.

Kolb, D. G. (1992). The practicality of theory. *Journal of Experiential Education, 15*(2), 24–28.

McLaren, P. (2000). Paulo Freire's pedagogy of possibility. In S. Steiner, H. Frank, P. McLaren, & R. Bahruth (Eds.), *Freirean pedagogy, praxis and possibilities: Projects for the new millennium* (pp. 1–21). New York: Falmer Press.

McLaren, P. (2003). *Life in schools: An introduction to critical pedagogy in the social foundations of education* (4th ed.). Boston: Allyn & Bacon.

McIntosh, P. (1989, July/August). White privilege: Unpacking the invisible backpack. *Peace and Freedom, 49*, 10–12.

Osborne, K. (1990). Is there a democratic socialist pedagogy? In D. Henley & J. Young (Eds.), *Canadian perspectives on critical pedagogy* (pp. 43–73). Winnipeg, Manitoba, Canada: The Canadian Critical Pedagogy Network with Social Education Researchers in Canada.

Pinar, W. F., Reynolds, W. M., Slattery, P., & Taubman, P. M. (Eds.). (2002). *Understanding curriculum* (4th ed.). New York: Peter Lang.

Richards, I. A. (Ed.). (1966). *The republic.* Cambridge, England: Cambridge University Press.

Russell, C. L. (2003). Minding the gap between methodological desires and practices. In D. Hodsom (Ed.), *OISE (The Ontario Institute for Studies in Education) papers in STSE education,* (Volume 4, 125–134). Toronto, Ontario, Canada: University of Toronto.

Shor, I. (1987). *Freire for the classroom: A sourcebook for liberatory teaching.* Portsmouth, NH: Boynton/Cook.

Shor, I., & Freire, P. (1987). *A pedagogy for liberation: Dialogues for transforming education.* South Hadley, MA: Bergin & Garvey.

Simon, R. (1992). *Teaching against the grain: Texts for a pedagogy of possibility.* South Hadley, MA: Bergin & Garvey.

Smith, M. (2002). *Plato.* Retrieved July 17, 2003, from www.infed.org/thinker/et-plato.htm

Weiler, K. (Ed.). (2001). *Feminist engagements: Reading, resisting, and revisioning male theorists in education and cultural studies.* New York: Routledge.

The Student-Directed Classroom: A Model for Teaching Experiential Education Theory

▾ ▾ ▾

Karen Warren

How can we teach a theory of what we practice? How can we come down off the ropes course, return from interviewing Aunt Arie, or put away our New Games props, and sit down in the classroom to learn experiential education philosophy? How can discussions about Dewey's ideas, lesson plans, Summerhill, moral development, ethics of teaching, motivation, and a host of other questions grounded in the basic foundations of experiential education come alive in a classroom setting? How can we give future teachers a sound theoretical framework to use in teaching experientially? The answer, of course, is experientially.

The Model

The student-directed classroom is the method I have used to introduce the theory of experiential education to college students, many of whom want to use experiential learning in their future teaching careers. This model has been in existence for five years at Hampshire College. It takes place within four walls, sandwiched in a two-hour time-block twice a week in a busy college schedule.

The experience in this model is the students' active creation of the class itself. Students determine the syllabus, prioritize topic areas, regulate class members' commitment, facilitate actual class sessions, undertake individual or group-inspired projects, and engage in ongoing

This chapter originally was published in the *Journal of Experiential Education*, with the following citation: Warren, K. (1988). The student-directed classroom: A model for teaching experiential education theory. *Journal of Experiential Education, 11*(1), 4–9.

evaluation. Because it is different from traditional educational theory courses that attempt to convey a body of knowledge that the teacher or the institution deems important, the student-defined curriculum promotes a shift from giving an education to, in the words of Adrienne Rich, "claiming an education."

In the student-directed classroom, the question often posed by the back-to-basics naysayers is, "Will students choose to learn what they are 'supposed' to learn in such a class?" I find it fascinating that during the five years of the Philosophy of Experiential Education course, an appreciable body of key concepts and questions has always been addressed.

Consistently, students want to learn what experiential education is all about and search through its historical and philosophical roots to arrive at a definition. They look at current developments in the theory by studying more recent program models: expedition education, cultural journalism, and various therapeutic, adventure, and alternative programs. Students are generally interested in the social issues that inundate educational theory. Issues such as oppression, multicultural perspectives, ethical and moral dilemmas, diversity, and social change all have become important subject matter. Teaching methodology and applications of experiential education are also primary topics. Finally, most students are curious about their own place within the experiential education movement and philosophy—how their own education and learning style can benefit from such an approach. In essence, they are striving to achieve a sense of themselves in an often vast and impersonal educational process.

So while the doubters question the magnitude and appropriateness of the content, the students have successfully devised a class experience rich in both content and process. An added benefit is that students are able to address the continuing questions that often override the content. Questions such as, "What is learning?" and "What are the goals of education?" which pervade and color all classes, can be explored in this format.

Power in the Model

The goal in the student-directed model is to empower rather than to hold power over. Therefore, the elimination of authority, the chief power dynamic in a teacher-directed situation, is a primary technique. This does not mean teachers withdraw from power by denouncing their authority. If a teacher abdicates power without transferring it to students, confusion results, the class lacks leadership and direction, and a miseducative void is created. Instead, the teacher needs to use the respect and position they enjoy at the onset of the class to promote student empowerment.

To foster this shift in the locus of power, the teacher introduces students to the tools of empowerment in the beginning class stages. (These tools are shown in the diagrams and explained later in the article.) Concurrently, the students accrue power as their initial promise of academic freedom becomes realized. The teacher relinquishes authoritarian influence and becomes an integral member of the evolving group.

After the students have attained self-determination, intervention by the teacher acting as a leader rather than a group member occurs only in situations when the group lacks the skills to deal with obstacles they encounter. For example, a student-led class meeting on the philosophical basis of experiential education was hopelessly jumbled one semester. I perceived the need for further focusing and for discussion about leadership skills and offered these to the class for future use.

There are situations where the students want to give power back to the teacher. The teacher then must decide whether they are giving power back legitimately. Do they need help with process tools, direction setting, or just a morale boost? Or do they in fact have the problem-solving capabilities but have declined responsibility by relying on the traditional power structure? The following sections on teacher role, student role, and evaluation will make it more clear how this power transformation is achieved.

Teacher's Role

The teacher's role in the student-directed classroom is challenging in its subtlety. I sometimes feel as if I'm tiptoeing the line between intervention and stepping back. As most experiential educators can affirm, it's an intuitive guess at times whether to: (a) actively facilitate the process either to maximize learning or to keep it from becoming miseducative, or (b) let the students' struggle with the experience serve as the didactic lesson. I have identified several components of the teacher's role in this model that may make this easier.

Informed Consent

Students need to know what they are getting into so they can make responsible choices. They make initial decisions based on a sketch the teacher provides of the student-directed classroom. A precise course description and detailed introduction to both the potentials and perplexities of the class are methods to provide this information.

Establishing a Concrete Vision

I remember my first exposure to an open classroom in junior high. The teacher pushed back the desks, promised us we were about to embark on an exciting educational journey, and told us we could do anything we wanted. As thrilled as I was by the prospects, I was totally lost as to how or where proceed. My classmates must have had similar trials because after a couple of weeks, this grand experiment fizzled, the desks were returned to rows, and we got down to the business of being taught English.

The lesson I took from that early exposure to a student-directed classroom was that students who are a product of a traditionally teacher-directed system need some assistance in making that exhilarating but unfamiliar jump to self-determination. The teacher's role, then, is to provide some initial structure and focusing.

In this model, the initial structure is the framework on which students can build their self-direction. The teacher conveys a concrete vision of the class by suggesting the course goals and what the students might expect from such an endeavor. The task of creating the curriculum then becomes the concrete focus. The teacher also facilitates the first several weeks of class to give direction and to set a model for future facilitation. Creative, well-organized class sessions set a standard for students to follow when they undertake their own facilitations.

Ground Rule Setting

In the introductory stages, the teacher sets the basic operating principles by both statement and example. These ground rules are the safety net that allows students to take risks to involve themselves in the frightening but compelling class maelstrom. Some ground rules stressed are: use of "I statements" to express feelings, active listening, commitment, use of inclusive language, constructive feedback, and intolerance of oppression.

Process Tools

Since interdependence reigns in this collective effort, students need the appropriate group skills to accomplish their goal of self-determination. The teacher is responsible for imparting the following process tools:

1. *Skills in thinking as a group.* In order to come up with what they want to learn, students are introduced to brainstorming and prioritizing strategies, and quickly find these to be of use in synthesizing their syllabus.

2. *Decision-making skills.* Consensus decision making is explained and tested out. Practicing with decisions at first, the group builds proficiency in the empowerment stage and is able to orchestrate very complex decisions in the self-determination stage.

3. *Leadership roles.* Since a group needs leadership rather than set leaders to function effectively, the teacher points out available leadership roles. Impelled by the situation, students actively take on the various roles of timekeeper, feelings articulator, group collective conscience, minority opinion advocate, question framer, summarizer, focuser, and gate keeper.

4. *Problem-solving skills.* Through a series of simple initiative problems, the group is equipped with the tools as well as the belief that they can creatively solve problems together.

5. *Feedback and debriefing skills.* Because debriefing is critical to experiential education, the teacher's job is to ensure it happens. Insisting on quality feedback time early in the course sets an expectation for continuation during the latter sessions.

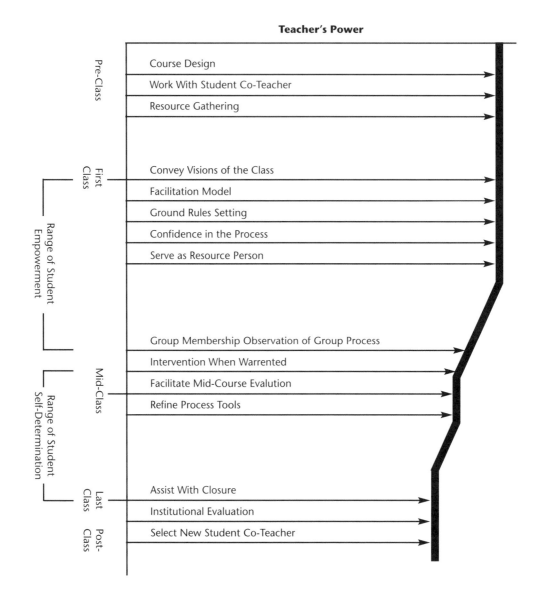

Teacher's Power

- Pre-Class
  - Course Design
  - Work With Student Co-Teacher
  - Resource Gathering

- First Class
  - Convey Visions of the Class
  - Facilitation Model
  - Ground Rules Setting
  - Confidence in the Process
  - Serve as Resource Person

- Mid-Class
  - Group Membership Observation of Group Process
  - Intervention When Warrented
  - Facilitate Mid-Course Evalution
  - Refine Process Tools

- Last Class
  - Assist With Closure
  - Institutional Evaluation

- Post-Class
  - Select New Student Co-Teacher

Range of Student Empowerment

Range of Student Self-Determination

Figure 1. **Teacher's role in the student-directed classroom.**

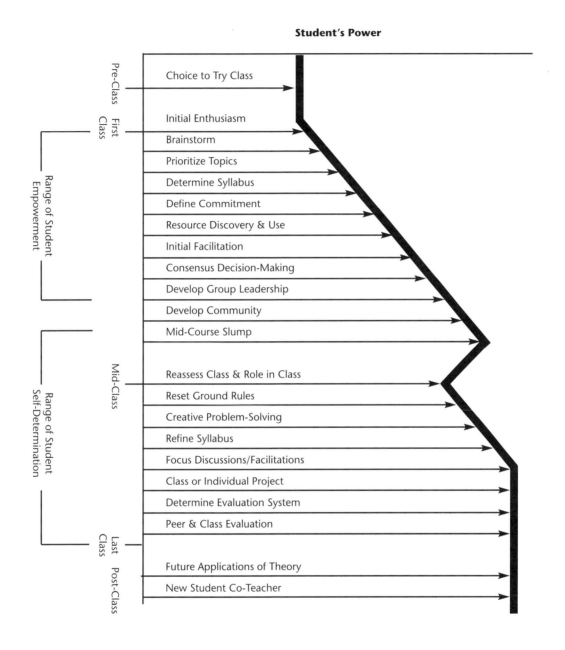

Figure 2. **Student's role in the student-directed classroom.**

Resource Person

After the students have brainstormed what they want to learn, the teacher becomes the resource for readings, speakers, films, and programs. By having a ready repertoire of provocative resources, the teacher can influence the quality of the course content.

This sequence of events often occurs. During the first few classes, students finalize an ordered list of topics for each class session. I then attach readings and other resource ideas to each subject. These ideas are presented to the group for acceptance and rearranging. Usually the give-and-take of resource selection helps refine the topics even further. Finally, the student facilitators have the option of adding to or changing the resources for their sessions.

Confidence in the Process

The importance of the teacher as cheerleader cannot be underestimated in this model. As students are learning that self-regulation can work, they often need someone to point out that the struggles are an important part of growth toward success. In this regard, the teacher can reframe the conflict in a positive light, have faith in the students, and exude a contagious delight with the process.

Closure Assistance

Termination can be a difficult time. The teacher assists in this stage by helping the students understand what they have accomplished. It's time to marvel at results. As they articulate their growth, students can better internalize what self-determination has taught them about experiential education theory. They can also postulate future applications of the theories learned. Asking for written and verbal self-evaluations and encouraging a closure celebration are ways the teacher can support the transition.

Student Role

The student role in this model is best elucidated by example.

Facilitation

The refinement of teaching skills resulting from the opportunity to facilitate are of great benefit to future experiential educators. Student-led class sessions are often a forum for innovation that illuminates experiential education theory far better than lectures or discussions.

For example, one year the class co-facilitators re-created the atmosphere of a traditional teacher-directed classroom with all its subtle nuances of authority. They dressed up in their best teacher clothes and put on an aura of professional aloofness to set the stage. We arrived at the classroom to find our usual circular seminar seating arranged in proper rows with assigned seats for all. Class started with a quiz on that day's reading, "A Process Guide to Teaching." Having focused on the ideas of teaching effectively outlined in the article, we had neglected to memorize the character names in each vignette that were the basis of our quiz questions. Even before we exchanged papers to be graded, we knew we were failures. Our only avenue was rebellion from the authority so perfectly play-acted before us. Spitballs flew and chaos reigned while our teachers finished their lengthy lecture on John Dewey. The lessons of student powerlessness in an authority-centered class were firmly entrenched by the enacted experience.

Develop an Effective Group

There is a noticeable increase in group efficiency as time passes in the course. As students risk more of themselves over time, discussions gain depth, facilitations find a focus, and the content becomes more compelling.

Project

Class or individual projects support an in-depth look at a particular aspect of experiential education theory. Individual projects have included experiential education applications to such topics as: cognitive learning, education in China, environmental ethics, women in the wilderness, the creative arts, and wit as a sign of gifted intelligence.

Some years the class decides to do a collective project. On one such occasion, an educational consortium was set up to create a school. After an overarching philosophy was determined, students worked in teams to establish different experiential education programs for the school. One team visited a junior high classroom to gather background resources. Another labored on lesson plans that would address the needs of disenfranchised kids. The project culminated with each team producing a comprehensive brochure of their program in the school.

Reassessments

The group finds itself reworking many class components as they learn from their experiences with self-regulation. They refine the syllabus: "If we want to see how experiential education theory works in practice, let's go to an alterative school." They focus discussion: non-productive tangents are more quickly identified and avoided. They reset ground rules. For example, the group typically has set time aside to redefine their commitment to the course. Collectively they determined what, specifically, being prepared for the class meant, agreed they wanted to start and end class on time, and verbally announced to their peers what their level of commitment was. Their expectations of each other were much more exacting than anything I would ever attempt to have a class follow.

Student Co-Teacher

Every year I enlist a student from a previous class to co-teach the course. Having participated in the struggles of self-direction firsthand the preceding year, the student co-teacher brings an invaluable voice of experience to the new group. Her/his perspective and credibility as a peer to the new class is yet another way to redistribute power.

Evaluation

Because evaluation in the traditional school situation is the primary way for the teacher to maintain power over the students, restructuring it in this training model emphasizes that students and teachers share equally in the learning process. It eschews the idea of evaluation as motivation in favor of its use in enhancing learning through immediate feedback.

In the student-directed class, evaluation takes three major forms. Facilitation feedback—where students in charge are critiqued on how they ran the particular class—encompasses the debriefing stage of the popular experiential education models. It allows class members immediate access to ideas on how to structure future teaching attempts.

The second evaluation tool is the mid-course assessment. Invariably there is a mid-semester slump when other commitments, conflicts within the class, and lethargy arise. The mid-course evaluation is the device to get things back on track. Directed by the teacher, it's an opportunity to gauge satisfaction and frustrations with the class. We figure out what things we're doing well and what needs fixing. Because we do the repair work at mid-semester instead of waiting until the end, students feel as if they have power to change their immediate educational experience.

The final major form to measure progress is peer evaluation. Class members record observations of other individuals' growth in the class and write evaluations to be used as part of the institutional evaluation.

While I realize that institutional constraints of traditional evaluation sometimes serve as barriers, with some effort student involvement in the evaluation procedure can be creatively incorporated. At Hampshire College, accepted evaluation practice is for the instructor to write a short course synopsis, followed by an evaluation of the student's work in the course. One-year students in the experiential education class decided they wanted to write the course synopsis collectively so it would truly reflect what the class had meant to them. They decided to represent the class diagrammatically—a dramatic departure from the institutionally accepted practice. Speculating on what this would look like in their permanent record and if it would be accepted by the powers that be at the college, there ensued an intense discussion about the goals and purposes of assessment in education and how we can faithfully document experiences as education. This dialogue was far more complex and intriguing than if I had come in that day and said the topic was evaluation of experiential education.

Conclusion

To integrate experiential education into the mainstream of American education, it is essential to validate its theoretical base. We must move beyond simply giving teachers-to-be the tricks of the experiential education trade. Additionally, we must challenge these students to discover a comprehensive understanding of the theories behind the techniques. This article has suggested one model to experientially convey the underlying theory to future teachers.

A word of caution is necessary. There is no pat formula for success in the student-directed classroom. As stated in the course catalogue description, "This unique educational collaboration requires that students be willing to struggle through the perplexities and frustrations of the responsibility of creating a refined educational endeavor." Instructors who wish to utilize this model must decide that the students' experience in the process of claiming their education is more important than a perfectly crafted, smooth-flowing, predictable class. But after all, isn't taking risks and exploring options precisely what experiential education is all about?

Note: *I would like to acknowledge and thank all the students over the years who are the true co-creators of this model.*

References

Auvine, B. et al. (1977). *A manual for group facilitators.* Madison, WI: Center for Conflict Resolution.

Avery, M. et al. (1981). *Building united judgement: A handbook for consensus decision making.* Madison, WI: Center for Conflict Resolution.

Chrislip, D. (1980). *A process guide for teaching.* An unpublished paper of the Colorado Outward Bound School.

Katz, M. S. (1978). Teaching people to think for the future: Some guidelines for teacher education. *Journal of Teacher Education, 29*(4), 57–61.

Lockwood, L. G. (1979). What my students have learned about classroom ecology. *Journal of College Science Teaching, 9*(11), 80–82.

Rich, A. (1979). Claiming an education. In *On lies, secrets and silence.* New York: Norton.

Wigginton, E. (1985). *Sometimes a shining moment: The Foxfire experience.* Garden City, NY: Anchor Press/Doubleday.

The Personal Intelligences in Experiential Education: A Theory in Practice

▾ ▾ ▾

Wayne Regina & Steve Pace

The philosophy and methodology of experiential education is applied in a variety of educational settings ranging from ropes courses and wilderness trips to academic college courses and K-12 classrooms. No matter the setting, certain common threads distinguish experiential education from other types of educational models and learning experiences. Joplin (1995) offers a stage-based model to define experiential education. She articulates focus, action, support, feedback, and debrief as important components of the experiential education learning process. Her five-stage approach offers a guidepost to structuring the learning environment for maximal effectiveness: clarity of task; a challenging environment that introduces uncertainty and ambiguity in order to actively engage the learner; support for and feedback to the learner to better ensure a positive outcome; and opportunities for a public debriefing so that the learner can reflect on the experience and share what was learned.

Prominent researchers and theoreticians outside of the field of experiential education have articulated and defined educational and learning theories that are remarkably consistent with the theory and practice of experiential education as described by Joplin (Joplin, 1995). One such approach is Howard Gardner's theory of multiple intelligences (Gardner, 1983, 1993), which has wielded great influence on the field of education, providing a robust catalyst for education reform (Armstrong, 1994; Campbell, Campbell, & Dickinson, 1993; Gardner, 1993; Lazear, 1993). At its heart, multiple intelligence (MI) theory and practice provide a natural bridge to experiential education theory and practice as they integrate current knowledge of brain-based learning with active and challenging learning environments, a dynamic pedagogy, and opportunities for reflection and review.

Interestingly, Gardner (1983, 1995) did not initially conceptualize the practical applications of the multiple intelligences when he first wrote about his theory in the seminal work *Frames of Mind*. Nor did he envision that MI theory would provide a catalyst for education experimentation and reform. Nevertheless, Gardner's initial writings and follow-up work spurred a generation of educators who were restless to break free from the bonds of traditional education and eager to develop and implement curriculum based on multiple ways of knowing and learning.

Gardner's (1983) initial research led him to propose seven intelligences that describe ways individuals learn. They are: logical-mathematical, verbal-linguistic, visual-spatial, bodily-kinesthetic, musical-rhythmic, interpersonal, and intrapersonal. A decade later, Gardner added an eighth intelligence, the naturalist intelligence (Checkley, 1997). In proposing a theory of multiple intelligences, Gardner (1995) suggests that *all* of the intelligences are equally important. He identifies these intelligences from studies of brain functioning and defines them as based on "biological and psychological potential" (p. 2), emphasizing that they do not simply reflect a learning style. In an interview with Checkley (1997), Gardner describes intelligence as "the human ability to solve problems or to make something that is valued in one or more cultures ... (with) a particular representation in the brain for the ability ..." (p. 8). Further, Gardner (1983) theorizes that these potentials are "capable of being realized to a greater or lesser extent as a consequence of the *experiential,* cultural, and motivational factors that affect a person (p. 2, italics added). In effect, by promoting all eight intelligences, Gardner advocates that intelligence is not only based on cognitive processes such as reading, writing, and arithmetic, but also through the arts—visual, musical, and dance—as well as through knowing oneself and others.

Prior to Gardner's MI theory, the educational system in the United States was focused almost entirely on the verbal-linguistic and logical-mathematical intelligences. These dominant intelligences translated into curriculum models, delivery systems, and assessment structures that were, likewise, related almost exclusively to the logical-mathematical and verbal-linguistic intelligences. Even today, almost 25 years after Gardner first published the scientifically based *Frames of Mind*, despite pockets of innovation in a variety of school settings including charter schools, independent schools, and a handful of public schools, the dominance of learning and high-stakes testing is still principally based on the verbal-linguistic and logical-mathematical intelligences.

While the prevailing educational paradigm still reflects a popular belief in the supremacy of these two intelligences in content, delivery, and assessment, a growing body of research and practice, based on Gardner's work and those of other educators influenced by Gardner, as well as other theorists and reformers, is demonstrating the power of accessing the numerous intelligences to facilitate learning. MI theory further proposes that all individuals have strengths in certain domains, and they can thus learn more naturally through these intelligences. Furthermore, MI theory and practice suggest that an active and varied pedagogy promotes learning, retention, independent and creative thinking, and problem solving. Perhaps most importantly, MI theory and practice advocate that learning does not take place in a vacuum. Learning about self and others by fostering development in the intrapersonal and interpersonal intelligences prepares students to learn academic content and to make positive contributions to society. The core of MI theory lies in the interpersonal and intrapersonal intelligences, commonly referred to as the personal intelligences (Gardner, 1983). Similarly conceptualized as emotional intelligence by Goldman (1995) and differentiation by Bowen (Kerr and Bowen, 1988), strength in the personal intelligences is viewed as crucial to all other learning. That is, success in developing and strengthening the personal intelligences significantly influences learning in all content and process areas (Larriveer, 2000; Marzano, 2003). For example, managing oneself effectively in highly ambiguous and anxious situations; the capacity to hear, offer, and integrate support and feedback; and the ability to incorporate public debrief and reflection are all capacities associated not only with experiential education but also with the personal intelligences. In effect, by strengthening these intelligences, the more emotionally mature individual becomes a more capable and ready learner. And, perhaps most significantly, the personal intelligences of the educator, as leader of the classroom or educational system, most considerably influence the educational environment of which the learners are a part. In other words, learning environments that encourage development of the personal intelligences are best promoted by educators who themselves are dedicated to enhancing their intelligences. This is especially true for educators and students involved in experiential education.

This chapter explores how experiential methodology is used to teach the theoretical concepts and skills of the personal intelligences and the related constructs of emotional intelligence and differentiation. It traces the important theoretical and practical implications of focusing on developing the interpersonal and intrapersonal intelligences as a means of improving content and process learning. We investigate Goldman's work on emotional intelligence and Bowen's theoretical concept of differentiation and their intersection with Gardner's personal intelligences. Research and theory supporting the use of the personal intelligences as the basis for personal development and content learning are presented as well. We further demonstrate how developing the personal intelligences are a central component of experiential education, using examples from our Prescott College course, *Community Mediation and Alternative Dispute Resolution*, to highlight the theory in practice. In doing so, we also discuss how this approach is consistent with the basic tenets of experiential education.

The Personal Intelligences and Related Constructs

In *Frames of Mind,* Gardner (1983) defines the intrapersonal and interpersonal intelligences. He classifies the intrapersonal intelligences as the:

> development of the internal aspects of a person. The core capacity at work here is access to one's own feelings [about] life—one's range of affects or emotions: the capacity instantly to effect discriminations among these feelings and, eventually, to label them, to enmesh them in symbolic codes, to draw upon them as a means of understanding and guiding one's behavior.... At its most advanced level, intrapersonal knowledge allows one to detect and to symbolize complex and highly differentiated sets of feelings. One finds this form of intelligence developed in the novelist (like Proust) who can write introspectively about feelings, in the patient (or the therapist) who comes to attain a deep knowledge of his own feeling life, in the wise elder who draws upon his own wealth of inner experiences in order to advise members of his community. (p. 239)

As defined by Gardner, then, developing the intrapersonal intelligence allows the individual to know him/herself more fully and to use that knowledge to benefit the self and others.

Gardner (1983) describes the interpersonal intelligence as one where an individual:

> Turns outward, to other individuals. The core capacity here is the *ability to notice and make distinctions among other individuals* and, in particular, among their moods, temperaments, motivations, and intentions.... In an advanced form, interpersonal knowledge permits a skilled adult to read the intentions and desires—even when these have been hidden—of many other individuals and, potentially, to act upon this knowledge—for example, by influencing a group of disparate individuals to behave along desired lines. We see highly developed forms of interpersonal intelligence in political and religious figures (a Mahatma Gandhi or a Lyndon Johnson), in skilled parents and teachers, and in individuals enrolled in the helping professions, be they therapists, counselors, or shamans. (p. 239)

In the same text, Gardner acknowledges that although all of the intelligences are important, it is the personal intelligences that form the basis for success for both the individual and society. He writes:

> While the decision to employ (or not to employ) one's musical or spatial intelligence is not heavily charged, the pressures to employ one's personal intelligences are acute: it is

the unusual individual who does not try to employ his understanding of the personal
realm in order to improve his own well-being or his relationship with the community....
Armed with such a scheme of interpretation, he has the potential to make sense of the
full range of experiences which he and others in his community can undergo. (p. 241–242)

In effect, while the other intelligences are important for both personal and social advancement, developing the personal intelligences is the most fundamental for success in life and
for societal betterment.

Other theoreticians and researchers echo the centrality of the personal intelligences. For
example, Daniel Goldman and his colleagues have created an industry of promoting emotional intelligence (Boyatzis, 2002; Goldman, 1994, 2006; Goldman, Boyatzis, & McKee, 2002)
and, more recently, social intelligence (Goldman, 2006). Salovey and Mayer (as cited in Goldman, 1994) used Gardner's work in the personal intelligences as a springboard for defining
emotional intelligence. Goldman (1994) expounds on their work in defining emotional intelligence to include:

1. *Knowing one's emotions.* Self-awareness—recognizing a feeling *as it hap-*
   pens—is the keystone of emotional intelligence ... the ability to monitor feelings from moment to moment is crucial to psychological insight and
   self-understanding.... People with greater certainty about their feelings are
   better pilots of their lives, having a surer sense about how they really feel
   about personal decisions....

2. *Managing emotions.* Handling feelings so they are appropriate is an ability
   that builds on self-awareness ... the capacity to soothe oneself, to shake off
   rampant anxiety, gloom, or irritability.... Those who excel in it can bounce
   back far more quickly from life's setbacks and upsets....

3. *Motivating oneself....* Marshaling emotions in the service of a goal is essential for paying attention, for self-motivation and mastery, and for creativity.
   Emotional self-control—delaying gratification and stifling impulsiveness—
   underlies accomplishment of every sort.... People who have this skill tend to
   be more highly productive and effective in whatever they undertake.

4. *Recognizing emotions in others.* Empathy, another ability that builds on emotional self-awareness, is a fundamental "people skill."... Empathy kindles
   altruism. People who are empathetic are more attuned to the subtle social
   signals that indicate what others need or want. This makes them better at
   callings such as the caring professions, teaching, sales, and management.

5. *Handling relationships.* The art of relationships is, in large part, skill at managing emotions in others.... These are the abilities that undergird popularity, leadership, and interpersonal effectiveness. People who excel in these skills do well at anything that relies on interacting smoothly with others (p. 43–44).

Finally, prior to Gardner and Goldman's research and writings on the personal intelligences/emotional intelligence, Murray Bowen (1971) addressed the importance of the personal intelligences, as articulated in his family systems theory. Bowen articulates two fundamental life forces—individuality and togetherness—and proposes that the interaction of these life forces determine a person's core capacity to manage himself, his life, and his relationships with others and society (Bowen, 2002; Kerr & Bowen, 1988). Bowen describes individuality as a universal, biological life force that propels organisms toward separateness, uniqueness, and distinctiveness. He theorizes that all life forms express this drive toward becoming distinct entities. Bowen explains togetherness as the complementary, universal, biological life force that propels organism toward relationship, attachment, and interconnectedness. For Bowen, it is these twin life forces in motion that determine the organism's level of differentiation, or capacity to function as a distinctly separate organism, while remaining in intimate connection with others and the environment. Bowen and his associates conceptualize differentiation as the ability of the individual to clearly define a self, regulate one's behaviors and feelings, develop personal responsibility, and, simultaneously, relate to others, work with individuals and groups, develop empathy and compassion, and take a stand regardless of the emotional climate or reactivity in others (Bowen, 2002; Friedman, 1996, 2007; Kerr & Bowen, 1988; Regina, 2000). Synonyms for differentiation include emotional maturity, personal integrity, ability to adapt to life's various situations and challenges, and willingness to accept personal responsibility for one's being and destiny (Friedman, 1991, 1996, 2007; Kerr & Bowen, 1988).

Clearly, all of these theoreticians, educators, clinicians, and practitioners have developed a common, converging schema of successful human functioning: one's effectiveness in life, capacity to learn and grow, ability to effectively engage with others, and personal satisfaction are related to the development of the personal intelligences—the interpersonal intelligence and the intrapersonal intelligence. Interestingly, these are many of the same outcomes sought and achieved through experiential education.

Most educational systems in the United States only glimpse the importance of developing these personal intelligences. While many schools and districts now implement character education programs—essentially programs designed to foster and promote the personal intelligences—these programs are usually relegated to secondary or tertiary importance in the average school day or school curriculum.

More innovative educational institutions and programs understand the importance of developing the personal intelligences and how fostering them not only increases a student's effectiveness in her life and within the life of the classroom but also facilitates learning in the other multiple intelligences. Sylwester (1995) states, "We know emotion is very important to the education process because it drives attention, which drives learning and memory (p 72)." Later he adds, "It's impossible to separate emotion from the other important activities of life (p 75)."

Caine and Caine (1997) go further, detailing how the brain functions when fatigued or feeling helpless. They offer the term "downshifting" to describe how learning suffers when students do not feel empowered or when they can no longer function adequately due to exhaustion. Their brain-based research model parallels Bowen's family systems theory, which describes how emotional reactivity increases as anxiety increases (Friedman, 2007, 1996; Kerr & Bowen, 1988). Bowen theory suggests that as long-term, multigenerational, chronic anxiety increases, levels of differentiation decrease. This, in turn, lowers resiliency, adaptability, and capacity to successfully learn to alter one's environment. Bowen theory proposes that the broadband, emotional "antibiotic" that best protects the "self" and promotes learning and personal development is increasing one's level of differentiation, (i.e. strengthening the personal intelligences [Friedman, 1987]).

Whether educators are guided by MI theory, emotional intelligence theory, Bowen theory, or other similar research-based theoretical systems, some of the most promising work in education reform utilizes an educational strategy that promotes developing the personal intelligences. In addition, effective learning strategies that promote the personal intelligences are largely based on an active pedagogy that bears all of hallmarks of experiential education as articulated by Joplin (1995). In fact, this was the theoretical underpinning for our course.

Curriculum-Based Applications

Community Mediation and Alternative Dispute Resolution

Education at Prescott College is experientially based. As such, students learn theory and practice through an active pedagogy designed to involve students directly in their own learning. Classes are small, usually between 10 and 14 students. Small class size allows for personalized learning, feedback, and training. The primary goal of the course *Community Mediation and Alternative Dispute Resolution* was to develop the skills necessary to effectively mediate disputes. To accomplish this goal, this 11-week course helped students develop their personal intelligences by combining theory and practice.

The focus of the course was on skill development, and experiential learning activities were integrated throughout. Through modeling, guided practice, and application, students developed skills in listening, reflecting, rapport-building, reframing, shifting from positions to interests, and agreement writing, among other exercises. This hands-on, skills observation and development component was supplemented by various readings and discussions around theories of conflict resolution and mediation, including a seminal journal article applying Bowen theory to mediation (Regina, 2000) and opportunities to apply principled negotiation in their own lives.

Several examples will highlight this approach. Initially, students and instructors shared why they were interested in the course. This structured activity was designed to begin the process of developing a sense of personal ownership in the course and its success. It provided the students with the opportunity to reflect on their personal interests and wants, as well as engage with others to formulate a common vision. In effect, the experiential exercise afforded the instructors and students with an initial assessment of each of the class participant's personal intelligences. Within the boundaries of the course description, the students and instructors co-created the learning goals that would be addressed during the course. The students were asked to brainstorm specific theories they wanted to cover and skills they hoped to attain. Topics were added and subtracted from the developing list until a consensus was reached. In its final form, the list included an understanding of conflict and conflict resolution, acquiring mediation skills, and improving interpersonal communication proficiency. Through the collaborative curriculum-building exercise, students began the process of developing personal and collective responsibility for the course. They helped formulate course topics and goals, and by so doing, they defined the course for themselves, self-managed their own emotional reactivity to the interests and wants of others, and worked cooperatively and collectively to take others' interests into consideration without losing the self in the process. This initial experiential activity was specifically designed to help students assess and develop their personal intelligences and set the stage for what was expected throughout the class.

Next, students were asked what attitudes and behaviors we expected from each other in order to successfully achieve our educational goals. This group norming exercise in developing clear and shared expectations as well as common agreements was critical to the success of the group as a learning community. Their responses included: say what you need, help others, have fun, actively participate, respect self and others, maintain confidentiality, take risks, arrive on time, be prepared for class, and so on. The students and instructors were then asked to commit to these common agreements and sign a group contract to hold each other accountable. The symbolic gesture of signing the agreement signified commitment. If a participant were to break an agreement later in the course, the class as a whole would be asked to respond to the transgression using the spirit of the contract as a rubric. This continued the process of creating a sense of group responsibility for the success of the course. In addition, this experiential exercise asked students to take personal and collective responsibility for their actions throughout the course, further promoting the personal intelligences.

In a second example designed to assess and interpret how students viewed conflict, students were paired together and given a bag of M&Ms. They were told the following: "You are going to play a fun game of arm wrestling. The winner of each arm wrestling contest can eat one M&M. Please play until all the M&Ms are eaten." During the activity, much laughter ensued as students began competing. After a brief period of time, many of the pairs discovered that if they cooperated they could share the M&Ms by taking turns winning. The activity was debriefed around the concepts of cooperation, competition, and conflict. Students were asked to reflect on how they managed the activity, the level of conflict and cooperation they created, and their degree of anxiety and comfort around competition. Through the debriefing process, the students discussed what they learned about themselves regarding the central topics. In other activities, which occurred throughout the term, students learned the specific skills of mediation. While the personal intelligences provided the theoretical "vehicle" for traveling down the road of skill development and improvement, students had to master a set of specific mediation skills along the way in order to successfully complete the course. These skills were introduced in sequence and included:

Stage 1 – Introductions: review, writing, and practicing introductions

Stage 2 – Uninterrupted Time: review and practice

Stage 3 – Developing Connections: review and practice

Stage 4 – Building Agreements: review and practice

Stage 5 – Concluding Comments: summing up, managing disputants who are not successful in formulating a common agreement

Developing specific skills for implementing each stage followed a consistent pattern. First, students read about the stage. Next, the instructors presented the micro-skills for each stage through either demonstration or through examples that were discussed and processed. Finally, students practiced each stage and specific skill through sample vignette mediations. As students developed the skills necessary for each stage, the subsequent stage was layered on, so that students learned the sequence of mediation as well as the skill set required for successfully implementing each skill and each stage. Students rotated through the roles of disputants and co-mediators so that each student experienced every role in the mediation process. Also throughout the training, the instructors observed each mediation group, provided critique and feedback to the participants, as well as inserted themselves into the mediation process as co-mediators as necessary to redirect a mediation that had lost its focus, to demonstrate a particular technique or skill, or to prompt the mediators into examining issues and interests that they may have missed.

In sum, at all times, the integration of experiential activities throughout the course fostered the development of the personal intelligences such that a feedback loop occurred through presenting the material, discussing the stages and skills for the lesson, implementing the activity through role plays, receiving individual practice, and debriefing with the entire class. As students progressed through the stages, new vignettes were introduced to keep the mediation role-plays fresh and to give students an opportunity to implement entire practice mediations.

Students "exposed" themselves to structured environments with highly ambiguous outcomes. That is, students needed the personal strength to develop and implement new skills in a public arena where they were critiqued by other students and by the instructors. The courage that students constantly displayed throughout the learning process was inspiring. They realized that the best way to learn was through an active, structured pedagogy. This provided opportunities to directly experience and thus learn the material; risk-take in environments and through activities that would naturally raise their anxiety levels; and debrief their learning in both private venues (such as portfolio reflections), as well as public arenas (such as small-group critiques and large-group discussions). This approach was consistent with the authors' experiences with other courses they had taught where strategies were employed to raise the personal intelligences of students.

Through growing the personal intelligences, students learned about themselves, developed increased capacities to work cooperatively with each other and, in doing so, acquired academic, theoretical knowledge along with specific skill sets useful for accomplishing the goals of the course and transferable to the world outside of the classroom.

The Personal Intelligences of Educational Leaders

Effectively developing the personal intelligences in educational settings must occur holistically throughout the learning community. Students cannot, nor should they be expected to, take risks in isolation. In particular, as educators, and thus leaders of the educational environment, we must be willing to subject ourselves to the same scrutiny and trials that we expect of our students. In his book, *Multiple Intelligences in the Classroom,* Thomas Armstrong (1994) reinforces this point when he writes,

> Before applying any model of learning in a classroom environment, we should first apply
> it to ourselves as educators and adult learners, for unless we have an experiential
> understanding of the theory and have personalized its content, we are unlikely to be
> committed to using it with students. (p. 16)

This practice is central for practitioners of experiential education. As educational leaders, our willingness to "walk our talk" is not simply a matter of fairness and balance. It is, rather, a function of setting an emotional atmosphere and tone in which learning is prized through a challenging environment that introduces uncertainty and ambiguity to engage us as learners and asks students to support our role as learners through offering constructive feedback and providing opportunities for us, as instructors, to publicly debrief our own experiential educational challenges so that we, as co-learners, can reflect on our experiences and share what we learned as well.

In fact, Friedman (2007) and Goldman (2006) suggest that leaders in any human system are the most significant individuals in influencing others and creating the emotional field in which learning and leading occur. If leaders in educational environments are capable of promoting a "positive resonance" or differentiated presence such that they are viewed as equal partners in learning, while maintaining their position of leaders in the system, then classroom and other educational environments can be more readily transformed into communities where learning is better promoted throughout the educational system (Boyatzis, 2002).

In other words, a leader with high levels of the personal intelligences who is committed to developing his differentiation capacity is a more emotionally mature leader. The more emotionally mature the leader, the greater the capacity for her to promote emotional intelligence in the educational endeavor. For many, this is the most important variable in successful learning and leading (Bowen, 2002; Friedman, 2007; Goldman, Boyatzis, & McKee, 2002; Regina, 2000). Who among us has not experienced this firsthand, where the self-responsible, nondefensive educator with a high capacity to engage others creates the necessary and sufficient conditions for learning, while the less emotionally mature leader fails regardless of the sophistication of the lesson plan?

As instructors, we wanted to set the emotional tone for risk-taking, learning from students and accepting their feedback, since they were to receive ours throughout the course. We did this through demonstrating two role-play mediations developed by students. For each mock mediation, two volunteers were selected to create the conflict scenario and role-play the parts of disputants. The instructors then demonstrated the stages of mediation through a "stop-and-go" process, whereby we debriefed each stage with the entire class before proceeding to the next stage. At the end of each role-play mediation, the entire activity was debriefed from both a personal and theoretical perspective.

These two classes were particularly important to developing a class culture that promoted the personal intelligences. They were examples of instructors actively participating in experiential education activities where they exposed themselves to the same scrutiny and risk-taking that they expected from students. As instructors, we entered the mock mediations with a substantial degree of uncertainty about the process and outcome. We conducted the mediations and solicited feedback, support, and critique from the students in the form of a public debrief. All the while, we were providing a forum for students to learn how to give and receive feedback, and promoting our own personal intelligences as we managed our performance anxiety, developed rapport with the participants, defined and clarified roles and guidelines for the mediation, and provided a template for conducting a community mediation.

As discussed earlier, the emotional tone of the learning environment is largely set by instructors through their willingness to be both co-learners in the educational process and honestly accept personal responsibility for managing their own personal intelligences. These class activities were specifically designed to help set the correct emotional tone for the course.

Conclusion

In sum, integrating development in the personal intelligences with academic and skill-based knowledge acquisition has yielded extraordinary results. This approach to education demonstrates all of the hallmarks of experiential education, through a theoretical system that promotes the intrapersonal intelligence and the interpersonal intelligence as foundational to ongoing success in learning inside and outside of the classroom setting. In an interview published in the book *The Project Zero Classroom* (Hetlan and Chalfen, 1999), Gardner reiterates this point when he says, "Personal intelligences are important because life consists significantly in understanding other people and in understanding yourself, and being able to use those understandings productively." An education that effectively focuses on developing and strengthening the personal intelligences is an education that elevates emotional maturity. More emotionally mature people can, in turn, more efficiently integrate and synthesize knowledge and information to become more productive citizens in the world. Experiential education, because of its emphasis on action and reflection, is a perfect crucible for developing the personal intelligences. The authors believe this is one of the primary reasons experiential education can be a life-changing methodology and philosophy.

The success of experiential education can be witnessed through the proliferation of theory and research articulating its effectiveness as well as its congruence with other theories of education and learning. In particular, this chapter provides a rationale for including MI theory, with specific emphasis on the personal intelligences, as a theory of experiential education. As educators provide multiple ways to instruct a variety of populations, experiential learning is ultimately effective when learners learn about themselves, others, the world in which they live, as well as specific content that is a part of a given curriculum.

References

Armstrong, T. (1994). *Multiple intelligences in the classroom*. Alexandria, VA: ASCD.

Boyatzis, (2002, April 24). Positive resonance: Educational leadership through emotional intelligence. *Education Week, 52*, 40–41.

Bowen, M. (2002). *Family therapy in clinical practice*. Northvale, NJ: Jason Aronson.

Bowen, M. (1971). Family therapy and family group therapy. In H. Kaplan & B. Sadock (Eds.), *Comprehensive Group Psychotherapy* (pp. 384–421). Baltimore, MD: Williams & Wilkins.

Caine, R. N. & Caine, G. (1997). *Education on the edge of possibility*. Alexandria, VA: ASCD.

Campbell, L., Campbell, B., & Dickinson, D. (1993). *Teaching and learning through multiple intelligences*. Tucson, AZ: Zephyr Press.

Checkley, K. (1997, September). The first seven ... and the eighth: A conversation with Howard Gardner. *Educational Leadership, 55*, 1: 8–13.

Friedman, E. (2007). *A failure of nerve: Leadership in the age of the quick fix*. New York: Seabury Books.

Friedman, E. (1996). *Reinventing leadership: Change in an age of anxiety*. New York: Guilford Press.

Friedman, E. (1991). Bowen theory and therapy. In A. Gurman & D. Kniskern (Eds.), *Handbook of Family Therapy, Vol. 2* (pp. 134–170). New York: Routledge.

Friedman, E. (1987, May–June). How to succeed in therapy without really trying. *Family Therapy Networker*, 27-–34.

Gardner, H. (1983). *Frames of mind*. New York: Basic Books.

Gardner, H. (1993). *Multiple intelligences: The theory in practice*. New York: Basic Books.

Gardner, H. (1995). Reflections on multiple intelligences. *Phi Delta Kappan, 77,* 200–208.

Goldman, D. (2006). *Social Intelligence: The new science of human relationships*. New York: Bantam Books.

Goldman, D. (1995). *Emotional intelligence: Why it can matter more than I.Q.* New York: Bantam Books.

Goldman, D., Boyatzis, R., & McKee, A. (2002). *Primal leadership: Realizing the power of emotional intelligence*. Boston, MA: Harvard Business Press.

Hetlan, L. and Chalfen, K. (1999). *The project zero classroom: New approaches to thinking and understanding*. Harvard, MA: Project Zero Harvard University.

Joplin, L. (1995). On defining experiential education. In K. Warren, M. Sakofs, & J. S. Hunt, Jr. (Eds.), *The Theory of Experiential Education* (pp. 15–22). Boulder, CO: Association for Experiential Education.

Kerr, M. E. and Bowen, M. (1988). *Family evaluation: An approach based on Bowen theory*. New York: Norton.

Larriveer, B. (2005). *Authentic classroom management: Creating a learning community and building reflective practice. Second edition.* Boston, MA: Allyn and Bacon.

Lazear, D. (1993). *Seven Pathways to learning: Teaching students and parents about multiple intelligences*. Tucson, AZ: Zephyr Press.

Marzano, R. (2003). *What works in schools: Translating research into action*. Alexandria, VA: ASCD.

Regina, W. (2000). Bowen systems theory and mediation. *Mediation Quarterly, 18*(2), 111–128.

Sylwester, R. (1995). *A celebration of neurons: An educator's guide to the human brain*. Alexandria, VA: ASCD.

The Design of Intellectual Experience

▾ ▾ ▾

Donald L. Finkel & Stephen Monk

Why Teach?

Beneath the conscious goal and motivations that drive a teacher's daily activities lies a basic human impulse: the desire to share intellectual experiences. Most teachers have felt for themselves the striking pleasure that results from the work of intelligence, whether experienced as insight, beauty, connectedness, or resolution. Ideally, they would like to lead their students to such pleasures; yet the accomplishment of this ideal is rare.

Few teachers adopt the explicit goal of sharing experience, and those who do must be struck by the difficulty of actively pursuing such an aim. This is not the sort of pedagogic goal about which one's colleagues talk. Moreover, what kind of methods could be formulated for achieving such a personal and insubstantial goal? Too easily, the dimension of experience is ignored altogether, leaving teachers with only the products of their disciplines to present. Yet it is the processes that lead to these products that yield the intellectual excitement they wish to share. For students to experience such excitement, the formal systems of knowledge must be undone, so that students can feel what it is like to put those systems together for themselves. Thus, *teachers must learn how to convert academic subject matter into activities for students.* Because it is just these intellectual activities that lead to understanding, the students' gains and the teachers' gratification stem from the same process.

This chapter originally was published in the *Journal of Experiential Education*, with the following citation:

Finkel, D. L., & Monk, S. (1979). The design of intellectual experience. *Journal of Experiential Education, 2*(2), 31–38.

This article will describe a framework for converting formal knowledge into structured activities for students. We shall examine an example and draw from it six principles for designing such activities. This discussion should make concrete the goal of sharing intellectual experience and indicate its benefits to both students and teachers. We must begin, however, by confronting the dilemma that faces any teacher who takes this goal seriously.

The Dilemma of Sharing

Suppose you return home from a trip to Nepal. You are brimming with the excitement of the experience and wish to share it with your friends. Your first inclination is to describe to them in detail all you can about the people, the landscape, and the customs, illustrating your adventures with as many slides as possible. Your first impulse is the *Impulse to Tell.* After several hours of slides and talk, you cannot avoid a conclusion: Since your friends have never experienced anything like Nepalese culture, they cannot possibly get from your description what you feel you are putting into it, or anything like what you got from the trip.

Perhaps it is impossible to tell about important experiences, to give them directly to others. Maybe you should wait until your friends' lives naturally take them to Nepal. Then, when they return, you will finally be able to share the experience. The Impulse to Tell has given way to the *Impulse to Let It Happen.* Following this impulse is not satisfying either, since you may have to wait forever, and you want to share your trip now. Compromises are possible, and you may urge your friends to travel. Yet even if amenable, they will probably experience Nepal quite differently. More likely, however, your urgings will awaken a long buried desire in them for travel up the Nile, and then you will be faced with the inevitable evening of Egyptian slides and monologues.

These two opposing impulses, The Impulse to Tell and the Impulse to Let It Happen, are inherent in the attempt to share experiences, and each has the unfortunate tendency to drive you to an extreme. If you sense you are telling unsuccessfully, you are likely to tell more and more, and to tell it in greater and greater detail. If you withdraw to let something happen, careful to avoid imposing your own experience on others, and nothing happens, then you will withdraw even further to leave a wider arena free for the others' experience. The dilemma of sharing is this: What do you do when you have discovered that neither telling nor refraining from telling is a successful mode of sharing?

Teachers also find themselves caught in this dilemma. In the classroom, the Impulse to Tell leads to lecturing or expository methods of presenting subject matter. The Impulse to Let It Happen is found in various, nondirective teaching modes that have arisen in reaction to exposition. We do not oppose these forms in themselves but rather the results that flow from them. Teachers who seek change by following one of these impulses find themselves either expounding in ever more exquisite detail or refining even further the role of non-leader. Since telling does not provide a genuine experience and letting things happen does not produce the particular experience you had in mind, neither of these impulses leads to the genuine satisfaction that comes from sharing an intellectual experience.

This claim immediately raises two questions. What are *intellectual* experiences and what does it mean to *share* them? Does going to a Beethoven concert with your friend constitute sharing an intellectual experience? What about watching a football game together? Returning to the previous example concerning the trip to Nepal, you cannot be sure that even bringing your friends with you to Nepal would have satisfied your desire to share the experience. To address these questions, we must distinguish between the external events or objects (the musicians, the musical sounds, the football game, the people of Nepal) and what we make of them (our perceptions, ideas, interpretations). These mental constructs are what we *use* to interact with the external events: without them we can have no experience. Thus, events in themselves are neither intellectual nor nonintellectual. These terms refer only to the nature of our interactions with events. Interactions may be characterized as more intellectual to the degree that they may engage and promote the development of more elaborate and comprehensive systems of ideas. Listening to Beethoven can be nonintellectual depending upon *how* one is listening, while watching a football game might be a most intellectual activity if it were part of a comparative analysis of games.

Sharing Intellectual Experiences

The solution to the dilemma lies in the intriguing possibility that a teacher can design an experience that has intellectual consequences for students, the very consequences the teacher wished to share in the first place. Our central thesis is that such pedagogic activity is possible and that teachers can best share intellectual experiences by designing them.

Now, what does it mean to share an intellectual experience? Suppose you are listening to a record of a Beethoven quartet with which you are not familiar, and you suddenly become aware of a structural similarity among all of Beethoven's late quartets. Full of excitement, you invite a friend over to hear your new record. You have had an intellectual experience and wish to share it. As you listen to the record together, are you sharing an intellectual experience? It is most unlikely that your friend will make the same discovery you made by just listening to the record. When the record ends, you look at your friend expectantly to see if "it happened," and then you recall that for a teacher to merely expose students to archetypal examples is precisely to yield to the Impulse to Let It Happen. It is tempting to think that something fruitful must result from such exposure. After all, how could one read Shakespeare and not be improved by the experience? However, teachers who simply trust in such invisible and delayed effects forgo a sense of direct contribution to their students' understanding. Implicit in the idea of sharing is that we teachers have something valuable to give, not Beethoven or Shakespeare, but ways of thinking about them, ways of understanding and ultimately of interacting with music and words. We would like to give our students the systems of ideas, the perspectives, the concepts that make possible these interactions with music and words. Yet, to adopt such an approach sounds as though we are back to Telling. If only we could collar our students, reach into their heads with a mental hand, and alter their patterns of thought! Once again, we face the dilemma of sharing.

To resolve this dilemma, we must focus on two crucial propositions about these patterns of thought we would like to alter. First, there is no way to interact intellectually with anything in the environment except through such mental patterns. Every student brings some form of conceptual system to new material: The student initially understands the material in the best way he or she can, interpreting it according to his or her present patterns of thought. This proposition is encouraging because it means the teacher is not attempting to get students to elaborate complex theories from nothing. It can also be discouraging, because it means that the teacher must work with students' systems no matter how primitive, fuzzy, or ill-conceived those systems may seem when compared to the system the teacher would like the students to develop. The second proposition is that the structure of the system of ideas that engages with an external event will never match perfectly with the structure of the event. One's own mental system will inevitably influence the way one "sees" the event. At the same time, interaction with the event can influence the system of ideas.

It is possible to influence someone else's patterns of thought by means less direct than a mental hand. *The teacher can design an environment, and activities for students within that environment, which will engage their current conceptual systems in such a way that these systems will be induced to develop.* These activities must aim to create a kind of mismatch between internal structure and external event that leads the student to refine, differentiate, and restructure the conceptual system. This approach to teaching is neither Telling nor Letting It Happen. In designing such experiences for students, the teacher must draw upon personal intellectual experiences, but the students will have their own experiences in working through the activities. No one can directly engineer an experience or guarantee the outcome for another person. However, designing focused activities within a concrete environment makes the chances of converging experiences likely, and such a convergence is as close as we can come to sharing.

We thus propose designing intellectual experiences for students as a means for sharing the pleasures of the mind with them. To design, in this sense, is to structure a specific environment for student interaction in order to promote the restructuring of the students' systems of ideas. We take the goal of conceptual restructuring to be of paramount importance because it is the students' systems of ideas that stay with them and shape their vision of the world. Moreover, it is the act of restructuring such systems that provides the pleasures of intellectual work we assume teachers wish to share with their students.

An Example

The most prominent feature of teacher-designed intellectual experiences, or "workshops" as we call them, is that students work on their own in groups ranging in size from two to seven. The teacher roves from group to group, observing, guiding, questioning, and "teaching," in response to the needs of specific groups or individuals. The students' work is directed by a set of written instructions and questions that we call a "worksheet." Thus, the teacher is present in the students' environment only through the written worksheet and occasional interactions.

The following worksheet is for a college-level workshop in developmental psychology, sociology, or the philosophy of education. The intellectual experience it attempts to share is the understanding that the way one thinks about child development is inextricably linked to one's conception of society. The authors hoped to induce their students to make this connection and to crystallize it by formulating alternative versions of the possible relations between society and the developing child.

There are four parts to the worksheet. As you read them, try to picture a classroom full of students engaged in these activities. Further, try to determine how each part of the worksheet requires a different style of work from the students. Finally, ask yourself these questions: Is the worksheet likely to engage the students' current patterns of thought about development and society? Is it likely to result in a restructuring of the students' ideas on this topic?

Eloise and the Philosophers

There are four parts to this workshop. Part I is to be performed in pairs. Parts II and III are to be done in groups of six, formed by combining three of the previous partnerships from Part I. Part IV will be completed with the class together as a whole.

Part I

Eloise is an ll-year-old girl who has decided to keep a diary during her sixth-grade year, which she has just begun. You will find attached the first entry in her new diary, written during the lunch hour of the first day of school. After reading the entry [which appears below, after Part IV], agree on and write down the answers to the following five questions.

List the five different activities in which Eloise participated during her morning.

For each activity, describe what you think were the teacher's underlying goals (or strategies) in having the children participate in such an activity.

Now consider that the school and its teachers are primarily agents of society, and that one of society's tasks is to employ the school to affect children's emotional and intellectual development in such a way that they are prepared to enter society and be useful members. Then each of Eloise's activities can be viewed as meeting society's goals well or badly, but on *two* levels: on the level of *content* (fractions, writing skill, ecology, etc.) and on the level of *form* (the way the activity is organized). Ignoring the content of Eloise's morning, describe how society is affecting her through the form of each of the activities. Why is each activity structured the way it is?

Note the basic similarities and differences among the five activities, based upon your responses to Question 3. Overall, do the forms of the different activities tend to be consistent with each other or inconsistent?

What are some different ways to view the possible relationship between the developing child and society? List at least three different relationships.

Part II

Form groups of six by combining three partnerships. Each group should choose a scribe to keep a written record of its results. The group will be given a set of 14 index cards, each with a quotation on it. [See below for example.] These quotes are from philosophers and educators, old and new.

Each quote implies a certain relationship between the developing child and society. Sort the quotes into a small number of categories (between three and five) that reflect the differing relationships. Try to agree on the groupings.

Formulate and agree upon descriptive labels for each of your categories.

You will probably have to go back and forth between questions 1 and 2, sorting some cards, deciding upon a tentative label, and re-sorting some of the original cards. If you cannot reach agreement, record minority opinions.

Part III

Remain in the same group of six.

1. Together with your original partner from Part 1, share your answers to Part 1, Question 5, with the group. Compare these answers to the categories your group devised in Part II. Did categorizing the quotes alter your original views significantly? If so, in what ways? Compare the effects of Part II on your views with its impact on other partnerships in your group, and have the scribe record general trends.

2. Using your current set of categories from Part II, your group should place each of the following systems into the appropriate category:

   (a) Summerhill (as seen in the film last week),

   (b) the school you are now attending,

   (c) the way your parents treated you (in general),

   (d) the way you intend to treat your children,

   (e) today's workshop.

Part IV

The class will reassemble as a whole. We will hear the results of each group's work from the scribes, and then discuss the entire exercise

Eloise's Diary

Dear Diary: It was great to get back to school and see my friends again, especially Susan. Before the bell rang, I told her all about our summer trip to Mexico, and about Manuel, and our trip to the beach together. This year I got Mrs. Morgan. She's okay, but I wanted Mr. Brown. Susan's so lucky she got him! After attendance, the first thing we had to do was write a paper about what we did over summer vacation. Why do teachers always give that dumb assignment? Well, I wrote about Mexico City, and the market place, about all the things you can buy there. Some people read their papers out loud, but I didn't. Then we had math. Mrs. Morgan explained about multiplying and dividing fractions. We had all that stuff last year, but no one seems to remember it. Even Mrs. Morgan made a mistake at one point! Of course, everybody loved that. We learned a little poem, so we know when to flip the fraction upside down, and when not to. (I forgot the poem already! I never was good in math!!) Then we saw a movie about a lake in Africa—like the ones on TV. Mrs. Morgan said for science we are going to learn a new thing called *ecology.* The first thing we had to do was list all the animals we saw using the lake and tell how they used it. Then Mrs. Morgan asked us what would happen to all the plants and animals if the hippos got killed and could never bathe in the lake. Richard said there would be a lot of dead hippos around and the whole class laughed. Richard's so dumb! But Mrs. Morgan wouldn't tell us the answer, even after we tried. Then we had gym. I love gym, but Mr. Brown's class creamed us in volleyball. If only I could get those creeps in our class to set up the ball, I'm sure we could win. When we got back, there was a policeman waiting in our room. Everyone was excited for a minute, but it turned out to be a lecture on drugs. He showed us all these pills and needles and stuff and said it was all bad. *Borrring!* Now it's lunch time. Oh, here comes Susan—see you tonight, Diary.

Sample Quotes

We include the following three quotations to give the reader of this article a flavor of the quotations used. We have chosen three rather extreme cases, but the full group of 14 index cards presents a formidable task of differentiation and categorization.

"Give your scholar no verbal lessons: he should be taught by experience alone; never punish him, for he does not know what it is to do wrong; ... May I venture at this point to state the greatest, the most important, the most useful rule of education? It is: Do not save time, but lose it."

"Having thus very early set up your Authority, and by the gentler Applications of it, shamed him out of what leads towards any immoral Habit ... (for I would by no means have chiding used, much; less Blows, till Obstinacy and Incorrigibleness make it absolutely necessary)...."

"What is the least that we can say about an organism's development? Everybody admits that two things must be said: First, it develops by getting habits formed; and second, it develops by getting new adaptations which involve the breaking up or modification of habits."

To appreciate the experiential flavor of the workshop, you should now switch gears and actually *do* the problems that make up Part 1. Readers usually tend to resist becoming more active in this way, but you will sense the power of this approach only if you overcome this resistance.

Principles of Design

The most striking quality of this worksheet on first reading is its variety. The students work in pairs, groups, and as a whole class. They read the imaginary diary of a sixth-grader and later classify quotes from philosophers. In addition to reading and sorting cards, they must express themselves to classmates, argue for their views, and reflect upon their own experiences. In order to reveal the orderly design within this apparent kaleidoscope of educational activities, we must break down the overriding goal of workshops into a set of interlocking principles. Recall that the teacher's goal is to convert an intellectual product into a sequence of activities for students. The six principles that follow will suggest how such a conversion may be facilitated and will illustrate why the authors of the worksheet designed it as they did.

A worksheet must always set forth an environment, and activities for students in that environment, which engage their current conceptual systems in such a way that these systems will be induced to develop. We will first examine the nature of that *environment,* then describe the structure of the *activities,* and finally discuss the resulting role of the *teacher.* Our six principles emerge from the discussion of these three elements of workshops. They are italicized in the text and summarized in a list at the end of this section.

Environment

The student's environment in a workshop has two chief components: an external shared event and the other students in the group. The external event can take many forms; in the above example it was Eloise's diary and then the quotes on index cards. Whatever the form, *the event must be specific, concrete, and present.* These features are required to engage effectively the students' conceptual systems. Any material (texts, data, graphs, journals) with which the students are going to work must be ready at hand in manageable quantities. The material must be sufficiently challenging to engage the students at diverse levels of sophistication, but not so complicated as to overwhelm them.

The group of students working together on a worksheet provides a second aspect of the environment. Students can help one another in a number of ways: They can provide mutual support and a sense of common purpose; their exchanges can promote the externalization and articulation of ideas; finally, the diversity of points of view provides a continuing source of puzzlement and constructive friction. This last feature of group work propels the card-sorting task in *Eloise,* while externalization and clarification of ideas lies behind the use of partnerships in Part I, the analysis of the diary. The teacher designing a workshop must think through these issues in advance in order *to exploit consciously the collective potential of the group.* Such devices as requiring agreement, fostering debate, inviting exchange of work, and assigning specialized roles use the group productively. With whatever techniques you use, your instructions must implicitly communicate your trust in your students' capacity as a group and your genuine expectation that together they have the resources to complete the task.

However, simply to place your students on their own in groups to explore a stimulating event is insufficient. Beyond the group and the event, a third aspect of the environment is required. *Specific questions and instructions must be written in advance and given to each student.* These questions and instructions constitute the worksheet itself. Sometimes the activities required will not be clear unless they are written. Even when the instructions could be communicated orally or on the board, it is important to distribute them to each student. With the worksheet at hand, the students can interact directly with the event and each other without the need for the teacher's constant personal mediation. These written questions and instructions embody the teacher's wisdom on the subject, yet in this form, they permit the students to take the initiative.

Activities

A great deal of activity can be generated by placing students in an environment that contains concrete events, other students, and specific written questions about these events. However, student activity in itself is not our goal. We wish to induce intellectual change in order to allow the sharing of intellectual experience. To effect intellectual change, activity must have a particular structure. This structure may be summarized by saying that *every worksheet requires the students to solve a problem.*

The best way to alter someone else's thought is to provide a problem that cannot be solved with his or her present conceptions. This requires a three-phase process. First, the student must be made to see the problem as a genuine problem that is disturbing and requires resolution. Such a problem must be formulated from the student's own view of the phenomenon. Thus, the first phase requires *activities that elicit the student's current mental structures.* People always have common-sense concepts, intuitions, or general rules of thumb for exploring anything new. These are what must be elicited by the first phase of the worksheet, because it is only from these mental constructs that intellectual change can proceed. The problem itself only comes into consciousness as a result of *questions that force upon the student the inadequacy of his or her present conceptions.* This is the worksheet's second phase. It must throw the student into a state of intellectual disequilibrium. Conflict between the students' differing conceptions or between obdurate phenomena and unsophisticated theories must make the student feel the problem in all of its perplexing force, and lead him or her to want to solve it.

It is not enough to perplex students and leave them hanging. Relevant information, guides, questions, and examples must be provided so that the students have a reasonable chance of making new distinctions and tying ideas together in a different way. *Activities that lead to intellectual restructuring* mark the third phase, which should result in the creation of a new mental equilibrium. The teacher must strike a balance between withholding too much information, on the one hand, and giving out a prepackaged solution, on the other. Repeated experience in workshops watching students restructure their ideas will guide most teachers to this balance.

In *Eloise,* the single problem that organizes the activities is this. How can we describe the system of mutual implications between views of child rearing and conceptions of social organization? As a question, this is very abstract and is unlikely to lead to a productive discussion. With this problem serving as a focus, the teacher must ask: What activities or tasks would be most likely to lead students to understand these implications? In this case, the authors decided to use a categorizing task. By articulating different ways in which a view of child development contains a conception of society (or vice versa), students will be forced to make distinctions and ask questions that are new to them. The workshop now has a central activity, one that will constitute the second phase (disequilibrium) of the three-phase structure. Sorting quotes almost inevitably reveals the inadequacy of students' intuitive views about children and society, and may well produce intellectual conflict as the students argue over which cards belong in which piles and why. Indeed, the card sorting is the center of this workshop and will perplex students and challenge their current thinking.

However, to present the student with 14 wordy quotes with no preparation might well throw them too far off balance. First, they need to have their own ideas about children and society elicited in a more familiar and concrete context. The questions about Eloise's diary fulfill this function. By the end of Part I, the students' own ideas would have been articulated, clarified, and written, so they can face the test of the card sorting.

If the workshop were to end after Part II, the students would have only their own shaky products, the set of categories, which might well seem ad hoc and of little significance. The students now need to use the categories, applying them to phenomena to see if they shed new light. In addition, they need to bring their ideas into the public arena of the class to present them to their peers and teacher. Parts III and IV of *Eloise* address these needs: They supply the resolution and closure to the experience. Certainly a total restructuring of ideas will not occur as a result of *Eloise,* but a first step will be made in the process. After the groups have compared their categories in Part IV, they will try to resolve their differences through synthesis in the ensuing discussion. Their original ideas (e.g., about free children and harsh societies) will have been shaken, and they will be on their way toward a more refined and complex system of ideas.

In all this, it is important to remember that, intellectual or otherwise, *a genuine experience has a style and texture* as well as an organization. Matters of rhythm and timing must not be neglected. Moreover, it is essential that the worksheet not speak to the students in a voice that is didactic or pedantic; it should speak in the author's natural voice. The finished worksheet should bear the teacher's personal stamp, reflecting a sense of play and purpose. *Eloise* requires students to shift activities repeatedly. It does not try to exhaust the meaning contained in any one source: it progresses, allowing for student work in new modes and in new combinations. The authors attempt to write in the style of a sixth-grade girl and provide physical props, the cards with quotes, so that some of the action can be physical. The important point to remember when you are composing a worksheet is that students will actually be doing the things you ask of them, and you must try to envision what it would be like to experience the activities you are designing.

Teacher

In writing a worksheet, you have provided a blueprint for an experience. By working backwards from the products of your discipline to activities for students, you have drawn on some of your most creative and pedagogic impulses. Yet your presence at the workshop itself will still be necessary, both to facilitate the students' interaction with the worksheet and to give you the necessary information upon which to base future worksheets. However, your role will be quite different from that of the conventional teacher. Most teachers are held captive by the need to continually direct and organize the activities of the class. The students' attention is almost always focused on the teacher. S/he is bound in place by the students' conviction that the teacher is the vital link between themselves and the subject matter. This traditional role puts the teacher at the hub of the wheel, the common source of support and cohesion. In contrast, the teacher's role in the workshop may be summarized by the phrase: *The teacher is there, but out of the middle.*

In a workshop, it is the worksheet, and not you, that provides the "carrying energy" for the students' work. They are in direct contact with the material and one another, so that you remain outside of their immediate experience. This is just what you need in order to be free to move around and respond to groups of students in a flexible fashion, tailoring your contribution to the needs of the moment. No matter how exquisitely you have designed your worksheet, some students will become stranded in irrelevant details, while others will skim over all that is interesting. Still other students will approach the problem from a point of view you never imagined. All of these students, and many others as well, will benefit from direct interaction with you. As you engage them, getting them started again, deepening their approach or leading them to a new angle of attack, you will feel the most immediate gratification of the sharing of intellectual experiences.

To summarize, the six principles of design are the following:

Environment:
1. The shared event must be specific, concrete, and present.
2. Specific questions and instructions must be written in advance and given to each student.
3. The teacher should exploit the potential of the group.

Activities
4. The worksheet must have within it an underlying problem to be solved.
   To make the problem genuine and solvable requires activities that:
   (a) elicit current mental structures;
   (b) point to the inadequacy of present structures;
   (c) lead to intellectual restructuring.
5. The workshop must have the texture of a genuine experience.

Teacher:
6. The teacher is there, but out of the middle.

Diverse Applications

We cannot convey in this brief article the variety of forms that workshops and worksheets may take. The interested reader should refer to our more complete treatment of the subject[1] where numerous examples are given, as well as more detailed guidelines for designing workshops. To suggest this variety, we present here several examples of workshops written by

---

[1] Finkel, D. L and Monk, G. S. (1978) *Contexts for learning: A teacher's guide to the intellectual experience.* Olympia, WA: The Evergreen State College.

us and our colleagues. Many of these have been composed in collaboration, because we have found that the most effective method of converting intellectual products into activities is for an expert in the subject to join forces with an intellectually inquisitive but naive partner.

1. *Hot Tips:* An exercise that starts with graphs of the prices of four stocks and moves toward an understanding of rate of change at a point—used in a calculus course for social science majors.

2. *The Ideal Gas Law:* A reconstruction of the Ideal Gas Law in chemistry, which starts with questions about balloons and pistons, and progressively builds toward an understanding of the regularities stated mathematically in the law—used in an introductory chemistry course.

3. *Examination of Assumptions:* An exercise in philosophical analysis, based on the extraction of assumptions in a fellow student's written argument, and using several written exchanges between the two partners—used in an introductory philosophy course.

4. *How Children Form Mathematical Concepts:* A set of questions used to help students digest a *Scientific American* article read prior to the workshop and brought with them to class—used in an advanced developmental psychology course

5. *The Problem of Identity in A View From the Bridge."* An exercise in applying to the characters in a play a psychological concept previously studied, based on the students re-creation of each character's point of view in a closing monologue—used in an interdisciplinary social science and humanities course.

Workshops can fulfill quite a variety of functions within a course. The following is a partial list:[2]

1. Have students parallel the work of an author before reading about that work.

2. Help students gather and organize a wealth of detailed and confusing information.

3. Articulate an intellectual structure by providing a shift of context.

4. Give practice translating between languages within a discipline to show power of a new language.

5. Help students crystallize their knowledge in preparation for a test.

6. Let students experience physically something they have studied or will study more abstractly.

---

[2] See Finkel & Monk, *Contexts for learning,* pp. 38–43, for amplification.

Conclusion

We began by addressing a question all teachers must eventually face: Why teach? We have ended with a proposal for improving instruction, a response to the question: How can I improve the learning that takes place in my class? We believe that these two questions are inextricably linked. Many teachers are quick to make superficial changes in their courses, employing new curricular packages, new kinds of tests, and new texts, in the hope of improving their students' education. We are proposing an alteration in the very structure of the teacher's experience with students. To suggest such a step would be futile without addressing a teacher's most basic needs and hopes. We focused on the goal of sharing intellectual experiences because we have found in our own collaboration with numerous teachers that it is precisely this consequence of designing and running workshops that is so gratifying and sustaining. Calling for such broad and unspecified goals as "significant educational change" or "faculty development" strikes us as unproductive because such sweeping appeals do not address teachers' immediate desires. Teachers don't want to "develop": They want to have intellectual exchanges with their students in a way that lets them see their students' progressive understanding. We have proposed one way of creating such exchanges, one that we believe is a significant educational innovation, and one that does result in development—for students and for teachers, too.

We have listed elsewhere[3] the detailed benefits to students and teachers of this workshop approach. Here we can only summarize by saying that virtually all students with whom we have worked have thrived in workshops. Because their teachers have removed themselves from "the middle," they have been able to apply their own intellectual powers to concrete problems, thus gaining an awareness of and a confidence in their own intelligence. Moreover, because their teacher's expertise has not been withheld, the students have felt neither abandoned nor manipulated. Able to interact with an environment constructed by their teacher and to work together in a collaborative atmosphere with their peers, they have made conceptual advances that have altered their mental landscape.

One of the dramatic consequences for teachers who write worksheets first and run workshops based on them is their strikingly sharper view of the effects of their pedagogical thinking on students. Having completed the intellectual work before the workshop, teachers can then see more clearly the quality of their students' thinking. Such a vantage leads to a ready understanding of how better to design the next workshop. Moreover, in having to work backwards from the intellectual products of their discipline to the activities that lead to them, teachers find they have to rethink many fundamental questions in their field. Their own intellectual excitement in this process parallels the students' enthusiasm in accomplishing the workshops. And within this interactive cycle occurs the genuine sharing of intellectual experience.

---

[3] Finkel & Monk, *Contexts for learning,* pp. 99–108.

The Paper Mirror: Understanding Reflective Journaling

▾ ▾ ▾

Delaura L. Hubbs & Charles F. Brand

Counselor education students learn to interact with clients while monitoring their own cognitive and emotional processes; relate to clients in a nonjudgmental, open, and caring manner; and maintain appropriate boundaries. In addition, these graduate students are expected to learn and grow while producing results appropriate to specific academic, professional, and ethical standards. Counseling programs endeavor to develop in students the concrete and measurable knowledge of psychopathology and mastery of skills necessary to apply diagnostic criteria to clients. However, development of a knowledge base, as well as professional skills, includes tacit processes internal to the student that are often difficult for an instructor to discern and measure. To address this dilemma, instructors may require students to write reflective journals that chronicle the students' internal processes about a course, an experience, a personal value, or a belief. The reflective journal holds potential for serving as a mirror to reflect the student's heart and mind. The journal assignment can be a structured and purposeful tool allowing access to the students' internal "making of meaning." This article explores several psychological and educational theories that explain why and how reflective journals work, common types of reflective journals, and a method for critiquing students' journal entries.

This chapter originally was published in the *Journal of Experiential Education*, with the following citation:

Hubbs, D. L. & Brand, C. F. (2005). The paper mirror: Understanding reflective journaling. *Journal of Experiential Education, 28*(1), 60–71.

Theories Behind the Paper Mirror

The rationale for using reflective journaling in higher education is grounded in general learning theory, adult learning theory, experiential learning theory, and in the importance of the counseling student's personal growth and professional development. Education theorist John Dewey (1938) espoused an educative experience that fosters meaningful (i.e., purposive) learning. He viewed an effective learning condition as one that actively engages the student with the content in an intensely personal way and advocated experiential learning as a resourceful means of achieving that end. Under effective learning conditions, according to Dewey, learners are inherently motivated. Subsequent research, such as Tough's (1968) landmark nationwide study of adult learners, supported Dewey's contention, as Tough highlighted the significance of the mature learner engaging in independent, self-selected, and self-directed learning projects.

Drawing from Dewey's notion of active learning, Kolb (1984) promoted experiential learning, highlighting the reflective process as a necessary part of engaging the learner. Kolb posited a four-stage model of experiential learning: (a) concrete experience, (b) reflective observation, (c) abstract conceptualization, and (d) active experimentation or application. Reflective journaling, selectively guided by the instructor, can help the student progress through Kolb's four stages. In stages one and two, respectively, the student's journal entry may begin with a description of, and subsequent reflection on, a specific experience. In stage three, the student may explore explanations or questions regarding the meaning of the experience. Finally, in stage four, the student concludes the entry by applying new meanings, interpretations, or understandings of the event. Reflective journals used in this way create effective learning conditions that can result in the types of meaningful or purposive learning that was first put forth by Dewey, and has come to be further refined by adult education theorist Kolb and psychotherapist Carl Rogers (1982).

Believing that learners are the experts in their own learning and developmental processes, psychotherapist Carl Rogers (1982) voiced ideas that support the use of journals as a tool for learning, personal growth, and professional development. Rogers presented his emerging ideas about the importance of learning that results from self-discovery saying, "The only learning which significantly influences behavior is self-discovered, self-appropriated learning" (p. 223). If educators accept the importance of self-discovered, self-appropriated learning, then creating conditions for students' self-discovery becomes central to developing competent practitioners. Journaling, as a learning strategy, provides opportunities for students to mull over ideas, uncover inner secrets, and piece together life's unconnected threads, thus creating a fertile ground for the significant learning to which Rogers referred.

Psychologist and learning theorist Len Semtonovitch Vygotsky (1986), may have explained how reflective journaling helps students develop an understanding of connections between themselves and the world around them. According to Vygotsky:

> Thought is not begotten by thought; it is engendered by emotion, i.e., by our desires and
>
> needs, our interests and emotions. Behind every thought there is an affective-volitional
>
> tendency, which holds the answer to the last "why" in the analysis of thinking. (p. 252)

The reflective journal provides a vehicle for inner dialogue that connects thoughts, feelings, and actions. Journaling may provide a medium for the student to access the affective-volitional tendency to which Vygotsky referred, and so prompts thought and action.

Whereas Vygotsky (1986) focused upon the interplay of thoughts, feelings, and actions, Knowles (1983), in explaining his theory of *androgogy,* highlighted the importance personal experience plays in the process of adult learning. According to Knowles, "Because of our experience we have often developed habitual ways of thinking and acting; preconceptions about reality, prejudices, and defensiveness about our past" (p. 4). Knowles continued, "To overcome this problem, adult educators are devising strategies for helping people become more open-minded" (p. 4). Boud (2001), Goldsmith (1996), and Moon (1999) believed that reflective journaling is an especially successful strategy for helping move the adult learner toward higher levels of critical (i.e., analytical) thinking and personal insight.

Similarly, Mezirow's (1998) *transformative learning* theory explained how one's deeply held values and chosen perspectives form mental frameworks that govern an individual's interpretations of the world and her or his place in it. Mezirow labeled automatic thinking as "habits of mind" or, in other words, conclusions and judgments to which people tend to jump without thought or question. Mezirow (2000) stated:

> Transformative learning refers to the process by which we transform our taken-for-
>
> granted frames of reference (meaning, perspectives, habits of mind, mind sets), to make
>
> them more inclusive, discriminating, open, emotionally capable of change and reflec-
>
> tive so that they may generate beliefs and opinions that will prove more true or justified
>
> to guide action. (pp. 7–8)

Because transformative learning is thoughtful learning adopted deliberately by the learner, reflective journals can be significant adjuncts in the transformative learning process. Transformative learning requires the student to question the foundations and prior learning that went into the formation of a given belief. In other words, transformative learning prompts the learner to consider whether a given belief came about as a result of concepts tacitly accepted, or as the result of a deliberate thought process. Mesirow (2000) adopted the term *assimilative learning* to describe the process of absorbing knowledge tacitly from the environment. Thus, assimilative learning is our unchallenged and untested acceptance of a belief as true, factual, or real. Transformative learning, then, involves examining an "assimilative" learned belief. The iterative process of examining the belief, testing it, and exploring alternatives to the belief results in transformative learning when the learner is ultimately changed, or "transformed" through the process. Thus, the learner's prior patterns of thinking would ultimately grow and change, or "transform."

Reflective journaling can provide ways to illuminate automatic thinking and habits of mind, and can lead students through a transformative process, especially when the instructor engages the student in mutual dialogue. Journaling provides students practice in the art of reflection that is important in learning new material and essential for transformative learning. Journaling also provides an opportunity for students to move past an intuitive adoption of patterns of thinking, or unquestioned beliefs, and encourages students to progress from *assimilative learning* to *transformative learning*. Reflective journals provide a structured way for the instructor and student to examine the student's thinking patterns or belief systems, and this examination process encourages relevant assimilative learning and supports transformative learning.

The Ethics of Assigning Reflective Journaling

The ethical implications of journaling in higher education programs should not be ignored, especially when personal disclosures could be used to assess suitability of the student to continue in the program. Counselor educators are governed by strict ethical codes designed to provide guidance to clinical practitioners (American Counseling Association, 2005; Gladding, 2004). Educators from other disciplines may follow ethical codes that govern their profession and may provide guidance applicable to the use of reflective journals. However, several general guidelines may be applied to the use of reflective journals as a learning and professional development tool in most educational programs.

Guidelines on the Instructional Use of Reflective Journals

Kerka (1996) suggested three conditions necessary for reflection in the use of reflective journals including: (a) perceived trustworthiness of the journal reader, (b) clarity of the expectation, and (c) quantity and quality of the feedback. Each condition guides the instructor when assigning reflective journals in the classroom. Students may be initially fearful of possible judgments or reprisals from the instructor as a result of what is written in their journals (Elbow & Clarke, 1987). To combat this, the instructor may need to dialogue with students about the purpose of the journal and the importance of self-knowledge in learning. Clarification of the purpose of the journal as a professional development tool in which the students and instructor share ideas about the students' experiences may mitigate some students' anxiety. We have also found it helpful to clarify in the syllabus the specifics of the journal assignment and to include a statement specifying how information contained in reflective journals will be treated. It is important for students to know if the information contained in their journals is written for a private audience, such as a private dialogue between the student and instructor, or if the journal assignment will be shared with another audience. It is important, after all, for the journal writer to be confident of the trustworthiness of the reader.

Reflective journal assignments may become a key factor in the student's development of reflective skills and are often not limited to classroom content. Journal writing as classroom assignments treads the fine line between personal issues and professional development. Although it is easier for instructors to deal only with classroom content, many educational and training programs require a level of competence from students that transcends content and touches on the "person" of the student (English, 2001). Rather than passing judgment on values and beliefs shared by students in their reflective journals, the instructor is tasked with maintaining an objective focus on the reflective process and unfailingly adhering to the guidelines specified in the journal assignment.

Instructors using reflective journals can clarify their expectations by initially providing students with guidance, explaining that the purposes of journaling are self-reflection and professional development. The instructor may then provide feedback that is focused upon the student's reflections *about the issue,* rather than the issue itself. The instructor encourages students to focus on what the journal reflections say about their reactions, their perceptions, and themselves.

Finally, just as students are expected to devote time, effort, and thought to writing journal reflections, instructors should find ways to demonstrate that students' efforts are monitored by the instructor throughout the semester. In our experience, students appreciate both written and verbal feedback about their journal entries. As students reflect upon issues, course content, and learning experiences, instructors can observe student responses and give feedback that reinforces reflections compatible with the goals of the journaling assignment. Conversely, reflective journals give instructors an opportunity to guide less-than-optimal comments into forms that are appropriate for developing professional skills.

Effective Journals for the Classroom

Reflective journaling can provide instructors with glimpses of the inner workings of the students' mind. Journal entries allow the instructor to view, through the student's words, the quality of comprehension and mastery of the material, as well as affective responses to the content. The reflective journal can be a vehicle for the student to define, question, and interact with content, concepts, ideas, values, beliefs, and feelings. In addition, reflective journaling invites students to articulate their understandings of course content and clinical experiences. In this way, reflective journaling can serve to link the students' understandings and feelings.

A review of the literature suggests that reflective journaling methods have not been qualitatively or quantitatively studied to any great extent. The literature does not disclose systematic attempts to assess the efficacy of any single journaling technique over another. However, anecdotal evidence suggests that the use of reflective journals can hone students' reflective skills, assist students in applying course content, help students process experiential learning activities, and encourage personal growth and professional development.

Reflective journals can take several forms. This article will focus on three described by Goldsmith (1996): (a) the dialogue journal, (b) the class interactive (team) journal, and (c) the personal journal.

The Dialogue Journal

The dialogue journal provides a means for the student and instructor to maintain a private dialogue with one another around any number of issues. The instructor comments in writing on a student's initial dialogue journal entry. In turn, the student may respond to the instructor's comments or proceed to the next journal assignment. This iterative process is repeated, creating a dialogue between the student and instructor.

The instructor should recognize that the student may experience the desire to please the instructor, to say the right things, or to seek approval and validations of his or her feelings, thoughts, and values. The desire to please may impact the journaling process. Consequently, instructors using journals may want to view students' dialogues in light of this effect. This interplay between journal writer and instructor models the interactive nature of counseling, and through this parallel process should come permission to air issues, thoughts, values, and beliefs without concern for judgment. The journaling process allows for examining and analyzing beliefs in a manner that encourages openness to alternative interpretations. This interactive procedure provides the student an opportunity to challenge his or her habits of mind, which is the critical thinking process described by Mezirow (1998) and Brookfield (1998).

The Class Interactive (Team) Journal

Whereas the dialogue journal facilitates a conversation between student and teacher, the class interactive journal provides a forum for students to interact among themselves. In a class interactive journal, the student shares his or her written reflections with classmates, receives feedback, and subsequently constructs a written reflection considering classmates' input. A variation of the class interactive journal is the *team* journal identified by Goldsmith (1996). This serves as a method for communicating, and sharing ideas and events between, and among, small groups of students. Because the team journal requires entries from each group member, it must be accessible by all members and, thus, serves as an ongoing record of team progress and learning. This type of journal is especially useful when group dynamics are important learning goals.

In addition, team journals are suited for use with electronic message boards, such as Blackboard, where messages can be posted and team members can respond.

Another feature of the dialogue journal and the class interactive journal is based on the fact that they are both iterative in nature, in that they evolve as a result of interactions between the student and others. The interactive nature of these types of journals is an inherently social process that provides the writer an opportunity for testing beliefs and assumptions—a sounding board, if you will, that allows students to examine values, concepts, and issues beyond their personal filters.

The Personal Journal

The personal journal is generally a narrative description of the student's inner processes. Personal journals (i.e., personal diaries) conjure the image of the little pink book with a flimsy lock kept by adolescent girls for recording secrets and dreams to be read by none other than the author. The solitary nature of a personal journal does not contain the sounding board effect inherent in dialogue and class interactive journals, and the writer of the personal journal may well process and reprocess the same concepts repeatedly with little challenge to his or her accepted beliefs or ideas. This intrapersonal looping of ideas may be self-affirming but not necessarily productive, as Brookfield (1998) posited:

> A self-confirming cycle often develops whereby our uncritical accepted assumptions
> shape actions that then only serve to confirm the truth of those assumptions. We find it
> very difficult to stand outside ourselves and see how some of our most deeply held val-
> ues and beliefs lead us into distorted and constrained ways of being. (p. 197)

The private nature of a personal journal, although possibly valuable as a tool for reflection, may mire the writer in those endless loops of self-modulated introspection against which Brookfield (1998) cautioned. Though practiced journal writers extol the virtues of this form of reflection, the personal journal may have limited application for classroom use or professional development. In our experience, because the personal journal does not allow feedback from others, the critical self-assessment that is a necessary skill for many professionals is unlikely to be developed through keeping this type of journal. Consequently, *class interactive* journals and *dialogue* journals hold more potential than *personal* journals for students' personal growth and professional development.

Critiquing Reflective Journal Entries

For purposes of collaborative review, the instructor and student seek together to discern the nature and quality of reflection represented in a student's journal entry, to determine whether students have moved past a simple understanding of course content and have progressed toward integrating the content into professional practice. In order for the instructor and student to critique a journal entry collaboratively, they must share a common understanding of how content relates to process, and how the student can move from superficial reflection to critical, or analytical reflection. The use of the 2 x 2 matrix (see Figure 1) provides the needed structure for the instructor and student to create a common understanding, or language, for examining journal entries.

With a given journal entry, both the instructor and student first determine whether the entry is a content or process statement. For the purposes of this method of critique, a *content* statement focuses "outside" the student, whereas a *process* statement discloses the student's level of introspection. For example, "Rogers' Person Centered Therapy lets the client take the lead," is based upon a fact or event, focused outside of the student, and, as such, would be a content statement. A process statement that incorporates the student's thoughts, feelings, or attitudes might sound like, "I felt awkward using person-centered techniques." Analyzing journal entries in this manner can assist the instructor and student in creating a mutual understanding of what comprise content statements and process statements. In addition, the matrix

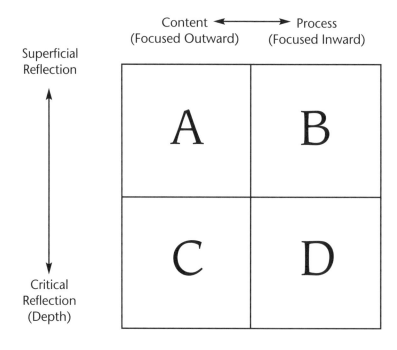

Figure 1. The diagram illustrates two continua merged into a 2 x 2 quadrant with context of the journal entry forming one axis and level of reflection forming the other.

helps the instructor identify misunderstandings or misinterpretations of course content, and provides a means for instructors and students to review journal entries collaboratively.

Using the 2 x 2 matrix (see Figure 1), the instructor and student can plot a journal entry on the content-process continuum. Following the content-process decision, the student and instructor judge where on a continuum, from *superficial* to *complex,* the journal entry appears. For example, a student's superficial entry would focus on content with no emotional value, but an entry that integrates theory with personal and introspective insights would suggest movement toward understandings of greater complexity. An entry falling into Quadrant A represents the student's superficial reflection of the content, and a Quadrant D entry demonstrates the student's ability to reflect upon the topic with a level of consideration that transcends superficial.

With practice, students' journal entries should indicate movement toward a level of introspection that integrates theory, concepts, and practice into the student's personal and professional development. The goal is for the student's writing to demonstrate progress toward reflective and inwardly focused entries. For instance, "Because I was quite directive and failed at staying person-centered when working with my client, I'm afraid I'll never be a good counselor," would be an example of a complex, inwardly focused entry. This statement demonstrates the student's understanding of a counseling theory. It also acknowledges recognition of his behavior and describes his emotional state. A journal entry combining these components in this way transcends superficial reflection and is, thus, categorized as a Quadrant D statement.

In our experience, students often begin their early journal entries with Quadrant A statements but, with practice and encouragement, move incrementally to deeper, more profound critical reflections that naturally fall into Quadrant D. It should be noted that students do not necessarily move through the four quadrants sequentially, but rather move from quadrant to quadrant influenced by level of maturity, development of reflective skills, and comfort with the topic. Consistent use of Quadrant D statements suggests that the student is demonstrating skills necessary for insightful or critical reflection, the same traits counselor educators strive to instill in their students. Just as counselor educators strive to instill a set of skills and ways of thinking in their students, instructors of other disciplines have embedded ways of thinking, skills, and methods appropriate to that discipline. Instructors in any field can use reflective journals to dialogue with students, and in so doing, model the language and methods appropriate for that discipline

Conclusion

The strength of reflective journaling lies in the collaborative opportunities for the instructor and student to employ common criteria to critique the student's reflective skills through journal entries. Consequently, because the instructor is not the sole reviewer, the student learns necessary skills of self-reflection and self-assessment. As Baldwin (1991) stated, "Writing bridges the inner and outer world and connects the paths of action and reflection" (p. 9). Thus, students who master the skills of reflective journaling gain an ability to connect their internal processes with their external realities. The connecting of inner and outer world experiences is a process that demands self-awareness and self-knowledge necessary for the practice of counseling, as well as other professions.

As a glass mirror reflects a visual image, the paper mirror reflects students' inner worlds and making of meaning. By providing a means for sharing student reflections, coupled with instructor feedback resulting in ongoing dialogue, the paper mirror can provide the instructor and students valuable information about students' progression and development. An ultimate goal in professional education is for students to synergize theories with their personal styles, broaden their repertoires of professional methods, inculcate professional ethics into their practices, and develop a base of knowledge that is the foundation for becoming well-rounded, model practitioners. The paper mirror reflects the student's struggles, questions, frustrations, and successes. As Dewey stated (1933), "The function of reflective thought is, therefore, to transfer a situation in which there is experienced obscurity, doubt, conflict, disturbance of some sort, into a situation that is clear, coherent, settled and harmonious" (p. 100–101).

References

American Counseling Association. (2005). *ACA code of ethics and standards of practice.* Retrieved May 5, 2005, from http://counseling.org/Content/NavigationMenu/RESOURCES/ETHICS/ACA_Code_ofEthics.pdf

Baldwin, C. (1991). *Life's companion: Journal writing as a spiritual quest.* New York: Bantam Books.

Boud, D. (2001). Using journal writing to enhance reflective practice. *New Directions for Adult and Continuing Education, 90,* 9–17.

Brookfield, S. (1998). Critically reflective practice. *Journal of Continuing Education in the Health Professions, 18,* 197–205.

Dewey, J. (1933). *How we think: A restatement of the relations of reflective thinking to the educative process.* Boston: D.C. Heath & Co.

Dewey, J. (1938). *Experience and education.* New York: Simon & Schuster.

Elbow, P., & Clark, J. (1987). Desert island discourse: The benefits of ignoring audience. In T. Fulwiler (Ed.), *The journal book* (p. 23). Portsmouth, NH: Boynton/Cook.

English, L. (2001). Ethical concerns relating to journal writing. *New Directions for Adult and Continuing Education, 90,* 28-35.

Gladding, S. (2004). *Counseling: A comprehensive profession* (5th ed.). Upper Saddle River, NJ: Pearson.

Goldsmith, S. (1996). *Journal reflection: A resource guide for community service leaders and educators engaged in service learning.* Washington, DC: The American Alliance for Rights & Responsibilities.

Kerka, S. (1996). *Journal writing and adult learning* (ERIC Digest No. 174). Washington, DC: Office of Educational Research and Improvement.

Kolb, D. (1984). *Experiential learning: Experience as the source of learning and development.* Englewood Cliffs, NJ: Prentice Hall.

Knowles, M. S. (1983). Adults are not grown-up children as learners. *Community Service Catalyst, 13*(4), 4–8.

Mezirow, B. (1998). On critical reflection. *Adult Education Quarterly, 48*(3), 185–198.

Mezirow, B. (Ed.). (2000). *Learning as transformation: Critical perspectives on a theory in progress.* New York: Jossey-Bass.

Moon, J. (1999). *Learning journal: A handbook for academics, students and professional development.* London: Kogan Page.

Rogers, C. (1982). Now I am only interested in learning. In R. Gross (Ed.), *Invitation to lifelong learning* (pp. 222–225). Chicago: Follett.

Tough, A. (1968). *Why adults learn: A study of the major reasons for beginning and continuing a learning project.* Toronto: Ontario Institute for Studies in Education.

Vygotsky, L. (1986). *Thought and language* (Rev. ed.). Cambridge, MA: MIT Press.

Girls' Outdoor Adventure Programs:
History, Theory, & Practice

▼ ▼ ▼

Priscilla McKenney, Nadine W. Budbill, & Nina S. Roberts

In the early 1990s a proliferation of research and popular literature sounded the alarm about the challenges of growing up female in the United States. The adventure education field responded as a handful of organizations and programs were established around the country addressing the developmental needs of adolescent girls. For more than 15 years, these programs have developed and defined intentional, research-based adventure programming for girls. However, despite what has grown into its own programmatic niche, there is still a relative dearth of research on the subject of girls and adventure education.

There are currently a substantial number of programs in the United States offering some type of adventure activities specifically for girls. Many of these programs have developed from the following two facets of research: (a) the comprehension that girls struggle with self-esteem, depression, body image, and other challenges as they enter and move through adolescence; and (b) the knowledge that participation in adventure programs can affect positive change in individuals. Perhaps most importantly, as these programs developed, they focused on supporting girls to develop and express their strengths and, theoretically, it is this strengths-based approach that guides the work of these programs today.

This chapter illuminates the historical context of single-sex programs and gender-based assumptions in adventure education with girls at the core. Knowledge gained from research on boys and/or mixed-gender programs is valid and has its place; nonetheless, the focus of this current segment relates to experiences of girls. It also provides current theoretical frameworks relating to two key questions that continue to surface: Why adolescent girls? Why adventure education for girls' positive development? We will explore key conceptual foundations of girls' adventure programs and include profiles of four leading organizations that have created effective frameworks for developing best practices in working with adolescent girls in this arena.

Historical Context

Single-Sex Outdoor Adventure for Girls and Women

There is a long tradition of single-sex outdoor adventure inspired and created by women. As early as 1902, Laura Matoon sparked the girls' camping movement by offering private-school girls opportunities to sleep outside in tents, hike, canoe, swim, and engage in nature studies in the mountains and lakes of New Hampshire. Her camps emphasized character development, creative arts, and skill development in outdoor activities. Mattoon "wished to show her students a kind of growth and adventure that only the outdoors could offer" (Martin, Cashel, Wagstaff, & Breunig, 2006; Miranda & Yerkes, 1996). In 1914, Abbie Graham, a private camp director, wrote an essay about the girls' camping movement suggesting that girls sought the outdoors because they wanted an experience with "a bit of swagger in it" (Graham, 1914). The camping movement, which preceded the boys' scouting movement, was one of the earliest forms of experiential and adventure education that had an intention of character development (Martin et al., 2006; Miranda & Yerkes, 1996).

A woman in pursuit of adventure "alone without a man" is also not a new phenomenon. For example, in 1923, Mariam Obrien Underhill, an American Alpinist, chose to climb in the Alps not only guideless but also "manless" (DaSilva, 1998). Fifty years later, in the 1970s, Arlene Blum organized the first American women's team ascent of Denali and, in 1985 she led the first American women's team to the Himalayan summit of Annapurna I (DaSilva, 1998). Girls also have a history of adventure pursuits. For example, in 1891, Susan Longmire became the second female to reach the summit of Mt. Rainier—at 13 years of age! Three years later, in 1894, Helen Holmes, a 15-year-old, also made a successful ascent of Mt. Rainier (Molenaar, 2000).

The historical involvement of women and girls in outdoor adventure pursuits continues to provide significant influence for working with girls today. First and foremost, these pioneering adventurers laid the foundation for modern-day participation for both girls and women. Despite the social progress that has been made in the realm of gender equality, girls and women today face many of the same barriers and challenges that our foremothers faced as they took to the outdoors (Da Silva, 1998; Henderson, Bialeschki, Shaw, & Freysinger, 1989). Historically, girls and women had to confront and overcome gender-based expectations in order to participate in outdoor adventures, defying gender stereotypes and roles as they took to the mountains, especially in single-sex groups without the assistance of men (Da Silva, 1998; Bialeschki & Henderson, 1993). This experience remains true for many girls and women to this day.

One of the prevailing early reasons for single-sex outdoor programs was simply the need to be in the presence of one's own gender. The value of this has been demonstrated by the strong tradition of programs such as Girl Scouts and Boy Scouts (Yerkes & Miranda, 1985). Since its inception in 1912, the Girl Scouts organization has provided single-sex outdoor experiences for girls to become better prepared to serve their communities and develop leadership skills through residential camp programs during the summer, as well as ongoing activities during the school year (Yerkes, 1999). Historically, Girl Scouts wanted their programs to emphasize "the aesthetic and spiritual kinship of girls to nature and of girls to one another," to give girls tools to thrive and "become a new type of woman, the politically active citizen" (Miranda, 1987).   Yet, some program activities offered through programs such as Girl Scouts, Campfire Girls, and the YWCA emphasized skills that supported the socialization of girls into socially accepted gender roles. According to Yerkes & Miranda (1985), girls were taught domestic skills such as sewing and cooking, which reinforced the idea of female servitude. Girl Scouts, and other similar programs, have since expanded their goals to include a commitment to helping girls develop their confidence, determination, and leadership skills through a broader range of activities, such as sailing, rock climbing, and challenge course experiences as these activities have become culturally popular (Girl Scouts, 2002).

In the mid-1960s, females began to participate in U.S. Outward Bound and National Outdoor Leadership School (NOLS) programs (Miner & Boldt, 2002; NOLS, 2008). At this time, rather than integrating female participants to create co-ed groups, cohorts were formed along gender lines, creating single-sex groupings for the entire program. Beginning in the 1970s, co-ed courses became the norm, which remains true to this day, with the exception of some courses for adolescents and women (Minor & Boldt, 2002). As female participation increased, very few questions were raised about the needs of girls and women as potentially different than those of their male counterparts (Hardin, 1979; McKenney, 1996). In the context of these U.S. Outward Bound schools, girls and women often have participated in adventure programs that operated under a philosophical framework designed for the male population (Hardin, 1979; James, 1980; Miner & Boldt, 2002; Warren, 1985).

In the 1980s, the emergence of women's outdoor programs began a new trend in the adventure education community. Since then, the literature has been substantial and varied, including writings on various theories, methods, and benefits of wilderness programs for women (Bialeschki & Henderson, 1993; Hardin, 1979; Henderson et al., 1989; Henderson & Bialeschki, 1987; Hornibrook, Brinkert, Parry, Seimens, Mitten, & Priest, 1997; Mitten, 1985; Pohl, Borrie, & Patterson, 2000; Warren, 1985; Yerkes & Miranda, 1985).

Central to the development of these programs for women was an "ethic of care." The ethic of care is a well-known theory of women's development (Gilligan, 1982) proposed in response to popular, male-centric models of moral development. Examples of typical "male-centric" models can be seen in the classic work of Piaget, Kohlberg, and Freud, all well-known psychologists. All their subjects were boys and men and their theories were developed based on interviews purposefully with males only (e.g., life stages of moral development).

Gilligan (1982) wanted to assert the inadequacy of their findings and show that women are not inferior in their personal or moral development, but they are simply "different" and the difference may be more complex than realized. She determined women and girls develop in a way that focuses on connections among people (rather than separation) and with an ethic of care for those people (rather than an ethic of justice). Furthermore, Gilligan produces her own stage theory of moral development for women and the transitions between the stages are fueled by changes in the sense of self rather than in changes in cognitive capability as indicated in the models where only males were the subjects.

This concept of "care" was later explored and further developed by Mitten (1985) as it relates to outdoor leadership; she advocated for leadership, for example, that honors relationship and choice for participants.   An ethic of care seeks to respond to the relationship-based and interpersonal nature of girls' and women's ways of being. This framework also aims to recognize, celebrate, and honor women for their strengths and goals, which are often varied and diverse. The accommodation of diverse strengths and goals is often overlooked in outdoor programs based in a more traditional philosophical model that emphasizes predetermined outcomes and the accomplishment of tasks over the process of being in the outdoors with others (Mitten, 1985, 1995).

Competence in outdoor leadership, technical skills, and physical strength has been, and typically continues to be, promoted primarily as male domains (Warren & Loeffler, 2006). Images and descriptions of outdoor adventure in the media, for example, portray a white, male-dominated culture where value is based on extreme accomplishments rather than on the quality of the experience (Loeffler, 1995; Roberts, 1992). Women's experiences and voices in the adventure education field, and in the culture in general, have often gone unrecognized and unheard, as have the voices of people of color. Because of this, women of all races often choose single-sex programs for a more supportive setting in which to learn technical outdoor skills, take risks, participate in decision-making, and develop their leadership skills (Henderson & Bialeschki, 1987; McClintock, 1996; Warren & Loeffler, 2006). This type of setting is effective for learning because, in order to participate in outdoor adventure pursuits, women often are required to overcome society's constructions of femininity and gender role stereotypes (Warren, 1985). Whittington (2006) defines cultural constructions of femininity by stating:

> In contemporary Western society, femininity emphasizes beauty; girls are valued for
> being compliant, sweet, nice, cooperative, upbeat, and sincere (Brown, 1997, 1998).

Notably, the dominant conception of femininity is shaped by the white, middle-class, heterosexual, male model of gender construction (p. 206).

Due to the reality of living in a highly gendered culture, it is beneficial for many women to come together in single-sex programs to support one another, gain skills and confidence, and experience adventure, all while free from the constraints of gender often present in co-ed groups. Inspired by the foundation that has been laid for women's programs and our foremother adventurers, today's programs seek to support girls to discover themselves outside of cultural constructions of femininity, to give them the opportunity to experience the limitless possibilities of who they are and who they can be, and to help girls realize and claim their own authentic power.

Why Adolescent Girls?

The 1990s saw the emergence of a plethora of research and various publications on the "crisis" of female adolescence. With titles such as *School Girls: Young Women, Self-Esteem, and the Confidence Gap; Shortchanging Girls, Shortchanging America*; and *Reviving Ophelia: Saving the Selves of Adolescent Girls*, the research pointed to a "developmental crisis" and "loss of self" for adolescent girls (Brown & Gilligan, 1992; Greenberg-Lake, 1994; Orenstein, 1994; Pipher, 1996). These findings acted as a call to action for those who work with and care about girls. A decade later, girls began to outperform boys in most academic subjects (Tyre, 2006) yet still face barriers to a positive self-concept, as indicated by troublesome reports about gender stereotypes, self-esteem, depression, body image, eating disorders, self-harm, and exposure to violence (Centers for Disease Control and Prevention, 2005; Girl Scouts, 2004; Girl Scouts 2006; Girls Incorporated, 2006).

In the first part of the 21st century, popular literature and culture fixated on girls' "relational aggression" with titles such as *Girl Fighting: Betrayal and Rejection Among Girls; Odd Girl Out: The Hidden Culture of Aggression in Girls*; and *Queen-Bees and Wannabes: Helping Your Daughter Survive Cliques, Gossip, Boyfriends and Other Realities of Adolescence* (Brown, 2005; Simmons, 2002; Wiseman, 2002). Such behavior, including gossip, teasing, bullying, cliques, policing each other's bodies, clothing styles, and trends, has come to be accepted because "girls will be girls," yet this behavior is more accurately framed in the context of girls' anger and struggle for power, voice, safety, and legitimacy within a culture that often denies girls these basic rights (Brown, 1999; Kilbourne, 2000). While the sensationalism of girls' aggression garnered public attention, it also became evident that there is still a crisis in the very nature of being female and adolescent in our media-saturated society.

In a 2006 report commissioned by Girls Incorporated, it was found that girls face intensifying pressure to be "everything to everybody:" smart, athletic, attractive, thin, a good friend, daughter, and girlfriend (Girls Incorporated, 2006). While there has been some progress in the past decade, and many girls perceive fewer limitations regarding their capacity for leadership and career prospects, gender stereotypes still persist and permeate their lives (Girls Incorporated, 2006; Lamb & Brown, 2006). For example, girl's still report lingering pressure to please everyone, dress "right," and be skinny. They also report a great deal of worry and concern about appearance, social pressures, pressure to have sex, and becoming pregnant (Girl Scouts, 2002; Girl Scouts, 2006; Girls Incorporated, 2006). Additionally, girls are up against stereotypical and limiting images of girlhood that are "sold" to them by clever marketing that is seemingly unconcerned with girls' healthy development (Lamb & Brown, 2006). In the face of this mounting pressure, some girls respond with amazing strength and resiliency; they find ways to resist and remain true to themselves. Others, however, respond with behaviors and attitudes such as low self-esteem, depression, poor body image, poor eating habits, and self-harm. Although it has been rightfully acknowledged by researchers and educators that boys are also under tremendous pressure as they navigate a culture rife with unhealthy messages about masculinity (Kindlon, 2000; Pollock & Pipher, 1999), this does not negate the challenges of growing up female in what Pipher (1996) has called a "girl-poisoning" culture.

It is important to note that the experience of adolescence is not mediated by gender alone. Race, class, and culture have a significant bearing on one's experience of adolescence and may be equally as important to one's identity development as gender (Girl Scouts, 2006; Girls Incorporated, 2006; Leadbeater & Way, 1996). Research by both the Girls Scouts (2006) and Girls Incorporated (2006) found that there are significant differences in body image and self-esteem between African American, Latina, Asian American, and White girls. These findings confirm earlier reports (American Association of University Women, 1992; Orenstein, 1994) that indicated that, overall, African American girls have higher self-esteem and a more positive body image than White and Latina girls. In areas of academic competence, however, African American girls consistently rated themselves lower than girls in other ethnic groups. These findings demonstrate that while girls from all backgrounds are in need of support, culturally competent programming and services that recognize girls' strengths and their challenges are needed to effectively respond to girls' diverse realities.

Consequently, Table 1 identifies girls' developmental needs (as cited throughout this chapter) and provides samples of program design, including curriculum and outcomes.

Why Adventure Education for Girls' Positive Development?

Historically, adventure education programs (not necessarily gender specific) have shared a common vision: To provide experiences that focus on self-discovery and personal growth. The main programmatic goal of many outdoor adventure organizations has been to help students gain self-confidence and discover their personal potential through the challenges of their experiences; one intended outcome is for participants to transfer this learning

Table 1.
How Girls Outdoor Adventure Programs Respond to Girls' Developmental Needs

Developmental Needs[1]	Programmatic Response
Self-expression; the nurturing of one's authentic voice	Girls' voices are valued. Use of "I feel" statements. Reflection time encourages girls' real voices. Creative expression activities
Meaningful and authentic connections with other girls; healthy relationships that include being an ally to one another.	Program includes structured time for building relationships, connecting, and sharing with others. Instructors monitor group dynamics and intervene when necessary.
Positive risk-taking opportunities	Girls learn risk-analysis, decision-making, and engage in positive risk taking activities, such as rock climbing, backpacking, leadership, and speaking one's truth.
Physical activity: to know one's body as a subject of one's own experience, not an object of others'	Girls are physically active, engaged in activities that demand their bodies to be strong. Program provides them an experience in which what their bodies can do is more important than how their bodies look.
Skill development; competency	Program makes sure technical skill development is central and demystifies competency in outdoor skills. Skill development is based on progression and experiential learning.
Leadership opportunities	Girls get to be leaders! They take turns practicing being in a leadership role, share what they know, and learn about their own feelings toward leadership. Cultural attitudes toward "women in charge" are explored.
Safe spaces for identity development	Girls' diversity is recognized and valued. Reflection time includes opportunities to share the many aspects of one's self.
Development of a sense of self from inside-out; opportunities for less self-consciousness; healthy body image and awareness	Girls are removed from mirrors, media, and the public scrutiny of peers. Activities build resistance to cultural/social messages about gender roles and beauty.
Learning effective ways to handle conflict	Conflict resolution is taught to girls. Conflict is normalized and embraced. Understanding the difference between assertive, passive, and aggressive behavior.
To be a valued and contributing member of a community	Each and every girl is seen, heard, and valued. Program structure ensures that girls are not left out and mediates social dynamics.
Exposure to a range of ways of being a woman; challenges to cultural constructions of femininity	Girls work with strong and diverse women role models and leaders. Exposure to activities that many perceive as "masculine" and "white."

[1] Developmental needs as reflected in the following: Brown, 2005; Brown & Gilligan, 1992; Culp, 1998; Gilligan, 1982; Gurian, 2001; Henderson & Grant, 1998; Lamb & Brown, 2006; McKenney, 1996; Mitten, 1992; Ponton, 1997; Sabo et al., 2004; Sax, 2005; Warren, 1996; West-Smith, 2000; Whittington, 2006.

back to their everyday lives. This tradition, of using challenge-based activities and wilderness opportunities as a method to promote self-esteem, continues to be an accepted programmatic theme in adventure education and an increase in self-esteem has been widely documented as a positive outcome of adventure education programs (Arnold, 1994; Aubrey & MacLeod, 1994; Cason & Gillis, 1994; Hattie, Marsh, Neill, & Richards, 1997; Moote & Wodarski, 1997).

Given the research that indicates adolescent girls need opportunities to bolster and further develop their self-esteem, self-efficacy, and overall self-concept, it is logical that adventure education programs have the potential to positively impact girls' development as well. Studies on the outcomes of girls' experiences with outdoor adventure programs have shown there are many benefits to their participation. From better body image (Edwards-Leeper, 2003), and increased self-esteem and self-confidence (Culp, 1998; Mitten, 1992) to resistance of gender role stereotypes and opportunities for genuine connections with other girls (Whittington, 2006), adventure education programs can offer girls a range of experiences that support healthy development. Other benefits include opportunities for positive risk-taking (Ponton, 1997) and genuine self-expression (Culp, 1998; McKenney, 1996).

In a study of *Connecting with Courage*®, a program of the Thompson Island Outward Bound Education Center for 12- and 13-year-old girls, McKenney (1996) found that participants demonstrated an increase of self-esteem from course start to post-course testing. Likewise, a study of the Women's Wilderness Institute's (WWI) *Girls Wilderness Programs* (Edwards-Leeper, 2003) found that girls who participated in one of WWI's summer programs experienced positive improvements in their body image, self-worth, and perceived academic, social, and athletic competence. An experience of physical efficacy, opportunities for leadership, as well as the value that is placed on self-expression and authentic voice, all contribute to increased self-esteem for girls. Skill development in adventure programs can also support these outcomes as the development of technical skills supports girls' sense of accomplishment and competency.

Even as girls experience progress and power in some aspects of their lives, the pressure to be thin and attractive to others continues to gain cultural momentum and significance, particularly in the lives of adolescent girls. Body image issues, unhealthy weight loss strategies, and eating disorders are highly prevalent in the lives of girls and young women (Centers for Disease Control and Prevention, 2005; Girl Scouts, 2004; West-Smith, 2000). Sixty-eight percent of female students in grades 9–12 say they are trying to lose weight and 55% of female students in grades 9–12 report moderating their diets (eating less food, fewer calories, or low-fat food) in order to lose weight; this is more than double the number of boys who say the same (Center for Disease Control & Prevention, 2005).

Involvement in adventure programs provides girls an escape from the daily inundation of messages about cultural standards of beauty and can provide a shift from a focus on how one's body looks to a focus on what one's body is able to do (West-Smith, 2000). In addition to this escape, adventure programs provide girls with an opportunity for participation in non-traditional and noncompetitive forms of physical activity. Consequently, recent research supports the benefits of physical activity for girls: improved mental health and well-being, better body image, decreased substance use, better sexual and reproductive health, and improved academic performance (Sabo, Miller, Melnick, & Heywood, 2004).

In a study exploring one particular girls' outdoor adventure program, Whittington (2006) investigated the ways in which the program challenged adolescent girls' constructions of femininity. She found that through participation in this program, girls gained an enhanced sense of pride, accomplishment, perseverance, strength, and determination. Results indicated that girls' gender-based assumptions about their own abilities were also challenged by their participation. For instance, as stated by one participant: "It's so empowering. It shows you that you don't need help, like those times we canoed by the boys and they wanted to help us with our gear and we didn't need them. It shows you what you can do" (Whittington, 2006, p. 5). Girls reported that during the program they felt liberated from the cultural conventions of beauty and cleanliness that required them to spend significant time each day tending to their physical appearance. They also reported enjoyment in seeing food as a source of nourishment and a necessity to maintain strength to accomplish the day's goals. This "freedom to eat" was a welcomed respite from the ways in which many girls modified their eating to achieve the perceived ideal image of beauty. Results also showed that involvement allowed girls to build and maintain authentic relationships with other girls; this was apparently achieved in a way that girls reported was difficult to do in their daily lives. Whittington concluded:

> The benefits of an all-girls program, particularly during adolescence, are that it allows girls to experience the outdoors and the wilderness with other females and to view the outdoors as a feminine sphere. These programs offer girls the opportunity to resist social stereotypes and promote positive gender identity development. These "hardiness zones" (Leopold, Brown, Wesson, & Brookings, 1999) offer girls interaction with caring adults, opportunities to take risks and challenges, and time away from the media and society (p. 8–9).

The Emergence & Growth of All-Girls Outdoor Adventure Programs

The value of single-sex outdoor adventure programs for women (and girls to a lesser extent) has been established and well documented by research since the 1980s (Roberts, 1997). Support for single-sex programs for adolescent girls also has begun to be established by research specifically on girls. Single-sex programs in traditional educational settings have also experienced resurgence in recent years due to the apparent benefits of this type of learning environment (Sax, 2006; Steiner, 2002). Studies focusing on single-sex educational programs indicate a potential to break down gender stereotypes, foster a freedom to build skills without the intimidation and self-consciousness inherent in many co-ed groups, and create a learning environment in which girls become players rather than spectators (Girl Scouts, 2004; Girl Scouts, 2006; Girls Incorporated, 2006; Sadker & Sadker, 1995; Sax, 2006). Additionally, when the element of adolescence is added to co-ed learning dynamics, gender roles generally become more rigid, since adolescence is a time when individuals face strong social pressures to conform to gender roles and expectations (Dillow, Flack, & Peterman, 1994; Sadker & Sadker, 1995; Sax, 2006).

Single-sex programs can provide girls positive experiences with outdoor adventure pursuits. This does not diminish the worth of co-ed programs. Instead, it rightfully suggests the value of being in the company of one's own gender. Especially for adolescent girls, as reported by girls themselves, single-sex programs facilitate greater participation (Culp, 1998; McKenney, 1996). Girls report that in single-sex groups they are more likely to share feelings and talk openly. According to Culp (1998), this candidness is particularly true with self-expression and technical skill development, as evidenced by the following interview comment: "If it was all girls and I saw some of them do it, I'd feel confident because they're girls and I'm a girl and I'd be like, 'I can do that,' versus if I saw boys do it, I wouldn't feel confident that I could do it" (p. 374). Furthermore, McKenney (1996) found that "an all-girls experience created a safer place to explore new skills and take risks on both a physical and emotional level, especially when sharing feelings and speaking out were involved" (p. 57).

All-girls outdoor adventure programs can provide adolescent girls a safe space in which to develop technical and interpersonal skills, build relationships, practice authentic self-expression, and connect with nature. As mentioned, the early 1990s saw the emergence of more adventure education programs for girls, in part, derived from both evidence-based (or outcome-based) evaluation and empirical research. Therefore, the predominant all-girls program model is founded upon the fusion of three key concepts: (a) the perceived value of adventure education programs, (b) a developing body of research on girls' development, and (c) the demonstrated effectiveness of single-sex educational programs.

Theoretical Underpinnings: Best Practices for Girls' Empowerment

A variety of conceptual frameworks have been discussed thus far. In the coming section, we will review best practices that create successful outdoor experiences for girls and how those practices have their theoretical roots in outdoor programs that have been successful for women. As noted by Mitten (1992), five key concepts, adapted from the theories of effective women's programs, are essential to set the stage for empowerment. They are:

1. A program philosophy that respects girls' experiences and is strengths-based;

2. Leadership guidelines that require instructors have the necessary competence, experience, and understanding of the needs of adolescent girls;

3. Respect for the value of "choice" so that girls can make choices about, and within, their experiences;

4. A continuum of action and reflection that provides opportunities for technical skill development; and

5. Relationship-building and self-expression.

Strengths-Based Framework

Girls possess numerous strengths, including courage, creativity, leadership, intuition, body wisdom, and compassion, to name a few. They can be outspoken, passionate, silly, serious, and empathetic. These qualities have prompted educators to adopt a "strengths-based" or "asset-based" approach to working with girls (Lerner & Benson, 2003). This is in contrast to the traditional "deficit model," which looks at young people as problems to fix, rather than as strong people to be seen for their potential (Lerner & Benson, 2003; Rose, 2006). For example, a strengths-based framework honors and respects the importance of relationships in the lives of girls and sees this as an asset, rather than a detriment. *Connecting with Courage*® allows, and welcomes, girls with prior relationships to do the course together as long as they are open to making new friends (Porter, 1996). This is a departure from some programs, such as the traditional Outward Bound model, in which friends are deliberately placed on separate courses.

Girls' resiliency has been demonstrated by their ability to withstand and thrive despite the many pressures and cultural contradictions they face (Brown, 1998; Leadbeater & Way, 1996, 2007). Many girls find ways to maintain their innate qualities of strength, though at times these strengths may be buried beneath the surface and not evident to those on the outside (Brown, 1998). Additionally, girls' strengths are often not recognized or valued as such by the dominant culture that often defines strength and success in individual, achievement-oriented ways. In short, while girls are up against a tremendous tide of challenges, they should not be seen as victims. Today, this philosophy of recognizing strengths and fostering resiliency provides a key theoretical underpinning for adventure education programs for girls (Leadbeater & Way, 1996, 2007).

The Role of Leadership

Adventure programs for girls must engage leaders who possess competence, experience, and an understanding of the unique needs of adolescent girls. It is not enough to simply have technical expertise. Equally important is for these individuals to have the ability to model both authentic self-expression and conflict resolution. Leaders should recognize the importance of the social aspect of girls' programs (Jordan, 1992). Concurrently, vigilant management of social and emotional dynamics is critical so all participants feel accepted and included. Negative social dynamics should be proactively addressed through discussion and problem-solving within the group. Ultimately, leaders should empower girls to manage conflicts themselves; this allows them to invest in the creation of their own positive community. Additionally, leaders must possess the ability to maintain a structured environment for a youth program to be successful.

An effective leader will "help girls stretch their limits, encouraging them to learn technical skills, while also allowing time for sharing and connecting with others" (McKenney, 1996, p. 22). Furthermore, leaders can empower participants through the demystification of technical competency and the promotion of transparency in the technical aspects of leadership (Warren, 1996). This allows girls to see that they, too, are capable of developing technical skills and assuming positions of leadership. Finally, leaders must embrace the ethic of care that calls for creating a sense of safety and compassion for all participants (Hardin, 1979; Martin et al., 2006; Mitten, 1995). This approach is in accord with feminist models of outdoor programs and leadership (Mitten, 1999; Henderson, 1996; Warren & Rheingold, 1996), which strives to create a positive environment for girls' and women's experiences, in part, by decreasing stress and anxiety, and by encouraging authentic risk taking (Estrellas, 1996).

Feminist models are in alignment with the transformational approach to leadership (Ewert & Hayashi, 2006; Jordan, 1992; Henderson, 1996) and also feminist pedagogy, or the manifestation of feminist theory in educational settings (Warren & Rheingold, 1996). In contrast to the traditional male-oriented model of leadership, in which all the power and knowledge rests within the leader, the transformational model of leadership shares power between leaders and participants. This is done with the goal of empowering participants to discover and bring forth their own experience and voice (Ewert & Hayashi, 2006; Henderson, 1996; Jordan, 1992). When working with adolescents, this approach can be used in an age-appropriate manner. Feminist pedagogy, as applied to experiential education, calls for an examination of power in the teacher/learner relationship, the use of personal experience as a valid teaching tool, and work for social justice (Warren & Rheingold, 1996). Effective leadership of girls' programs synthesizes all of the aforementioned elements, thereby attempting to create an emotionally safe environment in which girls can experience and thrive.

The Concept of Choice

"Choice" is a fundamental concept of best practices in many programs today. This concept originated in early grounded theory developed for girls and women's programs (Hardin, 1979; Mitten, 1985; Roberts, 1997). Consequently, choice—specifically *informed choice*, in which participants are given adequate information to make decisions—should permeate the program experience (Mitten, 1992, 1995). Choice is essential to programs that respond to adolescent girls' developmental needs because it decreases stress and anxiety and develops important life skills for girls such as setting boundaries, honoring one's own needs, and being one's own authority.

The notion of choice as a regular practice is essential in outdoor adventure programs (Estrellas, 1996; Hardin, 1979; Mitten, 1985, 1992). This feminist model encourages authentic risk taking, which can occur when stress is minimized and risk is transparently discussed in a framework of empowered personal choice. This model is supported by the work of Davis-Berman and Berman (2002), and in their more recently conceptualized work (Davis-Berman & Berman, 2008), who challenge adventure educators to move away from pushing participants out of their comfort zones in order to affect change and growth. Rather, they suggest that the best environment for positive growth and change is one in which participants feel "safe, secure and cared about" (2002, p. 308). This is particularly important for girls as research shows they tend to perform best in low-stress environments (Sax, 2006).

For example, rock climbing can create a lot of stress and anxiety for some girls. The expectation, explicitly stated, is that everyone must actively learn the basic instructions of the harness, knots, and mechanics of belaying. Each girl, however, can decide whether or not she climbs and is encouraged to define her own challenge; this might include becoming a competent belayer or climbing a series of rock faces to the top. What is constant is an expectation of active participation, regardless of the choice that is made. Theoretically, choice relieves some stress for girls and offers them an opportunity to determine when they are physically, mentally, and emotionally ready to try something new or different.

Providing participants with choices is fundamental to empowerment because doing so implies the participants' ideas, feelings, and perspectives are valued. This validates each individual as the creator of her own destiny and the purveyor of her own truth. Programs for girls must offer choices and honor girls as they make their own decisions. This process supports girls to set their own boundaries and practice saying "no" in an environment in which these assertions of authority are respected. This approach provides girls with opportunities to practice critical life skills while cultivating authentic self-assessment and decision-making. These skills are not always encouraged by a youth culture in which trends and peer pressure often guide individual decision-making.

Reflective Technical Skill Development

A continuum of action and reflection is a theoretical framework that provides girls and boys opportunities for positive technical skill development. This continuum of action and reflection is at the very core of experiential education and the roots of adventure education (Martin et al., 2006). The importance of technical skill development in girls' programs, however, should not be overlooked (Jordan, 1992), as it is often within the technical domains where girls may feel intimidated and incompetent. This can be attributed to the fact that girls often are not encouraged to acquire technical skills and that, in co-ed environments, girls often stand by and watch while boys advance in their skills development. According to Warren and Loeffler (2006), women's technical skill development is highly influenced by gender role socialization and the resulting cultural conceptions of "activity appropriateness." It can be assumed that girls are similarly influenced by the process of gender role socialization and, as such, come to the outdoor adventure program with preexisting notions about what girls can and cannot do.

Warren and Loeffler (2006) also illuminate the misalignment that often occurs between women's (and girls') actual competence and sense of competence. Actual competence is the ability to perform a skill, on a continuum from beginner to expert; sense of competence is one's perception and self-assessment of competence. Often, due to a lack of experience with technical skills and risk analysis, women and girls' sense of competence is much lower than their actual competence. Leaders must encourage, model, and create space for authentic self-assessment and reflection so that girls can progress toward an alignment of their perceived and actual competence. It is also important that girls are supported to reflect upon why it is that they have under-perceived their own abilities. It is through this genuine self-assessment and reflection that girls can feel supported to recognize and claim their competence.

And finally, four chief strategies that support girls' technical skill development include: (a) the creation of a supportive and collaborative learning environment in which competition is minimized (Warren & Loeffler, 2006); (b) the use of intentional curriculum by instructors who understand the importance of developing girls' sense of competence through technical skill development; (c) opportunities for reflection in which girls can process their experiences as they develop technical skills; and (d) the presence of female role models who demonstrate technical competency, yet also demystify that competency and share their own struggles and challenges with participants, as appropriate (Warren, 1996).

Table 2.
Four Preeminent All-Girls Outdoor Adventure Programs in the United States

Organization Name, Location, and Website	Year Established	Ages Served	Primary Programs
Connecting with Courage® (A program of the Thompson Island Outward Bound Education Center) Boston, MA www.thompsonisland.org	1991	12–13	Connecting with Courage® *Sailing* *Rock Climbing* *Sea Kayaking* *Backpacking*
GirlVentures San Francisco, CA www.girlventures.org	1997	11–14	Summer Courses: *Project Courage* *Transitions* School Year Programs: *Rock and Dance* *Urban Trek* *Girlz Climb On* *Self Defense* Community Courses: Leadership Development Program for High School Alumnae
Passages Northwest Seattle, WA www.passagesnw.org	1997	10–17	Girls Wilderness Programs: *Spring/Summer Adventures* *Parent/Daughter Programs* *Partnership Programs* After School Programs: Girls Rock! And Girls Rock On! *Afterschool Rock Climbing Programs & Girls Group* Alumnae Programs: *Girls Advisory Board* *Alumnae Climbing Nights* Custom Designed Workshops and Trainings
The Women's Wilderness Institute Boulder, CO www.girlswilderness.org	1998	12–17	Girls Wilderness Programs: *Adventure Camp* *Rock Camp* *Wild Voices* *Latina Girls' Course* *Leadership Course* *Wild Moves* *Wild Things* *Custom Courses*

Relationship-Building and Self-Expression

Theoretical foundations relevant to work with girls must value authentic relationship-building and self-expression (Brown, 1992; Culp, 1998). The importance of relationships in girls' lives was elucidated by the relational theory developed by Gilligan (1982). Activities that incorporate and encourage relationship-building and self-expression should be interwoven throughout the outdoor adventure program. It is critical that girls be supported, through purposeful curriculum and facilitation, to build sincere relationships in which they can speak honestly about their feelings and experiences. Subsequently, conflict resolution skills should be taught to girls in an effort to empower them to confront interpersonal conflict directly and independently, rather than allowing behaviors associated with "relational aggression" to occur (Brown, 2005).

Relationship-building and self-expression can transpire through creative means of processing experience such as verbal sharing, journal writing, visual arts, and expression-based activities such as art, dance, theater, writing, and structured time that encourages positive bonding (team-building, conflict resolution, sharing). As tested by McKenney (1996), these are effective tools for reflection and can support the process of discovery and learning-transfer as it applies to girls' daily lives. While technical skill development should be a cornerstone in girls' outdoor adventure programs, it is the ventures in relationship-building and self-expression that become the heart for girls' experiences in the outdoors and is of the essence.

Four Girls' Programs That Model Best Practices

While it is important to not overlook the significant contributions of the Girl Scouts and other such long-standing programs for girls, the emphasis here is on four programs that emerged, in part, from the research on girls as well as through sound practices in the adventure education field. While there are a number of programs in the United States that now offer some type of adventure programming explicitly for girls, we have chosen to focus on four that are considered to be effective, well established, and widely recognized across the United States: Connecting with Courage®, The Women's Wilderness Institute, Passages Northwest, and GirlVentures. The year established, primary programs, ages served, and locations of these four organizations/programs are presented in Table 2. The program descriptions cited below for Connecting with Courage®, The Women's Wilderness Institute, and Passages Northwest have been partially excerpted from the program collateral. The description of GirlVentures was written by the authors.

Connecting With Courage®

Connecting with Courage®, a program of the Thompson Island Outward Bound Education Center, was founded in 1992 to encourage girls, ages 12 and 13, to speak their minds, share their ideas, express their emotions, be creative, and challenge themselves through sensible physical risks. On a Connecting with Courage® expedition, girls get physically stronger by sailing, backpacking, or sea kayaking, and build mental muscles by exercising their imaginations. In addition to learning technical outdoor skills, girls are given the opportunity to take on leadership roles and make independent decisions. Girls develop new friendships, enhanced confidence, a greater ability to express themselves, and a clearer sense of their strengths (Thompson Island Outward Bound, 2007).

Passages Northwest

Since 1996, Passages Northwest has inspired more than 5,400 program participants to discover courage within themselves through outdoor exploration. Passages Northwest is dedicated to educating and motivating girls, ages 10–17, and women to develop leadership and courage through the integrated exploration of the arts and the natural environment. Activities include: rock climbing, sea kayaking, backpacking, hiking, snowshoeing, ropes courses, creative arts projects, service projects, girls group, parent/daughter programs, community partnerships, and workshops/trainings. Programming is grounded in experiential education and all endeavors are framed as community activities designed to develop teamwork and leadership skills. Creative, inquisitive, and physical courage are emphasized, as well as relationship-building and communication (Passages Northwest, 2007).

The Girls' Wilderness Program (Women's Wilderness Institute)

The Girls' Wilderness Program, a project of the Women's Wilderness Institute, offers outdoor programs for girls, ages 12–17, which emphasize creative self-expression, leadership, and community projects. The Women's Wilderness Institute's mission is "to strengthen the courage, confidence, and leadership qualities of girls and women, through the support and challenge of wilderness and community-based experiences." Since 1998, the Girls' Wilderness Program has recognized the unique strengths and needs of girls, and has sought to balance challenge and physical activity with the development of the healthy relationships that are crucial for girls' confidence and self-esteem. The Girls' Wilderness Program is rooted in the tradition of experiential education and girls are taught outdoor skills to gradually assume the responsibilities of the expedition, including navigation, cooking, setting up camp, and making decisions, with the support of the group and two leaders (The Women's Wilderness Institute, 2007).

GirlVentures

GirlVentures, established in 1997, is an adventure education organization whose mission is "to empower girls to develop and express their strengths." The following detailed description of GirlVentures provides an illustration of how various theoretical models described in this chapter have been put into practice. (One of the authors of this chapter, Priscilla McKenney, has been the Program Director of GirlVentures since 2002.)

GirlVentures offers intensive outdoor adventure programs to girls, ages 11–14. Each program involves: (a) a group of 10–12 girls from diverse backgrounds around the San Francisco Bay area; (b) two experienced outdoor instructors; and (c) one assistant instructor who is a GirlVentures' alumni and is enrolled in their Leadership Development Program. The group is removed from social and technological influences and dependencies such as phone, computer, TV, media, close friends, and family and placed in an environment that seeks to empower girls to develop and express their strengths, explore identity, and live simply in nature. Central to the program experience is outdoor adventure, self-expression, leadership opportunities, conflict resolution, and the creation of a model community in which everyone is heard and seen. The program provides a continuum of activities that includes technical skill development (such as rock climbing), reflection (such as "courage beads"), and transference (such as the activity "how is this like life?"). Throughout this continuum leaders use and model an "ethic of care," through which girls are supported to take positive risks and engage in activities within a "challenge by choice" framework. The program is completed with a graduation that celebrates the girls' strengths and accomplishments with family and friends. Throughout the school year girls return to participate in program opportunities that include community-building and leadership.

By creating an environment in which girls explore their strengths and learn a language of self-expression within a community of peers, GirlVentures seeks to provide adolescent girls with experiences that are relevant to their personal lives. A strengths-based model and girl-centered curriculum aims to prepare girls for their changing worlds and entry into adulthood. GirlVentures' program evaluations over the past five years have found that girls often return to their lives after the program with an increased sense of confidence, self-assurance, and a renewed ability to relate to others. Additionally, GirlVentures provides opportunities for girls and their families to stay involved with the program throughout their teenage years, and often beyond.

GirlVentures is committed to creating a multicultural organization that facilitates adventure education for a racially and socioeconomically diverse community of girls. At GirlVentures, diversity is actively explored through community-building activities that both celebrate and critique the notion of "difference." A priority at GirlVentures is the ethnic diversity of field staff. This commitment to break stereotypes and encourage participation among populations that have traditionally not been served by the adventure education field is also apparent in the Leadership Development Program that supports, trains, and encourages young women of color to pursue outdoor leadership. Through these programmatic and administrative commitments, GirlVentures seeks to provide culturally competent, intentional, and relevant programs to girls.

Conclusion

There is a theoretical and historical context that persuasively makes the case for girls' involvement in outdoor adventure pursuits, generally, and in single-sex programs more specifically. The research that exists continues to provide evidence of the benefits for girls who participate in adventure programs, from increased self-esteem and body image, to opportunities for positive risk-taking and genuine self-expression. Over the past 15 years, adventure education programs have developed a body of knowledge and best practices that facilitate girls' positive experiences in the outdoors. It is important to acknowledge that while we have focused on girls in this chapter, many of the best practices discussed here have become standard practice in programs for a wide spectrum of populations, including boys; the benefits of these practices have been widely seen and are certainly not limited to girls and women.

Fundamentally, girls' programs must embrace a philosophy, and aligned activities, which are grounded in theory and based on the available research about girls. This link, between adventure education and research, also lays the foundation for culturally competent programs that address the known challenges faced by girls as they enter and move through adolescence. While the case has been made for such programs, and a selection of studies have documented the theories, practices, and benefits of girls' outdoor adventure programs, there remains a definite need for more empirical research on this subject (e.g., pre- and post-tests, longitudinal studies).

Adventure education has the potential to give girls the tools they need to confidently navigate the world in which they live and become powerful women in their adult years. Many strong girls and women, as adventurers, scholars, and leaders, have blazed the trail for girls in the adventure education field. It is certain that girls will continue to reclaim the outdoors and adventure pursuits as territories of their own, as well as through co-existence with male allies. This will happen as more programs are designed with the strengths of girls in mind and as more girls are encouraged to resist the constraints of stereotypes in favor of their true selves that are strong, unique, and resilient.

References

Arnold, S. C. (1994). Transforming body image through women's wilderness experiences. *Women & Therapy*, 15, 43–54.

Aubrey, A. & MacLeod, M. J. (1994). So … what does rock climbing have to do with career planning? *Women & Therapy, 15,* 205–216.

Bialeschki, M.D., & Henderson, K. (1993). Expanding outdoor opportunities for women. *Parks & Recreation*, *28*(8), 36–40.

Brown, L. M. (1998). *Raising their voices: The politics of girls' anger.* Cambridge, MA: Harvard University Press.

Brown, L. M. (2005). *Girl Fighting: Betrayal and rejection among girls.* New York: New York University Press.

Brown, L. M. & Gilligan, C. (1992). *Meeting at the crossroads.* Cambridge, MA: Harvard University Press.

Cason, D. & Gillis, H. L. (1994). A meta-analysis of outdoor adventure programming with adolescents. *Journal of Experiential Education*, *17*, 40–47.

Center for Disease Control and Prevention. (2005*). Youth risk behavior surveillance.* Surveillance Summaries. MMWR 2006; *55*(SS-5).

Costa, D. M. & Guthrie, S. R. (1994). Feminist perspectives: Intersections with women and sport. In Women and sport: Interdisciplinary perspectives (pp. 235–252). Champaign, IL: Human Kinetics.

Culp, R. (1998). Adolescent girls and outdoor recreation: A case study examining constraints and effective programming. *Journal of Leisure Research*, *30*(3), 356–379.

Da Silva, R. (1998). *Leading out: Mountaineering stories of adventurous women.* Seattle: Seal Press.

Davis-Berman, J. & Berman, D. (2008). *The promise of wilderness therapy.* Boulder, CO: The Association for Experiential Education.

Davis-Berman, J. & Berman, D. (2002). Risk and anxiety in adventure programming. *Journal of Experiential Education, 25*(2), 305–310.

Deobold, E., Brown, L. M., Wessen, S., & Brookins, G. K. (1999). Cultivating hardiness zones for adolescent girls: A reconceptualization of resilience in relationships with caring adults. In N. G. Johnson, Roberts, M.C., & Worell, J. (Eds.), *Beyond appearances: A new look at adolescent girls.* (pp. 181–204). Washington, DC: American Psychological Association.

Dillow, K., Flack, M., & Peterman, F. (1994). Cooperative learning and the achievement of female students. *Middle School Journal*, (Nov.), 48–51.

Edwards-Leeper, L. (2003). *Evaluation of girls' wilderness program.* Boulder, CO: The Women's Wilderness Institute.

Estrellas, A. (1996). The eustress paradigm: A strategy for decreasing stress in wilderness adventure programming. In Warren, K. (Ed.), *Women's voices in experiential education* (pp. 32–44). Dubuque, Iowa: Kendall/Hunt.

Ewert, A. & Hayashi, A. (2006). Outdoor leaders' emotional intelligence and transformational leadership. *Journal of Experiential Education*, *28*(3), 222–242.

Gilligan, C. (1982). *In a different voice: Psychological theory and women's development.* Cambridge: Harvard University Press.

Girl Scouts of the United States of America. (2002). *The ten emerging truths: New directions for girls 11–17.* New York: Girl Scouts of the United States of America.

Girl Scouts of the United States of America. (2004). *Helping girls be healthy today, healthy tomorrow.* New York: Girl Scouts of the United States of America.

Girl Scouts of the United States of America. (2006). *The new normal: What girls say about healthy living.* New York: Girl Scouts of the United States of America.

Girls Incorporated. (2006). *The super girl dilemma.* New York: Girls Incorporated.

Greenberg-Lake: The Analysis Group. (1994). *Shortchanging girls, shortchanging America.* Wellesley, MA: AAUW Educational and National Education Association.

Gurian, M. (2001*). Boys and girls learn differently: A guide for teachers and parents.* San Francisco: Jossey-Bass.

Hardin, J. A. (1979). *Outdoor/wilderness approaches to psychological education for women a descriptive study.* Unpublished doctoral dissertation (Ed.D.), University of Massachusetts, from UMI #80–4934.

Hattie, J., Marsh, H. W., Neill, J. T., & Richards, G. E. (1997). Adventure education and Outward Bound: Out-of-class experiences that make a lasting difference. *Review of Educational Research, 67*, 43–87.

Henderson, K. (1996). Feminist perspectives on outdoor leadership. In Warren, K. (Ed.), *Women's voices in experiential education* (pp. 107–117). Dubuque, Iowa: Kendall/Hunt.

Henderson, K. & Bialeschki, M.D. (1987). *A qualitative evaluation of a women's week experience. Journal of Experiential Education*, *10*(6), 25–29.

Henderson, K., Bialeschki, M.D., Shaw, S., & Freysinger, V. (1989). *A leisure of one's own: A feminist perspective on women's leisure.* State College, Pennsylvania: Venture Publishing.

Henderson, K. A. & Grant, A.E. (1998). Recreation programming: Don't forget the girls. *Parks & Recreation*, *33*(6), 34–40.

Hornibrook, T., Brinkert, E., Parry, D., Seimens, R., Mitten, D., & Priest, S. (1997). The benefits and motivations of all women outdoor programs. *Journal of Experiential Education*, *20*(3), 152–157.

James, T. (1980). *Education at the edge.* Denver, CO: Colorado Outward Bound School.

Joplin, L. (1992). On defining experiential education. In Warren, K., Sakofs, M & Hunt, J.S. (Eds.), *The theory of experiential education* (pp. 15–22). Dubuque, Iowa: Kendall/Hunt.

Jordan, D. (1992). Effective leadership for girls and women in outdoor recreation. *Journal of Physical Education Recreation and Dance*, *63*(2), 61–64.

Kilbourne, J. (2000). *Can't buy me love: How advertising changes the way we think and feel.* New York: Simon & Shuster.

Kindlon, D. (2000). *Raising Cain: Protecting the emotional life of boys.* New York: Random House.

Lamb, S. & Brown, L. (2006). *Packaging girlhood: Rescuing our daughters from marketers' schemes.* New York: St. Martins Press.

Leadbeater, B. & Way, N. (Eds.). (1996). *Urban girls: Resisting stereotypes, creating identities.* New York: New York University Press.

Leadbeater, B. & Way, N. (Eds.). (2007). *Urban girls revisited: Building strengths.* New York: New York University Press.

Lerner, R.M. & Benson, P.L. (Eds.). (2003). *Developmental assets and asset-building communities: Implications for research, policy, and practice.* New York: Kluwer/Plenum.

Loeffler, T.A. (1995). *An interpretive qualitative analysis of factors which influence women's career development in outdoor leadership.* Unpublished doctoral dissertation, University of Minnesota.

Martin, B., Cashel, C., Wagstaff, M., & Breunig, M. (2006). *Outdoor leadership: Theory and practice.* Champaign, IL: Human Kinetics.

McClintock, M. (1996). Why women's outdoor trips? In Warren, K. (Ed.), *Women's voices in experiential education* (pp. 18–23). Dubuque, Iowa: Kendall/Hunt.

McKenney, P. (1996). *A program evaluation of an all-girls' outdoor adventure program.* Unpublished master's thesis, Prescott College, Prescott, Arizona.

Miner, J. L. & Boldt, J. (2002). *Outward Bound USA: Crew not passengers.* Seattle, WA: The Mountaineers Books.

Miranda, W. (1987, February). The genteel radicals. *Camping Magazine,* 12–15, 31.

Mitten, D. (1985). A philosophical basis for a women's outdoor adventure program. *Journal of Experiential Education,* 8(2), 20–24.

Mitten, D. (1992). Empowering girls and women in the outdoors. *Journal of Physical Education, Recreation and Dance, 63*(2), 56–60.

Mitten, D. (1995). Healthy expressions of diversity lead to positive group experiences. In Warren, K., Sakofs, M., & Hunt, J.S. (Eds.), *The theory of experiential education* (pp. 187–194). Dubuque, Iowa: Kendall/Hunt Publishing Company.

Mitten, D. (1999). Leadership for community building. In Miles, J. C., & Priest, S. (Eds.), *Adventure programming* (pp. 253–261). Pennsylvania: Venture Publishing.

Molenaar, D. (2000). *The Challenge of Rainier.* Seattle: The Mountaineers.

Moote, G. T. & Wodarski, J. S. (1997). The acquisition of life skills through adventure-based activities and programs: A review of the literature. *Adolescence, 32,* 143–167.

National Outdoor Leadership School. (n.d.) Retrieved February 5, 2008, from http://www.nols.edu.

Orenstein, P. (1994). *School girls: Young women, self-esteem, and the confidence gap.* New York: Bantam Doubleday Dell.

Passages Northwest. (n.d.) Retrieved July 19, 2007, from http://www.passagesnw.org.

Pipher, M. (1996). *Reviving Ophelia: Saving the selves of adolescent girls.* New York: Random House.

Pohl, S. L., Borrie, W. T., & Patterson, M. E. (2000). Women, wilderness, and everyday life: A documentation of the connection between wilderness recreation and women's everyday lives. *Journal of Leisure Research, 32*(4), 415–434

Pollock, M. & Pipher, M. (1999). *Real boys: Rescuing our sons from the myths of boyhood.* New York: Henry Holt.

Ponton, L. (1997). *The romance of risk: Why teenagers do the things they do.* New York: Basic Books.

Porter, T. (1996). "Connecting with Courage," an Outward Bound program for adolescent girls. In Warren, K. (Ed.), *Women's voices in experiential education* (pp. 18–23). Dubuque, Iowa: Kendall/Hunt.

Roberts, N. S. (1997). *A guide to women's studies in the outdoors: A review of literature and research with annotated bibliography.* Needham, MA: Simon & Shuster.

Roberts, N. S. (1992). *The portrayal of women in climbing magazine: A content analysis, 1970–1990.* Unpublished Master's Thesis (M.A.), University of Maryland at College Park, from UMI #1352487.

Rose, H. A. (2006). Asset-based development for child and youth care. *Reclaiming Children and Youth, 14*(4), 236–240.

Sabo, D., Miller, K. E., Melnick, M.J., & Heywood, L. (2004). *Her life depends on it: Sport, physical activity, and the health and well-being of American girls.* East Meadow, NY: Women's Sports Foundation.

Sadker, M., & Sadker, D. (1995). *Failing at fairness: How our schools cheat girls.* New York: Touchstone.

Sax, L. (2006). *Why gender matters: What parents and teachers need to know about the emerging science of sex differences.* New York: Broadway.

Simmons, R. (2002). *Odd girl out: The hidden culture of aggression in girls.* San Diego: Harcourt.

Stabiner, K. (2002). *All girls: Single sex education and why it matters.* New York: Riverhead.

Thompson Island Outward Bound Education Center. (n.d.) Retrieved July 19, 2007, from http://www.thompsonisland.org/english/youth/summer/courage.

Tyre, P. (2006). The trouble with boys. *Newsweek, 147*(5), 44.

Warren, K. (1985). Women's outdoor adventures: Myth and reality. *Journal of Experiential Education, 8*(2), 10–15.

Warren, K. (Ed.). (1996). *Women's voices in experiential education.* Dubuque, Iowa: Kendall/Hunt.

Warren, K. & Rheingold, A. (1996). Feminist pedagogy and experiential education: A critical look. In Warren, K. (Ed.), *Women's voices in experiential education* (pp. 118–129). Dubuque, Iowa: Kendall/Hunt Publishing Company.

Warren, K. & Loeffler, T. A. (2006). Factors that influence women's technical skill development in outdoor adventure. *Journal of Adventure Education and Outdoor Learning, 6*(2), 121–134.

Wellesley College Center for Research on Women. (1992). *How schools shortchange girls.* Wellesley, MA: AAUW Educational Foundation and National Education Association.

West-Smith, L. (2000). *Body stories: Research and intimate narratives on women transforming body image in outdoor adventure.* Edgewood, Kentucky: Adventurehaven Press.

Wiseman, R. (2002). *Queen bees and wannabes: Helping your daughter survive cliques, gossip, boyfriends and other realities of adolescence.* New York: Three Rivers Press.

Whittington, A. (2006). Challenging girls' constructions of femininity in the outdoors. *Journal of Experiential Education, 28*(3), 205–221.

Women's Wilderness Institute. (n.d.) Retrieved July 19, 2007, from http://www.womenswilderness.org.

Yerkes, R. & Miranda, W. (1985, March). Women outdoors? Who are they? *Parks and Recreation*, 48–52.

Yerkes, R. (1999). Dancing on the shores of the future. *Journal of Experiential Education, 22*(1), 20–23.

Beyond Book Learning:
Cultivating the Pedagogy of Experience
Through Field Trips

▼ ▼ ▼

Lisa Marie Jakubowski

Teach me and I will forget.
Show me and I may remember.
Involve me and I will understand.

(An ancient Chinese proverb, as cited by Reissa)

I begin with a quotation from a student who used this proverb to sum up her December, 2000, immersion field trip experience to Manzanillo, Cuba. This quotation succinctly reflects the central theme of this paper—learning through involvement. In a general sense, this has been my most effective strategy, to date, for engaging students in a process of teaching and learning about diversity and social justice. By connecting classroom and community, by taking learning beyond the text, students cultivate their appreciation of diversity by actually experiencing it.

The notion of participation or involvement in education is not new. When Dewey (1963) wrote about "progressive education" he noted that participatory, active learning was essential for individuals to gain knowledge and develop as citizens (p. 67). Today, learning through involvement reflects a commitment to a pedagogy that is "engaged" (hooks, 1994), "transformative" or "critical" (Shor, 1992, pp. 189–190; Wink, 2000, p. 123;), and "community-based"

This chapter originally was published in the *Journal of Experiential Education*, with the following citation:
Jakubowski, L. M. (2003). Beyond book learning: Cultivating the pedagogy of experience through field trips. *Journal of Experiential Education, 26*(1), 24–33.

(Mooney & Edwards, 2001). Such a pedagogy is "activist in its questioning of the status quo, in its participatory methods, and in its insistence that knowledge is not fixed, but, constantly changing" (Shor, 1992, p.189). Here, there is an orientation toward "change-agency," that is,"learning and acting for the democratic transformation of self and society. It can take place at work, at home, in school, and in community, wherever people take responsibility for rethinking and changing the conditions they are in" (Shor, p. 190). Jasso and Jasso (in Wink, 2000) actually describe critical pedagogy as "a way of life," where "living"critical pedagogy means relating teaching and learning to the real world as well as connecting that which we learn to our communities (p. 129).

This paper explores one example of living critical pedagogy, specifically—service-learning. According to Jacoby (1996):

> Service-learning is a form of experiential education in which students engage in activi-
> ties that address human and community needs with structured opportunities intention-
> ally designed to promote student learning and development. Reflection and reciprocity
> are key concepts of service-learning. (p. 5)

The immersion field trip, as a service-learning project, is presented as a "critically responsive" component of experiential education that is designed to facilitate the building of an "engaged learning community" (Warren, 1998, p. 135). A discussion regarding elements of the "critically responsive" pedagogical alternative will be presented here, namely—articulation of experience, critical thinking and reflection, and action. The compatibility of this approach with service-learning will then be highlighted. More concretely, the December 2000 field trip to Manzanillo, Cuba, is offered as an example of an international service-learning project allowing students, professors, other members of the Brescia University College Community, and our Cuban friends to work together toward a common goal. Reflections on the successes and challenges of this particular experience are discussed throughout.

Experience and the
"Critically Responsive" Approach

Traditionally, educational institutions have been viewed as places through which knowledge is transmitted to members of society. Described as "banking" (Freire, 1970, p. 58), or the "student-as-sponge" model (Waldstein & Reiher, 2001, p. 7), this more conventional approach to teaching and learning "objectifies" students and "marginalizes" knowledge stemming from personal life experience.

In contrast to banking is a Freirian process of "education" that conceptualizes students as active participants in their learning. In his vision of education, Freire began "with the conviction that the role of men and women was not only to be in the world, but to engage in relations with the world—that through these acts of creation and re-creation, we make cultural reality and thereby add to a natural world that we did not make" (Freire, 1998, p. 82). Education, through "a constant unveiling of reality," invites students to develop a critical awareness of their social worlds. Toward this end, a more balanced teacher-student relationship must emerge, a relationship in which teachers and students are jointly responsible for and simultaneously engaged in learning (Freire, 1970). Independent and critical thought is encouraged. Consciousness-raising and societal intervention is promoted. Through a problem-posing process, students receive challenges relating to themselves in the world and are urged to respond those challenges (Freire, 1970, pp. 68–69). Arguably, if we "educate" in this way, we are "living critical pedagogy."

In striving to relate classroom to community, theory to action, "community-based learning [CBL]" has become an increasingly popular option among sociologists. According to Mooney and Edwards (2001), CBL refers to "any pedagogical tool in which the community becomes a partner in the learning process ... all CBL initiatives are experiential, and in that way active learning" (p. 182). The integration of active learning into the curriculum is a dialectical process. Critical reflection and dialogue are used to highlight how: (a) course content can impact our understanding of community, and (b) community-based learning shapes and/or reshapes how we view course content. "The sense of knowing that emerges from this type of process transcends the knowledge attainable by either mastering the content or independently experiencing the community" (Mooney & Edwards, p. 186).

To facilitate this pedagogical process, it is helpful to adopt some variation of Freire's (1970) problem-posing model (see for example Joplin, 1981; Wallerstein, 1987; Wink, 2000). In Wallerstein's five-step questioning strategy, students are asked to: (a) describe what they see, (b) define the problem, (c) share similar experiences, (d) question why there is a problem, and, (e) strategize what they can do about the problem (p. 38). A variation on the five-step strategy is Wink's (2000) four-phase approach: (a) begin with the students' own experiences; (b) identify, investigate, pose a problem within your own life; (c) solve the problem together; and (d) act (pp. 140–141). Irrespective of the approach selected, education, in this Freirian sense, generally involve: the articulation of experience, critical thinking and reflection, and action.

Experience Critical Thinking, and Reflection

Critical thinking is more than an intellectual skill cultivated through higher education (Drake, 1976; Meyers, 1986; Stice, 1987; Young, 1980). In this context, critical thinking is understood to be a process that occurs among adults in their everyday interactions. Specifically, by choosing to regularly question and explore the most commonsensical details of their social experiences—in relationships, at work, in political involvements—when interpreting mass media (Brookfield, 1987, p. 12), critical thinking represents "a lived activity, not an academic pastime" (p. 14).

Critical thinking involves reflection: "the process of internally examining and exploring an issue of concern, triggered by an experience, which creates and clarifies meaning in terms of self, and which results in a changed conceptual perspective" (Boyd & Fales in Brookfield, 1987, p.14). Hutchings and Wutzdorff (1988) define reflection as "the ability to step back and ponder one's own experience, to abstract from it some meaning or knowledge relevant to some other experiences" (p. 15). It is "the link that ties student experience in the community to academic learning" (Eyler & Giles, 1999, p. 171). This process of reflection can also foster a new understanding about one's social world that is often accompanied by behavioral change. In this sense, critical thinking is by itself "a form of social action because of its transforming potential, its challenge to the dominant culture inside and outside us" (Shor, 1992, p. 195).

Given the previous statement, how can we facilitate critical thinking in order to make the relationship between student community experiences and academic learning more meaningful? One alternative is to adopt a "critically responsive" philosophy and model of teaching (Brookfield, 1990). Specifically, for the instructor, this reflects "a strongly felt rationale but which in its methods and forms responds creatively to the needs and concerns expressed by students. … The responsive component [represents] the willingness of teachers *to adapt their methods, content and approaches, to the context in which they are working and to the ways in which students are experiencing learning*" (Brookfield, pp. 23–24, emphasis added). Two integral components of this critically responsive alternative are: (a) the use of journals as a tool for reflection (Sullivan-Caitlin, 2002, p. 44), and (b) discussion.

While immersed in an experience, students' ongoing "journaling" provides a medium through which "they describe their activities and observations and reflect on their own reactions (intellectual and emotional) to these experiences" (Sullivan-Caitlin, 2002, p. 45). Starting with what people know, (i.e., their experience) provides an important statement to those who are experiencing learning. While emphasizing the value of experience, it also "helps people to recognize their own personal resources; how much they can learn from each other; how much they already know about a theme" (Arnold, Burke, James, Martin, & Thomas, 1991, p. 52). Once individuals concretize their experiences in the form of journal entries, it is possible to move from individual meditation on an experience to something more structured.

Discussion, "the theory and practice of group talk" (Brookfield & Preskill, 1999, p. 6), provides a means for engaging in structured reflection. Structured reflection includes an interactive group dimension that begins with discussion. Through discussion, experiences get "collectivized," allowing more voices to be heard, and similarities and patterns among experiences to be identified (Arnold et al., 1991, p. 54). The value of discussion[1] is fourfold:

---

[1] Brookfield and Preskill (1999) note that if discussion-based classrooms are to be "crucibles for democratic processes and mutual growth" (p. 8), both students and teachers need to practice certain dispositions, including: hospitality, participation, mindfulness, humility, mutuality, deliberation, appreciation, hope and autonomy. For a more detailed review of these dispositions, see Brookfield and Preskill (1999, pp. 8–19).

1. To help participants reach a more critically informed understanding about the topic or topics under consideration.

2. To enhance participants' self-awareness and their capacity for self-critique.

3. To foster an appreciation among participants for the diversity of opinion that invariably emerges when viewpoints are exchanged openly and honestly.

4. To act as a catalyst to helping people take informed action in the world (Brookfield & Preskill, 1999, pp. 6–7).

On the Question of "Action"

Central to learning through involvement is some form of action that links classroom and community. As a way of enriching their sociological education, my students have, for a long time, expressed a strong interest in applying their sociological knowledge to the living community. Through the process of critical reflection, the movement toward action might begin with individual "commitment statements" (Wink, 2000, pp. 155–156) by those students participating in a problem-posing process. As an example, around the issue of intolerance for diversity, an individual commitment statement might be: "I commit to approaching, with more openness, learning situations about diverse cultures and political systems." But what happens to these commitment statements? Do they translate into action? And if so, what form does this action take?

Arguably, the way(s) in which learning comes to be linked with social action is dependent upon the comfort level of the respective participants. The challenge, for me, becomes how to get students more actively involved in their educational experience, without imposing my preferences upon them.[2] Like others who strive to build an action component into their pedagogy (see for example Solorzano, 1989, p. 223), I will try not to impose a particular course of political action on students who are not comfortable with it. Instead, I try to remain mindful of the fact that the willingness of a student to experience action is influenced by a number of factors, including: the student's degree of comfort with the dynamics of the teaching and learning process, the student's level of self-confidence, cultural experiences, how well the student understands the problem under consideration, and previous experience working for social justice and change in community.

As I strive to more consistently build "learning through involvement" into my pedagogy, I have readjusted my personal expectations of what action ought to be. Experience has taught me that the nature of student engagement is contextual, and my success as a teacher in

---

[2] Later in this paper, I discuss various forms action can take in the context of this international service-learning project.

challenging students to become more active in their learning will vary with each group of students I teach. While efforts are continually made to bridge classroom and community, I recognize that it is more important to have "modest 'action' expectations for students than to alienate them from the teaching and learning process because of their resistance to a particular course of ... action" (Jakubowski, 2001, p. 72). Ultimately, as Wallerstein (1987) notes, whatever the level of action taken, students learn "through the experience of action itself" (p. 43) that social or political transformation of their realities is a possibility.

Keeping this in mind, the discussion will now shift to a more concrete example of how the immersion field trip, conceptualized as an international service-learning project, can facilitate critical thinking and reflection, and cultivate socially just forms of action. Specifically, immersion field trips, as one type of service-learning,[3] give students a break from the norm, and provide instructors with a way of linking subject matter in courses to the social world in which we live.

Critically Responsive Pedagogy,
Service Learning, and Social Justice

As sociologists strive to better prepare students for life beyond the university, service-learning, as an instructional methodology, has become increasingly popular (see for example, Hondagneu-Sotelo & Raskoff, 1994; Jacoby, 1996; May & Koulish, 1998; McEwen, 1996; Mooney & Edwards, 2001; Parker-Gwin, 1996; Sullivan-Caitlin, 2002; Warren, 1998; Wink, 2000). While more traditional pedagogical approaches aim to enrich the student's appreciation of society by "bringing the real world into the classroom" via films, newspapers or guest speakers, service-learning, as a more innovative approach, "seeks to enhance the learning process by bringing students into social or cultural settings that they might not otherwise confront" (Hondagneu-Sotelo & Raskoff, p. 248). While it can take different forms, service-learning generally involves activities designed to address human and community needs. These activities serve to complement course content and promote learning through reflection and social action (Hondagneu-Sotelo & Raskoff, p. 248; Jacoby, 1996, p. 5; Parker-Gwin, 1996, p. 97; Sullivan-Caitlin, 2002, p. 45).

---

[3] While recognizing that there will be exceptions, Mooney and Edwards (2001, pp. 184–185) suggest that there is a hierarchy of CBL options, with "out of class activities," such as field trips at one of the spectrum, and "service learning (advocacy)" at the other end. Here, I will argue that the immersion field trip to Manzanillo, Cuba, is one such exception, because it contains components more typical of service-learning (i.e., students are immersed in the community; they render a service; some received curricular credit; there is some application of course content to the real life setting; structured reflection occurred; and, in the gathering and distribution of humanitarian aid, there was social action) (Mooney & Edwards, 2001, p. 184).

According to Fertman (1994), "service learning rightly has been called the education of empowerment. It builds self-esteem, renews curiosity about learning, develops interpersonal skills, stirs leadership development, rekindles work and service ethics, and brings the world of careers closer to home" (p. 7).

Service-learning, as an instructional methodology, has four basic elements: preparation, service, reflection, and celebration (Fertman, 1994, pp. 11–16). First, *preparation* involves linking the activities in the field/community to specific learning outcomes. Second, the *service* must be both challenging and meaningful, and address a "real need." There are three types of service activity: direct, indirect, and civil action. Direct service is that which involves personal contact with individuals in need. Indirect service channels resources to solve a problem (e.g., gathering humanitarian aid for a country or community in need). Finally, civic action emphasizes active participation in "democratic citizenship." Action includes informing the public about the problem to be addressed and working toward solving the problem (Fertman, pp. 13–14). The third element of service learning is *reflection*: "the active, persistent and careful consideration of the service activity: the student's behavior, practice and accomplishments." Reflection is designed to connect the service activity to learning, helping students to understand the meaning and impact of their efforts by linking "what they have learned with what they have done" (Fertman, p. 15). As service-learning unfolds, reciprocity occurs between the server and the person or group being served. Through reciprocity,

> Students develop a great sense of belonging and responsibility as members of a larger community. Community members being served learn how to take responsibility for their own needs and become empowered to develop mechanisms and relationships to address them. (Jacoby, 1996, p. 8)

Thus, as Kendall (1990) notes: "Reciprocity creates a sense of mutual responsibility and respect between individuals involved in the service-learning exchange" (p. 22).

Finally, there is *celebration*. Celebration involves sharing, among various partners involved in service-learning, the achievements of the students and the benefits to communities in need resulting from the service (Fertman, 1994, p. 16). The field trip to Manzanillo, Cuba, provides a clear illustration of how service-learning does indeed reflect an empowering form of education.

Experiencing Political Diversity and Social Justice Through Field Trips

The Trip in Context

The impetus for organizing the December 2000 field trip to Cuba really began in the 1994–95 academic year. During that year, the author coordinated a Humanitarian Aid Drive for Cuba, which was co-sponsored by the London Branch of the Canada-Cuba Friendship Committee. As a community-based, college-wide social justice project, it succeeded in both: (a) raising student awareness of the economic, social, and humanitarian implications of the American embargo against Cuba; and (b) gathering more than one ton of aid for Cuba in the form of school and medical supplies (Geigen-Miller, 1994, p. C7).

While the students were thrilled with the success of this Aid Drive, they expressed one main regret: "It's too bad that we could not go to Cuba to deliver our school supplies and medicines, and experience Cuba, first hand, for ourselves." I was moved by their comments and set out to see what I could to do to make such a trip a reality. As Scarce (1997) notes, "students are motivated to learn when they concretely experience social phenomena through the every day setting of field trips" (p. 220). And, like Boyle (1995), I feel that one of our most important responsibilities, as teachers, is to "mak[e] students think beyond the four walls of the classroom" (p. 153). Accordingly, since the Humanitarian Aid Drive of 1994–95, I had been trying very hard to work out with my friends/contacts in Cuba, the logistical details for such an experience at a university college that had not previously sponsored an international field trip. Ultimately, with the encouragement of a very supportive administration, my long-time dream of taking students to Cuba materialized in December of 2000.

Pretrip Planning and Action

Recognizing that this would be a long and complicated project, long-range planning became vital. Even with amazing cooperation from two Cuban friends, who were invaluable in helping me coordinate activities and visits to various locations, there were many challenging details to attend to, including: (a) selection of the site; (b) visiting the site prior to the field trip; (c) selecting dates for travel; (d) establishing a screening process for potential student participants; (e) arranging for transportation and housing; (f) planning the itinerary; (g) preparing students for what they would greet on arrival, as well as reinforcing the academic expectations of the trip; (h) attending to administrative details around insurance and acknowledgement and assumption of risk; (i) facilitating on-site involvements, daily debriefings, and discussion groups; and (j) evaluating the trip (Scarce, 1997, pp. 221–225).

From the outset, I recognized that there would be a limit to the number of students who could participate in such a field trip, given the supervisory implications. Ten seemed like a reasonable number for a first-time endeavor. The College Chaplain, Theresa, was immediately invited to accompany me, as she had an interest in Cuba dating back to the Humanitarian Aid Drive of 1994–95. Furthermore, students would be selected, not from one particular class of mine, but from among my various courses; and those students interested in participating were formally interviewed. Those with some background or involvement in global development and/or social justice issues were invited to participate.

Beyond having an interest in Cuban development and social justice, other factors would impact the degree of involvement a student could have in this project. First of all, the timing of the trip proved to be a complicating factor. For financial reasons, early December was the estimated date for departure. This was a less expensive time to go, and cost is obviously a factor for university students. But even with the reduced rates, the cost was still a bit overwhelming for the budgets of some eager students, and they were unable to participate. Beyond budget, problems arose around the writing of mid-year exams. Specifically, our time away overlapped slightly with the start of Christmas exams, and therefore some students who had exams at this time were not comfortable with the option of seeking, with my assistance, special permission to write their scheduled exams upon their return. They, therefore, decided not to participate in the field trip. Finally, there were those students who were unable to travel with us because their parents were not comfortable with them travelling to a "Communist" country. With these various criteria factored in, our tentative list of 10 was reduced to a small but enthusiastic list of four: Ashley, Kalyan, Reissa and Onica.[4] It is important to point out that action or involvement in this project took various forms and no one form of action was more legitimate than another.

While only four students would ultimately make the journey overseas, we were determined to build on the enthusiasm for this project that was growing throughout our college. As noted above, there were various reasons why students could not travel overseas to Cuba. However, every effort was made to actively involve all interested people at the college in the pretravel phases of the trip. The Social Justice Club, for instance, played a pivotal role in raising awareness of the need for humanitarian aid. This student group spent considerable time and energy increasing community awareness and understanding of the economic, social, and humanitarian implications of the U.S. Embargo against Cuba. They initiated a Humanitarian Aid Drive, soliciting and gathering donations from both Brescia University College and the London, Ontario, community. They gathered school supplies, vitamins, and medicines for the rural Cuban communities we would be visiting, and made these donations "travel-ready" by sorting, packaging, and labelling the boxes. The Social Hope Committee at our college also contributed to the cause by donating funds to support our travel in and around the Manzanillo area. These actions were vital to the overall success of our international service-learning project. Finally, acting as "ambassadors" for the college, our small but enthusiastic group of students began their Cuban experience, which included delivering what had been gathered during the Humanitarian Aid Drive that preceded the trip. This aid, in the form of supplies for village schools, and vitamins and medicine for community doctors' houses, was graciously received. Throughout our stay, we were

---

[4] With their permission, I am using the real names of the four participating students. These four young women were representatives of Brescia University College's Social Justice Club. Two of them were also students of Community Development.

exposed to rather spontaneous doses of Cuban hospitality. Teachers and students, community doctors, and average Cuban families, welcomed us into their homes and their hearts. Through "journaling," students reflected daily about their experiences. These reflections became more structured during regularly scheduled discussion sessions throughout the week.

Without a doubt, one of the most memorable days for all of us was the visit to a fisher-woman's house and the town of Marea. As we walked in to explore a local village, hoping to visit the local school and doctor's office, we met a fisherwoman by the seaside. For purposes of anonymity, she shall be called "J." J generously became our host for the day, walked us through town introducing us to family, friends, teachers, and the doctor, insisting at the end of it all that she prepare lunch for us. Lunch was her catch for the day—lobster. Here are a sampling of comments from the journals of my students.

The Fisherwoman and Our Visit to Marea

> After J showed us around the village she brought us back to her home.... She gave us her whole day, without a second thought. I have never eaten so much lobster in my life.... She insisted that we finish everything. I was overjoyed, tears almost came to my eyes. J didn't speak English, but we felt the love in every word that she spoke. As we walked back to the hotel I was overwhelmed with love in my heart. The trail was even more beautiful than before. (Ashley)

> [J] cooked us an abundance of lobster and made coffee. She gave us all the food that she had. Onica can't eat shellfish and this is when I realized that J had no other food, even for her family to eat. She was determined to give Onica something so she made her a glass of lemonade.... It was so wonderful to meet people who truly give from the bottom of their hearts. Perhaps the "first world" countries need to learn a lot from these people, as opposed to trying to force them to conform to the well known way of life in the "better" countries. (Reissa)

> Today we went to a little village called Marea. We walked around the town. It was interesting to see how poor the people in the village were, how run down the buildings were ... and yet the people seemed so happy. Why should they be? Who says that material things make us happy? ... What was even more unforgettable was when we went to J's house and she made us a fabulous lobster lunch but, unfortunately, I can't eat lobster. She went out of her way to find something that I could eat. So, she made a tomato salad, but, I don't eat tomatoes. J then found limes and made me lime juice. I couldn't believe

how nice she was; I could not believe that she would go out of her way for me, a stranger. She dropped everything to make us lunch and made us feel very comfortable. We had such a great time that the condition of the house never came into our thoughts. There was no reason to pity these people; their surroundings didn't seem to have an effect on their happiness. (Onica)

From the time we got to the gate of J's home, I felt so welcome there. The saying *mi casa es su casa* didn't need to be voiced because I am sure we all felt like we were at home right away, just because of how welcoming she and her husband were. J's entire home is about the size of my parents' bedroom, but, it had me thinking, do we need such big houses anyway? Unlike any of our homes, her home had no Internet, no telephone, no television, no running water and no electricity … and her family is so happy and so giving! I think that since there are no frivolous material things to occupy your time, you must spend your time doing things that really count. I also think you genuinely love people around you when you are in a community like J's. You see them all without the frills of "development" and you get them as pure human beings. Not necessarily that they are super-human and all good because that is not the case, but, people are so genuine and with that tends to come respect and love. (Kalyan)

There were so many other experiences—our ecological hike, the day in Santiago de Cuba during which we travelled to sites of religious and political significance like El Cobre, and Antonio Maceo Revolution Square. On other occasions, we visited schools and classrooms in the towns of Duran and Marea. Through these experiences, the students gained a new understanding and critical insight into the concepts of difference and privilege (see McIntosh, 1995). Through journaling and structured reflection, students began "reaching in" (Jakubowski & Visano, 2002, p. 107), searching for a better understanding of themselves. They acknowledged their respective positions of privilege and began to see how their comprehension of the world had been filtered through those positions. They came to realize that remaining attached to their positions of privilege would be "self-censoring" and limit learning. In essence, experiences like the trip to Marea, described above, triggered reflection and ultimately, growth, among the students. By entering another world—that of the average Cuban citizen—they began to recognize the role of privilege in their lives, and were thereby able to work at breaking down barriers. By becoming conscious of their own privilege, the students could begin to learn and work effectively from within those positions (Jakubowski & Visano, pp. 107–109).

They regularly interacted with workers in the tourist industry and trusting relationships evolved. Our students spoke of how wonderful it was to talk to "the real person," rather than simply the service provider. Their candid conversations highlighted for the students, how the tourist industry can negatively impact Cuban citizens. For instance, when the students realized that Cubans, in general, are not welcome in the hotels as guests, Onica asked, " Why is it that Cubans are treated as second class citizens when tourists go to Cuba? Why shouldn't they be allowed in hotels? What makes them different? They should have first preference to the hotels and any other facilities in Cuba; after all they are Cuban!"

Finally, beyond these various experiences, the students found particularly moving and meaningful their encounters with Cuban doctors. They saw a group of professionals who performed their duties with dedication, skill, and compassion, striving to overcome the hardships that have befallen the island. In Marea, in particular, the doctor took the time to talk to us about community healthcare. We had a tour of his office, and his home, which were in the same building. He spoke at length about the "Family Doctor Plan" in Cuba, where an assigned family doctor lives in a given community, and attends to 120 families in the area. He shared with us his history in Marea, a community which he has adopted as his permanent home. He talked about his various responsibilities, ranging from maintaining health records, performing regular examinations, counselling and prevention, to pre and postnatal care.[5] We learned that medicines are often in short supply, and yet, doctors make do with what they have.

The level of commitment of the doctors was reinforced for us en route home from a trip to the city of Santiago, when in the evening, our driver saw a torch in the distance and realized someone was in distress. He backed up the van, and we were told by our friend and guide that someone needed our help. When we got closer we saw three men, one of whom was a doctor, carrying an elderly, and obviously ill, woman. We quickly made room in the van, picked them up and drove them past the doctor's house, to the local hospital, where she could be X-Rayed. While the journey was very short by van, we realized that the doctor had been travelling most of the day on foot, first to reach this woman, and then to get her to where she could receive treatment. Along the way, different people helped to carry her part of the distance, because no one had access to a vehicle in this rural, mountainous area. Everyone was exhausted, but nevertheless, remained determined to help this woman in need. The doctor explained to us the additional hardships associated with administering care in this mountainous area, having to travel by horse or mule to reach many of the families for whom he was responsible. Ashley reflected on this unexpected experience noting, "it was amazing to see

---

[5] For a more detailed discussion of the "Family Doctor Plan," see Bernal (2000) and Waitzkin et al. (1997). For a summary of Cuba's "country health profile," see Pan American Health Organization (1999) and the New Internationalist's World Guide (2001, p. 195).

us all pull together when there was an elderly woman being carried on the side of the road. There were two men attempting to carry her miles to the hospital. We saw such dedication on the doctor's part. He lovingly held her hand during the drive. I am happy we were able to help in such a big way."

As our week drew to a close, we engaged in a very rich dialogue with some of our Cuban friends around the most meaningful moments of our trip, and general reflections on Cuba. Below are some student comments that emerged from this structured reflection and discussion.

General Reflections on Cuba

Almost everything I heard about Cuba isn't true (e.g., that every Cuban wants to leave Cuba). Almost every Cuban I spoke to seems to love Cuba very much. Even though it's so poor, [they] want to stay and help it become a better place. They seem to be very proud to be Cuban,...Visiting Cuba has made me realize that maybe I should not put so much emphasis on material things. Instead, I should try to put emphasis on simpler, perhaps more meaningful things. (*Onica*)

I didn't want to leave that beach once I sat down and felt the sand between my fingers and the heart beat of the earth. It felt so untouched and natural.... I was so sad to leave that most welcoming piece of earth.... As we reflected on our most meaningful moments of the trip ... we were all touched to tears. We have such soft hearts.... After this experience we are connected so closely to each other. (*Ashley*)

I have read about Cuba and learned statistics on the island through research, however there are still assumptions and stereotypes that come with ignorance. I have realized that all the books in the world could not have taught me more about Cuba than I learned on this field trip. I am very grateful that I was fortunate enough to have such an enlightening educational experience. This popular proverb sums up my field trip experience: *Teach me and I will forget. Show me and I may remember. Involve me and I will understand.* (*Reissa*)

Without a doubt, one of the greatest accomplishment of this trip was the way in which it brought closer together, myself, Theresa, and our four participating students, creating a more enriching, overall learning experience. Barriers found in most classroom teaching situations were drastically reduced, as the students began to raise critical questions about the concepts of difference, privilege, development, justice, stereotypes, and political diversity that they had previously encountered only in their classroom studies. Nowhere was this more evident than during structured reflection and discussion circles that occurred in the evenings after dinner. As I facilitated these sessions, I was moved to see how students were making connections between this field trip experience and their own personal and academic lives. As the previous quotations suggest, it was clear that the students were deeply affected by their Cuban encounters, and as Theresa noted, the reflection and discussion circles became the place where they began to "put things together."

The international field trip experience reinforced how fostering positive relationships between the university classroom and wider community empowers students with the skills and confidence necessary to advocate for social justice. Beyond its preparatory, service, and re-flective stages, this immersion field trip was celebratory. In Cuba, we celebrated with our Cuban friends and colleagues, the active learning that had occurred on a daily basis in the community, the pedagogy of experience that had enhanced our knowledge and understanding of issues related to difference, privilege, development, social justice and respect for political diversity. We also celebrated the way in which our humanitarian aid, in the form of school supplies, vitamins and medicine, brought assistance to communities in need. When we returned home, our new understanding of privilege enabled us to work effectively to dispel myths and stereo-types about Cuba and its people. We offered displays reflective of Cuban culture, showed slides of our adventures and dialogued about our many experiences. It was truly a celebration!

Conclusion

Throughout this paper, I have suggested that cultivating a pedagogy of experience can be facilitated through the use of a critically responsive approach to teaching and learning that is grounded in experience, critical thinking, reflection and action. As a service-learning project, the immersion field trip to Manzanillo, Cuba is offered as one example of experiential learning. This example illustrates how classroom and community can come together in a way that invites students to engage in meaningful, active forms of learning about diversity and social justice.

Building a service-learning component into one's pedagogy makes for a more mean-ingful teaching and learning process. It encourages instructors to recognize student knowl-edge and experience as a valuable element of the educational process. Furthermore, through service-learning, students develop a greater awareness of their abilities to work for change and social justice. As studies reveal, there is a positive relationship between education-based community service, personal development, and a stronger sense of civic and social respon-sibility (e.g., McEwen, 1996; Vadeboncoeur, Rahm & Aguilera, 1996; Waldstein & Reiher, 2001, pp. 7–13; Wang, Greathouse, & Falcinella, 1998; Waterman, 1997, p. 3). In essence, a critically responsive pedagogy that incorporates service-learning:

is a critical-democratic pedagogy for self and social change. It is a student-centred pro-gram ... [that] approaches individual growth as an active, cooperative and social process because the self and society create each other.... The goals of this pedagogy are to relate personal growth to public life, by developing strong skills, academic knowl-edge, habits of inquiry and critical curiosity about society, power, inequality and change. (Shor, 1992, p. 15)

References

Arnold, R., Burke, B., James, C., Martin, D., & Thomas, B. (1991). *Educating for a change.* Toronto, Ontario, Canada: Between the Lines and Doris Marshall Institute for Education and Action.

Bernal, S. (2000). *Women's health care in Cuba: Observations of medical facilities in Cerro, Havana.* http://wwwdesignerwebs.org/CubaTripEducation.htm

Boyle, C. E. (1995). Seeing gender in everyday life: A field trip to the mall. *Teaching Sociology, 25,* 150–154.

Brookfield, S. (1987). *Developing critical thinkers: Challenging adults to explore alternative ways of think-ing and acting.* San Francisco: Jossey-Bass.

Brookfield, S. (1990). *The skillful teacher: On technique, trust, and responsiveness in the classroom.* San Francisco: Jossey-Bass.

Brookfield, S., & Preskill, S. (1999). *Discussion as a way of teaching: Tools and techniques for democratic classrooms.* San Francisco: Jossey-Bass.

Dewey, J. (1963). *Experience and education.* New York: Collier. (Originally published 1938).

Drake, J. (1976). *Teaching critical thinking.* Danville, IL: Interstate Publishers.

Eyler, J., & Giles, D. E. (1999). *Where's the learning in service-learning?* San Francisco: Jossey-Bass.

Fertman, C. (1994). *Service learning for all students.* Bloomington IN: Phi Delta Kappa Educational Foundation.

Freire, P. (1970). *Pedagogy of the oppressed.* New York: Herder and Herder.

Freire, P. (1998). Education for critical consciousness. In A. M. Araujo Freire, & D. Macedo (Eds.), *The Paulo Freire reader* (pp. 80–110). New York: Continuum.

Geigen-Miller, P. (1994, November 5). Cuba to get school supplies: Brescia College is taking a major role in the effort. *London Free Press,* C7.

Hondagneu-Sotelo, P., & Raskoff, S. (1994). Community service-learning: Promises and problems. *Teaching Sociology, 22*(3), 248–254.

hooks, b. (1994). *Teaching to transgress: Education as the practice of freedom.* New York: Routledge.

Hutchings, P., & Wutzdorff, A. (1988). Experiencing learning across the curriculum: Assumptions and principles. In P. Hutchings, & A. Wutzdorff (Eds.), *Knowing and doing: Learning through experience* (pp. 5–19). San Francisco: Jossey-Bass.

Jacoby, B. (1996). Service-learning in today's higher education. In B. Jacoby (Ed.), *Service-learning in higher education: Concepts and practices* (pp. 3–25). San Francisco: Jossey-Bass.

Jakubowski, L. (2001). Teaching uncomfortable topics: An action-oriented strategy for addressing racism and related forms of difference. *Teaching Sociology, 29*(1), 62–79.

Jakubowski, L., & Visano, L. (2002). *Teaching controversy.* Halifax, Nova Scotia, Canada: Fernwood.

Joplin, L. (1981). On defining experiential education. *Journal of Experiential Education, 4*(1), 17–20.

Kendall, J. C. (1990). Combining service and learning: An introduction. In J. C. Kendall (Ed.), *Combining service and learning: A resource book for community and public service–Volume 1* (pp. 1–33). Raleigh, NC: National Society for Experiential Learning.

May, M., & Koulish, R. (1998). Joining academy and community in an educational venture. *Teaching Sociology, 26*(2), 140–145.

McEwen, M. K. (1996). Enhancing student learning and development through service-learning. In B. Jacoby (Ed.), *Service-learning in higher education: Concepts and practices* (pp. 53–91). San Francisco: Jossey-Bass.

McIntosh, P. (1995). White privilege and male privilege: A personal account of coming to see correspondences through work in women's studies. In M. Anderson, & P. Hill Collins (Eds.), *Race, class and gender: An anthology* (pp. 76–87). Belmont, CA: Wadsworth.

Meyers, C. (1986). *Teaching students to think critically: A guide for faculty in all disciplines.* San Francisco: Jossey-Bass.

Mooney, L. A., & Edwards, B. (2001). Experiential learning in Sociology: Service learning and other community-based learning initiatives. *Teaching Sociology, 29*(2), 181–194.

New Internationalist. (2001). *The world guide: An alternative reference to the countries of our planet, 2001/2002.* Oxford: New Internationalist Publications.

Parker-Gwin, R. (1996). Connecting service to learning: How students and communities matter. *Teaching Sociology, 24*(1), 97–101.

Pan American Health Organization. (1999). *Cuba: Basic country health profile, summaries.* http://www.paho.org/English/SHA/prflcub.htm

Scarce, R. (1997). Field trips as short-term experiential education. *Teaching Sociology, 25,* 219–226.

Shor, I. (1992). *Empowering education: Critical teaching for social change.* Chicago: The University of Chicago Press.

Solorzano, D. (1989). Teaching and social change: Reflecting on a Freirian approach to the college classroom. *Teaching Sociology, 17,* 218–225.

Stice, J. (Ed.). (1987). *Developing critical thinking and problem solving abilities: New directions for teaching and learning.* San Francisco: Jossey-Bass.

Sullivan-Caitlin, H. (2002). Food, hunger, and poverty: A thematic approach to integrating service-learning. *Teaching Sociology, 30*(1), 39–52.

Vadeboncoeur, J. A., Rahm, I., & Aguilera, D. (1996). Building democratic character through community experiences in teacher education. *Education and Urban Society, 28,* 189–207.

Waitzkin, H., Wald, K., Kee, R., Danielson, R., & Robinson, L. (1997). Primary care in Cuba: Low and high technology developments pertinent to family medicine. Retrieved at: http://www.cubasolidarity.net/waitzkin.html

Waldstein, F. A., & Reiher, T. C. (2001). Service-learning and students' personal and civic development. *The Journal of Experiential Education, 24*(1), 7–13.

Wallerstein, N. (1987). Problem-posing education: Freire's method for transformation. In I. Shor (Ed.), *Freire for the classroom: A sourcebook for liberatory teaching* (pp. 33–44). Portsmouth, NH: Boynton/Cook Publishers.

Wang, J., Greathouse, B., & Falcinella, V. M. (1998). An empirical assessment of self-esteem enhancement in high school challenge service learning programs. *Education, 1*, 99–106.

Warren, K. (1998). Educating students for social justice in service learning. *The Journal of Experiential Education, 21*(3), 134–139.

Waterman, A. S. (1997). An overview of service-learning and the role of research and evaluation in service-learning programs. In A. S. Waterman (Ed.), *Service-learning: Applications from research* (pp. 1–11). Mahwah, NJ: Lawrence Erlbaum Associates.

Wink, J. (2000). *Critical pedagogy: Notes from the real world.* (2nd ed.). New York: Addison-Wesley Longman.

Young, R. (Ed.). (1980). *Fostering critical thinking: New directions for teaching and learning.* San Francisco: Jossey-Bass.

About the Editors

▾ ▾ ▾

Karen Warren, Ph.D., has taught courses in experiential education, outdoor leadership, wilderness studies, and social justice at Hampshire College for the past 25 years. Her books include *Women's Voices in Experiential Education* and *The Theory of Experiential Education,* as well as many publications on experiential education practice and social justice issues in adventure education. She has served AEE as a Board member, Professional Group and Publication Advisory Committee chair, a member of the *Journal of Experiential Education* (*JEE*) Journal Advisory Committee, various conference committees, and the committee that created the AEE definition of experiential education. Karen has been honored to receive the 1998 Michael Stratton Practitioner Award and the 2006 Outstanding Experiential Teacher of the Year Award from AEE.

Denise Mitten, Ph.D., teaches at Ferris State University, where she developed an MED program in experiential education. Her writing and research includes decision making and ethics, teaching and learning styles in a social context, nature and wellness, legal issues, group dynamics and gender issues. Starting with the Girl Scouts in the 1960s, Denise has worked in adventure and environmental education with many populations and has led trips from SCUBA to mountaineering. For 19 years, she worked with Woodswomen, Inc., developing and guiding trips in nine countries. In 2007, she received the Michael Stratton Practitioner Award from AEE. Denise has served AEE as Board president and treasurer, as a *JEE* Journal Advisory Committee member, and in other capacities.

TA Loeffler, Ph.D., brings 20 years of expertise leading people through life-changing experiences to every facet of her work. As a Professor of Outdoor Recreation at Memorial University of Newfoundland, TA has received several awards for excellence in experiential education. TA is the author of *More than a Mountain: One Woman's Everest* and numerous scholarly articles. TA's current research interests include women's involvement in outdoor adventure, photo elicitation, competency development, and the use of communications technology in the wilderness. TA currently serves on the *JEE* Journal Advisory Committee and is a past chair of the Women's Professional Group of AEE.

Contributor Biographies

▼ ▼ ▼

Katie Asmus, M.A., L.P.C., is an experiential adventure educator, body-centered wilderness therapist, and founder of Namaste Healing Arts. Katie trains others in therapeutically collaborating with the natural world and has a psychotherapy practice in Boulder, Colorado.

Molly Ames Baker, co-director of Colgate University Outdoor Education for 12 years, now works as a full-time mom of three, helping her kids to connect with the northern Michigan landscape.

Martha Bell, Ph.D., a Research Fellow at University of Otago, New Zealand, does social science contract research on families, bodies, and ability/disability. She recently assisted colleagues in teaching experiential learning to medical students.

At the time of authoring the article, **Almut Beringer** was a faculty member, School of Outdoor Education and Environment, La Trobe University, Bendigo, Australia. She currently serves as the Director of Environmental Studies and Sustainability at the University of Prince Edward Island, eastern Canada.

Dene Berman, Ph.D., is a practicing psychologist and a Clinical Professor in the School of Professional Psychology at Wright State University. His specialty is working with children and adolescents, which he does through Lifespan Counseling, the counseling practice he and Jennifer Davis-Berman launched in the early 1980s. He is co-author of *The Promise of Wilderness Therapy,* published by AEE in 2008.

Jason Berv has been a teacher, consultant, and researcher, and is the founder and director of The Watershed School in Boulder, Colorado.

Charles F. Brand is an associate professor of education at Marymount University; his scholarly interests include reflective practice and its application to experiential learning.

Mary Breunig, Ph.D., is an assistant professor of outdoor recreation in the Department of Recreation and Leisure at Brock University in St. Catharines, Ontario.

Mike Brown, Ph.D., is a Senior Lecturer in the Department of Sport and Leisure Studies at The University of Waikato, New Zealand. His career has combined academic appointments with industry experience.

Nadine W. Budbill, M.A., is the co-founder and director of Dirt Divas, a girls' mountain bike program in Vermont. She has extensive experience developing and implementing programs for adolescent girls.

Rebecca Carver, Ph.D., was a scholar, a compassionate human being, and an advocate of experiential education working for social justice. At the time of her death she was an Assistant Professor in the Department of Educational Leadership and Cultural Foundations at the University of North Carolina at Greensboro.

Chris Cashel, Ed.D., retired from Oklahoma State University as a professor of leisure studies in 2004. She worked for the Wilderness Education Association (WEA) for 22 years as an instructor and board member.

Kate Cassidy is Director of Community Adventure Training Initiatives (C.A.T.I.) and Youth University at Brock University. A Ph.D. candidate, Kate's research interests include group development, experiential education, sense of community, and youth engagement.

After 20 years teaching and administrating in private schools, **Steve Chapman** founded Broad Reach Strategies, a consulting firm located in Tennessee that helps organizations align their cultures with their missions and values.

April Crosby retired from the University of Alaska in 1997 and currently runs Crosby and Associates Consulting, specializing in organizational development for nonprofit and public agencies.

Jennifer Davis-Berman is an academic and practicing social worker. After earning her MSW at the Ohio State University in 1982 and her Ph.D. from Ohio State in 1985, she joined the faculty at the University of Dayton, where she has been a professor of social work since 1986. She is co-author of *The Promise of Wilderness Therapy,* published by AEE in 2008.

Cindy Dillenschneider is a professor and coordinator of Outdoor Education at Northland College in Ashland, Wisconsin. Her professional endeavors focus on universal design and inclusion in outdoor environments and activities.

Alan Ewert, Ph.D., is currently a Professor and holds the Meier Endowed Chairship in Outdoor Leadership at Indiana University. He also has instructed for Outward Bound, NOLS, and the WEA.

Karen Fox, Ph.D., is an Associate Professor in the Faculty of Physical Education and Recreation, University of Alberta, Edmonton, Alberta, Canada.

Dan Garvey is President of Prescott College. Before that he had a 25-year career as an administrator and educator focused on education reform and improvement. He is a former President and Executive Director of AEE.

Michael Gass, Ph.D., has been the Coordinator of the Outdoor Education Program in the Department of Kinesiology at the University of New Hampshire for the past 21 years. He also is one of the creators and principals of UNH's Browne Center, a program development and research center for experiential learning serving over 9,000 clients a year.

Randy Haluza-DeLay, a former Outward Bound instructor and environmental educator, now teaches sociology at The King's University College in Edmonton, Alberta. He is editor of *Speaking for Ourselves: Environmental Justice in Canada.*

Paul Heintzman, Ph.D., Leisure Studies Professor at the University of Ottawa, previously worked at outdoor centres across Canada. He received the SPRE Teaching Innovation Award for experiential learning activities on leisure and spirituality.

Delaura L. Hubbs is a therapist in private practice and has used reflective journals extensively in teaching university counselor preparation courses as well as with clients in therapy.

Jasper S. Hunt, Jr. is Professor of Experiential Education and Leadership Studies at Minnesota State University in Mankato, Minnesota. Jasper has written several books and published numerous publications largely specializing in ethics in experiential education.

Christian M. Itin, M.S.W., is an associate professor of social work, an author and presenter focusing on the advanced facilitation of experiential processes, and an active AEE member serving as President of the Board.

Lisa Jakubowski is an Associate Professor in the Department of Sociology at Brescia University College, where her teaching and research centers around Community Service-Learning and the Sociology of Law.

Thomas James is Provost and Dean of the College at Teachers College, Columbia University. His interests include history of education, public policy, and the role of experience in education

Anne C. Lindsay is Associate Professor in Teacher Education at University of Arkansas at Little Rock. Anne has extensive experience in evaluating and developing programs for young children; her research interests focus around the language of teaching across varied settings.

Mary McClintock, M.Ed., is an award-winning freelance writer, editor, book indexer, researcher and community activist who educates about peace, justice, and environmental issues through her writing.

Priscilla McKenney, M.A., is Program Director for GirlVentures, a girls' outdoor adventure program. She's a Graduate Advisor for Prescott College and serves as an Advisor for the Pacific Leadership Institute.

Pam McPhee, Faculty and Director of the University of New Hampshire's Browne Center, enjoys supporting deliberate cultures, whether it be in adventure programming, education, or organizational development.

Steven Pace, M.S.W., has been teaching experientially since 1974. He has worked extensively with Prescott College, the Association for Experiential Education, and the Voyageur Outward Bound School.

Bill Proudman is the founder of White Men as Full Diversity Partners, a consultancy building courageous business leaders and inclusive work cultures. Bill served for 11 years on the AEE Board in the 80s and 90s, and has been an experiential educator for over 35 years.

John Quay is a lecturer in the Graduate School of Education at the University of Melbourne. His doctoral studies follow Dewey in seeking a way out of educational confusion.

Wayne Regina, Psy.D., is a licensed psychologist, family therapist, and certified mediator. He is the former dean and current peace studies professor at Prescott College and Director of Skyview School.

Jay Roberts is the Director of Wilderness Programs and an Assistant Professor of Education at Earlham College. He has also directed brain-based summer educational camps for teens.

Nina S. Roberts, Ph.D., is a faculty member at San Francisco State University. She is also the Project Director of the Pacific Leadership Institute and is on the Advisory Council of GirlVentures.

Diane Samdahl is a professor in leisure studies at the University of Georgia, with expertise in research methodology and critical theory. She often challenges researchers to ask more critical questions.

Jayson Seaman works at the University of New Hampshire, where he teaches classes in outdoor education and educational foundations. His research interests presently include participants' use of language and other modes of communication in nonformal diversity education programs.

Cheryl A. (Estes) Stevens is a committed experiential educator who has been facilitating experiential learning and service-learning in recreation and leisure, outdoor leadership, and organizational development for more than 25 years.

Laura Tyson has been an outdoor educator and wilderness therapist for 25 years. She is the founder and former director of The Women's Wilderness Institute, and holds an MA in Contemplative Psychotherapy.

Mark Wagstaff, Ed.D., is a professor of Recreation, Parks and Tourism at Radford University in Radford, Virginia. Mark has worked in the outdoor education field since 1981.

Brian Wattchow, Ph.D., is a senior lecturer in the Sport and Outdoor Recreation degrees program at Monash University, Australia. He is also a founding member of the Movement, Environment, Community research group.

Brent Wolfe is an assistant professor of Therapeutic Recreation at Georgia Southern University, with a background in challenge course facilitation and training. He desires to positively impact those around him.

Rita Yerkes is Dean Emeritus of the School of Experiential Leadership at George Williams College of Aurora University. She is an author, Kurt Hahn presenter, and has served both as an AEE Board president and Accreditation Council chair.

Editors' Note: We were unable to track down the following authors and thus have not been able to include their biographies: **Donald L. Finkel, Laura Joplin, Kate Lehmann, Stephen Monk, Gordon W.A. Oles.**

ASSOCIATION FOR EXPERIENTIAL EDUCATION (AEE)

 AEE is a nonprofit, member-based, professional organization dedicated to experiential education. AEE provides professional development, skill building, information resources, standards, and best practices.

AEE's vision is to contribute to making a more just and compassionate world by transforming education.

AEE's mission is to develop and promote experiential education. AEE is committed to supporting professional development, theoretical advancement, and the evaluation of experiential education worldwide.

The AEE Board of Directors developed the following Ends Statement to (a) portray how the world will be changed because AEE exists and (b) to provide guidance for association work. The Ends Statement reads:

The Association for Experiential Education exists so that educators and practitioners have access to a professional learning community dedicated to enriching lives through the philosophy and principles* of experiential education.

1. The learning community is inclusive of diverse peoples and professional practices, collaborative with other communities, and accessible within reasonable means.

2. Authoritative information for implementing and advancing the philosophy and practice of experiential education is accessible.

   a. Standards are identified to improve professional practice and to safeguard the well-being of participants.

   b. Research about experiential education is coordinated and conducted.

3. Decision-makers value and support experiential education.

as articulated on the AEE website: www.aee.org

Who AEE Members Are:

AEE members are students, professionals, and organizations engaged in the diverse application of experiential education in:

education • adaptive programming • recreation • leadership development
physical education • adventure programming • corporate training
environmental education • youth service • mental health • corrections

Membership Benefits

Scholarly Journal and Relevant Publications

AEE publishes the peer-reviewed, professional *Journal of Experiential Education (JEE),* a collection of academic research, articles, and reviews; the *Horizon* association newsletter; regional and professional group newsletters and publications; and other materials showcasing experiential education research, articles, reviews, initiatives, techniques, programs, and more. A subscription to the *JEE,* as well as discounts on AEE publications and educational tools, are included with membership.

Networking and Professional Development

Members enjoy discounted fees for annual and regional conferences and can take advantage of AEE's online member directory.

Industry Standards and Risk Management

AEE works continuously with experts in outdoor and adventure programming to establish safety, efficiency, and general best practices. Organizational members who achieve AEE accredited status provide evidence that their program meets the highest industry standards.

Leadership Development

AEE members are afforded the opportunity to learn leadership skills through volunteer training and development throughout the association.

Discounts on Events, Goods, and Services

AEE members receive discounts on all AEE-sponsored conferences and events, and on experiential education–related gear, tools, and services from a variety of vendors.

Career Services

The AEE Jobs Clearinghouse offers online job postings for experiential education employment, from internships to directorships. Additionally, AEE conferences offer career workshops, mentoring, résumé postings, and more.

How You Can Participate

Annual Conferences

Every November, the association convenes an annual conference of more than 900 attendees, with hundreds of workshops, internationally recognized speakers and presenters, and more. Our signature event provides professional development and renewal, skill building, continuing education units, and unsurpassed networking and community-building opportunities.

Regions and Regional Conferences

AEE's eight regions sponsor regional conferences, playdays, seminars, and other activities so members and the local experiential education community can participate and network in smaller, more accessible and intimate settings.

Professional Groups

AEE professional groups represent specific areas of practice and offer opportunities for members to share knowledge and build skills with others who share similar professional interests within experiential education.

Involvement in any of the above activities, at any level, is a great way to become more involved in the association, expand your network, and get the most out of an AEE membership.

Join Us!

Memberships are available at different levels and benefit structures.
See all the details and join online.

www.aee.org